THE Great Psychologists

THE Great Psychologists
Fourth Edition

ROBERT I. WATSON, Sr.
University of New Hampshire
and University of Florida

J. B. LIPPINCOTT COMPANY

New York   Philadelphia   San Francisco

THE GREAT PSYCHOLOGISTS, Fourth Edition

Copyright © 1978, 1971, 1968, 1963 by Robert I. Watson.

Library of Congress Cataloging in Publication Data
Library of Congress Catalog Card Number: 77-12990

Watson, Robert Irving, 1909–
    The great psychologists.

    Includes indexes.
    1. Psychology—History.   I. Title.
BF81.W35 1977   150'.92'2   77–12990
ISBN 0-397-47375-3

To
E. G. B.
*my teacher, under whom
I have never studied*

PREFACE to the Fourth Edition

Unlike the cutting edge of a date-collecting research field, the "facts" of history change primarily with shifts of emphasis. It is hardly surprising, then, that after three previous editions many of the details still stand. What has changed most in this edition is that an overall pattern of attitudes called in my other writings, prescriptions, has been used. The major modification, then, is a shift of focus from the individual contributors to psychology to individuals *and* a pattern of attitudes or prescriptions. As a consequence of this analysis, the last two chapters and epilogue have been entirely recast and the first chapter now carries a preliminary survey of what is meant by prescriptions and how they shall be used. For the other chapters a prescriptive summary has been added.

Aside from the thousand changes of a few words here and there to try to improve meaning and clarity and some cuts where even I perceived tedium or prolixity, some other revisions are worth mentioning.

A misplaced emphasis on Galen's contribution to the theory of humors has been corrected. The relation of Newton to the British empiricists, especially Locke, has been clarified. Some particulars of the interpretation of Wundtian system have been recast. Some misinterpretations concerning the life of Titchener have been corrected. To Alfred Blumenthal and Rand Evans respectively go my thanks for their reading of the chapters on these last two matters. Needless to say, the errors that remain are my responsibility.

Professional developments and clinical psychology had been covered inadequately; discussion was sacrificed to allow inclusion of more new material.

Since reliance on primary sources had been heavy previously, relatively few new references have been added. Care was taken, however, to refer to significant new biographical material.

Over the years my wife, Hazel, has helped in the preparation of many books and editions. As always, she supplied a sharp eye to at least some of my awkwardness of phraseology and errors of grammar.

My thanks also go to Mrs. Cheryl Phillips, of the clerical staff of the Department of Psychology of the University of Florida, Gainesville, for typing the final manuscript.

Permission to quote material in this book is gratefully acknowledged both to the publishers and to the authors or translators: from L. H. Blum, *Psychoanalytic Theories of Personality,* Copyright 1953, by McGraw-Hill Book Company, Inc.; from E. G. Boring, *A History of Experimental Psychology,* 2nd edition, Copyright 1950 by Appleton-Century Crofts, Inc.; from R. Descartes, *Discourse on the Method of Rightly Conducting the Reason,* translated by E. S. Haldane and G. R. T. Ross, Copyright 1911 by Cambridge University Press; from Theophrastus, *Characters,* translated by J. M. Edmonds, Copyright 1929 by Loeb Classical Library and Harvard University Press.

Robert I. Watson

Gainesville, Florida
February 1, 1977

PREFACE to the Third Edition

Since it seems to have worked reasonably well, the general outline of the second edition has been preserved. Major attention has been devoted to clarification of countless passages. Many chapters have been expanded considerably. Others have been rewritten extensively. Hardly a page of text has escaped some changes. Factual errors have been corrected, and important current references have been added.

The tedium of page after page of type unbroken by headings has been relieved in many chapters. It is hoped that a certain amount of increased comprehension results. It is fitting that the one section on which I tried to find suitable headings and failed deals with the life and interests of William James. Here too much orderliness would have been false to the subject.

Present academic affiliations of our contemporary peripatetic psychologists are reported rather than those of some years ago.

Robert I. Watson

Durham, New Hampshire
March 1, 1971

CONTENTS

xi

Chapter 1

Thales TO Hippocrates:
BEFORE PSYCHOLOGY

"All men by nature desire to know."[1] So reads the first sentence of
Aristotle's *Metaphysics*. A desire to know has served to motivate
philosopher-scientists in their absorption, not only with psychological
matters, but with all fields of knowledge. We can discern other motives
but the search for knowledge is the basic drive implicit throughout this
book.

Aristotle's remark introduces his history of the earliest
science-philosophy, which came into being about 600 B.C. in Ionia,
on the coast of Asia Minor and spread from there to the rest of ancient
Greece. To some extent its study was indebted to even more ancient
civilizations.[2] Fragments of scientific knowledge, what we would call
astronomy, medicine (particularly surgery), and mathematics, were
known to the Egyptians and Babylonians. The recorded achievements of
these civilizations, however, lack continuity and what survives is
inextricably mixed with magic and superstition.

In what sort of world did these Greeks, who desired to know, live?
Ancient Greece, until very recently, had been composed of tribal villages,
and activities still consisted of tilling the fields, bartering in the markets,
engaging in mercantile sea voyages, and tending flocks. People
worshipped in the temples of their choice, went to war, gossiped in the
square, bought and sold slaves, maligned rulers (if the times permitted it),
visited courtesans, and engaged in or watched athletic contests.

Of these aspects of daily life only religion calls for further
examination. It was not that the Greeks (and the Romans after them) were
less religious than the still earlier Egyptian or Oriental peoples. Their
cities abounded with temples and statues of the gods but there was this
difference: the Greeks had no priestly caste to preach a dogma and to
wield political power. Moreover, the priests were not intellectually
influential. In all the written material that has come down to us from the

Graeco-Roman period, there is not a single work by a priest. Men worshipped the family and city divinities and accepted or rejected other gods more or less at individual discretion. Under the circumstances, the possibility of a conflict between the claims of natural and of supernatural knowledge was tremendously reduced. "Naturalism," the belief that nature requires for its operations only principles inherent in nature without appeal to supernatural factors, found a favorable social setting in this environment.

The fragments of the writings of early Greek thinkers show both the breadth of their interests and their cheery obliviousness to incipient divisions between the specialized fields of philosophy and science.[3] Their conception of nature was all-embracing. Science and philosophy were one. To be sure, there were a few different practitioners—physicians, lawyers, and engineers—but philosopher-scientists took as their province the whole of the universe and of man, speculating, observing, and thinking about the universe—every aspect of it that struck their fancy. Their "philosophy," as we would call it, would be distinguished by us from their "science," only by the broad sweep and vagueness of the philosophical assertions. Man, with the whole glorious world before him, was busy surveying the scene, not working out the details. A synthesis of all knowledge seems to have been the goal. In this, the desire to know far outstripped what could be known.

Purism, Nomotheticism, Naturalism, and Qualitativism

To orient ourselves to these beginnings of philosophy-science, let us consult its first history as given by Aristotle. Proceeding from his statement about the desire to know, he makes it clear that the early thinkers were seeking knowledge about nature for its own sake.[4] An attitude favoring purism was advocated, as distinguished from the utilitarian attitude of seeking knowledge for its application. Aristotle also considers the relative values of science, as we would call it, and experience.[5] The former is a knowledge of universals, the latter of individuals. Although, as we shall see, he did not entirely dismiss information about individuals, knowledge and understanding, as he sees them, come from the study of universals. Many, many centuries later this attitude would be called "nomothetic," emphasizing the discovery of generalities, (and general laws), rather than dealing with particular events or individuals (hereafter referred to as "idiographicism"). Aristotle also indicates that the ancients who framed the myths of the gods had a somewhat similar view of nature. The myths may overlap the earliest material he deals with,[6] but he concludes that the childlike quality of these stories minimizes their importance.[7]

A naturalistic attitude prevails in the writings of the first philosophers; also, it is evident that they did not share to any appreciable degree in the anthropomorphic interpretation of the gods put forth by many of their Greek contemporaries.

There are other implicit attitudes guiding their search for wisdom which Aristotle does not discuss. They had a tremendous confidence in their superior ability to reason as compared to relatively little reliance on knowledge obtained from observation through sense perception. They preferred to correct the theories of their predecessors, not by empirical use of new observations, but by pointing out errors in reasoning. This faith in reasoning introduces the conviction that "rationalism," as it came to be called, is the major, if not the exclusive, source of knowledge. Knowledge based on experience, or "empiricism," occurred casually and incidentally while experiment, later the preferred form of empirical methodology, was used very rarely.[8]

The last of these guiding attitudes is so central to the discussion that it may be overlooked. This is the thoroughly qualitative outlook: the early thinkers were searching for the "essence" of things as Aristotle was to call it.[9] A qualitative attitude was advocated rather than a quantitative one based on measurement.

Thales and Molarism, Vitalism, and Deductivism

The first philosopher-scientist, whose thinking exemplified adherence to nomotheticism, naturalism, rationalism, qualitativism, and purism was Thales of Miletus. Virtually nothing is known of his life with any degree of certainty. The facts are intertwined with legends of heroic proportions. He gained his greatest fame by predicting an eclipse that occurred during a battle between the Medes and the Lydians. Even this feat has been demonstrated to be just another legend.

Thales was born about 636 B.C. and was a much older contemporary of Croesus. In fact, he probably embarked with Croesus on the latter's ill-fated attack of Persia. In Miletus, he led what was apparently a very active and, to some extent, a very practical life. Aristotle recounts how Thales took advantage of his knowledge of the stars to foretell a great harvest of olives in the coming year.[10] He managed very cheaply to make deposits on the use of all olive presses during the time of harvest. When his fellow citizens wanted to use these presses at the same time, he rented them at a large profit. Aristotle draws the somewhat disingenuous conclu-

636 B.C.
Contemp.
of
Croesus

sion that Thales did this to show that philosophers could easily be rich if they so desired, but that their true ambitions are of another sort. It is also possible that Thales carried out the transaction in order to make a living. Neither he nor his successors were paid for their philosophical or scientific efforts. They either worked at something else or were supported by inherited wealth. The apocryphal story of how Thales once fell into a well because he was so intent upon gazing at the stars may counterbalance the shrewdness illustrated in the earlier story. At any rate, this anecdote is likely to have launched the first absent-minded professor joke.

We owe to Thales the recognition that to solve a problem, one must look for principles on which to base a solution. In this spirit he approached the problem of the nature of the world itself. Despite the multiplicity of appearances, he assumed that there must be some basic unity of substance in the universe. He reached the conclusion that water is that original substance, because from water all other things—earth, air, and living things—are derived. The reasons for his choice cannot be established with any assurance, although some of the phenomena on which he must have based his conclusions seem evident. Water is the only substance readily known to man in the three states of solid, liquid, and gas. Rising steam had been recognized as the same substance as the water within the kettle since that historic occasion when the first kettle boiled over. There are manifestations of water in snow, ice, clouds, fog, dew, rain, hail, and in the seas and rivers. Water indeed appears to be everywhere.

At the very dawn of philosophic-scientific thinking a molaristic attitude of such embracing totality as never to be surpassed had been advanced. The definition of a molaristic attitude, a preference for wholes rather than parts, for relatively larger rather than smaller units, seems pallid against the sheer scope of this order. The very boldness of the view that everything is water does help to bring out what is meant by this attitude. To be sure there were molecular units in the various examples advanced. But they were but parts of the whole which was that which received emphasis.

The early Greeks held the conviction that man is composed of the same substance as other entities and, along with all animate beings, is part and parcel of the material world. The characteristics of man were used by them to elucidate the nature of world, just as other matter was shown to help explain the nature of man. They saw the world as macrocosm, man as microcosm, each serving to give some account of the other.

It is not surprising that Thales' choice of the ultimate matter—

water—was influenced by biological observations. A passage from Aristotle suggests that Thales viewed the whole world as alive and animated.[11] "All things are full of gods." Aristotle believed that Thales thought water the ultimate substance because all living things depend on water for nourishment, and because the sperm is moist. Considerable evidence from mythology shows that water was believed by the Greeks to be the generative or life-giving fluid.[12] According to Aristotle, Thales thought that the magnetic stone must possess life because it is able to move iron; and that the soul is motivational in nature as well. Thales is said to have reached this view not only from knowledge of the properties of a magnet but also from studying the attraction of briskly rubbed amber for straw and dried leaves. Working with both the magnet and amber and finding the same manifestation of movement, he may have concluded that *all* objects had the power of movement provided one could hit upon the way to bring that movement about, and inanimate objects, through this power must be alive. This line of reasoning probably led Thales to adopt a "vitalistic" position, a belief that living things possess some sort of life principle, since their activities are not explicable by what we would call physical-chemical constituents. (The opposite approach is commonly termed "mechanistic.")

Although the evidence is scanty, Thales seems to have proceeded deductively, that is, having decided that water was the universal principle of all things, he sought out instances that supported this view. Aristotle credits Socrates, who came later, with being the first to use induction,[13] that is, proceeding from individual cases to the universal.[14]

Thales had propounded the problem of the nature of matter and indicated the direction for those who followed.

Later thinkers offered alternatives to Thales' premise that water was the basis of all matter. The nature of the primary substances was disputed by many who came after him.[15] Anaximenes (c. 540 B.C.) argued that air was the primary material since, aside from its basic state, it existed in the more rarified condition of fire and in the more concentrated forms of earth and of water. Heraclitus (c. 500 B.C.) opted for fire, prompted probably by a desire to account for change, which concerned him more than stability. "Everchanging" seems to have been his metaphor for change, epitomized in by far the best known Heraclitean fragment, "It is not possible to step twice into the same river."[16] Empedocles (c. 400 B.C.) brought together the earlier claims for a primordial substance by advancing the argument that each of the four elements—earth, air, fire, and water—was a primary substance. In the centuries to come, he was to receive the greatest continued agreement.

The nature of the soul concerned many thinkers. It was often dealt with as an aspect of this problem of the constituent character of the universe.[17] The question arose of whether or not there are two fundamentally different substances, body and soul (referred to as dualism), or one substance, either body or soul (monism).

Before considering the answers to this question something should be said about the Greek views of the soul at this time. It cannot be overemphasized that "soul" is one of the most elusive and complicated terms in the history of thought. The Greeks in all walks of life regarded the soul as the source of consciousness and life. A man was thought to be alive if he could move his limbs and other parts of his body; fainting meant that his soul had withdrawn temporarily; and death, that his soul had withdrawn permanently. Soul was often thought of as a vital principle or life force and had no necessary connection with theological considerations. Rather, soul epitomized the essence of life. The Greeks' view of soul shaped their perspective on the process of living things. Succinctly, conscious experiences were thought to relate to a source, the soul, which initiated movement.

The Greeks accepted what came to be called a two-aspect theory of soul, although it sometimes seems as if two distinct souls were being discussed.[18] One aspect of the soul, *thymos*, especially concerns us, as students of psychology. It is involved in thought and emotion, and perishes with the body. The "diaphragm" or the lungs were often conceived of as organs of consciousness. How could such a view be held? As Onians put it, to the ancient Greeks, thoughts are words, words are breath (*pneuma*), and the organs of the mind, consequently, are the lungs.[19] Such a theory, bizarre though it may seem to us, is rendered somewhat more plausible when it is remembered that it arose at a time when words were always spoken, and never written down.

The other aspect of the soul, *psyche*, was considered to be immortal, but in the earliest traditions—in Homer, for example—after death *psyche* maintains no memory of its earthly existence and, in fact, in life has no concern with waking experience. It follows that psychologists, whose very name is derived from the word *psyche*, more accurately should have been called "thymotologists," since conscious experience is their concern, while immortality is not!

What was the interest of the philosopher-scientists in this matter of the soul? Their concern was the actual construction of the soul, whether it was made up of one or more of the elements. As noted before, Thales held that "all things are full of gods."[20] Life properties were an integral part of his conceptions of all matter. He is also credited by many philosophers with the idea that soul has its essence in moving and is, in itself, self-moving.[21] Those who came after him are more specific.

Anaximenes assigned a bodily function to the soul, conceiving of it as the life-giving principle of his basic constituent, breath.[22] To others, the soul's locus of function was found in cosmological molar principles. In searching for unity in the diversity that makes up the world, Heraclitus arrived at the conclusion that the essence of all things must be fire, which transforms and consumes heterogeneous matter into itself. Aristotle notes that this fire is soul to Heraclitus.[23] In keeping with the prevailing opinion, Heraclitus related soul to movement, however, he is not known to have given the soul a specific bodily locus.

Democritus and Empiricism, Determinism, and Mechanism

Although "rationalism," a method of using reasoning to achieve wisdom, was almost unanimously accepted, there was some doubt about its effectiveness. Philosophers could argue that opponents were fallacious in their reasoning but they could do no more. Moreover, no matter how personally convinced of the truth of their particular position, they did not necessarily convince others. Its major alternative, which showed hesitant beginnings at this time, was "empiricism," the conviction that a major source of knowledge was experience. During this period empiricism did not reach the level of a methodological imperative. Instead, it was treated as a problem of knowledge—that is, whether or not the contents of the mind are derived from experience. Experience and the mind, as it were, were being considered rationally! According to earlier claims, knowledge is derived only through the doorway of sense. Heraclitus accepted empiricism as a guide, but went on to say that, while the senses are necessary, the mind alone can apprehend the law that governs change.[24] Protagoras (c. 430 B.C.), a Sophist and an older contemporary of Plato, reduced all psychic life to sensations. His famous saying, "man is the measure of all things,"[25] has been interpreted to mean that a given individual's perceptions are true for him but if there are several opinions about the same external object, there is no way of deciding which is true.[26]

Democritus was another older contemporary of Plato whose thought flourished about 420 B.C. He did not agree that all sensations are relative to the sentient subject, for instance, that an object could be truly sweet for X and truly bitter for Y. *All* sensations are false, declared Democritus, for there is nothing real corresponding to them outside the subject, nothing that we can know for sure. There is color, sweet, cold, and the like, true enough, but they are caused by something else, the atoms in the void, which are not established by sense.[27] Democritus felt that the senses give us no information about reality, that tastes and smells are subjective. Nearly 2000 years later these sensations were christened "the secondary qualities" and became important for Galileo, Descartes, Locke, and other moderns. We shall return to this issue of the fallibility of the senses after going into Democritus' theory of atoms in greater detail.

In his search for the ultimate principle, Democritus postulated the existence of atoms—tiny particles of matter in ceaseless motion.[28] He conceived of the matter of the universe as being entirely made up of these atoms, and all else as merely empty space. The interaction of atoms was the exclusive source of all phenomena. The world of Democritus ran itself. Naturalistic movement alone was sufficient; there was no necessity for postulating a prime mover, or a vitalistic principle. The service of atoms was accountable for and determined all movement and contact between atoms. There is little doubt that Democritus must be identified as an exponent of "determinism," the attitude that explains events in terms of antecedents. He is a "mechanist" as well, since physical atoms to him are all that is necessary to account for nonliving and living things alike, without appealing to a vitalistic principle.

When applied to the problem of perception, Democritus's mechanical concept gives us what may be called the first psychological theory of the mind. Sensation and perception involve contact of nonbodily atoms with those of the body. Their interaction produces an impression which spreads or reverberates throughout the body. An external object is perceived because its atoms pass in this way through the organs of the body to the "mind."[29] The mind itself is made up of atoms distinguishable from other atoms in terms of degree only, being of a spherical shape, having greater rapidity of motion, and showing a "subtlety" of action.[30] For the atoms of the external object to make an impression on those of the body, the former must possess a certain minimum strength. Although it was not understood in this fashion at the time, much later this theory was conceptualized as the sensory threshold (See Fechner, page 245). The mind itself rises from the senses and there is no absolute separation of sense and thought.[31]

To Democritus the various senses reduced to touch because no matter what the sensation—vision, smell, taste, or whatever—the atoms of the object being sensed were interpreted as having come into contact with the atoms of the body of the perceiver. Objects were thought to produce tastes in accordance with their shapes: a sour taste, for example, being produced by atoms that are angular, thin, small, and winding.[32]

Because the source of the sensation is at a distance from the observer, vision demanded a more elaborate account. He said that the seen object sends off images that mold the atoms of the air to the shape of the object; this air "figure-copy" touches the atoms of the eye from whence it is conveyed to the mind.

This is the original statement of the "representative" theory which holds that perception represents an object by being similar to it. A faint representation of the object emanates from the object and is conducted to the experiencing element of the body, the mind. Variations of this theory that the perception of an object is similar to the object proved so appealing as to linger in scientific circles until the end of the last century, despite repeated cogent objections. It may still be the view of the man in the street to suppose an object gives off some sort of emanation that forms a pattern of size, shape, and color, and that this pattern once impressed on the eyes is carried to the brain where this unchanged pattern is "seen."

Democritus argued that the senses are deceptive and not even true to the individual having the perception. His reasoning was that, because all matter is composed of atoms, there are always atoms in immediate proximity to any object. The atoms from a sounding object, for example, may mix with extraneous atoms that lie between the perceiver and the object, interfering with the person's perception. The senses are therefore deceptive: neither always nor under all circumstances do they portray the external world correctly.

The early Greek philosopher-scientists considered the senses singly and collectively and in relation to reason. What we would call feeling, experiencing pleasure and pain, was neglected by them; at least they did not recognize it as an issue worthy of attention. At the time there was no single word that existed in ancient Greek to define feeling as an effective experience.[33] One word carried not only the affective or pleasure-pain motif but also a cognitive meaning. It was similar to what in English is expressed by the word "feeling" when we combine the two connotations: "I have a feeling of danger"—which conveys the sense of impending danger as well as the expression of an unpleasant emotion. These early thinkers did explore cursorily the nature of man's desires, but specific emotions, such as courage, were dealt with only in passing. Nothing approaching a detailed, systematic, or ordered view of the interrelation of sense, thought, desire, and emotion was presented.

When Aristotle wrote the history of these first philosophers about one hundred years after their heyday, he referred to them as advocates of a "type of philosophy."[34] If one focuses on the individuals in their collective aspect we can speak of a group united by a common desire for knowledge and the acceptance of certain shared attitudes. It follows that a process of socialization had taken place. They had learned their roles as philosophers from those who went before. True, it was a tenuous group, scattered along two centuries of time and various parts of Greece. Any record of communication that took place is lost in obscurity, but a role group they were. In addition to those named or yet to be named, there were at least a dozen or so others within the group. Some were known to have been students of Thales, Heraclitus, and others. Moreover, there were surely silent followers, some silent because that was their role, others because their contributions were lost to time.

Meanwhile thought and events of significance to psychology were emerging from another source—medicine.

Hippocrates and the Naturalistic Contribution from Medicine and the Beginnings of Idiographicism

Medicine and psychology share an interest in the functioning of the human body and mind, and by the very nature of their art, medical practitioners must pay attention to the individual. The physician is committed to an idiographic attitude—he must explain and treat the problems of individual patients. Treatment was to be determined by symptoms, not by some deduction from an abstract principle of the nature of man. This stands in sharp contrast to the nomothetic attitude of earlier philosophers who sought general understanding rather than knowledge of particulars. But the psychology to come would encompass both attitudes. Moreover, modern psychology includes within its scope mind-body problems of a psychosomatic nature. On these two counts, then, medicine is relevant to the history of psychology.

It is in the *Odyssey* of Homer that we first hear of Greek medical practitioners. They made their way through the land—coming into homes to sell their services to those who had use for them, and then moved on.[35] The sign of a highly successful practitioner was the fame that preceded him wherever he went and that lingered until his return. Asclepius, the first Greek physician of whom we have knowledge, was just such a physician. His fame was so great that after his death he was deified with over three hundred temples erected in his honor. His priests jealously guarded their knowledge, passing it on only to those of the next generation whom they initiated into its mysteries. Persons from all walks of life went to the temples of Asclepius. Indeed, Socrates' last words dealt with his debt to Asclepius: "Crito," he said, "we owe a cock to Asclepius; will you remember to pay the debt?"[36]

Although instances of surgical operations were not uncommon, the percentage of cures of blindness and of lameness reported in records that survive seems very high, which suggests that many of these maladies had a psychosomatic basis. A favorable receptivity to the suggestive influences of temple healing may have been due to the reports of wonderful cures, and the use of rituals such as the wait to be received, the period of purification before admission to the sanctuary, the wearing of special robes, and the drinking of sacred waters.[37] The peak of the treatment was the incubation, a period of sleep in the sanctuary. Several characteristic phenomena were associated with this. The patient for example might see an apparition of a god and receive from him a message specific to his illness. He might have a dream in which a priest or a god would tell him what to do (an oracle), a dream foretelling the future (a vision), or even one in which the cure itself occurred. A certain amount of rational treatment, such as occasional use of drugs, was combined with these magical practices, but surgical treatment, bleeding, and massage were left to lay hands. As a consequence, the medical experience accumulated by the priests was almost exclusively "psychological" in nature. Faith healing, tempered by a bit of scanty scientific observation, epitomized the approach of temple medicine.

Gradually, a new and more naturalistic and rationally based medicine, relatively divorced from the supernatural and irrational aspects of temple medicine, began to emerge. One of its founders was Alcmaeon of Croton, a physician who lived at the beginning of the fifth century B.C. Almost nothing is known of his life and only sparse fragments of his writings remain. Many of these fragments are of psychological and physiological import. After discovering passages from the eyes to the brain, Alcmaeon[38] boldly concluded that not only did the brain receive perceptions of vision, audition, and olfaction, but it was also the seat of thought. And because he considered it the central organ of intellectual activity, Alcmaeon called the brain the soul. This was his way of naming the vital principle or source of life. Alcmaeon did not use the word "soul" in a theological sense and there was no necessary connotation of immortality. Soul was a convenient name for the central psychological agency. As a matter of fact, he did accept the immortality of the soul, for he considered it to be self-moving,[39] but his naturalistic description of it was divorced from his speculations about immortality.

Alcmaeon made the advance of unifying the two entities or aspects of the soul, formerly localized in the head and lungs, into one entity centering in the head—one soul, which performed all mental functions. Alcmaeon taught that the brain, where all sensations are "somehow fitted together," contains the governing faculty of the soul.[40] This brain is also the seat of thought; it serves to store and arrange perceptions, and is responsible for memory and belief. Alcmaeon held that sensations reach the brain through the medium of channels which start with the organs of sense. These passages were not the nerves as such, but, rather, channels for breath, the *pneuma*, mentioned earlier in connection with the *thymos*.

Thinking and perceiving were recognized by him as separate processes. To put it in his terminology, Alcmaeon made a distinction between intelligence and sensation, claiming that man alone understands, whereas other creatures have sense perception but are without understanding.[41] This distinction between perception, or what is acquired through sensory experience, and understanding, which is independent of sensory experience, was to become a major concern for the Greeks, reaching its culmination in the formulations of Plato.

Alcmaeon's work on the senses was based upon empirical observation of surgical operations. Tradition has it that he was the first to undertake the excision of a human eye.[42] His anatomical studies led him to the statement that the eye is enclosed in a membrane and is connected with the brain by "light-bearing paths" that join behind the forehead. That these paths (the optic nerves) join, he showed by dissection. He also observed that the eyes move together, not separately. The function of seeing, he stated, was brought about by the water and fire in the eye. Fire was thought to be present because when the eye is struck by a blow one sees light (intraocular light); the "water" of which he speaks is the aqueous humor. His theory attempted to combine the concept of vision as a radiation from the eye and the idea that it is an image reflected in the eye. Actually, these two notions are incompatible. The visual ray hypothesis, which concludes that seeing is an act of the eye, and the theory that the water of the eye, the aqueous humor, is a mirror that reflects objects cannot be reconciled.

In Alcmaeon's medical philosophy, health and disease are matters of equilibrium—the first a balance, the second, a rupture of that balance. This equilibrium, or lack of it, rests upon paired qualities—wet and dry, cold and hot, bitter and sweet. If each pair is in balance, we have health; if one quality predominates, we have sickness. Health viewed as equilibrium was to have far-reaching influence in the centuries to come through the Hippocratic doctrine of humors.

Although Hippocrates was an older contemporary of Plato—he was born about 460 B.C.—our information about his life is astonishingly meager. A few facts seem clear if we trust the account of Plato, who wrote that Hippocrates was a native of Cos and an Asclepiad, i.e., a member of a family or guild that could trace its origin back to Asclepius.[43] A number of medical schools had grown up in Greece in the course of the fifth century. The one of greatest fame was on the island of Cos where Hippocrates had apparently studied. He became well known as he traveled from city to city practicing and teaching. Although he had been a student at an Asclepiad school, no traces of Asclepiad mysticism can be found in his works.[44] Seemingly, he never recommended the use of temple medicine, despite his firm belief in the healthful influence of the environment as exemplified in air, water, and place.

Over the centuries his fame grew. A host of legends about him developed. These legends would add to his already distinguished descent from Asclepius an ancestry going back to Hercules as well. One account of his clinical acumen involves his remedy for plague-ridden Athens. Because blacksmiths alone seemed immune to the disease, Hippocrates suggested that fires be lighted in all public squares. The plague disappeared and his reputation increased. By the time of Galen, Hippocrates had become the prototype of all physicians.

The Hippocratic *Writings* consists of materials that today would be called textbooks, papers, case histories, speeches, extracts, aphorisms, monographs, and manuals; they encompass the entire field of medicine.[45] The Hippocratic Oath is probably universally known. The *Aphorisms,* with adages concerning symptoms, diagnosis of disease, and the art of healing, opens with its most famous sentence, "Art is long and life is short." It includes the history of medicine; the influence of air, climate, and locale upon disease; the treatment of acute disease; epidemics; injuries to the head; ulcers; and hemorrhoids.

In his history, *On Ancient Medicine,*[46] he states unequivocally his objection to earlier medicine: it depended upon the rationalistic method of the philosophers of the past who "first laid down for themselves some hypotheses to their argument, such as hot, or cold, or moist, or dry, or whatever else they choose. . . ."[47] This dogmatic starting point is false, he asserts. Medicine has a long-established existence of its own as an art. Each physician starts by learning what others have learned and then goes on to apply the empirical procedure. Of particular relevance to the history of psychology is his paper, *On the Sacred Disease,*[48] which provides illustrations of his empirical interpretation of disease. This "sacred disease" was epilepsy, then as now frightening to the beholder. The seizure of *grand mal,* the falling, the frothing at the mouth, the loss of consciousness, can easily strike terror in witnesses to an attack. On regaining consciousness, the victim often complains of being buffeted by blows from an unknown source. These dramatic phenomena suggested the intervention of a spirit possessing the body of the sufferer. One must therefore admire the author who wrote sturdily and without compromise that "this disease seems to me to be no more divine than others, but it has a nature, such as other diseases have, and a cause whence it originates, . . . hereditary, like that of other diseases."[49] He indicates that epilepsy is caused in the brain. Even more specifically he relates it to a humoral congestion in the brain that makes affected individuals phlegmatic, and which, in turn, brings on epileptic attacks.

The functioning of the humors just alluded to gave rise to the major theory of individual bodily function that was to dominate medical thought for many centuries to come. Polybos, who was Hippocrates' son-in-law, is supposed to have written the Nature of Man, the Hippocratic treatise concerning the theory of humors.[50] In propounding the theory, this Hippocratic writer implicitly accepts the view of Empedocles that the universe is composed of air, earth, fire, and water, which combine to produce all substances. These entities are unchangeable; water cannot become earth, nor earth water. By mingling, they form concrete objects. Corresponding respectively to these elements are the four combinations of qualities; warm-moist, cold-dry, warm-dry, and cold-moist. With this as its base, the theory postulates that these elements and qualities take bodily form in the respective humors—blood, black bile, yellow bile, and phlegm. These humors make up the constitution of the body and cause both disease and health. Deficiency or excess of one or another of the humors causes pain. Some disorders are evidenced by the appearance of liquid excretions from the body of the sick person, as from a cold in the head; or when the skin is broken and blood comes forth; or, in the case of severe injury, where other fluids of the body become visible. Relatively direct reasoning would lead one to conclude that these fluids are of considerable importance in the economy of the body. To Hippocrates, the theory of humors was a theory of disease. Only much later did Galen relate it to personality, by adding to it in a relatively systematic fashion the theory of physical temperaments (p. 84).

According to Hippocrates, therefore, a disease of an individual is a disturbance of the harmony of the elements as manifested in the humors. Hippocrates agreed with Alcmaeon that cures depend upon restoration of the disturbed harmony. The humors tended toward equilibrium, a state to which they ordinarily returned because of the body's inherent tendency to recover from illness or injury. The concept of the crisis, or critical turning point, was utilized; it was the task of the physician to assist nature by bringing his remedies to bear upon the patient at these critical times.[51]

The Hippocratic school was the first to relate to the brain the conscious life in its entirety, including the emotions.[52] It discussed this relation of the emotions to the brain in specific terms. Over-heating of the brain was thought to cause terror and fear, as shown by the flushed face. Conversely, when the brain is unduly cold, anxiety and grief result. Too much bile causes overheating; too much phlegm causes overcooling.

Nerves had no place in the Hippocratic writings, and there was no distinct concept of the functioning of muscles; in fact, muscles and tendons were often confused.[53] The coordination of parts of the body in movement was explained by the doctrine of "sympathy," or "consensus," an immaterial connection between the parts of the body which brought about movement. Knowledge of the structural basis of sympathy was lacking; it did not even occur to these theorists that such structure might be sought.

Overview

The philosopher-scientists and physicians of ancient Greece were concerned with natural rather than supernatural explanations of life and matter. They were convinced that both the world and man could be understood in terms of nature. According to Aristotle, theologians had treated science as myth while the philosopher-scientists set forth their theories in a demonstrable form.[54] Life for Thales and those who came after him was not, as it was for Homer, explained by the capricious whims of the gods. The Hippocratic writers similarly rejected supernatural influences in the causes and treatment of disease. A naturalistic attitude was becoming evident.

Thales and the other Greek pioneers were the first to pursue an interest in nature for its own sake—a puristic attitude. Before them, thinkers such as the poet Hesiod, and, undoubtedly, farmers and sailors, had been interested in natural events. But their interest in nature must have been secondary, for it was dominated by other more important utilitarian interests. Physicians also adopted a utilitarian attitude. In psychological matters this was to become, never the dominant attitude but, rather, counter-dominant to an emphasis on purism.

The philosopher-scientists advocated a nomothetic approach in their search for the basic constituent of the universe. In some measure the idiographic attitude of the physicans served as a balance. Both attitudes had their first champions at that time, although, then as now, the nomothetic-idiographic distinction was a matter of emphasis, not an absolute distinction. As was to happen again and again, a pattern of nomotheticism with purism, coexisted with another pattern of idiographicism accompanying utilitarianism. Emphasis upon rationalism and a deductive attitude, that is, still another pattern starting with a general principle and then finding incidents, also seemed to characterize the way of proceeding.

This early scientific and philosophical thought was thoroughly qualitative in that it took into account only similarities and differences in kinds or essences. It was not the way of thinking alone that prevented adoption of a quantitative attitude, that is, a demand that what is dealt with be countable or measurable. This modern facet of scientific thought was also prevented by the early Greeks' inability to conceive of, or to apply to scientific problems, the mathematics at their disposal, and the absence of any appreciable number of measuring instruments, aside from a few for astronomical calculations and devices. Attitudes would have to change before even the need for such instruments would be appreciated fully. At any rate, it was not until the dawn of modern science that quantitativism became an integral part of scientific investigation.

The experimental method was used very rarely. To the very limited extent that they adhered to an empirical attitude, these pioneers may be said to have depended upon "nature's experiments," the phenomena of the earth, of the stars, and of man that occurred naturally. Observation, as yet almost unaided by instruments, was the method from which most of our first scientific knowledge was derived. After all, the function of experiment is to direct observation, not replace it. Observation may occur without experimental variations of conditions, and some of the Greeks certainly were acute observers. Hailing them as the first scientists in the modern connotation of the word would be a mistake; they did not generalize cautiously from observation and experiment. On the contrary, they proceeded by analogical reasoning to reach fantastically extensive generalizations. Sometimes there was a lucky hit, sometimes not. Democritus, for example, allowed his reason to outrun his senses, having no means of observation by which to verify his views concerning the atom. The first inquiries about scientific problems nevertheless had been made. These scientist-philosophers wanted to account for the basic nature of the world, which they interpreted as mechanical. The mechanistic theory of Democritus was the most significant for the future—atoms differing only in size and shape, their contact accounting for movement.

Only the first gropings toward a dualism involving man and world or body and mind as separate entities was evident. The predominant view is exemplified by the lack of distinction between matter and what we today would call the secondary qualities of matter. To the early Greeks, "heat" had as much reality, in the sense of existing independently of the observer, as did the motion of the flames; to those who came later, heat was an experience. On the other hand, the view of Democritus that both body and mind are composed of atoms gave a rather clear expression to a monism of a mechanistic-materialistic sort.

Many of the problems of importance to the philosopher-scientists, in point of fact, were psychological in nature, provided one recognizes that the dominant contents of psychological study well into the modern period were conceived as subjective. Contentual subjectivity is an attitude implicit in much of what has been discussed—in dualism of soul or mind and body and in perception, to name two obvious examples. Contentual objectivity as expressed in the study of behavior so characteristic of current psychology, received some incidental mention in the symptomatology of disease but hardly anywhere else in Greek thought.

Hereafter, these and other attitudes expressed will be referred to as prescriptions, the term adopted by the writer since these attitudes serve a guidance function.[55]

Some prescriptions are primarily methodological, expressing favored ways of proceeding, such as the use of rational rather than empirical means of study. These methodological preferences are shared by later scientists and philosophers. Other prescriptions are concerned with definition and classification of psychological phenomena. For example, contentual subjectivism, the idea that psychological data is mental, will be found to dominate for many, many centuries; contentual objectivism, that is, considering psychological data as behavioral, became prominent only during this century.

Many, but not all, prescriptions have already been referred to in this account. For convenience they are all presented in Table 1 (p. 18). The arrangement of these prescriptions in contrasting pairs makes for clarity, since one is given not only a summary of what the attitude is, but what it is not. In almost all instances, at one time or another, the pairs were seen as diametrically opposed to one another. However, it must be added that on other occasions interrelation within pairs and in patterns of prescriptive allegiance exist which are not bipolar. In what follows some of these other relationships will be identified briefly.

In succeeding centuries, as the nature and the form of expression of both methodological and contentual prescriptions change, their relation with one another shift, new names are used, different patterns of dominance among prescriptions occur, and polarity, so far stressed, gives way to integration. But there is still discernible continuity of attitudes. A prescriptive attitude as conceived here has, in addition to its already familiar guidance function, a second essential characteristic—

Table 1   The Prescriptions of Psychology Arranged in Contrasting Pairs

---

Conscious mentalism–Unconscious mentalism (emphasis on awareness of mental structure or activity/unawareness)

Contentual objectivism–Contentual subjectivism (psychological data viewed as behavior of individual/as mental structure or activity of individual)

Determinism–Indeterminism (human events completely explicable in terms of antecedents/not completely so explicable)

Empiricism–Rationalism (major, if not exclusive source of knowledge is experience/is reason)

Functionalism–Structuralism (psychological categories are activities/are contents)

Inductivism–Deductivism (investigations begun with facts or observations/with assumed established truths)

Mechanism–Vitalism (activities of living beings completely explicable by physiochemical constituents/not so explicable)

Methodological objectivism–Methodological subjectivism (use of methods open to verification by another competent observer/not so open)

Molecularism–Molarism (psychological data most aptly described in terms of relatively small units/relatively large units)

Monism–Dualism (fundamental principle or entity in universe is of one kind/is of two kinds, mind and matter)

Naturalism–Supernaturalism (nature requires for its operation and explanation only principles found within it/requires transcendent guidance as well)

Nomotheticism–Idiographicism (emphasis upon discovering general laws/upon explaining particular events or individuals)

Peripheralism–Centralism (stress upon psychological events taking place at periphery of body/within the body)

Purism–Utilitarianism (seeking of knowledge for its own sake/for its usefulness in other activities)

Quantitativism–Qualitativism (stress upon knowledge which is countable or measurable/upon that which is different in kind or essence)

Rationalism–Irrationalism (emphasis upon data supposed to follow dictates of good sense and intellect/intrusion or domination of emotive and conative factors upon intellectual processes)

Staticism–Developmentalism (emphasis upon cross-sectional view/upon changes with time)

Staticism–Dynamicism (emphasis upon enduring aspects/upon change and factors making for change)

---

persistence over time. We are at the very beginning of a temporal span but even in this period many prescriptions have made their first appearance and even exhibited change. Many will still be evident when we consider the contemporary scene.

Reference Style

A full reference is given the first time a work is cited, including the particular edition consulted. Whenever possible, the date of original publication is given. When the work is cited again, either the author and an abbreviated title or the author's surname is repeated.

Editions from *The Great Books of the Western World* are used, except when more suitable editions were found (e.g., with Berkeley). Psychologists should feel a certain pride in their field since fifteen of the fifty volumes in this series are pertinent. Moreover, James and Freud are the most modern included.

If more specificity seems appropriate, the authors' division in terms of part, section, chapter, and part chapter are given. Direct quotations carry a page reference to the particular edition cited. References to Plato are given in the numbering system of Stephanus which is standard in almost all editions and translations. For the works of Aristotle, following the usual convention the page and column numbers are of the Berlin edition of the Greek text, edited by Immanual Becker.

Excerpts from the collection of readings, R. J. Herrnstein and E. G. Boring, eds., *A Source Book in the History of Psychology* (Cambridge: Harvard University Press, 1965), are cited whenever relevant. The full reference is not repeated; only the numbers of the excerpts are given.

In this book somewhat more than seventy individuals no longer living receive detailed attention during the modern period of the last four centuries. The major primary references of and secondary references to their work are to be found in R. I. Watson, *Eminent Contributors to Psychology*, Vols. 1 and 2 (New York: Springer, 1974, 1976).

References

1. R. M. Hutchins, ed., *The Great Books of the Western World*, Vols. VIII–IX, Works of Aristotle (including *Politics, Metaphysics, Topics On the Soul*), translated under the direction of W. D. Ross (Chicago: Encyclopaedia Britannica, 1952) (c. 340–322 B.C.). *Metaphysics*, 980a.
2. A masterly exposition of Babylonian astronomy and mathematics is in Otto Neugebauer, *The Exact Sciences in Antiquity*, 2nd ed. (Providence: Brown University Press, 1957). He shows that there was little contact with the Greeks before the diffusion of culture created by the conquests of Alexander the Great which did not begin until the third century B.C.

3. The primary sources are most completely and carefully collected in H. Diels, *Fragmente der Vorsokratiker*, W. Krantz, ed., 5th ed. (Berlin: Weidman, 1934–1938). An English translation of the fragments by Kathleen Freeman is available in her *Ancilla to the Pre-Socratic Philosophers* (Cambridge: Harvard University Press, 1957). She also gives a detailed exposition of these fragments and early reports in *The Pre-Socratic Philosophers: A Companion to Diels, Fragmente der Vorsokratiker*, 3rd ed. (Oxford: Basil Blackwell, 1953). The most complete and therefore the most important work on the lives of the Greek philosophers that has survived from antiquity is Diogenes Laertius' *Lives and Opinions of Eminent Philosophers*, trans., R. D. Hicks (Cambridge: Harvard University Press, 1925), III. Although frequently inaccurate, it remains our only source for many details. Most of what appears here concerning the works of Thales, Democritus, Heraclitus, Parmenides, Empedocles and Alcmaeon is derived from these sources and from the Works of Aristotle, cited above.

4. Aristotle *Metaphysics* 983.

5. *Ibid.*, 981a 13–982b 27.

6. *Ibid.*, 982b

7. *Ibid.*, 1000a

8. For discussion of this point see W. A. Heidel, *The Heroic Age of Science* (Baltimore: Williams & Wilkins, 1933), and M. Clagett, *Greek Science in Antiquity* (New York: Abelard–Schuman, 1955).

9. *Ibid.*, 1028a 10ff.

10. Aristotle *Politics* 1259a 8.

11. Aristotle *On the Soul* 411a 8.

12. B. B. Onians, *The Origins of European Thought, About the Body, the Mind, the Soul, the World, Time and Fate* (Cambridge: Harvard University Press, 1951).

13. Aristotle *Metaphysics* 1078b.

14. Aristotle *Topics* viii, 156a.

15. See reference 3.

16. Heraclitus, in Freeman, *Companion*, No. 91

17. Aristotle *On the Soul* 430b–411a.

18. Onians, *op. cit.*

19. *Ibid.*

20. Aristotle *On the Soul* 411a.

21. Freeman, *Companion*.

22. Anaximenes, in Diels, *Vorsokratiker*, Nos. 22, 23.
23. Aristotle *On the Soul* 405a 25–28.
24. Heraclitus, in Freeman, *Ancilla*, p. 118.
25. Protagoras, in Diels, *Vorsokratiker*, No. 1.
26. Freeman, *Companion*, p. 348.
27. Democritus, in Diels, *Vorsokratiker*, No. 9.
28. Freeman, *Ancilla*, pp. 299–303.
29. Aristotle is the authority for the statement that Democritus conceived mind and soul as one and the same (*On the Soul* 405a 8–13).
30. *Ibid.*, 403b 28–404a 16.
31. Democritus, in Diels, *Vorsokratiker*, No. 125.
32. Theophrastus *De Sensu* Sec. 49–83.
33. J. I. Beare, *Greek Theories of Elementary Cognition from Alcmaeon to Aristotle* (Oxford: Clarendon Press, 1906).
34. Aristotle *Metaphysics* 983b 21.
35. H. Gomperz, "Problems and Methods of Early Greek Science," *Journal of the History of Ideas*, IV (1943): 161–176.
36. R. M. Hutchins, ed., *The Great Books of the Western World*, Vol. VII, Plato, *Dialogues*, trans. B. Jowett (Chicago: Encyclopaedia Britannica, 1952) (c. 390–348 B.C.). *Phaedo* 118a.
37. H. Ellenberger, "The Ancestry of Dynamic Psychotherapy," *Bulletin of the Menninger Clinic*, XX (1956): 281–299.
38. Alcmaeon, in Diels, *Vorsokratiker*, Nos. 5–11.
39. Aristotle *On the Soul* 405a 29–34.
40. Alcmaeon, in Diels, *Vorsokratiker*, No. 5.
41. Alcmaeon, in Freeman, *Ancilla*, No. 1a.
42. Alcmaeon, in Diels, *Vorsokratiker*, No. 10.
43. Plato *Protagoras* 311; *Phaedrus* 270.
44. E. T. Withington, "The Asclepiadae and the Priests of Asclepius," C. Singer, ed., *Studies in the History and Method of Science* (Oxford: Oxford University Press, 1921), pp. 192–205.
45. Writings of Hippocrates, trans. F. Adams, in R. M. Hutchins, ed., *Great Books of the Western World*, Vol. X., (c. 400 B.C.) pp. 1–160.
46. Hippocrates *On Ancient Medicine*, pp. 1–9.
47. *Ibid.*, p. 1
48. Hippocrates *On the Sacred Disease*, pp. 154–160.
49. *Ibid.*, p. 155
50. Hippocrates, "The Nature of Man," J. Chadwick and

W. N. Mann, eds., *The Medical Works of Hippocrates* (Oxford: Blackwell, 1959), pp. 202–213.

51. Hippocrates *Of The Epidemics*, pp. 44–63.
52. Hippocrates *On the Sacred Disease*, pp. 159–160.
53. F. Fearing, *Reflex Action* (New York: Hafner Press, 1930), p. 10.
54. Aristotle *Metaphysics* 980a–993a.
55. The most pertinent references on prescriptive theory by the writer are "Psychology: A prescriptive science," *American Psychologist*, 22 (1967): 435–443; "The individual, social, educational, economic and political conditions for the original practices of detection and utilization of individual aptitude differences," (*Colloques: Textes des Rapports XIIe Congrès International d'Histoire des Sciences*. Paris: Michel, 1968), pp. 355–368; "Prescriptions as operative in the history of psychology," *Journal of the History of the Behavioral Sciences*, VII (1971): 311–322.

Chapter 2

Plato:
BEFORE PSYCHOLOGY

Plato lived during the Golden Age of Greece and saw it come to an end. His lifetime spans the period between the death of Pericles and Athenian acceptance of Macedonian rule.[1] During most of Plato's life, Athens was acknowledged as the intellectual center of the Greek world. His contemporaries included Sophocles, Aristophanes, Hippocrates, Thucydides, and Phidias. In short, he lived at a time when philosophy, poetry, theater, sculpture, and architecture flourished as never before. Trade and commerce were at their height as well. The quickening of the intellectual life was matched by a great deal of political and military activity. During Plato's youth, the Peloponnesian War was fought, and he himself was later involved in the struggle between democratic and oligarchic factions in Athens.

Socrates: Rationalism, Contentual Subjectivity, and Dualism

Plato's teacher, Socrates, had been born about 470 B.C., into a middle-class family; his mother was a midwife and his father may have been a sculptor. He dedicated his life to the search for knowledge, looking for it everywhere, in the gymnasium, in the marketplace, at dinner tables, wherever he could find persons willing to engage in conversation with him.

In these conversations he devised what later came to be called the Socratic method. Some general term, widely but loosely used— "friendship," "justice," or "piety"—would be advanced in the course of one of the conversations. Socrates would then ask for a definition of the idea. After his companion had given a definition he would draw him out in such a way as to get him to admit exceptions to that particular definition. A cross-examination of questions and answers would follow until either a clear, final definition was reached on which both could agree or, seeing the shortcomings of his particular definition,

Socrates' companion would have to acknowledge that what he had accepted as true was not true at all. This procedure applies reason to the matter in hand, and may be considered a classic example of the rationalistic method.

The Socratic method combined induction and deduction, as these processes of thinking are called today. Thinkers before him had most often started with general propositions from which they deduced particulars. Socrates' insistence on examining particular instances in order to arrive at a general statement made him a founder of the inductive method, although he also used deduction.

In Athens his opponents were the Sophists, itinerant professional teachers who taught virtue for a fee, and who promised their pupils worldly success. They held that true knowledge cannot be attained, however, because sensory life is entirely subjective. The Sophistic contention of Protagoras, cited in the previous chapter, that "man is the measure of all things," was interpreted to mean that what a man thinks determines what is true for him—which shows an emphasis on individualism. This attitude and their instructions on how to achieve worldly, i.e., personal success, meant that the Sophists were fostering an idiographic philosophy in spirit not too dissimilar to the self-help schemes of today.

Socrates differed from the Sophists in two major respects. He held that one could not teach virtue and so directed his inquiries toward universal (nomothetic) and constant moral norms. The Platonic dialogue, *Protagoras*, shows the Sophist of that name and Socrates locked in argument over whether or not men can be taught basic values.[2] Here and elsewhere, in order to debate Sophist doctrines, Socrates sought to elicit the knowledge inherent in each person. Knowledge to him was an activity of the mind. Self-knowledge resulted from the discovery of one's own ignorance. Once this discovery is made one can go on to knowledge by use of the Socratic method, for truth already resides in the mind. Socrates felt that his method permitted one to find the truth, the abiding reality that lies behind the apparent flux and relativity that the Sophists made so much of.

Socrates made rationalistic self-examination a philosophic method. "Know thyself" took on the meaning that the mind could turn to itself for knowledge. He called for methodological subjectivity precisely because if one did look into oneself, other persons would also find the same truths. The verification of truth was left to private experience and, indeed, could be found in no other way. This was one of the first instances of the systematic use of meditation, which was later to serve as a major psychological method, leading to the more specialized and rigorous introspection of Wundt, Titchener, and others allied with them. But Socrates did not intend to make the human mind the object of a distinct science; rather, it served him as a tool and as a means of finding the Good.

Socrates was primarily concerned with the relationship of virtue to knowledge, and this led him to a preoccupation with conduct. His emphasis on ethical conduct has sometimes been misunderstood. Cicero held that Socrates "called down philosophy from the heavens."[3] This felicitous expression was remembered and repeated for centuries. Yet it is no more than a half-truth. Socrates saw man as the proper source of study; this was true only in the sense that he directed attention to ethical problems, and not to psychology as such. Man had been very much the center of interest for the Hippocratics, the pre-Socratic philosopher-scientists, and even the Sophists, who had turned away from cosmology to human affairs and were intensely practical in endeavoring to teach a way of life. Socrates merely asked questions about man that were different from those these others had asked.

To Socrates the true concern of man was not for the body but for the soul. A soul using a body is a popular formulation. Socrates said, one must look to Man and tend his soul. The typical Athenian of the time of Socrates conceived of the soul (the *psyche*) as an airy, unsubstantial double of the body that at death became either a shadow going to Hades or a breath to be dissipated on the air.[4] In the common view, man's consciousness faded and disappeared with death. The body, not the soul, was the concern of the ordinary Athenian, who was astonished to be told by Socrates that the soul was more important.

In furthering the primacy of the soul, Socrates was the first to relate consciousness of self to the soul. By means of the self-knowledge of the soul, man has the insight to tell good from evil. If the soul can discern what is good, it will choose what is good. The soul not only allows us to see the good but is also the means whereby we choose that good. Hence, knowledge is a virtue, and no man intentionally does wrong; improper conduct is the result of ignorance. Although he advanced this important distinction, instead of further idiographic concerns, primarily the distinction was used to turn back the discussion to the nomothetic, i.e., not Callias, the man, but man in the abstract.

As a consequence of the very nature of his quest for knowledge, Socrates never recorded his thoughts. Plato did this for him in the *Dialogues*, in which Socrates is often the major speaker.[5] Consequently, the views of the two men are mingled. It is unnecessary for our purposes to differentiate further the thinking of Socrates from that of Plato.

Socrates' very style of living and his ability to puncture the weak spots of pompous and hollow men gained him many enemies. In 399 B.C., when he was seventy years old, he was accused of corrupting the youth of the city and of neglecting the city gods. He was convicted and sentenced to death. Despite an opportunity to escape, occasioned by a delay in carrying out the sentence, Socrates acknowledged that the punishment, although unjust, had been ordered by a legitimate court to which he owed obedience and he accepted its dictates. His last days have been recounted by Plato in the *Phaedo*, in which the tranquil dignity and courage of Socrates in the face of death are movingly presented.[6]

The Life of Plato

Plato was born in 427 B.C. to Ariston and Perictione, members of old and aristocratic Athenian families. Plato shared his family's interest in politics and was assured of sponsorship in the oligarchic party with which his family was allied. His relationship with Socrates, however, caused him to become disillusioned with politics when the oligarchists tried to force Socrates to implicate himself in a particularly unsavory phase of their political machinations. This incident led Plato to give up any further thought of an active political life in Athens.

Although a matter of some dispute,[7-9] it seems that Plato traveled a lot during the next few years. Shortly after his return to Athens, he founded the Academy. This was a society of scholars and students concerned with the study of certain branches of knowledge. Philosophical interests predominated, but some attention was paid to mathematics and a little to astronomy. Some who came to study under Plato remained at the Academy for the greater part of their lives, devoting themselves, after their probationary years, to the advancement of knowledge. Others came only for relatively short periods, and afterwards returned to their homes. They undoubtedly paid dues of a sort, but certainly not tuition. Plato, an aristocrat, was disdainful of the Sophists who taught for a fee. The Socratic method was probably used by Plato for much of his teaching. Despite recent opinions to the contrary, it is probable that Plato also gave formal lectures which revolved around the systematic and continued exposition of a particular topic. There is some indirect evidence that teaching might have been at more than one level. Advanced lectures may have been interspersed with others more popular in character. An anecdote suggests that sometimes there were members of his audience relatively unfamiliar with Plato's teachings.[10] A lecture entitled "On the Good" was announced. The audience came to find out how they might secure worldly goods, and were disappointed to hear about such matters as the "definite" and "indefinite" concepts essential to Plato's idea of the Good. United in place and time, unlike the pre-Socratic philosophers, Plato's followers formed another scholarly group. Their interaction is a matter about which, unfortunately, we know very little.

Very little is actually known with any degree of certainty about the activities of Plato's later years. According to "The Seventh Letter,"[11] he became involved in Syracusan politics as the supporter of a former pupil who aspired to the throne. But Plato could only dream that a philosopher might be king, for disaster, not victory, was the final result. Plato died in 347 B.C. He was over eight-one years of age. He is said to be buried in the ground of the school in which he served for forty years.

The Philosophical Basis of Plato's Psychological Contentions

Plato's psychological views are not systematically presented. The dialogue form, a conversation cast in a dramatic setting, is hardly conducive to systematic presentation, so that his views on ethics, religion, metaphysics, politics, social theory, and psychology are intermingled. His psychological contentions were always subordinate to what he considered as much more important and fundamental problems. At one point he seems to apologize for turning away from the eternal to indulge in the recreation of dealing with psychological matters.[12]

There are two major themes that express his interest in what were to become matters of psychological concern. Plato wished to find knowledge about which he could be certain. He decided that the ideas or forms that he sought were to be found in a reality which lay beyond the shifting phenomena of human conduct and physical processes. He was also eager to demonstrate the immortality of the soul.

Plato was influenced by Socrates' admonishment to care for the soul and also by Socrates' insistence that there was a definite meaning to things which one could penetrate by using the Socratic method. Plato was also influenced by the Pythagoreans, a religious cult which taught that the soul was immortal, that death was a release from the bonds of flesh, and that after repeated reincarnations a man could rise to know the Divine. The Pythagoreans attached considerable importance to number, and more or less incidentally made an important contribution to mathematical knowledge. According to Aristotle, the Pythagoreans devoted themselves to mathematics and thought its principles were the principles of all things.[13] In Pythagorean thought, all things are numerable. The relation between things is also expressible numerically, such as the musical intervals between the notes of a lyre. Just as musical harmony is dependent upon number, so also is the harmony of the world itself. And so the Pythagoreans contended that the first principle of the universe is number—that the world in a sense is based on number. Plato's absorption with mathematics based on an all-sufficient rationalism did not however lead to a quantitative attitude embracing a desire to measure. He was interested in the manipulation of mathematics for its own sake, glorying in the aspects of reasoning which lay within the field itself. He did not use mathematics as a tool for studying something else, except as an incidental or quasi-verifying application to astronomical problems already solved by reason.

   In his reaction against the new emphasis on materialism as exemplified by the teachings of the Sophists, Socrates had rejected science in favor of spiritual concerns. Plato shared this view. His attitude toward science can be characterized as negative. He denied the value of experiment.[14] He says, for example, that those who would attempt to verify color mixtures by experiment would be ignoring the difference between human and divine nature. For Plato, only God has the knowledge and power either to combine or to resolve color mixtures. Plato warns the astronomer that knowledge of the heavens will not be gained by observation but rather from a *priori* deduction from the heavenly idea.[15] Plato's rejection of scientific observation is rendered less harsh if he is interpreted to mean that the astronomer's task should be to record the real and not merely the apparent movements of the stars. In the *Timaeus*, he says explicitly that an account of the material world should not be expected to be more than "likely," that is, not exact or even self-consistent.[16]

   It would seem that Plato rejected quantitatively and inductively derived empirical knowledge. But this is only one side of the coin. While he may have had a negative attitude toward what many of us today would consider crucial prescriptions of modern science—induction, quantification, and empiricism—yet he also did much to provide a particular theoretical background for science in his rationalistic search for the Forms that give order to the universe.

   Plato laid part of the groundwork for the conceptualizations of scientists to come. When a modern biologist, physicist, or chemist works on a physical object—whether that may be a horse, a falling ball, or a sample of sulphur—he is thinking about, not that object, but something resembling a universal nontemporal, nonphysical version of the object, which Plato called a Form. The world of the universals of Plato was to give way to the world of natural law that was its direct descendant.

THE NATURE OF FORMS

To put it succinctly, Plato conceived of a world of phenomena and a world of Forms or Ideas.[17] By the former he meant the changing and essentially unreal world of appearances, which corrupts, decays, and dies. The world of Forms is real and eternal. A perceived tree is but the appearance of a tree, whereas the Form of the tree, although not perceived directly, is known through intuition and truly exists.

Plato used Form and Idea interchangeably. However, "idea" has been rendered singularly inappropriate to convey what Plato meant, since the word has come to be used for that which exists in the mind only. This is precisely the opposite of Plato's meaning. Plato specifically mentions that Ideas are not created by thought.[18] An Idea to him is a reality with an independent existence, and not a thought. The term, Form, is capitalized in order to indicate its technical usage.

How did he arrive at what to "common sense" must appear an extravagant and bizarre belief—that the world of appearances is but a shadow, masking the reality that lies beyond? One source must surely have been the Socratic search through specific instances of justice, courage, and virtue for essences. In the *Republic*, it is assumed that whenever a number of individual qualities have a common name, they also have a corresponding Form.[19] To Plato these were not subjective concepts—as we might call them—but real essences in the qualitative sense.

Something of what is meant by Form may also be envisioned by considering the role of mathematics. Plato did this in a fashion similar to that which follows.[20] Suppose a geometrician is working out a theorem to demonstrate that the interior angles of the triangle equal two right angles. Plato reasoned that the geometrician is not inventing something here, but is, rather, making a discovery. What is discovered is not the physical triangle that the geometrician has drawn, with all its minute imperfections of surface, drawing instrument, and lack of drawing skill. The physical drawing is not a triangle but something like a triangle. This universal object, this nonspatial, nontemporal object of thought, which the sensed physical triangle resembles, is the Form of a triangle.

So far there has been no discussion of the problem of how man may recognize Forms; consequently, one may have the impression of their existing somewhere "out there," divorced from human means of comprehension. This omission is to be remedied by an explanation of the relation of the soul to the Forms.

THE SOUL AND THE FORMS

The soul is the means whereby man apprehends the Forms.[21] Through the senses, the body knows the changing and essentially unreal world of appearances; only the soul is capable of knowing rationally the world of the Forms. Not only was Plato's method of finding knowledge a rational one, the knowledge he sought was contentually subjective in character, it was knowledge derived from the reasoning aspect of the soul.

The essential character of the soul is expressed in movement. Since the soul is self-moved, it is immortal.[22] On the other hand, whatever is moved by the motion of something else, such as the body, cannot be immortal. Ceasing to move, the body also ceases to live.

Platonic Forms have a reality distinguishable from sensible objects.[23] They exist in their own right; they are different from the things we sense. The "objects" that are sensed are impermanent; they can be the objects of opinions but cannot be the objects of true knowledge. Sensory experiences are always changing. Only appearances can be seen and they are similar, as Plato put it, to shadows in a cave.[24] Human beings, as it were, live in a cave, chained in such a fashion that they cannot move but must look at a wall. Light (truth) behind and above them streams into the cave. They see only the shadows of reality projected on the walls (sensory experience).

What was called reminiscence by Plato serves both to demonstrate the independent existence of the Forms and also shows how the soul functions in relation to them. Reminiscence, to Plato, is the faculty of the soul to recover the Forms it knew before it became united with the body. Knowledge of the Forms is latent in the soul, and is brought forth by effort. An illustration is Socrates' questioning of a slave boy about geometrical figures.[25] The boy was ignorant of geometry but by asking him certain questions, Socrates drew out of him the solution to a difficult geometrical problem. Since the boy could solve the problem under questioning, Plato argued that he had known the answer all the time, and that knowledge of the Forms is independent of body and is present at birth. In other words, learning consists of drawing out of the mind what is already present in the mind. Education is recollection.

This doctrine is not founded on the existence of innate ideas. Knowledge is not ready-made; to arrive at it and to remember it requires effort. Nor is reminiscence a depository of past experiences or remnants of learning from the senses. Plato admitted that a certain amount of remembering does take place this way, but is of negligible import. In this connection he introduced the famous simile of the wax tablet.[26] The minds of men are akin to wax tablets that vary in size, hardness, moistness, and purity, just as the minds of men vary in accuracy of recognition, retentiveness, and ease of learning. Plato minimized the importance of such learning in favor of reminiscence. Further along in the same dialogue, he even rejected his own tablet theory, since it is unable to account for error.[27] The wax tablet theory, he said, would make sensory experience the basis of truth and error. Since many errors, such as adding 6 + 5 and getting 12, are not misinterpretations of experience, but are nonetheless not correct—the wax tablet does not account for all errors. It is therefore a relatively insignificant explanatory device.

More specifically, it is reason, as an aspect or part of the soul, that makes the Forms intelligible. At long last, we come to a statement of general method which expresses Plato's desire to know. His method shows adherence to the rationalistic prescription, that the source of knowledge is to be found primarily, if not exclusively, through reason.

Psychological Views

To us, it is readily apparent that for Plato the soul is independent of the body. It follows that Plato's psychological views are dualistic, a theme running through all the discussion to follow. A vague, implicit dualism had been latent in the studies of body-soul functions by the pre-Socratic Greeks. Plato, following the lead of Socrates, gave the problem explicitness, precision, and subtlety. Broadly speaking, the dualistic prescription in this context is based on the conviction that soul and body are fundamentally different and are therefore separate entities. Moreover, since soul was thought to be more important, contentual subjectivity, the idea of psychological data as mental, continued to be promulgated.

SOUL AND BODY

To Plato, when the body becomes an unruly instrument, it hinders the performance of the soul.[28] Strong natural appetites of the body upset the functioning of reason. The action of the humors of the body affects the mind. Madness and ignorance are diseases of the mind brought about by the body. But excessive pain and pleasure are the greatest diseases of the mind, for a man in great joy or great pain cannot reason properly. Sense perception, desire, feeling, and appetite are products of the body and at war with the mind; in this way they interfere with apprehension of the Forms.

Plato believed that the seat of —or physical link between—the three aspects of the soul (reason, feeling, and appetite, as they are to be called in a later discussion of the structure of the soul) is the cerebrospinal marrow on which they are "strung."[29] The immortal (rational) soul has a separate place in the brain while the mortal (irrational) souls of feeling and appetite are located in the thoracic and abdominal cavities.[30] The heart serves as an advance post of the immortal soul; when wrong is committed, the heart is stimulated to anger and this emotion is carried by the blood vessels to all parts of the body. According to Plato, the blood vessels serve as the means for conveying sensations through the body.

The question of the independence or dependence of the body and the soul may now be clarified. As an entity, the soul is independent; when it is related to the body, however, the two act in unison. The soul itself is immortal, but certain relations and functions it assumes when it is connected with the body are not.[31] These disappear when the soul is again independent of the body. The vital principle of the soul is imperishable. Hence, a vitalistic prescription was adhered to unequivocally.

MOTIONS AND THE SOUL

In explaining sensory and other bodily processes, Plato makes use of a somewhat vague concept of motion.[32] It will be remembered that the essence of the soul to Plato is movement. Nevertheless, in discussing movement he uses a concept that is to some degree disconnected from his theory of the soul. This concept of movement is the nearest Plato came to a functional theory, i.e., an emphasis upon activities, rather than structures. The psychology of Plato always returns to the soul, and this instance is no exception. Plato says that psychological activities are related to various inner motions. He probably arrived at this conclusion by drawing an analogy between the motion of objects in the external world, and sensory experience. The instrument is the body; the function and source belongs to the soul, which directs the acts of the body. A sensory organ is the means whereby the motion of the external world interacts with the motion of the soul so that external nature is apprehended. Sensation comes about whenever some motion affects a sense organ. This outer motion is communicated to an inner motion, which is carried to the seat of consciousness in the soul. Thus, sense qualities, such as color, emerge from the interaction of environmental motion and the internal motion of the body. Diversity in the qualities sensed is caused by the difference in the motions that the impression communicates to the soul.

The movements of the soul include motions other than those related to sensations—will, pleasure, consideration, deliberation, pain, confidence, fear, hatred, love, and other similar motions. Thinking (mind) is a functioning (motion) of the soul, in that it is selective, spontaneous, and self-moving.[33] Emotion and drive are also explained on the basis of motion. Thinkers before Plato conceived of sensation as movement and emotion, as merely a more violent form of movement. Plato could not accept this relative and mechanical doctrine outright.[34] As he modified it, sensation is accompanied by emotion when the more violent degree of motion occurs, but the direction of movement—whether toward the natural or unnatural—decides whether the experience is pleasant or painful. If the violent motion conforms to nature, it is pleasant; if it does not, it is painful. When it is added that to Plato "natural" means productive of the Good and "unnatural," productive of the Bad, we see that here again psychology is subordinate to other considerations, in this case to ethics. What is called *drive* today Plato also relates to motion and to the soul.[35] Inner motion is spontaneous or self-active. The highest form of such movement is reserved for purposeful action directed toward a goal of some sort. Hence, purposive behavior is derived from the soul and expressed in movement.

THE STRUCTURE OF THE SOUL

Plato expressed three pertinent views dealing with the structure of the soul. In the *Phaedo* the soul is conceived of as unitary and simple.[36] At one point in the *Timaeus* the soul is described as twofold: the rational soul, concerned with the aspect of reasoning, or mind, and the irrational soul, consisting of desire and appetite.[37] A little later in the *Timaeus*,[38] in the *Republic*,[39] and in the *Phaedrus*,[40] the soul is tripartite—reasonable, spirited, and appetitive. Although some authorities find these three ways of describing the soul contradictory, it is possible to reconcile them: the first view emphasizes the essential unity of the soul, and the second and third views describe *aspects*—not parts—of this unitary soul. Thus the soul as a vital principle is unitary, but certain aspects or modes emerge when the soul is present in the body. Plato varied the classification of soul —reasonable, spirited, and appetitive or rational and irrational—as circumstances seemed to require. The emphasis that Plato placed upon the unity of the soul is important because consistency and integration of psychological structure are thereby made explicit.

REASONING IN THE DUAL AND TRIPARTITE SOUL

The first and highest aspect, reason, is the intellectual facet of the soul. To Plato, reason is the very essence of man; one is a man insofar as he is rational. This does not mean that rational man does not also possess the lower aspects of the soul, but, rather that he can be guided by reason. Reason has been discussed in connection with the theory of Forms and the theory of reminiscence. To review, reason is the means whereby we know intuitively the Forms, and reason, as reminiscence, is only indirectly dependent upon the natural world or its phenomena.

To go more deeply into Plato's conception of reason it is necessary to compare and contrast reason, as he sees it, with sensory experience. As we saw in discussing the Pre-Socratics, this controversy over whether reason or sense is the means of securing knowledge existed before Plato. Plato denied that sensation gives knowledge. To him, reason, not sense perception, is the means by which we synthesize our experiences. We do not see with the eyes but through them. We do not hear with the ears but through them. Common characteristics of diverse objects are not perceived by the separate organs of sense but by reason. Sense perceptions give only particulars; these particulars are formed into a pattern and by the nature of that pattern, yield some intelligibility. Reality is revealed when reason provides the interpretation of perceptual experience. Sensations supply some of the occasions for perceiving knowledge or serve as one of the tools for determining knowledge. An activity of the mind, the faculty of reason reveals the Forms behind sense experience, and it is the soul that makes one aware of the meaning of what is sensed.

Reasoning is related to processes other than reminiscence and sense. Memory plays a role in reasoning, although from what has already been said, it is not surprising to find it is a relatively minor one. Plato says that the soul is like a book into which memory inscribes our perceptions.[41] This record may be true when the "secretary" inscribes correctly but false when the opinion expressed is false. But there is another force at work—the "painter," imagination, who uses the records in his own characteristically creative way. Reasoning is carried on or worked through by a process of dialectic essentially similar to that of Socrates and using the three processes of reminiscence, memory, and imagination.

SPIRIT AND APPETITE IN THE TRIPARTITE SOUL

The second aspect of the tripartite division of the soul is the notion of spirit. Spirit is contentious, assertive, pugnacious, and forceful and in its drive toward action carries out the directives of reason. In so doing, spirit is the mediator between reason and appetite, the third aspect.

Both the role of spirit as a mediator and its differentiation from appetite are best shown by using Plato's own illustration.[42] One Leontius was present at a place of execution. He felt a desire to see the dead bodies and yet had an abhorrence and fear of them. He struggled for a time, but desire won, and Leontius "ran up to the dead bodies saying, 'Look, ye wretches, take your fill of the fair sight.' " He was angry with himself for his action, showing that spirit was on the side of reason, but nevertheless, appetite won out. This was proof to Plato of the existence of different aspects of soul, for how otherwise could he both want to look and yet not want to look at the bodies? The spirited element is therefore not the same as appetite because it can be used against it; since spirit and appetite are sometimes antagonists, they must be distinguished from one another.

Appetite, the third aspect, above all is undiscriminating desire. Appetite wants something, and it wants it now, without delay and without any consideration for the other aspects of the soul. The goal of appetite, as Plato sees it, is attainment serving as a replenishment. Thirst, for example, arising from deprivation of water, leads to a striving for water that when satisfied results in repletion.[43]

CONFLICT AND HARMONY AND THE TRIPARTITE SOUL

That the soul is unitary does not mean that it cannot have aspects which are at odds with one another.[44] Plato's awareness of the nature of the conflict is shown in the story of Leontius, but an even more dramatic illustration is given in Plato's example of the charioteer in the *Phaedrus*.[45] Plato likened man to a chariot team. In the team there is a powerful, unruly horse intent on having his own way at all costs (appetite). The other horse is a thoroughbred, spirited but manageable (spirit). On catching sight of his beloved, the charioteer (reason) attempts with some difficulty to direct the two horses toward the goal, which he alone (not they) can comprehend.

What Plato seems to be demonstrating in this story is a theory of conflict based upon reason, emotion, and drive. Man's attitude toward his objective is swayed by affective impulses and inhibitions over which reason, the charioteer, has some control. Reason acts as a check upon the affective aspect. For the ends of spirit or appetite to be met, reason must guide. Spirit or appetite need not be eliminated; instead they should be controlled. An attempt by reason to oust appetite and spirit would be as "irrational" as for appetite and spirit to banish reason. And although there is conflict among the aspects of the soul, sometimes they agree.[46] Reason is the natural harmonizer. Balance and proportion among the three aspects is sought, with the others subordinate to reason. Order consists in harmony and this subordination.

DRIVE AND THE TRIPARTITE SOUL

Drive characterizes all three aspects of the soul. Reason, spirit, and appetite—each is a drive, of and by itself, an endeavor toward a thing, a striving toward attainment of a goal.[47] The reflective aspect seeks understanding and wisdom; the spirited seeks success; the appetite, the lowest form of desire, seeks bodily pleasures or the means to them—money, food, drink, sex, etc. Reason may long for the realization of its own drives and assent to them. On other occasions reason may dissent, as it does with many of the drives of spirit or appetite. But this should not obscure the fact that reason has a characteristic drive of its own.

The *Symposium* of Plato is a dialogue concerned with *Eros*, or love, in which each participant offers his own interpretation.[48] Plato's position seems to be that there are two kinds of love—profane and sacred. The first sort is concerned with the body and the second with the soul, mind, and character. Physical sexual desire is interpreted, not as a desire for intercourse itself, but as a masked desire for parenthood, an attempt to perpetuate oneself. This passion for physical parenthood is the most elementary or rudimentary fruition of the good and eternal.

Only the higher love can lead to happiness. Love, as Plato conceived it, is in its highest form the love of wisdom. Whether one knows it or not, what one seeks is the beauty of the eternal Forms. This love is a longing for union, not only with the partner through reason, but beyond this, a union with the pure Form, or the essence of love itself. Thus the higher or immortal soul has its own enjoyment, its particular *Eros. Eros* is popularly translated as "love," but may often be more meaningfully called "life force." This is something akin to the biological will to live, the life energy, a concept of which we shall hear again.

Drives have an affective coloring of pleasure and pain. As we have seen, pain is what is contrary to nature; pleasure is what is in accord with nature. One class of pleasures derives from the restoration of the natural state of equilibrium. At the level of the appetite, depletion causes need (lack of pleasure), which when satisfied is followed by repletion (pleasure).[49] This process of a return to normal on the part of the organism is one form of pleasure.[50] Under excess heat or chilling there is a disturbance of equilibrium, and recovery or return to the natural state is pleasant. This is a form of pleasure in which there is an agreeable return to a normal bodily condition.[51] There is a second class of pleasures dependent upon mental processes themselves (not upon a balance within the organism). These are pleasures that we anticipate or remember mentally, such as anticipating recovery from a painful illness and remembering past pleasures that we look forward to enjoying again.

THE IRRATIONAL IN THE DUAL SOUL

While Plato was not the first to recognize the irrational in man, he considerably amplified, extended, and gave a rationale for it. He located this lower or irrational aspect within the soul itself and thought of it in terms of psychological conflict. The already familiar accounts of the passions, the tripartite division itself, and the story of Leontius all point to an appreciation of this aspect.

Emotions are related to the mortal (irrational) soul, which is endowed with courage, passion, and a love of strife. The wild beast in man may slumber or be restrained but is never tamed. Passion is irrational, liable to excess, expanding until it becomes a form of mania. A graphic illustration is given by Plato when he speaks of the "unnecessary" pleasures and appetites that everyone seems to have, although some can control them by reason. With everyone, when reason

. . . is asleep, then the wild beast within us, gorged with meat or drink, starts up and having shaken off sleep; goes forth to satisfy his desires; and there is no conceivable folly or crime—not except incest or any other unnatural crime or parricide, or the eating of forbidden food—which at such a time, when he has parted company with all shame and sense, a man may not be ready to commit.[52]

Overview

Plato's rationalistic theory of Forms and his dualistic convictions determined his attitude toward science. Science deals with the physical world. By definition, the objects of its inquiry belong to what Plato saw as the shifting and relatively unintelligible world of sensation. According to him, one could never trust these phenomena to give true knowledge. His distrust of the physical world, including sensory processes, helped to turn his philosophical thought away from science, including psychology. To Plato, only an understanding of the Forms, another class of existence entirely, could give us truth. The Forms are the objects of knowledge, material things are not, and inductive, empirical, and quantitative matters belong to the material world.

But this was a rejection of science on the basis of its use of empirical *led to notion of 'Natural Law'*

and inductive methods; the rational way in which science draws conclusions was acceptable to him. In his rationalism Plato gave us the beginning of a belief in natural law—law as basic nature far removed from
mere phenomena. When we understand the Forms, Plato said, we understand their natural relationship with one another. This interrelationship
was later to be conceptualized as natural law. It should be evident that
Plato did not himself formulate anything approaching this modern conception. He did, however, lay the groundwork from which it was to
emerge.

Ironically, Plato, who glorified reason, showed keen insight into the
functioning of the unconscious, irrational aspect of man. The irrationalis-
tic prescription, expressing intrusion into or domination over the intellectual processes by what we would call emotive and drive factors, received
varied and subtle consideration from him. His distinction between the
rational and irrational aspects of living function (soul); his appreciation of
the nature of conflict and, correlatively, of the nature of harmony; his
primordial concept of *Eros;* his conception of drive as related differ-
entially to the various aspects of living function; his realization of the
perniciousness of repression and his advocacy of controlled expression;
all are indicative of his deep insight into the irrational aspects of human
nature. His understanding, however, was but one among a few isolated
instances occurring before the modern period and without immediate
impact.

Unconscious mental life had been exploited in the suggestion and
incubation of Greek temple medicine but there is no indication that the
practitioners themselves understood it. Without intending a paradox,
Plato made it evident that he was aware of this mental unawareness, that
is, of unconscious mentalism, as the prescription will be called in considering later developments. The significance of unconscious mentalism
was not to be more fully appreciated until the time of Jung and Freud.
Jung's conception of libido is actually closer in spirit to Plato than it is to
Freud, for Jung stressed its general, nonspecialized drive character (pp.
534–35). Freud signalized his more specific debt to Plato by utilizing the
very term *Eros* in his systematic formulation. To Freud personality was
subject to reciprocal urging and checking forces akin to Plato's reason,
emotion, and drive. Freud, in his theory of personality structure, sees
personality as dependent upon id, ego, and superego (pp. 508–12).

To some extent Plato, too, was advocating a dynamic prescription,
an emphasis upon factors making for change in man. But in a larger and
much more influential sense, his overall conception of man in relation to
the unchanging Forms was static.

Coexisting with this emphasis on the irrational aspects of the soul was the transcendental view of a rational soul whose unity is a guarantee of immortality. The gulf between immortal (rational) and mortal (affective) aspects of soul corresponds to the gulf which Plato says exists between man as he is and man as he should be. According to Dodds,[53] this dichotomy represents two diverse strains in Plato's thinking about the nature of man—a pride and faith in human reason, a heritage from the Golden Age, also, a recognition of human worthlessness forced upon him by his experiences in Athens and Syracuse. Dodds points out that a psychologist might see this not as simple opposition but as a compensatory reaction on Plato's part in which the first tendency became a compensation for the second—the less Plato cared for men in the flesh, the more noble he thought the soul to be.

The influence of his far-reaching and multifaceted dualism has yet to be considered. In his theory of Form, Plato broke away from implicit pre-Socratic monisms or dualisms. He acknowledged a reality that could be comprehended by the senses, but also described an immeasurably exalted realm where intelligible beings gained true knowledge by understanding the Forms. Plato established the character of the dualism that was to prevail for many centuries. This was modified at the hands of his followers, the Neoplatonists, especially Plotinus (p. 93). Later the Church fathers, particularly St. Augustine (p. 100) and St. Thomas Aquinas (p. 121), with all their emphasis upon the soul's immortality and varying degrees of contempt or disparagement of body, were to make dualism a central doctrine of Christian orthodoxy. The Platonic tradition was to reach still another climax when it was redirected at the hand of Descartes into a dualism of body and mind (p. 154). Descartes sought the same goal of intuitive insight leading to knowledge, not based on the Forms or Ideas of Plato, but on innate ideas within the mind which interact with the body—a concept that for Plato would have been hardly more than an illustration of his broader dualism of soul and body.

In summary Plato was above all dualistic and rationalistic in outlook and yet showed keen insight into the irrational aspects of man. He was non-naturalistic in that he depended upon transcendent guidance, although not of a religious kind. He conceived of psychological problems in a structural way, as psychological categories and contents, not as activities.

In the work of Plato, psychology still had not emerged as a separate philosophical discipline. Plato's subordination of psychological matters to other issues is abundantly clear from his espousal of the theory of Forms, his desire to demonstrate the immortality of the soul, his conviction of the subordination of the body to the soul, and his distrust of the empirical evidence of the senses. He used psychology only as a means of dealing with these other, to him, more important problems. Momentous though he is in the history of thought, Plato lived and worked before psychology began to emerge as a separate field. His pupil, Aristotle, was the first philosophical psychologist.

References*

1. Major sources for the lives of both Socrates and Plato are Diogenes Laertius, *Lives and Opinions of Eminent Philosophers*, A.D. III, trans. R. D. Hicks (Cambridge: Harvard University Press, 1925); G. C. Field, *Plato and His Contemporaries* (London: Methuen, 1920); A. E. Taylor, *Plato: the Man and His Work*, 6th ed. (New York: Meridian Books, 1956); and G. Boas, "Facts and Legends in the Biography of Plato," *Philosophical Review*, LVII (1948): 439–457.
2. R. M. Hutchins, ed., *The Great Books of the Western World*, Vol. VII, pp. 1–799, Plato, *Dialogues*, trans. B. Jowett (Chicago: Encyclopaedia Britannica, 1952) (c. 390–348 B.C.). *Protagorus.*
3. Cicero, *Tusculan Disputations*, trans. J. E. King (Cambridge: Harvard University Press, 1927), Vol. IV, p. 10.
4. J. Burnet, "The Socratic Doctrine of the Soul," *Proceedings of the British Academy*, VII (1916): 235–259.
5. *Dialogues.*
6. *Phaedo.*
7. E.g., Taylor, *Plato.*
8. E.g., Boas, *Facts and Legends.*
9. Plato, "The Seventh Letter," trans. J. Harward, in R. M. Hutchins, ed., *Great Books of the Western World*, Vol. VII, pp. 800–814 (c. 367 B.C.).
10. Field, *Plato and his Contemporaries*, pp. 35–36.
11. "The Seventh Letter."
12. *Timaeus* 68.
13. Works of Aristotle, trans. W. D. Ross in R. M. Hutchins, ed., *Great Books of the Western World*, Vols. VIII–IX, (c. 340–322 B.C.). *Metaphysics* 985b 23–986a 3.
14. *Timaeus* 67–68.

*See p. 19 for description of reference style.

15. *Republic* 530.
16. *Timaeus* 27d 5–28a 4; 29b 3–d 3.
17. *Phaedo* 79.
18. *Parmenides* 132.
19. *Republic* 596a 6–7.
20. *Ibid.*, 510.
21. *Phaedo* 66 and *passim*; *Phaedrus* 247c.
22. Plato affirmed the immortality of the soul on several occasions, e.g., *Phaedo* 85e–86d and *passim*; *Phaedrus* 245cff; *Laws* 893b–896d; and *Timaeus* 69c–e.
23. Aristotle *Metaphysics* 987b 27.
24. *Republic* 514–521.
25. *Meno* 82–86.
26. *Theaetetus* 191.
27. *Ibid.*, 194–196.
28. *Timaeus* 86.
29. *Ibid.*, 85–86.
30. *Ibid.*, 69d–70a.
31. *Phaedo* 64ff.
32. *Laws* 894–896; *Cratylus* 400e; *Phaedrus*, 245b–c.
33. *Laws* 896.
34. *Timaeus* 64–65.
35. *Phaedrus* 245c–246a.
36. *Phaedo* 78ff.
37. *Timaeus* 69.
38. *Ibid.*, 70–71, 77.
39. *Republic* 439–440, 580–594.
40. *Phaedrus* 253–254.
41. *Philebus* 38.
42. *Republic* 439–440.
43. *Philebus* 31.
44. *Republic* 436, 440, 588.
45. *Phaedrus* 253–254.
46. *Ibid.*, 237.
47. *Republic* 580ff.
48. *Symposium.*
49. *Timaeus* 81.
50. *Philebus* 31.
51. *Ibid.*, 72.
52. *Republic* 571.
53. E. R. Dodds, *The Greeks and the Irrational* (Berkeley: University of California Press, 1951).

Chapter 3

Aristotle:
THE FOUNDING OF
PHILOSOPHICAL PSYCHOLOGY

Only fragments of the earliest Greek speculations on psychological problems exist today, and these speculations were made within a nonpsychological context. Similarly, Plato, for all his brilliant excursions into so many different aspects of psychological matters, always approached these ideas from a nonpsychological position. The first to develop a systematic psychology was Aristotle, who may therefore be regarded as the first philosophical psychologist.

Aristotle's life and works are best considered in relation to one another because of their developmental interplay, especially since it is now known that his thinking went through various stages. This will help to combat the literary myth that Aristotle's views are static and unchanging.[1] This myth was enhanced by the fact that, many centuries later, his collected works were arranged by editors as they saw fit. All works on logic or biology, for instance, were neatly grouped, to the point where even parts of different works were arbitrarily put together. One work got its title, *Metaphysics,* for no other reason than that it was grouped after physics. Contradictory views in different works or in different parts of the same work, including various ideas about the soul, were once treated by scholars as contemporaneous. Did Aristotle or did he not accept the Platonic theory of Forms? When his writings are treated as contemporaneous with one another, this becomes an insoluble question, since affirmative and negative answers coexist; but when it is understood that his views show development and change with time, such problems become much more capable of solution.

Early Life

Aristotle was born in 384 B.C. in Stagira, a provincial town in northern Greece.[2] His father, who was the physician to the King of Macedon, followed the Asclepiad tradition of the family and began training his son as a doctor. But his father died prematurely, and Aristotle's early education was continued by a friend of the family. Aristotle visited Athens for the first time in 367 B.C. By then, Socrates had been dead for thirty-two years, Plato was sixty-one years old, and the Academy had been in existence for two decades. Aristotle did not leave Athens for twenty years, but less is known of these years than of any other period of his life. It is even a matter of scholarly dispute as to what is meant when it is said that he "studied" under Plato. He himself makes no mention in any of his writings either of the Academy or of having studied under Plato.[3] Nevertheless, he probably did enter the Academy either immediately upon his arrival in Athens or else shortly thereafter, and it is likely that at some time during these twenty years he became a "colleague" of his former teacher, Plato.

In his early years, Aristotle was an enthusiastic Platonist. His first works, surviving only in fragments, were written in the popular form of the dialogue during this period at the Academy. Devotion to the Platonic theory of Forms, and all that it implies, seems to have characterized this stage of his intellectual development. For example, he held that the soul exists before the body, leads an unnatural existence when connected with the body, and is released by death to return to its real existence.

In 347 B.C. Plato died at the age of eighty-one. His successor as head of the Academy was Speusippus, an inferior thinker, but Plato's nephew and legal heir. Speusippus had strong mathematical and Pythagorean leanings, both of which Aristotle probably found incompatible with his already changing viewpoint.

Middle Life

Whatever the reason, Aristotle at this time left Athens for Asia Minor, and did not return for twelve years. He settled first in Assus, a town near Troy, and attached himself to the court of Hermias, the Tyrant of Assus. He stayed in Assus for three years, during which time he continued to study, to write, and to collect biological specimens. He also married Hermias' niece and adopted daughter, Pythias, and if the story that he devoted his honeymoon to collecting seashells is true, it certainly betrays a severely scholarly turn of mind. After leaving Assus he went to Mitylene in Lesbos where he lived until 343–342 B.C. Here, he taught and wrote as before. He also went on with empirical research on animals. It was probably here too that he was joined by Theophrastus, who later succeeded him as head of the school he would in time found.

Under the influence of Hermias, whose territory was on the periphery of the Greek world bordering on lands under Persian influence, Aristotle had become a Pan-Hellenist, a protagonist for a Greece united against the Persian Empire. He was invited to Pella, the court of Philip of Macedon, to become tutor to Philip's son, Alexander, then a boy of twelve, who was to become Alexander the Great. It is altogether likely that the offer was made not because Aristotle was a philosopher, but because he was a learned, Pan-Hellenist patriot. His tutorship ended when Alexander became regent for Philip. The assassination of Philip in 335 B.C. threw the court at Macedon into a state of turmoil. Intrigue and counter-intrigue became rampant, and Aristotle decided to return to Athens.

His tutorship must have been valued. During Alexander's monumental march of conquest through the East, he gave instructions to his subordinates that biological specimens were to be collected and sent to his former teacher, and according to legend, Aristotle's influence was responsible for Alexander's strong but short-lived passion for spreading Greek ideals at this time.

While he was away from Athens, Aristotle's thinking began to differ from Plato's. Experts disagree as to precisely when these differences began to manifest themselves, but it is generally agreed that they arose during Aristotle's years of travel and developed further during the first few years after his return to Athens. He became increasingly concerned with collecting empirical data, and when his empirical conclusions contradicted Platonic or other philosophical thinking, he did not hesitate to modify the older concepts, or even to disavow what had formerly been his own convictions.

Plato's interest in science was limited to mathematics and astronomy, and was probably inspired by a Pythagorean belief in the fixed and universal character of these disciplines. Biologically inclined, Aristotle was more interested in the variable and the particular. Aristotle himself defined one major aspect of the difference in attitude between him and Plato. In his *Physics* he points out that both mathematics and physical science deal with planes, lines, and points;[4] but he adds that a mathematician studies them not as the limits of a physical body (which in reality they are) but as abstractions. The mathematician ignores for his purposes the specific physical body. Not so the physical scientist, who deals with actual physical bodies that show motion, that is, change. Change is an essential part of both animate and inanimate nature. Change can be ignored in mathematics where one unit is exactly like another of its kind forevermore; it cannot be ignored in science, for change prevents nature from ever repeating itself. In the same section of the *Physics* he refers to those "holders of the theory of Forms" who followed the same procedure as the mathematicians but with less justification, thus indicating his disagreement with Plato.[5]

Because of his greater dependence on empiricism, Aristotle had also to disagree with Plato on the question of the trustworthiness of the senses.[6] Plato's rationalism is in sharp contrast here with Aristotle's more empirical outlook; Aristotle had turned to biology, with its imperfect but living and changing organisms, and away from the perfect but static and lifeless mathematics that was the science of Plato.

Aristotle repeatedly criticized Plato for incorrectly separating form from matter and for giving a kind of separate existence to universals.[7] In contrast to individual subjects, universals are names of classes that predicate many subjects. To Aristotle, the subject matter of physics is *both* form and matter,[8] that is, form embodied in matter.[9] Although substance is individual, we can treat a universal or a general type, that is, a form, as if it were a substance. For instance, we can speak of human nature, and the statement is meaningful. A universal may be arrived at by abstracting from a class of objects whatever it is they have in common. Thus a general notion is a useful tool in science even though only the individual object has a separate existence. Plato insisted on the reality of ideas apart from objects; Aristotle found Form resident in physical bodies.

Aristotle denied the existence of the Forms apart from the particular and tangible things embodying them. A lump of wax will serve as an illustration. The shape of the lump cannot perish without the material also perishing; if form ceases, matter ceases. The lump may change its form, but form, as such, cannot disappear without matter also disappearing. Form and matter may be conceptualized separately by an act of abstraction, but we cannot imagine a substance without form or a form without substance.

To Aristotle, therefore, form exists in the particular, and not apart from it. His is the common-sense notion that the substantial reality of things resides in the things themselves. Nothing can exist without matter, and matter cannot exist without form. The individual object as we know it is that which has separate existence—this man, this horse, this plant. Each is a man, or a horse, or a plant insofar as each has both matter and form.

The substantial reality of things lies in the things themselves, not in another order apart from them. Aristotle argued that by attributing an independent existence to Forms, Plato made it impossible to explain the changing, moving character that objects exhibit. Platonic Forms do not contribute to the exploration of changes in the sensible world. What exists is not the ideal, but the imperfect drawing marked off on the ground: not the ideal of justice but the faulty justice carried out by men. The Forms exist when realized in matter. To each Form there corresponds, as Aristotle put it, "a special matter."[10]

Aristotle thus denied Plato's dualism of two worlds; he regarded it as an unnecessary duplication. For him, there was but one world, that of actual things, with the role of form merely an aspect of this world. The reality of forms was not denied and could be studied, but through philosophy, not science.

Although one of his works on logic dates from the earlier period, the rest quite possibly were written during these middle years, as were his works on ethics. Aristotle virtually founded the field of logic, and to this day the term "non-Aristotelian" logic is used to designate contributions to that science that did not follow his tradition. His works on logic are referred to collectively as the *Organon*, meaning "instrument" in the sense of a tool for philosophic and scientific investigation.[11] The ethical treatises of Aristotle were the earliest formal works of this kind. Ethical considerations had been discussed before by Plato and others before him. But these accounts were not systematically organized. It was Aristotle who performed this service. Some of his biological works also date from this period, but it will be more convenient to examine these later.

Aristotle on his Return to Athens

Aristotle was forty-nine years old and at the height of his powers when he returned to Athens. Shortly thereafter he founded his school, the Lyceum. The name "Peripatetic," which came to be attached to his point of view, arose from his habit of walking with his pupils in the school's covered walk.[12]

We know somewhat more about the organization of the Lyceum than we do about the organization of the Academy. Aristotle probably devoted the mornings to lecturing on logic and metaphysics. During the afternoons he is supposed to have given public lectures on ethics, politics, and rhetoric. Along with this teaching, he and his students actively engaged in research. The school had a rudimentary organization and something of a staff, a library and specimen collections, and even special dinnerware.

The atmosphere of the Lyceum appears to have been more scientific than philosophical. Aristotle had collected zoological specimens during his years of travel, but his most extensive research took place after his return to Athens. Observational studies were made, students prepared collections, and in general the resources for research were augmented quite deliberately. The *History of Animals* shows clear traces of different authors. The work was apparently distributed among various persons, each having an assignment that had been schematically developed in advance. Aristotle was a powerful organizer. He was the first of a long line of individuals who, quite apart from their own direct contributions to science, were able to direct and to stimulate scientific work in their associates.

During these years, although he was engaged in intense intellectual labor, he found time to pursue other interests and concerns. He adopted the orphan son of his former guardian. After the death of his wife he formed an attachment with Herpyllis, a native of Stagira. They never married, but apparently their union was a happy one and he lavished care on Nicomachus, the son he had by her.

His past tutorship and his continued connection with the court of Alexander made Aristotle unpopular with the very strong nationalist party in Athens. In 323 B.C. the news of the death of Alexander was received in Athens while Aristotle's political protector was absent from the city. Anti-Macedonian feeling ran strong in the city. Rather than allowing the Athenians "to sin twice against philosophy," (the first sin being the execution of Socrates), Aristotle retired to his mother's former country estate in Chalcis, a stronghold of Macedonian influence.[13] Here in the same year he died of some form of stomach disorder. He was sixty-two years old. His will, which is extant, shows his concern for every relative and dependent and includes provision for the emancipation of several of his slaves.

Much of Aristotle's more strictly scientific work, except some biological treatises, was completed during the years after his return to Athens. These years also saw the completion of many sections of his major philosophical work, the *Metaphysics*. His research in botany, zoology, and anatomy, through which he tried to solve many of the fundamental problems of biology, clearly established him as a great pioneer in these fields. His research on the structures and functions of living things was more exhaustive and greater in scope than that of anyone who lived before him. He was familiar with more than 500 different animal species and had dissected or investigated fifty of these with some thoroughness. In his work, then, he was often the naturalist, the field worker collecting specimens so as to classify them in some framework, more than the philosopher.

In examining the extant works as a whole, one is impressed by the amount of space devoted to the biological-psychological works—calculation shows that 30 percent of the pages are given over to these subjects.[14] No other topics are treated so extensively.

It was also during this second stay in Athens that most of his definitive works on psychology were written or completed.[15] The predominantly psychological works include the master work, *On the Soul*, and shorter works, known collectively (and rather misleadingly) as the *Short Physical Treatises,* including *On the Sense and Sensible, On Memory and Reminiscence, On Sleep and Sleeplessness*, and *On Dreams*.

Because it deals with the functioning of the individual organism as a whole, Aristotle's *On the Soul* must be regarded as the first book to treat psychology as a systematic philosophy. Psychology's emphasis on the whole organism serves to differentiate it from its biological neighbors, particularly physiology, the study of the functioning of organs; and its focus on the individual differentiates psychology from what later became its social science neighbors.[16] With this book psychology came into existence as a discipline consciously differentiated from other fields, and in writing it Aristotle became the founder of philosophical psychology.

Aristotle's already familiar account of earlier Greek thinkers in Book I of *On the Soul* gives us our first history of psychology.[17] His analysis is detailed and sharply critical. He felt that previous thinkers had failed to recognize the unity or oneness of the *psyche* or soul and so had divided it into parts. They had also misstated the soul's relation to the body by separating one from the other. Moreover, they had limited the soul to man instead of extending it to all living things.

Aristotle's Aim

We know of Aristotle's claim that he and other men desire knowledge above all else.[18] According to him, every kind of knowledge is to be prized.[19] There is a sheer delight in the exercise of the senses, quite apart from their usefulness,[20] (a notion Plato could never have accepted.)

Aristotle held that all men wonder why things are as they are.[21] It was this human habit of wonder that caused man to philosophize.[22] Knowledge, an understanding of the causes of things, ends this wonder by abolishing ignorance.[23] The very definition of *psyche* or soul is, "a substance capable of receiving knowledge."[24] More specifically, intelligence is the faculty of soul that enables the soul to receive knowledge.[25] Man alone is capable of intelligence or deliberation.[26] It follows that man is the only animal capable of acquiring knowledge.[27] Not only did Aristotle himself seek knowledge, he also saw man as uniquely fitted for such a search.[28]

While Aristotle's aim was knowledge of all kinds, he made distinctions between theoretical knowledge, practical knowledge, and productive knowledge.[29] In turn, he divided theoretical knowledge into three different sciences. Pride of place goes to "first philosophy," which in the Middle Ages came to be called metaphysics. The other two theoretical sciences were mathematics and physics. Physics, which was concerned with material nature, included what we would call biology and psychology.

Aristotle supported the distinction between knowledge of universals and knowledge of individuals.[30] Theory leads to the former, Aristotle explains, experience to the latter. Experience is not inferior to theory in dealing with matters of action. But this is not the case with knowledge, which belongs "rather to art than to experience,"[31] while wisdom belongs to theory. Similarly, the senses give knowledge only of particulars, since knowledge is based on principles and causes. He defended the nomothetic attitude, and although he did not reject the idiographic view, he relegated it to inferior status. In the same discussion he holds that rationalism is superior to empiricism, but experience is by no means disregarded. Theoretical science deals with that which could not be otherwise; that is to say, science admits of but one true answer to a particular problem.[32] Art and practical wisdom involve situations that are variable, in which more than one solution is possible. This emphasis upon one true answer, something occurring without exception, is indicative of Aristotle's groping toward a concept of scientific law. Not only is scientific knowledge universal in character, according to Aristotle it follows from first principles and emerges as conclusions from demonstrations.[33] There are basic and indispensible characteristics of science. In discussing them we turn to the issue of scientific method.

Knowledge and Scientific Method

In the Physics, his major account of scientific inquiry, Aristotle considers what one first encounters when thinking scientifically.

> We must advance from generalities to particulars; for it is a whole that is best known to sense-

perception, and a generality is a kind of whole, comprehending many things within it, like parts. Much the same thing happens in the relation of the name to the formula. A name, e.g., 'round', means vaguely a sort of whole: its definition analyzes this into its particular senses. Similarly a child begins by calling all men 'father', and all women 'mother', but later on distinguishes each of them.[34]

Out of this welter of sense experience emerges the first of the basic or indispensible characteristics of science: principles, or basic truths. These serve as starting points from which one proceeds to particulars. While sense perception is concerned with particular instances, its content yields the rudimentary general principles from which we proceed inductively to higher and higher levels of principles, until the "true" principles are established. Knowledge is not possible through sense perception alone, since the senses give us only particulars without demonstration.[35] Sense perception is nevertheless necessary for the acquisition of knowledge.[36] To have knowledge, one must grasp the primary or first principles or, as Aristotle elsewhere puts it, the "why of it."[37]

For Aristotle, the locus of the growth of knowledge from primary principles is the soul. This is in keeping with his definition of the soul as a substance capable of receiving knowledge.[38] He says elsewhere that first principles themselves do not require demonstration and could not be demonstrated.[39]

Induction provides deductive reasoning with basic principles (as do sense perception and habit).[40] Thereafter, one sometimes proceeds from induction and at other times from deduction.[41] There is no question, however, that Aristotle encouraged deduction, describing it as demonstration, already identified as the indispensible characteristic of science.

The basic premises of demonstration are definitions.[42] Having exempted first principles for reasons just given, he proceeds on the assumption "that all (scientific) events we do know by demonstration."[43] But what exactly is demonstration?

Demonstration is a kind of syllogism, although not all syllogisms are demonstrations.[44] A syllogism, in turn, is defined as a "discourse, in which certain things being stated, something other than what is stated follows of necessity from their being so."[45] This is a very wide definition covering any valid deductive argument, including, for example, Euclid's theorems. Passing over certain slight inaccuracies that need not concern us, we might use as an illustration of a syllogism: All theories based on empirical evidence deserve rational consideration. All psychological theories are based on empirical evidence. Therefore: All psychological theories deserve rational consideration.[46]

The sciences have communion with one another because of this common element of demonstration.[47] However, the scientist need answer only questions that fall within his own field and not concern himself with other fields indiscriminately.[48]

Despite his allegiance to syllogistic logic and his contributions to the field, Aristotle saw that induction alone, without syllogisms, may also give proof. His frequent substitution of letters of the alphabet for major, minor, and middle terms, and his use of explicit statement, show he was also aware that the subject matter of deductive arguments is quite irrelevant to their validity.[49] In other words, if false premises are used, a conclusion will be reached, but one which is untrue. His critics in the centuries to come triumphantly, and mistakenly, proclaimed that poor Aristotle never knew that one could not go beyond the truth of one's original premises by syllogistic reasoning.

Experience and observation are tests of his astronomical and biological theories. Observation of hundreds of species of animals were carefully reported in his biological treatises. He even contrasted observation and theory. He comments that observation, not theory, will reveal the method of generation of bees, for example, and that we should accept theories only if they agree with observation.[50]

In practice, Aristotle would sometimes seize on the few available facts and make sweeping generalizations. Naturally, he made mistakes. His driving search for knowledge did not allow time to make sure of his grounds before proceeding to the next question. Sometimes he was not too critical of the facts he accepted. He might even believe, without any attempt at verification, old wives tales and the accounts of credulous or sensation-seeking travelers. But the major source of difficulty was that enough facts simply were not available to him or to anyone else of his time.

His emphasis upon classification, often considered by historians of science to be a stage of science that must precede experiment, calls attention to this sheer lack of other information. Membership of an object to a given class was of crucial importance. This knowledge decided its essential nature or essence and marks Aristotle's distinctive contribution to biology.[51]

SCIENCE AND CAUSE

According to Aristotle, we also know by means of causality.[52] In fact, knowledge of causality is the essence of scientific knowledge. Four causes determine everything—the material cause, the motor or efficient cause, the formal cause, and the final cause.[53] Aristotle describes in considerable detail their nature and interrelation.[54] The material cause is what a thing is made of (e.g., the bronze of a statue); the motor or efficient cause is what sets into motion the process leading to its production (e.g., the sculptor); the formal cause gives the definition of its essential character (e.g., the horse itself); and the final cause is that aim or end toward which a thing develops (e.g., serving to decorate a temple). One of Aristotle's expositions of cause took place in his criticism of Thales, Empedocles, and the other pre-Socratic philosophers' views on the basic material constituent for the universe. They had given inadequate answers because of their preoccupation with the material cause and relative neglect of the other causes.[55] A major issue for Aristotle is whether the final or the efficient cause has priority.[56] Clearly, he asserts, it is the final cause, that for the sake of which the thing is formed.

Aristotle's meaning may be compared with the contemporary more or less unsophisticated view of the matter. Today when we speak of "cause" in an unqualified fashion we generally have in mind what Aristotle called efficient cause. "Final cause" is also occasionally referred to but almost always in this qualified two-word fashion. These two meanings meet the contemporary requirements for cause as something both necessary and sufficient to produce an effect. True, some persons today would accept one of these meanings and reject the other but they would do so on the basis of these two requirements, arguing that the one meaning or the other be rejected because it did not meet these criteria. Matter and form are not considered as causes today but as static aspects or characteristics of a thing, necessary but not sufficient as a cause. To Aristotle none of the four causes alone was sufficient; all were necessary. Thus to him cause meant conditions, none individually sufficient to account for the existence of a thing. It is not surprising that he would consider matter and form causes, since, without them, nothing could be or come to be.

Final cause and purpose are not synonymous; to call them so is misleading, because not all final causes have consciously foreseen ends, an implication of purpose often considered essential today. To Aristotle, human purposes do exist, people do display foresight and conscious intention, but purpose is just one aspect of final cause. No conscious purpose exists outside human actions. Natural processes are final ends, but not conscious intentions.

The prominence of end gives Aristotle's views a teleological character. To say that Aristotle was a teleologist is to say that he believed there was a plan or design to the universe. The teleologist holds that all things, including man, develop and move to an end, the final cause of their motion. Every instrument, including the human being, depends upon the nature of that for which it is designed. Anaxagoras had said that man was the most intelligent animal because he had hands; Aristotle said that man had hands because he was an intelligent animal.[57]

To make its meaning clear, the teleological position is often contrasted with explanation by sufficient cause. Those who accept the teleological position are said to deny efficient causes; those who accept efficient causes are said to deny final causes. In accepting both final and efficient causes (as well as formal and material causes), Aristotle was clearly more than a teleologist.

Insofar as he was a teleologist, Aristotle was also a functionalist (p. 67). A search for end is also a search for function or for what something does. For example, the eye, is designed for seeing. The explanation that Aristotle gives of its structure is based on its function. It exists for seeing. The life history of the organism as a whole seems decided from the outset by a prevision of the form which is the actual outcome. Little acorns grow into mighty oaks if nothing hinders that growth. There is no wrong turn; no beech or maple comes from the acorn. This functionalism dominates his views of biology and psychology.

Biological and Psychological Functions

It was mentioned in connection with Aristotle's classification of knowledge (p. 50), that physics, one of the theoretical sciences, has both biological and psychological aspects. Generally speaking, physics concerns natural things that are in motion.[58] What physical sciences tend to have in common is that they deal with things that have in themselves a principle of movement.[59]

Living things have a particular movement that arises from psyche.[60] Movement in this case should not be interpreted literally. Psyche is not self-moved; it does not transport itself in space (except incidentally as the body moves about). Its motion is more figurative, more a principle of movement than a literal movement. Psyche does manifest itself in movements of various sorts, however, for example, locomotion, alteration, diminution, growth, sensation, and thinking.[61] Inclusion of what we would call both biological and psychological activities is evident. Psyche is of primary interest to Aristotle, who wrote that all knowledge is valuable, but that knowledge of the psyche is to be prized above all (p. 50).

The word *psyche* is both more and less than "soul" for Aristotle. It means more in that *psyche* is integrated with matter. It is less in that the term soul later acquired a variety of religious significances quite absent from Aristotle's thinking. Although soul is the customary translation of *psyche*, it is best to use the word without translation to avoid both the subtractions and the whole host of accretions "soul" has acquired over the centuries since Aristotle used it in his own way.

His conception of life as *psyche* marks Aristotle as a vitalist, one who believes that there is a principle peculiar and essential to the phenomena of life. Vitalism stands in contrast to mechanism. For example, Democritus was a mechanist, since his theory of atoms encompassed living and nonliving objects alike; life was capable of mechanical expression. This is not the case with Aristotle, who postulated the special principle, *psyche*, necessary for life and absent from nonanimate things.

To Aristotle, body is what living matter is composed of; *psyche* that gives living its essential character. But what is its essential character? Life in this perspective is defined in terms of entelechy. Aristotle considers *psyche* "the first grade of actuality of a natural body having life potentially in it."[62] This is the first entelechy. Similarly, he defines the second entelechy as the operation of the function. The first entelechy deals with possession of a function not being exercised, or the potentiality of a function; the second entelechy involves the exercise of that function. An illustration of the first entelechy would be the acquisition of knowledge while asleep; and of the second entelechy, the exercise of that knowledge while awake. It is the latter with which we are concerned primarily. The sequence itself may cause confusion, since, in effect, the more important entelechy is the second, not the first. Yet Aristotle was being quite logical, since the capacity for a function must exist chronologically prior to the actual exercise of that function. Moreover, the first entelechy (*psyche*) is the subject and source of operations, which are known through the process of living. *Psyche* is the principle of these operations.

Entelechy has been variously defined in translation—the last stage in the process from potentiality to reality, the fullest realization, the culminating end, and the actuality. Here, the complete expression of some function would seem to be the most apt way to express its meaning. The teleological implications of this way of thinking are plain: it is the end toward which the *psyche* moves, that principle which Aristotle stressed.

To Aristotle, *psyche* basically meant living. In this, it is again evident why psychology should be considered an aspect of biology, since all psychological phenomena are included among living activities. This view is what Nuyens calls the biological conception of *psyche*.[63] It also makes clear that *psyche* is operative throughout the whole scale of animate things and is not confined to man alone. *Psyche* marks the distinction, not between thinking and unthinking beings, but between the organic and the inorganic.

It will be remembered (p. 46) that Aristotle distinguished between matter and form. In this context, body is matter; *psyche* is form.[64] The illustrations used before of man, horse, and plant as matter and form now become illustrations of body and *psyche*. The constituents of the body are matter; the form is composed of *psyche*. The living individual consists of both together: they form a unity. A dead body is only matter having no form of man.

A recasting of the traditional four causes is thus indicated. Instead of keeping them distinct and separate, Aristotle suggests that the *psyche* functions not only as the formal, but also as the efficient and final causes of the body.[65] *Psyche* is the efficient cause because it sets the process going in the body; it is the formal cause because the existence of the body means life; and it is the final cause because a body exists for living. His description of the final cause is Aristotle's way of saying that the body was made for *psyche,* that it exists for the sake of *psyche*. Psyche therefore coincides with three of the causes. The final, formal, and efficient causes all function as form and thus in an extended sense are formal, while the material cause is the passive recipient of form.

It follows, then, that when a natural state of affairs prevails, *psyche* dominates the body; in a corrupt state, the body dominates *psyche*.[66] Although he refers to it only casually and incidentally, Aristotle goes so far as to compare movement originated by *psyche* to that which animates automatic puppets.[67] This idea was to be developed by Descartes many centuries later (p. 159).

Body and *psyche* are not, as in the Platonic dualistic sense, a contrast of reality and form; they constitute a unity. To Aristotle they are aspects of the same living thing. Here again Aristotle disagrees with Plato. To Aristotle, *psyche* was essentially form in his own sense of the word. He views the unity and inseparability of body and *psyche* as an instance of matter and form.

The form of the body cannot exist without the matter of the body, with which it has an organic connection. What happens then to the *psyche* when the body is gone? One interpretation is that body and soul are so inextricably joined that one cannot survive without the other. Soul cannot exist disembodied. This straightforward, logically derived, and not unexpected view is clearly stated by Aristotle in Book 1 of *On the*

Soul.[68] Body and psyche are an inseparable unit but they can be distinguished for the sake of discussion. As Zeller,[69] a nineteenth century German philosopher, put it, "They are separable in thought, inseparable in reality." This particular way of thinking about body and psyche is still acceptable.

There is, however, another view which Aristotle holds that is logically discordant with this position. It is found in the part of On the Soul which some authorities believe was written in the earlier, Platonic phase of his thinking; it is consequently not representative of Aristotle's mature position. Here he seems to say that the highest element in man, Nous, which is not dependent upon the body, is immortal in that it survives the body. This divergent view was the cause of one of the most tangled controversies, both of the thinking of the Middle Ages and of modern scholarship. The rejection or acceptance of the immortality of the psyche are both defensible interpretations of Aristotle, although the former is adopted in discussing his psychology.

Aristotle's view of the relation of psyche and body should not be confused with a modern materialist or epiphenomenalist position in which life is considered an emergent characteristic—a resultant of the particular composition of the body. Life is thus subordinate, and antecedent in time, to the body. In Aristotelian terms this would mean that form is subordinate to matter, an impossible state of affairs. Despite the fact that in the modern view of the generative process, the matter of the body exists prior to psyche, Aristotle could not have accepted this position.[70]

A body is composed of organs needed for the body's functions.[71] An organ, in turn, is there to fulfill a function.[72] The concept of something being "organic" we owe to Aristotle. According to him, even plants have rudimentary organs, since roots are analogous to the mouth and serve to take in nourishment.[73] In contrast to Aristotle's functional definition, today we use the distinction between organic and inorganic structure to differentiate animate from inanimate things. This distinction on the basis of structure was to Aristotle only an incidental bit of information helping him to differentiate life from nonlife. The different ways living and nonliving things behave was more important to him than the existence of differences in bodily structure.

Aristotle argues that psyche is diffused in every part of the body. This diffusion of psyche becomes less marked in higher animals; the greater the degree of organization in the animal, the greater the degree of centralization and the less need for psyche in each part.[74] Despite the diffusion of psyche throughout the living body, a center for it in the body was sought. This center, the point at which psyche actuates the body,

Aristotle found in the heart, for the following reasons: diseases of the heart are fatal; psychological experiences, such as joy or sorrow, cause a disturbance of the heart; the heart is the first organ formed in the embryo, and its palpitation shows that the embryo has life.[75] In identifying life with *psyche* and *psyche* with the heart, Aristotle rejects the Platonic doctrine of the brain as the organ of the soul. He uses as one argument for doing so the fact that he found the brain insensible to direct stimulation.[76] It is ironic that Plato was right on the basis of the "wrong" argument. Plato assigned reason to the brain because of several irrelevant speculations, typical of which was the fact that the brain was the part of man nearest the heavens. Aristotle, on the other hand, was wrong for the "right"—that is, naturalistic—suppositions.

Aristotle referred to parts of the *psyche*, just at Plato did.[77] Neither meant "parts" in a literal sense. The term "aspects" was used instead of "parts" because it better reflected the structural view of Plato. In the same way, "functions" catches more accurately the train of Aristotle's thought. *Psyche* exhibits inclusive or general functions; these in turn may be broken down into specific functions.

According to Aristotle, *psyche* may be divided into an indefinite number of general functions. In practice the number of divisions most often used by him seems to range from two to five, depending on his particular intent. He divides functions into the rational and the irrational; into growing, sensing, remembering, desiring, reacting, and thinking; and into growing, sensing, and knowing. This last tripartite division referred to in a less functional way as nutritive, sensitive, and rational *psyche*, is the one most commonly used by later scholars to summarize the views of Aristotle.[78] But the more functional conception of growing, sensing, and knowing will often be used in the present account, especially when a quick, convenient way to summarize the functions of *psyche* is desired.

In living things there is an unbroken developmental hierarchy among levels of functioning; each higher level incorporates the lower levels of functioning—it cannot take place without them. The lower functions exist potentially in the higher function; to use Aristotle's own illustration, they exist in the same manner as the triangle does within the quadrilateral.[79] The highest act of thinking is at the top of a chain of continuous development in which sensing is the lowest form of discrimination.[80] This hierarchy serves to demonstrate that *psyche* has a unity with several related functions. This argument for the unity of *psyche* may be seen from a slightly different perspective as a theory of development. The growth *psyche* is included in the sensing (or animal) *psyche,* and the sensing *psyche* is part of the knowing (or human) *psyche.*

It would be a serious misunderstanding of his point of view to conclude that Aristotle had arrived at a theory of evolution. Two major considerations show that he did not anticipate such a theory. The modern view of evolution teaches that species are not fixed, but mutable. Furthermore, the more complicated structures are seen as having come later than the simple ones and as developing from them. On both these counts Aristotle took a diametrically opposed stand. Species had no origin for Aristotle; they were merely existent. A fully developed member of a species existed before young of that species were generated. In terms of that old puzzle, "Which came first, the chicken or the egg?" Aristotle's answer would have been unequivocal—the chicken came before the egg. Aristotle's conception of the developmental hierarchy reverses present-day evolutionary thinking. Aristotle said that the simpler function exists potentially in the more complex; evolutionary theory would say the more complex exists potentially in the simpler one. To Aristotle reality precedes potentiality in that the simpler function exists potentially in the more complex reality. The higher, more developed function stands first. This view is not only nonevolutionary, it is teleological in that the higher stage represents the realization of the lower; it is its end. In every sphere of reality the higher levels include the lower.

While living was the fundamental activity, the master function as it were, there were also various other expressions of *psyche.* The more specific biological-psychological functions of growing, sensing, remembering, desiring and reacting, and thinking now merit examination. It is in keeping with Aristotle's functional, active, and individually oriented point of view, that they are referred to in this grammatical form rather than in the more static and passive form of "growth," "sensation," and "thought."

GROWING

Progressive change of the organism is brought about by more specific activities that are included in the general function of growing. Briefly, these specific functions are persistence of the living entity, its accession of things from its surroundings, and the increase in size of every particle of it.[81] Growing is the most widely distributed general function exhibited by plants, animals, and men. Plants differ from other living things in that they possess this general function, but not sensing.[82] It is because of the relation of growth to plants that the term "vegetative soul" was applied to this general function in the Middle Ages.

SENSING

The specific function of sensing is possessed by animals and men, but not by plants.[83] Indeed, the ability to sense (in what Aristotle considers to be its most primitive manifestation of touch) is the means of distinguishing an animal from a plant.[84] To Aristotle, sensing objects means in modern terminology that perceiving is involved.

Aristotle specifies that by the external senses, he means the traditional five senses—sight, hearing, smell, taste, and touch—and no other. His argument for the existence of only five external senses runs somewhat as follows: If we assume that all objects in this world are known to us through these external senses, then the assumption of an additional sense would mean either that it merely duplicates an existing one or that it has no object. These are both unthinkable consequences in a world in which each thing is designed with an end in mind.

The senses each receive detailed consideration by Aristotle. He sees touch as more complex than the others, no matter how we subdivide the original five senses. Each sense organ responds to one or more sets of qualities. For example, the eye is sensitive to color, including black and white.[85]

Sensing and growing alike depend on alteration or movement from without.[86] Sensitivity is an activity aroused in the organism by the environment. This need for the dual functioning of organism and environment is based upon Aristotle's basic premise of movement or change, that the senses are related to the environment. But the organism's relation with the environment in sensing is different from what takes place in nutrition. Through nutrition, the material object is taken in from the environment; plants and animals devour the nutritive object. A sweet fig nourishes the organism through the matter of the fig: the form, sweetness, does not enter. In sensing, not the object itself, but its form is received from the environment, just as the wax receives the form of the seal without assimilating the metal of which it is composed.[87] In sensing, the body responds to the form of the external object without being acted upon by the matter.[88] The environmental effect is formal, not material.

Sensing is actualized by the sensible quality of the object,[89] but it is not merely the passive process of assimilating form. At this point the sensing of the organ becomes "like" the object sensed. The sense quality that is a potentiality of the object is actualized by the activity of the sense organs. The sky has the power to be seen as blue: the power of being visible to the eyes as blue. Hence, for Aristotle one does not see in the eyes but *with* the eyes.

The particular nature of sensing needs further clarification. Guthrie does this admirably in commenting on Aristotle's view of the nature of sensing. He writes: "The peculiarity of life is that *when* the bodily organ is materially altered by an external object, *then* another, totally different result supervenes, which we call sensation."[90] The objective stimulus is the cause of motion: a change that proceeds through a medium in the sense organ or some other part of the body becomes transformed or, to use Aristotle's term, is actualized into consciousness. The sounding in the object and the hearing of the animal are different, but when the process occurs, they are merged into one.[91]

The question arises as to how sensations of qualities—white, sweet, and so on—give a perception of concrete things? Moreover, there are perceptions that are not peculiar to any one of the senses. Movement, rest, shape, size, number, and duration are not experienced by any one sense alone. How, then, does one experience these so-called common sensibles? They seem to belong to or to be common to all senses, but are not peculiar to any one of them. When one says, "I smell smoke," he means not only that the smell is experienced but also that he is aware he is smelling it. These considerations led Aristotle to postulate that there was a common sense that carries out the functions of synthesizing the sensory elements into perceptual units, including both perception itself and con-sciousness that one is perceiving.

The particular argument of Aristotle for a composite functioning of the special senses in sensing self-perception may be stated as follows: If I do not perceive that I perceive the stimulus in a single indivisible act, then there would be another sense required in order for me to know I was sensing. But this would require a third to unite the previous ones. This, in turn, would require another sense to unite the three, and so on, by infinite regress. To cut this short, Aristotle asserts that the sense perceives itself. Hence the common sense depends on the combined functioning of the various senses in order to account for what it does.

The distinction of form and matter that has been applied to the relation of *psyche* and body, and sense and sense organ may be applied to self-perception. In this instance the knower perceives the qualities of an object and is aware that he has done so. *Psyche* has form and apprehends form; the sense organ has form and apprehends form; the person has form and apprehends form.

Aristotle concerned himself with the issue of whether a common sense was a sixth sense or a composite of the single senses.[92] Despite some disagreement among authorities, Aristotle's naturalistic spirit and his argument about perceiving incline one to believe that he thought common sense was a composite and not another sense.[93] The common sense functions through the common nature of all five senses and assures that we perceive one world, not one for each sense. It is not another or sixth sense, rather it is a name for certain functions of the five senses collectively. The alternative interpretation that would distinguish common sense from the five external senses will be taken up in the chapter on Aquinas.

The conscious being is always active. An admirable illustration may be found in Aristotle's account of sleeping, a function he related to the common sense.[94] After all, one does not sleep with some senses awake (i.e., active) and the others asleep. They function in common. Sleep is caused by fatigue of the common sense, which loses vitality. Sleep therefore has a restorative function.

Aristotle was a shrewd observer who let few details escape him. For example, he argues that sleep may also be brought about by food in the stomach. This last point would be corroborated by all who have observed the effects of a heavy meal. But instead of attributing sleep to blood being withdrawn from the brain, Aristotle had to account for it in terms of the heart, his center for *psyche*. He did so in the following fashion: Digestion causes gases to descend to the heart, which results in the heat of the body collecting around the heart. According to Aristotle, sleep is in a sense due to "heartburn."

In sleeping only the growth functions are active; sleep is inhibition of conscious functioning. How, therefore, is a dream to be accounted for?[95] Aristotle holds that it is similar to sensation yet not the same since there is no object sensed. He concludes that in dreaming there is a persistence of the effects of sensory stimulation that occurred during the waking state but that are carried over into sleeping.

REMEMBERING

Memory is related to former sense perception.[96] There is a persistence of the effect of sense impressions, and this allows us to make use of knowledge already acquired.[97]

Remembering, like dreaming, arises from the effects of sensing that persist after the object is removed. Sensory stimulation stamps in, as it were, an impression of the percept.[98] These traces of former movements, images, form one of the bases for remembering. There is a fainter continuation of the original movements through images. One also recognizes through memory the originally sensed object or event. Memory consists, then, of remaining aware of a perception of some event that occurred in the past. To have memory one must have awareness both of duration (time) and of a particular perception. Remembering, in the strict sense, is related to the general function of sensing and is therefore shared with animals. But memory is also a faculty in and of itself, for its object is distinct and separable—the past precisely as past.

Recollection (recall) is not the same as remembering.[99] Remembering is the spontaneous reproduction of past perceptions, i.e., a retention of the effect of past experience. Recall is the active search to recover these past perceptions. This demands hard thinking, in this context called by Aristotle deliberation, since it involves a search in which one reasons that he has had the experience in question. Hence, unlike remembering, recollection is limited to man, who alone has the power of deliberation.[100]

It was in connection with recall that Aristotle systematized the now famous doctrine of the laws of association. Recall occurs because we are able to call up a series of associations in regular order,[101] i.e., according to specified principles. Plato implied that similarity and contiguity are two of the means by which recollection operates, but he did not develop the idea.[102] Aristotle was the first to develop it systematically. He believed that three sorts of relationships serve as links in the chain of associations—similarity, contrast, and contiguity.[103] Recall occurs insofar as experiences succeed one another in memory. This is to say that the recall of one object tends to be followed by the recall of that which is like it (similar to it), contrary to it (contrasted with it), or accompanying it (contiguous with it) in the original learning. Similarity, contrast, and contiguity as sketched by Aristotle were historic 'ly to form the basis for the doctrine of association in the centuries to cume. Three other factors relevant to modern learning theory also are mentioned by Aristotle, to which little attention was paid until the modern period. Aristotle was aware of the contention that the more often an experience is repeated, the better it will be remembered.[104] He spoke of "some" events as being better remembered after a single experience than others experienced many times. Remembering after only a single experience is a qualification of the more general norm, not specifically verbalized, that the more an experience is repeated, the better it will be remembered. "Bonds of association" also are seen by Aristotle as acquiring special strength from emotion. He indicates that when excited by love or by fear, the person can see a desired one or a feared one approaching despite there being little resemblance.[105] He goes on to state that the more one is under the influence of emotion, the less "similarity" is necessary for this to happen. Aristotle also spoke of things arranged in a "fixed" order as more easily recalled than items "badly" arranged.[106] Something approaching the distinction between meaningful and rote materials is suggested in this identification of order of materials as a potent factor in recall. All of these factors were to be subjected to research scrutiny in the modern study of learning.

DESIRING AND REACTING

In some of his writings Aristotle raised desiring (appetite, conation) to a status equal with growing, sensing, and knowing and spoke of it as one of four general functions.[107] Desire is related to sensation and pleasure-pain (which gives rise to it) and has consequences in reacting.

Sensing, pleasure-pain, desire, and self-motion form a sequence. The process is as follows: pleasure and pain follow upon sensing, although they are not a part of sensing itself. Rather, they are consequences of sensory experiences.[108] As explained earlier, sensing is the means whereby objects in the environment are perceived. Some objects are perceived as pleasurable, others as unpleasurable. Once these feelings are experienced, desire is introduced. Where there is sensing, there is pleasure and pain; where there is pleasure and pain, there is desire.[109] Ignoring pain for the moment, what the organism desires is the satisfaction that the perceived object will give. It should be noted that desire is related to sensing in a circular fashion since sensing is followed by pleasure and pain, which in turn arouse desire, and desire is a craving for the pleasant and a cringing from the painful. So far, sensing, pleasure-pain, and desiring have been accounted for sequentially. Reacting (locomotion) must now be brought into this sequence.

Aristotle says that desire is the immediate and efficient cause of movement.[110] Locomotion is also related through pleasure and pain to desire since it takes us toward an object we desire or away from one we desire to avoid. As Aristotle puts it, unless moved by compulsion, an animal is moved only insofar as it seeks pleasure or avoids pain.[111] Pleasure and pain are not simple impressions following upon sensing; they incite desire, which brings about locomotion and completes the process. This sequence, however, is subject to an important qualification in that thinking is also a source of movement (p. 66).

Aristotle's theory of the nature of pleasure and pain is a statement of the doctrine that pleasure is that which is according to nature and pain that which is contrary to nature.[112] Pleasure and pain are therefore the concomitants or accompaniments of activities. Aristotle holds that pleasure accompanies the free expression of activity, an unimpeded exercise of the functions of the *psyche*. If the experience is painful, it is so because it conflicts with the natural state of the functioning of the *psyche*. The realization of any natural function is pleasurable and the pleasure is proportional to the completeness of the realization. Pleasure is moreover related to the exercise of a function. When an activity is pleasurable, it tends to be exercised—those who delight in geometry become geometricians.[113] Instances of pathological pleasure do not contradict the claim that freedom and naturalness characterize pleasure since Aristotle held that these abnormal pleasures come about from a kind of diseased condition of the body and not from psychological activities.

In his analysis of psychological motion, or of psychological field forces, to put it in more modern terms, Aristotle appealed to the concept of an "unmoved mover."[114] Its use in connection with desire is straightforward and objective. In the relation between the desiring individual and the desired object, the latter serves as a stimulus, or mover, as he called it. But this mover is not similarly affected by desire. Consequently it is an "unmoved mover." In a sense, then, the object of desire, the unmoved mover, is outside the process of the functioning organism. Aristotle argues that every action has an unmoved mover. As a consequence the number of unmoved movers is countless.

The concept of the unmoved mover was seized upon by scholars in later ages in their search for God in Aristotle and a single "supreme unmoved mover" was lifted to theological heights. His remarks lend credence to this position.[115] His highest order attempt at unification reduced the number of kinds of motion, to either forty-seven or fifty-five kinds of unmoved movers. But in this same discussion he speaks on one eternal mover whose essence is actuality. It would seem that his analysis of unmoved movers took place in two different realms—one concerned with kinds of motion, the other with a theological necessity. His use in psychology of the concept of the unmoved mover was singularly free from theological complications. In baldest terms he seems to mean that for every reaction there is a stimulus.

It is convenient at this point to add emotions to the discussion of desire. Aristotle's Rhetoric[116] and his Nichomachean Ethics[117] contain most of the relevant material. An illustration of how he assigns psychological implications to philosophical concerns is found in his treatment of emotions and desires as they relate to moral virtues. These virtues include courage, which necessitates a psychological discussion of fear; temperance, which requires that desires be considered in a psychological setting; and good temper, which demands consideration of the psychology of anger. Other psychological matters are discussed in a similar vein. Various emotions are analyzed in terms of the disposition that gives rise to the particular emotion of the person towards whom it is directed, and of the occasions that give rise to it.[118] An essentially practical description of the emotions emerges.

His comments concerning emotion extend even into his theory of the fine arts, including the theatre. In discussing the nature of tragedy, he claims that its function is to arouse pity and fear, but only in such fashion and in such amounts that will allow us to purge ourselves of these emotions.[119] This is the famous doctrine of catharsis. Catharsis is brought about by transferring to the tragic hero our own sufferings. In him we see ourselves, and in his fate our doom. But since this is not the actual situation, since his particular fate is not ours, we shift our fear for ourselves into fear for him. This emotional involvement allows us to release our apprehensions and to deflect our psychic burdens onto another's shoulders. Self-pity gives way to compassion, and we are better for this emotional experience.

THINKING

A man may desire and thus act; he may also think,[120] and thought may or may not be followed by action. In other words, not only desire but also thinking, in which calculation of the means toward an end becomes part of the sequence, may precede action.

Action by no means implies all sorts of movement. Consistent with what has been said, action is a kind of movement in which an end is involved.[121] All other movements are just that and nothing more, since they do not involve an end and are therefore not complete. Again Aristotle is being both functional and teleological in approach.

Some animals have the ability to sense and also the ability to imagine, but none have the ability to think. Imagination in animals is the *highest* of their functions. In Aristotle's opinion man is the only animal that thinks.[122]

To Aristotle, thinking is a process that depends upon the hierarchically lower general functions. It is not completely separable since each higher level presupposes lower ones. Those functions that bear a hierarchical relation to thought are sensation, imagination, and memory. Thought requires sensory experiences with which to work; and sensation reverts to its derivative, imagination, which in turn leads to memory. The materials for thought are supplied by the imagination. In this context, images serve as perceptions.[123] Thinking depends upon the retention of images, which are molded by thought into relations and patterns, so that there is not merely a flux of images but a meaningful organization of them.

Aristotle's insistence that images are necessary for thought is worth stressing. He leaves no doubt of his position—thinking takes place in images,[124] never without them.[125] The influence of this Aristotelian dogma of no image-no thought was to last well into the modern period—indeed, until the turn of the twentieth century and the Würzburg School (pp. 308–9).

By a shift of perspective from memory to thought, association becomes an integral aspect of thought (p. 63). Similarity, contrast, contiguity, and the rest bring about associations that we refer to as thought.

Thought is not seen by Aristotle as a means of suppressing natural impulses. Suppression of any natural human function he considers a distortion[126] of the natural. Fear and anger and other emotions have suitable occasions when they are appropriate. There are things we ought to fear, and there are occasions when we should be angry. Thought does not suppress emotions: it helps to determine right conduct.

Overview

Aristotle gave us the first functional view of mental processes. The *psyche* is not isolated from the thing known. This yields a functional definition of it. *Psyche* is a *process*; *psyche* is what *psyche* does. The inner structure of *psyche* is supported and partly guided by a field of external relations. This field, the environmental world, cannot be defined unless we consider as an integral part of it what we do in response to it. Organism, a concept he introduced, and environment are two aspects of the same interacting process. Psychological functions are understood in terms of some object or objective toward which they are directed. A psychological activity is a response directed to this object or objective; desiring is understood in terms of that which is desired; thinking is understood in terms of that which is thought.

No doubt it would be pleasing to claim Aristotle as the first psychologist interested in contentual objectivity (behavior), and therefore a precursor of the present behavioral emphasis. However, this hope must be dashed in view of his contentions that actions are the only motions of psychological significance. Nevertheless, reacting does play a small but essential part in biological and psychological functions. Actions are always particular to Aristotle and, as we have seen, science is not concerned with particulars, but with universals.[127] To put the same point in a somewhat different way, actions relate to individuals, and knowledge of all actions is the result of experience and not of theorizing.[128] Further, actions involve practical knowledge, not philosophical wisdom.[129] From Aristotle's point of view, behavior, as such, is not open to scientific study. Contentual subjectivity is still paramount.

The continuity of psychobiological development is another major guiding concept in the thinking of Aristotle. His account of psychological functioning from thinking, the highest level, down to growing, the lowest level, is consistent throughout. Developmentalism in reverse, as it were, was being advanced as a prescriptive attitude. The pre-Socratics had considered change but not development; Plato held to a static prescription with his Forms. Aristotle, however, conceived of development as essential to the understanding of living things. As he conceived it, the functional character of each process lends itself to a dynamic conception.

He also did much to advance an empirical point of view. Before Aristotle, some of the pre-Socratics and Sophists had taken a position of extreme sensationalism; Plato's position can be characterized as extreme rationalism. Reconciling these two points of view, Aristotle took a mediating position of empiricism *and* rationalism. He held that knowledge was gained from sense experience and thinking. Indeed, in matters involving action, he said that "men of experience succeed even better than those who have theory without experience."[130] But experience is still knowledge of individuals, not of universals; as such, it is dependent upon theory, and theory is derived from reason. Experience is therefore inferior to reason.

The process of moving from generalities to particulars, i.e., deduction, is stressed in his discussion. However, there is as much emphasis on collecting facts, only later to be put in a theoretical framework, so that there is no doubt that induction was used in considerable measure as well.

Aristotle was more naturalistic in outlook than Plato. He tended to keep within the realm of the natural world, i.e., within the natural processes of living, sensing, and thinking. When he ventured beyond physics, as all the Greeks did, his position was commendably cautious, although not without fire and conviction.

So far as a psychological orientation is concerned, unity of body and *psyche* made Aristotle a monist; in terms of epistemologial knowing, Aristotle was a dualist in that he separated body and *psyche*. In the centuries to come Aristotle's teachings on epistomological knowing were to be adopted by the church, particularly through the theological doctrine provided by Aquinas (Chapter 6).

Determinism, the theory that human events are explicable in terms of antecedent events, had been known before Aristotle. In fact, he chided the pre-Socratics for their preoccupation with material causes. But it was Aristotle who systematically developed the concept in terms of the four causes. More than any other single factor, Aristotle's insistence upon the primacy of final cause, teleology, over efficient cause was to result in the overthrow of his ideas during the scientific revolution of the sixteenth and the seventeenth centuries. In that period the physical description of natural processes concerned itself more with efficient cause and consequent effect. To be sure, the more biologically-minded Leibniz and Harvey fought a valiant rear-guard action in defense of purpose and teleology. Gradually, thereafter, this doctrine disappeared, or rather merged with a more general functional viewpoint.

On psychological matters, in summary, Aristotle was: functionalistic, contentually subjectivistic, developmentalistic, rationalistic and empiricistic, deductive, deterministic (with a teleological emphasis), and monistic. It is also apparent that in the main, his outlook was naturalistic, nomothetic, and puristic. He followed the trends already established in Greek philosophy-science but sharpened them and gave them more explicit recognition than they had previously received by writing their first history.

Study of Aristotle is rewarded by a feeling of wonder at the modernity of much of what he says about psychological matters. It is with Aristotle that we have for the first time a reasonably complete picture of a whole psychology. He was, of course, wrong in many of his "facts" and he omitted important topics; but his overall framework of growing, sensing, remembering, desiring, reacting, and thinking, with but a few changes, bear more than a resemblance to modern psychology. Aristotle was the first philosophical psychologist. The advent of a scientific psychology was still far in the future.

References*

1. The account of Aristotle's life, works, and chronology leans heavily upon information from J. H. Randall, *Aristotle* (New York: Columbia University Press, 1960) and W. Jaeger, *Aristotle: Fundamentals of the History of His Development* (Oxford: Clarendon Press, 1934). The chronology of his works given by Jaeger is followed and supplemented by that of F. J. Nuyens, "The Evolution of Aristotle's Psychology," *Proceedings of the 10th International Congress on Philosophy* (Amsterdam, 1948), pp. 1101–1104.
2. *Ibid.*
3. T. W. Organ, *An Index to Aristotle: in English Translation* (Princeton: Princeton University Press, 1949).

*See p. 19 for description of reference style.

4. R. M. Hutchins, ed., *The Great Books of the Western World*, Vols. VIII–IX, Works of Aristotle, trans. W. D. Ross (Chicago: Encyclopaedia Britannica, 1952), (*c.* 340–322 B.C.). *Physics,* 193b 22–194a 18.

5. *Ibid.,* 193b 35, p. 270.

6. *On the Soul* 428a 11.

7. *Metaphysics* 990a 33–993a 16, 1040a 9, 1078b 6–1079b 11, 11086a 188–1087a 25; *On Interpretation* 17a 38.

8. *Physics* 194b 12.

9. *Ibid.,* 324b 5–22.

10. *Ibid.,* 194b 9, p. 271.

11. *Categories; On Interpretation; Prior Analytics; Posterior Analytics; Topics; On Sophistical Refutations.*

12. From *peri,* a prefix meaning "around," and *patos,* meaning "a path."

13. W. D. Ross, *Aristotle; a Complete Exposition of His Works and Thought,* 5th ed. (New York: Meridian Books, 1959), p. 14.

14. In the edition used *(op. cit.)* the total of his complete works are given in 1415 printed pages. The so-called "Biological Treatise" occupies 331 pages, while *On the Soul* and the other psychological works occupy 98 more for a total of 429 pages or 30 percent of the works.

15. For the purposes of this presentation Jaeger's *(op. cit.)* opinion about the dating of the books of *De Anima* is followed instead of Nuyens' *(op. cit.)* This means that the discussion of *Nous* in *De Anima* III, Chapters 4 and 5, is considered an earlier position in harmony with earlier ethical and metaphysical views, but not expressive of his final thinking. The doctrine of the *Nous* as making all things and being separate, deathless, eternal, and impersonal is questioned. This is a matter of a judgment with which, at least, Nuyens would disagree—and he has some cogent arguments that this doctrine represents a final phase of Aristotle's thinking. This author is in agreement with both Nuyens and Jaeger that some of the physical treatises date from the transition period.

16. *Metaphysics* 1040b 5.

17. *On the Soul* 404a 1–411b 30.

18. *Metaphysics* 980a 1.

19. *On the Soul* 402a 1–4.

20. *Metaphysics* 980a 22.

21. *Ibid.*, 983b 14.
22. *Ibid.*, 500a–501a.
23. *Ibid.*, 501b–c.
24. *Topics* 151b 1 p. 206.
25. *On Dreams* 458b 3.
26. *On the Soul* 443a 12; *On the Parts of Animals*, 642b 18; *Politics*, 1332b 5.
27. *Topics* 130b 8, 132a 20, 133a 21, 134a 15, 140a 36.
28. *Nicomachean Ethics* 1097b 25–1098a 20.
29. *Metaphysics* 1025b 25ff.
30. *Ibid.*, 981a 12–982a 4.
31. *Metaphysics* 981a 25.
32. *Nicomachean Ethics* 1140b 2.
33. *Ibid.*, 1140b 31–1141a 1.
34. *Physics* 184a 21–b 14, p. 259. This description of psychological "individuation within a mass," as it might be called, showed Aristotle's appreciation of the Gestalt properties of perceptual wholes long before that point of view became prominent on the psychological scene.
35. *Posterior Analytics* 87b 28–88a 17.
36. *On Dreams* 458b 2.
37. *Physics* 195b 19, p. 271; *Metaphysics*, 983a 25, 993b 23, 994b 29.
38. *Prior Analytics* 99b 15–100b 17.
39. *Nichomachean Ethics* 1141a 8.
40. *Ibid.*, 1098b 1–8.
41. *Ibid.*, 1139b 18–35.
42. *Posterior Analytics* 90b 24.
43. *Ibid.*, 72b 16, p. 98.
44. *Prior Analytics* 25b 28.
45. *Ibid.*, 24b 18–20, p. 39.
46. J. Lukasiewicz, *Aristotle's Syllogistic*, 2nd ed. (Oxford: Clarendon, 1957), Chapter 3.
47. *Posterior Analytics* 77a 26.
48. *Ibid.*, 77b 7.
49. *Rhetoric* 1356b 8.
50. *On the Generation of Animals* 760b 70.
51. E.g., *On the Parts of Animals* 639a 1–642b 4.
52. *Posterior Analytics* 94a 20.
53. *On the Generation of Animals* 715b 3–5.
54. *Physics* 194b 16–195b 30; *On the Soul* 415b 8–11; *Metaphysics* 1013a 24–1014a 25.
55. *Metaphysics* 983b 7–985b 22.
56. *On the Parts of Animals* 639b 12–640a 12.

57. *Ibid.*, 687a 8.
58. *Physics* 185a, 12.
59. *Metaphysics* 1064a, 17.
60. *On the Soul* 415b 8–28, 432a 14–434a 22; *On the Motion of Animals* 700b 4–701a 6, 701a 35, 702a 35, 703a 2.
61. *On the Soul* 406a 13, 413a 24, 415b 19–27.
62. *Ibid.*, 412a 30, p. 642.
63. F. J. Nuyens, *L'évolution de la Psychologie d'Aristotle* (Louvain: Institut Supérieur de Philosophie, 1948).
64. *On the Soul* 412a 12–413a 10.
65. *Ibid.*, 415b 8–11; *On the Parts of Animals* 645b 15; *On the Generation of Animals* 715b 3–5; *Metaphysics* 1044a 37–1044b 1.
66. *Politics* 1254a 31–b 4.
67. *On the Motion of Animals*, 701b 1–5.
68. *On the Soul* 403a 2–b 19, 407b 15–16.
69. Zeller, E. *Aristotle and the Earlier Peripatetics*, Vol. 2. (New York: Longmans, Green, 1897).
70. *Politics* 1334b 20.
71. *On the Generation of Animals* 716a 25.
72. *On the Parts of Animals* 687a 11.
73. *On the Soul* 412b 3.
74. *On the Motion of Animals* 703a 38.
75. *On the Parts of Animals* 657a 25, 656a 30; *On the Motion of Animals* 703b 24; *On the Generation of Animals* 734b 26.
76. *On the Parts of Animals* 656a 18–28.
77. *On the Soul* 402b 1–8.
78. E.g., *On the Generation of Animals* 736b 15.
79. *On the Soul* 414b 29.
80. *Posterior Analytics* 99b 35.
81. *Generation and Corruption* 321a 19–b 12.
82. E.g., *On the Soul* 424a 33; *On the Parts of Animals* 666a 35.
83. The major discussion of the five senses occupies Chapters 5 through 12 of Book II of *On the Soul*, 416b 31–424b 19. (Hernstein and Boring, Excerpt No. 1 gives a major portion of these chapters).
84. *On the Sense and Sensible* 436b 10.
85. *On the Soul* 418a 27ff.
86. *Ibid.*, 415b 24–416b 32.
87. *Ibid.*, 424a 16–24.
88. *Ibid.*, 425b 22–24.
89. *Ibid.*, 417a 10–418a 6, 418b 27–419b 11.

90. W. K. Guthrie, *The Greek Philosophers: from Thales to Aristotle* (New York: Harper and Brothers, 1950), p. 149.
91. *On the Soul* 425b 27.
92. *Ibid.*, 424b 20–427a 15.
93. E.g., *ibid.*, 424b 20–22.
94. *On Sleep and Sleeplessness* 953b 12–958a 32.
95. *On Dreams* 458b 1–464b 18.
96. *On Memory and Reminiscence* 449b 1–453b 11. (Herrnstein and Boring, Excerpt No. 65, gives the portion devoted to associative memory.)
97. *Ibid.*, 450a 14, 541a 16; *Posterior Analytics* 99b 36–100a 8; *On the Sense and Sensible* 441b 23–24.
98. *On Memory and Reminiscence* 450a 31, p. 691.
99. *Ibid.*, 451a 21–453b 11.
100. *Ibid.*, 453a 13.
101. *Ibid.*, 451b 11, p. 693.
102. R. M. Hutchins, ed., *The Great Books of the Western World*, Vol. VII, Plato, *Dialogues*, trans. B. Jowett (Chicago: Encyclopaedia Britannica, 1952) (c. 390–348 B.C.). Phaedo, 73c.
103. *On Memory and Reminiscence* 451b 19–21.
104. *Ibid.*, 451b 11.
105. *On Dreams* 460b 2.
106. *On Memory and Reminiscence* 452a 3.
107. *On the Soul* 432b 3.
108. *Ibid.*, 414b 5.
109. *Ibid.*, 413b 23.
110. *Ibid.*, 433a 5–434a 22; *On the Motion of Animals* 701a 35, 703a 5.
111. *On the Soul* 432b 17.
112. *Nicomachean Ethics* 1174b 4.
113. *Ibid.*, 1175a 34.
114. *On the Soul* 434b 33.
115. E.g., *Metaphysics* 1071b 3–1075a 14, *passim*; *On the Motion of Animals* 699a 12–700a 26.
116. *Rhetoric* 1378a 20–1388b 30.
117. *Nicomachean Ethics* 1105b 19–1106a 14, 1108a 30–1109b 27, 1111b 4–18.
118. *Rhetoric* 1378a 20.
119. *Poetics* 1149b 27.
120. *On the Soul* 433a 5–434a 22; *On the Motion of Animals* 701a 1–b 33.
121. *Metaphysics* 1048b 22.
122. *On the Soul* 433a 12.

123. *Ibid.,* 432b 14.
124. *Ibid.,* 431b 2.
125. *Ibid.,* 431a 16.
126. *Nicomachean Ethics* 1103a 14–1109b 27.
127. *Nicomachean Ethics* 1110b 6.
128. *Metaphysics* 981a 1.
129. *Nicomachean Ethics* 1141b 21.
130. *Metaphysics* 981a 13–15.

Chapter 4

Theophrastus AND Galen:
THE HELLENISTIC AND ROMAN PERIODS

With the deaths of Aristotle and Alexander, Greek history, philosophy, and science entered a third phase known as the Hellenistic Period, which extended from about 300 to 100 B.C. It followed the conquest of the Near East by Alexander, when Greek culture was carried eastward and Oriental culture spread westward. The Hellenistic Period is often referred to as the twilight of Greek thinking, but the decline was by no means abrupt. Progress continued to be made, but by men who stood in the giant shadow of Aristotle. Psychology was most advanced by Theophrastus, who was a lesser figure than Aristotle but whose views were more modern—at least in spirit—than those of his master.

Theophrastus

Theophrastus was born in 372 B.C. He first came to Athens in order to study under Plato, but he became the friend of Aristotle, whom he joined in his travels and whose interest in natural history he shared. When Aristotle was obliged to leave Athens in 323–322 B.C., he appointed Theophrastus his successor as head of the Lyceum, and though only twelve years Aristotle's junior, Theophrastus lived long enough to serve as head of the Lyceum for thirty-five years. He died in 287 B.C. complaining that life was too short: a man had to leave it just when he was beginning to understand its mysteries.

Theophrastus was particularly interested in the study of botany. His two treatises on plants make him the founder of that science. As if this were not enough of an accomplishment for one man, no less than 227 treatises on such varied topics as religion, politics, education, rhetoric, mathematics, astronomy, logic, natural history, meteorology, ethics, and psychology are ascribed to him![1] He showed an unflagging zeal in his scientific inquiries and continued the pattern laid down by Aristotle of systematically collecting and reviewing his material, sometimes with the aid of other experts.

In most matters he followed Aristotle faithfully, but he tended to be even more empirical. He sought an empirical basis for scientific theories and argued that facts should not be forced to fit into a theory.[2] He reacted against the major role assigned by Aristotle to the search for final causes, and held that science is concerned more with efficient causes than with final causes.[3] This was an anticipation of an advance not actually made until the time of Galileo, when it was realized that final causes are in fact scientifically irrelevant.

In expressing these objections and reservations he shows a more naturalistic and modern spirit than Aristotle. Theophrastus went into much more detail in describing the observable processes of the mind— sensation, perception, pleasure and pain, emotion, and temperament.

These tendencies of Theophrastus were expressed in *On the Senses,* a treatise on physiological psychology.[4] Aristotle notwithstanding, he returned the seat of the intellect to the brain. His treatise contains not only valuable criticisms of earlier thinkers but also a statement of his own views. His specific findings and assertions on vision, hearing, smell, taste, and touch are given in such detail as to defy summarization.

Throughout this work, he shows the spirit of critical scientific thinking that characterized his general attitude. Perceptions to him reveal external nature, and external nature exists independently of our perception of it. Theophrastus also recognized that it was not enough to pay attention to the stimulus alone, since the same stimulus may have different effects according to the conditions present in the sensory organs.

But how does an object act upon the sense organ? Theophrastus rejected the theory of emanations for several reasons, among them that effluences would not explain taste, touch, and smell; this would require a wasting away of such objects over time, and many objects that are sources for these experiences are characterized by the short duration of the sensory impressions they create. He also rejected the theory that the sensed object comes into contact with the sense organ directly. In his view nothing actually penetrated the organ. He then adopted Aristotle's position that sensory objects act upon the senses through media and not by direct presence. He disagreed with Aristotle, however, concerning the locus of sensory qualities. Theophrastus argued that whatever the effects of the objects on the sense organs, these effects are carried to the brain before they have the quality of sensory experiences. Aristotle believed this to be true only for some sense modalities; for others he held that the sensory qualities are generated in the sense organs themselves. From a modern standpoint, Theophrastus had the better of this argument.

According to Theophrastus, pleasure is a natural accompaniment of that which is in accord with nature. But unlike certain of his predecessors, he did not believe that pain is also involved in all sense impressions. He based this denial on what he called the plain facts of observation. Excessive stimulation sometimes causes pain because it disturbs the correspondence between sense organs and object, but this is not usually the case. He had no patience with the view of Plato that one's pleasures may be false. All pleasures are true in the sense that they are pleasures, no matter what our ethical or other judgments about them may be.

Theophrastus is best known today, however, for his *Characters,* a collection of personality sketches.[5] This was a quasi-literary contribution, and before we consider it, something should be said about the literary tradition upon which he built.

Centuries earlier, Homer had used the device of attributing a master personality trait to certain characters; thus he refers to "crafty Ulysses" and "brave Hector." Aristotle had rather casually inserted descriptions of character types in his *Ethics* and *Rhetoric.* But what to his master was a passing illustration became in the hands of Theophrastus a new psychological genre—the description of types of character. He was not content to use a single descriptive term for a person, as Homer had been. Instead, he deduced from a particular attribute of personality the variety of consequences that would follow in the diverse circumstances in which that trait might be exhibited. He therefore demonstrated the interdependence among the behaviors described. But by selection, within the limitation of a personality attribute, there were neither incongruities nor combinations of more than one master trait. It followed that he imposed unity upon the personality but did not allow incongruity. In this respect, at least, the Greek dramatists Aeschylus and Sophocles were immeasurably superior in giving subtlety to their portrayal of personality. Nevertheless, it would appear that this subtlety was utilized with literary aims in view; the efforts of Theophrastus, though relatively one-dimensional, were carried out with some awareness of their scientific interest. He says as much in his dedicatory letter to the *Characters,* indicating that his interest in the subject was aroused when he considered that, while the whole of Greece had the same climate and all Greeks had the same upbringing, they did not all have the same character.

Each vignette emphasizes one or another major trait. Dissembling, flattery, garrulity, boorishness, penuriousness, tactlessness, and surliness are some of the thirty character traits sketched. The one on flattery follows.

Flattery might be understood to be a sort of converse that is dishonourable, but at the same time profitable, to him that flatters; and the Flatterer will say as he walks beside you "Are you aware how people are looking at you? No man in Athens gets such attention;" or this, "You were the man of the hour yesterday in the Porch; why, although there were more than thirty present, when the talk turned to who was the finest man there, the name that came to every lip both first and last was yours." And while he says such things as these, he picks a speck from your coat; or if so be a morsel of chaff be blown into your beard, plucks it out and then says with a smile "D'ye see? because you and I be not met a whole day, your beard's full of grey hairs—though I own your hair is singularly dark for your age." He will desire silence when his friend speaks, or praise the company for listening to him; when he comes to a stop, he will cry in approbation "Quite right;" and if he make a stale jest will laugh, and stuff the corner of his cloak in his mouth as if he could not hold his merriment. Moreover, any man that comes their way is bidden stand awhile till the great one be gone past. He will buy apples and pears and bring them in for the children, and giving them before their father will kiss them and cry "Chicks of a good strain." When he buys shoes with him at the cordwainer's, he will tell him that the foot is shapelier than the shoe. And if he go visiting a friend of his, he will run ahead and tell him he is coming, and then face round and say "I have announced you." He is the man, you may be sure, to go errands to the women's market there and back without stopping for breath; and of all the guests will be first to praise the wine; and will say in his patron's ear "You are eating nothing"; or picking up some of the food upon the table exclaim "How good this is, isn't it?" and will ask him whether he is not cold? and will he not have his coat on? and shall he not draw his skirts a little closer about him? and saying this, bend forward to whisper in his ear; and will speak to another with his eye on his friend. He will take the cushions from the lackey at the theatre and place them for him himself. He will remark how tasteful is the style of his patron's house; how excellent the planting of his farm; how like him the portrait he has had made.[6]

It may be noted that this and the other characters were concerned with the less admirable aspects of human nature. Lest a misanthropic point of view be attributed to Theophrastus, there are several references in the ancient literature to a lost companion volume, devoted to "good" characters.

On the death of Theophrastus, his successor as head of the Lyceum was Strato of Lampsacus. Strato was also a worker faithful to the naturalistic spirit of Aristotle. His numerous writings, now lost, dealt with so many of the problems of natural science that he gained the title of "the Physicist." The many successors to Strato at the Lyceum over the centuries appear to have been of relatively little importance. More and more they became involved in specialized investigations in grammar, literature, and ethics; and the earlier keen interest in the sciences disappeared almost completely. It was not until the sixth century A.D., after a span of 860 years, that the school finally closed its doors. However, even during the lifetime of Theophrastus and Strato, the intellectual center of the Hellenistic world shifted to Alexandria, and in doing so the character of that world changed.

Alexandria and Science

The great empire of Alexander had disintegrated at his death, various parts falling into the hands of his generals. A few large monarchies replaced the empire. Of particular importance in the history of science was Ptolemaic Egypt.[7] Ptolemy I, a Macedonian general, proclaimed himself king and founded the Ptolemaic dynasty that was to last for three centuries. The last of his line was Cleopatra, upon whose death Egypt fell to the Romans. Ptolemy's capitol was Alexandria, a city founded a few years before by Alexander himself. Under the aegis of Ptolemy and of his son, Ptolemy II, both the great library—the largest in the ancient world—and the museum at Alexandria were organized. The museum was primarily a research institute. It eventually comprised living accommodations for the scientists and their assistants, seminar rooms, laboratories, botanical and zoological gardens, and an observatory. The Ptolemys made still another contribution to science, indirect but not unimportant. The stipends they paid the museum scientists were the first financial support scientists had received.

The first head of the museum was the same Strato who on the death of his master returned to Athens from Alexandria to lead the Lyceum. In his dozen or so years in Alexandria, he so emphasized science (at the expense of philosophy) that the future course of the institution was assured.

During the first century of existence of the museum much important scientific work was done. Alexandria became a center of specialists, for it provided an opportunity for sustained work in narrower fields. This approach survived only briefly and did not reappear on such an extensive scale until the modern period. Among the mathematicians at the museum was Euclid. Archimedes may also have visited Alexandria from Syracuse, and was in any event directly influenced by its school of mathematics. Advances in mechanics, astronomy, geography, medicine, and anatomy were made as well.

These specialists were indifferent to philosophical issues rather than actually hostile toward them. But their indifference increased in direct proportion to the success of their methods of specialization. In this respect they were the first modern scientists! These men realized that the earlier attempts at syntheses of knowledge had been premature. As scientific Candides they resolved to cultivate their own gardens, though they intended to talk with their neighbors over the fences they were erecting.

From the Alexandrian point of view, psychological matters were not scientific. Apparently, they were considered outside the realm of naturalism, while anatomical and physiological concerns were not. Psychology and physiology, heretofore intermingled, were now separated. The work of Herophilus and Erasistratus, which we are now to consider, must therefore be referred to as work in anatomy and physiology. From the perspective of today, their work is relevant to psychology itself, but from the perspective of Alexandrian science it was not.

Herophilus of Chalcedon, who lived about 300 B.C., a contemporary of Euclid, was one of the founders of anatomy. In the scientifically free atmosphere of Alexandria, he not only dissected the human body, but did so publicly. The anatomy of man he compared explicitly to that of animals. He recognized the brain as the center of the nervous system and as the seat of intelligence. He distinguished tendons from nerves; the name he gave to nerves (neura-aisthetica) implied a recognition of their function of sensitivity.

Erasistratus, a younger contemporary of Herophilus, clearly distinguished among the arteries, veins, and nerves. He regarded the nerves as vehicles for carrying the pneuma for sensation and motion. He thought the shortening of muscles was due to distention of the animal spirits as conveyed by the nerves. He distinguished motor from sensory nerves, but this finding was lost to those who came after him and had to be discovered all over again.

Still another contribution deserves mention. It was made by a nameless physician, probably also from Alexandria, in a volume of lectures entitled the Book of Medicine.[8] He suggested that the nerves have exits from the spinal cord, that they radiate throughout the body, and that the powers of sensation and motion are both located in them. He also distinguished voluntary powers from what he called natural powers; these natural powers include attraction, growth, digestion, and expulsion, and have in common the ability to take place whether we want them to or not. In some slight measure, this view anticipates the concept of reflex action and marks a distinct advance over the theory of "sympathy" that was accepted at the time (p. 15).

The Background of the Hellenistic and Roman Periods

While these advances were being made in Alexandria, the rest of the Mediterranean world was sinking into an intellectual decline. In fact, the same process of deterioration was also at work in Alexandria itself, where a concerted interest in alchemy first became manifest. Among the causes of this decline were a growth of skepticism, a growing sense of futility, and intellectual disillusionment. Above all, there was an increased acceptance of supernaturalism in its more extreme forms. Superstition had been a part of the daily life of the earliest Greeks, but its influence had waned for a time, only to return in the wake of the political and military disasters and epidemics which later afflicted the Greeks. Oriental mystery religions began to flourish alongside the ancient Greek faiths, because its easy-going paganism could not meet the challenge posed by these new problems. Thus, the growth in appeal of the mystery cults, astrology, and magic, most of which came from the East, were related either as cause or effect to the shifting perspectives of Hellenistic man.[9]

The Roman Period

It was during these years that the Roman conquest of the Hellenic world took place. This ushered in the fourth and final phase of ancient science, which is commonly known as the Graeco-Roman period and which extended from about 100 B.C. to 500 A.D.

It is remarkable that the Romans are not even mentioned until this relatively late date, for they had emerged into history in the seventh century B.C. from their status as one of many city-states. Their prosperity and their military and governmental power had increased steadily through their defeat of the independent city-states, but their contributions to art, drama, philosophy, and science remained negligible. Roman culture was in fact derived from Greek sources. Changes took place nevertheless, for when Greece was incorporated into the Roman Empire, one might say that Greek thought assumed a Latin dress.

The general intellectual climate became intensely practical. The Romans had little interest in the theoretical issues that had so excited the Greeks. The engineers and architects who covered the hills of Rome with mighty buildings, roads, and aqueducts were essentially practical in outlook, relying heavily on rules of thumb.[10] The Romans had also a definite flair for law, for the maintenance of order, and for conquest. Their sense of order did extend to commenting on Greek science and adapting it but they hardly advanced it in either scope or depth. To use the words of Bertrand Russell, the period of the Roman Empire was a period of "subjection and order."[11] The doctrines from Greece and the East excited only a few Romans; the larger proportion went about their business— economic, military, and governmental—more or less unheeding. Since there was no applied psychology as yet, psychological matters would not have interested them.

Roman philosophy, as represented by Stoicism and Epicureanism, was directed toward providing a means of personal escape from the evils of the world. "Wisdom for the conduct of life," to use a phrase of Wilhelm Windelband's, became the fundamental philosophical quest.[12] In their search for this wisdom the two schools of thought contributed continuity to psychological thinking. They maintained, for example, the representative theory of perception advanced by Epicurus[13] that had been derived from Democritus (p. 8).

Galen

The next great figure in the medical-philosophical tradition was Galen, born about 130 A.D. in Pergamon, a town in Asia Minor.[14] He was a Greek subject of the Roman Empire and his birthplace was then second only to Alexandria as a center of learning in the Western world. He received as complete an education in both philosophy and medicine as the time and place could afford. At twenty he began traveling and studying abroad, and during a stay in Alexandria, he began to concentrate on anatomy. Dissection of the human body was no longer allowed in Alexandria, but the anatomy of apes and other large mammals was studied. Many of Galen's errors, perpetuated over the centuries, were based upon attributing to the human organs what in fact were to be found only in nonhuman species. Also at this age he began writing and remained a prolific writer for the rest of his life. At twenty-eight, he returned to Pergamon and was appointed surgeon to the gladiators. This gave him an excellent opportunity to further his knowledge of anatomy by working with both the living and the dead. Subsequently, he went to Rome to practice. His fortune and his movements were bound to the court and to a whole series of emperors. Meanwhile, his eminence as a medical teacher was recognized, and he lectured to large crowds. His works on anatomy, physiology, and kindred subjects were written in these years. It seems clear that knowledge of the body's structure was conceived of as essential to an understanding of its working.

It should be emphasized that Galen was a skilled and astute practitioner. An anecdote[15] illustrating his clinical shrewdness anticipates by nearly two thousand years a measure now used in so-called lie detection. One day, Galen observed that a female patient of his had a quickening of the pulse when someone mentioned the name of a male dancer. On her visit the following day Galen arranged for someone to enter and tell of having seen the performance of still another dancer. A similar test was performed on the third day. Neither the second nor the third name produced a quickening of the pulse. On the fourth day when the first dancer's name was again mentioned, the pulse became rapid once more. He diagnosed her malady as the sickness of love and he went on to comment that physicians seem to have no conception of how bodily health can be affected by the *psyche's* suffering.

According to Galen, the basic physiological principle of life is spirit or *pneuma*. On the basis of this principle, he divides living things into the classes of plants, animals, and men—plants can grow, animals can move as well as grow, and men cannot only move and grow but can also reason. The three grades of life had their characteristic adaptations of the *pneuma*.[16] The first adaptation became natural spirit and brought about growth; the second became vital spirit and caused locomotion; the third became animal spirit and caused thought. Lest there be confusion between the second and third adaptations, "animal" spirit, possessed by man alone, was derived from the word *anima,* meaning soul. With regard to the seat of the soul, Galen remained faithful to Plato: the brain and nervous system were the seat of his distinctive intellectual life.

Galen integrated the existing knowledge of anatomy and physiology.[17] On cutting open the solid-looking organ that is the brain of the ape or man, Galen was struck by the four hollow intercommunicating chambers containing clear fluid.[18] He reasoned that they must serve some function, and decided that they constituted the place of generation and assembly of the animal spirits of the soul (mind). The animal spirits were thought to flow along nerves throughout the body, in accord with the now general acceptance of nerves as prerequisites for motion.[19] The belief that the animal spirits cause movement was reinforced for Galen by his observation that the living brain seemed to rhythmically pulsate. This dogma was not successfully challenged until the Renaissance. This doctrine of animal spirits was related to and expressed by the terms "sympathy" or "consent." Communication in this manner, animal spirits flowing from one part of the body to another, accounted for the appearance of symptoms in one organ when the disease was in another.[20]

Galen completed Hippocrates' four-fold classificatory system of ours by his theory of the four temperaments.[21] It will be remembered that Hippocrates had associated Empedocles' four elements with the humors or bodily juices—blood, black bile, yellow bile, and phlegm. A vaguely formulated theory of four temperaments had been accepted more or less incidentally, particularly among the Stoics, even before Galen.

Later workers have emphasized the psychological aspects of the theory of temperaments to such an extent that sometimes the theory is not recognized for what it was to Galen—a classification of medical-pathological types. It must be remembered that Galen was not deliberately developing a psychological theory; temperament was for him simply one of the three principle causes of disease—the others were climate and other external factors. To use typical medical examples of the system, he argued that foods that are naturally warmer produce more bile and that a person whose nature is warmer is more subject to biliousness than others. A distinctly secondary consideration for Galen was the explanation of individual differences in behavior and emotion. Such was his fame however, that even to this day he is credited with taking the decisive step of systematizing the view and emerging with a full-blown theory of temperament. The story is much more complicated than that, and has been told in recent years particularly well by Klibansky and his associates.[22] The common extension of this view is that a person with a predominance of the blood is said to be sanguine in temperament (warmhearted, volatile); when there is an excess of black bile, a person is thought to be melancholic (sad); excess yellow bile indicates that one is choleric (quick to anger and to action); a preponderance of phlegm leads to the phlegmatic humor which has so little changed over the centuries that it needs no explanation. Only with these later, non-Galenic additions to the Hippocratic doctrine, do we have a complete theory of temperamental humors.

The theory of the four temperaments formed a part of the mainstream of intellectual thinking, until the rebirth of medicine in the Renaissance 1,400 years later. Although the doctrine of humors has now faded from the medical scene, vestiges of it in expressions such as "good humor," "humorous," and their derivatives persist. It also survives in theories of personality type, in which a person is said to be characterized by the possession of a particular temperament.

What occurred in connection with the Galenic theory of humors is indicative of Galen's influence during the centuries that followed. A variety of circumstances fostered a reliance upon Galen's work after his death in 200 A.D. His strongly devout theistic attitude appealed alike to Christendom and Islam. He held that all things were determined by God and that the structure of the body was formed by God for an intelligible end, which was consonant with Christianity. He was not a Christian, although for centuries people believed that he had been. Moreover, his writings were confident and dogmatic in tone. His philosophical speculations, especially on the soul, were considerable and added to his appeal. His bulky writings, far too difficult for general study, were summarized and commented upon by many lesser men, and their works, not his, were read. Wretched treatises not even based on his works became popular whenever they bore his name. Meanwhile his best works were lost or fell into oblivion. This compounded the errors and further reduced the general quality of the medicine of that time.

Overview

The temporal period from Theophrastus to the death of Galen extended from about 300 B.C. to 200 A.D. Their work and that of their contemporaries made it a period of consolidation and strengthening of certain already established prescriptions. Rationalism and nomotheticism were still dominant; empiricism and idiographicism showed an increased strength and refinement and then declined. Naturalism, still strong among the individuals with whom we have been concerned, was, nevertheless, under increasing attack from nonphilosophical and nonscientific sources. Theophrastus and Galen were empirical and yet did not neglect the value of rationalism. They advocated idiographicism as well, despite their preference for dealing with types rather than with idiosyncratic differences among individuals. The structural prescription expressed in anatomy was seen as a prerequisite of the functional understanding of its workings.

There was increased specialization. This becomes evident when we compare the interests of the individuals of the time with those of pre-Socratic Greeks. An increased separation of science and philosophy was also apparent. Psychology was still seen as a branch of philosophy.

Greek science extended over a period of 800 years. It had begun with the speculations of the earliest philosopher-scientists of the sixth century B.C. and had continued until the second or third century of the Christian Era. The rate of progress slowed and finally stopped; some would say it even went backward. Greek scientific thought did not die, however, but was transmitted to the Arabs. In the late Middle Ages, it returned to European paths, modified and changed, but still recognizable and forceful.

References*

1. Diogenes Laertius, *Lives and Opinions of Eminent Philosophers,* trans. R. D. Hicks (Cambridge: Harvard University Press, 1925). (III, A.D.)
2. Theophrastus, in C. J. DeVogel, *Greek Philosophy: A Collection of Texts with Notes and Explanations; Aristotle, the Early Peripatetic School and the Early Academy* (Leiden: Brill, 1953) (c.300 B.C.), II, 230–240.
3. *Ibid.*
4. Theophrastus, in G. M. Stratton, *Theophrastus and the Greek Physiological Psychology* (New York: Macmillan, 1917).
5. Theophrastus, *The Characters,* trans. J. M. Edmonds (London: Heinemann, 1929), pp. 43, 45.
6. *Ibid.,* pp. 43, 45.
7. Sources for this account of Alexandrian science are G. Sarton, *Ancient Science and Modern Civilization* (Lincoln: University of Nebraska Press, 1947); and *A*

*See p. 19 for description of reference style.

History of Science and Culture in the Last Three Centuries B.C. (Cambridge: Harvard University Press, 1959); B. Farrington, *Science in Antiquity* (London: Home University Library, 1936); and two more general books that nevertheless contained valuable material on this period—C. Singer, *A Short History of Medicine, Introducing Medical Principles to Students and Non-medical Readers* (New York: Oxford University Press, 1928); and W. Windelband, *A History of Philosophy; Greek, Roman and Medieval* (New York: Harper and Brothers, 1901), I.

8. *Book of Medicine,* trans. E. A. W. Budge (London: Oxford University Press, 1913) (*c.*300 B.C.).

9. W. C. Dampier, *A History of Science, and its Relations with Philosophy and Religion,* 4th ed. (Cambridge: Cambridge University Press, 1949).

10. M. Clagett, *Greek Science in Antiquity* (New York: Abelard-Schuman, 1955).

11. B. Russell, *A History of Western Philosophy* (New York: Simon and Schuster, 1945), p. 218.

12. Windelband, *History of Philosophy,* p. 157.

13. Epicurus, Letter to Herodotus, from the original text of Diogenes Laertius, trans. C. Bailey, W. J. Oates, ed., *The Stoic and Epicurean Philosophers: Complete Extant Writings of Epicurus, Epictetus, Lucretius, and Marcus Aurelius* (New York: Random House, 1940) (*c.*300 B.C.), Herrnstein and Boring, Excerpt No. 22.

14. Sources used were C. Singer, *A Short History of Medicine;* H. E. Sigerist, *The Great Doctors: a Biographical History of Medicine* (London: Allan and Unwin, 1933); G. Sarton, *Galen of Pergamon,* (Lawrence: University of Kansas Press, 1954); and O. Temkin, *Galenism: Rise and Decline of a Medical Philosophy* (Ithaca, N. Y.: Cornell University Press, 1973).

15. L. Thorndike, *A History of Magic and Experimental Science During the First Thirteen Centuries of Our Era* (New York: Macmillan Company, 1923), I.

16. B. Farrington, *Greek Science: its Meaning for Us* (London: Penguin, 1953), pp. 297–298.

17. Galen, *On Anatomical Procedures: Translating the Surviving Books With Introduction and Notes,* trans. C. Single (London: Oxford University Press, 1956); Galen, *On Anatomical Procedures: the Later Books,* trans. W. L. H. Duckworth; M. C. Lyons and B.

Towers, eds., (Cambridge: Cambridge University Press, 1962).

18. C. S. Sherrington, *Man on His Nature*, 2nd ed. (London: Cambridge University Press, 1951), pp. 198–199.

19. F. Fearing, *Reflex Action: a Study in the History of Physiological Psychology* (Baltimore: Williams and Wilkins, 1930), p.12.

20. J. F. Fulton, *Physiology of the Nervous System*, 3rd ed. rev. (London: Oxford University Press, 1949), p. 202.

21. R. M. Hutchins, ed., *The Great Books of the Western World*, Vol. X, Galen, *On the Natural Faculties*, trans. A. J. Brock (Chicago: Encyclopaedia Britannica, 1952) (200 A.D.), pp. 163–215.

22. R. Klibansky, E. Panofsky, F. Saxl, *Saturn and Melancholy: Studies in the History of Natural Philosophy, Religion and Art* (New York: Basic Books, 1964).

Chapter 5

Plotinus AND Augustine:
THE PATRISTIC PERIOD

Before considering the work of the next two great contributors to psychology, it is necessary to turn back some two centuries from the time of Galen to the beginnings of the Christian Era. An examination of the link between philosophy and early Christianity, and the alleged influence of Christianity on the fall of science, provides a necessary introduction to Plotinus, the greatest exponent of Neoplatonism. Despite his paganism, Plotinus profoundly influenced Augustine, the greatest "psychologist" of the nearly thousand years to follow.

Christianity and the Fall of Science

Christianity did not lead directly to the fall of Greek scientific-philosophical endeavors; the decline had started even before the advent of Christianity. Until the end of the second century A.D., the Christians were a small, obscure, but persecuted sect with no seeming influence on the class of individuals who might be expected to study science or philosophy. In fact, in their thought science was held in low estate. In the centuries that followed, Christianity did nothing to promote science, and in many ways discouraged its revival. The practical attitude of the Romans and the later invasions of the barbarians contributed to the fall of science; the church maintained the situation and to some degree aggravated it. Early Christian teaching indirectly abetted the decline by diverting to theological speculation individuals of scholarly temperament who might otherwise have turned their interests to science and philosophy as it was known in the past.

89

Philosophy and the Beginning of Christianity

Jesus, the Apostles, and their immediate successors were concerned with spreading the Gospel, not with promulgating philosophy or science. Jesus was a man of simple faith, who had an intuitive vision into the hearts of men but no interest in formalizing and systematizing the assumptions implicit behind his practices. An artist in the broadest sense, even a psychotherapist (if such a term may be permitted), he epitomized the viewpoint of art, not that of science.

But once their period of comparative obscurity was over, Christians found it necessary to defend their new religion against non-Christian thinkers. Therefore, insofar as philosophy was studied, it was used for the defense of religion, for apologetics, as the written tracts were called. The second century also began the period of the church fathers, those writers who in later ages were used as sources of reference for points of doctrinal orthodoxy. The Patristic Period, as it came to be called, spanned the centuries devoted to the formation of Christian orthodoxy.

A detailed history of these early Christian views would be a history of Christian dogma, not of philosophy. Some Christian thinking of the period was antirational. Tertullian, a church father, not only held that his faith was unphilosophical, but was proud of the fact.[1] He took the position that the content of revelation is not only above reason, but in a sense contrary to reason. The Gospel was incomprehensible in terms of worldly discernment. Tertullian took an extreme position, but in varying degrees others shared this shift of focus, not to an interest in the irrational which Plato had maintained, but to an antirational stance.

Origen, born in Alexandria in A.D. 185, was one of the intellectual leaders of the church at that time. His attitude toward science is noteworthy in its contrast to the antirationalist view. He held that all knowledge is good because it is a means toward perfection and that philosophy and science are compatible with Christianity.[2] This attitude eventually entered into the formulation of church dogma.

Both the Edict of Milan, issued by Constantine in 313, and the recognition of the Catholic church as the official religion of the Roman Empire, following shortly thereafter, made imperative the development of an authoritative system of theology; Christianity was no longer a small outcaste sect but a state religion.

There was one paramount intellectual consequence of the official sanction of Christianity. Heresy was born. Unlike the easygoing religions of old whose guardians were content to allow one to worship how and when one pleased if only token obeisance were made to the gods of city or state, Christianity demanded uncompromising adherence to the one

God who, through the voices of the Hebrew prophets and through Christ, had made manifest the Truth. This revelation could not be disputed. To do so was heresy. One was no longer free to speculate on any and all matters. Certain truths were revealed, and one could not challenge these without being accused of heresy.

Philosophers could no longer inquire about a given point, once dogma was settled by the ecumenical councils. These councils decided by majority vote what were henceforth to be regarded as revealed Christian truths. The minorities on these votes, now faced with heresy, could either agree or, as sometimes understandably happened, break off to form heretical sects. Insofar as they drew their inspiration from the same source, these heretics were still Christian, but they denied some point of dogma. Sometimes these differences were introduced by continued adherence to one or another now-banned aspect of the old religions of the classical era, such as a belief in magic. Often they arose over the interpretation of the Trinity, especially over the particular nature of the relation of the Son to the Father.

What was the effect of Christianity on psychological thought? Concisely, supernaturalism, in the sense of going beyond nature, was to dominate. A preoccupation with the world to come developed. Naturalistic interests were suspect precisely because they dealt with matters of this world.[3] Since the immortal soul was elevated as a result of this pattern, soul-body dualism became a major issue. An intense preoccupation with the problems of sin and guilt, a reaction to feelings of helplessness and doom, prevailed among Christian and non-Christian mystics. An attempt was made to suppress any suggestion of a relationship between human nature and the animal kingdom. The position of animals was degraded and a sharp dichotomy was drawn between mankind and the beasts that perish. This change in attitude was demanded since animals might otherwise be thought to have reason, implying in turn that they were morally responsible beings. Psychological contributions were hereafter made only within the context of these concerns.

Plato's world view had called for the supremacy of transcendental reality, and the inferior status of sense. This tendency in Plato was now even more in focus because the best known dialogue in the centuries to come was the atypical *Timaeus* (p. 110) which pictured the universe as a living thing with a soul penetrating its body.

At the time of the rise of Christianity, philosophy was dominated by the Neoplatonists who stressed precisely these aspects of Plato's thinking. The adaptation of their views to Christian dogma was almost inevitable. One of these Neoplatonists was the pagan, Plotinus, who would have a profound effect upon Augustine, ultimately influencing the entire course of Christian philosophy.

The aspect of Platonism which most appealed to Plotinus was the anti-rationalism that earlier neoplatonists had fostered. He ignored the major argument of Plato's teaching—that real knowledge could be obtained. But he turned, not to scepticism, but to faith, a faith that wanted rationalism to fail. The more it failed, the more persuasive his mystic path would appear to be.

Plotinus

Plotinus was born in Egypt about A.D. 205 and in his youth became a disciple of Ammonius Saccas in Alexandria, with whom he remained for eleven years.[4] He and other students swore to keep secret their master's teachings, which had not been set down in writing. When he was thirty-nine years old, Plotinus left Ammonius with the intention of traveling to the East in order to learn Persian and Indian philosophy. The expedition of the Emperor Gordian, which he joined for this purpose, reached Mesopotamia, but ended with the assassination of the emperor. This was the occupational hazard of emperors at the time; no less than eleven died in this fashion during the sixty-five years of Plotinus' life.

Plotinus arrived in Rome in 245, and remained there the rest of his life. His austere and ethical teaching soon won him influence over many of the leading Romans of his time. He functioned not only as a teacher of philosophy, but also a counselor on ethical problems. His moral principles were high and his character unimpeachable; his advice on moral problems was eagerly sought.

During his first years in Rome he wrote nothing. It was only after repeated urgings on the part of Porphyry, his student and biographer, that he began to write—in the last six years of his life—the major portion of his only work. After Plotinus' death in 270 A.D., Porphyry arranged the essays, according to some numerological quirk, in sets of nine works each, as a consequence of which he named them *The Six Enneads* (Six Groups of Nine).[5]

The central theme of Plotinus' teaching is mystical reunion with the world soul. Plotinus seems to have been dominated by a desire to map out the world beyond sense reality and to try to live in that world as fully as the bonds of flesh would permit. It would be easy at this point to simply dismiss him as a mystic and move on. But he was also something more. His was not a crude mysticism based merely on habitual trances. In fact, according to Porphyry, Plotinus attained a state a vision only four times in the six years they worked together. In these states he felt himself to have risen to the world beyond the world of experience. At the same time, although careless of dress and hygienic considerations, he was in great demand as the executor of estates of minor children! The practical Romans would hardly have so trusted him if he had fitted the stereotype of the mystic. When chided for performing this business service, seemingly discordant with his philosophical teaching, Plotinus is said to have re-marked that the children would need the money if they did not find philos-ophy. It was not that he was oblivious to the world; he simply valued things other than those that the majority of men hold dear. He saw material life as a play acted out by the shadows of men, whose comings and goings were irrelevant.[6]

There is a calmness to his writing, not the heat so often accom-panied by confusion that characterize so many mystical excursions. Consider how he describes his mysticism:

> But there are earlier and loftier beauties than these [from sense]. In the sense-bound life we are no longer granted to know them, but the soul, taking no help from the organs, sees and proclaims them. To the vision of these we must mount, leav-ing sense to its own low place.[7]

His intention was to demonstrate to those who had not had such transcendental experiences that there were realities beyond the world of sense.[8] Consequently, he appealed to experiences that were open to the understanding of the uninitiated, and this made his thinking relevant to the history of psychology. He adopted as his approach the analysis of the forms of mental activity. This was the rational method through which to obtain information about the soul, since, by definition, the soul is imma-terial. But such analysis was only incidental to Plotinus' major thinking and did not constitute an attempt to systematize a psychology. Neverthe-less, throughout all his work he used a meditative method, and thus helped to establish this approach to psychology. Despite himself, he made a modest contribution to psychology in an otherwise barren age.

He espoused a doctrine of the development of man toward perfec-tion. His goal was the independence of the soul from the body, or as close an approximation of this as possible. He considered matter to be the obstacle to this. The Platonic doctrine of the body as the prison of the soul is central to his thinking, thought he altered the relationship between the two. Plato had conceived of the soul as being within the body, but Plotinus believed that although the body existed in space—after all, space is defined as a container for bodies—the soul could not be so contained because it is incorporeal.[9] It gives the body life but does not combine with it. Soul and body are united but never fused, mixed, or spatially connected. The soul uses the organs of sense of the body; motions are of the body, not of the soul. His central point is that the soul is correlative with but independent of the body. The emotions, for example, are known to the soul, but it is the body that is perturbed.[10] The body experiences the emotion; the soul perceives it.

The soul has three major classes of activity. First, it performs the functions of perceiving the world of sense. Second, it reflects. That is, there is a division of consciousness into subject and object: the soul not only thinks, but it also thinks it thinks. In the first and second kinds of mental activity, there is a state of excitation, which is sensation; reflection is conscious perception of this excitation. Third, there is the pure activity of contemplation, without such a separation of subject and object, in which the soul transcends its immediate location in order to dwell on the eternal and changeless. This changelessness was Plotinus' goal, the ineffable state toward which he strove. It is at its highest level the experience of the "One."[11]

Psychological interest centers, however, not on his goal, but on the second function, reflection. His concept of this function, in which "we" (his word for self) is operating, gives us the first clear statement of self-consciousness.[12] Unlike union with the One, which is without consciousness of self, "we" become aware at this level of the object and, apart from this, of ourselves. We are self-conscious in that the object and thinker are distinguished by us.[13] As he puts it, "we know, and it is ourselves that we know. . . ."[14] He even uses blushing as an illustration of heightened self-consciousness. To Plotinus, self-consciousness is but a means of contrast with the ineffably higher plane of contemplation of the changeless. He hit upon self-consciousness as an effective means of casting this higher level into relief; once it served its purpose, he said no more about it.

Augustine

Augustine lived in a world overwhelmed with troubles.[15] In his youth the barbarians had poured into the empire; in his middle age Rome was sacked by the Goths; and in his declining years, while all around him the whole western Roman Empire was facing its final ruin, he helped prepare for the defense of his diocese against the Vandals. Augustine did not advance science generally, and probably even impeded its development, but his subjective attitude, with its consequent attention to the self and to introspection, and his stress upon the functioning of the will, make him important in the history of psychology.

LIFE OF AUGUSTINE

Aurelius Augustine was born in 354 at Tagaste, a small town in the Roman province of Numidia in northern Africa. Many years later, he described his childhood and youth in his *Confessions*,[16] his spiritual autobiography. He tells us that at an early age he had learned something about Christianity from his mother but that her teachings had made little impression on him at the time. When he did well in his first schooling, his father aspired to make him a lawyer; so he was sent to Carthage at about the age of sixteen to study rhetoric. Again he did well in his studies, but the frivolity of student life led him into dissipation of various sorts, which he describes in detail in his *Confessions*. Since he was now sixteen, he took a mistress to whom he remained faithful for years. She bore him a son, Adeodatus, which means "Given of God." The custom of taking a concubine, sanctioned by pagan morals and Roman law, was thought to be a step above promiscuity, and his was a deeply passionate nature. "Give me chastity and continency," he cried out, "only not yet."[17] This plea occurred many years later in Milan after his mistress had returned to Africa, and before his planned but never-contracted marriage to another.

His intellectual life was also intense. His reading of *Hortensius*, a work by Cicero that is now lost, led him to a love of philosophy, and over the years he became increasingly conversant with the Roman pagan literature. Though fascinated by both Plato and the Neoplatonists, and loving Latin, he disliked Greek and never mastered it. Roman Africa at that time was also a place where many diverse Christian, heretical, and pagan religious strands intertwined. Augustine became involved with several of these and at age nineteen converted to Manicheanism, which told of a world of opposed substances of light and darkness. The external opposition of good and evil was a battle fought on many levels. Man on earth would strive to become part of the kingdom of light and could become part of that domain. This doctrine was submerged in a morass of esoteric teachings including, for example, dietary prescriptions: meat belonged to darkness and was forbidden; vegetables were of light and could be eaten. Since Manes, the Persian who founded the system, claimed direct authority from Jesus Christ, his doctrine was technically a perverted form of Christianity, in fact, from the orthodox Christian point of view, it was a particularly offensive form of heresy. During Augustine's time, Manicheanism had a large numer of adherents and exercised considerable temporal power.

On the completion of his studies in Carthage in 373, Augustine decided to follow the career of a teacher of rhetoric, rather than that of a lawyer. After a year in Rome, he accepted the municipal post of rhetoric in Milan. This post was in the control of the Manicheans and was secured for him precisely because he was one of their adherents. But by this time he was in the process of discarding their doctrine.

Augustine was increasingly forced to adopt a skeptical position.[18] He began to doubt whether reality could be known at all. Neoplatonism freed him from this difficulty and through the Neoplatonists he was led to accept as legitimate an order of reality beyond the material world.

In his later writings he adapted the Neoplatonic conception of reality to a Christian context.[19] This was to have a profound effect upon all subsequent Christian theological and philosophical thinking. Many of his ideas—about God, matter, the ascent of the soul, freedom and evil and the relation of God to the world—show the impress of Neoplatonism, especially as expressed by Plotinus. It was this conception of reality that he inserted into Christian theology and philosophy. His views on the spiritual nature of the reality accessible to the human soul were derived from the Neoplatonists. Like them, he believed there was a supreme author of being and like them, he desired to transcend the material world. There were, of course, differences in outlook. In contrast to the Neoplatonists, Christian thinkers insisted on a voluntary act of creation by God; existence was temporal, not eternal; and God was on a level entirely different from that of his creatures.

Augustine next came under the influence of Ambrose, the Bishop of Milan, and his relationship with Ambrose had a decisive influence on the development of his thought. Dissatisfied with what he saw as the incompleteness of Neoplatonism and philosophy, he found in Ambrose someone to fill his needs, someone to help him find peace. In his Confessions he says, "That man of God received me as a father, and showed me an episcopal kindness on my coming. Thenceforth, I began to love him, at first indeed not as a teacher of the truth, but as a person kind towards myself."[20] It is noteworthy that an important stride in the development of the intellectual forces of Western Christendom should have started in an interpersonal relationship that later flowered into a religious conversion.

There were other influences at work to help bring Augustine into the church. There was the scene in the garden of his house in Milan, movingly described in the Confessions.[21] He tells us in impassioned words of his conflict of will over whether or not to renounce the joys of the flesh for the sake of God. After an intense struggle, the conflict was resolved when he was commanded over and over again by a voice that sounded like that of a child to "take up and read." He took up the Bible and read from St. Paul: "Not in rioting and drunkenness, not in chambering and wantonness, not in strife and envying: but put ye on the Lord Jesus Christ, and make not provision for the flesh to fulfill the lusts thereof."[22] He proceeded to reread Paul's *Epistles* and found in him a kindred spirit who had passed through a thousand doubts as to the Divine Word. This was not the pale abstraction of the Platonic *logos* but something that was to him, as it was to Paul, much more vital, warm, and deep.[23]

After a period of intellectual and spiritual preparation, he was in 387 baptized in Milan by Bishop Ambrose. He had resigned his professorship of rhetoric the year before, primarily because of dissatisfaction with what he had to teach, but also partly because he was suffering from a chest ailment. Although never formally a teacher again, he did not cease teaching, though now he pursued a different goal. After his conversion, he returned home to Africa. He sold his property and gave the proceeds to the poor. He and some friends organized a monastery in Tagaste, where he lived the life of an ascetic. In 389 his son, on whom he had lavished great care and affection, died. Augustine shortly thereafter was ordained a priest in Hippo. Here, in what was to be his home for the rest of his life, he founded another monastery.

In 395 or 396 Augustine was consecrated a bishop—a post he held until his death. His quiet monastic life was now over. The successful administration of a bishopric in the fifth century in northern Africa among pagans and heretics was no light task. Practical shrewdness and forceful leadership, as well as piety, were necessary. Above all, skill in human relationships was required. Religious controversies within the church, church councils, combats against heresy, and even lay legal activities occupied much of his time, and he continued to be in poor health. Nevertheless, he was able to find time to engage in enormous literary activity as well as prolific correspondence with other church leaders.

Vandals were at the gates of Hippo in 430 when Augustine died at the age of seventy-six. A few months after his death his parishioners were either slain or scattered and less than fifty years later, in 476, the empire of the western Caesar was abolished.

Augustine's major works were written during the later part of his life, that is to say, in the first quarter of the fifth century. The two best-known are his *Confessions*,[24] finished in 406, and the *City of God*,[25] completed in 426. Augustine gave the classic statement of the Christian philosophy of history in his *City of God* in the form of a contrast and comparison of the earthly and the heavenly cities. Eventually the terrestrial city would have to yield to the heavenly city, and the course of history could be defined as the struggle between the two.

ATTITUDES TOWARD SCIENCE

The attitude Augustine took toward faith explains both his philosophical and his scientific views. He held that it is necessary to believe in order to know, that understanding comes from faith. Nevertheless, there are many things we cannot believe unless we understand them. Supplementing the primacy of belief, therefore, is the subordinate principle that we also know in order to believe.

Knowledge of any sort is valuable to Augustine only insofar as it brings one closer to understanding God, the soul, and the human self. God is the source of all causation. Miracles are simply unusual occurrences, and require no more and no less explanation than any other event.[26] If they were not rare, they would not cause surprise. Often knowledge of this fact is enough, thereby denying any need to understand miracles rationally. Eyes fastened on God have little care for the transitory mundane affairs of the world.

His views toward science were ambivalent. Deprecatory remarks abound. For example, scientific knowledge, such as the ability to predict eclipses, he says, may puff a man up with pride.[27] After a short account of the work of Thales, he complains that Thales did not relate his theories to the divine mind,[28] yet Augustine also praised Thales. The apparent discrepancy is considerably dissipated when it is remembered that he considered science good whenever it served religious ends, but irrelevant, and hence bad, whenever it did not. The positive value of scientific knowledge would be not only to understand the Bible, e.g., the flora and fauna of the Holy Land, but also to be able to refute pagan arguments. When comparing profane knowledge with Scripture, he writes, "For whatever man may have learnt from other sources, if it is hurtful, it is there condemned; if it is useful, it is therein contained."[29] By and large, the effect of Augustine upon science was to impede rather than to advance its progress. However, his ambivalent attitude toward science in general went hand in hand with a firm conviction in the certainty of inner experience.[30] As a consequence Augustine is important in the history of psychology, although not in the history of the other sciences.

Philosophical and Personal Background of Augustine's Psychology

For Augustine, revelation and inner experience were the two sources of truth. His most systematic statement of the principles of sacred theology—a guide to the interpretation of Scripture—is his "On Christian

Doctrine.''[31] References to inner experience are repeatedly cited in developing particular aspects of the doctrine. In his dependence on subjective knowledge, his second source, he made use of a concept of self, and focused on the issue of freedom of the will as an experienced phenomenon. The relation of self and freedom of the will to his philosophical views will be detailed briefly here.

Augustine wished to rise to the heavenly city by the love of God. In order to do this there had to be contempt of self.[32] This ascent of the soul to God, vividly described in his *Confessions*,[33] required various steps involving passing from body, to sense, to inner sense, and ultimately to the final place of abiding with disregard of self. The direct relation of his thinking to that of Plotinus is obvious, while his indirect debt to Plato may also be discerned.

From Augustine's point of view, there were several compelling theological reasons that made the problem of will a primary issue.[34] For one, Adam's fall, although in a sense brought about by Satan, would not have occurred had Adam not already had a deficient will. Moreover, the problems of the relation of absolute predestination to freedom of the will, Divine Grace, and sin all occupied central positions in his theological thought. Equally compelling were his experiences as a youth when passion overwhelmed his will—for which he later reproached himself severely. In one dramatic instance, he remembered with shame that in his youth he and some friends had stolen some pears, only to throw them away uneaten. He did more than register his harrowing repentance. He analyzed his motives for what might be called today a typical act of juvenile vandalism.[35] In the first place he recognized that he had committed this act because he was with friends. Alone, it would not have occurred to him to steal the fruit. More important for our use of the illustration, he believed that he did it precisely because it was forbidden; he experienced a sense of power in doing what he was not supposed to do. Will, or motivation, as it may be called, is the crux of his understanding of the episode.

Concerning these matters, Augustine held a subjective view. But why, it may be asked, was Augustine interested in the inner man—in psychological topics? The direction his interests took, focusing on the inner man, followed from the sort of man he was and from the experiences he had had. Augustine illustrates in an admirable fashion that a man turns to reflection when he becomes aware of difficulties within himself.

Augustine had no conception of psychology as a separate discipline, so what is to follow may give an impression of greater integration than is warranted by his own presentation.

SOME ASPECTS OF THE PSYCHOLOGY OF AUGUSTINE

Augustine's contentually subjectivistic approach is best illustrated by his psychological description of time.[36] Time was created when the world was created and has no reality apart from created existence. Neither the past nor the future really exist experientially when they are actually in the past or in the future. Yet there is time past and time future. Augustine resolves the contradiction by arguing that time is thought of in the present, but the past is identified with memory, and the future with expectation. There are three times, in other words: a present of things past, a present of things present, and a present of things future. Time is not of the external world but is an inner experience. Time is phenomenological.

[handwritten in left margin: cf the idea of Fritz Perls (Gestalt Therapy)]

Augustine's subjective emphasis led naturally to a consideration of the proof of the reality of self-existence. He argues that even to doubt one's own existence is to assert it anyway: to doubt is to think, and to think is to exist. Under these circumstances, a man cannot doubt his existence, for to do so would be to talk nonsense. Instead of the expression of Descartes, "I think, therefore I am" (p. 152), Augustine's formula was, "For if I am deceived, I am."[37] Of all knowledge, the existence of one's own thought is most certain. Sense perception does not give us knowledge. The mind knows the external world only indirectly. What it does know directly is awareness of self, not from contact with the world but from contact with itself, by knowing itself. The mind produces its experiences from within the self. Life is a unity known through self-consciousness. One important consequence of this view is that the automatic functions of the body, grouped together as lower functions, are not part of this self, but are negligible and can safely be disregarded.

From this primary awareness of existence one can advance to an awareness of ideas in the mind. These ideas are universal and real concepts—goodness, being, number, and the like. In his way of expressing universals, Augustine followed Platonic thinking, but differed beyond this point. The source of ideas was in God; these ideas were grasped by God's gift of illumination. The mind, when considering things of this world, including the body, can recognize its own superiority to them. At the same time, it realizes that it falls short of knowledge of eternal things and thereby recognizes its own shortcomings.

Soul is regarded by Augustine as an immaterial spiritual entity; man is a dualistic union of body and soul. Body *and* soul make up human nature.[38] The soul was considered immaterial and indestructible. It did not pre-exist from eternity but was a product of creation. Since nothing was created after the six days of creation, body and soul must both have been created then also.

The soul is immaterial but acts in and through the body, which it animates and directs. It has the form of the body but can be separated from the body after death and become immortal.[39] Both the immateriality and immortality of the soul are demonstrated by its power of grasping the eternal. Augustine's proof of the existence of the soul is an extension of what he said about self-existence: to have a thinking existence is to have a soul.

The unity of the mind does not preclude the coexistence of different functions. Augustine attributes to the mind three faculties—reason, memory, and will.[40] Imagination, which mediates between memory and reason seems to be treated as still another but lesser faculty. Each of these functions is relatively independent. Augustine handles them as entities that in and of themselves explain the facts. This is especially true of will. His view is brought out clearly in the following illustration. Speaking of a youthful temptation he wrote, "My will the enemy held, and thence made a chain for me, and bound me. For of a froward will was a lust made: and a lust served a custom; and custom not resisted became necessity."[41] The will created a habit; habit became necessity. In so doing will functioned as an entity in itself.

The reality of the freedom of the will has been affirmed in the previous quotation. It is the human will that makes possible a choice between good or evil.[42] On more than one occasion Augustine affirms that will is a matter of freely determined choice;[43] it concerns us because of the problems of human freedom in relation to the will of God,[44] and to sin and salvation.[45]

The psychological faculties of reason and memory also receive attention from Augustine. A partial summary of their functioning may be offered in terms of one form of interrelationship of the three faculties. Even the simplest act of apprehension has three components: the mind is conscious of itself (memory); it is aware of the possibility of many objects potentially available to attention (reason); and it selects the one with which it becomes involved (will).

Overview

So far as psychological issues are concerned, a dualism of mind and body supplied the general intellectual background for the period. More specifically, the transcendent goal of Plotinus and the religious goal of Augustine mark their dependence on supernaturalism as a prescription.

The pejorative connotation this term assumed over time is unfortunate. Simply, supernaturalism refers to accepting what lies beyond nature. Antirationalism was strong; a commonly accepted test of faith was to believe that which one could not believe because of reason, a conviction in which Plotinus shared but which Augustine did much to combat because of his personally strong faith in reason. Contentual subjectivism and purism concerning psychological matters maintained a tacit dominance over the thinking of both men without explicit discussion.

Until the rise of the scholastic Aristotelianism of Aquinas 800 years later, Augustine was the chief authority of the church on psychological matters. St Augustine was the most subtle contentually subjective thinker before Freud. He gave an interrelated account of unity and of conflict as expressed in the will. In this and the other faculties, he presented a functional view of human nature, all the while emphasizing a dynamic attitude. His insistence on the truth of his contentions based upon the immediate certainty of inner experience did much to foster a contentually subjectivistic approach to psychological problems. His defense of the primacy of will helped to counteract too exclusive a stress on the intellectual phase of human experience. On the other side of the ledger, when combined with his negative attitude toward science, the sheer charm of his writings, his brilliantly insightful expression, and his striking metaphors probably served to help slow down and delay the advance of psychology as a science.

References*

1. W. Windelband, *A History of Philosophy: Greek, Roman and Medieval* (New York: Harper and Brothers, 1901), Vol. I.
2. A. C. Crombie, *Medieval and Early Modern Science*, 2nd rev. ed. (New York: Doubleday, 1959), 2 vols.
3. G. Murphy, *Historical Introduction to Modern Psychology*, rev. ed. (New York: Harcourt, Brace, 1949).
4. Sources for the account of his life are those of his student, Porphyry, On the life of Plotinus and the arrangement of his works, in *The Enneads*, trans. S. MacKenna. (New York: Pantheon Books, n.d.) and J. Katz, *The Philosophy of Plotinus* (New York: Appleton-Century-Crofts, 1950).

*See p. 19 for description of reference style.

5. R. M. Hutchins, ed., *The Great Books of the Western World*, Vol. XVII, Plotinus, *The Six Enneads*, trans. S. MacKenna and B. S. Page. (Chicago: Encyclopaedia Britannica, 1952) (*c.* 270), pp. 1–360.

6. *Ibid.*, Trac. II, 15.

7. *Ibid.*, I, Trac. VI, 4, p. 23.

8. This view permeates his discussion. A good secondary discussion is to be found in Katz, *Philosophy of Plotinus*.

9. Plotinus *Enneads* IV, Trac. III, 20.

10. *Ibid.*, IV, Trac. IV, 28.

11. *Ibid.*, V. Trac. I, 2.

12. *Ibid.*, IV, Trac. III.

13. *Ibid.*, Trac. IX, 3.

14. *Ibid.*, p. 137.

15. Augustine, *The Confessions;* trans. E. B. Pusey, in R. M. Hutchins, ed., *Great Books of the Western World*, Vol. XVIII, (*c.*400) pp. 1–125. This is the major source for details about his life. It is supplemented by R. W. Battenhouse, "The Life of St. Augustine," R. W. Battenhouse, ed., *A Companion to the Study of St. Augustine* (New York: Oxford University Press, 1955, pp. 15–56); V. J. Bourke, *Augustine's Quest of Wisdom* (Milwaukee: Bruce, 1945); and B. Russell, *A History of Western Philosophy* (New York: Simon and Schuster, 1945).

16. Augustine *Confessions*.

17. *Ibid.*, VIII, 17, p. 57.

18. E.g., Augustine, *The City of God*, trans. M. Dods, in R. M. Hutchins, ed., *Great Books of the Western World* Vol. XVIII, (*c.*413–426), pp. 127–618, VIII.

19. M. H. Carre, *Realists and Nominalists* (London: Oxford University Press, 1946).

20. Augustine *Confessions* V, 23, p. 33.

21. *Ibid.*, VIII, 19–22, 30.

22. *Ibid.*, p. 61.

23. *Ibid.*, VII 27.

24. *Ibid.*

25. Augustine *City of God*.

26. *Ibid.*, XXI, 8.

27. Augustine *Confessions* V, 3–5, 8.

28. Augustine *City of God* VIII, 2.

29. R. M. Hutchins, ed., *Great Books of the Western World*, Vol. XVIII, Augustine, *On Christian Doctrine*, trans. J. F. Shaw, (*c.*427), pp. 619–698.

30. Augustine, *The Trinity*, trans. S. MacKenna, in J. Deferrari, ed., *The Fathers of the Church: A New Translation* (Washington, D.C.: Catholic University of America Press, 1963) Vol. XLV, (c.416), pp. 281–282.
31. Augustine *On Christian Doctrine*.
32. Augustine *City of God* XIV, 28.
33. Augustine *Confessions* VII, 23.
34. Augustine *On Christian Doctrine* II, 46.
35. Augustine *Confessions* II, 9–18.
36. *Ibid.*, XI, 17–40.
37. Augustine *City of God* XI, 26, p. 337.
38. *Ibid.*, XIV, 5.
39. *Ibid.*, XIII, 19, XIV, 2–3, 5–6.
40. Augustine *Confessions* X, 6, 10–11, 17, 18, 26–27, 37; *City of God* IX, 4–5, XIV 6–9, XIX, 18.
41. Augustine *Confessions* VIII, 10, p. 55.
42. Augustine *City of God* XIV, 6.
43. Augustine *Confessions* IX, 1; *City of God* XXII, 30.
44. *Ibid.*, II, 14; *City of God* I, 36, IV 33, V, 1, 9–10, XVIII, 2.
45. Augustine *Confessions* VII, 5; *City of God* V, 9–10, XII, 21, XIV, 11–12, 15, XXII, 1, 30.

Chapter 6

Aquinas:
THE MIDDLE AGES,
RATIONALISM, AND FAITH

[handwritten annotations: CLASSICAL ERA / PATRISTIC ERA / — EARLY 400-500 to 900 (DARK) / — HIGH / Ends c 1450, 1500]

A long period of preparation was necessary before Thomas Aquinas could emerge as the great philosophical psychologist of the Middle Ages. Consideration of the Dark Ages, the rise and fall of Islam, and the intellectual climate of the later Middle Ages will provide background for his contributions.

The Dark Ages

After the classical twilight and the patristic period came the early Middle Ages. They extended from about A.D. 400 or 500 to 900, and are often referred to as the Dark Ages. Although there were still some fathers of the church to come, some scholars argue[1] that the creative patristic epoch had closed with the death of Augustine in 430. In the fifth century the world empire of the Romans collapsed and was broken up. From then on the West was divorced from the empire in the East. In 529 the Emperor Justinian closed the Academy of Athens, and one may find this event more emotionally satisfying as the date that brings to a final close both the Greek era and the early period of Christianity.

During the Dark Ages, the material preconditions for scientific advancement no longer existed. Misgovernment, top-heavy bureaucracy, civil wars, and the encroachment of neighboring barbarian peoples led to a steady decline. The uniformity of Roman law gave way to a maze of discordant local customs. The universal monetary system of the Romans disappeared. Land became the basic unit of value. Lack of order among the new kingdoms, further invasions by barbarians, and an utter lack of culture among the rulers produced chaotic systems of government and low standards of living. There was little leisure time, widespread illiteracy, and few towns, let alone cities. Most of the European population lived in self-sustaining but marginally surviving villages, armed both against their neighbors and invading bands of marauders from afar. Science and culture inevitably suffered. To be sure, there were little enclaves in Ireland and at Monte Cassino where some religious scholarship survived. But the church did not go under and the Bishops of Rome as Popes successfully claimed spiritual authority over all Christendom and asserted more and more temporal authority. There was no psychological advance made during this period and insofar as there was any interest in psychology—and there was little—it was based on Augustinian doctrines. The works of Aristotle and Plato had, by and large, been lost. They were to return later from the East, where the Arabs, armed with the new religion of Mahomet, were already developing into a formidable cultural and political power.

Islam

Mahomet was born in Mecca in Arabia in 570. In middle age, he received a revelation from God that he began to preach. He fled to Medina in 622 to escape persecution for his teachings. Known as the Hegira, his flight marks the beginning of the Mohammedan era. He called his religion Islam, which means a surrender to God, and his followers were known as Muslims. His message is contained in the Koran.

The development of Islam was remarkably fast.[2] From the Hegira in 622 and the death of the prophet ten years later, to the conquest not only of Arabia and Syria but also of Egypt and Persia in another twenty years, an irrevocable change was wrought upon the face of the Near East. Sicily and Spain soon came under the domination of Islam. One hundred years after the death of Mahomet, the Muslim empire extended over an area larger than that of the Roman Empire at its height.

Muslims assumed positions of leadership in governmental, military, and religious affairs, but scholarship at first fell to non-Muslims. A series of historical forces had been at work making these non-Muslim scholars available in lands that fell under Muslim rule.[3] Egypt and Syria had been Hellenized and had Greek-speaking schools and strong philosophical traditions. In Persia an ancient oriental culture came under Muslim domination. With their ties to the ancient civilization still unbroken, the scholars of these lands contributed a great deal to the cultural and scientific advances of the area. Pagan and heretical Christian scholars, especially the Syrian Nestorian Christians and the Greeks of the

Byzantine Empire, fled the Christian empire in the West to take refuge in this region, and helped to graft Hellenic civilization onto Muslim culture. Christian physicians, driven out of Constantinople, brought their knowledge to the Arabs.

The jostling proximity of many tongues made translation extremely important for the diffusion of knowledge. Naturally, the most important translations were from Greek sources. Material from Greek philosophy and science was available to the Arabs from the newly conquered lands. By the end of the fifth century much of Aristotle and some of Plato had been translated into Armenian and Persian. In the eighth century this non-Muslim material became a major portion of the secular intellectual provender of the Muslims. Aristotle held a particular fascination and his writings were very popular, along with Neoplatonic works often not attributed to their correct sources. The works of Aristotle in going through several translations, were often, if not always, garbled. To add to the confusion, many works were falsely attributed to him. For example, the so-called *Theology* of Aristotle was actually an abridgement of the last three books of Plotinus' *Enneads*. Moreover, Aristotle was often known through the biased works of commentators, rather than from first-hand study. Hippocrates and Galen were also much translated. Despite the confusion in the materials available to them, from the middle of the eighth century until the twelfth century, Muslim culture completely overshadowed that of the Latin West.

The Muslims assimilated Greek and Hellenistic material and then went on to make distinctive contributions of their own. The philosophical speculation received from the Greek world had much the same effect upon Islam that it was to have upon Christianity. Attempts at a reconciliation of revelation and reason became a major problem. Hotly contested arguments arose concerning the question of heresy. Mystical movements, similar in spirit to those in the Christian world, also appeared.

Our knowledge of the original contributions made to psychology by Islam is only superficial. It would appear that by and large even the greatest of the Muslim philosophers, Alkindi, Avicenna, Alfarabi, and Averroës,[4] were primarily imitative of the Greeks, and often showed a strong Neoplatonic strain. Insofar as they were naturalistic, they tended to follow Aristotle. None of the Muslim scholars can now be seen as qualifying as great philosophical psychologists. Nevertheless, their contributions to psychology deserve more study than has so far been given them.

This same neglect has befallen the Jews who lived during these centuries in the Muslim world. Treated by the Muslims more often than not in an enlightened fashion, they experienced one of the high points of their scholarship. Between the ninth and the thirteenth centuries, especially in Spain and Egypt, lived several Jewish scholars who presented psychological thinking of originality and power. The psychological views of the Jewish philosophers, including Abraham Ibn Daud, Solomon Ibn Gabirol, Abraham Ibn Ezra, Ibn Zaddik, Isaac Israeli, and especially Moses Maimonides, have been shamefully neglected.[5] Although their influence on later developments in psychology is, to say the least, obscure—their work will not be examined here—they are well worth serious study.

In fields other than psychology and philosophy, the Muslims made some scientific advances.[6] Fired with enthusiasm by Greek and Hindu sources of knowledge, they made contributions in mathematics, astronomy, chemistry, technology, and medicine. Instead of being members of the clergy, as were scholars in the West, Muslim scholars were often physicians. With them the study of philosophy, medicine, and some of the rudiments of natural science went hand in hand. Advances continued even until the fifteenth century, but by the twelfth century Muslim supremacy had come to an end.

The High Middle Ages

By the eleventh century in Europe, the social characteristics often associated with the Middle Ages had emerged more or less clearly.[7] The spread of feudalism gave a measure of personal safety to individuals of all social classes and tended to stabilize social relations among them. There were three major social classes—the clergy, the aristocracy, and the rural farm workers. The church was influential not only because of its spiritual authority but because of its extensive landholdings. It was beginning to challenge successfully the secular authority on its affairs and to make its appointments increasingly free from these influences. It also wielded considerable political power. The aristocracy was by and large a military caste depending for its revenues upon its estates. Knighthood had already emerged with its code of chivalry. The rural population worked the estates and was levied for war service, and in return received protection from their liege lords. In the eleventh century, because of a growth in population, greater political stability, more extensive trade, and increased social mobility, the towns became increasingly important. These conditions made a growth in scholarship possible.

COMMON CHARACTERISTICS OF THINKING

The thinking of the Middle Ages must be understood in context. Greek philosophy-science had been based on an attempt to see the world rationally; Christian doctrine is based on faith. One solution, the one popularly attributed to the men of the Middle Ages, was to deny rationalism and embrace faith in the supernatural. Although this attitude was indeed widespread, there was also an attempt by some churchmen to reconcile faith and reason. But of the two, faith was primary and fixed; and reason was secondary and precarious. The dominance of one over the other was never in doubt. No matter how precise the reasoning, if the conclusion did not conform to revelation, it was not true. Errors in faith, no matter how they were introduced, were heretical. Conformity was expected and enforced.

This common attitude led to a considerable amount of uniformity in intellectual life. There was a preoccupation with death. The pilgrimage of man to the grave, with life but a fateful probation either for blissful life everlasting or eternal woe, was a dominant theme. Large segments of intellectual life were guided by a contempt for earthly matters, a despising of human joy, a longing for eternity, a sense of *memento mori*.⁸ But life was not uniformly gloomy. There were rays of simple joy that penetrated the dark gray and made the Middle Ages less grim than it is often thought to have been.

Medieval thinking was not all of a piece. It did not consist of a single integrated system any more than modern philosophy does. The uniformity of thinking was greater than it is today, but was not all-pervasive. As Gilson has reminded us, not all Christian philosophy was either Christian or philosophy.⁹ Fortunately, there were many authorities and these authorities often disagreed with one another. There was variation and change according to the style of the writer and the particular problem, and contrary to popular opinion the scholastic method did allow for some freedom of thought.

On the whole, the spirit of the age was not conducive to psychological concerns. The union of theology and philosophy that gave us Christian philosophy in its spirit of otherworldliness was foreign to psychology. Most of its problems dealt not with man, but with the relationship between God and man—a quite different proposition. Only incidentally did the question of man as man occupy these thinkers. In this small fragment, in this isolated part of the pattern, there were some matters of psychological concern.

SOURCES OF KNOWLEDGE

Most of the intellectual heritage of the West was derived from the scriptures, from the writings of the church fathers, including Augustine, and from a smattering of Neoplatonism. In the early Middle Ages the largest and most important compilation of fact, and of fiction masquerading as fact, was the *Natural History* of Pliny (23–79 A.D.).[10] This work served as a textbook and encyclopedia for the medieval scholar, having within it all sorts of miscellaneous information on what were thought to be facts about nature.

The Latin writer Chalcidius, who was a contemporary of Plotinus, translated a part of the *Timaeus* into Latin and also wrote a commentary on it. Up to the twelfth century, this was the only work of Plato known to the Latin world. Otherwise, Plato was known through Neoplatonic writers rather than directly. Only much later, in about 1150, were two other dialogues, the *Meno* and the *Phaedo,* made available in Latin. The remainder of Plato's works received little attention until the humanist translations of the fifteenth century.

The *Timaeus* is Plato's poetic vision of the world, of the universe, and of God. Its central theme is that the world and man are but incidents or manifestations within the ideal patterns that reside in the mind of God. The things of the world, the visible things, are not real. They have significance only to the extent that they conform to the ideal.

Unfortunately, the *Timaeus* is Plato's least typical dialogue; it is a mixture of the serious and the fanciful, not always easy to tell apart. The astronomical lore that it contains—each soul is said to have both a star and a numerical relation among the planets—later contributed to a lot of harmful astrological nonsense. Because of the style in which it is written, there are problems of interpretation, and the *Timaeus* probably causes more perplexity among scholars than any of Plato's other dialogues. Sarton even goes so far as to say that the influence of the *Timaeus* was largely negative.[11]

Insofar as Aristotle had been known to earlier Christian thinkers, he was seen as definitely secondary to Plato and in fundamental agreement with him. Logic was the one area in which he was acknowledged to be original. The earlier and more elementary portion of his *Organon* had come down from the early Middle Ages in the direct tradition. It was studied along with a widely used commentary by Boethius. These works were staples of dialectic training; together they formed one of the three subjects of the *Trivium;* the others were grammar and rhetoric. The rest of the *Organon* was translated as early as 1150, two generations earlier than those of his works that are of more direct psychological interest. In the Middle Ages there was a search for premises about which one can be certain, and according to Schiller,[12] this goes far to account for the relative neglect of experience during the years since Aristotle.

Ideas derived from Platonic sources dominated Christian philoso-

phy. The fundamental theme in Platonism—the dualistic contrast between things of the senses and things of the mind, between body and
spirit—was preserved. Ever the resident of two realms, man can choose
either one or the other—he can either take the tangible but temporal
things of the senses or turn upward to God and eternal life. For the
Christian the correct choice was clear.

SCHOLASTICISM

The patristic period, dedicated to the formation of orthodoxy, had
passed long before scholasticism made its appearance. The task of
scholasticism was to elaborate a recognized and accepted orthodoxy, to
build upon accepted dogma a system of principles. The scholastic began
with this doctrine and then traced its implications for various theological
questions. Along with consciousness of a need for divine salvation, Henry
O. Taylor considers two of the common characteristics of medieval
thought to be a deference to authority and an all-pervasive scholasticism
leading to work that was diligent and receptive rather than original.[13]
Reverence for the past was a predominant attitude of the scholastic.

The scholastic method in its generic form is defined by Wilhelm
Windelband as follows:

a text used as the basis for discussion is broken up
by division and explanation into a number of
propositions; questions are attached and the possible answers brought together; finally the arguments to be adduced for establishing or refuting
these answers are presented in the form of a chain
of syllogistic reasoning, leading ultimately to a decision upon the subject.[14]

Naturally, there was variation in detail from writer to writer. In more
general terms, oral discussion of question and answer, a form of dialectic,
characterized the scholastic method. Scholasticism was especially congenial to the medieval mind because it permitted acceptance of authority
and yet proceeded from that point by dialectic. It was the medieval
version of eating the cake and having it too.

The scholastic had considerable freedom within the framework of
his method, which was limited in latitude by the stipulation that dogma in
no way must be put to question. It should be noted that the scholastic did
not merely make an appeal to authority, as is sometimes alleged. As R.
McKeon indicates, an adroit scholastic could find authority for either side

of a question and then proceed to find truth by examining the interplay of both sides.[15] The scholastic might know the ultimate answer on the basis of revelation and faith, but he did not necessarily, nor even often, cheat to make it come out right. If his claim led to erroneous conclusions, he did not insist that it did not. Instead he went back over his earlier arguments for the sources of his error and perhaps sometimes couldn't find them! Being human, he could delude himself that his doctrine was not contrary to dogma and proceed to argue the point. He, of course, did so at his peril because his position might eventually be judged heretical.

During the Middle Ages philosophers were almost always theologians, but it is usually overlooked that they often considered problems that had no theological import whatever. A philosopher as philosopher, then, could depend upon reason alone, limited only by his skill and the knowledge available to him.

The Universities

Although some had been founded the century before, the universities did not come into real prominence until the thirteenth century.[16] They had not been important before because there was simply not enough learning to justify their existence. They came into being with the expansion of knowledge. Favorable conditions for their presence now prevailed. Both the gathering together of people into larger communities and the increased ease of travel helped set the stage for them. The youth of the eleventh century had entered monasteries; those of the thirteenth attended universities. The universities at Bologna, Paris, and Oxford were among the most important, and Paris was a truly international institution; men came there to study from all over France, as well as from the Low Countries, and from Italy, England, and Germany. There were, of course, other universities: Cambridge in England; Padua, Naples, and the medical school at Salerno in Italy; Montpellier, Toulouse, and Orleans in France; Salamanca and Valladolid in Spain; and Lisbon in Portugal.

Their curricula consisted of an arts course and higher courses in theology, law, and medicine. Each of these had separate faculties. The arts course usually involved a study of the seven liberal arts and the "three philosophies"—natural philosophy (natural science), ethics, and metaphysics. Masters and scholars were usually clergymen, but not always ordained priests. The newly founded orders of friars, the Dominicans and the Franciscans, both controlled professorships and did much to further the cause of the church. They also served to supply many of the most distinguished professors.

The universities became a potent intellectual force. They aided intellectual progress by supplying a setting that made time and resources for study possible and provided a less involved and more disinterested point of vantage than the monasteries from which to approach fields of knowledge.

THE RECOVERY OF ARISTOTLE

It was to Spain and to Sicily, recovered by the Christian world in the twelfth and thirteenth centuries, that scholars from the West came to work on translations from the Arabic.[17] Such translations could have been done directly from the Greek sources and, as a matter of fact, some of them were, but Arabic sources were usually used. Use of these sources reflected glory upon the Arabic commentaries and the original Arabic works that were translated at the same time. Along with the recovery of Galen and Hippocrates, the West acquired the medical works of Avicenna and the philosophical teaching of Averroës, and these immediately became important. In medicine the Arabic scholars had added valuable observations, and in philosophy they were responsible for a variety of distinctive new perspectives. The translations from Arabic sources included not only religious, philosophical, and medical works, but also works in the fields of science, such as optics, geology, and mathematics. Original contributions in alchemy, magic, and astrology (sometimes attributed to Aristotle) had a considerable effect both for good and for ill. From the end of the twelfth century and for the next hundred years, the proportion of texts translated directly from the Greek gradually increased, and in the fourteenth century translations from the Arabic virtually ceased.

Renan[18] goes so far as to claim that the introduction of these texts into the West divided the Middle Ages into two distinct periods: the earlier, without knowledge of Greek, the later, with ancient science restored. This sweeping generalization is not without merit as a summarization. Certainly a major task of the scholars was to assimilate and study ancient knowledge and to express it in a fashion that would be acceptable when viewed against the imperatives of their time.

As important perhaps for the intellectual history of the West as all other works combined was the recovery of the works of Aristotle. The first medieval scholar supposed to be familiar with Aristotelian treatises was Alexander of Hales (d.1245). The works of Aristotle were imported into the universities of Paris and Oxford between 1200 and 1270. With this recovery the times were ready for the appearance of Aquinas.

Thomas Aquinas

The reconciliation of supernaturalism with rationalism was the task of Aquinas. He carried on this task with intricate but massive tools: the teachings of the church and the recovered works of Aristotle.

It is perhaps fitting that so far as places and events are concerned, the life of Thomas Aquinas bears an impersonal stamp, an objectivity without many of the towering heights and dark shadows of other great men. The fire was there, but it burned with a steady glow, not in a great shower of sparks and flame. He was known to have been really angry only twice in his life. He led an intense intellectual life, and his solitary mind was always hard at work beneath a placid bulk that won for him from his fellow students at the University of Paris the nickname the "Dumb Ox." A story is told that characterizes his imperturbability and abstractedness in the service of scholarship, irrespective of circumstances. Obedient to the orders of his superiors, he had gone to a state dinner at the court of the King of France, Louis IX, later known as St. Louis. He sat at table, a huge man in the black and white habit of the Dominicans, unheeded and unheeding, surrounded by the pomp, the colors, and the jewels of the most brilliant court of Europe. All around were people engaged in gossip, intrigue, and idle, inconsequential chatter. He said little or nothing. Suddenly a huge fist crashed down on a table, and his voice rang out clearly above the discreet hubbub, "And *that* will settle the Manichees!" He had been elsewhere, using his time for his task in life.

Besides being a great scholar, Aquinas was also a Christian saint. This sketch does not even pretend to illustrate this side of his nature. The omission is mentioned as a warning since some would say that Thomas the scholar cannot be understood apart from Thomas the saint.[20]

The family of Aquino was a distinguished and aristocratic one. The Castle of Roccasecca where Thomas was born in 1225 was midway between Naples and Rome. His father, Landulfo, was Count of Aquino, a town nearby, and an official in the service of Frederick II, the King of Sicily. His father had considerable influence at the Benedictine Abbey of Monte Cassino, which was only a few miles from the castle.

At about age five, Thomas entered the abbey and remained there as a student for nine years. In 1239 the monks were forced to leave the abbey because of a war between Pope Gregory II and Frederick II, whose kingdom included that portion of Italy. Thomas enrolled as a student at the University of Naples, a state institution founded only a few years before by the same Frederick whose warmaking had forced him out of the abbey. At Naples he completed his study of the liberal arts.

In 1243 his father died. The next spring Thomas took the habit of the Dominican order. This step caused considerable consternation in his family, not because of his intention to become a priest—they had expected him to return to Monte Cassino, where in the normal course of events and with his family's influence, he would have become abbot—but because he had joined a mendicant order, one made up of begging friars. In deciding to become a beggar, he was not only throwing away wealth and power, but also ecclesiastical ambition. This decision went against the aristocratic grain of the family. Their anger and exasperation were known to John the Teuton, General of the Dominican Order, who decided to take Thomas to Paris so that he might complete his philosophical and theological studies at a more comfortable distance from his family. His mother was not one to have the family wishes flouted and at her direction a group of relatives boldly abducted him from the party traveling to Paris and took him to the family castle, where he was held prisoner for about a year. He was not angry with his family at this imprisonment and, indeed, had so persuasive a tongue that he converted his oldest sister to Saint Benedict. But one thing did make him angry. His brothers, barbaric nobles of their age, conceived a scheme of trying his chastity. They slipped into his prison apartment a prostitute, presumably selected for her seductiveness. On seeing her, he seized a brand from the fire and his expression was such that she fled without saying a word. He then took the flaming log and drew a cross upon the door of his prison. G. K. Chesterton says that his anger rose as much from a feeling of insult over his brothers' belief that something so cheap would tempt him, as from the particular nature of the temptation.[21]

Even the pope intervened on the side of the family, but Aquinas was adamant in his resolve to be a Dominican. The Dominicans continued to appeal to both the pope and the emperor. Finally, in 1245, Aquinas regained his liberty and once again donned the habit of the order. He went to Paris to study under Albert the Great.

Albert was already known as a champion of Aristotle, whose works were coming into general use at the university. In anything more than a sketch of the greatest psychologists, Albert would have an account of his own.[22] More of a scientist and a more original observer than Aquinas and equally if not better versed in psychological matters, he did not have his student's gift for synthesis. The influence of Aquinas upon subsequent developments was the greater, and so the student, not the teacher, is discussed.

In 1248 Albert went to Cologne to establish a Dominican House of

Studies, and Thomas, his favorite pupil, accompanied him. After four years, Thomas returned to the University of Paris for still further study and to begin his career in teaching. As a teacher, he was extremely popular; as a student, he was prodigious. According to regulations, he could not receive his magistrate (doctorate) in theology until after his thirty-fourth birthday, but a papal dispensation was granted him, and he took it at thirty-one. He was also appointed to one of the two Dominican chairs at the University of Paris. As a master, he continued to teach for three additional years at Paris. For ten years after that he was a teacher of theology in various places in Italy.

Sometime between 1261 and 1264 Aquinas wrote the *Summa Contra Gentiles.*[23] Designed for use in missionary work, this "Summary Against the Gentiles" is a work addressed to those nonbelievers who are philosophically skilled and unimpressed by a call to believe—whose rationalism prevents an acceptance of revelation. This work gives not theological, but philosophical arguments, proven by reason alone. Since some of his arguments concern the nature of man, it becomes important as a source for his views on psychology.

Late in the year 1268 he returned to teach at the University of Paris only to find himself in a sea of academic troubles in which he took a leading and vigorous part. Despite his active academic battles, Aquinas found time during his stay in Paris to write additional works. It was during the Italian decade that he had met William of Moerbeke. At his suggestion, Moerbeke began a new translation of Aristotle directly from the Greek. Between 1260 and 1271 William translated or revised translations of nearly all of Aristotle's works. On the basis of this uncorrupted text, Thomas wrote various commentaries on the works of Aristotle, including *On the Soul.*[24]

A few years earlier, around 1266, Thomas had begun the *Summa Theologica,* which was destined to become his most important work.[25] It was designed as a summary for the training of beginners in theology. The first part is concerned with God and creation. His major treatise on psychology is placed between a discussion of the six days of creation and a study of man in the state of original innocence. This was a scriptural order of presentation; man was created last and is therefore treated last. Later parts are concerned with man's moral life and Christ and the sacraments. This work is more obviously theological than the *Summa Contra Gentiles.* But *The Treatise on Man,*[26] a part of it, is a detailed account of his psychology. It is supplemented in this regard by the *Treatise on Human Acts* and the *Treatise on Habits.*[27]

Certainly Aquinas was interested in psychology. In this connection he passed a test that most psychologists might fail; no matter his religious convictions a psychologist could not fail to be impressed by the incident. A friend of Aquinas, one Friar Romano by name, died.[28] Aquinas had a vision in which he saw his friend in Heaven. Out of all the questions on Heaven, Hell, the World, and Man that he might have asked, the question he put to his friend was this: "Do we retain our knowledge of this world in the next?" What more crucial projective test of the primacy of a psychologist's calling could be asked? Under similar circumstances, would even contemporary learning theorists do as well?

In 1272 Thomas left the University of Paris and returned to Italy, where he taught at the University of Naples and continued to work on the *Summa*. His career as a writer came to a sudden and dramatic end on December 6, 1273. He had been saying Mass that morning when a great change came over him. Afterward, whenever he was urged to continue writing his *Summa* he would merely say, "I can do no more; such things have been revealed to me that all I have written seems as straw, and I now await the end of my life." In January, 1274, he received instructions from Pope Gregory X to attend an ecumenical council in Lyons. On the way he fell ill and was forced to break the journey at the Cistercian Abbey of Fossanova, which was not far from his place of birth. There, on March 7, 1274, he died. Less than fifty years later   Thomas was canonized by Pope John XXII.

REASON AND FAITH

The interpretation of Aristotle in the chapter devoted to his views was essentially biological in nature. Little of what was said would have made Aristotle appealing to medieval theologians. What was considered irrelevant in this earlier discussion becomes relevant now, and before considering Aquinas further, we must first return to Aristotle.

From the perspective of psychology as a contemporary science, what follows is not a psychological issue at all. Nevertheless, it is important because in the opinion of Aquinas, anything that touched the issue of reason and faith had implications for psychology.

Before dealing with the interpretation of Aristotle by Aquinas, it might be desirable to state how certain matters are sometimes interpreted today by non-Thomistic scholars. First, we must face the issue of the inseparability of form and matter. If *psyche* is the form of the body, what happens when the body dies? The form must also be gone. The earlier chapter on Aristotle suggests that he rules out personal immortality completely. Here we get into one of the most tangled webs of modern scholarship. The very chapters of Book III of *On the Soul,* described as an interpolation of his earlier views and therefore inapplicable, provide an answer that should in fairness be stated.[29] *Nous,* the highest manifestation of the mind, is there held to be of a different order from the other functions.[30] *Nous,* as the entelechy of the body, is regarded as imperishable.

The individual object, including the human being, perishes. But here we face another perplexing problem; for in the same passage of *On the Soul*[31] where Aristotle speaks of *Nous* (mind) as imperishable, he also tells us that memory and love perish because they are parts of a complex that perishes, namely, the body-psyche unit. Hence, personal immortality seems to be denied in the very passage that is crucial to the argument in favor of it. (It was perhaps this very point Aquinas had in mind, when in his dream of Father Romano, he asked about memories of earthly existence in the life hereafter).

In a broad perspective, one can conceive of Aristotle as being concerned not with the problem of the immortality of the human soul, but with *Nous* as a human function capable of knowing truth, of rising above man's animal limitations to a direct vision of universals. He was arguing for the existence of some dominating source of intelligence outside the universe. It is hard to read religious overtones into what he has to say about movement and the unmoved mover.[32] Motion is eternal—it always has been and it always will be. We can trace movement back from one mover to another—A moves B, B moves C, and so on. Eventually we have to postulate a mover himself unmoved, a transmitter of movement not moved by an anterior movement. This unmoved mover Aristotle calls God. The unmoved mover is not an object of worship. He is not aware of man, nor in any way concerned with him. Divine providence is completely absent. God is a metaphysical necessity, not an object to be loved and worshipped. What modern science disregards as irrelevant to its enterprise, the cause-uncaused, Aristotle considers necessary to investigate because metaphysics cannot, in his view, be divorced from physics.

This striving toward higher existence as conceived by Aristotle was seen in the Middle Ages as a striving toward God. The scholars of the Middle Ages could not have known that in his later thinking Aristotle may have discarded this theory of a higher existence. Aristotle, as he was known, appealed to the Christian thinkers precisely because this postulation of a supreme intelligence was considered by them an integral part, even the capstone of his thinking. His work stressed the idea that all living creatures are subject to law, and was seen by the Christian thinkers as demonstrating that this law was personally decreed by God. The only alternative to His guidance known to thinkers of the Middle Ages was pure chance, to them an abhorrent possibility. It was not until the time of Galileo and Newton that natural law was put forth as still a third alternative.

Aristotle had posited four kinds of causality—material, motor, formal, and final—and had given weight to each of them (p. 52ff). It was therefore possible for those who came after him to stress one or the other according to their interests. It was this teleological strain in Aristotle that Aquinas raised to a position of primacy. There is an intelligent being who directs all things to their ends—and this was interpreted as God.[33] The other causes that Aristotle had used to complete the analysis were subordinated to it. Efficient causes, said Aquinas, are subordinate to final causes; this corresponds to a soldier's tactical disposition by a subordinate commander who is directed by the high command.[34]

Aristotle was interpreted by Aquinas and others as holding that all that exists and all that happens does so for the sake of some end. Every activity, all change, and all growth are to be understood in relation to the ends they serve. Everything is pervaded with change, and no change is meaningless. Change implies preparation, and preparation presupposes becoming. Hence, Aristotle's view was considered in the Middle Ages to be uncompromisingly teleological.

All we have just said was interpreted by Aquinas in a way that would reconcile it with Christian dogma. To his glory, he could do so in a fashion that still satisfies many contemporary thinking men and women who apply to his work their personal test of reason.

Nous, or active reason, minimized in the earlier naturalistic account of Aristotle, became the salient feature of Aquinas' view on man, in general, and on psychology, in particular. Moreover Aquinas did not divorce metaphysical considerations from those of psychology. The unmixed separable character of *Nous* was taken by advocates of religious Aristotelianism, especially that of Aquinas, to mean that *Nous* was capable of separate existence. Hence, it was considered to be the Aristotelian counterpart of the immortal soul.

As a consequence of espousing Aristotle, Aquinas laid himself open to attacks on two fronts. On one side the church conservatives saw his corroboration of Aristotle as an attack on Augustine and the other church fathers and the Neoplatonism with which their views had been so hopelessly intermingled. From Aquinas' point of view the second source of attack was the crucial one; it came in the form of apparent agreement rather than opposition to him. These opponents were themselves Aristotelians. Their leader was Siger of Brabant, who followed to some extent the Averroist interpretation of Aristotle and taught that *Nous* was capable of a separate existence but was conjoined in the individual with a "material intellect." Both *Nous* and the material intellect were necessary for thinking, and since the material intellect was corruptible, this pre- cluded personal immortality. Siger thought that matter exists from eter- nity, and that after the impersonal *Nous* left the matter of the body, it became part of a universal and common intelligence.

Irrespective of one's own interpretation of Aristotle's views about personal immortality and the exact nature of *Nous* (and it would seem that Russell[35] is right and that Siger may have had a case), it is possible, as stated earlier, to take the position of Aquinas and argue for the soul's immortality. The views of the Averroists concerning the eternity of matter, although definitely expounded by Aristotle, disagree with the teaching of the church on creation. On all three counts the position of the Averroists was incompatible with Catholic doctrine. When this was called to their attention, Siger and his followers agreed that perhaps these teachings of Aristotle did contradict the teaching of faith. Ostensibly in the interests of defending reason and faith, Siger suggested the compromise known as the doctrine of two truths. He argued that there were two truths: the truth of the material world and the truth of the supernatural world. When being naturalistic, one may hold in abeyance the other truth; on turning to religion, one accepts this truth. Aquinas, too, followed Averroës in dis- tinguishing faith from reason. To Aquinas, Siger said in effect, "You speak of reason and faith as both giving truth; so also do we, but with this differ- ence, one does not need to trouble about reconciling the two. This fine distinction is all that divides us."

This doctrine, seeming so near and yet actually so far from what he was teaching, was a flat contradiction of all that Aquinas stood for. To him, it was merely a subterfuge. For the second time in his life he was aroused to anger,[36] and in his reply to Siger his usually temperate style gave way to such expressions as "puffed up with false knowledge," "if he dares," and "false teaching."[37]

To his eternal credit, he also opposed the opposite error, namely, that one's views about other matters are irrelevant as long as one's religious attitude is correct.[38]

What Aquinas championed was the doctrine of the *one* truth. There are two paths to the *same* truth, not two truths. Nothing that is philosoph- ically demonstrated will ever contradict or ever be contradicted by what is taught to man through revelation. This position of Aquinas may be made clearer if we deal more specifically with the issue of reason and faith as he saw it. Truth in reason and faith (in science and religion) are one; this concept is so important to him that he opens the *Summa* on this

Both Reason + Revelation lead to the same truth.

theme.[39] Theology is the noblest of the sciences because of the worth of its subject matter. The knowledge that we arrive at from the evidence of our senses is not enough to know the essence of God but what we sense does come from God and this permits us to know that he exists.[40] It is not that there is no distinction between theology and philosophy—there is. Theology concerns faith, that which is known immediately and without doubt; philosophy is known only after consideration of the other possible alternatives.[41] Because certain truths, such as the mystery of the Trinity, cannot be known by reason, they are matters of consideration for theology alone. There are many other truths, however, that are within the province of both reason and revelation.[42] The theologian and the philosopher both consider the same truths, but from different points of view: the theologian regards them as given; the philosopher regards them as in need of demonstration. The philosopher, for example, may, through a process of reasoning, arrive at an acceptance of God as the Creator; the theologian, on the other hand, accepts that God is the Creator because He has revealed Himself as such.

As far as church orthodoxy was concerned, Aquinas decisively disposed of the arguments of Siger. Nevertheless, during and after his lifetime, Aquinas' teachings continued to be brought up for condemnation by church authorities.[43]

PHILOSOPHICAL PSYCHOLOGY

Three factors make it possible to be briefer in discussing the psychological views of Aquinas than some of the other great philosophical psychologists. The previous discussion of reason and faith is part of Thomistic psychology. Moreover there are much more complete modern statements readily available, which is not the case for the earlier thinkers.[44] Most important of all, Aquinas followed Aristotle in much of his psychology, and Aristotle has already received rather detailed treatment. A possible misunderstanding must be disposed of in this connection. To put it succinctly, Aquinas followed Aristotle, not because he was Aristotle, but because much of what he had said Aquinas thought was true. Aquinas did not hesitate to disagree with Aristotle where he thought the Greek philosopher was wrong. But since the terminology of Aquinas is different from that of Aristotle, some restatement must be made even of points on which they were in agreement.

SOUL AND BODY

To Aquinas, man as a species has one substantial form, the rational soul.[45] Man is neither soul alone, nor body alone, but soul and body, a united or composite substance. There are no vegetative sensitive substantive forms or souls. The person is a unity; the rational soul has not only the function particular to itself but also encompasses the vegetative and sensitive functions. The human soul thus exercises the functions of the lower forms of life, which have vegetative or sensitive souls. The rational soul as a totality is united with its body in order to carry on its natural functions. Unlike some earlier thinkers, Aquinas taught that the soul is neither imprisoned nor carrying out a sentence of punishment; it is doing what is natural and good. It's union with the body is not to the detriment of the soul but to its enrichment.[46] The soul completes human nature and also confers the incidental benefit of allowing the achievement of knowledge through the senses. It is acting according to its nature, in which matter exists for form, and not *vice versa*.[47]

This view is not materialistic in the sense that soul or mind is made to depend on material substances (or if you prefer, cortical substances). Nor is it, to use a Thomistic term, angelectic, with mind or soul interpreted as a purely immaterial entity or as an independent spiritual being.

For Aquinas there are a multiplicity of corporeal substances; that is to say, a multiplicity of substances that have matter in their nature. Four species may be distinguished—nonliving bodies, plants, animals, and men.[48] Inanimate objects perform material activities alone; plants have material and vegetative activities; animals, these two and sensory activities; and man has rational activities in addition to the three lower activities.

SOUL AND ITS FACULTIES

In one of his most sustained and detailed psychological statements,[49] Aquinas distinguishes between the unity that is soul and its faculties or powers. He makes further divisions among these faculties or powers. The soul is not its faculties. The soul does not exercise these functions directly through its essence as such, but through powers with which it is endowed and that are distinct from its essence. There is an order or priority among these faculties related to the corporeal substances of which they are composed. The rational faculty is conceived of as higher than the sensitive and, therefore, as embracing and controlling the sensitive, while the sensitive faculty is above the nutritive one. The vegetative faculty embraces the powers of nutrition, growth, and reproduction. The sensitive faculty embraces the five exterior senses, the four interior senses (a description of which follows), sensitive appetite, and locomotion. The rational faculty comprises the active and passive intellect, and the will. The vegetative faculty encompasses the subject's own body-soul combination. The sensitive faculty has as its object, not the body of its sentient subject alone, but every sensible body. The rational faculty has as its object not only sensible body, but being itself. The higher the faculty, the more comprehensive its scope, extending from a particular body-soul composite, to sensed bodies, to being in general.

There is no need to review the powers of the vegetative faculty nor the exterior senses of the sensitive faculty since they are treated in a manner similar to that used by Aristotle. This is not the case with the interior senses of the sensitive faculty. In using the expression, interior sense, Aquinas was not referring to additional sense modalities arising from stimulation within the organism but to operations at the level of sensitive life and, consequently, to psychological functioning not involving reason. For example, a bird goes beyond the outer senses in using vision to select twigs for nest-building because, while the exterior senses give awareness of color, they do not inform that the twig is useful for the particular task. Since the bird does not reason, he must have an interior sense by which to apprehend the utility of the twig.

Reception of sense data involves the already familiar common sense for reception of those qualities, such as softness, that cannot be perceived by one sense modality alone. But reception also includes the particular interior sense illustrated in the preceding paragraph. It becomes necessary because the data received transcends the qualities of the common sense. It is called *via aestimativa,* or estimative power. Animals are dependent on it because they are without the aid of reason. When a lamb sees a wolf and "estimates" it is to be avoided, this is done, to use a modern term, by instinct. Estimating is a power of sensing what is harmful and what is useful to the organism; it is a power that does not depend on previous experience or training. In man, estimating is allied to mind, since there is always a background of abstract knowledge and universal principles derived from reason with which it interacts. This is analogous to instinctive estimating, but because it is effected by reason, it must be distinguished from it also. It is given a distinctive name, *via cogitativa* or cogitative power.

In addition to reception of sense expressed in the common sense and estimative or cogitative power, both animals and humans conserve the data of sense. Because it produces sense images, Aquinas refers to imagination as the conservation of sense data. As for the conservation of those estimative or cogitative powers that transcend sense, such as the recognition of an image as an item of personal experience in past time, this requires still another power. It is called sensory memory. Thus the four interior senses are the common sense, the sense of estimation and cogitation, imagination, and memory.

In considering sensation, Aquinas almost echoes Aristotle, despite differences in terminology. He holds that sensed material things exist only in the sensing individual, not as material but as immaterial, and the ability to sense is the ability to receive form (species) without matter.

According to Aquinas, the power of appetite is twofold and involves sensitive appetite at the sensitive level and volition or will at the rational level. Sensitive appetite desires objects that are sensed. There are two major kinds of sensitive appetites, the *concupiscible,* so called because they desire the objects of sensible pleasure, and the *irascible,* whose function is to urge a fight for the objects in question when there are difficulties in securing them. The *concupiscible emotions* include love, desire, joy, hatred, aversion, and sorrow, while the *irascible* embrace hope, despair, courage, fear, and anger. Aquinas calls the act of a sensitive appetite a *passion.*

In keeping with his teleological emphasis, Aquinas asserts that at least some knowledge of purpose must be present for an activity to be called voluntary.[50] Perhaps the most typical of the arguments that Aquinas advances for freedom of the will is that it arises from freedom of the intellect; as he puts it, free choice is free judgment. Some activities forced on one give rise to coercive necessity, but these are involuntary. Free will is evidenced in voluntary activities about which judgments are made.

Because it is an appetitive faculty, the will cannot be understood apart from its natural object. We desire happiness, which is found in the good, by our very nature, proceeding from the will in itself. This means the desire comes from the will itself and is not imposed upon us from without, as by violence. We cannot help desiring because we are the creatures that we are. This naturalness of the desire for happiness does not mean one is not free to make his own individual choices. In the relation of will and intellect, will is subordinate. Intellect is dominant. "Nothing is willed unless known," is a dictum of Aquinas.

The functioning of the rational faculty as such needs to be considered. The power of the so-called agent intellect or active intellect is concerned with abstraction; and the power of the possible intellect is concerned with understanding, judgment, and reasoning. The first power is active or creative; the second is passive or receptive. Because it is material, a sensible object is only potentially intelligible. Aquinas is empirical in that he holds with Aristotle that natural knowledge begins with sensation.[51] But in order to make sensory experience intelligible, the activity of the active intellect of the mind is necessary. With the operation of the active intellect we extract the form from the individual substance in which it is embedded and experience "color" or "horse." When the agent intellect acts, the concrete nature of the datum is laid aside and what remains is something capable of being understood. It is no longer material but is intelligible, an object of intellect. The agent intellect renders sensible natures intelligible by abstraction for use by the possible intellect. Sense experience provides the stimulus for setting in operation the agent intellect. It makes "possible" the realization of the truth that the possible intellect potentially contains. Prior to sensory experience the possible intellect is a *tabula rasa,* devoid of ideas. To a certain extent this task is performed by the senses themselves in that through them we perceive the *species* to which the objects belong, i.e., a green flower and a green glass have the color green, which is its species. To understand, we must penetrate sensible species to intelligible terms.

PSYCHOLOGY AND THEOLOGY

In closing discussion of these aspects of the psychology of Aquinas, a return to theology is particularly fitting. So far as the teachings of psychology are concerned, a reconciliation with dogma becomes imperative in connection with revealed doctrines about the resurrection of the body and its eventual reunion with the soul. This, in turn, requires the immortality of the soul. The issue at hand is how Aquinas reconciled his previously stated views on psychology with these theological imperatives. To do so Aquinas drew upon previously established teachings. It will be remembered that Aristotelian *Nous,* the active reason or active intellect, has been interpreted by Aquinas as deathless. Aquinas extended this contention of immortality to the rational soul as a unit. It will also be remembered that Aquinas himself made a distinction between the soul and its faculties. Both of these points are made use of in the reconciliation.

To Aquinas, some of the faculties belong to the soul as such. These faculties transcend the power of matter. For the rational faculties, the body is not necessary as the organ of activities. The rational faculties are not intrinscially dependent upon body, even though when united with the body they draw upon sense experience, which is dependent upon the composite. Other lower faculties, when in the soul-body composite, do depend upon the body for the way in which they are exercised in the composite, and cannot be exercised in that way without the body. Relying as they do upon the body, the sensitive and vegetative faculties, in the form they functioned in while part of the soul-body composite, perish with the composite. But the soul is a unity. It therefore follows that the human soul cannot be said to depend intrinsically upon the body for its existence. Consequently, the whole substance of the soul shares in the deathlessness of the active intellect (the *Nous* of Aristotle). The soul, as distinguished from its faculties, is a unity, and this unity survives separation from the body.

Self-consciousness, that is, the ability of the active intellect to reflect upon itself, shows the immateriality of the rational soul as contrasted with the body. So it may be added that while the lower functions may be lost, *we* do not perish. Self-awareness, reason, and the will, integral aspects of the rational soul, do survive.

THE INFLUENCE OF AQUINAS

Some would call this period the Age of Thomism.[52] But though Thomas was well known in his time, he certainly was not universally acclaimed. On the contrary, his views met with considerable opposition. His originality was recognized, but often this realization was accompanied by the suspicion that his ideas were dangerous.

The victory of Thomism did not occur overnight. Thomas's fellow Dominicans were the first to accept him in a more or less official fashion, but opposition continued to be vigorous. As Sarton reminds us, the gradual triumph was an advantage, stirring less jealousy and opposition when it reached the stage of almost being taken for granted.[53] The victory of Aquinas, when it came, was complete. It set the prevailing position of later Catholic philosophy to this very day.[54] The Thomist philosophy was eventually established as the official philosophy of the Roman Catholic church.[55] The Papal Encyclical of 1897 confirmed the teachings of St. Thomas Aquinas as the true Catholic philosophy. This does not mean, as it is sometimes mistakenly alleged, that his views must be accepted by Catholics. Serious consideration of his teachings is required, but not unthinking acceptance of them.

From the modern perspective, the reconciliation of faith and reason performed by Aquinas still has an intellectual appeal. For those to whom it is important and relevant, he still provides a means of reconciling faith and reason without compromising the value or nature of either the one or the other. According to this view, experimental psychology, even psychophysical investigation, is legitimate. In no way does psychology detract from faith, and faith is neither subordinated to nor contradicted by psychology.

The work of Aquinas enhanced the stature of both rationalism and empiricism. The senses were described as the means by which man attained the basis of knowledge. In accepting the senses, Aquinas was accepting man's ability to use the knowledge that he obtained from them. He was also saying that man's reason is sovereign while he is in the human state. The world may be transitory, but reason does have its own domain. Reason supplements faith; it does not deny it—and while empiricism is a useful tool, rationalism is thus paramount.

The appeal to reason argued so eloquently by Aquinas was highly successful, though sometimes in ways not intended by Aquinas or the church. Others after him were able to draw the conclusion that reason and faith could exist side by side as two separate realms. Although this did happen, it was not intended by Aquinas. On many occasions his work was used to help justify the separation of faith and reason, or religion and philosophy. This controversy foreshadowed the separation of science and theology that was to come.

Meanwhile supernaturalism had been persuasively defended by the closely reasoned appeal of Aquinas who considered nature a part, but an important part, of man's earthly existence.

Science in the Later Middle Ages

The recovered works of Aristotle played a double and antithetical role in the scientific development of the later Middle Ages. It was as if thinkers of the time could not let him alone—they were either for Aristotle or against him. They never ignored him. In these developments his various works served different purposes. On one hand, the works supplying information about biology and physics formed the basis of knowledge for many scholastics. On the other, his newly recovered methodological works, with their teachings of logic, gave the opponents of the first group of Aristotelians a potent weapon. When complemented by the recovered Greek and the new Arabic mathematical works, the methodological works became a tool for the development of new ideas on induction and experiment and the use of mathematical demonstration.[56] This was especially true in the field of physical dynamics where the greatest scientific advances in these centuries were made. It was precisely Aristotle's views of motion and space that were most sharply criticized. The methodological Aristotle was used to demolish the contentual Aristotle.

In general, the great advance of the twelfth century was a dawning realization "that a particular fact was explained when it could be deduced from a more general principle."[57] A mathematical-deductive method was beginning to emerge, reinforced by the mathematical advances that took place during the thirteenth and subsequent centuries. At Oxford there was a reaction against the almost exclusive attention to theology, logic, and philosophy. Robert Grosseteste (c. 1170–1253) was the most prominent teacher and the founder of the mathematical-scientific tradition of that great institution.[58] He realized, albeit dimly, that a distinction could be made among the inductive, experimental, and mathematical approaches to science.

Duns Scotus

William of Ockham

Developments within philosophy thereafter made it more possible to apply the scientific approach to nature. This was the developing gap between reason and faith as expressed in the rise of skepticism. Duns Scotus[59] and William of Ockham,[60] two Franciscan friars of Oxford at the end of the thirteenth and the beginning of the fourteenth centuries, were very important in this connection. Both contributed to the trends then emerging, which entered on a desire to separate reason from faith. Scotus and Ockham were at opposite poles in the struggle between realism and nominalism. Both probably believed that they were working for the greater glory of faith, but the overall effect of their thinking was actually to make easier the separation of faith from reason. As a consequence, scepticism toward faith went hand in hand with a greater independence of faith. It was increasingly possible thereafter for reason to go one way and faith another.

THE EXPERIMENT

In view of the grip of scholasticism on the thinkers of the later Middle Ages, it is hardly surprising that observational study of the phenomena of nature was almost nonexistent during these years. A few observations were made by some scholars. The work of Albert the Great on botany is a case in point. More significant for the future than observational excursions were the scattering of halting and imperfectly understood attempts to develop an experimental approach to the problems of nature and man and thus to advance empiricism.

True experiments were rare in the Middle Ages and continued to be rare in the Renaissance.[61] Working in almost complete isolation from one another, a number of scholars tried to formulate in their writings this "new" way of studying nature. These lonely pioneers included Roger Bacon, Peter of Spain, Raymond Lull, and Arnold Villanova. Roger Bacon is by far the best known of these men today.[62] In fact, a myth of his singularity grew up among those who came after him. Bacon himself also believed that he alone in his day had a true appreciation of the scientific spirit. It is partly as a corrective for this that Peter of Spain, rather than Roger Bacon, is chosen for exposition.

Peter of Spain (c.1215–1277) was a remarkably versatile man. He was educated at Paris, became Rector of Medicine at the University of Sienna, physician to Pope Gregory X, Archbishop of Braga, and, in 1276, was elevated to the Chair of St. Peter, as John the XXI. He wrote a textbook on logic,[63] in use for centuries, and a compendium of medicine that was also very popular. But it is for two other accomplishments that he deserves to be rescued from the neglect of psychologists. Somewhere between 1245 and 1250 he wrote an original account of psychology, *De Anima*.[64] It must be emphasized that this was not a commentary on Aristotle (he did write such a commentary, however). Instead, it was perhaps the first avowedly independent work on psychology for over a thousand years; it was concerned with psychology alone. It even contained a chapter on the history of psychology. Peter devoted some attention to the relation between the psychological and medical aspects of the field. The "psychologist pope" has by no means received the attention that he deserves.

The second of the two accomplishments that make Peter of Spain worthy of our attention more relevant to the issue at hand was his account of the experimental method. In his *Commentaries on Isaac*, a work on diets and medicines, Peter formulated his plea for something resembling an experiment.[65] He spoke of two methods by which dietary science might be investigated, *via rationis* and *via experimenti*. The path of reason and the way of experiment (or experience) are both necessary but different. The path of reason proceeds through the use of the intellect, studies causes, and uses syllogistic methods; the way of experiment proceeds through sense, studies effects, and applies induction. Reason again is a necessary further step to confirm what is found by experiment. Peter gives a series of six steps or conditions that he considers necessary to carry on medical experimentation. (1) The medicine should be free of foreign substances. (2) There should be assurance that the patient has the disease for which the medicine is intended. (3) It should be given without admixture with other medicines. (4) The medicine should be of the degree opposite to the disease. That is to say that if the disease causes an excess, the medicine should be such as to decrease it, as when a medicine cools off a heated condition. (5) It should be tested, not only once but many times. (6) The proper body should be used, the body of a man, not an ass. Through the simple and concrete language of his six steps shines a remarkable grasp of some of the implications of how an experiment is conducted today.

MEDICINE

After the classical twilight, medicine became largely overrun by folk-medicine.[66] The historical situation of medicine was similar to that of ancient knowledge in general—some medical knowledge persisted, particularly in commentaries on Galen, and much more had come back from the Arabs. The revival of Western medicine began in the eleventh century when the medical school at Salerno, founded a century or two earlier, came into prominence, perhaps stimulated in its pioneering by contact with the Arabian medicine of nearby Sicily. In the twelfth and thirteenth centuries, the university medical schools of Montpellier, Bologna, Padua, and Paris gained prominence. However, the church prohibited its clergy from carrying out surgery in support of its abhorence of bloodshed. This, coupled with a contempt for any form of handiwork, led to the appearance of barber-surgeons as assistants to the professors. Certainly, knowledge of anatomy was in a poor state, and most university medical teaching was of a theoretical and dogmatic character.

SCIENCE AND SUPERSTITION

In the late Middle Ages superstition, the dark underside of supernaturalism, as it were, had great appeal. The history of medieval science was inextricably bound up with magical, superstitious practices. Magic was so pervasive that Lynn Thorndike, the historian of science of the Middle Ages, found it eminently fitting to include magic *and* experimental science.[67]

Belief in demons and witches was widespread in the fourteenth century, though not to the terrifying extent to which it swelled in the fifteenth and sixteenth centuries. Astrology had many devotees; magic was performed everywhere. Divination by dreams was taken very seriously. These and similar superstitions were not confined to the ignorant peasant; a king might be as superstitious as his lowliest subject. Nor was the scholar-churchman exempt. The official policies of the church toward such matters took a complicated and circuitous course, impossible to trace in short compass. It is sufficient to say that in earlier centuries superstition was tolerated but generally discouraged, but later it became a matter of considerable concern and brought massive persecution of alleged witches on the part of Catholic and Protestant authorities alike.

An apt illustration of the combination of science and superstition prevalent in these times is to be found in the medical teachings of Arnold of Villanova (c. 1235–1316).[68] Simultaneously, he was a thorough Galenist and a believer in the Devil and demons. He combined Galenic humoralism with demonology in his diagnostic and etiological considerations. He believed that because the Devil likes warmth, the presence of warm humors in the body makes an individual susceptible to seizure by the Devil. Hence, warm humors are to be avoided. Arnold likewise brought Galen into accord with astrology. Accepting the Galenic contention that epilepsy is caused by the humors, he related the particular humor bringing on an attack to the particular quarter of the moon in which it occurred. The planet Mars he considered responsible for melancholia, because the planet's color and supposed heat was said to affect the color and heat of the bile, bringing on melancholia. While bleeding was recommended as a treatment, he argued that it must be applied in accordance with astrological portents involving consideration of the phases of the moon and constellations.

The End of the Middle Ages

The period of the medieval revival of learning had spent its force by the close of the first quarter of the fourteenth century.[69] Its contributions were again and again reproduced in the fourteenth through the sixteenth centuries, first in manuscript and then in printed form; but very little creative or original work was done until the new period of the scientific Renaissance came along.

To be sure there were changes presaging the future. In the second half of the fourteenth century there was an increase in the number of scholars who were not clerics.[70] This was indicative of changing times. Works also began to be written in native tongues instead of in Latin.

The fourteenth century and the first years of the fifteenth century saw many stirring events, the general effect of which was to destroy the synthesis of the thirteenth century. The Black Death wiped out perhaps a fourth of the population. The One Hundred Years' War compounded the usual wastefulness of war with its incredible length. There was the rise of the commercial classes, the decrease in importance of the feudal aristocracy, the rise of strong national monarchies, and a decline in the moral prestige of the papacy. The Babylonian captivity, the Great Schism, and the power politics of the church hierarchy helped to persuade people that papal autocracy must be held in check.

But when did this period end and a new one begin? Various dates have been advanced, but it is relatively unimportant to try to be precise here. With Sarton it is agreed that about 1450 is as good a date as any,[71] since this date saw the appearance of printing in the West.

References*

1. E.g., H. O. Taylor, *The Mediaeval Mind*, 4th ed. (Cambridge: Harvard University Press, 1959).
2. P. K. Hitti, *Arabs, a Short History* (Princeton: Princeton University Press, 1946).

*See p. 19 for description of reference style.

3. The influence of non-Muslim scholars and the assimilation of Greek and Hellenistic material is recounted by A. C. Crombie, *Medieval and Early Modern Science*, 2nd rev. ed. (New York: Doubleday,
1959), 2 vols; M. Desruelles, and A. Bersot, "L'assis-
tance aux alienes chez les Arabes du VIIIe au XIIe
siecle," *Année med. psychol.*, 96, (1938) 689–709; and
D. L. O'Leary, *How Greek Science Passed to the Arabs*
(London: Broadway House, 1948).

4. Averroës is perhaps the only one of the group who
has been studied from a psychological point of view.
J. Bakos, *Psychologie d'Ibn Sīnā (Avicenne) d'après son
oeuvre aš Sifá* (Prague: Editions de l'académie
Tchécoslovaque des Sciences, 1956). More peripheral but still interesting is the volume by E. Renan,
Averroës et L'Averrosime. (Paris: Alcan, 1869).

5. Dimly discernible in such works as I. Husik, *A History of Mediaeval Jewish Philosophy* (New York:
Meridian Books, 1958).

6. G. Sarton, *Introduction to the History of Science* (Baltimore: Williams & Wilkins, 1927–1948), 3 vols. in 5.

7. Major sources helpful in understanding the relevant
aspects of High Middle Ages were Taylor, *Mediaeval Mind*; Sarton, *Introduction to the History of
Science*; G. Leff, *Medieval Thought: St. Augustine
to Ockham.* (Baltimore: Penguin Books, 1958);
E. Gilson, *The Spirit of Medieval Philosophy.*
(New York: Charles Scribner's Sons, 1936); the
introductions to *Selections from Mediaeval Phil-
osophy*, R. McKeon, ed., 2 vols., (New York: Charles
Scribner's Sons, 1929); the article by the same
writer, "Aristotelianism in Western Christianity,"
Environmental Factors in Christian History, J. T.
McNeill et al. ed. (Chicago: University of Chicago
Press, 1939), pp. 206–231; and R. Klibansky, *The
Continuity of the Platonic Tradition During the
Middle Ages* (London: Warburg Institute, 1939).

8. E. K. Rand, "Medieval Gloom and Medieval Uniformity," *Speculum* I (1926): 253–268.

9. Gilson, *Spirit of Medieval Philosophy*.

10. Pliny the Elder, *Natural History*, 6 vols., trans. J.
Bostock and H. T. Dilly (London: Bell, 1855–1890),
(A.D. 77).

11. Sarton, *Introduction to the History of Science*.

12. F. C. S. Schiller, *Hypotheses*, in C. Singer, ed., *Studies*

in the History and Methods of Science (London: Oxford University Press, 1917), pp. 414–446.

13. Taylor, *Mediaeval Mind.*

14. W. Windelband, *A History of Philosophy, Greek, Roman and Medieval* (New York: Harper and Brothers, 1901), I, 312–313.

15. McKeon, *Selections From Medieval Philosophy.*

16. A standard source is H. Rashdall, in R. M. Powicke, A. B. Emden, ed., *The Universities of Europe in the Middle Ages,* 2nd ed., (Oxford: Clarendon Press, 1936).

17. A good succinct account may be found in O. H. Haskins, "Arabian Science in Western Europe," *Isis,* VII (1925), 478–485.

18. Renan, *Averroës et L'Averrosime.*

19. The major source for details and for all dates is the account of his life by V. Bourke, *Thomistic Bibliography, 1920–1940* (St. Louis: St. Louis University, 1945). Some material has also been drawn from F. C. Copleston's *Aquinas* (Baltimore: Penguin Books, 1955), G. K. Chesterton, *St. Thomas Aquinas* (Garden City N.Y.: Doubleday and Company, 1958), and M. Grabmann, *Thomas Aquinas: his Personality and Thought,* trans. V. Michel (London: Longmans, 1929).

20. E.g., Grabmann, *Thomas Aquinas.*

21. Chesterton, *St. Thomas Aquinas.*

22. Particularly relevant to psychology are his *Summa Theologiae* and *Summa de Homine* which form volumes 31–33, and 35 respectively of *Opera Omnia,* ed. A. Bourget (Paris: Vives, 1890). A good secondary source is G. C. Reilly's, "The Psychology of Saint Albert the Great, Compared with that of St. Thomas," *(Philosophical Studies, Catholic University of America,* 1934, No. 29).

23. T. Aquinas, *Summa contra Gentiles,* 5 vols., trans. English Dominican Fathers (New York: Benziger, 1928–1929). (1258–1264).

24. *Aristotle's De Anima in the Version of William of Moerbeke and the Commentary of St. Thomas Aquinas,* trans. K. Foster and S. Humphries (New Haven: Yale University Press, 1951). (1269–1270).

25. R. M. Hutchins, ed., *Great Books of the Western World,* Vols. XIX–XX, T. Aquinas, *The Summa Theologica,* trans. by Dominican Fathers and rev. by

D. J. Sullivan (Chicago: Encyclopaedia Britannica, 1952) (1266–1273).

26. *Ibid.*, First Part, QQ. 75–100, Vol. 1, pp. 378–522.
27. *Ibid.*, Part 1, Second Part, QQ. 1–48, 49–89, Vol. 1, pp. 644–826, Vol. 2, pp. 1–204.
28. K. Foster, *The Life of St. Thomas Aquinas: Biographical Documents* (Baltimore: Helicon Press, 1959).
29. Works of Aristotle, trans. under direction of W. D. Ross, in R. M. Hutchins, ed., *Great Books of the Western World,* Vol. VIII–IX (*c.*340–322 B.C.); *On the Soul* 429a 10–430a 25.
30. F. Nuyens, *L'evolution de la psychologie d' Aristote* (Louvain: Institut supérieur de Philosophie, 1948).
31. Aristotle *On the Soul* 408b 17–32.
32. Aristotle *Physics* 241b 24–245b 2, 252b 10–267b 26; *On Generation and Corruption* 334a 8–15; *Metaphysics* 1012b 22–31, 1018b 8–35, 1049b 4–1050b 5, 1072a 30–3, 1074b 14.
33. Aquinas *Summa Theologica* First Part, Q. 2, 3.
34. *Ibid.*, Part 1, Second Part, Q. 109, 6.
35. B. Russell, *A History of Western Philosophy* (New York: Simon and Schuster, 1945).
36. Chesterton, *St. Thomas Aquinas.*
37. Aquinas, The Unicity of the Intellect, in *"The Trinity"* and *"The Unicity of the Intellect.,"* trans. by R. E. Brennan (London: Herder, 1946) (1270).
38. Aquinas *Summa contra Gentiles* Vol. 2, 3.
39. Aquinas *Summa Theologica* First Part, Q. 1, 1–3.
40. *Ibid.*, Q. 12, 12.
41. *Ibid.*, Part 2, Second Part, Q. 1, 4.
42. Aquinas *Summa contra Gentiles* Vol. 1, 3.
43. F. Van Steenbergen, *The Philosophical Movement in the Thirteenth Century.* (New York: Nelson, 1955).
44. J. E. Royce, *Man and Meaning* (New York: McGraw-Hill, 1969); G. P. Klubertanz, *The Philosophy of Human Nature* (New York: Appleton-Century-Crofts, 1953).
45. Aquinas *Summa Theologica* First Part, Q. 75, 1–7, Q. 76, 3; *Summa contra Gentiles* Vol. 2, 56, 57.
46. Aquinas *Commentary on Aristotle's De Anima* 1 ad 7, 2 ad 14. (In reference 24)
47. Aquinas *Summa Theologica* First Part, Q. 76, 41.
48. Aquinas *Summa contra Gentiles* Vol. 4, 11.
49. Aquinas *Summa Theologica* First Part, QQ. 77–90. (With exceptions specified below, this is the source

for discussion of his psychological views hereafter.)

50. *Ibid.*, Part 1, Second Part, Q. 6.
51. *Ibid.*, First Part, Q. 12, 12.
52. Leff, *Medieval Thought.*
53. Sarton, *Introduction to the History of Science.*
54. Grabmann, *Thomas Aquinas.*
55. Sarton, *Introduction to the History of Science.*
56. A. C. Crombie, *Medieval and Early Modern Science,* Vol. 2; *Science in the Later Middle Ages and Early Modern Times,* 2nd rev. ed. (Garden City, N.Y.: Doubleday 1959).
57. *Ibid.*, p. 3.
58. A. C. Crombie, *Robert Grosseteste and the Origins of Experimental Science, 1100–1700* (Oxford: Clarendon, 1953).
59. John Duns Scotus, Selections from the Oxford Commentary on the Four Books of the Master of the Sentences, in R. McKeon ed., *Selections from Medieval Philosophers* (New York: Charles Scribner's Sons, 1930), (*c.*1300) II, pp. 313–350.
60. William of Ockham, *Studies and Selections,* ed. and trans. S. C. Tornay (Chicago: Open Court, 1938) (*c.*1322).
61. Sarton, *Introduction to the History of Science.*
62. Roger Bacon, Selections from the *Opus Majus,* in R. McKeon, *Selections from Medieval Philosophy,* Vol. II, pp. 7–110.
63. Petrus Hispanus, *The Summulae Logicales of Peter of Spain,* ed. and trans. J. P. Mullally (South Bend: Notre Dame University Press, 1945) (1268).
64. Pedro Hispano, *De Anima,* P. Manuel Alonso, S. I., ed., (Consejo Superior de Investigaciones Cientificas. Instituto Filosofico "Luis Vives." Serie A. Num. 1, Madrid: 1941).
65. L. Thorndike, *A History of Magic and Experimental Science During the First Thirteen Centuries of our Era,* Vol. 2 (New York: Macmillan, 1923).
66. Crombie, *Medieval and Early Modern Science.*
67. Thorndike, *History of Magic and Experimental Science.*
68. G. Zilboorg and G. W. Henry, *A History of Medical Psychology* (New York: W. W. Norton, 1941), p. 137.
69. Thorndike, *History of Magic and Experimental Science.*
70. Sarton, *Introduction to the History of Science.*
71. G. Sarton, *Six Wings; Men of Science in the Renaissance* (Bloomington: Indiana University Press, 1957).

Chapter 7

Descartes:
THE RENAISSANCE AND
THE BEGINNING OF
THE MODERN PERIOD

The one hundred and fifty years from the appearance of printing in the West in about 1450 to about 1600 has come to be called the Renaissance. Providing limiting dates for a given historical period is essentially a matter of convenience. In this case, the opening date marks the first time when learning could be transmitted in a stable fashion, and is a plausible one for our purposes, especially in regard to scientific and cultural history. Though often selected for other reasons, the terminal date has special appeal for psychology, for it was in 1596 that Descartes, the first philosophical psychologist of modern times, was born.

The Renaissance: a Period of Preparation

The Renaissance was a period of general and literary enrichment, not one of specific scientific accomplishment.[1] But the spirit of the age, although essentially literary, brought differences in outlook that were to influence the sciences, including psychology.

Some anticipation of the new outlook may be found in the thinking of Petrarch, a lonely pioneer who died in 1374, only one century after Thomas Aquinas, but nearly a century before the date of convenience used here for the beginning of the Renaissance.[2] This dawning outlook was expressed in his humanistic attitude—an interest in the freedom of the human spirit and freedom from the medieval traditions of scholastic theology and philosophy. Petrarch had a sense of living in a transitional period and was eager to recover and know the Latin classics. As heralded by Petrarch, the Renaissance was not a pagan movement, nor had it divorced itself completely from the Middle Ages, as it was later to do. Petrarch may have loved Cicero best, but he quoted Augustine frequently. A loyal churchman, he regarded the study of the classics not as a hindrance but rather as an aid to Christianity. From the start, however, he was contemptuous of Scholasticism. He scoffed at these interpreters of the works of others, "Like those who have no notion of architecture, they make it their profession to whitewash walls."[3]

During the Renaissance there was a mellowing of the scope of the still fundamental supernaturalistic framework. Concern for the humanness of man assumed greater importance; the value of man as an earthly being and as an integral part of the world of nature was held by a growing number to be almost as important as consideration of his destiny in the life beyond.

Specific manifestations were the discovery, preservation, and translation of ancient manuscripts; textual criticism; writing letters in the manner of Cicero; and concern with epigraphy, archaeology, grammar, and rhetoric. A paradox of the rebirth of classical humanism, with its emphasis on Latin and Greek, was the concurrent popularization of the vernacular tongues as vehicles of the literature of the day. Rabelais and Montaigne, for example, fought for the use of French as a language of literature. The fear of novelty, so characteristic of the Middle Ages, gave way in the Renaissance to an actual pursuit of novelty for its own sake.

During the Renaissance another form of discovery was also taking place—the voyages of discovery of Columbus, Diaz, da Gama, and the captains of Prince Henry the Navigator. In this way the known world was enlarged. Characteristically, other Renaissance men were rediscovering ancient geography through translations of ancient manuscripts.

The New Education was one of the innovations of the Renaissance. Impatient with the *Trivium* and *Quadrivium* of the Middle Ages, and eager to transmit the newly discovered heritage to others, the scholars of the time developed a new curriculum. The Englishmen, More and Ascham, and the Spaniard, Vives, were leading figures in espousing this brave new curriculum. Ironically, the curriculum that emerged resembled in many ways the liberal education of Latin and Greek, now so much decried by modern education. This curriculum had to be paid for dearly; it proved so popular that for centuries to come it effectively blocked the widespread teaching of sciences.[4]

The leading humanists, although well-read in the ancient classics, were not concerned with working toward new developments in philosophy. This does not mean that there were no philosophers. In fact, every school of ancient philosophy had its champions during the Renaissance.

Under the patronage of Cosimo de Medici, a Platonic Academy was founded in Florence in 1462. It was dominated by Marsilio Ficino (1433–1499), who along with others of this time, attacked the Aristotelianism of the Scholastics.[5] Regarding Plato equal in authority to divine law, Ficino set out to reconcile Platonic doctrine with Christian teaching.[6] In the battle of Plato versus Aristotle, it was Plato who triumphed. After all, Aristotle had been the philosopher of the schoolmen. Moreover, Plato's dialogues were in the process of being rediscovered, as Aristotle's works had been earlier, so that Plato's views seemed fresh and new while Aristotle's seemed musty and old-fashioned. Some students of the period have gone so far as to say that it was largely due to Plato's influence that the early humanists were not scientifically oriented.[7] Whatever the reason, many of the great men of the Renaissance were hostile to science. Petrarch, Erasmus, Rabelais, Ficino, and even Vives in one way or another had something disparaging to say about science.[8]

Neither the philosophy nor the science of that time owed anything to the Reformation, many of whose leaders detested "natural reason" and were hostile to science. Luther denounced reason as the mistress of the Devil; he taught that Aristotelian metaphysics, science, and ethics were false, and even that Aristotle's logic was inconsistent with theology.[9] On a convenient pretext, Calvin condoned the burning of Michael Servetus, the discoverer of the pulmonary circulation of the blood, because Servetus had described the Holy Land as a barren wilderness (which it was), thus contradicting the scriptural description of it as a land of "milk and honey."

No great philosophical psychologist emerged during this period, but there were some contributors of lesser rank. They are arranged here in the order of their birth. There were Pomponazzi (1462–1525), who interpreted Aristotle as agnostic concerning the immortality of the soul;[10] Niccolo Machiavelli (1469–1527), who forcefully presented his views that human beings were controlled more by passion than by reason;[11] and Juan Luis Vives (1492–1540), who espoused the education of women, the direct examination of our experience, and the use of psychology in education.[12] Philippus Paracelcus (1493–1541) identified the influence of unconscious motivation.[13] Jean Fernel (1497–1558) advanced a view of man as a work of nature.[14] Philip Melanchthon (1497–1560) introduced affectivity into the interpretation of consciousness, and made casual use of the term, "psychology."[15] Huarte of San

Juan (c. 1530–1592) pointed out the connection between psychology and physiology, and is known for his examination of differential capacities.[16] Michel de Montaigne (1533–1592) emphasized individual differences and the variability of human nature.[17] In 1590 Rudolf Goeckel (1547–1628) first made use of Melanchthon's term, psychology, in the title of a book.[18] Despite the lack of great psychologists, there seems to have been a noticeable broadening of the general field of psychology during the Renaissance. A certain amount of freedom from theological concern can also be observed. Psychological thinking about the soul and body was based on the division of the soul into vegetative, sensitive, and rational faculties intertwined with some version of Galenic humors.

It is hardly surprising that the most important scientific work during the Renaissance appeared relatively late in the period. The year 1543 saw the appearance of both of the scientific works heralding the modern period, the *De Fabrica corporis humani* of Andreas Vesalius (1514–1564)[19] and the *De revolutionibus Orbium Coelestium* of Nicolaus Copernicus (1473–1543).[20] Vesalius's work on anatomy had the tremendous advantage of being based on personal dissection and observation. He found that he had reason to disagree sharply with ancient authority, and specifically with Galen. What had been believed for centuries about details of gross anatomy just were not so. Copernicus reported that the Ptolemaic conception of an earth-centered universe did not agree with astronomical findings, and that the sun must be cast in the central role formerly ascribed to the earth. Even more importantly, Vesalius was giving a new emphasis to the use of direct observation for securing scientific data and Copernicus was giving the world a new cosmology. Although for generations afterward the characteristic medieval scientific doctrines continued to be taught in the schools, the ideas that Vesalius and Copernicus represented steadily gained wider and wider acceptance and extension.

The absence of a clearly understood scientific method placed a severe limitation on scientific work during the Renaissance.[21] It was the scientific movement of the seventeenth century, with its stress on methodology, that gave us the beginnings of the modern period in science.

The Beginnings of the Modern Period in Science

The modern period in science was coming into being at the turn of the seventeenth century. A distrust of the past and a desire for the new were prominent characteristics of the age. Whether they truly were or not, a remarkable number of works published in this century claimed either in title or in preface to be new.[22] Even as we do today, the thinkers of the seventeenth century prided themselves on their modernity, and, just as we are, were trapped in the past.

The scientists of the century did show a reluctance to accept rationalistic first principles, on the bases of which one was to deduce conclusions of what must happen. They were groping toward freedom from philosophical presuppositions. But there is no unanimity of opinion concerning their want of philosophical presuppositions. Burtt alleged that the Pythagorean-Platonic tradition can be seen as the foundation for and the justification of the beginning of modern science in these years.[23] Against this view, Strong has arrayed an impressive mass of evidence.[24] He takes the position that the choice of method by the scientists of this time took place prior to whatever metaphysics they might have used thereafter to justify their position. Philosophical precedents and distinctions were not fundamental to their work, but merely incidental and supportive. Strong argues that it was not knowledge of the Pythagorean-Platonic tradition that turned these scientific workers from classification to measurement. Theirs was the methodological problem of how to do the job at hand, not the metaphysical task of justifying it. They were pragmatic in that they developed working distinctions and definitions in order to handle the specific subjects with which they were concerned. A reluctance to accept first principles meant specifically that appeal to the authority of the ancients had lost its former almost paralyzing hold. It followed that if authority of the ancients was to be abandoned, a new procedure must replace it. This procedure was found in mathematics.

A variety of circumstances conspired to make mathematical operations characteristic of the science of the time. For one thing the appeal of the Aristotelian concept of nature as a hierarchy based on a qualitative prescription had lost its hold. The influence of Aristotle and his emphasis on classification was at its lowest point in centuries. This gave an opportunity for mathematics to regain its importance as a quantitative method. And there were other, more positive factors at work that strengthened the appeal of mathematics. The Greek mathematics of Alexandria had been rediscovered. The generality and complexity of mathematics had increased over the centuries and the useful tool of Arabic notation for mathematical expression had been introduced. A tremendous variety of practical problems in navigation and gunnery, for example, stimulated craftsmen and others to apply mathematics. The increased level of mathematical sophistication more than any other one factor, made possible the scientific advancement of the seventeenth century.

The mathematically oriented scientists of the sixteenth and seventeenth centuries followed the procedure of measuring the properties or motions of the bodies they studied.[25] These they generalized as the rules of operation in nature. The demonstration of physical relations in mathematical formulation was their contribution to physical science.

In the physical sciences but not in psychology, quantitativism as a prescription consequently was coming to the fore. From this time, it was not to be seriously challenged by qualitativism.

GALILEO, QUANTITATIVISM, AND METHODOLOGICAL AND CONTENTUAL OBJECTIVISM

Galileo Galilei (1564–1642) was perhaps the most important of these early modern scientists. In his *Dialogues Concerning the Two New Sciences,* which contain some of his most important studies, he used mathematics and concerned himself with the quantitative conditions of variations in quality.[26] He reasoned that if Copernicus and others found a pattern underlying the motion of the planets, perhaps he would discover a pattern of the phases of local motion here on earth. He proceeded to search for the regularities which would manifest this pattern—uniform motion, acceleration motion, violent motion, and related phenomena. The details need not concern us, but his approach is of direct relevance. The constants he assumed in his work were not absolute, but subject to correction by empirical means. If something were true, for instance, a certain specified result should occur. He proceeded to verify whether his conclusions did or did not hold true. This is a far cry from making these constants metaphysical imperatives.

Representative of the problems investigated during the period by Galileo and others are studies on the pitch, velocity, and transmission of sound; the origin of light and color and the wavelike properties of light; and the corpuscular theory of matter.

Those aspects of sound and light that were trustworthy, in the sense that they were open to investigation, come to be considered parts of physics, the aspects that were subjective in character were relegated to the study of the mind and philosophy. Cogent reasons to distrust the unaided senses had become apparent to thinkers, whether or not they were influenced by Neoplatonism. To those who accepted his findings, Copernicus' discovery that the earth moves showed that the senses were unreliable. Actually this phase of the emergence of the physical sciences was to help delay the appearance of a scientifically oriented psychology.

Then and later the reaction of many physical scientists to psychological phenomena was epitomized by Galileo's attempt to deal with the question of the separation of what we now call physics and psychology.

Galileo seized on Democritus' distinction between the perceptual world of sensory appearances and the conceptual real world as his focal point (p. 9). Galileo objected to considering qualities such as heat (in the subjective sense), as well as tastes, smells, and colors as having the same reality as shape and motion.[27] The former are names for qualities having their locus, not in the object, but in the responsive body. Remove the body, and these qualities would be annihilated. They are different from the primary and real. They do not exist as truly as phenomena with which a physical scientist deals. It can be seen that Galileo was in the process of excluding man's experience from the world of nature. Some fifty years later this separation would be called the distinction between primary and secondary qualities by Robert Boyle, one of the founders of chemistry and a contemporary of Locke. It goes a long way to explain the caution and suspicion with which psychology, as a science, is viewed to this day by physicists and others. Perceptions could not be trusted as sources of information about the world because they do not correspond to anything in that world. Somehow what a psychologist deals with in terms of experience is not as "real" as what the physical scientist works with. In the service of a prescription for a methodological objectivity for the physical sciences, Galileo was tacitly reinforcing the view that psychology was contentually subjective in nature.

FRANCIS BACON AND INDUCTIVISM

Another form of rebellion against philosophical presuppositions was expressed by a contemporary of Galileo, Francis Bacon (1561–1626) who in Novum Organum,[28] Advancement of Learning[29] and New Atlantis[30] sketched his views of what science should become. In Novum Organum and the Advancement of Learning[31] he proposes drastic changes in scientific procedures. His target was Aristotle, or rather the Aristotle of the Organon, Aristotle the logician. He did not see that Aristotle had insisted on the admissability of induction in research, although by no means to the exclusion of deductive logic. Bacon eagerly espoused an inductive method. He did not hold mathematics in particularly high regard as a scientific tool, and in failing to stress mathematics, he was out of tune with most of the great scientists of his time.[32] He did realize that mathematics was essentially deductive, but to him the appropriate method was primarily inductive, based upon the patient collection of instances.[33]

Bacon insisted on going beyond the simple enumeration of instances, a method that was well known long before this time. His goal was to bring into use a new and particular form of induction. He would have drawn up lists of facts with a given quality in common, lists of facts lacking the quality, as well as lists of those that possessed the quality in varying degrees. The particular character of a given quality he was sure could emerge from a study of such lists. His was a sweeping inductive method; he held that the collection of many facts would eventually lead to a generalization about them. His detestation of grandiloquent theories of the Middle Ages in which some broad rationally derived point would be declared truth with little factual support. His reaction against rationalism was so extreme and his dependence on empiricism so intense, that he did not believe that even tentative hypotheses must guide a scientist in the selection of facts to be gathered. He failed to realize, as we now do, that hypotheses are to be advanced and judgment suspended until the facts are gathered, and, then and only then, can we decide whether the hypotheses being tested are true, false, or unproved.

In his espousal of induction he was anticipating its success in fields where mathematics had as yet but little use. It was in biology that inductive procedure was to be most faithfully followed. But to use induction properly, one must have preliminary hypotheses as a guide in selecting instances, something that Darwin and the other great biologists recognized. In the long run, of course, both induction and deduction were found to be essential to the scientific enterprise.

Bacon enthusiastically but uncritically endorsed the use of experiments.[34] He argued that by prodding nature to take off her mask, as he put it, experiments make her reveal her struggles and help us to decide causes. We go from experiments to the isolation of causes, and conversely, from causes to the invention of new experiments.

Idols

In service of his method, Bacon advanced his famous account of the *Idols*, those preconceptions that blind men to truth.[35] There are four kinds: *Idols of the Tribe*, inherent, generally agreed-upon ways of thinking, such as our ways of perceiving; *Idols of the Den*, prejudices created by an individual's environment and education; *Idols of the Market Place*, deceptions arising from loose use of words; *Idols of the Theater*, blind acceptance of authority and tradition (all previous systems of philosophy seemed to him to create theatrical worlds, not deal with the real one).

Bacon also fostered another aim that became characteristic of the age—the seeking of useful knowledge, or as we have called it, the utilitarian prescription. Power over nature in the service of man is the most apt way to express the Baconian spirit of the age that was to come. It was so important to Bacon that he expressed it among the first aphorisms of *Novum Organum:* effects cannot be produced without knowledge of causes; with this knowledge, power and knowledge become one.[36] This view of power as the fruit of knowledge was shared to some slight degree with others of his time, including Descartes, who in his *Discourse on the Method for Rightly Conducting the Reason*[37] spoke of a practical philosophy that masters nature.[38]

Generally speaking, Bacon's forceful writings, his enthusiasm, and his position as one of the eminent figures of his time (he was Chancellor under James I) led to a wide audience for his writings and to increased knowledge of and respect for scientific methods. Especially important in this connection was his success in pleading the usefulness of science. Henceforward, science was to be judged both by the knowledge obtained and by the usefulness of that knowledge.

[margin note: Usefulness of Science]

BIOLOGY AND THE SCIENTIFIC REVOLUTION

The opening stages of the scientific revolution in biology lagged behind those of the physical sciences.[39] Contributions in biology in the sixteenth century were still hampered by insistence that the soul was the locus of origin of bodily action. The relative neglect of biology and psychology during these years was not entirely due to the lack of workers in these fields, but rather to the general scientific climate of the age, which was dominated by the physical sciences. Indeed, the emulation of physics by psychologists in the nineteenth century had its roots in the work of the seventeenth century.

Some noteworthy researches were carried out. As a natural extension of his interest in the primarily visual science of astronomy, Johannes Kepler (1571–1630) studied vision directly.[40] On examining the eye he found that an *inverted* image is cast upon the retina. This flatly contradicted the representative theory of vision of Democritus (p. 9), holding that objects give off images of themselves that impinge directly on the sense organs. How could this be the case if the image were inverted? Kepler was content to demonstrate the phenomenon and leave to others the reconciliation of his finding with a theory of perception.

Even more important was the demonstration of the circulation of the blood by William Harvey (1578–1657).[41] Before his time, there had been general acceptance of the thousand-year-old theory of Galen, calling for pulsation of the blood, which the body consumed as nutriment. According to this theory, the blood itself was not the substance we know, but included animistic and supernatural entities, "animal spirits." Harvey not only demonstrated conclusively that the blood moved, "as it were, in a circle,"[42] but that the heart functioned as a pump in the same manner as it did for water or other nonliving things. He also measured the amount of blood passing through the heart in one-half hour and found that it would exceed the weight of the body by more than three or four times; thus he very effectively demolished the consumption theory. However crudely, he measured a bodily function and thus brought a quantitative approach to physiology. He also weakened the belief in the occult qualities attributed to the blood. What made Harvey's work outstanding was his integration of scattered facts into a comprehensive generalization. His success in demonstrating, without appeal to either the soul or to any other vital force, that a bodily function could be explained solely by mechanical principles was a tremendous stimulus to later work along these lines.

At this time the biological sciences were still seen as part of medicine, and not as sciences in their own right. A. R. Hall, in his careful study of scientific development between 1500 and 1800, concluded that the biology of today as pursued in laboratories and in field stations, is essentially a creation of the nineteenth century.[43] Moreover, the closest of kin to modern psychology, the field of physiology, had to await further advances in the knowledge of anatomy before it could come into its own.

René Descartes

René Descartes was the first great psychologist of the modern age. This is not the same as saying that he was the first modern psychologist. Unlike some scientists of his day, he still made metaphysical assumptions, and consequently his psychology was subservient to his philosophy. Nevertheless, for the first time since Aristotle, a psychological system de novo was attempted.

He fondly believed himself to be independent of past authorities. Starting out to find truth from rock bottom was one of the ways he expressed the modern spirit. He prided himself on reading relatively little, for he wanted to turn away from the classics to "the great book of the world."[44] He seldom referred to the past either to acknowledge borrowing or to criticize. Of course, no more than anyone else could he entirely escape the past, and his thinking shows its influence much more than he was prepared to acknowledge.

A remarkable amount of scientific work had been done during the early years of the century, when Descartes was growing up and attending school. Exactly what scientific knowledge was available to Descartes in 1629, the year he began publishing? Over eighty years had elapsed since the works of Vesalius and Copernicus had appeared. William Gilbert (1540–1603) had published his experiments in electricity and magnetism twenty-nine years before. Francis Bacon had died three years earlier in 1626. His form of induction had enlarged the scope of knowledge, particularly through the control of nature that it gave. Tycho Brahe (1546–1601), whose observatory Descartes had already visited, had made his meticulous astronomical observations. Kepler, who had worked with Brahe, had advanced his three basic laws of planetary motion, and was to die a year later in 1630. In 1616, Galileo had been secretly condemned by the church for citing evidence supporting the heliocentric theory. If Descartes did not know of this condemnation, he had only to wait until 1633, when it was made public. Harvey, born before Descartes but destined to outlive him, had published the demonstration of the circulation of the blood that very year. Of all the great scientists of that time, only the greatest of them, Isaac Newton (1642–1727), was not contemporaneous with Descartes; his general theory of dynamics was to embrace Descartes' laws of motion in accounting for the motions of the whole universe, the planets, their satellites, and the comets.

DESCARTES' LIFE

Descartes was born in March 1596 at La Haye in Touraine.[45] The economic circumstances of his father and mother, both of whom came from professional families, allowed him an income sufficient to assure a modest financial independence throughout life. He never occupied ecclesiastical or academic office.

In the spring of 1606, he entered the college of La Flêche, founded a year or two before by the Jesuits. Because of his frailty, he was excused from morning religious duties and allowed to stay in bed. While abed he did his lessons and developed the habit of sustained reflection and analysis. He continued the habit of remaining in bed in the morning and working out his thinking for almost the rest of his life. The program of study he followed consisted of languages, mathematics, humane letters, physics, ethics, logic, and metaphysics. With one clear exception the subjects that he studied left him "embarrassed with so many doubts and errors that it seemed to me that the effort to instruct myself had no effect other than the increasing discovery of my own ignorance".[46] Mathematics was the only exception, "because of the certainty of its demonstration and the evidence of its reasoning."[47]

Little is known about his life during the six years following his departure in 1614 from La Flêche. It would seem he went to Paris, and after a brief period of sampling its pleasures found that they palled. As a result he went into studious seclusion. Then and later, the proximity of friends proved to be too much of a distraction. It was in pursuit of even more privacy that in 1618 he went to Holland.

He enlisted as a gentleman volunteer in the army of Prince Maurice of Nassau, but apparently did not see combat. In November of 1618 he met Isaac Beeckman, a mathematician and the rector of a small college. They became warm friends, and Beeckman's influence turned Descartes toward purely theoretical problems. The following year, 1619, Descartes was ostensibly engaged in military service; during that time he traveled to Denmark, Hungary, Austria, and possibly Bohemia.

His winter quarters in 1619–20 were in a small village near Ulm. There he spent his time in study and speculation. The next step of his intellectual journey was taken during this winter. It was at this time that an inspiration came to him. Somewhat of a mystical experience, it caused him to vow to travel in gratitude for divine inspiration to the shrine of the Blessed Virgin in Loretto. The gist of the inspiration was the conviction that mathematical methods could form the basis of all reasoning. He resolved to devote the rest of his life to the cultivation of reason through the method revealed to him.

In the spring of 1620 he again took to traveling for the study of *le grande livre du monde*. Between 1628 and 1649, Descartes lived in various places in Holland. Although he lived quietly, his thinking attracted considerable attention, but he tried to avoid personal contact. He was, however, a voluminous correspondent. He moved from town to town, requiring for his needs only proximity to a Catholic church and to a university.

Most of his important works were written and published in Holland, although much preparation preceded their composition. During his first years of residence in Holland, he wrote *Rules for the Direction of the Mind*.[48] By 1633 he had nearly completed his *Treatise on the World*, an account of the world and man. This work contained two heretical doctrines—a defense of the earth's rotation and an espousal of the infinity of the universe. However, he stopped work on the *Treatise*, and what he had finished of it was not published during his lifetime. Had the condemnation of Galileo intimidated him? Or did he simply want to continue his work in peace? Perhaps he had resolved to reconcile both science and religion, and had deferred publication until he could do more work. We simply do not know. His life-long religious orthodoxy may have been merely politic, but the evidence seems to indicate sincerity.

A portion of *The World,* called *L'Homme,* was posthumously published.[49] It has been called the first textbook on physiology. It is also useful for his views on physiological psychology. In 1637 he published his *Discourse on Method*[50] accompanied by three shorter pieces including *Dioptric,*[51] a study of optics, the first published statement of the law of refraction.

In order to secure criticism, he circulated in manuscript his *Meditations of the First Philosophy;*[52] in 1641, he published this book, including in it his answers to the criticisms of it that had been submitted to him. The *Discourse* and the *Meditations* both included accounts of his methodology of science based on his particular philosophical presuppositions.

An otherwise minor point in connection with the *Meditations* helps throw light on the shift in attitude toward theological and philosophical matters since the Middle Ages. Descartes was especially anxious to placate the church. He, accordingly, wished to dedicate the book to the dean and members of the faculty of Theology of the University of Paris. But in the second paragraph of this dedication, he remarks that he had always considered questions of God and of the soul to be matters of philosophical concern rather than theological argument.[53] This remark could not have been expected to endear the clergy; yet he surely would not have included a remark that would inevitably weaken his case. Nevertheless, he did have reason to feel anxious about the attitude of the church toward him, then and later. The age may have been somewhat more tolerant, but this is far from saying one could not get into trouble through philosophical and scientific teachings. In general, Cartesian teaching was to be criticized by both Protestants and Catholics as subversive and contrary to religious doctrine. As a consequence of living in a Protestant country, he learned that Protestant dogmatism could be as unyielding as Catholic had been to others. Intervention of powerful friends, however, prevented any serious consequences.

In 1649 he published the *Passions of the Soul.*[54] In accord with the times, psychological discussion early in the volume was followed by a development of the ethical significance of his psychological ideas. He held that the passions give rise to all good and evil of this life, and he wished to show how the mind might control the passions.

Queen Christina of Sweden had become interested in his views, and a correspondence developed that, when reworked, became part of his *Passions of the Soul.* In the fall of 1649, at the Queen's request, Descartes took up residence at the Royal Court. This change was to prove both incongenial and fateful. Descartes was used to spending his mornings in bed. His enthusiastic but not very competent pupil, however, set the hour for her instruction at five in the morning. It was an unusually cold winter in Stockholm that year. Before six months had passed, on February 11, 1650, he died of pneumonia.

THE RATIONALISTIC METHOD OF DESCARTES

Rationalism had been a tool since the beginning of intellectual history. It had been used (and abused) but without too much explicit attention to it as a method. This Descartes remedied through explicit attention. In his hands, the method turned out not only to be rationalistic but also deductive and to have as its ideal, treatment of all matter in the "spirit" of mathematics.

He first came upon the mathematical aspect of his methodology during that winter spent near Ulm. His discovery was to emerge as analytic geometry, the reciprocal application of algebra and geometry. He was not the first to do this,[55] but Descartes helped to unite and extend the relation between the two. He made it possible to express the properties of whole families of curves by means of simple algebraic equations. If these two apparently disparate fields of knowledge could be combined, he reasoned, could not all the fields of knowledge be so combined? The method of analytic geometry could then be applied to all knowledge and a unity of all science might be achieved. He believed that the methodological assumptions of the physical sciences formed a unity that he was making explicit and could defend with examples. In his adherence to the point of view that there was a basic unity to all the sciences, Descartes was fortified still further by a conviction that it is more efficient to study them all together, than to deal with them one at a time.[56]

As Descartes saw it, the particular value of the mathematical method was the possibility of starting with the simplest ideas and then proceeding to draw careful inferences from them. He contrasted this deductive method with a negative view of the syllogism. Descartes recognized that the syllogism did not directly adapt itself to learning what was new, but was more useful in restating and in clarifying what was already known.[57] The use of accumulated experience (empiricism) as a source of scientific knowledge, as he saw it, allows deduction but is otherwise methodologically weak. For if one depends up empiricism, one must necessarily start with highly complex objects. Inferences may be drawn, but they may be wrong. Mathematical deductions which start with self-evident truths cannot lead to error.

How does one use this deductive method? Descartes cites several possibilities. His *Rules for the Direction of the Mind* gives a way of applying it in terms of twenty-one rules.[58] In the *Discourse on Method,* he allows that there are four essential rules of procedure.[59] These four rules are: 1) never accept as true anything that is not known clearly to be such; 2) divide difficulties into as many parts as possible; 3) proceed from what is simplest and easiest to understand to what is more difficult; 4) make the connections so complete and the reviews so general as to insure that nothing is overlooked. His manner, here and elsewhere, was formally clear and simple and a far cry from scholastic technicalities. These rules are neither as self-evident nor as free from the possibility of error as Descartes thought, but to explore this further would take us too far afield.[60]

4 RULES

Descartes placed the problem of knowledge at the center of his inquiry. He held a rationalistic prescription of knowledge: by means of unaided reason one can know truth. At times he seems to say that men have, to an equal degree, the intelligence to distinguish the true from the false.[61] But he admits that individuals are born with different degrees of discernment.[62] He adds that this discernment can be made much more expert by practice, and he insists that all sciences should proceed from matters that are easy to understand.

Knowledge

Truth and falsity come from thinking alone.[63] This is his plea for rationalism: through thought, one can know truth. Experience is available but is fallible.[64] But his paradigm of geometry misled him into thinking that clarity and distinctness are a guarantee of truth. The history of science is littered with self-evident truths that have had to be abandoned. The geocentric hypothesis, for example, is a shining example (if one may be permitted a pun). Descartes failed to see, as Galileo saw, that principles should first be treated as hypotheses and that hypotheses, as such, are tentative, and can be tested on whether or not the consequences deduced from them agree with empirical observations. In short, he did not insist in his methodological account upon the experimental check required by Galileo and Bacon.

DESCARTES' SEARCH FOR CERTAINTY

In keeping with the temper of his age and with his own distrust of knowledge inherited from his predecessors, Descartes asked himself throughout his *Discourse on Method,* what he could be certain of without any possibility of doubt.[65] He was not a sceptic; he merely insisted that doubt is the proper place to start constructing a system that would answer the sceptic. He wanted to doubt in order to find out what he could be certain about.

I resolved to assume that everything that ever entered into my mind was no more true than the illusions of my dreams. But immediately afterwards I noticed that whilst I thus wished to think all things false, it was absolutely essential that the "I" who thought this should be somewhat, and remarking that this truth *I think, therefore I am* was so certain and so assured that all the most extravagant suppositions brought forward by the sceptics were incapable of shaking it, I came to the conclusion that I could receive it without scruple as the first principle of the Philosophy for which I was seeking.

And then, examining attentively that which I was, I saw that I could conceive that I had no body, and that there was no world nor place where I might be; but yet that I could not for all that conceive that I was not. On the contrary, I saw from the very fact that I thought of doubting the truth of other things, it very evidently and certainly followed that I was; on the other hand if I had only ceased from thinking, even if all the rest of what I had ever imagined had really existed, I should have no reason for thinking that I had existed. From that I knew that I was substance the whole essence or nature of which is to think, and that for its existence there is no need of any place, nor does it depend on any material thing; so that this "me," that is to say, the soul by which I am what I am, is entirely distinct from body, and is even more easy to know than is the latter; and even if body were not, the soul would not cease to be what it is.[66]

This quotation indicates that the central core of his solution is the certainty of his thinking and, therefore, of his existence. He found the last limits of doubt and the starting point of his system in the application of his first procedural principle, which was to accept nothing as true unless it were clearly evident.

In the *Meditations,* he used a somewhat different approach to the same problem.[67] He first asked what he formerly had considered himself to be. He answered that he had believed himself to be a man—with face, hands, arms, flesh, and bones; that he had been nourished; that he had been able to walk; and that he had been able to think and to feel.

He proceeded with his argument by asking one to suppose that there was a certain powerful "genius," or demon, who was intent on deceiving him. Under these circumstances, could he, Descartes, affirm as certain these things that he had just described about the body? After thinking this over carefully, he realized that none of what he said of the body pertained to his awareness of "me." Moreover, if he had no body about which he could be certain, he could not be certain about walking or taking nourishment or perceiving. But what of thinking? Here is something, he said, about which I can be certain.

I am not more than a thing which thinks, that is to say a mind or soul, or an understanding, or a reason, which are terms whose significance was formerly unknown to me. I am, however, a real thing and really exist; but what thing? I have answered: a thing which thinks.[68]

For both approaches the starting point of the system of Descartes is the certainty we have of our own existence. Doubt itself is a kind of thought. I doubt, but in so doing I also think. I know I exist because I perceive the fact distinctly. This doubting self is conscious. Descartes is not separating self and thought as in subject and verb; rather, he is affirming the existence of a thinking self as a unity, something whose "essence" consists in thinking. Thinking is not meant here in the abstract; it is a person he is talking about. One is reminded of Augustine's somewhat similar expression (p. 100). But Augustine advanced the idea only incidentally, while Descartes used it to deduce the principles fundamental to his overall position.

His doubt was only provisional. He retrieved the world, which his doubt had denied him, by first proving to his satisfaction the existence of God, starting from his axiomatic self-certainty. Going beyond the primary axiom that man is a being whose nature it is to think, he proceeds to examine another clear idea, that of perfection, which leads him to the concept of the perfect being and the consequent proof that God exists. Although this proof of God's existence is complicated, the major points of his argument are clear.[69] 1) everything has a cause, including our ideas; 2) we have the idea of God; 3) to cause us to have an adequate idea of God nothing less than God is necessary; therefore, 4) God does exist. God is the most perfect of beings and would not deceive us. We may therefore examine natural reality confidently.[70]

While not denying its existence, he held that the concept of final cause should not be utilized in science.[71] This, too, was a conclusion reached by appeal to his principle of clarity. We can form no clear idea of the end to which God made the world, so we have no right to attribute to him some special reason for creating it. In science, final cause—explaining things by attempting to ascertain God's purpose—is worse than useless. It is apparent from Descartes' discussion that inadmissibility of final cause extends beyond the physical to include biological and physiological events. Organs may perform their function admirably but this does not entitle one to draw the conclusion that they were created to serve this purpose.

Comparing himself to Archimedes who said that, given a fixed point in space, he could lift the earth, Descartes claimed that he had found the bedrock upon which to construct a whole system of science.[72] He built his system upon what he considered to be essential philosophical certainties. But despite the originality of his demand for basic philosophical assumptions, he resembles his philosophical predecessors, rather than the great modern scientists who were his contemporaries. Now that his method has been explained, we can turn to the way he applied it to a crucial psychological question—the relation of mind and body.

MIND AND BODY AND DUALISM

His major argument for the separation of mind and body was related to the subjective certainty of the self that he had found after his sceptical journey. But Descartes also asserted that we know mind and body are separate because if something is taken away from the body, say a foot, nothing is considered to have been lost to the mind.[73] Since we clearly perceive mind as different from body and vice versa, there is a real distinction between them; and they can exist apart from one another.[74] Fundamentally, created reality is composed of two materially exclusive natures—extension and thought; it therefore follows that they are subject to different laws. Mind is free: matter is subject to natural law. Moreover, this dualism implies two parallel worlds either one of which may be studied without reference to the other.

The rational soul and the mind are synonymous. Mind is the soul insofar as it thinks.[75] In order to avoid ambiguity, Descartes considered mind the preferred term, instead of soul. His choice will be followed hereafter, not only in this chapter but in all of those that follow. It was Descartes whose voice was most effective in separating philosophy and theology (p. 149). His thinking on these matters more than that of any other person gave us the philosophical tradition of mind that subsequent thinkers have had to come to terms with, either in agreement or dissent. His views encouraged naturalistic interpretations of mind more than supernaturalistic interpretations. Therefore, mind, not soul, will signify the central content of psychological considerations in succeeding chapters.

MIND

Descartes made several succinct statements on the nature of mind that may help us to grasp more clearly what he meant. Mind, he said, is a thing that thinks; it is identical with the thinking thing:[76] this thing is unextended substance;[77] this nonbodily substance has the characteristic of thought;[78] the power by which we know things is purely spiritual;[79] the purely spiritual is called mind.[80] The mind is outside of the physical order of matter and is in no way derived from it.[81] Such, then, is the Cartesian nature of mind.

There still remains one major argument for dualism.[82] *WATSON himself*

What was merely a methodological distinction for Galileo, became for Descartes an argument for a dualism of two worlds. In support of the immateriality of the mind, he happily enlisted the distinction between primary and secondary qualities and phrased it that odors, smells, and tastes became mere sensation, "existing in . . . [one's] thought."[83] Bodies exist only in the shape and motion. He goes so far as to say that sensations represent nothing outside of our minds.[84] They are not in the objects, but in our minds. Instead of sensible qualities residing in bodies, actually it is quite possible that sensible qualities and the objects are not at all similar.[85] In approaching fire and first feeling heat, then moving still closer and feeling pain, far from compelling one to believe that "heat" and "pain" are somehow in the fire itself, on the contrary, suggests that they are not. The upshot, then, was that secondary qualities were relegated to the mind of the perceived while primary qualities were the properties of nature and the features of the world requiring mechanical explanation and, to be, by definition, the only essential properties, of the scientific concern.

A rigid separation of body and mind, contrasted and separated entities, was insisted on by Descartes. All reality of the human being, Descartes was saying, is either spatial (body) or conscious (mind). The relationship is disjunctive; what is spatial is not conscious, what is conscious is not spatial. It follows that mind or body each can be studied without reference to the other. The physical world, including body and its mathematically measurable relationships, is in one realm, the mind with its thoughts, sensations and free will is in another. The body's behavior is determined by mechanistic laws, but in the mind there is purpose and freedom of will, making a person's actions subject to praise and blame. As distinguished from body, man's mind then cannot be reduced to an aspect of a mechanical system because man's mind transcends the material world and the efficient causality which governs therein.

Descartes' dualism had important implications for the sciences in general and for psychology in particular. Matter, including body, was to be treated mathematically and explained mechanically. The two substance view, mind and matter, simplified physical science by means of what it excluded, while at the same time, it introduced a major problem for psychology. From the present perspective the effect of dualism was more pernicious than helpful. The dualistic view of psychology, so firmly established by Descartes, was to dominate even into the twentieth century.

MIND AND ITS FACULTIES

While it is clear that Descartes regarded the mind primarily as structural, "a thing", as he put it, he also had a subsidiary functional view of the matter. Thus, the mind is a unity, but it does have functions, powers, or faculties.[86] The faculties are not parts of the mind since it is one and the same mind that employs itself in these faculties. He usually speaks of thought as embracing the functioning of mind. He uses the term broadly, considering it to include all kinds of mental experience: doubting, denying, willing, imagining, and feeling.[87] In fact, as he uses the term, thought includes all that we are conscious of.[88] He usually discusses the mind in relation to thought or understanding, imagination, memory, and sense, and does not relate it to the will. Only in relating mind to will does he vary from this position.

Powers of the Mind
1) will
2) understanding

What amounts to another classification of the modes of thought is the dual classification into will on the one hand, and understanding with all of its ramifications on the other.[89] Volition is one of the two basic powers of the mind; the other is understanding. To Descartes, one of the certain ideas we have is of freedom of will.[90] Will is related to understanding as a means of accounting for error.[91] The will is unlimited and has freedom of choice; understanding, on the other hand, is limited. This dominance of will is demonstrated by the fact that we do not always connect the same action with the same thought. Willing has intervened, causing movement in the way required by the act of will. The will then directs the action. Will gives assent or dissent to what has come into our understanding. This is a free choice.[92] One errs, not in failing to understand properly, but in willing, which is wider in compass and range than understanding. One may not will properly and may therefore fall into error. For example, if the principle of clarity is disregarded and will is allowed to precipitate a decision, error can occur. In a way this makes understanding subordinate to will. But in the same context, Descartes speaks of choices made by necessity, thereby obscuring the issue somewhat.

In view of the relation of the self to will, it is plausible to consider at this point Descartes' conception of self. As was established to Descartes' satisfaction by considerations already discussed, the self is known directly; he could conceive of not having a body but could not conceive of not having a mind aware of itself. That the self participates in willing (as well as in discriminating and judging) is shown in the experience of having made a choice. Self is known through consciousness.

Thought gives rise to ideas, which are of two sorts: those that might be called derived and those that are innate. Derived ideas are occasioned by external stimuli. More important than these, however, are the innate ideas. They are a special class of ideas; they are the ideas that give form to universal truths.[93] Unlike ideas arising from sensations, they are not preceded by organic impressions. Ideas are innate because they are developments of consciousness alone, and not transmitted by objects in the eternal world. It is not surprising that for Descartes, the idea of the self, the idea of God, and the axioms of geometry are among the most important innate ideas. Perfection, substance, quality, infinity, and unity are also innate to the mind and are not derived from sensory experience. To be sure, sensory experiences may remind us of these ideas, but they are not due to the sense perceptions. These ideas are innate in the sense that they are potentially capable of being developed into a form of

innate ideas

conscious experience. They exist potentially and become actual in the presence of experience. Descartes had little occasion to consider memory or association as mental processes since for him the doctrine of innate ideas included them as well.

Understanding to him is the basic instrument of thought; imagination, memory, and sense are aids to understanding.[94] Understanding alone is capable of perceiving truth, but others may help when used correctly. Understanding derives directly from mental activity, uninfluenced by the body. Although imagination, memory, and sense are also purely mental in themselves, they are influenced by bodily activities and are therefore a product of the interaction of body and mind. In the section that follows, their mental nature will be considered, but discussion of the body will be deferred until the interaction of body and mind is examined.

We are exposed to error in direct experience, not through failure of the understanding, but in a fashion similar to that occurring in the case of will. We fail to take into account that sense, imagination, and memory may err. Descartes' search for certainty is the setting in which he handles the problem of errors caused by the senses (p. 151). It will be remembered that Descartes had concluded that God would not deceive us about the reality of the world of matter. In a sense Descartes proved too much; after all, errors and illusions do exist. How are we to account for them? Here he falls back on his procedural rule of clarity. We can be sure of what we apprehend clearly. Error comes when we neglect this precaution. Sensory experiences are not among the clearly thinkable ideas and are therefore among those prone to error. The same is true of imagination and memory. If we forget that these three ways of gaining knowledge may err, our conclusions may be wrong because of our failure to take their tendency to error into account. Otherwise, our understanding would have served us correctly.

Sensing, as distinguished from understanding, is the perception of qualities—colors, sounds, odors, and the like.[95] These sense experiences are less than real as we have seen earlier (p. 155), but are convenient signs that allow us to get about in the world. Thus the sound of horses' hooves warns us of the approaching object, and we can step out of the way; but it has told us nothing about the true reality of matter. The image we have of the horse does not copy the natural object, as men before Descartes believed; rather, our image signifies or stands for the object. This was a considerable step forward from the naïve representative theory of perception that calls our experience nothing more than a copy of a picture of the object.

What Descartes says about the specific senses needs only brief summary. There were seven senses to Descartes: the usual five, the internal sense by which we localize sensory happenings within the body, and the passions. Further discussion will be foregone until the consideration of body and the interaction of mind and body.

MOLAR MECHANISTIC THEORY

The molecular level of mechanistic theory, traceable historically to the atomic theory of Democritus, had been reintroduced into the thinking of the seventeenth century by Pierre Gassendi (1592–1655) a priest, mathematician, and scientist who made it acceptable to religious belief by arguing essentially that all phenomena may be reduced to atoms— except the immortal soul.[96]

Although Descartes made some use of a variant of this molecular point of view, the so-called corpuscular theory, the primary thrust of his thinking was at the molar level of mechanistic theory; his was the pioneer modern formulation of it, conceptualizing the body of man as the unit of study.

The body of man, as distinguished from his mind, is composed of matter and has the common characteristics of all matter. The body is extended in space and is capable of movement.[97] Fundamentally, Descartes' mechanistic principle states that all natural phenomena can be reduced eventually to local motion. Action by physical contact is a special instance. Hence, the behavior of the bodies of men is determined by mechanistic laws, that is, the law of the movement of bodies in space, and is to be studied in light of this.

From the point of view of movement, the human body is a machine with more parts, to be sure, but not more alive, than any man-made *automata,* meaning a machine that moves itself.[98] An *automata* with the outward form of a monkey and with organs resembling those of a monkey would be indistinguishable from a real monkey.[99] If a similar machine were made in the likeness of man, however, we could detect that it was a machine, because the machine would not speak appropriately to the particular situation (even though a machine could be made to say words); moreover, we would soon discover "it" did not act from knowledge. These two criteria are also those by which we distinguish man from beast. Since even the deaf and dumb are able to invent signs, and since very little reason is required in order to learn to talk, brutes have no reason at all.[100] Moreover, the same example demonstrates that man is more than body.

Descartes was especially intrigued by the flow of water in fountains, which he compared to the flow of vital spirits.[101] Some of the statues in the royal gardens of his time were so arranged as to perform certain activities when someone stepped on their hidden pedals. Once set into motion, a sea monster would squirt water, or Neptune would appear to threaten the passerby with his trident. Tunnel rides in amusement parks and some of the props used at Disneyland are appropriate modern illustrations. In a description of the body of man as a machine, Descartes writes of the actions of clocks, mills, and similar machines as duplicating the body's behavior.[102] He then asks the reader to compare these forms of motion with the functions of the body, such as digestion, heart action, respiration, sleeping, sensory experiencing, common sense, imagination, retention in memory by imprinting, the appetites, and the internal movements of the members. He concludes that these functions, which are forms of motion, follow naturally from the arrangement of the component parts, and that all that is necessary to set them in motion in the body is the heat of the vital spirits, which itself is in no way different from that of other fires. The body performs functions arising from the presence of vital heat and is thus similar to animals in the functions it exhibits.[103]

He holds that most muscular action does not depend on the mind at all.[104] Heartbeat, digestion, respiration, even walking and singing are performed without the mind attending them. A falling man who thrusts out his hands to break his fall, does so merely because the sight penetrating the brain drives the animal spirits into the nerves in such a way that the motion is carried out. Mind is not involved. Descartes also uses as an illustration our inability to control the enlarging of the pupil by thinking; nature does not make this connection but instead connects its movement with looking at far or near objects.[105]

We have here something approaching a statement of what we would later call reflex behavior. Motion follows predictably from the stimulation of nerves. There appear to be fixed channels for the behavior repertory. This is a conception akin to reflex behavior. Descartes is sometimes given too much credit in the area of reflex theory. True, he uses the words undulatio reflexa in describing the absence of voluntary action, but he was referring to the analogy between mechanical and physiological action expressed in the resemblance of the reflection of light and the reflux of water to what he thought happened in the flow of vital spirits.[106] This involves a "rebound" of particles. Moreover, when writing in this fashion, he generally refers to activities that have a considerable degree of coordination and integration; for example, all animal behavior and in man, walking and talking.[107] On both counts modern neurology would disagree.

Before considering how Descartes handles the problem of the interaction of mind and body, it is worthwhile to pause and consider both the state of the knowledge of physiology in his day and some of his own research in what was to become physiological psychology. It will be remembered that Descartes came after Vesalius and was familiar with the contemporary work of Harvey. Descartes himself demonstrated through using the excised eye of a bull that an inverted image is actually formed by the lens in the retina at the back of the eye.[108] He also found that sensations of hearing vary in harshness or softness according to the force with which the ear is struck and the harmony or discord of sound depends upon agitations or vibrations of the air. He studied the functioning of muscles and knew that they worked in opposing pairs. He knew something about the anatomy of the brain and argued that, since the construction of the brain differs from man to man, we have individual differences among men in mental activities.[109] Nerves were known, but the nature of the neural impulse was not. His physiological equivalent for the neural impulse was still the vital spirits. Vital spirits were a kind of rarefied blood or subtle wind,[110] and the nervous system had a series of valves—like those affixed to water pipes—that allowed their passage. The motor force of the nerves was thought to reside in the brain.[111] Despite his limited knowledge, however, Descartes did give us the first systematic attempt at a physiological psychology since Theophrastus.[112]

DUALISTIC INTERACTION OF BODY AND MIND

To Descartes, man was a mind united with a body,[113] the two interacting with each other. His position, therefore, came to be called *interactionism;* this term distinguishes it from another form of dualism, referred to as parallelism, which will be discussed later. Mind and body interact, and each affects the other. The interaction of mind and brain is merely a more specific instance of the overall interaction. The mind sometimes acts independently of the brain (as illustrated by innate ideas), sometimes in interaction with it.[114] Thought, originating in the mind, may have consequences, such as movement. These movements are not thoughts, but activities of the body.[115] In other instances the mind is present in what today might be called a sensory-motor process. In this instance, mind affects the machinery at the critical point of transmission from sensory to motor channels.[116] In both kinds of mental activity—thought as such affecting the body, and sensorially derived functioning of the mind in turn affecting the body—mind directs the vital spirits that pass from the heart through the brain to the muscles.[117]

Although each movement seems to be joined by nature to a particular thought, it may be directed "by habit." He illustrates this by the fact that sounds are understood as words.[118] Those movements and thoughts naturally joined can also be separated. This separation comes about from custom. Custom does not require long usage for the separation to be effected and may even be acquired by a solitary action as when we are unable to eat any food that has once made us ill. The same separation by custom may be noticed in brutes since a setter may be trained to stand still on hearing a gun, instead of fleeing, which he does naturally.

A bodily locus for interactions of mind and body was thought by Descartes to be necessary. He found it deep within the recesses of the brain,[119] the point of contact being the pineal gland, actually a vestigial organ of no functional significance. As the mind is unitary, a unitary structure was needed. The pineal gland was chosen by Descartes in part because it was the only organ in the brain that was single, that is to say, not divided into a right and a left half. Moreover, it was adapted for ready accessibility to all parts of the body because of its strategic location.

Movement of the vital spirits in the nerves produces an impression on the pineal gland as a seal might on wax, and from this impression the mind produces a sensation. In effect, a quantity of motion becomes a mental quality. The reverse also occurs; the mind makes an impression on the pineal gland, though in a way never made clear. At any rate, the mind affects the flow of animal spirits by changing their course in the direction of this or that muscle. To Descartes, there was still a complete dualism; the pineal gland was merely the point of contact.

The soul is united with the body, which it uses as an instrument.[120] The pineal gland is not the container or seat of the mind or soul; it is associated with the body, and the soul is not confined within the pineal gland at all. In order to have sensations and appetites the mind must be united with the body.[121] It is not merely lodged as would be a pilot in a vessel, but united with it, in fact, intermingled with it, as a consequence of which pain, hunger, and the like are felt.[122] If there were only lodgement one would not feel pain, but merely perceive something external, as when a sailor knows that his ship is damaged but does not himself feel pain.

Important for understanding the interaction of body and mind, as Descartes conceived it, were what he called "the passions."[123] The term is used by Descartes much more broadly than it might be imagined from its connotation today. Those motions from the vital spirits of the body that have effects on the perceptions, feelings, and emotions of the mind, he speaks of as the passions.[124] From the perspective of the mind, they are experiences taking place in the mind. This is their mental aspect. On the other hand, the affective aspects, feelings, or actions are in the body.[125] Although sometimes the movements of the passions are accompanied by thoughts they need not be because they can arise in spite of one's intentions.[126] This is additional evidence that they are of the body.

These psychological experiences require activity of the brain prior to that of the mind. The psychological phenomena that depend, not upon the *activity* of the mind initiated by the mind, but rather upon its *passivity,* upon its being affected from outside, are the passions. The passions include not only feelings and emotions, but perceptual effects as well. It is true that Descartes also used a narrower definition of passions when he called them feelings or emotions that are brought about by the spirits. That definition would bring passions closer to the present-day meaning of affective states.[127] In general, however, feeling and emotion are to Descartes distinguished from the other passions because they arise from considerable agitation of the animal spirits but do *not* refer to objects outside the body.[128] The movements of the spirits nearly always create an "agitation" that remains in our thoughts until it dies down.[129]

Since the passions are received from outside the mind and are not willed to appear, this differentiates them from the will. The function of a passion is to excite the will to action, although the passions should remain under the will's control.[130] The conflict is not between lower and higher levels of the soul, as it was with Plato, but between two sets of tendencies, one arising from the will, and the other from the action of the vital spirits on the passions.[131] In other words, the passions arise from the mind's opposition to bodily impulses. Without a body related to a mind, there would be no passions. It is the effect of body on mind that produces passions.

A comparison of emotion in man and animal is enlightening. Because he is an *automata,* a sheep fleeing from a wolf is not afraid, but he behaves in a way that we interpret as terror. This is because we are afraid when our bodies are in the same condition. In the same situation, our bodies would go through the same mechanical actions, but because we have minds, those motions would cause us to feel passion as well.

Descartes discussed six primary passions.[132] These are wonder, love, hatred, desire, joy, and sadness; all other passions, and there are many, are derivatives or combinations of these. From wonder, an intellectual passion, are derived esteem, contempt, generosity, pride, humility, veneration, and disdain. All the other primary passions are forms of desire in a broad sense, since they incite to action. Passions of desire (in the narrower sense) arouse hope, fear, jealousy, confidence, courage, and cowardice. Joy and sadness lead him to advance the theory of pleasure and pain, for the latter are predecessors of these passions and serve to produce them—joy is agreeableness and sadness disagreeableness. Joy and sadness are also related to secondary passions, specifically derision, envy, anger, shame, regret, and joyfulness.

The work of Descartes was a catalyst for many later trends in psychology. A summarization of his psychological views should be placed within a setting of the later developments that they influenced. Especially important are the reactions to his dualism of body and mind and to his emphasis on the cognitive aspect of the human mind. There were also reactions against his inclusion of the body of man in the mechanistic world and against his corresponding exclusion of the mind of man. Despite their deep-seated difference, advocates of both the phenomenological and the mechanistic approaches owe much to Descartes. This will become clear after we examine the Cartesian reaction to dualism and the contributions of Benedict Spinoza and Gottfried W. Leibniz, who are important in their own right as well as for their reactions to Descartes.

The Cartesian Reaction to Dualism

Descartes' formulation of a basic dualism—that there is a real world from which an equally real thinking self is separate and exempt—was influential for centuries to come, even though later formulations that were proposed to handle this dualism often differed greatly from Descartes' original view. His dualism of body and mind, with the former subject to mechanical laws and the latter exercising free will, was to become the commonsense viewpoint of many millions of persons who have never heard his name.

One of the first problems arising from his dualism that Descartes' immediate successors and followers, the so-called Cartesians, became concerned with was his treatment of interaction. Descartes had formulated what he considered to be a complete dualism—a total separation of mind and body. His followers were anxious to support this basic point, but his formulation made certain difficulties apparent. He had defined his two substances—body and mind—in a fashion which would make in-

His definitions precluded interaction
└ Yet he claimed it .

teraction impossible; nevertheless, he held that there was interaction. He had asserted that a quantity of motion became a mental quality but had not explained how this could happen. How could two substances, body and mind, by definition utterly different, the one extended and the other unextended, actually interact? The pineal gland is, after all, a bodily organ in space; how could it interact with an immaterial mind? The last was a problem never completely solved by Descartes, even to his own satisfaction.

Some of the Cartesians who stressed the spiritual element in his teaching—Arnold Geulincx[133] (1625–1669) and Nicolas de Malebranche (1638–1715),[134] for example—solved the problem by denying that there could be contact. They held that all causal action originated with God, who was neither body nor mind but embraced both in his infinite being. With interaction denied, the problem now shifted to explaining the appearance of interaction when actually none existed. Why, for example, if I "will" (a mental act) my arm to move, does it appear to me that the arm does so (a physical act)? This was the problem they faced. Both explained the appearance of interaction by arguing that instead of event A causing event B, what actually happens is that A furnishes the occasion for God to produce B. They differed on how God acts in these circumstances: according to Geulincx, He acts upon the body, which then acts upon the mind; according to Malebranche, God acts directly upon the mind without the intervention of body. As an *occasionalism* analogy to the seeming interaction, Geulincx advanced the theory of the "two clocks." In effect, he said, "Imagine there are two clocks that keep perfect time and that while you look at one you hear the other strike." You would think that the first caused the second to strike. This, he continued, is what happens with the mind and the body. They are so perfectly attuned that events in one realm keep time with the other. On occasion, such as in willing movements, the will seems to cause the movements; however, it is purely physical laws that cause movement and the will does not really act on the body. While denying *reality* to interaction he was accounting for the *appearance* of interaction. This view came to be called "occasionalism" because either a mental or a physical event became the occasion for Divine intervention: it was a form of dualistic parallelism, so-called because, while admitting the two realms of the mental and the physical, it denied that they interacted, and insisted that they functioned in parallel.

Other attempts at solving the Cartesian mind-body problem were made by Benedict Spinoza and Gottfried Leibniz. Although profoundly influenced by Descartes, both are too important and too original to be referred to as Cartesians.

Benedict Spinoza and Monism, Rationalism, Deductivism, and Determinism

Benedict Baruch Spinoza (1632–1677) lived out his life as a lens grinder in Amsterdam.[135] He was relatively obscure and uninfluential during his lifetime. The *Ethics,* his most important work,[136] was published posthumously. The title of this work reflects his central aim: he wished to establish a way of life that was ethically correct and satisfying. In this context, psychology was a necessary step toward ethics.

Methodologically, Spinoza was both rationalistic and deductive. Sharing Descartes' enthusiasm for a geometric ideal, Spinoza began with self-evident axioms from which he proposed to deduce the nature of reality. He presented his views in geometrical form, that is, each new point was derived from preceding points. His conception of science admirably reflects his rationalistic method. The order of natural objects and the order of knowledge of them are coextensive; *"the order and connection of ideas is the same as the order and connection of things."*[137]

Spinoza's views are firmly rooted in his conception of God.[138] God is infinite and is the only substance. Thought and extension are but attributes of God. To think of "things," i.e., the objects of the world as we know them, is incorrect; instead of things, there are modes of substance, and whatever is, is a modification of the one substance that is God. A body is an abstraction, a finite way of regarding the infinite substance that is God. The human mind is no more than an aspect of the mind of God.[139]

Man is a unitary individual and has the modes or forms of attributes of body (extension) and mind (thought).[140] To Spinoza, mind and body are not separate, as they are to Descartes. They are one; they are two aspects of the same reality. Neither body nor mind is autonomous; man has modes of the attributes of both extension and thought. This is a form of parallelism—monistic parallelism. Every bodily event coexists with and is coordinate to a mental event. Body and mind correlate, but they do not cause one another any more than the convex side of a glass causes the concave. Apparent interaction arises from ignorance on our part and shows only the coincidence of actions; it is a matter of appearance, not a reflection of reality.[141] Spinoza clearly states that it follows from this that the body cannot determine the mind to think nor can the mind determine the body to motion or rest.

Unlike Descartes, Spinoza thought of the mind as an automaton, a term he explicitly applied to it.[142] Mind and body both were to be studied deterministically. Spinoza was perhaps the first modern thinker to view the world, including man, from a strictly deterministic standpoint. Both mind and body are of equal status, and both are subject to natural law.[143] Spinoza saw clearly that his deterministic view of man required that there be laws of nature which are applicable to man. He mentions, for example, remembering by similarity and by contiguity as examples of the laws which we should seek.[144]

Time and again he tells us that the will is not free.[145] The mind has no free will; it is determined by a cause that in turn is determined by another cause, and so on.

Although something of a digression, it may be of interest to consider the apparent dilemma that Spinoza seems to have brought upon himself. How can man be ethically influenced—and ethics is after all, his main theme—if there is strict determinism? Throughout his works the answer is offered that man's nature may be improved by improving his understanding and by encouraging him to follow ethical principles that may be learned. The behavior of ignorant man is determined from without while the wise man can act in line with greater knowledge of nature. Acting in the light of necessity is man's highest freedom,[146] and freedom is one with necessity.

In contrast to Descartes' view of the mind as primarily cognitive, Spinoza emphasizes the conative or drive aspect of mental life. Central to Spinoza's psychology is his concept of *conatus*, something similar to what we would call an impulse toward self-preservation.[147] The striving for self-preservation is desire when it is conscious of itself; it is appetite when it is not.[148] In another place he speaks of man being led more by "blind desire" than by "reason."[149]

When unconscious desire is coupled with his emphasis on conation in general and his acceptance of determinism, it is hardly surprising that he should be seen as anticipating Freud.[150] But although this may be of some incidental interest, it must be pointed out that Spinoza's thinking was arrived at from a perspective vastly different from that of Freud; and although he was familiar with the works of Spinoza,[151] Freud shows no evidence of a direct influence.

According to D. Bidney, Spinoza was the first modern to present psychology as the science of the laws of the mind.[152] While a science of psychology would not have been an entirely alien conception to Spinoza, it is also possible to argue that his interest in psychology was too peripheral, and his influence on later developments in psychology of too little moment, for this claim to be given much credence.

Gottfried W. Leibniz and Molecularism, Monism, Conscious and Unconscious Mentalism

Gottfried Wilhelm Leibniz (1646–1716), one of the inventors of the calculus, was also a philosopher, scientist, historian, diplomat, logician, and lawyer, and after his death, a leading intellectual force in Europe.[153] Among his many concerns, he investigated the issue of body-mind relationships.

Leibniz's unique contribution to our understanding of the nature of the mind is to be found in the theory of the "monad," his term for the individual units of all substances, indicating that he was guided by a molecular prescription. He held that the world consists of an infinite number of monads.[154] As a unit, each monad is unextended. Extension is rejected by Leibniz as an attribute of substance, and this leaves the monads—all monads—with mind as their essential attribute. Each monad is a psychic entity. In denying substance, he denied the reality of matter also, and in its place substituted an infinity of monads. Although mental, each of the monads has some of the properties of a physical point, and when collected into an aggregate, they create an appearance of extension.[155] The tree and the stones of everyday life, although appearing to the senses as objects, are actually aggregates of monads, and in themselves are not phenomenal. Thus, Leibniz satisfied the need for an explanation of at least the appearance of extension in the world.

Each monad acts independently, but is created by God to act in pre–established harmony with other monads.[156] The monads may appear to interact, but they do not. This takes the place of the untenable position that they influence one another.[157] There is no causality between monads. There is no causal relation between monads, not even between those of the mind and those of the body. For our present discussion this is most important. Noninteraction of body and mind is but a special case of the parallelism of monads. Mind and body follow their own laws but show perfect agreement, and give the impression of interaction. But actually there is a parallelism. The situation is similar to the interplay of the instruments of a symphony orchestra, in which each player follows the score and yet gives the impression of one instrument responding to another. In a similar manner God composed the score, which is then played out according to pre–established harmony.

Stripped of the trappings of the monads, Leibniz's conception of parallelism was a forerunner of the doctrine of psychophysical parallelism that was to be so important to Wundt and others (p. 276). All units of the world are endowed with life and motion and so are somewhat akin to consciousness. Even lifeless matter is only relatively unconscious; it has the least possible degree of consciousness.[158] Living organisms are composed of monads with varying degrees of consciousness.

Mental events, that is to say, the activity of monads, have degrees of clarity ranging from the totally unclear to the most definitely conscious or clearly grasped.[159] To Leibniz, this was more a matter of focal and peripheral attention than of consciousness as we would use the term.[160] Nevertheless, in view of the closeness of meaning, it was later seen as a conception of the continuum of consciousness-unconsciousness. At one extreme there are mental events of which we are totally unconscious, while at the other extreme are those that are clearly grasped or to use the technical term, apperceived.

The degree of consciousness is a relative matter.[161] The supposedly unconscious has the possibility of becoming conscious. There are lower degrees of consciousness—*petites perceptions,* to use Leibniz's term. These, when actualized, are apperceived. Hearing the roar of the surf is apperception, because it is the sum of all the drops of water we would not be conscious of if they were heard only one by one. The sound of a single drop is unconscious perception; sum up many drops at once and there is apperception.

The Phenomenological Approach

As a consequence of the emphasis upon the cognitive part of the human mind by Descartes and those who followed him, two points of view—the phenomenological and the mechanistic—were to emerge. Descartes' *Meditations,* Edmund Husserl (1859–1938) asserted centuries later, is the prototype of reflection in which the philosopher turns within himself as the source of immediate experience.[162]

The introduction of "immediate experience" as a way of characterizing the rationalistic approach of Descartes may cause some ambiguity which should be eliminated immediately. Empiricism, as it has been presented, comes into direct conflict with rationalism, and yet places so much emphasis on experience as to be said to depend upon it. The confusion comes about because, unlike German, we do not have words to distinguish between the effects of cumulative experience and the awareness in consciousness of immediate experience. "Experience" must suffice for both, but one concept refers to experience as given, and the other to the effect of repeated experiences. Rationalism depends upon the immediate experiences, empiricism upon cumulative experiences.

The phenomenological approach which Husserl discussed sees the mind as most appropriately studied through the analysis of immediate experience, with the mind separate from the body. The mechanistic approach deals with causal relations, rather than description, and consequently must pay attention to bodily functions in order that psychological processes may be brought into accord with natural laws. It would appear that Descartes is chiefly responsible for the clear separation of these two views of psychology, although Leibniz and, to a lesser degree Spinoza, as well as others, had a share in it. A phenomenological psychology was hereafter to exist side by side with a mechanistic psychology. Ever since Descartes, we have had to face the mind-body problem of how to render an adequate account of the relation of mental experiences to the corresponding neurophysiological processes.[163] In modern times there has been a division of labor between philosophy, with its concern for its logical and epistemological components, and psychology—more specifically, psychophysiology—with its talk of relating the phenomenal patterns to the processes of the organism.

The method of Descartes is rationalistic, and his psychological views emphasize intellectual factors. Both these trends have worked together to help produce the phenomenological approach. Through reason one can know truth. The passions, for example, originated in bodily perturbation and in a sense do hardly more than disturb the mind. The criticism that is sometimes made that Descartes treats the passions in too intellectual a fashion could be made more precise by saying that, since passions by his definition include the intellectual, he leaves no room anywhere in his position for elements that could be called purely affective irrational, or even motivational. To Descartes, psychology is almost exclusively cognitive.

A major influence of Descartes was an intellectualism with a bias in the direction of cognitive over conative processes.[164] This helped start a trend that persisted until the end of the nineteenth century, when biological findings and conceptions redirected interests toward conative matters. In this regard, Spinoza, who emphasized the conative, was a voice not to be echoed for some time to come.

In sharp distinction from his treatment of the study of the body, Descartes did not suggest that the mind could be studied by use of quantitative techniques but only through the process of meditation. In the whole world of nature Descartes was rigidly deterministic with one exception—the mind. But mental events, too, were seen as determinate in the phenomenological approach that was beginning to emerge. Spinoza supplied the deterministic correction, while Leibniz presented the argument that activity is the essential of consciousness.

The Mechanistic Approach

Descartes had advanced his theory of animals as automata in order to create a greater cleavage between man and brute in support of religious convictions. But others saw that to admit the validity of this argument was uncomfortably close to admitting that the old foundations for religious belief were to some extent inadequate. A vast controversy on the religious implications of his position resulted, extending over many years and many books.

More relevant to psychology is the reaction against his view that man's mind must be excluded from the mechanical sphere. Many of those who came after Descartes were so convinced of his view that mechanical activity accounted for the actions of animals and the body of man that they disagreed with his carefully made distinction between human mind and human body and held that human psychology was also to be accounted for on mechanical grounds. This was done simply by considering not only animals but also man as automata. This interpretation, abhorrent to Descartes though it would have been, unwittingly made him the father of the modern mechanistic approach to human nature. This "correction" happened in the eighteenth century[165] and was promulgated by several scholars.

Julien Offay de la Mettrie (1709–1751), the most influential of those who would render Cartesian views consistently mechanistic, published *Man a Machine* in 1748.[166] He regarded his thesis, given in its very title, as a natural extension of Descartes' teaching that animals are machines.[167] He arrived at his point of view not merely through reading, but from observation, including self-observation. During a severe illness he had noted that his bodily infirmity was associated with a mental disturbance. After recovering, he proceeded assiduously to collect psychological and medical evidence that supported his materialistic thesis. His theoretical view was that matter is endowed not only with the attribute of motion, but also with that of consciousness. To him, body was the only human reality.

It should not be imagined that even the more general mechanistic view of animal and human bodily function went without challenge. A reaction against mechanism came about from within physiology itself. Georg Ernst Stahl (1666–1734) took the position that the chemical activities within the living organism are essentially different from those reactions in the laboratory and in nonliving matter.[168] The soul permeates the entire organism and controls all functional manifestation. The soul is a force—a living force. To him the very fact that the body is alive proved his point. We have in the work of Stahl the beginnings of modern vitalism, to a less mystical form of which such an eminent man of the nineteenth century as Johannes Müller subscribed (p. 257).

LaMettrie
Mechanism

STAHL
vitalism

References*

1. Good general sources concerning the relevant aspects of the Renaissance are the volumes by E. Cassirer et al., eds., *The Renaissance Philosophy of Man* (Chicago: University of Chicago Press, 1948); G. Sarton, *Six Wings: Men of Science in the Renaissance* (Bloomington: Indiana University Press, 1957); and A. R. Hall, *The Scientific Revolution; 1500–1800: the Formation of the Modern Scientific Attitude* (Boston: Beacon Press, 1956).
2. Petrarch, "On His Own Ignorance and that of Many Others," trans. H. Nachod, E. Cassirer et al., eds., *Renaissance Philosophy of Man*, pp. 47–133 (1368).
3. *Ibid.*, p. 108.
4. J. H. Randall, *The Making of the Modern Mind*, rev. ed. (New York, Macmillan, 1940).
5. P. O. Kristeller, "The Platonic Academy of Florence," *Renaissance News*, XIV (1961): 147–159.
6. M. Ficino, "Five Questions Concerning the Mind," trans. J. L. Barroughs, E. Cassirer, et al., eds., *Renaissance Philosophy of Man*, pp. 185–214 (1476).
7. J. D. Bernal, *Science in History*, Vol. 1 (New York: Cameron, 1954).
8. R. M. Blake, et al., *Theories of Scientific Method: the Renaissance Through the Nineteenth Century* (Seattle: University of Washington Press, 1960).
9. R. McKeon, "Aristotelianism in Western Christianity," J. T. McNeill, et al., eds., *Environmental Factors in Christian History* (Chicago: University of Chicago Press, 1939), pp. 206–231.
10. P. Pomponazzi, "On the Immortality of the Soul," E. Cassirer, et al., eds., *Renaissance Philosophy of Man*, pp. 257–384 (1516).
11. N. Machiavelli, "The Prince," trans. W. K. Marriott, in R. M. Hutchins, ed., *Great Books of the Western World*, (Chicago: Encyclopaedia Britannica, 1952), Vol. XXIII (1513), pp. 1–37.
12. Major references are J. L. Vives, *On Education*, trans. F. Watson (Cambridge: Cambridge University Press, 1913) (c. 1521–1532); J. L. Vives, *Opera Omnia* (Farnham-Surrey: Dawson, 1965) (c. 1520–1540); *Tradado del alma*, Span. trans. José Antanon of *De Anima et Vita* (Buenos Aires: España Calyse, S.

*See p. 19 for description of reference style.

A., 1942) (1538); and F. Watson, "The Father of Modern Psychology," *Psychological Review*, XXII (1915): 333–353.

13. Paracelsus (Theophrastus von Hohenheim), "The Diseases that Deprive Man of His Reason," H. Sigerist, ed., *Four Treatises* (Baltimore: Johns Hopkins University Press, 1941), pp. 127–212 (*c.* 1512); Paracelsus, *Sämmtliche Werke*, 4 vols., (Modern German Translation by B. Aschner) (Jena: Fischer, 1926–1932) (*c.* 1526–1541).

14. Two major secondary sources are C. S. Sherrington, *The Endeavors of Jean Fernel* (Cambridge: Cambridge University Press, 1946) and C. S. Sherrington, *Man on His Nature*, 2nd ed. (Garden City, N.Y.: Doubleday, 1951).

15. P. Melanchthon, "*Commentarius de Anima*," C. G. Bretschneider, ed., *Opera Omnia*, Vol. 13 (Halle: Schwetschke, 1834–1840) (1540).

16. Huarte y Navarro, Juan de Dios. *Examen de Ingenios: or, The Tryal of Wits. Discovering the great Difference of Wits among Men, and what Sort of Learning suits best with each Genius*, trans. Mr. Bellamy (London: Richard Sare, at Grays-Inn-Gate in Holborn, 1698) (1575).

17. M. E. de Montaigne, "The Essays," in R. M. Hutchins, ed., *Great Books of the Western World*, Vol. XXV, pp. 3–543 (1580–1592).

18. R. Goeckel, *Psychologia–Hoc est de Hominis Perfectione,* cited in G. Zilboorg, and G. W. Henry, *A History of Medical Psychology* (New York: W. W. Norton, 1941), p. 178 (1590).

19. Vesalius, *De humani corporis fabrica* (Basel: Oporinus, 1543); Vesalius, *The Epitome*, trans. L. R. Lind (New York: Macmillan, 1949) (1543).

20. N. Copernicus, "On the Revolution of the Heavenly Spheres," trans. C. G. Wallis, in R. M. Hutchins, ed., *Great Books of the Western World*, Vol. XVI, pp. 505–838 (1543).

21. Recently it has been argued that more continuity existed between medieval and seventeenth century science than had previously been thought. The seventeenth century science was a culmination of cooperative efforts of generations of scientists, particularly at the School of Padua as J. H. Randall, Jr. demonstrates in *The School of Padua and the*

Emergence of Modern Science (Padova: Editrice Atenore, 1961).

22. L. Thorndike, "Newness and Novelty in Seventeenth Century Science and Medicine," *Journal of the History of Ideas*, XII (1951): 584–598.
23. E. A. Burtt, *The Metaphysical Foundations of Modern Physical Science* (Garden City, N.Y.: Doubleday, 1932).
24. E. W. Strong, *Procedures and Metaphysics* (Berkeley: University of California Press, 1936).
25. *Ibid.*
26. G. Galileo, *"Dialogues Concerning the Two New Sciences,"* trans. H. Crew and A. de Salvio, in R. M. Hutchins, ed., *Great Books of the Western World*, Vol. XXVIII, pp. 129–260 (1638).
27. G. Galileo, *Il Saggiatore*, quoted in J. W. Reeves, *Body and Mind in Western Thought* (London: Penguin Books, 1958), pp. 106–107 (1623).
28. F. Bacon, "Novum Organum," in R. M. Hutchins, ed., *Great Books of the Western World*, Vol. XXX, pp. 105–195 (1620).
29. F. Bacon, "Advancement of Learning," in R. M. Hutchins, ed., *Great Books of the Western World*, Vol. XXX, pp. 1–104 (1605).
30. F. Bacon, "New Atlantis," in R. M. Hutchins, ed., *Great Books of the Western World*, Vol. XXX, pp. 199–214 (1614–1617).
31. Bacon, "Novum Organum," "Advancement of Learning," *esp.* Second Book.
32. Bacon, "Advancement of Learning," Second Book, XVII, 4.
33. *Ibid.*, Second Book, VIII, 2.
34. Bacon, "Advancement of Learning," Second Book, VII, 1. "Novum Organum," First Book, Aphorisms, 71, 95, 98–106.
35. Bacon, "Novum Organum," First Book, Aphorisms, 39–68.
36. *Ibid.*, Aphorism 3.
37. R. Descartes, "Discourse on the Method of Rightly Conducting the Reason," trans. Elizabeth S. Haldane and G. R. T. Ross, in R. M. Hutchins, ed., *Great Books of the Western World*, Vol. XXXI, pp. 41–67 (1637).
38. *Ibid.*, VI.
39. Sherrington, *Man on His Nature*, Chapter 4.

40. J. Kepler, *Ad Vitellionem paralipomena, quibus astronomiae pars optica traditur*, (Frankfurt) Chapter 5, trans. A. C. Crombie, I. B. Cohen, and R. Taton, eds., *Mélanges Alexandre Koyré; L'Aventure de la science* (Paris: Hermann, 1964) (1604) (Herrnstein and Boring, Excerpt No. 23).

41. W. Harvey, *An Anatomical Disquisition on the Motion of the Heart and Blood in Animals*, trans. R. Willis, in R. M. Hutchins, ed., *Great Books of the Western World*, Vol. XXVIII, pp. 265–304 (1628).

42. *Ibid.*, Chapter 8, p. 285.

43. Hall, *The Scientific Revolution*.

44. "Discourse on Method," I, p. 44.

45. "The Discourse on the Method of Rightly Conducting the Reason" gives an autobiographical statement of some of the events of his life, while A. G. A. Balz, *Descartes and the Modern Mind* (New Haven: Yale University Press, 1952) and S. V. Keeling, *Descartes* (London: Oxford University Press, 1934) contain good secondary accounts.

46. "Discourse on Method," I, p. 42.

47. *Ibid.*, p. 43.

48. R. Descartes, "Rules for the Direction of the Mind," trans. Elizabeth S. Haldane and G. R. T. Ross, in R. M. Hutchins, ed., *Great Books of the Western World*, Vol. XXXI, pp. 1–40 (1629).

49. R. Descartes, "Treatise on Man," in R. M. Eaton, ed., *Selections* (New York: Charles Scribners Sons, 1927), pp. 350–354 (1662) (Part given in another translation in Herrnstein and Boring, Excerpt No. 57).

50. "Discourse on Method."

51. R. Descartes, "Dioptric," trans. N. K. Smith, *Descartes' Philosophical Writings* (London: Macmillan Ltd., 1952), pp. 167–179 (1637) (also in another translation in Herrnstein and Boring, Excerpt No. 27).

52. R. Descartes, "Meditations on First Philosophy," trans. Elizabeth S. Haldane and G. R. T. Ross, in R. M. Hutchins, ed., *Great Books of the Western World*, Vol. XXXI, pp. 69–293 (1641).

53. *Ibid.*, p. 60.

54. R. Descartes, "Passions of the Soul," *Essential Works of Descartes*, trans. L. Bair (New York: Bantam Books, 1961), pp. 108–210 (1649).

55. Keeling, *Descartes*.

56. "Rules," I–II.
57. "Discourse," II.
58. "Rules."
59. "Discourse," II.
60. A good critique is available in Keeling, *Descartes*.
61. "Discourse," I.
62. "Rules," IX.
63. *Ibid.*, VIII.
64. *Ibid.*, VIII, XII, XIII; "Meditations," I, VI, *Second Objection, Fifth Objection; Passions*, Part II, 3.
65. "Discourse," esp. IV.
66. *Ibid.*, pp. 51–52. Quoted by permission.
67. "Meditations," II.
68. *Ibid.*, p. 79.
69. W. T. Jones, *A History of Western Philosophy* (New York: Harcourt, Brace, 1952).
70. "Meditations," VI.
71. "Meditations," IV.
72. *Ibid.*, II.
73. *Ibid.*, VI.
74. *Ibid.*, Arguments, IV.
75. *Ibid.*, Reply to Fifth Set of Objections.
76. *Ibid.*, Preface to the Reader.
77. *Ibid.*, IV.
78. R. Descartes, *Principles of Philosophy*, trans. Elizabeth S. Haldane and G. R. T. Ross, *Philosophical Works* (Cambridge: Cambridge University Press, 1911), Vol. I, pp. 203–320, (1644) Part I, 53.
79. "Rules," XLI.
80. "Discourse," III, V.
81. *Ibid.*
82. R. I. Watson, "A Prescriptive Analysis of Descartes' Psychological Views," *Journal of the History of the Behavioral Science*, VII (1971): 238–239.
83. "Meditations," Reply to Sixth Set of Objections.
84. *Principles*, Part 1, LXVI–LXX.
85. "Meditations," VI.
86. *Ibid.*
87. *Ibid.*, II.
88. *Ibid.*, Arguments, Definition I.
89. *Principles*, Part I, XLII.
90. *Ibid.*, I.
91. "Meditations," IV; "Passions, XXXV.
92. *Principles*, Part I, XXXVII.
93. "Discourse," V, VI; "Meditations," Reply to Fifth Set of Objections.

94. "Rules," XII.
95. "Meditations," Reply to Fifth Set of Objections.
96. P. Gassendi, *Syntagma Philosophicum*, in F. N. Magill, ed., *Masterpieces of World Philosophy in Summary Form*, Vol. 1 (New York: Salem Press, 1961) pp. 404–410 (1658).
97. "Meditations," Arguments, Definition VII.
98. "Passions," VI.
99. "Discourse," V.
100. R. Descartes, "Letter to Henry More," in R. M. Eaton, ed., *Selections*, pp. 358–360.
101. "Treatise on Man," Part II.
102. *Ibid.*
103. "Discourse," V.
104. "Meditations," Reply to Fourth Set of Objections.
105. "Passions," XLIV.
106. *Ibid.*, XXXVI.
107. "Meditations," Reply to Fourth Set of Objections.
108. "Dioptric" (Herrnstein and Boring, Excerpt No. 27).
109. "Passions," XXXIX.
110. *Ibid.*, VII.
111. "Rules," XII.
112. For a discussion of how he conceived the mechanism of human action, see Herrnstein and Boring, Excerpt No. 57.
113. "Treatise on Man;" "Meditations," Reply to Fourth Set of Objections; "Passions," *Essential Works* XXXIV. (Herrnstein and Boring Excerpts, No. 44, 103).
114. "Meditations," Reply to Fifth Set of Objections.
115. *Ibid.*, Argument, Definition 1.
116. R. S. Peters, ed., *Brett's History of Psychology* (London: Allen and Unwin, 1953), p. 351.
117. "Meditations," Reply to Fourth Set of Objections.
118. "Passions," LX.
119. *Ibid.*, XXXI–XXXIV.
120. "Meditations," Reply to Fifth Set of Objections.
121. "Discourse," III.
122. "Meditations," VI.
123. "Passions."
124. *Ibid.*, XXVII.
125. *Ibid.*, II.
126. R. Descartes, "Letter to Marquis of Newcastle," in R. M. Eaton, ed., *Selections*, pp. 355–357.
127. "Passions," XXVII.
128. *Ibid.*, XXVIII.

129. *Ibid.*, XLVI.
130. *Ibid.*, XLVII.
131. *Ibid.*
132. *Ibid.*, LXIX–XCVII.
133. Geulincx, *Ethica*, J. P. N. Land, ed., *Opera philosophica*, Vol. 3 (The Hague: Nijhoff, 1892) (1675).
134. N. de Malebranche, *De la recherche de la vérité où l'on traite de la nature de l'esprit de l'homme et de l'usage en doit faire pour éviter l'erreur dans les sciences*, ed. F. Bouillier (Paris: Garnier, 1879–1880) (1674–1675); N. de Malebranche, *Dialogues on Metaphysics and Religion*, trans. M. Ginsburg (New York: Macmillan, 1923) (1688).
135. Primary sources are mentioned later. Good secondary sources on Spinoza are those of H. A. Wolfson, *The Philosophy of Spinoza*, 2 vols. in one (New York: Meridian Books, 1934); R. McKeon, *The Philosophy of Spinoza; the Unity of his Thought* (New York: Longmans, Green, 1928); G. H. R. Parkinson, *Spinoza's Theory of Knowledge* (Oxford: Clarendon Press, 1954).
136. B. Spinoza, *Ethics*, trans. W. H. White, rev. A. H. Stirling, in R. M. Hutchins, ed., *Great Books of the Western World*, Vol. XXXI, 355–463 (1677).
137. *Ibid.*, Part II, prop. 7, p. 375.
138. Spinoza, "Ethics," Part I.
139. *Ibid.*, Part II, prop. 11.
140. *Ibid.*, Part II.
141. *Ibid.*, Part III, prop. 2.
142. B. Spinoza, "Treatise on the Correction of the Understanding," trans. A. Boyle, E. Rhys, ed., *Spinoza's Ethics and de intellectus Emendatione* (New York: E. P. Dutton, 1910), pp. 228–263 (1677).
143. Spinoza, "Ethics," Part III, Preface.
144. B. Spinoza, "A Theologico-Political Treatise," R. H. M. Elwes, ed., *Chief Works* (London: Bell, 1909), Vol. I, pp. 3–278 (1670) IV.
145. Spinoza, "Ethics," Part I, props. 17, 28, 36, appendix, Part II, props. 1, 48–49.
146. Spinoza, "Theologico-Political Treatise," Chapter II, Sec. 11.
147. Spinoza, "Ethics," Part III, props. 4–8.
148. *Ibid.*, Part III, prop. 8.
149. B. Spinoza, *"Political Treatise,"* R. H. M. Elwes, ed., *Chief Works*, Vol. 1, pp. 280–387 (1677).

150. W. Bernard, "Freud and Spinoza," *Psychiatry*, IX (1946): 99–108.
151. *Ibid.*
152. D. Bidney, *The Psychology and Ethics of Spinoza; a Study in the History and Logic of Ideas* (New Haven: Yale University Press, 1940).
153. Good secondary sources include B. Russell, *A Critical Exposition of the Philosophy of Leibniz*, rev. ed. (London: Allen and Unwin, 1937); and H. W. Carr, *Leibniz* (New York: Dover Publications, 1929).
154. G. W. Leibniz, "The Principles of Nature and Grace, Based on Reason," P. P. Wiener, ed., *Selections* (New York: Charles Scribner's Sons, 1951), pp. 522–533 (1714).
155. G. W. Leibniz, "The Monadology," P. P. Wiener, ed., *Selections*, pp. 533–552 (1714).
156. G. W. Leibniz, "New Essays on the Human Understanding," P. P. Wiener, ed., *Selections*, pp. 367–480 (1704), Preface.
157. Leibniz, "The Monadology," 61.
158. G. W. Leibniz, "Considerations on the Principle of Life and on Plastic Natures by the Author of the Preestablished Harmony," P. P. Wiener, ed., *Selections*, pp. 190–199 (1705).
159. Leibniz, "New Essays," Preface.
160. Leibniz, "Principles of Nature and Grace," 4, 16.
161. Leibniz, "New Essays," Preface.
162. E. Husserl, *Cartesian Meditations: an Introduction to Phenomenology* (The Hague: Nijhoff, 1964) (1931).
163. H. Feigl, "Mind-body *not* a Pseudo Problem," S. Hook, ed., *Dimensions of Mind* (New York: New York University Press, 1960), pp. 24–36.
164. Peters, *Brett's History of Psychology*, p. 348.
165. L. C. Rosenfield, *From Beast-Machine to Man-Machine: animal Soul in French Letters from Descartes to La Mettrie* (New York: Oxford University Press, 1941).
166. J. O. de la Mettrie, *Man a Machine*, trans. G. C. Bussey and Mary W. Calkins (La Salle, Ill.: Open Court, 1912) (1748) (Herrnstein and Boring, Excerpt No. 58).
167. *Ibid.*, p. 72.
168. G. E. Stahl, *Theoria Medica Vera* (Halle: Orphonotrophei, 1707–1708).

Chapter 8

Locke AND Berkeley:
BRITISH EMPIRICISM
AND ASSOCIATIONISM

In considering Spinoza and Leibniz we have moved into the latter half of the seventeenth century. Important events in the physical sciences meanwhile were taking place in Great Britain. This was the age of the founding of the Royal Society; of the Newtonian synthesis; of Locke's struggle to find the limits of human knowledge by the study of human nature; and of a general increase of interest in science. More specifically for psychology it was the period in which empiricism as a method led to associationism as a major contentual problem in psychology.

The Royal Society was chartered in 1662, although informal meetings of the "Invisible College," an informal network of scholars who corresponded and met with one another from time to time, had been taking place as early as 1645.[1] The doctrines of Francis Bacon were the central force binding the founders together (although without entirely realizing it, they turned more to the experimental method of Kepler and Galileo). Their meetings were not confined to reading papers; public demonstrations of the most varied experiments were carried out also. The society also served to create favorable public opinion and its journal, *Philosophical Transactions,* fulfilled the need for a publication source. While many of the articles were of a scientific nature the majority were practical and dealt with such matters as shipbuilding, navigation, and mine pumping. Utilitarianism, so highly valued by Bacon, was being practiced.

Isaac Newton (1642–1727) was elected a Fellow of the Royal Society in 1671. In 1703, he was made its president, which he remained until his death, in the meantime assuming the dominant position not only within the Society but within British science in general. Under his domination the utilitarian character of the activities of the Royal Society tended to diminish. His two major publications were the *Opticks*,[2] primarily concerned with the composition of matter as shown by experiment, and *The Mathematical Principles of Natural Philosophy*,[3] concerned with quantity of matter as shown by mathematics. He had philosophical presuppositions, to be sure, but they were not decisive in his scientific work. Despite personal religious devoutness his integration of mechanical principle, particularly gravitational principles, could and were interpreted naturalistically. The lesson drawn by others was that the solar system kept going on its own momentum and followed its own laws. The question of whether God started the gears that were to drive the mechanism could be disregarded by others although not by Newton himself.

In the mathematization of science he was just as profoundly influential. To quote the gist of his position as he expressed it,

> the whole burden of philosophy seems to consist in this—from the phenomena of motions to investigate the forces of nature, and then from these forces to demonstrate the other phenomena; and to this end the general propositions in the first and second books are directed. In the third book I give an example of this in the explication of the System of the World; for by the propositions mathematically demonstrated in the former books in the third I derive from the celestial phenomena the forces of gravity with which bodies tend to the sun and the several planets.[4]

As for experiment, years before the appearance of his *Opticks*, he had given a paper to the Royal Society concerning his demonstration of the composition of white light.[5] Using a prism and white light as a source, he found that the spectrum of color broke down into violet, indigo, blue, green, yellow, orange, and red (memorized to this very day by the mnemonic device of VIBGYOR). Later it was to be shown that, instead of seven, there were an infinitude of degrees of refraction but his findings were the basis for all future work. He also worked out the laws of color mixture.[6] He showed that hue and saturation (but not brightness) are related so that in the mixture of two colors the hue that results is intermediate between the hues and the saturation is stronger the closer together the colors are to each other in the circle.

Newton resolved physical nature into five fundamental categories—material particles which exist in absolute space and absolute time, propelled into motion or change of motion by force. These are the categories from which he would derive the laws of nature.

Nomotheticism, naturalism, empiricism, and quantitativism, four prescriptions basic to all science, were furthered by Newton perhaps more than any other man, before or since. That the thinking of Newton was an inspiration to British empiricism is borne out by the repeated references to his work in that which follows.

The appeal to rationalism, nevertheless, was still an intellectual rallying call to the men of the seventeenth and eighteenth centuries. But rationalism was a term loosely used. During these centuries reason was the means of combatting the dogmatism and authoritarianism of the past. With their faith in cool objectivity, impartiality, and intellectualization, Locke and some of the other British empiricists were in this extended sense also rationalists, but others—Hobbes and Hume, for example—shared considerably less in the tendency to glorify reason.

The major point of agreement uniting the British associationists was their empiricism, which stood in contrast to still another and crucial facet of the rationalistic view. Rationalism in its major sense meant starting with assumptions and then deducing rationally the place of the human mind in that system. Rationalism as a means of achieving certainty of truth had characterized Descartes, Spinoza, and Leibniz. English empiricists, methodologically speaking, relied primarily on what could be learned from cumulated sense experiences and tended to be skeptical of achieving absolute certainty in any field. They were seeking a more "down-to-earth" philosophy in contrast to what they considered the speculative character of the philosophy of the continent. They accepted the Baconian proposition that scientists must start from observations that are collected carefully and from which relatively cautious generalizations are made. Contentually, the psychological generalizations which they fostered center on the laws of association—the ways in which mental events are connected. The great psychologists of this British empirical and associationist tradition are Locke and Berkeley, but chronologically preceding their work was that of Hobbes.

Thomas Hobbes

Thomas Hobbes (1588–1679) lived just before the period under consideration. He was a contemporary of and a correspondent with Descartes. He was also the first of the British empiricists. Despite this, he lived long enough *not* to be elected to the Royal Society, an omission that will become understandable shortly. Hobbes followed the careers of tutor and minor diplomat; he therefore spent considerable time traveling on the continent. For a short time he served as Bacon's secretary-translator.

He was an implacable foe of supernatural and religious beliefs. His favorite tactic was to assert his orthodoxy and then slip in a devastating criticism. He piously asserted that one must, of course, accept divine revelation—provided one has experienced it personally—otherwise it is only a belief.[7] It is small wonder that he incurred the wrath of the orthodox majority.

Hobbes is best known as a political philosopher but is relevant here because psychology formed the foundation for this work. His *Leviathan*[8]—so named because he saw the microcosm of man writ large in the macrocosm of the state—and his shorter work—significantly named *Human Nature*[9]—are the most important as statements of his psychological views.

Hobbes considered psychology a field to be investigated prior to making any attempt to understand the state and government.[10] Consequently, his interest in conduct was specifically in social conduct. He held a somewhat cynical view of human nature. Men originally lived in a state of mutual warfare and it was only enlightened selfishness that permitted cooperation. Without government" . . . the life of man [is] solitary, poor, nasty, brutish, and short."[11] On the basis of self-interest and the fear of attack, men agreed to live under government. The doctrine that self-interest is the basis of conduct came to be referred to as "psychological hedonism."

Influenced by Galileo's conception of motion, Hobbes held that everything that happens is matter in motion; mental activities are motions of the nervous system arising as reactions to motions in the external world.[12] Thinking is, in reality, nothing more than movement excited in the brain.[13] Motions account not only for cognitive processes but also for action and emotion. Everything in nature is material. Thinking implies a thinking thing, just as walking implies a walking thing; in both instances this thing is the body. Consequently, Hobbes rejected Cartesian interactionistic dualism in favor of a materialistic monism. Blithely disregarding all difficulties and inconsistencies, Hobbes conceived of sensation, thought, and consciousness as due to the motion of atoms in the brain. He offered no explanation of how the connection between atomic motions and mental processes, two apparently different activities, came about. They simply did. In this assumption he anticipated a behavioral position for psychology. His defense of a contentual objectivity as characterizing psychological phenomena did not go so far as to reject the concept of the mind, as we shall see in a moment.

According to Hobbes, the content of mind arises from sense experience, not from innate ideas;[14] this marks him as an empiricist. All complex experience is derived from simple experience, and all simple experience is derived from sensation. In other words, the cognitive powers of the mind are derived from the senses and the senses alone. Cognitions are merely corruptions of the original sense elements. For example, imagination and memory are "decaying" conceptions in that they are slowly fading sensations.[15]

Hobbes argued against the common belief that the qualities of our experience—color, for example—are inherent in the object.[16] He insisted that in all instances "the subject of their *inherence* is not the *object,* but the *sentient.*"[17] Psychological experiences, in other words, are subjective and are not counterparts of the objective stimuli that give rise to them. He goes so far as to call psychological experiences "apparitions," but adds that they come about as the result of the objects working on the brain.

The notion of association he did little more than partially outline, leaving its development and extension to others. The processes of association or, as he referred to them, "the trains of thought," are of two sorts.[18] There are those that are unguided and without design. In addition, there are those that are regulated and orderly, as when one thought introduces the one that follows or when design or desire regulate thought. This distinction contains a clear differentiation between what was later to be called free and controlled association. Moreover, he was showing that coherence (or contiguity, as it would be called today) is one of the bases of sequences of association. Desire and habit serve as agents of selection. More or less incidentally, in the quite different context of the necessity of impressing people with knowledge of the laws, he suggested periodic repetition as a means of making sure that laws are remembered.[19] Frequency as a factor in learning was thus acknowledged.

Hobbes stressed the influence of the passions and desires, which he saw as motions arising from within man.[20] The basis of human action is "a perpetual and restless desire for power after power."[21] He distinguished between the appetites and aversions with which one is born and those that are acquired from experience.[22] Although he devotes a chapter to the passions, it is unsystematically presented and digressive. A fair number of passions are mentioned, but in no sense can it be seen as an exhaustive statement. He does make it clear that passions may sway reason.[23] As a consequence, passions are regarded as infirmities of man.[24] The passions serve to sustain and direct thought. Deliberation is simply a choice from among appetites and aversions.[25] Pleasure, pain, pride, and fear are prime determiners of conduct.

Notwithstanding the incompleteness, the inconsistency, and the obvious vagueness of his views and despite his lack of direct influence upon his successors, Hobbes was prophetic of an emerging empirical, monistic, materialistic conception of mind. Many later developments followed along lines he had marked out, for he argued that man is an integral part of the natural world, not just physically, as Descartes believed, but mentally as well, and held out the hope for a science of human physics that was to be worked out in more detail by Hume in the next century.

John Locke

John Locke (1632–1704) was an older contemporary of Leibniz and Newton, and though he lived most of his life in the seventeenth century, he belonged in spirit to their eighteenth century.[26] Although anticipated in a few particulars by Hobbes, English empiricism really was launched by Locke, who thus became the founder of psychology as the empirical science of the mind.

In January 1649, John Locke was a seventeen-year-old scholar at Westminster School. Close to the abbey and the school was Whitehall Palace Yard. Here on January 30, Charles I, King by Divine Right, was executed as a traitor to the Commonwealth. For some years both before and after the execution, which he may have witnessed, the young Locke lived in the midst of the Great Rebellion that was so crucial to English history. Small wonder, then, that he and more than one of his fellow students of this severely studious school—all of whom were within sound of the tumultuous doings outside its walls—were moved in later years to concern themselves with matters of government.

Locke was born in Pensford, a village near Bristol, ten years before the outbreak of civil war. His father, a small landowner and a lawyer by profession, was a captain in a volunteer regiment under the Long Parliament. The unsettled conditions of the times reduced the already modest family fortunes considerably, but through the influence of his father's colonel, Locke was sent to Westminster School in 1646. After remaining at Westminster six years, he was granted a junior studentship at Christ Church, Oxford, in 1652. Locke remained at Oxford after taking his bachelor's degree in 1656. He took a master's degree and then had academic appointments successively in Greek, rhetoric, and moral philosophy.

He was perhaps most influenced by Robert Boyle who was at Oxford during Locke's years of residence. Robert Boyle (1627–1691) was part of the group which founded the Royal Society, and one of the founders of modern chemistry, doing much to clear away the mysticism that had surrounded the field. Above all, he wished to foster the alliance between chemistry and mechanical science. His general contribution to Locke's education was to show him how to approach matters empirically; one of the more specific contributions was to provide Locke with the conception of primary and secondary qualities. This was a distinction made before by Galileo (p. 143) but it was also arrived at and named by Boyle.

Boyle

It was only later that Newton, who was only ten years old at the time Locke arrived at Oxford, made an impression; but Newton's influence was so important that in the "Epistle to the Reader" of his major book, along with Boyle and one or two others, he spoke of the "incomparable Mr. Newton."

The founding of the Royal Society at Oxford, of which Locke became a member, led him to some studies and demonstrations in chemistry and meteorology. He also began the study of medicine. At Oxford he took an interest in political questions, particularly the relation of church and state and the importance and desirability of religious toleration. In the meantime, he had largely outgrown his Puritan upbringing. Given Cromwell's dwindling power, and repressive measures, he saw more hope for religious and political liberty under Charles than under the government of the Rump Parliament. So when Charles II was crowned in 1660, Locke welcomed the change in government, and for some years had no reason to regret it.

In 1667, he left Oxford for the political world of London. He had made the acquaintance of Lord Ashley, afterwards the Earl of Shaftesbury, and took up residence with him in London as his confidential secretary, tutor to his son, personal physician, and eventually his trusted confidante and friend. In 1669, in his capacity as confidential secretary, he was charged with helping to draft a constitution for the colony of Carolina, and he managed to have embodied in it some of his permissive views concerning religious toleration.

Shaftesbury became involved in a plot against Charles II and in 1681 fled to Holland where he died early the following year. Although apparently not a party to the plot, Locke was also suspected and he also sought refuge in Holland. Meanwhile he continued working on the *Essay*. It appears probable that he was involved to some degree in the planning of the bloodless Revolution of 1688 that crowned William of Orange as King of England. At any rate, he returned to England in 1689 on the same ship that carried Princess Mary, wife of William of Orange. Shortly afterward he was offered several ambassadorships, but took instead a post that offered considerable leisure, that of the Commissioner of Appeals.

toleration

He was now in a position to work toward implementing some of his favorite ideas fostering tolerance of differences of opinion. In his pleas for religious toleration, Locke[27] went much beyond most of the individuals of his time. He would have extended toleration to all outside the church with the exception of atheists, Catholics (because of their presumed allegiance to a foreign power), and those who would use religion as a pretext to put forward social or political views at variance with the best interests of the community.

Up to the time of his return to England in 1689 at the age of fifty-six, Locke had published little of importance. In the next few years a whole series of works appeared. There was his *Letter Concerning Toleration*[28] published the year of his return; *An Essay Concerning Human Understanding,*[29] which appeared the year following; and works on government, economics, education, and Christianity, between then and 1695.

For psychology, interest in his work centers on *An Essay Concerning Human Understanding.*[30] Aside from the posthumously published *The Conduct of the Understanding,*[31] essentially all of his psychological views are contained in this one work. Locke tells us in the "Epistle to the Reader," that the *Essay* was conceived and the resolution to write it in the following fashion:

> I should tell thee, that five or six friends meeting at my chamber, and discoursing on a subject very remote from this, found themselves quickly at a stand, by the difficulties that rose on every side. After we had awhile puzzled ourselves, without coming any nearer a resolution of those doubts which perplexed us, it came into my thoughts that we took a wrong course; and that before we set ourselves upon inquiries of that nature, it was necessary to examine our own abilities, and see what *objects* our understandings were, or were not, fitted to deal with.[32]

This and his other writings that followed rapidly made Locke famous both in England and on the continent and he became the acknowledged voice of philosophical and governmental liberalism. Voltaire

Views embraced by Voltaire

(1694–1778), who developed an unbounded admiration for Locke, and placed him on the same exalted plane as Newton, did much to spread a favorable opinion of his views on the continent, and especially in France.

THE ORIGIN OF LOCKE'S PSYCHOLOGICAL VIEWS

In proposing, as Locke did in his "Epistle to the Reader" (p. 188), that the examination of our ability to understand ourselves is basic to later investigation in other fields, including the sciences, he was making psychology fundamental. But he also made explicit the limits he would set to his inquiry. In the introduction to the *Essay*, he specifically disavowed any concern with the physical aspects of understanding.[33] In a similar vein he indicated that such speculative matters as the essence of understanding would also be disregarded. He took understanding for granted, and carried on his inquiry in order to see how far understanding could take him and where it would fail him, so that he would be more cautious thereafter in meddling in matters beyond comprehension.

In order to carry out his intention of looking into the origin, certainty, and extent of human knowledge, Locke proposed a psychological inquiry into the ideas, "which a man observes, and is conscious to himself he has in his mind; and the ways whereby the understanding comes to be furnished with them."[34] An "idea" was defined very broadly as anything about which the mind can be employed in thinking. In other words, an idea denoted any sort of experience.

INSISTENCE ON NONEXISTENCE OF INNATE IDEAS

Locke plunged immediately into his task by arguing that there are no innate ideas, a position that seems to have gone hand in hand with adherence to the rationalistic prescription since the time of Plato.[35] With his stand on innate ideas, he began his attack on the still dominant rationalism. Although he did not mention Descartes by name, his attack was probably directed against him, even though Descartes held a moderate position involving acceptance of potentially innate ideas that are actualized by experience, rather than the extreme position that Locke attacked. Certainly his views were contrary to those professed by the contemporary Cambridge Platonists whose thinking dominated English academic circles. Such ideas as "what is, is" or "it is impossible for the same thing to be and not to be" are, Locke said, not imprinted upon the mind. We are not born with these or any other moral, theological, logical, or mathematical principles. Despite his denial of their existence, Locke tried to account for how these false opinions could have arisen. When a

*good
a discovery!
of
Egocentrism*

man once grasped some general proposition that he could not thereafter doubt, he was inclined to think this now self-evident proposition must have been innate.[36] Locke held that those fostering a belief in the innate were the intellectually lazy and the dogmatically minded, the latter because they recognized that unquestioned propositions could be thrust upon others. In his crisp way of putting the matter, acceptance stops the inquiry of the doubtful.[37]

The argument for innate ideas based on the sheer existence of ideas commonly agreed upon and universally accepted is given short shrift by Locke; his argument is that their universality does not demand innateness if some other way can be found to account for the presence of such ideas. If ideas be universal, he asks, how is it that children and idiots do not have them? Moreover, he points out that children can reason long before they appreciate the truth of maxims they were given earlier as illustrations.

What a child is told and retold by nurses or others, he accepts.[38] When he becomes an adult, as a consequence of being unable to remember a time when he did not accept these principles, he believes he must have held them all along. So where do generally agreed-upon ideas come from? To answer this Locke set upon himself the task of demonstrating that all knowledge is derived from the effects of experience, thereby declaring his allegiance to the empiricistic prescription.

SENSATIONS, SIMPLE IDEAS, AND PRIMARY AND SECONDARY QUALITIES

Ideas come from sense impressions in the form of "particular" ideas. The mind, "the yet empty cabinet" (so-called because of what he considered the false analogy of the well-stocked cabinet filled with innate ideas), is furnished with ideas by experience.[39] Sensing takes place when the impression from the sense organs is transmitted to the mind. These sensations are simple ideas, and in receiving them, the mind is essentially passive; it must sense when it senses and cannot refuse impressions or blot them out.[40]

Sensible qualities are simple ideas; that is, they are not divisible into different ideas.[41] Some simple ideas are admitted through one sense, while others depend upon combinations of the senses—for example, ideas of space and extension, rest and motion.

What we know through the senses is not known immediately but through the intervention of ideas.[42] Knowledge is real only to the extent that our ideas conform to the reality of objects. With simple ideas, there is at least a rough correspondence, for these ideas are the products of things outside ourselves operating on the mind. But all our ideas are not exactly identical to the images and do not exactly resemble any object.[43]

Sensible qualities are of two kinds: solidity, substance, figure, and mobility are primary; they are inseparable from their objects no matter how much the latter may change in other ways. Color, sounds, and tastes are examples of secondary qualities which do not really exist in the objects themselves but which do have the capacity to produce sensations in the observer.[44] The secondary qualities exist only as modes of the primary qualities. Illustrative is the failure of objects to have color in the dark. But the most famous illustration is the experiment of the three basins of water: if, after placing one hand in a basin of cold water and the other in a basin of hot water, both hands are now placed together in a basin of tepid water, one hand will feel warm, and the other will feel cold. To Locke, this proved the subjective character of perception. The objective nature of the cause and the subjective character of the effect in consciousness had been established.

Although using this and other illustrations to drive home his point about secondary qualities, Locke was no idealist. The tepid water was real enough, as were whiteness and bitterness and other secondary qualities. There is an external reality that lies behind the ideas that we have, Locke was convinced. This is the crucial issue on which his successors were to seize. How, they would ask, if we are aware of ideas for primary and secondary qualities alike, can we know that there is such a reality (p. 199)?

REFLECTION, SIMPLE AND COMPLEX IDEAS

Ideas arising from sensations are supplemented by reflection, which we carry on with our minds.[45] Ideas of sensation and ideas of reflection make up all ideas. These two together make up all mental activity, for they are the only sources of ideas. Reflection is the operation of the mind itself, as opposed to the operation of sensations upon the mind. Reflection gives rise to ideas, but these ideas are based on those already supplied from sensory experience. Ideas of reflection could not be innate by definition, since they use the materials of sensation. The operations collectively called reflection are perceiving, thinking, doubting, believing, reasoning, knowing, and willing.

Reflection comes later than sensation. Children reflect only after time spent in examining their "floating visions."[46] Apparently, Locke had some conception of development for he wrote that as experience increases, the mind has more to think about. Perception is the simplest level of reflection.[47] Children first have ideas of hunger and of warmth that exemplify perceptions. Even animals have perceptions. Perceptive reflection is the first step toward knowledge. Remembering is also present in children. When the same ideas again recur, without the operation of the object of the original sensation, we have remembering. Before mentioning the other ways in which reflection functions, it is useful to introduce another facet of Locke's psychological views, that of complex ideas.

Simple ideas are received passively, but the mind can actively make ideas by putting them together in combinations.[48] Complex ideas are derived from a combination of simple ideas of sensation and simple ideas of reflection.[49] All ideas, even the most abstruse, remote, and abstract, arise from these two sources.[50] All complex ideas derive from the repetition and joining together of simple ideas from sense or reflection.

It is now appropriate to return to the question of reflection in order to consider those particular operations of the mind that involve complex as well as simple ideas. The mind contemplates both simple and complex ideas, discerns similarities and differences between them, compares and distinguishes them, and composes them in new arrangements. The process culminates when the mind begins to treat these ideas as abstractions and to use them to form general ideas.

How Locke viewed abstract ideas deserves special consideration since his successor, Berkeley, offered a very important critique of them. Locke argued that we join together ideas derived directly from sense or from reflection to form abstract ideas by considering some attributes common to several particular ideas and ignoring those aspects in which they differ. A number of objects, such as a sail, a bone, and a bowl of milk, can give us an idea of whiteness when we ignore the differences among the objects and concentrate on the similarity of them.

Complex ideas have their origins in the thoughts of men more than in the reality of things. Ideas are of utmost diversity as Locke himself illustrates by placing in the same list whiteness, hardness, thinking, motion, man, elephant, army, and drunkenness.[51] Complex ideas may be analyzed into simpler ones. Systematically analyzed complex ideas, considered in some detail by Locke, include substance; relation, including cause and effect; identity and diversity, including personal identity; and proportion. With this analysis complete, Locke proceeds to consider such issues as clarity and obscurity, distinctions and confusions, reality and fantasy, adequacy and inadequacy, and the truth and falsity of ideas.[52]

Drawing upon what he had learned from Boyle and Newton, Locke extended the realm of natural law to the phenomena of the human mind. The material particles of Newton and the corpuscles of Boyle had their ideational counterpart in the ideas of the mind for which laws could be found. Without being explicit about it, to Locke, ideas serve the same function for the mind that particles and corpuscles do for the physical nature. Ideas cohere as do the particles to form complex ideas. In keeping with the Newtonian conception, Locke saw man as essentially static, pushed or pulled by external forces.

FEELINGS

Feelings play only a secondary role in Locke's psychological considerations. Pain and pleasure are simple ideas accompanying both sensation and reflection.[53] The passions are derived from the feelings. The passions are modes or manifestations of pleasure and pain and include love, hatred, desire, joy, sorrow, hope, and anger. Basically, the passions are derivatives of good and evil in that they are identified by reference to the pleasure and the pain to which they give rise. Each passion is related by Locke to good and evil. Desire, for example, is the thought of some attainable good, while envy is the uneasiness we experience when someone obtains a good before we do.

Pleasure and pain are therefore defined by the ideas one has. Locke's views, deriving complex emotions from a base of simple pleasures and pains, was to have considerable effect on psychological theories throughout the eighteenth century.

ASSOCIATION OF IDEAS

The fame that Locke has received for coining the phrase "the association of ideas" is undeserved to some extent. His chapter bearing this title was interpolated in 1700 only by the fourth edition of the *Essay*.[54] His system of psychology was fully developed without recourse to the association of ideas. It is therefore fitting and proper that this topic be treated as an appendix to the rest of his thinking.

Earlier he had held that ideas are fixed in the memory by attention and repetition, but above all, by pleasure and pain.[55] "Hurts" and "advantages" to the body are taken notice of because of pleasure and pain. Reflection, as we have seen, is a means by which one combines a number of simple simultaneous experiences into a compound but single experience. He thus anticipated a more precise formulation of what later was called simultaneous association. He likewise referred the origin of complex ideas, even those most abstract, to the repetition and joining together of simple ideas.[56] The changeableness of habits, as brought about by reflection, practice, application, and custom, is used by Locke to explain how we can change the agreeableness or disagreeableness of things.[57] So the topic of the nature of habit and association had not been completely neglected by Locke.

Aside from the title itself, the phrase "association of ideas" is used but once in this relatively short chapter.[58] He makes no reference either to Aristotle or to Hobbes and does not in any way refer to "laws of association." He approaches the topic by pointing out that there is something unreasonable in all men, for, although each of us can readily perceive flaws in the reasoning of others, we are blinded to even much greater inadequacies in ourselves. How does this come about? It is because of wrong connections of ideas that occurred by chance or by custom in a particular individual. An example he gives is that of teaching children that goblins have more to do with darkness than with light and, as a consequence, finding that they are unable thereafter to separate the idea of darkness from the idea of goblins, so that now the dark brings with it these frightful ideas.

A considerable proportion of the chapter is taken up with instances of this theme of wrong associations. Locke also offers an instance of more neutral tying together of ideas, pointing out that once a musician begins a tune, he will be able to continue it without further care or attention. In no way, however, does he show that he regards this as any more than another and similar illustration. As already mentioned, rationalism, in the form of a calm, impartial reason carrying on reflection, was defended zealously by Locke. Paradoxically, his chapter on association can be conceived as his defense of why individuals are unable to behave in the light of reason in this sense. It would seem that Locke used association only to explain errors of understanding; those who came after him were to use it to explain understanding itself.

INFLUENCE

The influence Locke had upon later developments in psychology was varied and profound. A summary of his views and their influence follows.

1. In making understanding central to his work, Locke organized the higher mental processes into a field of psychology broader in nature than anything that could be investigated by physiological methods alone.

2. Locke did much to set the limits of a psychology that was still relatively speculative, still contentually subjective in character and dualistic in nature, but that could later be separated more completely from philosophy.

3. After he denied the existence of innate ideas, his strategy of

starting with simple ideas that arise from experience and then trying to show that complex ideas are composed of simple ideas (with the aid of reflection) convinced many others of the validity and worth of empiricism. He may thus be said to have launched British empiricism.

4. He conceived of ideas of elements in a manner essentially similar to the particles of Newton. He held that the complex ideas of the mind were formed of these particles and were capable of *analysis* into units. This was clearly a molecular approach, one to prove important; it was in vogue in the nineteenth and twentieth centuries, as epitomized in the views of Wundt and Titchener.

5. While disavowing an intention to consider physiological mechanisms in his account, he did introduce the mechanism of ideas in a manner that seemed to indicate indebtedness to Newton's "minute particles" of matter. Like their physical counterparts, Locke conceived ideas as cohering to form aggregates in ways that have been detailed. Locke was successful in establishing a basis for mental mechanisms.

6. To meet the difficulty of accounting for the higher intellectual processes, Locke postulated reflection as coordinate with sensation in the formation of experiences. In solving this problem he altered his position to one that was not entirely empirical. In a sense, he substituted a native power of reflection for the innate ideas he had discarded. He made a concession to nativism that Hobbes had held was needless. Locke's concept of reflection was somewhat vague. Out of this very vagueness came a spur to others to find a means of extending his principle of association in order to account for how complex and derivative ideas came about.

7. In continuing the distinction between primary and secondary qualities and presenting them so graphically, Locke did much to draw attention to this distinction.

8. In a manner reminiscent of Aquinas, Locke referred to reflection as an internal sense. Locke made a distinction between being aware of an idea (reflection) and merely having an idea. The question of how the mind obtains knowledge of its own operations was thus solved; reflections were ideas about ideas. Act psychologists of the nineteenth century made this distinction an important part of their approach, in that they distinguished between the mental act of function on one hand and mental content on the other.

9. In originating and illustrating the phrase "association of ideas," Locke made explicit the possibility of working out the interconnections and sequences of ideas as expressive of experiences. A reduction of the entire mental life to association would follow. Association will be found

as one of the principal themes pervading psychology in an open or disguised form to this day.

10. The *Essay Concerning Human Understanding,* published in 1690, initiated a continuous sequence of subsequent publications extending from Berkeley, Locke's immediate successor, through Hume, Hartley, the Scottish School, the Mills, on to Alexander Bain, the last great philosopher psychologist of Great Britain who died as recently as the early years of this century. The rest of this chapter is devoted to an account of these developments, with emphasis on the themes of the cruciality of the distinction, or lack of it, between primary and secondary qualities; the subjective nature of all ideas; the crucial importance of empiricism which was to become a viable alternative to rationalism; the opening up of the study of association to account for some forms of learning, and to become important in perception; and encouragement of more cautious and parsimonious psychological interpretation required when trying to account for how ideas are associated with one another.

George Berkeley

George Berkeley was a deeply religious man. He became disturbed by the sceptical attitudes engendered by the materialistic thought that he believed was threatening to dominate the intellectual life of his time. The guiding themes of Berkeley's writing were defense of religion and the refutation of scepticism. Berkeley saw a danger posed to religion by the new materialistic Newtonian science. It was not science that he wished to banish, however, but a belief in the primordial character of matter which made it possible for impious persons to deride immaterial (spiritual) substance, to consider the soul corruptible, and even to deny providence.[59] He held that spiritual and intellectual confusion arose from the belief in something independent of mind called matter. To Berkeley, this belief was a chimera.[60] Pursuing his theme he asked, "What sort of world does this science of matter in motion depict?" He concluded that it was the world as revealed by the senses. In an effort to combat the source of danger to religion, he turned to inquiry about mental life.

George Berkeley (1685–1753) was born in Ireland and was educated at Trinity College, Dublin.[61] By the time he arrived, his college included in its teachings the works of Descartes, Hobbes, Locke, and Newton. His academic progress was swift; he entered at fifteen, took his bachelor's degree at twenty, completed his master's degree and became a junior fellow at twenty-two, and received ordination as a deacon of the Anglican church at twenty-four. At the same age, in the year 1709, he published the first account of his psychological-philosophical views in *An Essay Towards a New Theory of Vision.*[62] A year later he gave a more general statement in *A Treatise Concerning the Principles of Human Knowledge.*[63] In one sense his life after the age of twenty-five is an anticlimax, since these two works are vastly more important than anything else he wrote later. Nevertheless, he had a full life—teaching at Trinity; further writing; visiting the London of Swift, Addison, and Steele, where he captivated society by his charm; traveling on the continent; and endeavoring to further educational and missionary enterprises in the American colonies. In connection with these benevolent efforts, he settled for nearly three years at Newport, Rhode Island. When his hopes for support from governmental grants were not realized, he returned to London, leaving his house, farm, and library to Yale University. In fairness it must be added that on later occasions he also donated books to Harvard. For the last eighteen years of his life, Berkeley was Anglican Bishop of Cloyne in County Cork, Ireland.

PHILOSOPHICAL POSITION

The major arguments for Berkeley's philosophical position are psychological in nature. Before presenting them, a statement of this philosophical position is necessary, although the evidence is reserved for sections of the chapter that follow. To appreciate the full impact of his philosophical views, the psychological arguments are essential.

It is convenient to refer to Berkeley's philosophical position as "mentalism," a name given to it in later years because of his insistence that the mental aspects of life are paramount.[64] Berkeley, while stressing mental phenomena, did not deny the existence of a world of physical things. Others who came after him could and did make this specific denial. Their position, in distinction from his "mentalism," came to be called "subjective idealism," with which his view is sometimes confused. $\Re$(NO INFINITE PERCEIVER)   *mentalism*

To elucidate what is meant by mentalism, consider the nature of an object. Psychologically speaking, Berkeley said that an object is a collection, a sum of sensations that experience has given us together, and consequently habit makes it impossible to disassociate them in our minds. The world is the sum total of our sensations. To illustrate:

Take away the sensations of softness, moisture, redness, tartness, and you take away the cherry. Since it is not a being distinct from these sensations; a cherry, I say, is nothing but a congeries of sensible impressions or ideas perceived by various

> senses; which ideas are united into one thing (or have one name given them) by the mind because they are observed to attend each other.[65]

So mentalism is the theory that a collection of impressions and ideas makes up our experiences.

Berkeley was insisting on the primacy of consciousness. He declined to accept anyone else's perception, "so long as I myself am conscious of no such thing."[66] Only what one is conscious of is important. Man's knowledge of other men is derived only through ideas excited in him.[67]

Berkeley argued for direct observation of phenomena. These phenomena are real enough; their *esse* is *percipi*.[68] Perception is his definition of reality, that is, appearances to him are real.[69] This position places him close to what we would today call a phenomenologist.[70] That perceived objects do not exist independently of perception is almost as classic a formulation of the phenomenologist's position as we have. The qualifying phrase, "close to," is necessary because he escaped the position; as we shall see, the Infinite Perceiver assured him of the presence of objects. Anticipating much of Mach's analysis of Newtonian assumptions, Berkeley found no justification for Newton's conceptions of absolute space and time and argued that all motion was relative to the observer.[71] Not only matter but Newtonian motion, time, and space he declared unknowable.

Berkeley did not, however, deny the reality of matter merely because man's own prowess allows him to be certain only of mental events. It follows from his position on this issue that the unity of mental life cannot be explained by reference to the physical world. Berkeley raises some questions in this connection. The smell and the color of the rose are not "out there" to be experienced together. How then are they experienced together? Similarly two people report the same sequence of events, but Berkeley could not appeal in explanation to the "stimulus objects," as we would call them. How can this come about? Furthermore, what makes a unity of the collection of experiences that belong to an individual mind? In answer, Berkeley decided that what holds together experiences of this sort is the soul, a logically necessary but supernatural substratum to our experience. Moreover, there must be an active cause for the continued experience of the "works of nature." This Berkeley found in God.[72] There was a persistence of physical objects guaranteed by the "Permanent Perceiver"—God. This phase of his thinking is captured neatly in the famous pair of limericks by Ronald Knox:[73]

There was a young man who said, "God
Must think it exceedingly odd
    If he finds that this tree
    Continues to be
When there's no one about in the Quad."

Dear Sir:
    Your astonishment's odd:
I am always about in the Quad.
        And that's why the tree
        Will continue to be,
    Since observed by
            Yours faithfully,
            God.

His views on these matters created a sensation, not only in scholarly circles, but throughout literate society. To the man of common sense what he had advanced was a paradox because he was misinterpreted as saying that the object itself, say a rock, was imaginary. When Johnson was challenged by Boswell to refute Berkeley, he gave a stone a mighty kick, and replied, "I refute it *thus*." As is sometimes the way of the world, this refutation, irrelevant to the issue at hand, (because, to Berkeley, the idea of rock had among its associated ideas that of hardness) is perhaps better known than the doctrine that it was intended to demolish.

PSYCHOLOGICAL VIEWS

In the first section of the *Principles* Berkeley presented a short statement of the elements of his system of psychology.[74] He asserted that the objects of human knowledge could be reduced to: ideas imprinted on the senses, perceptions obtained by attending to the passions and the operations of the mind, and ideas formed by the help of memory and imagination. To Berkeley, these are the molecular elements of mental life. The collective acts of knowing the objects of knowledge or perceiving them and exercising such operations as willing, imagining, or remembering them, Berkeley called mind, spirit, soul, or "myself." This mind is not one of these ideas but something distinct from them.

EXPERIENCE AND REALITY

It will be remembered that Hobbes had denied that psychological qualities are actually inherent in the object (p. 185). Locke held that we know only through ideas, yet made a distinction between primary and secondary qualities, with only the former inhering in the object (p. 191).

Berkeley asked then, *how do we know the reality of the objects of the world?*[75] If we know everything through ideas, as Locke said, how can we know by means of ideas that some qualities inhere in objects while others do not?[76] Berkeley wondered how Locke could know from experience, what was not derived from experience. Locke had asserted something that he could not have experienced. The same arguments that are cogent in respect to secondary qualities, Berkeley argued, apply equally to primary qualities. Berkeley insisted that all ideas are similar to what Locke had called secondary qualities. Primary as well as secondary qualities are merely sensation—or ideas, as Berkeley calls them—and an idea exists in the mind perceiving it.[77] In one bold stroke Berkeley reduced primary qualities to secondary qualities. We never know anything but our experiences. So far as Berkeley is concerned, the world is a plausible but unproved hypothesis. Moreover, he held that it is a hypothesis that can never be proved by naturalistic means, since we know only our own experience. Berkeley's answer to the question of how we can ever obtain a belief in the existence of an external world, was to invert Locke's proposition that ideas enter into the mind from outside by means of the senses, since all we know are the ideas of which the mind is constituted.

EMPIRICISM AND SENSATION

In spite of his divergences from Hobbes and Locke, Berkeley was still an empiricist.[78] Although he disagreed with them on the nature of the outer and inner worlds, he still agreed that knowledge could be established by verification through direct experience derived from the senses. It is sometimes said that he denied the evidence of the senses. On the contrary, he accepted the evidence of ideas but considered himself forced to find the existence of the world behind subjective phenomena on other grounds. It will also be seen that his theory of space perception is uncompromisingly empiricist in nature.

The crucial role of experience is clearly established in his handling of the relations among sensory experiences. Ideas are classified by the separate sense departments. Hence, vision, touch, smell, taste, and hearing are five classes of sense ideas with which we are born. Berkeley insisted that ideas within each sense department are distinct, that is to say, separate and not overlapping. The smell of the rose and the color of the rose are distinct sensations, not innately intermingled in any way. The ideas to which they give rise are distinct from one another. There is no idea common to both, and yet somehow they manage to be combined. It is evident that Berkeley had to find a combinatory factor. He found it in experience. It is only loose terminology when we refer to both *seeing* and *hearing* a coach, as if they were a single experience. One says that one "hears" a coach half a mile away. Strictly speaking one hears only a certain *sound* that suggests a coach. The sound itself is no distance at all. Seeing is exactly analogous—I say that I see a coach in the distance, but what is actually seen serves merely to suggest a coach at that distance. Nevertheless, one can infer that it is the same coach because the ideas have been observed to go together constantly and are spoken of as one and the same thing. What one visualizes and what one hears are different things; but because they are united by experience, it becomes natural to treat them as one experience.

ASSOCIATION

Locke had doubted that a man born blind, but who by some circumstance was later able to see, would be able to distinguish by vision a cube from a triangle even though both were known to him by touch. Berkeley unequivocally agreed.[79] The blind man now having sight would have to have new experiences, wherein sight and touch would be associated, just as a man born blind would have no idea of distance by means of vision and would have need of experience before being able to see. In this and in his explicit discussion of association he made the point that ideas are associated when they are connected in experience.

His classification of the principles of association—although he did not use that term—was more inclusive than Locke's and, even more important, he used it to account for normal associations.[80] He neatly summarized the nature of simultaneous association in the first paragraph of the *Principles*.[81] He states that complex ideas are formed because the ideas of sight (light and color), touch (hardness and softness), smell (odor), and so on accompany each other and come to be marked by one name. As an illustration, a certain color, taste, smell, figure, and consistency which have been observed to go together, we call *apple*. Elsewhere he writes:

men combine together several ideas apprehended by diverse senses or by the same sense at different times or in different circumstances, but observed, however, to have some connexion in Nature either with respect to co-existence or succession; all which they refer to one name and consider as one thing.[82]

Contiguity of sensation is the basis for a simultaneous association of ideas. He also specifies successive association and distinguishes among association by similarity, causality, and coexistence.[83]

ABSTRACT IDEAS

Since ideas arise from within separate sense departments, it is not surprising that Berkeley denied the existence of abstract ideas.[84] An abstract idea must involve material derived from several senses; otherwise, even advocates of the reality of abstract ideas would have to deny altogether that sensory content is present. For Berkeley, ideas are restricted to perceptions and images—and these come from sense and are always particular. Under such circumstances, Berkeley could not admit that abstractions were images presented to the mind. Berkeley did agree that we can form general ideas that stand for whole groups of phenomena. However, we can form no ideas from common content since there is no common content. We merely have words to denote this common element, but have no new ideas of it, strictly speaking. We can have words to connote such common features of perceived objects, but we cannot have new ideas of a strictly abstract content. One can emphasize the triangularity of a figure without attending to its other qualities, but Berkeley could not, try as he might, frame a definite idea of a triangle abstractly without any of these qualities.[85]

Mental processes, he held, are always particular.[86] A general idea is just as particular as the idea of any single object. The idea simply becomes general by standing for or representing all other particular ideas of the same sort.

VISUAL PERCEPTION AND SPACE

Berkeley's first presentation of his psychological thinking was *An Essay Towards A New Theory of Vision*.[87] It is psychology's first monograph and, in many ways, his most important work. Accordingly, it will serve to integrate what has been said as well as to bring us back to his attack on materialism.

Berkeley embarked upon his famous analysis of the problem of distance perception because of an objection to immaterialism that can be stated as follows: It was argued that we actually see things at a distance from ourselves, and consequently things exist independently of the mind. Common man thinks external objects can be seen and that direction and distance, as such, can be seen. "Out there" is a road, and beyond the road, a tree, and in the far distance there is a range of hills. Objects seem spread out before him, making him rebel against a contention that he has no knowledge of space from direct perception of it. Locke had said that perception occurs only mediately or indirectly by means of images or resemblance. But these images are still images of external things. To be consistent Berkeley had to go further and deny these external things if his espousal of the immateriality of the external world was to gain credence. He did this by an analysis of visual perception.

Berkeley[88] argued that the various properties of depth perception—shape, magnitude, distance, and the relative situation of objects—are not perceived directly by the eye but are learned after visual sensations have been associated with sensations of "touch" (in which he included movement in space, as in reaching and walking). Berkeley goes on to say that pictures cast upon the retina are flat and give no suggestion of the distances of objects from the eye. Nor does the degree of convergence of the eyes (as visual receivers) give us a clue to distance. Earlier workers had emphasized the difference in visual angles in explaining differences in visual convergence.[89] On the basis of introspective evidence, he argued that neither he nor anyone else is conscious of calculating the angle at which the eyes are converging. Even though convergence is present, there is nothing in the visual experience, as such, that would give the viewer a reason for associating a sensation of less convergence with more distant objects and vice versa. Berkeley does not deny the phenomena of convergence. Quite the contrary, he depends upon it, but it is the sensing of the *movement* of the eyes, not the shift in angles, that aids in perception of distance through convergence. When looking at an object, we "alter the disposition" of the eyes as the object approaches or recedes.[90] This is accompanied by a sensation bringing to mind the idea of greater or lesser distance; this in turn was learned from experience with situations where objects producing the sensation were associated with a given distance. He goes on in a similar vein to elucidate other phenomena involved in the perception of distance. To explain the visual perception of magnitude, he cites sensations arising from convergence, accommodation (straining of the eyes in focusing), and the blurring that occurs when the focus is poor.

One part of his argument merits special attention. It will be noted that Berkeley objected to the discussion of visual angles as an aspect of seeing. Much of the work on vision after Newton had been concerned with such matters. Berkeley's analysis of depth perception avoided a confusion prevalent then and still occurring today—the confusion between the psychology of vision and geometrical optics.[91] He was not opposed to the physical sciences, including this subdivision, merely to the confusion of the two areas.[92] Speaking generally, space is not perceived as such; it "is suggested to the mind by the mediation of some other idea which is itself perceived in the act of seeing."[93]

In this work on visual perception he did not appeal to association as such, but to what he called "uniting" in experience. It is evident that it was association that he meant. To Berkeley, distance perception was not a "given," immediately experienced, but something mediate that had to be learned. Berkeley believed he had demonstrated that sight and touch as expressed in movement have nothing intrinsically in common; "customary connexion" leads them to a common result. Space is not known directly but through this "connexion." This is essentially an experiential theory of visual perception of distance based on empiricism.

Berkeley's theory of space perception is a definite contribution to psychology since he demonstrated that distance or depth is not a sensation but an additional aspect of visual data. He reduced an apparently simple experience to the more primitive psychological experiences on which it was based. By stating that our perceptions of distance and magnitude are capable of reduction into simpler elements, he served to encourage those who came after him to attempt to analyze other experiences into elements, thus perpetuating the molecular approach. Berkeley made clear that the problem of knowledge is not a philosophical problem alone, but a distinctively psychological one as well.

David Hume

David Hume (1711–1776) was born in Scotland and educated at Edinburgh.[94] As a youth he gave his family some cause for misgivings about his future; his mother said of him that he was "a fine, good-natured crater but uncommon weak-minded." She was probably wrong about his intelligence: at least he later became Undersecretary of State. After several false starts he found his field in philosophical writing. But he was never satisfied with the acclaim that his writings received. Indeed, the reception of A Treatise of Human Nature, published anonymously before he was thirty, although it sold fairly well, fell so far below his high expectations that he was led to exclaim that it "fell dead-born from the press."[95] He recast the first part of the Treatise into what was later called An Enquiry Concerning Human Understanding, which, during his lifetime, had little more impact than its predecessor.[96] But he enjoyed widespread popularity from other writings, particularly a history of England. While serving in various governmental posts, he was frustrated in his attempts to secure a professorship; his unorthodox religious convictions and the skepticism of his views made him suspect to the establishment.

In introducing his *Enquiry,* Hume defined his investigation as that of moral philosophy or the science of human nature.[97] Man was a natural object in a world of nature, to be studied by the methods of natural science; thus Hume clearly affirmed his adherence to a naturalistic prescription. Moral subjects, in contrast to physical subjects, included ethics, politics, criticism, and logic conceived of as the art of reasoning.[98] This new psychological science was advanced to show that some things previously taken as inalienable features of the universe were actually characteristics of one's own psychological makeup projected onto the world.

Hume argued that we can do more than merely describe the operations of mental life; we can find the principles upon which these operations are based.[99] Astronomers, he goes on to say, patiently studied the motion, order, and magnitude of the stars; finally, a philosopher (Newton) determined the laws and the forces by which they are directed. Can we not, given equal capacity and caution, do the same with mental life? He answered in the affirmative because he thought he had found the law that corresponded to the law of gravitation in the physical world, the law of association of ideas, which seemed to him the universal principle of human nature.

Mental contents, Hume held, are of two sorts—the impressions arising from sensing, feeling, and willing, which are vivid and strong, and the ideas (images and thoughts, we might call them) that are less clear and fainter copies of impressions.[100] He specifically refused to assign any ultimate cause to impressions. He probably did not wish to deal with the source of external objects; at any rate, he held that impressions are the given elements from which all else starts. Ideas are derived from impressions. As he put it, we must learn from experience that fire burns and that water is wet.

To Hume, memory and imagination are not faculties but names for the two different ways in which ideas work.[101] Memory is distinguished from imagination by its greater clarity and vivacity and by the fact that the order of memories repeats the succession of the original impressions. Imagination is not as clear as impressions nor does it follow the same order, but it is relatively free in the course its reconstructions may take. Imagination may be compounded by transposition, augmentation, or diminution, but is still dependent upon material afforded by experience.[102]

The three principles or laws of association to account for mental operations are resemblance (similarity), contiguity in place or time, and causality.[103] To use some of his illustrations, a picture leads our thoughts to the original (resemblance), the mention of one apartment in a building leads to mention of others (contiguity), and if we think of a wound, we can scarcely avoid consideration of the pain that follows (causality).

As Hume's thinking developed, he seems to have become aware that causality was not on the same level of operation as the other two forms of association, and, without eliminating it from the list of the three principles, he reduced it to a special case of the other two. The relation of causality, he concluded, is not an ultimate law of the association of ideas but rests upon the two primary relations of similarity and space-time contiguity. One phenomenon follows another, and we come to expect it to happen again.[104]

All reasoning about factual matters, Hume said, seems to be founded on the relation of cause and effect.[105] What is the origin of our notion of cause? A billiard ball moves and knocks against another billiard ball, that also begins to move. Hume held that, despite this sequence, there is nothing in the motion of the first ball to suggest the necessity of the movement of the second. No intuition reveals the power whereby one object produces another. All we comprehend is one phenomenon following another. The senses do not supply the ideas of a necessary connection. Can it, perhaps, be due to reflection?[106] Consider, he says, the motion of our bodies when following the command of our will. Throughout the succession of events we are completely conscious, but can we tell how this operation is affected? Hume held that we cannot, and considered that it must forever escape our most diligent inquiry. Reflection does not supply the answer. All that we know is that the command of the will is followed by the action. We observe the succession of two phenomena—nothing more.

The mind cannot find the effect in the supposed cause, no matter how acute the scrutiny since the effect is totally different from the cause.[107] Frequent and invariable sequences make us assume that the effect must occur because the cause has occurred. Actually, there is no necessary relation of phenomena as is ordinarily implied by the concept of causality. Adam could not tell from the transparency and the fluidity of water that immersion would suffocate him.[108] Instead, we know from experience that objects are conjoined with similar ones. Hence, we can formulate another definition of cause and speak of it as "one object followed by another, the appearance of which always conveys the thought to that other."[109] To Hume, cause is recurrent concomitance.

Causation as seen by positivism

Thus the relation of causality is reduced to similarity and succession. Causality is a habit of mind originating in experience and the association of ideas. Causal experience is nothing more than customary expectation. The consciousness of determination, which pervades our view of causality, is false. Objectively considered, causality is regularity of contiguous sequence. The necessity of cause-effect exists only in the mind, not in objects.[110] Hume is sometimes misinterpreted as denying causation. He did not: he merely shifted the locus of causality from the external world to the mind in keeping with his theme mentioned earlier.

Hume held that the principle of connection between our ideas is habit.[111] Habit is the universal law of mind. Not only our external perceptions, but all of our experiences are explained by habit. As it has been put, "empiricism becomes associationism."[112] When two objects or two events are found constantly joined together, we infer one from the other. For example, flame has in the past been conjoined with heat, and snow with cold, so the presentation of one part of these pairs will lead the mind to expect the other part. For this to take place one experience is not sufficient, several experiences are necessary to establish a habit.

The mind was reduced by Hume to impressions and association of impressions. On introspective examination, Hume stated that he always came upon particular impressions and never more than impressions.[113] What is termed the mind is essentially nothing more than a bundle of sensations.[114] This conception of mind was to have a long history, culminating in the structuralism of Wundt and Titchener.

Hume's clear recognition of the importance of association and his formulation of the laws of association were crucial. Locke had never even considered using association as an explanation of mind and its functioning, but had relegated it to an explanation for abnormal connection between ideas. His theory that compounds of impressions and ideas give us more intricate mental phenomena is a concept to which later psychologists owe a great deal.

The significance of what Hume called his "very curious discovery"—that our knowledge of causation results from experience of habitual sequences of perceptions of events—was not fully appreciated during his lifetime but has since had great influence.[115] Hereafter all individuals concerned with the problem of determinism had to take into consideration Hume's devastating criticism that we could not prove causality since experience gave us only concomitance or succession of events. Kant's reaction to it is especially noteworthy (p. 229).

There has been a clear-cut progression of thought about the nature of experience and mind from Locke through Berkeley to Hume. Locke held that experience arose directly or basically from sense impression, but he accepted the existence of objects similar to, although not identical, with our ideas. Berkeley denied the existence of objects insofar as we, know them is concerned, but held that soul or mind is necessary to make experiences cohere or hold together. Hume took the obvious next step of questioning the existence of mind, reducing it to a collection of impressions from which all else starts.

David Hartley

David Hartley (1705–1759) is more important for his systematization of what had gone before than for his originality. Clarity and comprehensiveness, rather than subtlety, mark the account of association contained in his *Observations on Man,* first published in 1749.[116] The deliberate omission of Locke, the idealism of Berkeley, and the scepticism of Hume had exempted them from any need to pay attention to the relationship between physiological and mental processes. It was Hartley's work that restored the body and its functioning as the physical foundation for mental interconnections. Unable to become a minister because of doctrinal scruples, Hartley had become a medical practitioner, as might be anticipated from the very first sentence of his introduction to "*Observations:* Man Consists of Two Parts, Body and Mind."[117] He was a contemporary of Hume but began writing and publishing in a minor way on psychological matters before the appearance of the latter's *Treatise.* He was most influenced by Locke and Newton, although he acknowledged the influence of John Gay, a clergyman, whose writings had called his attention to associationism.

The portion of his *Observations* that is of psychological interest was followed by sections devoted to ethical and theological considerations. In passing it might be noted that he prepared for the transition from the psychological to the social and religious sphere by taking the position that if we know how associations are formed, this gives us the power to see to it that good ones are cherished and that sinful ones are rooted out.[118]

Besides its intrinsic merit, events have conspired to keep alive the psychological portions of *Observations;* the theological has been forgotten. In 1775 Joseph Priestley arranged republication of the portion devoted to psychology, without either the physiology or the theology.[119] In 1791, fifty years after original publication, Hartley's son issued another arrangement that was widely recognized as a clear statement of physiology and psychology as associational.[120]

Hartley said that man consists of two parts, mind and body.[121] Both must be studied because body and mind are related.[122] In the arrangement of the material in the 1791 edition, thereafter most widely used, the mental and bodily spheres are presented by Hartley in consecutive propositional form, one proposition dealing with the mind and the following one with the body. Thus, one proposition states that sensations, often repeated, leave certain vestiges that may be called simple ideas.[123] The companion proposition holds that sensory vibrations, being often repeated, leave in the brain a disposition for repetition of similar but minute vibrations.[124] Often the pairs of propositions are identical in statement except that the psychological term is replaced in the second by a physiological one.

The doctrine of vibration suggested by Newton's account of motion, Hartley tells us, is his starting point.[125] Newton had spoken of physical impulses as vibratory. Hartley held that external physical vibrations set in motion the white medullary substance of the brain with which sensations are intimately associated.[126] Changes in the former entail corresponding changes in the latter. Hartley insists that the nerves are solid, and are not tubes; this made necessary his postulation that vibrations transmit movement from one part of the body to another.

Although not entirely clear on the issue, he apparently held that cerebral vibrations and ideas perform in parallel. One is not the cause of the other. They simply show consistent correspondence. Events in one are correlated perfectly with events in the other. As a consequence, Hartley's view may be interpreted as a simple form of what is called psychophysical parallelism.[127]

Hartley agreed with Locke that the mind at birth is a blank.[128] Simple sensations supply all states of consciousness. Sensations are internal states of the mind arising from impressions made by external objects; all other internal states are ideas.

Hartley's law of association, the law of the growth of sensation and ideas, is that of contiguity, both synchronous (simultaneous) and successive.[129] The passage from sensation to idea or from idea to idea occurs because of associative contiguity. One is able to induce the other provided the latter has occurred in the past frequently, in conjunction with the former. The recurrence of one induces a repetition of the other. By means of the law of contiguity, Hartley explained memory, emotion, reasoning, and voluntary and involuntary action. One or two illustrations might be given. When sensory vibrations subside, they leave their trace in fainter vibrations, the "vibratiuncles." Like Hobbes' "decaying sense," they are the sources of memory and imagination (seeing a tree and remembering a tree are two sets of vibrations differing only in intensity). Vibrations are aroused by means of association. This is to say, when two sensations occur, either simultaneously or successively, they become connected so that when one is re-evoked later, the vibrations extend to the other, and we have an idea of that other. Associations are strengthened when vibration is greater. The association, under these circumstances, will be "cemented" sooner and stronger than is the case when the vibrations are less powerful.

Since association is both simultaneous and successive, it becomes for Hartley the basis for mental compounds or "clusters and combinations," as he calls them.[130] Simple ideas mix to form compounds just as letters coalesce into syllables and words. However, if the simple ideas in a particular compound are numerous, they may not be discernible in the complex because each single idea is overpowered by the sum of all the rest.

Hartley also broadened the conception of association to include motor activities—a movement may recall an idea; an idea may recall a movement. Ideas associated with movements form the basis for voluntary action. Muscular movements repeated in this same sequence become associated into automatic habits. His discussion of voluntary and involuntary action[131] attempts to relate the two, asserting that association by contiguity explains both how automatic movements come under voluntary control and how voluntary movements become automatic.

The special senses are discussed in detail by Hartley in a manner that distinguishes the dual roles of vibration and association.[132] Color, excited by an object, is a vibration of the rays that extend to the eye. In the eye the external vibration is changed to a backward and forward vibration of the nerve that extends to the brain, the seat of intelligence.

Hartley proceeds to apply the twin doctrines of vibrations and association to a number of other topics, ranging over sexual desires, respiration, words and associated ideas, passions or affections, memory, and imagination.[133] In so doing, he appears to be reasonably consistent.[134] He closes the portion of the volume devoted to psychological matters with a defense of determinism, though he continues to maintain that there is a difference between involuntary and voluntary motions. He argues that to state that A and its contrary a can follow from similar previous circumstances, is the same as affirming that they occur without cause. If this were the case, he goes on, the foundations of all abstract reasoning would be destroyed.

Hartley was the first to explain all forms of mental life on the basis of association, in a manner that rendered plausible a mechanistic base. Associationism as a system of psychology was thus formulated. For those who came after him, especially for James Mill (p. 213), the nature and implications of association had been outlined. Because it is simultaneous (as well as successive), association was still another step toward the mental atomism that was to come.

Hartley's speculative physiological propositions may be of little value today, but his point that body and mind cooperate to function conjointly has become an integral part of much modern psychological thinking. Still lacking was anything approaching a detailed understanding of the actual functioning of the nervous system.

The Scottish School

Thomas Reid (1710–1792), Dugald Stewart (1753–1828), and Thomas Brown (1778–1820) were all professors at Scottish universities; this led to their distinctive doctrines being referred to as those of the Scottish School.[135] The school was more persistent than original or profound. Its basic doctrine was that associationism, especially as promulgated by the sceptical Hume, had degraded the nature of man; and these Scottish professors wished to restore man to a dignity that would conform with Christian dogma. To this end they either rejected or modified associationism. Physiological explanations of behavior, especially Hartley's, they likewise rejected as derogatory to human dignity.

But skepticism menaced man in another way; it destroyed the guarantee of the existence of outside objects. Although far from a skeptic, Berkeley had contributed to this position by inverting the Lockean solution and insisting that initially there is conscious experience and that the problem then becomes how the mind creates objects. The general answer of the Scottish School was that objects are restored by appeal to "common sense," which renders them self-evident and open to all men, a view that is opposed to the subtleties (or sophistries) of the empiricists. Common sense is a vague term, but its employment in this argument shows a significant shift from the position taken in earlier centuries, when authority was the defense offered for religious orthodoxy. By contrast, the new orthodoxy answered the empiricists with the empirical defense of common sense. The Scottish School also answered with more specific assertions this problem of objective reference. Reid[136] conceived that the existence of external objects is divinely implanted. In the course of this argument he utilized the distinction between sensation as the raw data of experience and perception, which involves reference to an object. Brown[137] used association to show that Reid's distinction, naming sensation and perception as *powers,* could be interpreted instead in terms of sensitive and associative powers. This made it unnecessary to consider perception a distinct power but accounted equally well for the way in which we know objects.

Reid's faculty psychology[138] is much like that of Christian von Wolff (p. 227). Dugald Stewart[139] largely echoed this position, but Brown,[140] who was more original in his approach, broke from the tradition. Reid and Stewart opposed Hume's skepticism and his view of causality. Brown, however, comes near enough to the Humean view of causality to pose a problem in deciding whether or not he belongs in the Scottish School.[141]

While rejecting the skepticism of their predecessors, the members of the Scottish School kept associationism alive. Brown in particular drew closer to his associationist predecessors by proposing so-called secondary laws of "suggestion"[142] (he avoided the term "association" as implying mere passive sequence). Mind was more than a combination of elements. Quite apart from association, there was in it the unity of an operating, controlling self. The different kinds of possible union, the primary laws of suggestion, were resemblance, contrast, and nearness in time and space. The secondary laws of suggestion, conditional in nature, were duration, liveliness, frequency, recency, degrees of coexistence with other suggestions, constitutional differences of mind or of temperament, differing circumstances of the moment, state of health or efficiency of the body, and prior habits. These modified the primary laws according to prevailing conditions and explained why under specified conditions a particular suggestion appeared rather than another—why, at this particular time and place, the thought of "cold" brought forth "dark" rather than "hot"; why "butterfly" produced sometimes "bird," and sometimes "moth." Until nearly a century later, when the experimental attack on problems of learning began, this insight lay fallow.

Brown also distinguished simple from relative suggestion.[143] The latter occurs when we experience feelings of relation as distinguished from simple connections. These feelings include resemblance, difference, and proportion. For example, we have the experience that this house is bigger than that one, that this particular class of objects has the relation of subordinate to superordinate, that there is an equality of the square of the hypotenuse of a right angle to the square of the two other sides, or that there is an incongruity between the shallowness of a posturing player and the drama of heroic proportions in which he appears. So Brown recognized a capacity for learning simple associations. This was a contribution of some originality, anticipating the day when the combination of simple mental elements would be recognized as insufficient to account for learning and perception.

Brown[144] also spoke of a mental chemistry but used the term in precisely the opposite fashion of what it would usually mean today—the mental analysis of mental elements in isolation. Brown meant the appearance of a psychological combination that is not present in the elements—the taste of lemonade is a blend, not a sum of sweet and sour. This conception was to be sharpened by John Stuart Mill a little later (p. 215).

The Mills

James Mill (1773–1836) and his son, John Stuart Mill (1806–1873) have been labeled not too inappropriately "Utilitarian philosopher" and "philosopher" respectively.[145] Both are remembered as social theorists, economists, and leaders of the Utilitarians. But John Stuart later emancipated himself considerably from Utilitarian teachings and also achieved eminence in the fields of logic and the philosophy of science. In their Utilitarianism they followed their friend, Jeremy Bentham (1748–1832). The Utilitarian creed, as Bentham described it, exalted the principle of "Utility," summarized in the words "greatest good for the greatest number,"[146] which held that people are ruled by self-interest, and that social, political, and legal action ought to lead to the acquisition of pleasure and the avoidance of pain for the common good.[147] The term "utilitarian" has heretofore been applied to an attitude reflecting an interest in practical application. It is evident, however, that Bentham and the others were using the word in an even wider context as a means of relating the motivations of men to social good. In doing so Bentham was making a considerable contribution to the psychological problem of motivation and the philosophical problem of ethics.

James Mill began his career by being licensed to preach in the Church of Scotland, but "abandoned theology after his acquaintance with Bentham."[148] He then made his living by literary journalism until 1819 when he entered the home service of the East India Company. He is best remembered for his *History of India* (1818), an immense and influential volume. He ended his career as Examiner, that is, head of the company's office.

James Mill's psychology is most accessible in the *Analysis of the Phenomena of the Human Mind*.[149] It is an associationism, closer to Hartley and Hume than to Brown,[150] simplified and consisting of only two classes of mental elements: sensations and, when these are removed, ideas. All association, even by similarity, can be reduced to contiguity alone. Mill slightly tempered this extreme view by admitting two subdivisions of contiguity, successive and synchronous. Thus the words of a poem are associated successively, in time; the objects in a room synchronously, in space.

Mill applied a similar reductive procedure to the causes of variation of strength of association and accepted only frequency and vividness. Differences in strength of associations are explained by these two classes alone. Strength is comprised of permanence, certainty, and assurance, or "correctness," spontaneity, and ease of formation, or "facility."[151]

Association has another function; it serves to bind experiences together. A complex state of association holds within it all the original elements. The complex phenomena of the mind are formed out of simple ideas and sensations. The ideas of any object are the fusion of the ideas of the components, nothing more. Thus, the complex ideas of wall are made up of ideas of brick, mortar, position, and quantity. Complex ideas of plank, wall, and nail, united with ideas of position and quantity, compose an idea of floor. Similarly, glass, wood, and the like yield window, another complex idea. The even more complex idea of house comes from these ideas combined. Mill then works through furniture and merchandise and other things to the most complex idea of all, that of "everything," which is made up of these and all other ideas.

James Mill felt no need for any synthesis of ideas. Experiences sometimes appear to be simple, but indissoluble association really explains this. Psychological analysis shows that behind "simple" experiences a welter of elementary associations will always be found. Compounding, he held, was an absurdity. As Boring says, the whole is less, as well as more, than the sum of its parts.[152]

For Mill, association is neither power nor cause. It is a passive process; mind has no creative function. Sensations occur in a certain way, and are reproduced mechanically as ideas in that same order, one following the other. This brings association as a doctrine to its nadir in logical, mechanistic, and molecular simplicity.

John Stuart Mill had been a child prodigy. According to Cox and her associates his I.Q. in youth was 190, the highest they had obtained in their careful reconstruction of the intelligence quotients of many eminent men.[153] He was educated at home by his father, on a plan devised by him and by Bentham. At three he learned Greek, at eight he read Herodotus and Plato in the original. He had no boyhood friends, never learned to play, and was dominated by his father. This father-domination contributed to the mental crisis of John's early manhood, and helped to delay the publication of *Logic*[154] until 1843. His account of logical induction and deduction, and especially his clear explanation of the methods of agreement, difference, concomitant variation, and residues (the "Canons") is classic in scientific method, although not original with him.

The contents of the volume are broader than the main title suggests, especially in two respects.[155] An issue he faces squarely is whether or not there is a science of human nature. He answers in the affirmative with due consideration to the problems of exactitude and the presence of laws. It hardly approaches the ideal of exactitude, but it does have laws, the laws of association. He also suggests that alongside a general science of human nature, there should be a science to-be, ethology, the science of character. This was an idea ahead of its time and fated to be almost totally disregarded by those who came after him. At that time of the publication of the *Logic* he was thirty-seven, young in years, old in thought, and affected by his relationship with Harriet Taylor, whom he married after the death of her husband. After *Logic*, his works were considerably influenced by her. His output was voluminous, and included works on philosophy, economics, political science, and psychology.

John Stuart Mill's more specific psychological views also appear as supplemental material to the expanded 1869 edition of his father's *Analysis*.[156] Besides editing, along with Alexander Bain and others, he contributed voluminous notes. But, as shown in his *Logic*,[157] he emancipated himself from the rigid, atomistic associationism of his father. He stressed activity in mind (i.e., it was more than the vehicle for adding new experiences), asserted that the combination of mental elements give rise to something new, something not present in the original. In the compound, the parts disappear and new properties emerge that bear little or no resemblance to their constituent elements. The whole is more than the sum of the parts. This was also to become a central problem for the Gestalt school (p. 473).

John Stuart Mill also contributed to that perennial problem of the reality of the existence of external objects by holding that the mind is aware of matter since it is capable of a permanent possibility of sensation, which is the same as saying that one believes in matter.[158]

John Stuart Mill was a gentler, more human, and less "dry" character than his father. Of the two, John is the greater in the history of thought, but as a psychologist he is of less consequence.

Alexander Bain

Alexander Bain (1818–1903) was born, lived, and worked for most of his life in Aberdeen, Scotland. He had brief schooling (until his twelfth year) and was trained as a weaver like his father. Continuing his education through night school and reading, he entered Marischal College in 1836, where he became assistant to the professor of Moral Philosophy. As a student he wrote for the *Westminster Review* and began a lifelong friendship with John Stuart Mill, later taking the lead in revising James Mill's *Analysis of the Phenomena of the Human Mind*. This contact in London resulted in his appointment as Assistant Secretary to the (London) Metropolitan Sanitary Commission, after a brief period he spent teaching in Glasgow.[159]

Bain's major work covers two volumes, *The Senses and the Intellect* (1855)[160] and *The Emotions and the Will* (1859).[161] These remained standard, as revised, for nearly half a century. Bain's thoroughness is evident in his coverage of previous literature, exhaustive for the British and more comprehensive than usual for the Continental. These texts were the first to link psychology to physiological knowledge other than in an imaginary fashion, as Hartley did. He paid particular attention to reflexes. He treated habit and instinct fully, and belief more pragmatically than others of his time did. His analysis of the origin and development of volition is penetrating.

These publications probably brought about the turning point in Bain's life. It is said that his radicalism (including a flirtation with positivism), and his refusal to become a church member helped to render abortive previous applications for university chairs.[162] But, in 1860, he was at last appointed professor of Logic and Rhetoric at the University of Aberdeen. He remained there in this capacity until 1880, and in various honorary offices until his death in 1903.

Bain's *Mind and Body*,[163] *A Manual of Mental and Moral Science*,[164] and *On the Study of Character*,[165] all belong to his professorial years. The first contains a discussion of his solution to the mind-body problem in which mind and body are seen as forming a unity, observed either objectively as matter or subjectively as mind. The second was a condensation and up-dating of the main works. The last was a pioneer work on personality, with a specially telling critique of phrenology. Bain was also the founder and the original proprietor of the journal, *Mind*, which first appeared in January, 1876. This was the first journal of philosophical psychology. But the time was not yet ripe for an experimental journal; this is why Wundt's journal, although seven years younger than *Mind*, is considered the first journal of modern psychology.

His later writings (barring revisions of his major texts) scarcely are of concern to us. They relate mostly to the other areas (rhetoric, grammar, education, administration) to which he contributed. It is as a psychologist that he is mainly remembered, being the only man in his day recorded as such.[166]

Argument has run high as to the nature of Bain's position in the history of psychology. Is he the last of the old psychologists or the first of the new? He was new in his stress on physiology, and his broadening and reworking of associationism to make it serve as the basis of a psychology assimilated to that discipline. But despite his forward-looking view of mind and body as a "double-faced unit," he was old in his cautious parallelism. His views on social psychology and individual differences were more modern than is usually realized.[167] He did not assimilate evolution the way Spencer did, however, although he gave great weight to Darwin's work on emotional expression in animals as illustrating the physical side of anger.[168] He also modified an edition of The Emotion and the Will to include a chapter on evolution as related to the emotions,[169] but he thought "the history of the highest races does not fall in with evolution",[170] by which he meant man from the Greeks onwards. The main forward-looking aspect of Bain's psychology is that it rests upon a genuine, thorough, and up-to-date physiology, not a mythical physiology like the one created by Hartley, who fit his to the psychological facts as he saw them.[171] Bain's Autobiography shows the care he took to read, visit with, and understand major physiologists and anatomists, in order to distinguish fact from conjecture.[172] For instance, his analysis of hunger shows how he achieved accuracy in his detailed appraisal of this area (perhaps Bain's dyspepsia also motivated him).[173] Yet he still regarded conscious data as primary and he was no reductionist. To him, the place of psychological experiment was limited.

Bain's modification of associationism had similar Janus-like qualities. According to Cardno, his principal statement in all four editions of The Senses and the Intellect is as follows.[174] "Actions, sensations or states of feeling, occurring together or in close succession, tend to grow together or cohere in such a way that when any one of them is afterwards presented to the mind, the others are apt to be brought up. . . ."[175] This cohesion embraced contiguity as the law of association proper. Similarity was considered the second principle of association. Bain's major innovation was to assimilate somewhat more adroitly what had been called "mental chemistry" when discussing Mill. Following Brown, Mill had introduced the principle into associationism, but in his system it had no more than the position of an attached foreign body.

Constructive association or imagination, as Bain called the principle, was seen as supplemental to association by contiguity and similarity:

"by means of association the mind has the power to form new combinations or aggregates *different* from any that have been presented to it in the course of experience."[176] Although it was not considered so by Bain, constructive association can also be interpreted as less than total reliance on association. This is not the only instance of this use of nonassociationistic factors. In detail, Bain is often forward-looking. Thus, in constructive association-making, new combinations required something more than associations to account for novelty. Moreover, infants possess reflexes, instincts, and differences in acuteness. True, there are no innate ideas, but there are innate behaviors prior to education. Heredity was accepted as operative by Bain, yet his adherence to association as a general principle, especially with the vocabulary he uses, is limited. He represents a culmination rather than a radical initiation. The nature of the culmination is indicated by the fact that Bain can be suitably discussed here, but Herbert Spencer, two years younger, can be discussed only after considering Darwin. After Bain, association would still live on but not under its old banner. If present-day interests of the philosopher in psychology are disregarded as not being in the mainstream of the history of psychology, then Bain was the last philosopher-psychologist in Great Britain. Probably the evaluation that his psychology is full of germinal ideas that he failed to develop is as near as we can come to a one-sentence appraisal.[177]

Overview

Newton was the seminal figure for the major English empiricists. He had demonstrated that material nature may be studied successfully by considering that one was dealing with particles propelled by force into motion or changes of motion. Without being too explicit about their source, Locke applied Newtonian materialistic conceptions to mental life; Berkeley directly attacked the materialistic implications of Newton by denying that matter was involved, but otherwise accepted his thinking; Hume directly and avowedly applied Newtonian materialistic conceptions to the mind.

The points concerning British empiricism and associationism presented in this chapter form a complex interlocking pattern to which many individuals contributed, so that only the very broadest of trends will be offered in summary. Empiricism, a prescription to which all of those discussed subscribed, became a viable alternative to rationalism. The quantitative and methodological objectivism of the physical sciences was evident to these students of human nature and they made some beginnings in following these leads. There was a skepticism about reaching absolute certainty either avowed or expressed implicitly. The caution they displayed in the kind of evidence offered moved in the direction of a greater methodological objectivism. Despite Berkeley's spirited and brilliant appeal to supernaturalism and the dogged defense of it offered by the Scottish School, naturalism was becoming more commonplace. The importance of ideas and the way they were combined resulted in the acceptance of centralism, dualism, contentual subjectivism and molecularism. Hobbes alone raised some incoherent objections to centralism, dualism, and contentual subjectivism. Interest in utilitarianism increased. Both inductive and deductive procedures were followed and clarified, especially from the time of John Stuart Mill.

References*

1. An excellent authoritative source for the early history of the Royal Society is the account of Dorothy Stimson, *Scientists and Amateurs, a History of the Royal Society* (New York: Schuman, 1948); while R. K. Merton's "Science, Technology and Society in Seventeenth Century England," *Orisis*, 4, (1938): 360–362, is a detailed quantitative study which brings out clearly, among other findings, the utilitarian character of much of the science and technology of the time.

2. I. Newton, *Opticks* (London: Smith and Walford, 1704).

3. I. Newton, "The Mathematical Principles of Natural Philosophy," in R. M. Hutchins, ed., *The Great Books of the Western World*, Vol. XXXIV (Chicago: Encyclopaedia Britannica, 1952) pp. 1–372 (1687).

4. *Ibid.*, pp. 1–2.

5. I. Newton, "An Hypothesis Explaining the Properties of Light Discoursed in My Several Papers," T. Birch, *History of the Royal Society of London* (London: Millar, 1757), Vol. III, pp. 262–263 (1675). (Herrnstein and Boring, Excerpt No. 2).

6. Newton, *Opticks*, Book 1, part 2, props. 5–6 (Herrnstein and Boring, Excerpt No. 3).

7. T. Hobbes, "Leviathan," ed. Nelle Fuller, in R. M. Hutchins, ed., *The Great Books of the Western World*, Vol. XXIII, pp. 49–283 (1651). Part 1, Chapter 26.

8. *Ibid.*

9. T. Hobbes, "Human Nature," ed. W. Molesworth,

*See p. 19 for description of reference style.

in R. S. Peters, ed., *Body, Man and Citizen* (New York: Collier Books, 1962), pp. 182–244 (1650).

10. *Ibid.*, Chapter 1, Conclusion; *Leviathan*, Introduction.
11. *Ibid.*, Part I, Chapter 13, p. 85.
12. *Ibid.*, Part I, Chapter 2.
13. *Ibid.*, Part I, Chapters 2, 7.
14. *Ibid.*, Part I, Chapters 1, 2, 7.
15. Hobbes, *Leviathan*, Part 1, Chapter 2.
16. Hobbes, *Human Nature*, Chapter 2, Sec. 4.
17. *Ibid.*, p. 185.
18. Hobbes, *Leviathan*, Part 1, Chapter 3 (Herrnstein and Boring, Excerpt No. 66).
19. *Ibid.*, Part II, Chapter 30.
20. *Ibid.*, Part I, Chapter 6.
21. *Ibid.*, Part I, Chapter 11, p. 76.
22. *Ibid.*, Part I, Chapter 6.
23. *Ibid.*, Part I, Chapter 5, Part II, Chapter 19.
24. *Ibid.*, Part II, Chapter 27.
25. *Human Nature*, Chapter 12.
26. An excellent account, not only of his life but also of his views on philosophy, psychology, ethics, education, and politics is to be found in R. I. Aaron, *John Locke*, 3rd ed. (Oxford: Clarendon Press, 1971).
27. J. Locke, "Letter Concerning Toleration," trans. W. Popple, in R. M. Hutchins, ed., *The Great Books of the Western World*, Vol. XXXV, pp. 1–22 (1689).
28. *Ibid.*
29. J. Locke, "An Essay Concerning Human Understanding," 6th ed., collated and annotated by A. C. Frazer, *Ibid.*, pp. 85–395 (1690).
30. J. Locke, "Essay."
31. J. Locke, *The Conduct of the Understanding* (New York: Alden, 1883) (1706).
32. Locke, "Essay," Epistle to the Reader, p. 87.
33. *Ibid.*, Introduction, 2.
34. *Ibid.*, Introduction, 3, p. 94.
35. *Ibid.*, Book I, Chapter I.
36. *Ibid.*, Book I, Chapter I, Sec. 25.
37. *Ibid.*, Book I, Chapter IV, Sec. 24.
38. *Ibid.*, Book I, Chapter II, Sec. 22.
39. *Ibid.*, Book I, Chapter I, Sec. 15, p. 98.
40. *Ibid.*, Book II, Chapter I, Sec. 25.
41. *Ibid.*, Book II, Chapter II, Sec. 1.
42. *Ibid.*, Book IV, Chapter IV.

43. *Ibid.*, Book II, Chapter II.
44. *Ibid.*, Book II, Chapter VIII (Herrnstein and Boring, Excerpt No. 5).
45. *Ibid.*, Book II, Chapter I, Secs. 1–4 (Herrnstein and Boring, Excerpt No. 104).
46. *Ibid.*, Book II, Chapter VIII, Sec. 8.
47. *Ibid.*, Book II, Chapter IX, Sec. 1.
48. *Ibid.*, Book II, Chapter XXII, Sec. 2.
49. *Ibid.*, Book II, Chapter XIII.
50. *Ibid.*, Book II, Chapter XII, Sec. 8.
51. *Ibid.*, Book II, Chapter I, Sec. 1.
52. *Ibid.*, Book II, Chapter XXIX–XLII.
53. *Ibid.*, Book II, Chapter XX.
54. *Ibid.*, Book II, Chapter XXXIII (Herrnstein and Boring, Excerpt No. 67).
55. *Ibid.*, Book II, Chapter X, Sec. 3.
56. *Ibid.*, Book II, Chapter XII, Sec. 8.
57. *Ibid.*, Book II, Chapter XXI, Sec. 71.
58. *Ibid.*, Book II, Chapter XXXIII.
59. G. Berkeley, "A Treatise Concerning the Principles of Human Knowledge," in R. M. Hutchins, ed., *The Great Books of the Western World*, Vol. XXXV, pp. 404–444 (1710) Sec. 93.
60. *Ibid.*, Sec. 87.
61. The definitive statement of his life and works is by A. A. Luce, *The Life of George Berkeley, Bishop of Cloyne* (London: Nelson, 1949).
62. G. Berkeley, "An Essay Towards a New Theory of Vision," A. A. Luce and T. E. Jessop, eds., *Works* (London: Nelson, 1949), Vol. I, pp. 159–239 (1709).
63. "Principles."
64. R. A. Tsanoff, *The Great Philosophers* (New York: Harper and Brothers 1953), p. 365.
65. G. Berkeley, "Three Dialogues Between Hylas and Philonus," A. A. Luce and T. E. Jessop, eds., *Works*, Vol. II, pp. 171–263 (1713). Third Dialogue, p. 249.
66. "New Theory," 12, p. 173.
67. "Principles," Sec. 145.
68. *Ibid.*, Sec. 3, p. 413.
69. *Ibid.*, Sec. 35.
70. G. A. Ferguson, "A Note on George Berkeley," *Canadian Journal of Psychology*, VII (1953): 156–158.
71. "Principles," Sec. 12, 98, 117.
72. *Ibid.*, Secs. 146–147.
73. R. Knox quoted in B. Russell, *A History of Western*

Philosophy (New York: Simon and Schuster, 1945), p. 648.

74. "Principles," Sec. 1.

75. *Ibid.*, Secs. 10, 14–15.

76. *Ibid.*, Secs. 9–15.

77. *Ibid.*, Sec. 1.

78. E.g., "Principles," Sec. 30.

79. "New Theory," 41–42, 50.

80. Another summarization of his way of conceiving the connection among ideas is given in G. Berkeley, "The Theory of Vision Vindicated and Explained," A. A. Luce and T. E. Jessop, eds., *Works*, Vol. I, pp. 251–276 (1733) (Herrnstein and Boring, Excerpt No. 68).

81. "Principles," Sec. 1.

82. "Dialogues," Third Dialogue, p. 245.

83. H. C. Warren, *A History of the Association Psychology* (New York: Charles Scribner's Sons, 1921), p. 245.

84. "Principles," Introduction, Secs. 6–25.

85. *Ibid.*, Introduction, Sec. 13.

86. *Ibid.*, Introduction, Sec. 10.

87. "New Theory," (Herrnstein and Boring, Excerpts Nos. 28, 36).

88. *Ibid.*, 16–28, 52–87, 111–112, 121–159.

89. *Ibid.*, 2–15.

90. *Ibid.*, 17, p. 175.

91. *Ibid.*, 14–24.

92. *Ibid.*

93. *Ibid.*, 12, p. 173.

94. F. C. Mossner, *The Life of David Hume* (London: Nelson, 1954).

95. D. Hume, *A Treatise of Human Nature*, 2 vols., ed. A. D. Lindsay, (London: Dent, 1911) (1739–1740).

96. D. Hume, "An Enquiry Concerning Human Understanding," ed. L. A. Selby-Bigge, in R. M. Hutchins, ed., *The Great Books of the Western World*, Vol. XXXV, pp. 449–509 (1748).

97. *Ibid.*, Div. 1, p. 451.

98. "Treatise," Preface.

99. "Enquiry,", 9.

100. *Ibid.*, 12 (Herrnstein and Boring, Excerpt No. 69, involves another edition of Div. 11–17).

101. Hume, "Treatise," Book I, Part I, Sec. III.

102. Hume, "Enquiry," Div. 13.
103. *Ibid.*, Div. 19.
104. *Ibid.*, Div. 59.
105. *Ibid.*, Div. 24–25.
106. *Ibid.*, Div. 48–57.
107. *Ibid.*, Div. 24.
108. *Ibid.*, Div. 23.
109. *Ibid.*, Div. 60.
110. "Treatise," Book I, Part III, Sec. XIV.
111. Hume, "Enquiry," Div. 36.
112. P. Janet and G. Seailles, *A History of the Problems of Philosophy*, Part 1, *Psychology* (New York: Macmillan, 1902) p. 369.
113. "Treatise," Book I, Part IV, Sec. VI.
114. *Ibid.*, Book I, Part IV, Sec. IV.
115. D. Hume, "An Abstract of a Treatise of Human Nature," A. Flew, ed., *David Hume: On Human Nature and the Understanding* (New York: Collier, 1962), pp. 287–302, p. 294 (1740).
116. D. Hartley, *Observations on Man, his Frame, his Duty and his Expectations*, 2 vols. (London: Richardson, 1749) (Scholars' Facsimiles and Reprints, 1966).
117. *Ibid.*, Introduction, p. III.
118. *Ibid.*, Sec. II, Prop. 14.
119. J. Priestley, *Hartley's Theory of the Human Mind, on the Principles of Association of Ideas with Essays Relating to the Subject of It* (London: Johnson, 1775) (1749).
120. D. Hartley, *Observations on Man*, 6th rev. ed., 3 vols. (London: Tegg, 1834) (1791).
121. *Ibid.*, Part 1, Introduction.
122. *Ibid.*, Chapter I.
123. *Ibid.*, Chapter I, Sec. I, Prop. VIII.
124. *Ibid.*, Chapter I, Sec. I, Prop. XIX.
125. *Ibid.*, Chapter I.
126. *Ibid.*, Chapter I, Sec. I, Prop. II.
127. There is good evidence (see e.g., Peters, *Body, Man and Citizen* pp. 423–424) that Hartley was at heart an occasionalist but this point was not appreciated by those whose work he inspired.
128. *Observations*, Part I, Introduction.
129. *Observations*, 1749, Vol. 1, Chapter I, Sec. 2, Prop. 9, 10, 12 (Herrnstein and Boring, Excerpt No. 70).
130. *Ibid.*, p. 73.
131. *Ibid.*, Vol. 1, Chapter I, Sec. 3, Prop. 18, 21 (Herrnstein and Boring, Excerpt No. 59).

132. *Ibid.*, Vol. 1, Chapter II, Sec. 1–5.

133. *Ibid.*, Vol. 1, Chapter II, Sec. 6–7, Chapter III.

134. *Ibid.*, Conclusion.

135. S. A. Grave, *The Scottish Philosophy of Common Sense* (Oxford: Clarendon Press, 1960).

136. T. Reid, *Essays on the Intellectual Powers of Man* (London: Macmillan Ltd., 1941) (1785) Essay 2, Chapters 5, 16. (Herrnstein and Boring, Excerpt No. 37).

137. T. Brown, *Lectures on the Philosophy of the Human Mind* (Boston: Hallowell, 1828) (1820) II, Lec. 25 (Herrnstein and Boring, Excerpt No. 38).

138. Reid, *Essays.*

139. D. Stewart, *Elements of the Philosophy of the Human Mind,* 3 vols. (London: Tegg, 1867) (1793–1817).

140. Brown, *Lectures.*

141. F. Copleston, *A History of Philosophy* (London: Burns, Oates, 1929), Vol. V, pp. 383–385.

142. Brown, *Lectures* (Herrnstein and Boring, Excerpt No. 71).

143. *Ibid.*

144. *Ibid.*

145. *Concise Dictionary of National Biography. Part 1, From the Beginnings to 1900* (London: Oxford University Press, 1961), pp. 875–876.

146. J. Bentham, *Works,* ed. J. Bowring (Edinburgh: Tait, 1838–1843), Vol. X, pp. 142.

147. J. Bentham, *Theory of Legislation* (Oxford: Clarendon Press, 1914) (1789).

148. *Concise Dictionary,* p. 875.

149. J. Mill, *Analysis of the Phenomena of the Human Mind* (London: Longmans and Dyer, 1829).

150. Warren, *Association.*

151. Mill, *Analysis* (Herrnstein and Boring, Excerpt No. 72).

152. E. G. Boring, *Sensation and Perception in the History of Experimental Psychology* (New York: Appleton-Century, 1942), p. 9.

153. C. M. Cox, *et al., Genetic Studies of Genius, Vol. II, Regarding Mental Traits of Three Hundred Geniuses* (Stanford: Stanford University Press, 1926).

154. J. S. Mill, *A System of Logic, Ratiocinative and Inductive, Being a Connected View of the Principles of Evidence, and the Methods of Scientific Investigation,* 8th ed. (New York: Harper and Brothers, 1874) (1843).

155. *Ibid.*, Chapters 4, 5.

156. J. Mill, *Analysis of the Phenomena of the Human Mind*, New ed. with notes, illustrative and critical, by A. Bain, A. Findlater, and G. Grote, ed., with additional notes by J. S. Mill (New York: Longmans, Green, Reader and Tyler, 1869).

157. Mill, *Logic*.

158. J. S. Mill, *An Examination of Sir William Hamilton's Philosophy* (London: Longmans, Green and Reader, 1865 (Herrnstein and Boring, Excerpt No. 39).

159. A. Bain, *Autobiography* (London: Longmans, Green, 1904).

160. A. Bain, *The Senses and the Intellect* (London: Parker, 1855).

161. A. Bain, *The Emotions and the Will* (London, Parker, 1859).

162. Bain, *Autobiography*, pp. 174, 196.

163. A. Bain, *Mind and Body*. London: King, 1873 (Herrnstein and Boring, Excerpt No. 108).

164. A. Bain, *A Manual of Mental and Moral Science* (London: Longmans, Green, 1875) (1869).

165. A. Bain, *On the Study of Character, Including an Estimate of Phrenology* (London: Parker, 1861).

166. J. A. Cardno, "Victorian Psychology: A Biographical Approach," *Journal of the History of Behavioral Sciences*, I, (1965): 165–177.

167. J. A. Cardno, "Bain and Individual Differences," *Aberdeen University Review*, XL (1963): 124–132; J. A. Cardno, "Bain as a Social Psychologist," *Australian Journal of Psychology*, VIII (1955): 66–75.

168. A. Bain, *The Emotions and the Will*, 3rd ed. (New York: Appleton, 1875) (1859).

169. *Ibid.*, Preface.

170. *Ibid.*, p. xiii.

171. J. A. Cardno, "Bain and Physiological Psychology," *Australian Journal of Psychology*, VII (1955): 108–120.

172. Bain, *Autobiography*.

173. J. A. Cardno, "Bain, Lewes, and Hunger," *Psychological Reports*, II (1956): 267–278.

174. *Ibid.*

175. A. Bain, *The Senses and the Intellect*, 3rd ed. (London: Longmans, Green, 1868), p. 327.

176. *Ibid.*, "Intellect," Chapter 4, Sec. 1, p. 570.

177. L. S. Hearnshaw, *A Short History of British Psychology: 1840–1940* (New York: Barnes and Noble, 1964), p. 13.

Chapter 9

Kant AND Herbart:
THE APEX OF RATIONALISM AND THE FURTHER DIFFERENTIATION OF PSYCHOLOGY

The field of philosophical psychology would have to take into consideration the thinking of Immanuel Kant as it did the work of Plato, Aristotle, and Descartes. How he viewed psychology had a profound effect upon both those who agreed and those who disagreed with him. A sharpening and clarification of the distinction between a rational psychology and an empirical psychology resulted. Before considering his viewpoint, it is necessary to examine the views of his teacher, Christian von Wolff.

Wolff and Faculty Psychology

Implicitly or explicitly, a doctrine of faculties has often appeared in earlier theories of psychology. The soul was conceived of as carrying on its functions, such as knowing, remembering, feeling, and willing, by making use of corresponding faculties. The first important proponent of eighteenth-century German faculty psychology was Christian von Wolff (1679–1754), for most of his academic life, a professor at Halle. To place him in temporal perspective, he was most influenced by Leibniz, his older contemporary. His view is representative of the several versions of faculty psychology prevailing on the continent in the period from the middle of the eighteenth century through most of the nineteenth century. In no sense is he to be counted among the greatest psychologists, but his influence on Kant would be sufficient reason to mention him. His two psychologies, rational and empirical, set the stage for Kant.

Wolff's *Empirical Psychology*[1] made its appearance in 1732 and was followed two years later by his *Rational Psychology*.[2] He saw the tasks of these two psychologies as interrelated. Rational psychology deduces from metaphysical conceptions and from the experience of the soul's activities; empiricial psychology is concerned with man, the composite of body and soul. This way of formulating the distinction between rational and empirical psychology has methodological implications based on emphasis, since in Wolff's view rational psychology depends more on reason and less on experience, and empirical psychology more on experience than on reason. For him this is primarily a contentual distinction. Soul is the concern of rational psychology; man (soul and matter) is the concern of empirical psychology. Both psychologies use the two methods but in varying degrees. Following similar thinking on the part of Leibniz, Wolff held that rational psychology gives clear and distinct ideas, while empirical psychology yields only obscure, confused ideas of things. Rational psychology depends on reason; empirical psychology, on sensation. At one extreme are the confused ideas of sensation; at the other are the clear ideas of reason. In short, mental activities consist of degrees of reason or clarity of ideas.

The major theme of his empirical psychology is that, while the soul is unitary[3] and lacks parts,[4] it has different powers and faculties. According to Wolff, faculties are "potencies of action" that are expressed in powers.[5] The major dual classification of groups of faculties are knowing, on the one hand, and feeling and desire, on the other.[6] Knowing is further subdivided into perception, memory, understanding, and reason. To take memory as an example: asked why something is remembered, Wolff would reply that it is remembered because one has a faculty of memory. Unfortunately, to ascribe a mental activity to a faculty serves to explain it and makes further analysis unnecessary. It was not apparent then that the doctrine of faculties is self-defeating and circular.

Wolff's distinction between empirical and rational psychology, though deviating from the usual (since it was not primarily a methodological one) was prophetic of changes to come. It clarified the existence of two psychologies, even though Wolff derogated empirical psychology and defined it in such a way as to make it subordinate to rational psychology.

Kant and Transcendental Mental Activity

Immanuel Kant (1724–1804), who never traveled more than sixty miles from his birthplace in East Prussia, lived the uneventful life of a philosophy professor at the University of Königsberg. Most of the stories his chroniclers tell concern nothing more than interruptions of his bachelor routines—the consternation of his neighbors when one day he failed to take his walk at the usual precise hour (he had been enthralled with Rousseau's *Emile*); or the crisis brought about by fast-growing poplars that obscured his view of the church steeple he habitually gazed at while meditating (the owner of the trees obligingly cut their tops); or the trouble he had avoiding sightseers after he became famous (which led him to find a new restaurant in which to take his noonday meal).

The influence of Kant upon continental thought proved to be enormous. Although not without opposition (his successors, in fact, set out immediately to "correct" his views), he dominated philosophical thinking for generations. His most influential work relevant to psychology, *Critique of Pure Reason,* appeared first in 1781.[7] This publication was followed in 1788 by his *Critique of Practical Reason,*[8] and in 1790 by his *Critique of Judgment.*[9] The very titles of these, his three most important works, show that they bear some relation to psychology. But to say that his inquiry was related to psychology is by no means the same as saying that his approach was psychological in nature. On the contrary, he repeatedly insisted it was not. As he conceived it, his philosophical task was concerned with the question of the validity of knowledge. He understood psychology as an empirical search for the laws of mental functioning. His empirical psychological views are contained in his *Anthropology,* just recently completely translated into English.[10] Although he had taught a course with the title for many years, beginning as early as 1772, it was not until 1798 that he prepared the lectures for publication.[11] His contributions of greater moment to psychology came from his critical philosophy, not from his psychology.

In his earlier years Kant did little more than critically elaborate Wolff's rationalist and faculty doctrines. Reading Hume, he was aroused from his dogmatic slumbers. For Hume, causality was neither self-evident nor capable of logical demonstration. Kant was not only convinced by Hume's argument, he also realized that this same lack of certainty must be true of all other principles fundamental to philosophy and science. There were two alternatives: either to accept Hume's skepticism or to find a *priori* principles free of the defect Hume noted. It is possible to arrive inductively at general laws only if it is also possible to establish independently a *priori* rational principles.[12] As a rationalist, Kant could not accept the alternative of skepticism, so his task became one of establishing that synthetic a *priori* principles are possible, despite Hume's cogent objection. He therefore set for himself the task of demonstrating the existence of these rationalistic principles.

Kant agreed with Hume that all known objects are phenomena of consciousness and not realities independent of the mind. But for Kant empiricism is not enough. The known object is not a mere bundle of sensations, for knowledge of it includes "unsensational" characteristics or manifestations of a priori principles. That is to say, in addition to sense data, phenomena would not be possible without the mind, which is inherently capable of ordering phenomena.[13]

Kant insisted that the scientist and the philosopher approach nature with certain implicit principles that underlie experience, and he understood his task to be finding these principles and making them explicit. He proceeded to derive them from careful rational inquiry into the logical forms of judgments that we make about the world.

These various transcendental principles, or "categories," as Kant[14] called them, are activities of the mind; to the extent that they are universal, necessary, and independent of sense experience, they are a priori. Consider the argument expressed in the following example: Events follow other events according to rules. Every event has a cause. Nature itself is a system of causal relations. These statements have always been accepted as valid, but they cannot be verified experientially. They are a priori because they are conditions for the possibility of experience, that is, without causality and the other categories one would have no way for ordering experiences into a phenomenal world of objects. So causality was naturally one of Kant's categories. This particular illustration was chosen because it also served to answer Hume. We cannot know causality from experience, but we do know it a priori.[15] Kant's twelve categories of understanding include unity, reality, totality, existence or nonexistence, and community or reciprocity.[16]

Kant reinforced the argument for his categories of understanding by claiming that intuitive forms of sensibility also exist prior to experience. Space and time are intuitively knowable, a priori.[17] Kant held that consciousness of time and extension in space are certainly real and not data of the bodily senses. All objects of pure perception are located in space and time, without which objects would not be perceptible. We go on from them to perception of content through experience. They are the forms of intuition as distinguished from the contents of experience. The forms of sensibility of space and time join the transcendental principles and, together with them, become the means of structuring and understanding the world.

With its concept of space as a priori, Kant's philosophy was a forerunner of what were to emerge as the nativistic theories of space.[18] It had definite ties with Cartesian notions of innate ideas, but it was not the same. Man is not born with ideas but with principles of ordering that provide the conditions for the possibility of experience.

Before dealing with the mind, the more general problem of Kant's view of mathematics and science must be mentioned. Kant was very much concerned with scientific problems. The profound impression science had made on him strikingly demonstrated in his emphasis upon space and time and causality. To him, mathematics is the source of scientific knowledge. This follows because much of mathematics represents *a priori,* absolute, nonempirical judgments requiring no further proof. He believed, and considered he had proved, that an empirical inquiry is as scientific as the amount of mathematics it contains.[19] To Kant, science is exact, quantitative, and mathematical, a view that dominates science to this very day.

Kant dealt specifically with the problem of the mind.[20] The great modern rationalists—Descartes, Leibniz, and Spinoza—although differing among themselves, sought to know mind through mind. Kant attacked what he considered their fallacious belief that mind is a substance, i.e., that it is "some thing." To state his argument in detail would be impracticable; it is enough to say he demonstrated to his own satisfaction that mind is insubstantial and a purely formal unity. Rejection of mind as substance had direct implications for psychology as a science. It followed that mental processes cannot be measured, since they have only the dimension of time and not space.[21] Psychology cannot possibly be an experimental science if it has but one dimension of time, because there is no other variable with which to relate temporal events.

This did not mean that Kant rejected the concept of the mind. As a formal unity he lifted it to the pinnacle of his system, for he held mind to be the means whereby the categories and concepts are known. Without being spatial, the mind orders perceptual phenomena through the innate principles of time and space and supplies us with the categories that make it possible to understand experience and to make incoming sensations meaningful. In a manner reminiscent of Plato, Kant posited that the mind is an active agency that composes the raw material of the world into an order of conceptualized phenomena. But Kant was no idealist; he did not believe that the mind creates the world; there are "things in themselves" with independent existences, but they are not knowable.

"Apperception" was Kant's philosophical term for the mind's process of assimilating and interpreting new experiences in order to give them meaning. There is unity in every act of perception. In recognizing an object, we can find the bits and pieces that are the elements of the associationists—the hearing elements and the seeing elements of the coach of Berkeley, for example—but these are meaningfully organized a priori, not through association: the mind has acted to form a unitary experience, to create an object within a meaningful context. There is an active mind that organizes the experience with the help of space and time and Kantian categories. Kant viewed the mind as active apperception; apperception is a process by which new experiences are taken hold of and brought into relation with other elements in the mind. This is not passive impression, but rather an active grasping. This ordering of experience in accordance with the categories or forms through appercep-tion is a philosophical analysis, not a psychological one.

"Things in themselves," the causes of things, are unknowable. Kant agreed with Locke and Hume that knowledge comes from sensory per-ception; this is perception not of things as they really are, but only as they appear to us (phenomena). We perceive phenomena the way our mind makes us see them. The mind selects, according to the structures arising from the categories, from the welter of impinging sensations, and imposes upon them the unity inherent in the principles.

It is not surprising that faculty psychology, which was simulta-neously rationalistic, relatively free from appeal to empiricism, and tended to lend itself easily to the support of religious views, proved congenial to Kant. From this perspective, the categories are forms of the mind. Kant classified mental faculties into cognitive (knowing), feeling, and desiring and subdivided the cognitive faculty into understanding, judgment, and reason.[22] His Anthropology also had three parts roughly comparable to the divisions of his three Critiques (Pure Reason, Judg-ment, and Practical Reason);[23] this lent further support to the threefold classification of mental powers.

The immediate effect of Kant's philosophical pronouncements about mind and the impossibility of experiment was to temporarily prevent psychology from becoming an experimental science. In the larger perspective and as a more delayed influence, he helped create a desire to make psychology both experimental and mathematical. Be-cause of his prestige, it would never again be forgotten that science was mathematical.

Kant also helped to keep subjectivism alive, for he stressed the importance of mental phenomena as such. By holding that events are appearances, he helped to direct psychology toward phenomenalism. His view that ultimate principles lie outside the context of experience made Kant the great champion of nativism, which agrees that human beings have innate "given" ways of knowing that are true but not dependent on experience. This stress on unity of organization, with its nativistic base, affects German psychology to this day.

Herbart and Experience, Metaphysics, and Mathematics

Johann Friedrich Herbart (1776–1841) was a professor at Göttingen and at Königsberg; in fact, he filled the chair vacated by Kant. While a tutor in Switzerland, he had made the acquaintance of Pestalozzi, the educator, who directed his attention to pedagogical problems, which thereafter formed a supplement to his already established philosophical and psychological interests. An account of his psychology is contained in the *Lehrbuch zur Psychologie*,[24] which appeared in 1816, and in his more extensive *Psychologie als Wissenschaft neu gegründet auf Erfahrung, Metaphysik und Mathematik*,[25] which appeared in 1824 and 1825. The qualifying terms in the title of this, his major book, give the clue to the nature of his psychology; it is a science based on experience, metaphysics, and mathematics. These three themes will become obvious in the account that follows.

Herbart's metaphysical starting point for psychology was his concept of being.[26] His general concept of the universe was that of independent elements called *reals*. To some extent he was following Leibniz, but, unlike Leibniz, he did not regard all reals as sharing the common characteristic of consciousness. Herbart's conception of mechanical interaction, is the antithesis of Leibniz's conception of preestablished harmony. Despite his dependence on metaphysics, he was led by his particular definition of being to define psychology as the "mechanics of the mind." In keeping with the trend of the times, which was to minimize the mind in favor of emphasizing consciousness, he explained mental states as an interaction of ideas. The mind is the stage on which the vastly more important players—the ideas—act their parts.

Herbart held that experimentation in psychology is impossible,[27] but to remain a science, psychology must, at least, be mathematical. He therefore prepared a series of equations that dealt with psychological matters. For example, to determine how much of an idea is suppressed, he postulated that o equals the suppressed portion of the ideas in time (indicated by t), and S is the aggregate amount suppressed. Then $o = S(1-e^{-t})$. He carried on no actual measurements. The mathematical values he assigned in any given equation were always guesses based on rational plausibility, and his mathematical formulations served only as illustrations.

Herbart's system of psychology concerned elementary bits of experiences, sensations in our terminology, which combined to form ideas. He held that ideas are the real contents of the mind. To this extent he followed the British associationists. But the mechanics of Leibniz's theory of ideas as activity supplied for him the means of making a substantial modification of British associationism—the concept of ideas as forces. According to British associationism, ideas combined in what he conceived to be entirely too passive a fashion. Herbart argued that associations are in reality much more complicated, digressive, and diversive than the associationists had described them.[28] The associationists had assumed, implicitly or otherwise, only the attraction of ideas, and had not paid particular attention to the nature of the force involved.

Herbart postulated both attraction and repulsion of ideas, particularly when ideas clash. Ideas become forces when they resist one another.[29] Some ideas do not resist one another, and for these associations a conventional explanation is sufficient. These are the ideas that are neither opposed nor contrasted with one another such as a tone and a color which unhindered form a complex.[30]

There are other ideas that contrast, such as red and yellow, which may become blended or fused, but which never form a complex. Sometimes ideas are so resistive that they do not form even loosely affiliated complexes. One ideas may be so much a hindrance to another that the second is not even available in consciousness.[31] This hindered idea, although not in consciousness, still exists. Inhibited though these ideas may be, they remain existent as tendencies. When the forces opposing the ideas are changed—when there is a change in the apperceptive mass—then the idea that has previously been kept out of consciousness returns.

This entering into consciousness requires the conceptionalization of a threshold of consciousness. Herbart also used the conception of threshold to explain sleep. If only a few active ideas are present, we have dreaming; if all active ideas are driven below the threshold, we have the unconsciousness that is deep sleep.[32]

According to Herbart, an idea is never lost once it has been created. The number of ideas a person is conscious of at any given moment is paltry in comparison with the number of ideas he is capable of having. The explanation for this poverty of ideas present in consciousness, as contrasted to the wealth of tendencies available, lies in the threshold of consciousness. Besides those few grasped at a given moment, a person can shift from below the threshold other ideas.[33]

Some ideas move into consciousness relatively readily; others do not. Submerged ideas move above the threshold to the full focus of attention if they are consonant with the apperceptive mass or dominant system of conscious ideas; this conception he derived from Leibniz. An idea that comes into consciousness combines with the existing ideas to the extent that it is congruent with those already in consciousness. There is a unity of consciousness—attention, one might call it—so that one cannot attend to two ideas at once except insofar as they will unite into a single complex idea. When one idea is at the focus of consciousness, it forces incongruous ideas into the background or out of consciousness altogether. Combined ideas form wholes, and a combination of related ideas forms an apperceptive mass, into which relevant ideas are permitted to enter while irrelevant ones are excluded.

Ideas are active and may struggle with one another for a place in consciousness; Herbart's concept of threshold and its corollary—that there are both conscious and unconscious mental processes—are distinct advances over earlier views, as was his account of how ideas held from consciousness could reappear. Herbart gave psychology the beginning of a theory of inhibition, or interference, in learning, which was to reappear in many guises and theories in times to come, extending from Pavlov's "conditioned reflex" to Freud's "repression." However, his contribution in this area should not be overestimated. Darwinism, medical psychology, and psychiatry contributed much more than Herbart did to the understanding of the dynamics of unconscious processes.

Herbart did much to make clear that psychology was crucial to educational theory and practice, where his theory of apperception had the most direct and influential application. Since it is against the background of previous experience that a new idea is assimilated in the apperceptive mass, it follows that if information is to be acquired as easily and as rapidly as possible, in teaching one should introduce new material by building on the apperceptive mass of already familiar ideas. This line of reasoning led educators to adopt the practice of planning lessons so that the pupil passed from already familiar to closely related, but unfamiliar elements. Herbart's work was also influential in exposing the shallowness and sterility of the faculty psychology that was so prevalent during this time.[34]

Overview

In addition to the omnipresent rationalism, prescriptively speaking, conscious mentalism prevailed because psychology was concerned with experience and a dualism of mind and body was exemplified in the thinking of von Wolff, Kant, and Herbart. Herbart, however, also emphasized unconscious mentalism by conceptualizing the threshold and related phenomena. Nomotheticism as a concern with the general and not the particular were accepted explicitly and implicitly by all three philosophers. Kant presented what, essentially, is a static view of human nature, while Herbart was to some extent concerned with dynamics, as seen in his conception of attraction and repulsion of ideas.

The philosophically rooted views of Wolff, Kant, and Herbart helped to prepare the way for a psychology separate from philosophy. Wolff espoused the separation of empirical from rational psychology. Kant made quantitativism the hallmark of a science, but denied psychology a place as a science because it could not be mathematical. Herbart made psychology a mathematical science but denied it could be quantitative. The two views, different as they are, sharpened the issue of the quantitative nature of psychology without resolving it. However, each made distinctions that would help psychology emerge as a separate science—once answers to their arguments could be found.

References*

1. C. von Wolff, *Psychologia empirica* (Frankfurt: Rengeriana, 1732).
2. C. von Wolff, *Psychologia rationalis* (Frankfurt: Rengeriana, 1734).
3. C. von Wolff, "Rational Psychology," sec. between 48–67, trans. E. K. Rand, B. Rand, ed., *The Classical Psychologists* (New York: Houghton Mifflin, 1912), pp. 229–231 (1734).
4. *Ibid.*, Sec. 57.
5. *Ibid.*, Sec. 54.
6. W. B. Pillsbury, *The History of Psychology* (New York: W. W. Norton, 1929), pp. 110–111.
7. I. Kant, "The Critique of Pure Reason," trans. J. M. D. Meiklejohn, in R. M. Hutchins, ed., *The Great Books of the Western World*, Vol. XLII (Chicago: Encyclopaedia Britannica, 1952), pp. 1–252 (1781).
8. I. Kant, "The Critique of Practical Reason," trans. T. K. Abbott, in R. M. Hutchins, ed., *The Great Books of the Western World*, Vol. XLII, pp. 291–361 (1788).
9. I. Kant, "The Critique of Judgment," trans. J. C. Meredith, in R. M. Hutchins, ed., *The Great Books of the Western World*, Vol. XLII, pp. 461–613 (1790).

*See p. 19 for description of reference style.

10. I. Kant, *Anthropology from a Pragmatic Point of View*, trans. and intro. Mary J. Gregor (The Hague: Nijhoff, 1974) (1798).

11. I. Kant, *The Classification of Mental Disorders*, trans. and ed. C. T. Sullivan (Doylestone: Doylestone Foundation, 1964) (1798).

12. "Pure Reason."

13. *Ibid.*

14. *Ibid.*

15. *Ibid.* (Hermstein and Boring, Excerpt No. 105).

16. *Ibid.*

17. *Ibid.*

18. *Ibid.* (Hernnstein and Boring, Excerpt No. 30).

19. I. Kant, *Metaphysische Anfangsgründe der Naturwissenschaft* (Riga: Hartknoch, 1766), Preface.

20. E.g., "Pure Reason."

21. *Metaphysische Anfangsgründe.*

22. *Judgment*, Introduction IX.

23. *Anthropology.*

24. J. F. Herbart, *Lehrbuch der Psychologie*, 2nd ed. (Königsberg: Unzer, 1834) (1816).

25. J. F. Herbart, *Psychologie als Wissenschaft Neugegründet auf Erfahrung, Metaphysik und Mathematik*, 2 vols. (Königsberg: Unzer, 1824–1825).

26. *Ibid.*, Chapter 2.

27. J. F. Herbart, *A Text-book in Psychology*, 2nd rev. ed., trans. M. K. Smith (New York: Appleton, 1891), Sec. 4. (1834).

28. *Ibid.*, Sec. 72.

29. *Ibid.*, Sec. 10.

30. *Ibid.*, Sec. 22.

31. *Ibid.*, Sec. 11.

32. *Ibid.*, Sec. 50.

33. *Ibid.*, Sec. 127.

34. *Ibid.*, Sec. 9, 53–125.

Chapter 10

FECHNER:
PSYCHOPHYSICS

Engrossed in philosophical and mystical interests, Fechner devoted several periods of his long life to speculation and to the investigation of what seemed to him the most fundamental problem of life—psychophysics, or the quantitative investigation of the functional interrelations of body and mind.[1] In spite of the arid quality of his psychophysical studies, his writings reveal a burning enthusiasm for grappling with the very nature of man.

Life and Careers of Fechner

Gustav Theodor Fechner was born in 1801 in a small village in the Wendish country of southeastern Germany.[2] His father was a Lutheran preacher; he died when Gustav was five years old, but not before he had given his precocious son a grounding in Latin. After attending a *gymnasium*, Fechner in 1817 matriculated at the University of Leipzig, an association that was to last for seventy years. He took his degree in medicine in 1822, but he decided against going into practice.

Even in his youth there were some glimmerings of humanistic interests. Under the pseudonym of Dr. Mises, he employed the weapon of satire against views with which he disagreed. The first of these satirical pieces appeared in 1821, before his graduation; it was directed against the medical fad at that time of using iodine and was called, *Proof that Man is Made of Iodine*. Occasional satirical pieces continued to come from his pen. Earlier in the century, there had been in Germany a resurgence of interest in materialism. To Fechner, materialism was a theory devoid of truth, and several of his satires were devoted to attacking the view that the universe is inert matter—the "night view," as he called it—and to a defense of the position that the universe can be regarded from the point of view of consciousness—the "day view."

This antimechanist position was to be a fixed point in what otherwise appears to be a series of shifts of interest. Throughout his life Fechner seemingly moved from one field to another, although in a larger sense there was a consistency and integration. The nature of this unity should become apparent as we touch on these careers. According to Boring, in the productive years between 1817, when Fechner started medical school, and 1887, when he died, he was successively a physiologist, a physicist, a psychophysicist, an experimental estheticist, again a psychophysicist, and, throughout most of the later years, a philosopher.[3] Following his aim steadfastly through these careers, he founded psychophysics, which in turn led to the founding of experimental psychology.

After graduation in medicine he began his second career by studying physics. In 1824, after a period without official appointment, he started to lecture on this subject and to conduct laboratory investigations in electricity. In 1833, he married. In 1834, when only thirty-three years old, he became a professor of physics. His academic future seemed secure.

During these years sheer economic necessity had led him into translating various French scientific works that served to add to his scientific knowledge; however, some of his means of increasing his income amounted to hack work, such as editing and writing a considerable share of an encyclopedia of household knowledge in eight volumes. He broke under the strain of work and became a "nervous invalid." In general, this could be characterized as a neurotic depression with pronounced hypochondriacal features.

In the winter of 1839–40, a painful eye disorder developed, and he resigned his chair in physics. Fechner had studied after-images by staring into the sun, which undoubtedly aggravated the condition, if it did not bring it on. Years of suffering followed. His eyes were so hypersensitive to light that he could not leave the house without bandaging them, and for the rest of his life he had to curtail his reading. Sometimes for weeks on end he could not eat at all; he eventually found that fruit, strongly spiced raw ham, and wine could be tolerated. He could not talk for long periods and he thought of suicide. Some slight improvement occurred late in 1843, but it was thought there was no chance of his regaining his health. In 1844, he received a small pension from the university, thus establishing officially his position as an invalid. However, hardly one of his remaining forty-four years went by without some serious contribution from his pen. There is no doubt that he really suffered, so it would be unfair to apply to him that grand phrase, "he enjoyed poor health."

Nevertheless, a defensive component in his illness was undoubtedly present, but it is fruitless to conjecture whether this was a secondary gain to an organic disorder or was primarily of psychogenic origin.

His inability to use his eyes resulted in many hours spent in contemplation. This reinforced his speculative turn of mind, which came to the fore as soon as he was able to resume working. He now entered the third phase of his career and became a psychophysicist with philosophical leanings. The reason for his inclusion among the great psychologists lies in his connection with psychophysics. Reserving details for later systematic and methodological discussion, it suffices to say that he became interested to the point of obsession in demonstrating that mind and body are aspects of a unity.[4] Since matter (body) is not to be denied any more than consciousness (mind), the two must be reconciled and made one. Fundamentally, to Fechner, the difference between mind and body, the dualism that some find, is nothing more than a difference in point of view concerning the psychophysical entity. The mind is related to the body as the inside of a circle is related to the outside. This makes his view a double-aspect theory—mind and body are but two aspects of a fundamental unity. Since the two aspects are identical, the view is also referred to as the "identity hypothesis."

The solution, he tells us, came with dramatic suddenness on the morning of October 22, 1850.[5] In bed, "before getting up," he realized that the law of the connection between body and mind is to be found in a statement of the quantitative relations between mental sensation and bodily stimulus, not in simple proportion, but such that increases in the former correspond to proportional changes in the latter.

Ten years later, his *Elemente der Psychophysik* appeared. For this book, Fechner ranks among the great psychologists. Here he discusses the functional relations of mind and body and reported investigations of his own and others on the various senses—sight, sound, and the cutaneous and muscular senses.

Some conception of Fechner's intent to measure psychological functions can be gained by turning to his next undertaking, the study of experimental esthetics, another field he founded. Fechner had had a deep and long-standing interest in art. His first paper in this new career appeared in 1865 and dealt with the "golden section," the most esthetically pleasing relation of length to breadth in an object. Here again, Fechner applied his exact method to a global goal. He rebelled against the attempt to develop an esthetics "from above down" by formulating abstract principles of beauty by which to judge the concrete object, in the manner of the Romanticists. Instead, he believed one must start with simple figures. In order to find the linear proportions an artist used, he measured endlessly and patiently the dimensions of pictures, cards, books, snuff boxes, writing paper, windows—in fact, any object that was purported to have esthetic appeal. Thus he sought to develop an experimental esthetics "from below."

Fechner also became very much involved in a *cause célèbre* of his day concerning the authenticity of two paintings of the Madonna, each attributed to Holbein. Although very similar, they differed in detail, and the authenticity of each was in dispute. Fechner inclined to the opinion that both were authentic. There was also a dispute over which was the more beautiful. Taking advantage of an exhibition in which both were exhibited together, he launched what may have been the first public opinion poll. He made arrangements for the public to be invited to record comments in a book placed alongside the paintings. Sparseness of returns with a disproportionate number from art critics, who had already formed opinions, made this particular venture a failure.

His major book on esthetics, *Vorschule der Aesthetik,* [6] appeared in 1876. Its appearance also served to close his participation in esthetics. Experimental psychology in the person of Wundt, now also at Leipzig, and the intense interest of many others, protagonists as well as antagonists, would not leave him in peace to pursue his still strong philosophical interest. He was drawn back to a second career in psychophysics, which lasted until his death in 1887. In that same year, he wrote a paper so well summarizing psychophysical research as to draw from Wundt the comment that it was the clearest extant summary.

The Aim of Fechner

The careers through which Gustav Fechner moved did not reflect a change in fundamental interest. His guiding aim was a search for an answer to an all-consuming question—the nature of the relationship between the spiritual and material worlds. He sought a unified conception of body and soul that, while based on mystical speculation, also had a scientific basis.

Post-Kantian philosophers had promulgated a "philosophy of nature" that was romantic, transcendentalist, and vitalistic. A characteristic tenet was that spiritual influences express themselves through physical symbols. This belief fired the imagination of Fechner and became an important aspect of what, in a somewhat oversimplified fashion, can be referred to as the mystical strain in his nature. And yet the vague symbolism upon which the philosophers of nature pontificated could not escape criticism from that other aspect of his personality, the scientific. From Herbart he had learned to respect both the conception of psychology as a science and the conceptual value of mathematics in this pursuit. However, he could neither go along with Herbart's metaphysics nor accept his denial of quantification and experiment to psychology. Fechner struggled with both the mystical and scientific sides of his nature, feeling it necessary to unify them. This union finds no great favor among psychologists today, but it must, nevertheless, be explored as the background against which Fechner's psychological contributions were made.

In the spirit of Plotinus, his spiritual ancestor of seventeen centuries before, Fechner saw the world as a system of souls appearing to each other as bodies. His mystical strain was reflected in the very title of one of his works, *Zend-Avesta on the Things of Heaven and the Hereafter*.[7] In this book, Fechner endowed all things with personal souls. The world is made up of external manifestations, bodies that are correlated with internal animate realities, souls. This is panpsychism, a theory of the world that endows plants as well as animals with some rudimentary kind of soul. Its relation to primitive animism is direct and obvious. But Fechner was no simple throwback to primitive views. He argued these and related problems with subtlety and enthusiasm.

Consonant with the two major influences that affected him, Fechner sought precise confirmation of these speculations. His was a nature that asked for a relation between poetical and speculative world-views, to be demonstrated by means of precise measurement. He made the mystical aspect his goal, and the scientific aspect his method. Actually it was his philosophical, even mystical views that led to the first precise measurements in psychology.

The starting point for measurement of physical stimulus and mental sensation he found in the research of E. H. Weber, who was also at Leipzig. He specifically disclaimed having in mind Weber's work when this idea occurred to him, though it is reasonably certain he knew of it before this date. At any rate, shortly thereafter he made Weber's work the basis of his subsequent investigation. It therefore becomes necessary to consider the influence of Weber upon his thinking and research.

The Influence of Weber

Ernst Heinrich Weber (1795–1878) had been appointed *Dozent* in physiology at the University of Leipzig in 1817, the same year Fechner arrived as a medical student.[8] The next year he was appointed Professor of Anatomy, and later in his career was made Professor of Physiology. For many years Weber and Fechner moved in the same academic circles and lived in the same community.

As a physiologist, Weber was particularly interested in touch and in the muscle sense, hitherto relatively neglected fields of research.[9] Weber's research interests will at first appear to be a far cry from Fechner's lofty aim. His work concerned the muscle sense. In investigating the part played by the muscle sense in relation to touch, he wished to find the smallest difference between weights, the so-called just noticeable difference, that his subjects could discriminate. Their task was simple. On each trial they lifted two weights, one a standard weight, the other a comparison weight; and they reported which one felt heavier. On subsequent trials the same or different comparison and standard weights were used. Large differences between the weights were obvious to all subjects and were reported as differences, but small differences in weight were often undetected by subjects who reported that the two weights were the same. When Weber studied the results of many trials and several standard weights in relation to weights just noticeably different, he found that for each standard weight there was a relation between sheer heaviness and the perception of differences between weights. This finding was expressed in the form of a ratio of one-fortieth to each of the standards. Suppose he were using standard weights of twenty, forty, and eighty "ounces" (actually, lighter weights by about half were used). He found that a weight of forty ounces could usually be discerned as different if there was a one-ounce disparity in the comparison weight but that usually the difference was not perceived when it was less than this amount. This gave a ratio of one-fortieth. This same ratio was found when the standard weight was cut in half to twenty ounces or doubled to eighty ounces. It needed only one-half ounce difference at twenty ounces (one-fortieth of twenty ounces), while two ounces were required at eighty ounces (one-fortieth of eighty ounces) for a just noticeable difference to be perceived.

Next Weber asked, suppose instead of being lifted, the weights were allowed merely to rest upon the skin; what would the ratio now be? When comparison weights were allowed to rest on the skin, a ratio was found, but now it was one-thirtieth instead of one-fortieth. In other words, one-thirtieth of the standard weight must be added to that of comparison weight if a difference just noticeable to the subject were to be detected. Since smaller differences in weight could be discriminated when the weights were actively lifted (one-fortieth) compared to when they were passively resting on the skin (one-thirtieth) he concluded that this difference demonstrated the influence of the muscle sense upon discrimination as compared to the lower degree of discrimination when touch alone was operative. Adding the muscle sense to touch increased accuracy of discrimination. Weber also tested capacity to discriminate length of lines and marshalled evidence on differences in the pitch of tones, and again he found constant ratios.

Weber generalized that for each of the senses there is a constant fraction for which a difference is just noticeable. He admitted that this ratio does not hold without exception for extremes of tone. It was later established that, irrespective of the mode of sensory stimulation, this ratio does not hold at the extremes, and that in general it is only approximately true.

Weber's second major contribution was the experimental determination of the accuracy of two-point discrimination of the skin.[10] Weber established how far apart two points must be in order for them to be felt on the skin as two. A blindfolded subject would be instructed to report whether he felt one or two points touching his skin. Using a drawing compass, Weber then stimulated the skin either with one or with two points simultaneously at varying distances apart. When the two points were a relatively small distance apart, a subject would report a clear and sharply defined "one"; at relatively great distances, he would report "two points"; and when the points were in the region between these two extremes he would report "uncertainty and blurriness." There was a threshold at which two points could just be discriminated. Weber showed that this "two-point threshold," as it came to be called, varied according to the part of the body stimulated. On the finger tips the subject would report discriminating the two points when they were but .220 cm. apart, but for the same discrimination on the small of the back the points had to be 4.06 cm. apart or many times greater. His explanation of this difference in sensitivity from one part of the body to another rested upon his hypothesis of "sensory circles," i.e., there are regions of the skin in which doubleness is not perceived because immediately adjacent tactile nerve fibers are stimulated. For doubleness to be sensed, at least one unstimulated fiber must lie between those stimulated. Regions with large thresholds would thus have touch fibers relatively sparse; the points stimulated had to be farther apart in order to skip an adjacent fiber.

Although peripheral to the problem of psychophysical measurement, it should be mentioned in passing that since the sensory circles were a matter of distribution of sensory nerve fibers, his findings could be interpreted as lending support to a nativistic theory of space perception.

More generally, it can be seen that Weber's studies are experiments in the strict sense of the term. Varying the intensity of weights and the length of lines and the distance between two points on the skin allowed the experimenter to study their differential effects on the perceptual experience of the subject.

Psychophysics

Weber held that when one distinguishes between objects, it is not the difference between them that is perceived, "but the ratio of this difference to the magnitude of the things compared."[11] He made it clear that the magnitude of stimuli just noticeably different from each other can be stated as a ratio between the intensities, and that this ratio is independent of the particular intensities used. Fechner grasped the implications that Weber's statement had for his own psychophysical problem and he proceeded to develop them.

Fechner construed Weber's results to mean that one could measure sensation as well as the sensory stimulus and state the relation between the two in the form of an equation.[12] After years of repeating and extending Weber's research, he formulated Weber's ratio into an equation: $\Delta R/R = K$; in which ΔR is the just noticeable stimulus increment, K is a constant, and R is the standard stimulus magnitude. In other words, when divided by the magnitude of the standard stimulus, a stimulus increment gives a constant value. Strictly speaking, this is Weber's law. Fechner was perhaps too generous when he applied this designation; not to this constant that actually Weber found, but to a more generalized formula, he himself arrived at only by carrying the reasoning several steps further. Nevertheless, the equation with which Fechner started will be referred to as Weber's law; the final equation, yet to be stated, will be called Fechner's law.

Instead of working Fechner's law through mathematically as Fechner did, let us try to get the general relation clear.[13] As one proceeds arithmetically by steps of one in the scale of sensation aspect—so Fechner's law asserts—one multiplies the value of the stimulus magnitude by a constant ratio. Stimuli of twenty, forty, and eighty ounces should give equal steps of sensation. A long and complicated argument was offered by Fechner about measuring sensations indirectly from direct measurement of the stimulus; we shall ignore this, however, and move to a discussion of direct measurement based on the assumption that just noticeable differences are equal. Fechner reasoned that it can be assumed that just noticeable differences, j.n.d.'s, as they came to be called, are equal through the range of the sense quality, that these j.n.d.'s are thus equal increments and measure sensation. Being equal, they can be added up to make magnitudes. There remained only the question of finding a zero point from which to start so that we can know when we are dealing with "one," "two," and so on—the number of units above zero as the j.n.d.'s are cumulated up the scale. This zero point Fechner took as the threshold stimulus, that value of the stimulus at which the sensation is just ready to appear. This value is zero on his scale. The j.n.d. appearing thereafter is one, the next j.n.d. is two, and so on.

The increase of the subjective intensity of a sensation varies directly with the increase of strength of the stimulus. The psychic increases arithmetically by a constant difference when the physical increases geometrically by a constant multiple. When one series increases arithmetically and the other series geometrically, we are dealing with a logarithmic relation. This was demonstrated by the mathematical manipulation of Weber's law, a process by which Fechner emerged with the equation $S = K \log R$ in which S is the sensation's magnitude, K is a constant, and R is the stimulus' magnitude. A sensation equals a constant multiplied by the logarithm of the stimulus. This is Fechner's law. Sensation had been measured, and the identity hypothesis, so Fechner thought, had been demonstrated. He had found his proof of his identity hypothesis in a table of logarithms!

To summarize Fechner's research and the researches of those who followed him, we may say that the experiments indicate that Fechner's law holds approximately for the middle range of stimulus intensity but does not hold for either small or very large intensities. Visual brightness has a ratio of about one-hundredth; lifting weights, one-fortieth; and tone, one-tenth. For instance, in visual brightness the ratio just given means that for a change in illumination to be perceived the total illumination must be increased by one-hundredth of its amount.

Fechner established what he considered to be the absolute stimulus threshold or limen, the value at which the subject's sensing of the stimulus is just ready to appear, as that value of stimulus that marks the limit of a sensory continuum. Anyone who is familiar with the fact that vibrations are heard as sound in the range between about 16 vibrations per second, the lowest audible tone, and about 20,000 vibrations per second, the highest audible tone, and anyone who knows that there are vibration rates both higher and lower not heard as sound is aware of the existence of thresholds. (The dog whistle of vibrations beyond 20,000, unheard by humans, shows that dogs have a higher tonal threshold than humans.) Subject to qualifications to be given later, one can speak of 16 and 20,000 vibrations per second as the stimulus thresholds of hearing.

Lower stimulus thresholds were established by Fechner and others for weights, brightness, and many other sensory intensities. No upper thresholds could be established since these are intensities capable of limitless increase.

Now that the so-called absolute threshold is familiar, it can be seen that in discussing j.n.d.'s, we were dealing with something that can be called the *differential* threshold. Fechner believed the differential limen to be the least amount of change in a stimulus necessary to produce a sensed difference. Changes less than this are not sensed as different, i.e., are below the differential threshold. The amount necessary to produce just the perceived difference is the differential limen. The differential threshold resembles the just noticeable difference enough to be frequently confused with it. Speaking more accurately than Fechner did, the differential threshold is a statement of the statistical quantity for the point between what is sensed as not different *and* the just noticeable difference. It is a statistical value representative of the point where the sensation is just as often not sensed as sensed.

In the course of his research, Fechner developed one and systematized two others of the three fundamental methods of psychophysics. These three are the method of limits, the method of average error, and the constant method. The method of average error that Fechner developed along with his brother-in-law is the most fundamental and will be used as an illustration. The subject himself adjusts a variable stimulus so as to fulfill the instructions given him—for example, to make one line equal to the length of a standard line. Before him he sees a length of line, the standard. Another line is to be adjusted by him to be as close to the standard in length as he can make it. No matter how closely he approximates the line, however, an error, large or small, will be made. Sometimes he makes the line too long, sometimes too short, but he always makes some error. After many trials, the average of his errors is found, the so-called average error.

After publication of the *Elemente* in 1860, interest was immediate, intense, and widespread. Many others, seeing the value of Fechner's work, proceeded to carry out similar experiments. Various controversies raged. One criticism directed against his work, the so-called quantity objection, is that we are not aware introspectively that sensations have magnitude. William James, a phrase maker, said in substance that our feeling of pink is not a portion of our feeling of scarlet.[14] Another argument centered on the question of whether Fechner was really measuring sensation, since he had assumed the equality of j.n.d.'s. From the vantage point of today it can be said that Fechner erred methodologically in the direction of treating psychophysical findings without full consideration of the various sources of complication present in the individual and in the conditions of the experiment.[15] As a matter of fact, 16 and 20,000 vibrations a second as stimulus thresholds for hearing are not constant limits for all people. Fechner was wrong; there are no absolute thresholds. Precise thresholds change from one individual to another and from one condition to another. Auditory sensitivity varies widely because of differences in native acuity, or because of changes occurring in the ear due to injury or the aging process; conditions such as the state of the background noise-level or the precision of the sound source delivering the particular pitch are also known to affect the results.

Significance of Weber and Fechner

Since Weber's work preceded Fechner's, it is plausible to ask why Weber is not stressed and why Fechner is treated as someone who later, more or less independently, worked in the same area? Precedence is given to Fechner because he was an "event-making" man; Weber was merely an "eventful" man in the felicitous terminology that Sidney Hook applied in somewhat similar circumstances.[16] As a physiologist, Weber carried on some research on a problem that interested him. It was a different problem, to be sure, from that occupying most of his fellow physiologists, but neither he nor they saw it as different in spirit. He did not realize that he had hit upon something that would profoundly effect future developments in psychology. But he had. In this sense, he was an eventful man. At a propitious time he worked on research that was to give him a prominent place in the history of psychology. But its larger significance escaped him. Unlike Weber, Fechner was an event-making man. He saw what others, including Weber, had not seen—the implications and consequences of psychophysics. Fechner's insight that October morning about measuring sensations and relating them to measurements of their stimuli was independent of Weber's researches. It was related to this prior work on magnitude of stimuli, which was recognized by Fechner as supplying a method; but the insight had to occur before recognition of the relevance of the method. Weber took the first step along a fork in the road, but did not realize he was walking a different road; Fechner did.

Ironically, with all the excitement his findings engendered, little attention was paid to Fechner's goal for psychophysics. His attempt to found a philosophy upon exact science was a failure, but his work did advance psychology as a science.

Overview

Sensory psychology was put on a quantitative basis with the introduction of Fechnerian psychophysics. No less a person than Wilhelm Wundt[17] said of Fechner that his was the "first conquest" in the field of experimental psychology. In all fairness it must be admitted that not all psychologists have held such a high opinion of Fechner's work. William James,[18] for example, some thirty years after the appearance of Fechner's major work, concluded that the yield of psychophysics in psychological outcome was precisely "nothing," and that Fechner's findings were "dreadful." He went on to point out that Fechner's successors, laboring mightily, could topple every one of his findings, but invariably they ended up praising him for his contribution to the scientific methodology of psychology. Indeed, his conclusions have not withstood the strain of later criticism; nevertheless, his methods are still not only serviceable and useful, but actually fundamental to sensory measurement.

But in a larger sense Wundt was right; psychophysics gave a quantitative expression to measurement of the mind. No longer could it be argued that mind could not be measured, nor that mathematics could not be applied to its research study. Quantitativism and the refinement of empiricism as expressed in a positive attitude toward experiment would hereafter be characteristic of the psychologist to come.

References*

1. G. T. Fechner, *Elemente der Psychophysik*, 2 vols. (Leipzig: Breitkopf and Härtel, 1860).
2. The major source for the details of Fechner's life was G. S. Hall, *Founders of Modern Psychology* (New York: Appleton, 1912), but the organization of the material about his life and his careers owes much to the presentation of E. G. Boring, *A History of Experimental Psychology*, 2nd ed. (New York: Appleton-Century-Crofts, 1950), pp. 275–283.
3. *Ibid.*, p. 283.
4. G. T. Fechner, *Elements of Psychophysics*, Vol. 1, trans. H. E. Adler, eds., E. G. Boring and D. Howes (New York: Holt, Rinehart and Winston, 1966), Chapter 1 (Herrnstein and Boring, Excerpt No. 107).
5. *Elemente*, II, p. 554.
6. G. T. Fechner, *Vorschule der Aesthetik* (Leipzig: Breitkopf and Härtel, 1876).

*See p. 19 for description of reference style.

7. G. T. Fechner, *Zend-Avesta, On the Things of Heaven and the Hereafter* (Leipzig: Voss, 1851).

8. Lest the emphasis on Weber and Fechner give a false impression about the initiation of research in the field, one aspect, that of threshold measurement, had not waited for their work. P. P. Bouguer, *Traité d'optique sur la gradation de la lumière* (Paris: Guerin & Delatour, 1760) (Herrnstein and Boring, Excerpt No. 15) had already measured the differential threshold for brightness; and C. E. J. Delezenne, "Sur les valeurs numériques des notes de la gamme" (*Recueil des travaux de la Société des Sciences, de l'Agriculture et des Arts de Lille*, 1827, pp. 4–6) (Herrnstein and Boring, Excerpt No. 16) had studied the differential threshold for pitch.

9. E. H. Weber, "Der Tastsinn und das Gemeingefühl," R. Wagner, ed., *Handwörterbuch der Physiologie* (Braunschweig: Vieweg, 1846), Vol. III, pp. 481–588 (Herrnstein and Boring, Excerpt No. 10); E. H. Weber, *De pulsu, resorptione, auditu et tactu: annotationes anatomicae et physiologicae* (Leipzig: Koehler, 1834). (Herrnstein and Boring, Excerpt No. 17).

10. E. H. Weber, "Ueber den Raumsinn und die Empfindungskreise in der Haut und im Auge," *Berichte der königlich-sächsischen Gesellschaft der Wissenschaften zu Leipzig mathematisch-physische Klasse 4* (1852), pp. 87–105 (Herrnstein and Boring, Excerpt No. 32).

11. *De pulsu*, p. 172.

12. G. T. Fechner, "Elements of Psychophysics," trans. H. S. Langfeld, in B. Rand, ed., *The Classical Psychologists* (Boston: Houghton Mifflin, 1912), pp. 562–572 (Herrnstein and Boring, Excerpt No. 18).

13. The mathematical derivation involves calculus. Those interested in tracing it through mathematically are referred to Boring, *History of Experimental Psychology*, pp. 287–289.

14. W. James, "The Principles of Psychology," in R. M. Hutchins, ed., *The Great Books of the Western World* (Chicago: Encyclopaedia Britannica, 1952), Vol. LIII, p. 356 (1890).

15. E.g., R. S. Woodworth, *Experimental Psychology* (New York: Henry Holt, 1938), Chapter 18.

16. S. Hook, *The Hero in History* (New York: John Day, 1943), pp. 181–183.

17. W. Wundt, "Zur Erinnerung an Gustav Theodor Fechner: Worte gesprochen an seinem Sarge am 21. Nov. 1887, *"Philosophische Studien,* IV (1888); 471–478.

18. James, "Principles," pp. 356–359.

Chapter 11

Helmholtz:
NEURAL PHYSIOLOGY

One of the sources from which experimental psychology was to emerge was experimental physiology, the study of the functioning of the organ systems of the body. It is customary to say that general physiology became a separate discipline with the appointment in 1833 of Johannes Müller to the first professorship of physiology at the University of Berlin. Here, between 1834 and 1840, Müller compiled his *Handbuch der Physiologie des Menschen*, a systematic organization of comparative anatomy, chemistry, and physics as related to general physiology.[1] More pertinent to psychology at this time, however, was the study of the nervous system by physiologists. In this field the giant among pioneer neural physiologists was Hermann von Helmholtz. But, as always, the way was prepared by other men.

Physiology before Helmholtz

During the latter half of the seventeenth century, as well as during the eighteenth century, physiology assumed many of its modern characteristics and went beyond the hypothetical science of Hartley and LaMettrie. Robert Whytt (1714–1766), for example, summarizing in 1751 the physiology of the reflex, formulated the beginnings of many modern concepts.[2] According to him, the "fundamental" experiment on the nature and existence of the reflex had been performed about 1730 by Stephen Hales. He made use of the already known fact that a decapitated frog responded to pinching by withdrawing the legs, and found that it failed to continue to do so when the spinal cord was destroyed. Whytt himself repeated and extended this experiment, in the course of which he introduced the terms "stimulus" and "response." In 1771, Unzer (1727–1799) used the word "reflex" to distinguish between this kind of action and that carried on volitionally.

The first half of the nineteenth century yielded a variety of developments that firmly established physiology as a science. Simultaneous with these was the rise of phrenology, which later proved to be a scientific blind alley, but did serve to bring attention to the mind and its relation to the brain.

THE BELL-MAGENDIE LAW

During the years 1811–1822 Charles Bell[3] (1774–1842) in Great Britain and François Magendie[4] (1783–1855) in France, working independently, performed the research that distinguished between the sensory and motor nerves. In a general way this distinction had been known to Galen, and others had from time to time rediscovered it. Prior to the work in question, however, the distinction had been lost sight of and the nerves were conceived as if all of them more or less indiscriminately carried on both motor and sensory functions. A controversy developed over the priority of the work of Bell and Magendie.[5] Bell published first, but it is not entirely clear that his original paper reported what he later claimed it did; while Magendie, when he published eleven years after Bell, stated the matter with unequivocal clarity. The important point is that through their work a clear-cut research distinction had been made.

Magendie established the distinction between motor and sensory nerves by cutting the nerve roots at the spinal cord and studying the functions that were lost. He found that it is through the posterior (dorsal) roots of the spinal cord that sensory fibers enter, while the anterior (ventral) roots are the path through which the motor fibers leave the spinal cord. For instance, when Magendie cut an anterior root, he found a complete paralysis, which was not present when the posterior root was cut. Since movement was prevented by this cutting, the anterior root must have been responsible for the movement.

One effect of this work was to separate clearly neural physiology into the studies of sensory and motor functions or, to use more obviously psychological terminology, to establish a physiological basis for a distinction between sensation and movement. This distinction between sensory and motor nerves, according to what came to be called the Bell-Magendie law, is still fundamental today in bringing order into the study of physiology and psychology.

GALL AND PHRENOLOGY

At about the same time Bell and Magendie made their important contributions, an interest in phrenology was rampant. Franz Joseph Gall (1758–1828) had worked, first in Vienna and then in Paris, on the physiological localization of the functions of the brain. But his research more and more turned to what others came to call phrenology, to which he devoted the rest of his life.[6] While still a boy, Gall had been impressed by what he thought to be a relationship between the mental characteristics of his schoolmates and the shapes of their skulls. Years later, when mapping out the location of centers for various functions on the surface of the cerebrum, the cerebral cortex, he tried to verify this impression. He reasoned that if a region of the cortex was well developed there would be a characteristic bump or protrusion of the skull at this point, or a comparable hollow if underdeveloped. Gall collected instances of what appeared to be over- and underdevelopment of areas of the brain as reflected in the shape of the skull, and thereby formed judgments of their possessors' striking characteristics. He did this by seeking out examples where he thought he might find them. Among pickpockets from the prisons he found the bump of acquisitiveness. Later he extended his search among friends and public figures. He also sought out persons who seemed to show a common trait to a striking degree and received permission to search their skulls for bumps and hollows. Once he found some sort of correspondence between one, two, or a few individuals in the possession of a certain characteristic and similar bumps or hollows, he named the trait and assumed that when the physical evidence was found thereafter the characteristic would also be prominent.

From a modern perspective one is struck by the glaring inadequacy of the method that Gall used. Today, any college sophomore in psychology would be able to tell him that his research called for taking an unselected sample of the population, measuring all their bumps, and, without knowledge of these measurements, estimating their standing on the psychological characteristics with which Gall was concerned. Then the two streams of data would have to be compared for the degree and nature of the relationship shown.

Nevertheless, it was not long before Gall's teaching excited popular attention, and soon he had disciples and fellow practitioners, including Johann Kaspar Spurzheim (1776–1832), who did much thereafter to extend the number of characteristics studied and to spread the phrenological doctrine.

When the mapping was completed, each characteristic had a definite place of localization in an area of the cerebral cortex. Thus, with the aid of a chart, the phrenologist could examine the subject's skull and plot the individual's strengths and weaknesses in abilities and personality.

Phrenology was a faculty psychology to end all faculty

psychologies; Spurzheim postulated thirty-seven characteristics or faculties.[7] He divided them into affective and intellectual faculties and further
subdivided these two classes into propensities and sentiments, and perceptive and reflective faculties. Some of the affective faculties were
destructiveness, amativeness, self-esteem, and benevolence; the intellectual capacities included calculation, order, and causality. As in all faculty
psychologies, the major task was naming and estimating the strength of
the function. Once done, this made further analysis superfluous. Thus, it
served as a block to further inquiry.

Phrenology was never generally accepted by scientists even when
it was still possible to regard its tenets as hypothetically plausible. It was
opposed by such familiar figures as Charles Bell and Thomas Brown in
Great Britain and Pierre Flourens in France. Spurzheim was most active in
spreading phrenological views in England and in the United States. His
visit to the United States in 1832 produced considerable interest among
physicians practicing in the mental hospitals.[8] Rather than necessarily
accepting his views *in toto,* psychiatrists found that phrenology offered
them general guidance in their thinking about the abnormal functioning
of the mind as it relates to the condition of specific areas of the brain. To
this extent phrenology was of value, and its appeal continued despite the
scientific opposition and lasted even into the present century. To this day,
popular magazines are devoted to it, and phrenological charts with their
neat squares superimposed on an outline of the head still appear at the
booths of fortune tellers at amusement parks and fairs.

Phrenology did serve the function of making the man in the street
aware that he had a brain. Even more important, it stimulated scientists to
take up research on the brain and helped to make explicit that psychological functions may be localized in the brain. This fostered a functional
approach destined to remain significant.

FLOURENS AND LOCALIZATION OF FUNCTION IN THE CEREBRUM

One of Gall's sharpest critics was Pierre Flourens (1794–1867),
who was also engaged in investigating the function of various parts of the
brain, but by performing experiments not collecting anecdotes. His research led him to the conclusion that removal of the cerebrum, while
leaving the reflexes intact, abolishes thought and volition.[9] Moreover, he
concluded that the cerebrum as a whole, and not limited portions of it, is
responsible for all thought and volition. He localized various functions in
the other major parts of the brain—the cerebellum and the medulla
oblongata, for example—but he said that each part, in its turn, functioned

as a whole. This theory was directed against phrenology, of course; the phrenologists localized each of their thirty-seven faculties in definite parts of the cerebrum. For years thereafter, Flourens's view that the cerebrum functions as a whole prevailed, strengthened, if anything, by being in opposition to the phrenologists.

It was not until 1861 that Paul Broca (1824–1880) the French surgeon and physical anthropologist, showed that the loss of speech in one individual was due to a lesion centering in the third convolution of the left frontal lobe.[10] This was the first successful challenge to Flourens's doctrine of the unity of the cerebrum; Broca had found a localization of function within a specific area of the cerebral cortex. That speech was too complicated a mechanism to be confined to one specific region, as later research showed, does not detract from the import of this first demonstration of specific localization. Direct electrical stimulation of the brain followed in 1870, first demonstrated by Fritsch and Hitzig;[11] this led to the concept of the existence of a series of motor centers and seemed also to establish (what was then accepted as fact) that there were a variety of brain centers. Needless to say, the functions isolated bore no resemblance to those named by the phrenologist.

MÜLLER AND THE SPECIFIC ENERGY OF NERVES

In 1833 Johannes Müller (1801–1858) was named to the newly-created chair of physiology at Berlin. This chair had previously been combined with that of anatomy. Müller's appointment signalized the recognition of physiology as an independent sphere of science. His major work, *Handbuch der Physiologie des Menschen,*[12] which appeared between 1834–1840, systematized and exhaustively summarized the knowledge of physiology of his time in a primarily inductive fashion (of which Francis Bacon would have approved). This work served to place general physiology on a scientific footing. In it, he brought comparative chemistry and physics to bear upon physiological problems. He accepted the concept that vital phenomena is fundamentally different from those of chemistry and physics not concerned with living substances. His adherence to a vitalistic prescription stands in sharp contrast with the mechanistic approach and was denied by even his students (p. 261). Müller may be said to have done for general physiology what Helmholtz in the next generation was to do for neural physiology.

The most direct contribution of Müller to psychology was his doctrine of the specific energy of nerves.[13] He arrived at the conclusion that each sensory nerve, however stimulated, gives rise to only one type of sensory process, and no other.[14] The sensation that is experienced is due, not to the nature of the stimulus as such, but to the sense organ, nerve, or brain center that is stimulated. For example, the optic nerve always responds by leading to the sensation of light whether it is stimulated in the usual fashion or pinched, heated, irritated by acid, or shocked by electric current. (An easily verified everyday illustration is that of pressing with the thumb against the closed eye, thus producing a flood of light). Müller was saying that every sensory nerve responds in its own characteristic way, no matter how stimulated. To paraphrase a statement of James,[15] if we were to interchange surgically the optic and auditory nerves, we would hear the lightning and see the thunder. Müller was a Kantian, and he saw his doctrine as offering unequivocal support for nativism. What is more innate than the nervous system itself? In a moment, however, we shall find Helmholtz using the same doctrine to support empiricism.

Where does the specificity arise? Müller considered seriously two possibilities, either that it was in the nerves themselves or in the centers in the brain where the nerves terminate; in an early publication he attributed specificity for vision to the portions of the brain it involved. Both views seemed to him to be defensible, but he decided in his later *Handbuch* in favor of the specific energies being in the nerves themselves. In view of the fact that Flourens's research discredited the doctrine of cortical localization, this conclusion is hardly surprising. Müller's version of specific energies was consequently not brought into question by the arguments concerning brain localization. Nowadays, with increased knowledge, we would assign the specificity to the brain, not the nerves.

It is agreed today that "specific energy" is the basic principle governing the physiology of the special senses. To take Müller's doctrine in its broadest perspective is to say that we are not aware of objects directly but only through some form of intermediary, in this case, the sense organs and nerves. For example, Müller[16] used his doctrine of specific nerve energies to solve that problem, encountered so often before, of how the eye could represent whatever object it received. In addition to the inverted image problem, he dealt with the question of the size of an object, especially how large objects are represented as such by the eye. His answer to both problems was that all the mind perceives is the state of the nerves leading to the brain. This principle of knowing only through an intermediary had been understood since Herophilus, and the British associationists had, in their various interpretations, made much of the fact. Müller's research, however, gave a scientifically solid footing that still prevails.

DONDERS AND REACTION TIME

The speed of reaction had been a research problem since the end of the eighteenth century when the Astronomer Royal at Greenwich dismissed his assistant for making errors in observing the time at which stars crossed the meridian.[17] A moment's reflection can show that this is a very serious matter because astronomical findings were calibrated by these observations.

A few years later, Friedrich Wilhelm Bessel (1784–1846), the Prussian astronomer, came upon an account of the incident and realized that the unluckly assistant might not be unique and that astronomers in general might differ in accuracy of their observation of the times of stellar events. When the problem was put this way, other astronomers agreed with Bessel, and the "personal equation," as it came to be called, became a matter of widespread interest among them. A variety of methods of comparing the personal equation of one astronomer to that of another came into use. That is, relative personal equations were established— astronomer A was shown to be one-tenth of a second slower than B, but two-tenths of a second faster than C in carrying out his stellar observations. A constant correction, the personal equation of $B-A=.10$ second could then be used in collating their astronomical observations.

After the discovery of electric currents and electromagnets, these relative personal equations became absolute measures through the invention and perfection of the chronograph and chronoscope. In the chronograph, a key is pressed, making a mark on a drum that receives constant marks from a tuning fork vibrating 500 times a second. The first ones measured the time accurately to less than a tenth of a second. But technical advances continued rapidly. By 1862, the Hipp chronoscope was being used to measure the personal equation to a thousandth of a second. The measurements these instruments supplied could now be stated in absolute terms—A took 300 milliseconds while B took 200 milliseconds to respond.

The absolute personal equation of the astronomer, when adapted to physiological tasks, came to be called reaction time. Franciscus Cornelius Donders (1818–1889),[18] a Dutch physiologist and a contemporary of Helmholtz, became interested. First in 1865 and then more fully in 1868, he extended the study by going beyond simple reaction time or the reaction to a predetermined stimulus by a given predetermined response. A reaction already agreed upon, pressing a key, for example, would be made when a light went on. The elapsed time was simple reaction time. If this reaction were to be made more complicated, Donders reasoned, the increased time taken to react could not be attributed to whatever was added to complicate the reaction. He performed experiments to study so-called discrimination and choice reaction times.

Simple reaction time had called for subjects to respond to stimulus A with response a. For discrimination time, Donders presented several stimuli—A, B, C, D—in irregular order, but his subjects were instructed to respond only to A, not to the others. Consequently, they had to discriminate A from all other stimuli before responding with a. In his new discrimination reaction, 'A' was to be made to a red light, but the subject was to withhold his reaction if a green light, B, or a yellow light, C, was flashed. As Donders predicted, his subjects took longer to make the discrimination reaction than they did to make the simple reaction. Subtracting simple reaction time from the discrimination reaction time gave him the discrimination time. This was called the subtractive procedure. Choice was even more complicated: subjects responded to A with a, B with b, C with c, and so on. This gave a still longer reaction time; the choice time was the total time minus the discrimination and simple reaction times. From the measures, Donders obtained three reaction times—simple, discrimination, and choice. The very time taken by mental events had been brought to heel and measured. Thus, the temporal study of various mental functions—"mental chronometry," as it was called—was launched, to be followed up by Wundt and others later.

Hermann von Helmholtz

The compartmentalization of knowledge is a limitation that most scientists, including psychologists, suffer gladly, human capabilities being what they are. They find one thing quite enough to do. The great abilities of Hermann von Helmholtz permitted him to disregard the convenient but artificial boundaries that had been set up between sciences.

By what resembled a process of natural growth, Helmholtz was led by his interest in research through physics (he was a coformulator of the law of the conservation of energy); neural physiology (he measured the rate of the neural impulse); optics (he invented the ophthalmoscope and advanced the theory of color vision associated with his name); acoustics (he formulated the theory of resonance as the basis for hearing); and other important, but less relevant work in hydrodynamics, electrodynamics, and meteorological physics. In all, he wrote more than 200 papers and books, a high proportion of which made important contributions to science.

Helmholtz conceived of psychology as a separate discipline, but as one allied to metaphysics insofar as it ascertained the laws and nature of the products of the mind.[19] He made an exception of the psychology of the senses because of its close alliance with physiology. Consequently, he had no hesitation in discussing psychological issues pertinent to his interests.

Helmholtz was empirical in the tradition of Locke and Hartley. He stated his major argument against nativism with admirable brevity. It was not that nativism was disprovable, but simply nonparsimonious.[20] In spite of his strong empirical tendencies, he was also influenced to some extent by Kant. For example, he accepted the law of causality as a *priori* and transcendental and not demonstrable from anything else.[21] Causality was not a law of nature but a regulative principle guiding the scientist in comprehending phenomena. How he related his empirical position to space perception is considered later (p. 267).

LIFE AND GENERAL SCIENTIFIC ENDEAVORS OF HELMHOLTZ

Hermann Ludwig Ferdinand von Helmholtz was born in Potsdam, Germany, in 1821.[22] His father taught in the *Gymnasium* of that city, and because of the son's delicate health, first tutored him at home. At age nine, however, the boy entered the *Gymnasium* and advanced so rapidly that he was graduated at seventeen. Lacking the financial means to study physics, an already formed major interest, Helmholtz continued his studies at the Medico-Chirurgical Friedrich-Wilhelm Institute in Berlin where no tuition was charged to those promising to serve as surgeons in the army upon graduation. Helmholtz was never a student at the University of Berlin, but Johannes Müller was the teacher who had the most profound effect upon him during these student days. Students under Müller, who became his friends, included Emil DuBois-Reymond, Rudolf Virchow, and Ernst Brücke. They all admired Müller immensely, but he was of an older generation, and although he had helped to win physiology away from the philosophy of nature, he still held to the prevailing vitalistic theory of biological activity. This his students could not accept. The spirit of their attitude is caught in a solemn oath that Brücke and DuBois-Reymond imposed upon themselves during their student days: they pledged themselves to prove and to expound the principle that "no other forces than common physical chemical ones are active within the organism."[23] Such was the temper of these young scientists, all of whom were under thirty.

Shortly after graduation in 1842 Helmholtz became an army surgeon at Potsdam. While carrying on his duties with the military, he

Brücke
Teacher
of Freud.

continued his studies in physics and mathematics, and wrote and published several papers. Already his tremendous energy, which never left him, was becoming evident.

In 1847, less than five years after his graduation, Helmholtz read before the Physical Society of Berlin his classic paper on the indestructibility of energy, giving mathematical formulation to the law of conservation. A few years earlier in 1842, Julius Mayer (1814–1878) had published a theoretical paper on the topic, along with the method for calculating the dynamical equivalent of heat. J. P. Joule, almost immediately after Mayer, published the results of the experiments which he had been conducting for several years and which led to a theory substantially similar to Mayer's. Controversy about priority sprang up. Helmholtz freely acknowledged their priority. But all three men actually deserve credit, Mayer for the theoretical formulation, Helmholtz for its mathematical statement, and Joule for its verification in research. It is worthy of note that this paper by Helmholtz was in the spirit of that oath taken by his friends a few years before, since the theory of the conservation of energy is simultaneously a denial of the existence of biological vital force and the substitution for it of the physical and chemical analysis of energy transformation.

After serving in the army for five years and after a short stint as an instructor in anatomy at a Berlin art school, Helmholtz was called to Königsberg as associate professor of physiology. Since he had a reasonably secure position, he married. He then turned to what proved to be his second major contribution, the measurement of the speed of the neural impulse, a topic to which we shall return presently.

During these years he also worked in physiological optics. In 1851 he invented the ophthalmoscope, which was a concave mirror with a small hole in the middle through which the observer looked as he reflected light into the eye of the patient. Once conceived, this relatively simple device to look into the eye itself was of enormous value in research and medical practice.

In 1856 the first volume of the *Handbuch der physiologischen Optik* appeared; the last of its three volumes appeared ten years later; it was issued as a unit in 1867.[24] Nearly sixty years later in 1924–25 it was translated into English, not just as a classic, but as an indispensible tool for the serious student of vision.[25]

In 1855 Helmholtz went to Bonn as professor of anatomy and physiology. While still at Königsberg he had become interested in acoustics. During his three years at Bonn, his first major research into hearing was carried out. In 1858, during the period in which he centered his attention on acoustical problems, he moved to an even more important position in the German university system, the professorship of physiology at Heidelberg, a chair he occupied until 1871. If anything, his already tremendous productivity increased during this period. In addition to the research on audition relevant to this particular account, he showed a remarkable ability to come to grips with important and crucial problems in hydrodynamics and electrodynamics. He ranged over many areas. Some of the papers he wrote between 1858 and 1871 were on such topics as afterimages, color blindness, the Arabian-Persian musical scale, relation between the natural sciences and the totality of sciences, the form of the horopter, the movements of the human eye, the regulation of ice, the axioms of geometry, and hay fever. His acoustical researches culminated in the appearance of *On the Sensations of Tone* in 1863.[26] Just as his book on vision did, this new book summarized his investigations, and sifted, summarized, and systematized the entire available literature. During this period, honors were showered on him, among them invitations to lecture, calls from foreign countries, and the prorektorship of the University of Heidelberg.

In 1870, when Helmholtz was fifty years old, the chair in physics at the University of Berlin became vacant and he was asked to set his own conditions of acceptance. He asked for and received a salary of 4,000 thalers (a huge sum for that day), a promise of a new institute of physics, its directorship, and living quarters in that institute. Until arriving at Berlin in 1871, Helmholtz had been somewhat cramped for space and limited as to apparatus. In 1887 he was made the first director of the new Physics-Technical Institute at Charlottenberg, near Berlin, while retaining his professorship at the University.

His desire to espouse empiricism led him, during the period from 1866–1894, to publish five papers on geometrical axioms with the intention of showing that, contrary to Kant, these are also products of experience. He did his job so well that his discussion of non-Euclidian space came to be cited by others after him as evidence for a (nonexperiential) fourth dimension.

Although he continued his interests in physiological problems, revised his books on hearing and vision, published papers on color vision, and made that spirited defense of empiricism mentioned earlier, his researches during these years tended to center on problems of physics less close to present interests. For example, he helped direct his pupil, Hertz, to problems whose solution made a crucial contribution to the founding of wireless telegraphy and radio.

He developed popular and elaborate lecture demonstrations and continued to give scientific lectures designed to be of a popular nature; four different collections of these lectures appeared in print. In 1877 academic freedom was the basis of one of his popular lectures in which he discussed the "admirable" state of German universities—where, with the yoke of the church thrown off, professors taught unhindered—as contrasted with the backwardness of British universities, which had not made these advances.

In 1893 Helmholtz went to the United States for the first and only time in order to attend the Chicago World's Fair as a delegate from Germany. While returning, he had a severe fall down the ship's stairs and he never fully recovered. He died from a cerebral hemorrhage in September 1894.

Some of the problems that influenced psychological thinking on which he worked call for relatively detailed statements. These are the speed of the neural impulse; vision, particularly his theory of color vision; space perception; and his theory of hearing. Each problem will be taken up in turn.

THE SPEED OF THE NEURAL IMPULSE

As exemplified by J. Müller, the prevailing view before the research of Helmholtz was that the speed of the neural impulse was instantaneous or at least so fast as to be incapable of measurement.[27] Estimates of speeds many times the velocity of light had been secured by assuming that the rate of flow of "animal spirits" would be similar for vessels of the same size and that speed varied inversely with the diameter of the conductor. Since the diameters of nerve fibers were very, very minute, indication of tremendous speeds were obtained. The method used by Helmholtz,[28] which would have been entirely inadequate had the previous estimates been true, was to take a motor nerve and attached muscle from a frog's leg, the so-called nerve-muscle preparation, and arrange it so that both the moment of stimulation and the resultant movement would be recorded on a drum revolving at a known speed. Helmholtz measured the time between stimulation and the muscle twitch for different lengths of nerve. The difference in time interval between stimulation of the nerve near the muscle and its recorded reaction and stimulation far from the muscle gave him the time taken for passage. Since he knew the distance between the points of stimulation, he could now calculate its speed per second. Helmholtz found the speed to be the very modest one of about ninety feet per second.

The Bell-Magendie law, which distinguished between sensory and motor nerves, made it unsafe for him to leave the problem as measured with motor nerves alone, so he now investigated sensory-motor nerves to find out whether their speed was similar or different. He also turned to human subjects. When stimulated on the toe and on the thigh, a man can respond with his hand. The difference in the time between stimulation and reaction over the differing lengths traversed in the two instances gave Helmholtz his measure of speed of reaction—something between fifty and 100 per second, but variability from trial to trial and subject to subject was so great that he did not follow up the original study. The individual differences, later to become so important in themselves, were for Helmholtz nothing more than an indication of inadequate control, as indeed they turned out to be. Nevertheless, these two phases of the study gave him rough measures of the speed of sensory and motor neural impulses. In general, later and more accurate research had demonstrated that the neural impulse varies enormously. The speeds Helmholtz found proved to be too slow. Nevertheless, it was Helmholtz who carried out the pioneer study.

The fact that the nervous impulse is not instantaneous but takes appreciable lengths of time signified that mental events were definitely limited by the properties of the body and that an analysis of bodily motion was relevant to psychological phenomena. Mental events that seem instantaneous may actually be temporal events. As Boring so aptly phrases it, "it brought the soul to time. . . ."[29]

This was the first "reaction-time" study as it came to be called. However, Helmholtz was interested only in the sheer speed of the neural impulse, and it was the work of Donders published some fifteen years later that showed a grasp of the psychological significance of the problem.

VISION

While integrating previously available research in the field of visual physiology, Helmholtz also did an enormous amount of original work in that field; this is presented in his *Handbuch der physiologischen Optik*.[30] The three volumes have been characterized respectively as physiological, sensory, and perceptual accounts of vision.[31] Some of his own specific research studies show a similar affinity for psychological problems.

He measured the optical constants of the eye, demonstrated how the eye accommodates for different distances, and developed and supported by research a theory of visual space. Most important of all was his theory of color vision.

As early as 1802, Thomas Young (1773–1829) had published a theory of color vision in which he postulated that the retina is equipped with three kinds of color sensitive points.[32] These three primary colors, working cooperatively, were said to furnish the range of experienced colors. The derivation of all colors from a limited number of colors was not new, as we know from Newton (p. 182). Going beyond Newton, Young's contribution was the suggestion of a physiological basis of three kinds of "particles on the retina" (receptors), each kind acting independently. This suggestion lay fallow until Helmholtz espoused the theory, to be known thereafter as the Young-Helmholtz theory of color vision.

In Helmholtz's theory three sets of fibers in the retina are said to give rise respectively to sensations of red, green, and violet.[33] There are supposedly three kinds of photochemically decomposable substances in the end organs, varying in degree of sensitivity to different parts of the visible spectrum. With disintegration of these substances, neural excitation occurs. The three kinds of excitation act differently on the brain only because, while playing the part of connecting wires, they are united to different functioning parts of the brain. Helmholtz then proceeded to suggest how these particulars of receptor and cerebral localization could be used to explain various psychological visual experiences. On stimulation of the red and green fibers together, yellow results. Other combinations produce other colors. When all three kinds of organs are stimulated in the right proportion, white results. Looking at a white surface after colored stimulation, we see negative afterimages because after one organ has been thoroughly fatigued by use, we see with the unfatigued organs alone. Color blindness (red-green blindness) could result from lack of either red or green organs, or both. An objection to the theory arose from critics: yellow, postulated as arising from stimulation of red and green organs, should not be seen by color-blind individuals, whereas actually they can see yellow. In spite of criticism, modification, elaboration, and correction, the Young-Helmholtz theory is still taken very seriously today.

Helmholtz held that this color theory is a particular application of Müller's general law of the specific energy of nerves, with "three nerve systems."[34] Müller himself had applied the principle of the specific energy of the nerves to the differentiation of one sense from another, but not to the separate qualities within a single sense, such as sweet and sour or red and green. Helmholtz was applying the rule within a single sense modality. If we speak of Müller's theory as one of specific *nerve* energies, then Helmholtz was proposing a theory of specific *fiber* energies.[35] Although Helmholtz did much to advance this theory of fiber energies, he had been anticipated by several other investigators, including Thomas Young himself. Young also anticipated Müller's more general doctrine by advancing his theory of specificity for different color qualities. Despite his citing of Müller, Helmholtz evolved a theory that turned out to be more a doctrine of the specific energies of *cortical areas* than of nerves. As we know, the cortical area alternative had been raised, but not accepted by Müller. In the location of specificity, later research was to support Helmholtz and not Müller.

SPACE PERCEPTION

In interpreting space perception, Helmholtz was also an empiricist. Here he saw as his opponent Ewald Hering, who held that every point on the retina was innately capable of perceiving height, breadth, and depth.[36] In part, Helmholtz defended an empirical position by use of Müller's doctrine of specific energies.[37] Helmholtz held that the various sense organs and nerves each have characteristic qualities that are not in themselves meaningful, being bare sense impression. At this point experience enters, for recurring association gives these sense impressions meaning.[38] The doctrine of specific nerve energies interpreted by Müller in support of Kantian nativism was now interpreted by Helmholtz as a defense of empiricism.

Helmholtz also stressed the importance of the empirical process of unconscious inference in space perception.[39] Perception of space, he said, is not inherent; instead we "infer" space from past experience, but without awareness that this process of inference is going on. Certain small cues together constitute a sign that the object is to be found at a certain distance. Without noticing the sign itself, we infer how far away the object is. To use an example—when we gaze at an object twenty feet away, intervening objects at various closer distances are actually seen as double, but we do not notice this. (This can be verified by anyone who takes the trouble. Hold a pen first a few inches from the nose and then at arm's length, while looking across the room. The double image will be evident in both instances but greatest when the pen is close up.) Closer objects are seen, while one looks at the far object, with varying degrees of doubleness. A specific degree of doubleness is unconsciously interpreted, without the viewer's noticing the doubleness at a certain distance to the object. This is what Helmholtz meant by "unconscious inference."

AUDITION

In the field of hearing Helmholtz made many contributions.[40] Among them were his clarification of the role of timbre to round out the major harmonic components and his theory of how hearing is mediated by the ear and the relation of this theory to the doctrine of specific energy of nerves. Each of these must be examined in more detail.

That pitch depends primarily on frequency of sound waves and intensity on the amplitude of the waves had been understood and explained in Müller's *Handbuch;* as yet timbre had received no similar explanation. The *fact* of timbre, that is to say, the existence of qualitative differences between tones other than pitch, was, of course, well known. Anyone hearing the same note played by different instruments realizes that something makes them sound different despite their identity of pitch. Helmholtz explained this experience of timbre by the presence, in addition to the fundamental pitch, of so-called overtones or vibration rates more rapid than the fundamental tone that fixes the pitch.[41] Most vibrating bodies vibrate not only as wholes, but also simultaneously as parts. It is these partial vibrations that give rise to timbre. The shape of waves making up a tone from a musical instrument, if visualized, would show that the main wave is the same as that for all other instruments and gives rise to the fundamental pitch when playing that particular note, but that part waves are unique to this particular instrument and result in the timbre. The more similar the tone of two instruments, the more similar are the characterizing overtones. Here again, Helmholtz was not content merely to advance a theory; he conclusively demonstrated his contention by building a series of tuning forks and resonators that permitted him to systematically vary the intensity of the overtones accompanying a fundamental tone. From these he produced synthetically the characteristic timbre of various musical instruments.

His theory of hearing evolved over the years and this is not the place to trace its modifications. It was essentially a theory of pitch; he assumed that intensity was more or less explained by varying degrees of excitation of the fibers.

Helmholtz marshalled evidence that a portion of the inner ear responds to an auditory wave stimulus by resonance, vibrating in tune with the frequency of the sound wave. The ear behaves like an unstruck tuning fork that begins to vibrate after another one has been struck. This is the theory of resonance.

After discarding the organs of Alfonso Corti as the basis of differential tuning, Helmholtz finally reached the conclusion that the basilar membrane with its many hair cells in the cochlea of the inner ear is the resolving organ of hearing. This basilar membrane is trapezoidal in shape (narrow at one end and increasing gradually in width). The hairs on its narrower end he thought were tuned to high pitches; the hairs on the wider portion, to the low pitches. Pitch, transmitted to the brain after analysis by resonance on the basilar membrane, is dependent on place of stimulation. The differential action of a portion of the basilar membrane is the means whereby the pitch of the heard sound is determined.

The resonance theory gave rise to many alternative theories.[42] The most formidable competition to the resonance theory has come from the frequency theory, in which the basilar membrane is said to vibrate as a whole, thus giving rise to nerve impulses that preserve unchanged the frequency of the stimulus. Thus the brain itself—not the basilar membrane—becomes the place where auditory analysis into different pitches takes place. Today each theory is seen as explaining some, but not all, of the evidence. It is clear that the old theories are too simple. Resolution of the present discrepancies is a task for future research.

The doctrine of specific nerve energies was regarded by Helmholtz as an important established fact. It was natural for him to apply it to hearing. Differences of quality *ipso facto* thus meant that there are differences in the conduction of sensory fibers. Research since Helmholtz's day had demonstrated the existence of between 1,500 and 11,000 distinguishable pitches.[43] Helmholtz was contending that there was about this number of specific energies in hearing alone! This bold step attracted attention and the issue of the specific energies in hearing became a prominent one for research in all sense modalities.

Overview

The acceptance of developments in physiological science during this period would influence the acceptance of modern psychological science. Methodological and contentual inspiration was transferred to the fledgling science.

Empiricism in the form of the experimental method unequivocally became the method of choice among physiologists during this period. Since it was capable of repetition by others the use of experiment increased methodological objectivism. Nomothetic interests still prevailed. The contentual problems of reaction time, sensory experience, and space perception were to be claimed by psychologists as also within their sphere of interest. Quantitativism, the use of measurement to specify results, was firmly established. Mechanism, a prescriptive allegiance to exploration in mechanical terms, had been espoused by most physiologists after the time of Müller. Determinism, the study of events explicable in terms of antecedents, was accepted as a matter of course. Appeal to events within nature, naturalism, was also now a matter of course.

The integrative work of Johannes Müller and Hermann von Helmholtz had a significance beyond that of bringing together items of a heretofore scattered research literature. So, too, did the appointment of Müller to a chair in physiology—which had become recognized as a scientific speciality. The task and the role of the physiologist had been recognized. Workers on tasks now seen as related, perceived a common-bond; the possibility of becoming a student in the particular subject became apparent; and making career in the field became possible. Physiology as a field of research and teaching was to have a profound effect on Wundt, the founder in his time of a new discipline, modern psychology.

References*

1. J. Müller, *Handbuch der Physiologie des Menschen*, 3 vols. (Coblenz: Hölscher, 1834–40).
2. R. Whytt, *An Essay on the Vital and Other Involuntary Motions of Animals* (Edinburgh: Hamilton, Balfour and Neill, 1751) (Herrnstein and Boring, Excerpt No. 60).
3. C. Bell, *Idea of a New Anatomy of the Brain: Submitted for the Observation of His Friends* (London: Strahan and Preston, 1811) (Herrnstein and Boring, Excerpts No. 6, 8).
4. F. Magendie, "Expériences sur les fonctions des racines des nerfs rachidiens," *Journal de physiologie experimentale et pathologique*, II (1822): 276–279; "Expériences sur les fonctions des racines des nerfs qui naissent de la moëlle épinière," *Journal de physiologie expérimentale et pathologique,* II (1822): 366–371 (Herrnstein and Boring, Excerpt No. 7).
5. L. Carmichael, "Sir Charles Bell: A Contribution to the History of Physiological Psychology," *Psychological Review,* XXXIII (1926): 188–217; J. M. D. Olmsted, *François Magendie, Pioneer in Experimental Physiology and Scientific Medicine In Nineteenth Century France* (New York: Schuman, 1944).
6. F. J. Gall, "Sur les fonctions du cerveau et sur celles de chacune de ses parties, Vols. 4, 6), W. Lewis, trans., *Gall's Works* (Boston: Marsh, Capon and Lyon, 1835) (1825) (Herrnstein and Boring, Excerpt No. 45).

*See p. 19 for description of reference style.

7. J. K. Spurzheim, *Phrenology or the Doctrine of the Human Mind* (Philadelphia: Lippincott, 1825).

8. E. T. Carlson, "The Influence of Phrenology on Early American Psychiatric Thought," *American Journal of Psychiatry*, LXV (1958): 535–538.

9. M. J. P. Flourens, *Recherches expérimentales sur les propriétés et les fonctions du système nerveux dans les animaux vertébrés* (Paris: Crevot, 1824) (Herrnstein and Boring, Excerpt No. 46).

10. P. Broca, "Remarques sur le siège de la faculté du langage articulé, suivies d'une observation d'aphémie (parte de la parole)," *Bulletin Société d'Anatomie*, VI (1861): 330–357 (Herrnstein and Boring, Excerpt No. 47).

11. G. Fritsch and E. Hitzig, "Ueber die elektrische Erregbarkeit des Grosshirns, *Archiv für Anatomie und Physiologie:* (1870), 300–332 (Herrnstein and Boring, Excerpt No. 48).

12. Müller, *Handbuch* (Herrnstein and Boring, Excerpt No. 9).

13. Charles Bell had anticipated Müller to some extent in a privately printed paper and many others had made use of the doctrine, but it was Müller whose authoritative publication made it an accepted and acceptable principle.

14. J. Müller, *Elements of Physiology*, trans. W. Baly (London: Taylor, 1837–1842) (1833–1840).

15. W. James, *Psychology: Briefer Course* (New York: Henry Holt, 1892), p. 12.

16. J. Müller, *Zür vergleichenden Pnysiologie des Gesichtssinnes* (Leipzig: Cnobloch, 1826), pp. 55–66 (Herrnstein and Boring, Excerpt Nò. 25).

17. E. G. Boring, *A History of Experimental Psychology*, 2nd ed. (New York: Appleton-Century-Crofts, 1950), pp. 134–142.

18. F. C. Donders, "Die Schnelligkeit psychischer Processe, "*Archiv für Anatomie und Physiologie*, VI, (1868): 657–681.

19. H. L. F. Helmholtz, *Treatise on Physiological Optics*, 3 vols., ed. J. P. C. Southall (Rochester, N.Y.: Optical Society of America, 1925) (1856–1866).

20. *Ibid.*

21. V. F. Lenzen, "Helmholtz's Theory of Knowledge," M. F. A. Montague, ed., *Studies and Essays in the History of Science and Learning. Offered in Homage*

to George Sarton on the Occasion of His Sixtieth Birthday, 31 August, 1944 (New York: Schuman, 1946), pp. 299–320.

22. The major source of details about his life was H. Margenau, Introduction, in H. L. F. Helmholtz, *On the Sensations of Tone* (New York: Dover Publications, 1954). This was supplemented by H. Gruber and Valmai Gruber, "Hermann von Helmholtz: Nineteenth Century Polymorph," *Scientific Monthly*, LXXXIII (1956): 92–99.

23. Quoted in Boring, *History*, p. 708.

24. H. L. F. Helmholtz, *Handbuch der physiologischen Optik* (Leipzig: Voss, 1867) (1856–1866).

25. *Treatise.*

26. H. L. F. Helmholtz, *On the Sensations of Tone*, trans. A. J. Ellis (New York: Dover Publications, 1954) (1863).

27. Müller, *Elements.*

28. H. L. F. Helmholtz, "On the Rate of Transmission of the Nerve Impulse," *Berichtn. König. Preussische Akadamie der Wissenschaften. Berlin* (1850): 14–15, reprinted in W. Dennis, ed., *Readings in the History of Psychology* (New York: Appleton-Century-Crofts, 1948), pp. 197–198.

29. Boring, *History of Experimental Psychology*, p. 42.

30. *Optik.*

31. Boring, *History of Experimental Psychology.*

32. T. Young, "On the Theory of Light and Colours," *Philosophical Transactions of the Royal Society*, XCII (1892): 18–21 (Herrnstein and Boring, Excerpt No. 4).

33. *Treatise*, Vol. 2, Sec. 20 (Herrnstein and Boring, Excerpt No. 11).

34. *Ibid.*

35. Boring, *History of Experimental Psychology.*

36. E. Hering, *Beiträge zur Physiologie: Zur Lehre vom Ortsinn der Netzhaut* (Leipzig: Englemann, 1861–1864) (Herrnstein and Boring, Excerpt No. 33).

37. *Treatise.*

38. *Ibid.*, Vol. 3, Sec. 26 (Herrnstein and Boring, Excerpt No. 34).

39. *Ibid.*, (Herrnstein and Boring, Excerpt No. 40).

40. *Sensations of Tone.*

41. *Ibid.*, Chapter 6 (Herrnstein and Boring, Excerpt No. 12).

42. R. S. Woodworth, *Experimental Psychology* (New York: Henry Holt, 1938), pp. 535–537.
43. E. G. Boring, *Sensation and Perception in the History of Experimental Psychology* (New York: Appleton-Century-Crofts, 1942), pp. 341–342.

Chapter 12

Wundt:
INTROSPECTION AND EXPERIMENT

Wilhelm Wundt is the first man one can call a psychologist without qualifying the statement by reference to another, perhaps stronger, interest. In terms of self-image he was a psychologist even more than a philosopher. This subjective criterion can be supported by a crude but adequate summary of his life's work. Although he wrote four major books in philosophy, running to perhaps twenty-one editions, in psychology he published six books that appeared in about thirty-six editions.

When he founded the modern science of psychology, Wilhelm Wundt was fully aware of what he was doing. In his preface to the first edition of his *Principles of Physiological Psychology*, dated 1874, he begins with the impressive statement that the work is being presented in order to "mark out a new domain of science."[1] He also states flatly that, as a science, psychology cannot be based on metaphysical assumptions of any sort.

To Wundt, the use of the experimental method, whenever possible, was mandatory. He replaced the age-old method of meditation with a more exact and exacting method of introspection. Prior familiarity with how Wundt interpreted introspection and experiment will help to clarify the events of his life and the experiments conducted in his laboratory.

The Meaning of Introspection and Experiment

Since Wundt referred explicitly to physiological psychology in the title of his book, what he meant needs careful clarification. Essentially, he held that the already available physiological methods might be used for psychological study whenever they appeared appropriate, although there was no a *priori* way of determining when these should be employed.

Parallelism

Despite Wundt's calling the new science "physiological psy-chology," he insisted that the psychic and the physiological processes are separate but parallel.[2] Because causality in natural science is a closed system, the phenomena that are studied by natural science cannot affect the mind or be affected by it. Outer experience (physics) and inner experience (psychology) differ in the point of view from which the experience is observed. The former is mediate, the latter is immediate. Conscious phenomena are therefore observable without reference to the body in which they occur, and "physiological psychology" does not imply an attempt to explain the phenomena of the psychical by examin-ing the physical life. Although he hesitated to use the term, since it smacked of metaphysical assumptions he had promised to avoid,[3] mind-body interaction was being rejected; instead, Wundt adopted a monism of the psychophysical parallelistic variety. His parallelism was methodological; physiology follows one method to achieve knowledge, psychology follows another. They are two bodies of knowledge. The manner of connection between elements in the subject's immediate experience is entirely different than the occurrences studied by physiol-ogy. Causality in psychology is different from causality in physiology or in any other physical sciences.

When psychology investigated the relation between the processes of physical and mental life, it was called psycho-physics. On this subject Wundt[4] explicitly acknowledged that he followed Fechner, but he denied Fechner's hope that psychophysical methods could be used for metaphysical purposes. Metaphysical implications, he admitted, may emerge from experimental research but only as an end result of research.

Although using psychophysical methods for many problems, Wundt disagreed with Fechner on what was being measured. Wundt held that to put the matter correctly one must state that two sensations are of equal intensity or one sensation is just noticeably different from another sensation. Wundt was seeking to study, not the relation between the body and the mind, but the relation between sensation on the one hand, and the process of psychological judgment on the other. A purely psychologi-cal interpretation with no appeal to the relation of stimulus and sensation resulted. To Wundt, data obtained from psychological study were illustra-tive of a law of psychological relativity. The degree to which sensations differ makes judgments of their relative magnitude possible. This point of view was consistent with his conviction that psychology concerned itself with contentual subjectivity and not with an alleged body-mind interac-tionism.

Wundt firmly established the method of introspection as psycholo-

Wundt's introspection
diff. them
*meditation_*

gy's characteristic procedure. The use of something resembling intro-spection was not new in itself, as even a fragmentary review will show. Socrates had made an appeal to introspection and Plotinus and Augustine had sharpened his approach. Descartes and the British empiricists were agreed on its use. Descartes' method, more properly called meditation, had been characterized earlier as contemplative meditation on problems that interested him (p. 169). Intuitive self-evidence of an entirely private sort was sought about cognition or the passions, both highly complex states, and Descartes' favorite topics. The English empiricists shifted their meditative interests from the area of these higher mental processes to that of sensations. The reduction by Hume of soul or mind to a bundle of sensations and his doctrine that images are faint copies of sensations illustrate this shift.

Despite resemblance to earlier exponents of introspection, Wundt proceeded in a significantly different fashion, and meditation can now be seen as the better term for these past efforts. Wundt launched introspec-tion, now properly so called, by refining the conscious elements of meditation and combining them with experiment. It is therefore crucial to be quite precise about what he was doing.[5] The Cartesian meditative tradition is to be replaced by experimental self-observation. Observations have no scientific usefulness unless they can be related to an external or measurable response—discrimination response, reaction time, emo-tional responses, and the like. How Wundt and his students succeeded in finding or inventing a vast array of apparatus for presenting stimuli and measuring responses will become clear when some of their typical re-search is examined (p. 282).

Methodological Rules

Wundt recognized that conscious contents are fleeting and in continual flux; he therefore laid down explicit rules for proper use of the introspective method:[6] 1) the observer, if at all possible, must be in a position to determine when the process is to be introduced; 2) He must be in a state of "strained attention;" 3) the observation must be capable of being repeated several times; 4) the conditions of the experiment must be such that they are capable of variation through introduction or elimina-tion of certain stimuli and through variation of the strength and quality of the stimuli. The first rule is necessary so that the observer will not be caught off guard. In terms of Wundt's arrangement for introspection, the observer knows when to expect the introduction of the stimulus and is ready to observe the state of consciousness. He is therefore capable of isolating the mental processes of that moment. As for the second rule, the observer must be conscious of every nuance of that which is presented. Repetition, the third rule, allows for the uncovering of omissions and

strained or trained.

distortions of earlier trials. The fourth rule makes it possible to study the effect of variation, that is, the effect of the change resulting from addition or subtraction of various aspects of stimulating conditions as shown in variations of the experience. This last rule takes us to his conception of an experiment.

Wundt held that, insofar as physiological psychology draws upon experiment, we can refer to it as experimental psychology.[7] It is perhaps from John Stuart Mill that he derived his conception of psychology as a science of observation and experiment.[8] But Mill only talked about experiments; Wundt carried them out. Wundt[9] asserted that in psychology pure self-observation is insufficient. It is only when additional recourse to experiment is made that exact quantitative results are possible. The essence of an experiment is to vary the conditions of a stimulus situation and then to observe the changes in the experiences of the observer. In advocating experimental control of conditions of introspection, Wundt was taking a giant step.

Herbart had urged using mathematics in the study of psychological problems, although he had denied the possibility of using experiment. Kant had not only denied the possibility of experiment in psychology, but had also held that the use of mathematics itself was impossible. He believed that the only dimension of consciousness was time and that with one dimension one could not carry out experiments; consequently, psychical processes were indeterminate.[10] Since practically all German philosophers of his time were either Kantians or Herbartians, it is to Wundt's credit that he overcame this formidable intellectual block and saw that both mathematics and experiment could be applied in psychology.

Wundt agreed that Kant was correct concerning the unidimensional nature of consciousness confined to internal experience. But when we turn to *external* stimuli, not only are units of measurement supplied, but also one more dimension that Kant had neglected is added, namely, intensity.[11] With the dimensions of quality and intensity, experiment becomes possible. Every simple sensation has a qualitative determinant, such as blue, warm, or sweet.[12] Qualities are not divisible into simpler units. Herbart, as we have seen, recognized that these classes of variables are present, but had not appreciated how they could be turned to experimental use.

Armed with intensity and quality as the two classes of variables, Wundt was prepared for the experimental study of psychological phenomena. It is true that in sound, for example, intensity is never separable from some quality of pitch, but it is possible to change either the intensity alone (loud-soft), or the pitch alone (high-low), while maintaining the other unchanged. Moreover, we may use two notes and consequently change the quality of the sound so that it is different from that of either note alone. Intensity and quality becames subjects for scientific study. On these premises Wundt was able to launch the experimental study of psychology.

Life and Research of Wundt (1832 - 1920)

Wilhelm Wundt was born at the village of Neckarau near Heidelberg in Baden in 1832; he was the son of a Lutheran pastor.[13] He was a solitary child, and he played little and absorbed himself in study. As a young child he stayed in the home of a Lutheran vicar who was his tutor. He formed so strong an attachment to this tutor, presumably at first his father's assistant, that when the vicar was transferred, he was inconsolable until allowed to board with him and to continue under his tutelage. At thirteen he entered the gymnasium, where he also boarded and was ready for the university at nineteen.

His medical studies took him to Tübingen, Heidelberg, and Berlin. It has been hazarded that Wundt went into medicine without any special call, but he did so in part because he wanted to continue away from home! It is doubtful whether he ever intended to practice medicine. As with many others before and after him, the study of medicine was the means of entering into a scientific career, which even at this age he seems to have had in mind. He did some work at the Berlin Institute of Johannes Müller in physiology, and a year or two later he shifted to physiology as an academic field.

In 1857 he was appointed *Dozent* at Heidelberg and began to lecture in physiology. His first announced course in physiology attracted four students! Between 1858 and 1864 he served as assistant to Helmholtz, who had just arrived from Bonn. Relations with the taciturn Helmholtz were nonexistent, according to Titchener. In 1864 Wundt was appointed assistant professor. In 1866 he was chosen to represent Heidelberg in the Baden Chamber, but he soon resigned because of the time required. There was a delay of academic advance until 1874, when he was called to Zürich to the chair of Inductive Philosophy. This, it should be noted, is only an apparent shift in field. In academic circles he had come to be viewed as a promising man for appointment to a post in philosophy. After all, psychology was formally still a branch of philosophy.

During these years, Wundt was very active in physiological research. In 1858 he published a study of muscular movement and elasticity during action, in which he reported investigating the effect of constant galvanic current and mechanical thermal and chemical stimuli upon muscles.[14] Not only was he working in this field, but a conception of psychology as a distinct science was beginning to emerge. Between 1858 and 1862 various sections of his *Beiträge zur Theorie der Sinneswahrnehmung* appeared.[15] This volume so much anticipated later developments in his thinking that Titchener, one of his greatest students, has asserted that it outlined the program of his entire life.

In the introduction of this work Wundt stresses the primacy of method as a means of scientific advancement. He also cited advances in apparatus, such as the laryngoscope and the ophthalmoscope, as a means of ushering in whole series of discoveries. Psychology, he goes on, has not yet felt the impulse of the new empirical method being used all around it. It has asked metaphysical questions first, concerning the essence, origin, and destination of the soul. These questions should be asked at a point where psychology may end, but not where it should start. It must take the simplest of experiences for its point of departure. Psychology should crawl before it tries to walk. Wundt marshals evidence primarily from vision and secondarily from touch. One may recognize in this work his struggle to utilize physiological methodology in dealing with psychological problems.

From 1867 onward, he gave a course at Heidelberg entitled "Physiological Psychology." This date establishes the formal offering of an academic course of this nature. As he "worked up" his lecture notes over the next few years, a new book, by general agreement his most important, began to take form. This was his *Principles of Physiological Psychology*.[16] The first half was published in 1873 and the second in 1874. It was destined to go through six editions, the last in 1911, and swell in size to three large volumes. (It was characteristic of most of his books that new, amplified, and revised editions would appear from time to time). The *Principles* changed in detail, sometimes very important detail, but it is remarkable how the expansion and change did not require major shifts in his systematic views. It is the one indispensible source for an account of his system of psychology. Wundt entered on the last, longest, and most important phase of his career in 1875. In that year he became professor of philosophy at Leipzig. Here he lived and worked for forty-five years.

At the University of Leipzig in 1875, Wundt established one of the first two experimental laboratories of psychology in the world.[17] For many years it has been customary to consider 1879 as the founding year for the first experimental laboratory in the world on the mistaken belief that it was in this year that Wundt's Leipzig laboratory was given formal recognition by university authorities. Formal recognition to a course in "experimental psychology" was not given by the university until the winter of 1883, when it also provided an appropriation for a laboratory; an "Institute for Experimental Psychology," as such, was not listed by university authorities until 1894. In this connection 1879 is notable only for the appearance of the first student to do publishable psychological research with Wundt, which may be the reason for saying that psychology was "founded" in that year. Actually, before Wundt's arrival in October, 1875, the Royal Ministry had set aside a room to be used by Wundt for his own apparatus and for demonstrations connected with his *Psychologische Ubungen* or "Psychological Practicum." A good case can be made for 1875 as the year for the establishment of the first laboratory in psychology—or rather of the two first laboratories—since William James also equipped a small laboratory in the same year (p. 373). Thus, we can see the subjectivity of deciding when or how gradually the founding of this important psychological agency took place.[18] Nevertheless, if psychology must have a date to celebrate its coming into full-fledged scientific status, 1875 is perhaps the best choice.

In 1881, Wundt began to publish a journal, *Philosophische Studien*, containing reports of experimental studies that had begun to flow from his laboratory. This was the first journal devoted as much to psychology as to philosophy. Lest the title be puzzling, Wundt thought philosophy should be psychological in nature. He did not support attempts to create a department for psychology separate from that of philosophy. Moreover, between 1880 and 1901 he published four books in philosophy—a logic, an ethics, a systematic philosophy, and an introduction to the field.

One of the results of the founding of the laboratory and the spreading fame of Wundt was the migration of students to Leipzig to study with him and to work in the laboratory. There gathered around him would-be psychologists using introspection and experiment to derive the laws of the human mind. In this way Wundt became the leader of a "school" of psychology. These students were united in their systematic views as well as in sharing a common purpose. Instead of each working alone, with his labors culminating in books, the laboratory atmosphere fostered specific research studies appearing as articles in journals. Wundt would then synthesize the results of the various studies in the successive editions of the *Grundzüge*.

The sheer availability of co-workers was important. Since the experimenter could hardly be the observer at one and the same time, the experimenter of one study was available as a subject for another. Lest this point be dismissed as trivial, it is pertinent to indicate that introspection as practiced in Wundt's laboratory was not a skill acquired without a period of rigorous apprenticeship. Getting at the elements of experience required arduous training. Moreover, even if nonstudent assistants could be trained as subjects, the nature of the tasks to which they were put would have demanded payment. One does not embark on introspection as a lark! Later, when simple report, not introspection, was needed, the problem was solved by American ingenuity through the use of a captive population of college students.

CHARACTERISTIC RESEARCH

The work of the Leipzig laboratory may illustrate what a major segment of experimental psychology was like before and at the turn of the century. About one hundred experimental studies appeared in the *Philosophische Studien* during its twenty-odd years, almost all of them carried out either in the laboratory or conducted by Wundt's students soon after they left Leipzig. Consequently, the research bore heavily the impress of Wundt's direction, since typically he assigned the problem on which a particular student was to work.

Boring's summarizing classification may be utilized to sketch the research coming from Wundt's laboratory.[19] In quick overview the studies may be classed as those in sensation and perception, reaction, attention, feeling, and association. About half the research concerned problems in sensation and perception, particularly in vision. Papers on the psychophysics of color, peripheral vision, color contrast, negative after-images, visual contrast, and color blindness are typical of those concerned with visual sensation; visual size and optical illusions are characteristic subjects of those papers on visual perception. Auditory sensation was investigated by psychophysical methods, and beats and combination tones were also studied. An attack was made on the problem of time perception by studying the ability of subjects to reproduce intervals of varying lengths in the comparison of "filled" times (time occupied with mental work or sensory stimulation) and unfilled time. Tactual sensation came in for investigation through the problems of the two-point threshold, using the already familiar methods of Weber and Fechner.

About one-sixth of the time and effort of the workers in the laboratory was devoted to the reaction experiment. The subtractive procedure of Donders was used (p. 260), although his times for choice and discrimi-

Sensation + Perception – 50%
Reaction time – 16%
Attention – 10%
Feeling – 10%
Association – 10%

nation were replaced by a more complicated classification of times for volition, perception, apperception, cognition, association, and judgment.

Hopes ran high in the Leipzig laboratory for a chronometry of the mind, since, by the additive and subtractive procedures, it appeared entirely feasible to work out the times necessary for each of these processes. These hopes were dashed, however, for as Boring notes, the times for a separate process were constant neither from person to person nor from study to study,". . . and later introspection showed that in a more complicated reaction the entire conscious pattern is changed and that the alteration is not merely the insertion of another link on a chain."[20] Oswald Külpe (1862–1915), the German philosopher and experimental psychologist, delivered the most telling blow against the view that the elements are additive.[21] He showed that changing the task does not merely add another unit; instead, it alters the whole process. Külpe interpreted Lange's results as showing that the subject's predisposition or attitude alters the perceptual-reactive process. Previously Lange's classical research study had established characteristic differences in speed between some subjects who attend to the stimulus as compared to other subjects who attend to the response, in favor of the greater speed of the latter.[22] This did much to solve the problem of the personal equation. Those who attend to the response react more quickly than those who must shift attention from stimulus to the reaction to be made.

[handwritten margin note: attention to response faster than attention to stimulus]

As interest in the reaction experiment waned, studies first of attention and then of feeling came to take its place, each including about one-tenth of the laboratory's studies. Lange's study, just mentioned, helped to create the interest in attention. To Wundt, attention was clear perception of a narrow region of the content of consciousness. An example of this is the word or words we are reading on this page relative to the rest of the page, to the adjoining page, and to much of the surrounding environment of the room. Whatever is in the focus of attention becomes distinct and separate from the rest of the field. Research in the area of attention was performed by means of the complication experiment, i.e., the range and fluctuation of attention were studied. Following the lead of Jacobs, Cattell was responsible for carrying out the classic study of attention span (meaning that which can be taken in at a glance) and found that four, five, or six units (lines, letters, or words) could be apprehended in an exposure that was of too short duration to allow a movement of attention.[23]

Studies of feeling, the work of the laboratory in the 1890s, involved the use of the method of expression through which feelings and correlated changes of pulse, breathing, muscular strength, and the like were studied. The method of paired comparisons was also developed. This method requires the subject to compare each particular stimulus with every other stimulus in terms of the subjective feeling aroused. Suppose the task were to judge the pleasingness of a variety of colored paper patches: patch A is compared to B, C, D, E, F; then patch B is compared to A, C, D, E, F, and so on. On each trial the observer was to say which was the most pleasing of each pair: A or B, A or C, and so on.

Studies of association make up another one-tenth of the total output of the laboratory during these years. Under Wundt's direction much was done to refine the method. As will be discussed in a subsequent chapter (p. 330), Galton, although using single words as stimuli, had often allowed his responses to take the form of a connected narrative description of the images. Wundt required each response to be a *single* word that made not only the classification of responses easier to handle, but also the time relations involved to be more susceptible to precise measurement. More exact instruments of measurement such as the lip key and the chronoscope, which measures time in thousandths of seconds, were used. The major categories of association derived by Wundt's students were two: "inner" and "outer." Inner associations are those showing intrinsic connections between the words, as in lion-animal, spear-shield, cow-milk, and white-black. Outer associations are those in which there are other purely extrinsic or "accidental" associations, as in curve-accident or book-concept; or in speech-habit associations, such as fur-fly or crash helmet. Cattell was chiefly responsible for discovering the importance of control in association. Instruction to give reactions that bore a definite relation to the stimulus word—an opposite or a subordinate or the like—made for quicker reactions than did free association in which there was freedom to choose any word that one wished. Giving the response "dark" to the stimulus word "light," when one had been told in advance to give the opposite of the stimulus word, resulted in a more rapid reaction than when no control on the associations to be given was exercised. It would appear that when there are many possible responses more or less equally associated with the stimulus word, there is a process of interference that delays the reaction. An everyday example is the interference met by one who speaks more than one foreign language in arriving at the correct word, especially if the languages themselves are similar, as in Spanish and French. The great German psychiatrist Emil Kraepelin (1856–1926), who studied under Wundt, extended the experimental use of association to problems in psychopathology.[24] He

Kraepelin (1856-1926)

found that under experimentally induced fatigue, alcoholic intoxication, and similar states, there is an increase in superficial, extrinsic, or outer associations dependent upon habit, an increase at the expense of inner associations, which depend upon meaning. The former resemble the associations of some psychotic patients, particularly the manics.

It becomes apparent from the survey of the research from his laboratory that Wundt did not occupy himself with developing new kinds of experiments; the methods he used are already generally familiar to the reader from the account of psychology *before* Wundt. Studies of the psychology and physiology of the senses owe much to the work that went before, particularly to Helmholtz. Reaction time studies again owe something, not only to Helmholtz, but also to Donders, while the association study can be attributed to Galton. Even the study of feeling, where Wundt was at his most original in a theoretical sense, depended on extension of Fechner's method of impression to paired comparisons; and studies of expression were linked to the utilization of already existing methods for studying pulse, breathing, and the like. Even for attention there had been antecedent studies, although there had been no occasion to discuss them. Wundt wished further to reduce to quantitative terms the research areas already extant. His view of the scope of experimental psychology was consequently a narrow one, practically confined to the five classifications of research in his laboratory.

LATER LIFE AND STUDENTS

Wundt began sponsoring doctoral dissertations as early as 1875.[25] By 1919 the total had reached an impressive one hundred and eighty-six, of which seventy were working on philosophical topics and one hundred and sixteen on psychological problems. Not all of the men he sponsored were destined to become leading psychologists. Struck by the number of unfamiliar names, one psychologist[26] tried to trace them down; astonishingly, eighty-six could not be found. A considerable number of the students were apparently content, after receiving the precious title, *"Herr Doktor,"* to sink back into the oblivion of the *gymnasium.*

His students came from all over Europe. Many were even American (to be considered in later chapters). The first of these was G. Stanley Hall, fresh from his studies at Harvard. This roving ambassador of American psychology-to-be "dropped in" for a time in the first year of the new laboratory and studied with Wundt. Ambivalent toward Wundt, he was careful to state that most of his time was spent with Ludwig, the physiologist.[27] But his story is best told in a later chapter. James McKeen Cattell, Wundt's first *bona fide* American student, studied at Leipzig on

G. Stanley Hall

JAMES McKeen Cattell

two occasions. It was on his second sojourn in 1885 that Cattell made his pronouncement to Wundt that the latter needed an assistant and that he, Cattell, was that assistant. Other American students of Wundt's were Edward W. Scripture, later director of the Yale Psychological Laboratory and a student of hearing; Edward A. Pace, for many years head of the Department of Psychology at Catholic University and the leading voice in interpreting the "new psychology" to Catholics; Lightner Witmer, the founder of the first psychological clinic at the University of Pennsylvania; and Charles H. Judd, the pioneer educational psychologist at the University of Chicago. Even this short list shows something of the breadth of activity that these Americans managed to show on their return to the United States after the severely rigorous "pure" training they had received. Born in England where there was no suitable post for an experimental psychologist such as he, Edward Bradford Titchener, another of Wundt's students, came to American to direct the psychological work at Cornell University. Among this group he was the most unswervingly faithful to the program of his teacher. The best known continental psychologists who worked in the Leipzig laboratory, besides Külpe, already mentioned, were Hugo Münsterberg, Alfred Lehmann, Ernst Meumann, Theodor Lipps, and Felix Krueger.

According to Titchener, Wundt was a quiet, unassuming, pleasant person whose life followed a totally regulated pattern. He worked on his current book or article in the morning, then had a consultation hour.[28] In the afternoon he paid a formal visit to the laboratory; he followed this with a walk, during which he cast his lecture into rough form; he delivered the lecture without notes and made a second, informal return to the laboratory. He was a very popular lecturer, apparently simplifying his material somewhat to suit his audience. As Hall puts it, Wundt's style of writing is as lusterless as lead—but as solid.[29] To perhaps a surprising extent, concerts and interests in current affairs occupied many of his evenings. He was a man of simple tastes who avoided public functions and virtually never traveled.

It is not surprising that from this background emerged the serious hard-working, hard-driving writer of so many books in so many editions; no single person would be humorless enough to read every work in every edition. If he did try to, what would he face? Boring wryly estimated that Wundt had produced some 53, 735 pages (averaging out to 2.2 pages per day for every day from 1853 to 1920).[30] At that rate, the consumer-reader, reading at the rate of sixty pages per day, would need nearly two-and-a-half years to go through the entire output.

In 1902, only twenty-eight years after the preface to the first edition of the *Principles,* in which he had expressed his intent of presenting a new science, he could say in the fifth edition that the material was now pouring in from all sides.[31] No longer was there any doubt as to the legitimacy of his endeavors. Instead, divergent trends within the field itself were becoming a cause of concern to him. European psychology was beginning to have centers of influence other than Leipzig and Wundt. The climate of the times was producing psychologists, inde-pendent of Wundt, who had drawn on their common cultural heritage and arrived at an experimental psychology by the end of the century. Some of them will be considered in the next chapter. Our present con-cern is with Wundt's reaction to work that deviated from his own.

ATTITUDE TOWARD OTHER BRANCHES OF PSYCHOLOGY

Wundt was unalterably opposed to the application of psychol-ogy.[32] When Meumann, a gifted pupil, turned to educational psychology, Wundt treated this as desertion in the face of the enemy. Kraepelin, another student, applied psychology to psychiatry, and was advised by Wundt to concentrate on psychiatry.[33] Work other than that of his own students came in for even more severe criticism. He was especially critical of the work of the so-called Wurzburg School. After securing the immediate response to stimulation, workers at Wurzburg proceeded to question their subjects about all that had gone on in their minds. Wundt considered this a blatant violation of the rules of introspection. Despite the admission that child (and animal) psychology were supplementary branches[34] of the field, he categorically rejected the beginnings of child psychology in the work of Preyer and Baldwin. Their work was not psychology since the conditions of study could not be adequately con-trolled.[35] In his laboratory, no work with animals was conducted. He was also very critical of French psychology, claiming that the work done in that country was reduced to studies of suggestion and hypnotism.[36] He argued that one cannot give the name "experimental psychology" to each and every operation that brings about a change in consciousness. Those studies lacked exact introspection, so they were not true psycho-logical experiments. Lest one get the impression that he could not tolerate differences of opinion, there were other students such as Hugo Münster-berg (p. 376), Felix Krueger (p. 556), and Eduard Spranger (p. 557), who disagreed with him sharply on various major theoretical points with whom he maintained cordial relationships; he was, in fact, personally helpful to them.[37]

The idea of a social psychology was part of the *Zeitgeist.*[38] Steinthal and Lazarus had devoted the first published issue of their journal to the topic in 1859–1860. At first, social psychology was seen by Wundt as only an auxiliary science. Not until 1893 was he convinced that social psychology deserved to be considered a coordinate branch along with experimental psychology. He believed that experiment is not feasible when problems more complex than those of perception and memory are considered. Beyond this point, experiment fails us and we must have recourse to cultural psychology. In making this division of labor, Wundt was also saying that the higher mental processes, incapable of direct experimental attack, should perforce be studied through the chief products of common mental life, that is to say, through language, myth, and custom.[39] Language, for example, he held as the major key to understanding thought. In order to consider the problems of the higher mental processes, he began writing the *Völkerpsychologie,* the first volume appearing in 1900 and nine more volumes between then and 1920.[40] Although there is a temptation to which many succumb to translate this term as "folk psychology," it would appear that "cultural" psychology captures his meaning much better.

Cultural psychology was conceived of as the investigation of the various, still-existing stages of mental development in mankind.[41] In this sense it can and has been called "genetic" psychology. To Wundt, mankind shows development through a series of successive levels: primitive man has the lowest grade of culture; next comes the totemic age; then the age of heroes and gods; and finally, the age in which we are now living, that of the advance toward humanity. Cultural psychology is differentiated from ethnology by Wundt; ethnology is concerned primarily with the external cultures and only in a very incidental fashion with the psychological characteristics that are at the core of cultural psychology.

As if according to plan, Wundt published his autobiographical reminiscences, *Erlebtes und Erkanntes,* in 1920.[42] He died on August 31 of that year, two weeks after his eighty-eighth birthday.

Some Systematic Views

Wundt's claim to greatness rests more upon his work as a founder of psychology than on his systematic views. His system amounted primarily to a classificatory scheme, and as Boring observes, this itself was not capable of direct or indirect experimental proof or disproof.[43] As new evidence appeared, Wundt revised his position on various issues. It would be impossible to do justice to these changes in a short space; unless otherwise specified, only his mature theoretical guidelines, as established in the fifth edition of the *Principles*, published in 1902,[44] and in the second edition of his *Introduction*,[45] published in German in 1911 and in English in 1912, will be examined along with a recent important reappraisal of his work by Blumenthal.[46]

To Wundt, psychology is the science that investigates the facts of consciousness. Mind is a process; and yet it has elements, although this is a somewhat ambiguous view of the matter. Consciousness supplies us the total of its immediate experience. The more specific immediate experiences involved, to name only the most important, are sensations, feelings, ideas, volitions, and apperceptions. None of these appears in an uncompounded state; they must be abstracted from the compound by introspective analysis. In fact, all of our experiences are complex and must be analyzed introspectively.

The elements of the mind, or the basic states of consciousness, are sensations and feelings. When abstracted by introspection, pure sensations are found to possess only intensity and quality and lack spatial or temporal aspects. Sensations are objective in the sense that they have reference to external things. Experiences directly aroused by external stimuli were often referred to by earlier systematists as sensations while those dependent upon internal conditions were called ideas. Wundt held this to be an error. The source for touch and organic sensations of our body are just as much a part of our outer world as is stimulation from external objects. Hence, these sensations, too, are external.

Feelings that accompany sensations are the subjective complements referring to states of consciousness itself. Sensations and feelings are simultaneous aspects of immediate experience. Sometimes the aspect of feeling is apparently negligible, but it is always present. If intensity is increased, feeling becomes apparent, as when a light is increased in intensity to the point at which it becomes dazzling. Wundt, nevertheless, considered feeling an experience that was distinct from that other conscious element, sensation.

Feelings cannot be described in terms of pleasantness-unpleasantness alone, as Wundt himself had held earlier. Two additional dimensions—tension-relaxation and excitement-depression—must also be used to account for the range of the experiences of feeling. Wundt had found that a given feeling experience involves three dimensions but in different combinations; for example, pleasant, tense, and excited in one case or unpleasant, relaxed, and depressed in another. Feeling experience is not a matter of simultaneity alone. The dimensions in the experience change through time: tickling at first might move along the dimension of pleasantness; but then tension and excitement would become apparent, and unpleasantness would come to predominate over pleasantness.

This tridimensional theory of feeling, as it was called, stimulated a tremendous amount of research in both his own and rival laboratories, but the theory was not borne out by immediate post-Wundtian research. The results of these studies were found applicable in contemporary research situations, however. It is in this way that psychology, having become an experimental science, advances. A theory may stand or fall; the experiments persist, either interpreted as isolated facts or worked into a modified or different system when they are congruent with it.

The concept that the mind is reducible to elements for purposes of study and the fashion in which these elements cohere is obviously a heritage from the empiricist-associationist tradition. But Wundt went beyond this level; the experiences we have are more than the sum of their parts—there is a creative synthesis of immediate experience.[47] This, especially in later writings, he came to stress. His was not a mental chemistry as is often alleged. Indeed, he specifically rejected Mill's view of the matter.[48] Besides analysis there is a constructive process of psychic synthesis. Once the systematic analysis into elements had been accomplished, their manner of synthesis could be carried out. Seeing a landscape, he was aware, did *not* add up to thirteen specified visual sensations of variant hues and the accompanying feelings of mild excitement, high pleasure, and low tension, meaningfully perceived. This synthesis was expressed by using concepts of combination, complexes, fusion, apperception, and volition.

When sensation and feeling are combined, they form ideas and perceptions. To Wundt, the term idea included such complexes as memory images and perceptions.[49] Ideas, including both sensations and feelings in composite, are representative of objects either in perception or in memory.

Wundt, chronologically following Mill, made use of association. However, it was but one principle of combination that he used.[50] He preferred to limit it to successive association, since he considered simultaneous compounds so much more tightly knit as to require a different principle of combination. This was fusion, of a kind that occurs in tones in the musical chord or in illusions.

Consciousness shows various degrees of apperception, of contexts, and of connections—the unification of the conscious contents. Children may run words together in something they recite without understanding what they are saying. Adults may parrot a difficult concept but not understand what is meant by it. Unification requires apperception, a combination of a complex and a unity. This doctrine of apperception is already familiar, but Wundt stressed its cognitive aspects more than his *apperception ;*

predecessors. To define it more fully, clearness of comprehension of conscious content—occurring through the combination of sensory experiences with preexisting ideas, and accompanied by feelings—results in apperception. Feeling enters into the process; the particular quality of the experience of the feeling of a compound is dependent on apperception. Easy, smooth-flowing reactions give rise to pleasure, conflictual discordant ones to pain.

Wundt made a distinction between the whole range of consciousness and the so-called fixation point of apperception. Only processes in the fixation point of apperception are apperceived. This does not mean that apperception cannot range over the complex of ideas, referred to as the apperceptive mass, but at a given moment the matter in the fixation of apperception is a selection from this mass. When apperceptions refer to any given content, Wundt says they are customarily called "states of attention."[51] Wundt preferred to discuss the phenomena in terms of apperception, possibly to bring out its active character in contradistinction to states of attention as a more passive process. But he knew, of course, that others could and did discuss this problem in terms of attention, a rather more familiar way of handling the issue.

Combinations of feelings alone with ideational processes give rise to the emotions. In some emotions, such as joy and delight, pleasure predominates; in others, such as anger and fear, displeasure is the stronger.

Volitional processes had a central position in Wundt's system. Voluntarism was his term for psychological causality and followed from his differentiation of psychological from physical causality. Psychological causality arose from volitional processes.

Closely related to the emotions are the volitional processes. To Wundt, volitions are primarily affective in nature. The feelings are the "determining factors" of volition. Sometimes feelings are not strong enough to produce volition, but volition is not operative unless they are present. Volition culminates in an action, as when an angry person strikes the object of his anger. Without the striking the process would be emotion alone.

In dealing with volition Wundt was considering action as differentiated from reception. The distinction between sensory and motor nerves that arose from the work of the physiologists carried over into Wundt's psychology at this point. Sensations are the psychological phenomena associated with the former; movements, called actions, are the psychological phenomena associated with the latter. There was a natural coherence between a sensation and an action which was modified through experience.

Overview

Wundt was the first modern psychologist—the first person to conceive of experimental psychology as a science. He founded the first psychological laboratory, and he edited the first experimental journal. In addition to these pioneering efforts, Wundt was the great synthesizer of research findings, both of the work that preceded him and of that carried on by his students. Wundt's *forte* was not to light up the dark corners with luminous ideas or to give us a dazzling new perspective. Rather, he refurbished the old incomplete picture, working over a thousand details, cleaning here, repairing there, filling a crack here, so that psychology as it left his hands was an improved, more coherent entity, but still reognizable.

The areas of investigation worked out by Wundt—sensation and perception, reaction time, attention, feeling, association—became firmly fixed as the very chapter titles in the textbooks that were to come, making this work a not inconsiderable portion of psychology. And yet his treatment of other areas of psychology was either nonexistent or, at best, woefully inadequate. The problem areas of learning (as differentiated from association), motivation, emotion, intelligence, thought, and personality were to be systematically brought within the scope of psychology by men who had other points of view.

Whatever one may think of the narrowness of Wundt's conception of psychology, it must be admitted that the course he chose had the effect of solidifying an independent field of psychology. If he had struck out on uncharted paths it is quite conceivable that the emergence of psychology as a separate discipline would have been delayed. It does not detract from his achievement to add that much of the history of psychology following Wundt consisted of rebelling against the limitations he had placed upon the field. In general, forward movement is most sure when it has something to push against.

The methodological prescriptive allegiances of Wilhelm Wundt are similar to that of the physiologists from whom he drew inspiration. Naturalism was accepted without question; he subscribed to methodological objectivism in the sense that he attempted to quantify experience so that others could repeat his procedures, and quantitativism itself. Since the combination of introspection and experiment was the method of choice, Wundt fostered empiricism. His rejection of empiricism's rival, rationalism, was equally straightforward. Psychology as a science, he held, could not be based on metaphysical, i.e., rationalistic assumptions. Nomotheticism had so compelling a hold on Wundt that he rejected attempts at idiographically oriented investigation even among his own students. Acceptance of determinism was implicit in all his research investigations.

Contentually, an adherence to contentual subjectivism of a conscious mentalist variety dominated. Wundt hardly conceived contentual objectivism to be possible, let alone advocated it. His methodological position of dual aspect parallelistic monism, caused him to insist that, for example, in psychophysical research one studies the relation between sensation on one hand and judgment on the other, and not the dualistic relation of body and mind. This made systematic his conception of psychology as contentually subjective in nature. The units were the elements of mental contents, and were thus molecular in that the isolation of these elements was the first task of psychology. It is important to add that a principle of psychosynthesis was advocated. Thus a molar view was also adhered to in which the sum of the elements was more than these elements. Wundt's was a structural view of the mind since parts, not functions, were stressed. It was static in that the enduring, not the changing facets of mind were sought. Purism of an almost snobbish variety was held to against any claims of utilitarianism.

References*

1. W. Wundt, *Principles of Physiological Psychology*, 5th German ed., Vol. 1, trans. E. B. Titchener (New York: Macmillan, 1904), author's preface to first edition (1874).
2. W. Wundt, *Lectures on Human and Animal Psychology*, 2nd German ed., trans. J. E. Creighton and E. B. Titchener (New York: Macmillan, 1894), pp. 440–450 (1892); W. Wundt, *An Introduction to Psychology*, 2nd ed., trans. R. Pintner (New York: Macmillan, 1912) Chapter 5 (1911); W. Wundt, *Grundriss der Psychologie* (Leipzig: Engelmann, 1896), Section 1, para, 2 (Herrnstein and Boring, Excerpt No. 109); W. G. Bringmann, W. Balance, and R. B. Evans, "Wilhelm Wundt 1832–1920: a Biographical Sketch," *Journal of the History of the Behavioral Sciences*, XI (1975): 287–297.
3. Principles, *Introduction*.
4. *Ibid.*, pp. 180 ff.
5. W. Wundt, "Selbstbeobachtung und innere Wahrnehmung," *Philosophische Studien* IV (1887–1888): 292–309.

*See p. 19 for description of reference style.

6. W. Wundt, *Kleine Schriften*, Vol. 2 (Leipzig: Engelmann, 1911).

7. *Principles*, Introduction.

8. E. B. Titchener, "Wilhelm Wundt," *American Journal of Psychology*, XXXII (1921): 161–178.

9. *Principles*, Introduction.

10. *Ibid.*

11. *Ibid.*

12. W. Wundt, *Outlines of Psychology*, 7th German ed., trans. C. H. Judd (Leipzig: Engelmann, 1907) (1896).

13. Some of the facts of his life and research as reported here were derived from Titchener, while the other source, unless otherwise specified, is Wundt's own psychological reminiscences, *Erlebtes und Erkanntes* (Stuttgart: Kröner, 1920).

14. W. Wundt, *Die Lehre von der Muskelbewegung* (Braunschweig: Vieweg, 1858).

15. W. Wundt, *Beiträge zur Theorie der Sinneswahrnehmung* (Leipzig: Winter, 1862).

16. W. Wundt, *Grundzüge der physiologischen Psychologie* (Leipzig: Engelmann, 1873–1874).

17. R. S. Harper, "The First Psychological Laboratory," *Isis*, XLI (1950): 158–161.

18. E. G. Boring, "On the Subjectivity of Important Historical Dates: Leipzig, 1879," *Journal of the History of the Behavioral Sciences*, I (1965): 5–9.

19. E. G. Boring, *A History of Experimental Psychology*, 2nd ed. (New York: Appleton-Century-Crofts, 1950), pp. 340–344.

20. *Ibid.*, 342.

21. O. Külpe, *Outlines of Psychology*, trans. E. B. Titchener (New York: Macmillan, 1909).

22. L. Lange, "Neue Experimente über den Vorgang der einfachen Reaktion auf Sinneseindrücke," *Philosophische Studien*, IV (1888): 479–510.

23. J. M. Cattell, "The Time it Takes to See and Name Objects," *Mind*, XI (1886): 63–65, reprinted in W. Dennis, ed., *Readings in the History of Psychology* (New York: Appleton-Century-Crofts, 1948), pp. 326–328.

24. E. Kraepelin, "Der psychologische Versuch in der Psychiatrie," *Psychologische Arbeiten* (Leipzig, 1895): 1, 1–91.

25. M. A. Tinker, "Wundt's Doctorate Students and

Their Theses (1875–1920)," *American Journal of Psychology*, XLIV (1932): 630–637.

26. S. W. Fernberger, "Wundt's Doctorate Students," *Psychological Bulletin*, XXX (1933): 80–83.
27. G. S. Hall, *Founders of Modern Psychology*, (New York: Appleton, 1912).
28. Titchener, "Wilhelm Wundt."
29. Hall, *Founders*.
30. Boring, *History*, p. 345.
31. *Principles*.
32. W. Wundt, "Ueber rein und angewandte Psychologie," *Psychologische Studien*, V (1910): 1–47.
33. Hall, *Founders*.
34. *Principles*.
35. H. Eber, "Zur Kritik der Kinderpsychologie, mit Rücksicht auf neuere Arbeiten, *Philosophische Studien*, XI (1896): 586–588.
36. *Principles*.
37. Bringmann, *et at.*, "Wilhelm Wundt."
38. Titchener, "Wilhelm Wundt."
39. *Ibid.*
40. W. Wundt, *Völkerpsychologie*, 10 vols. (Leipzig: Engelmann, 1900–1920).
41. W. Wundt, *Elements of Folk Psychology: Outlines of a Psychological History of the Development of Mankind* (London: Allen, 1916), pp. 4ff. (1912).
42. *Erlebtes*.
43. Boring, *History*, p. 328.
44. Principles, *Introduction*.
45. *Introduction*.
46. A. L. Blumenthal, *Language and Psychology: Historical Aspects of Linguistics*. (New York: Wiley, 1970); A. L. Blumental, "A Reappraisal of Wilhelm Wundt," *American Psychologist* XXX (1975): 1081–1088.
47. W. Wundt, *Gründzuge der physiologischen Psychologie*. 5th ed., Vol. 2. (Leipzig: Engelmann, 1902).
48. *Ibid.*
49. Principles, *Introduction*, p. 45.
50. W. Wundt, *Outlines of Psychology*, trans. C. H. Judd (New York: Macmillan, 1897) (1896) (Herrnstein and Boring, Excerpt No. 76).
51. *Principles*, p. 316.

Chapter 13

Brentano AND Ebbinghaus:
THE BROADENING OF PSYCHOLOGY

Despite the considerable dominance that Wilhelm Wundt exercised over German psychology, some psychologists embraced other prescriptive influences or investigated contentual areas different from those he espoused. Of Wundt's contemporaries and successors, two merit special attention: Franz Brentano, who advanced a view that psychology is properly concerned with acts rather than contents, and thus adhered to a functional prescription; and Hermann Ebbinghaus, who became the first psychologist empirically to study memory and learning, thus broadening the content of psychology. There were two others whose contributions showed a similar but also significant broadening effect. G. E. Müller carefully followed up and expanded the work of his predecessors on psychophysics, color vision, and memory; and Oswald Külpe, Wundt's erstwhile assistant, became the leader of the group of psychologists that came to be called the Würzburg school, the school that extended the use of introspection to the study of the higher mental processes.

Franz Brentano

In 1874, the year that saw the complete publication of the crucial first edition of Wundt's *Grundzüge*, another significant, but markedly different book appeared. This was *Psychology from an Empirical Standpoint*, written by a Catholic priest, Franz Brentano. While Wundt had drawn his inspiration from practically contemporaneous work, Brentano reached far into the past to the work of Aristotle and Aquinas, and thence to Locke and Mill. An account of Brentano's life will help one to understand his book's significance.

297

LIFE OF BRENTANO $\left(1838 - 1917\right)$

Franz Brentano was born in Marienburg on the Rhine in 1838.[1] When he was very young, his family moved to Bavaria. He lost his father early, and his mother, a devout Catholic, encouraged his early inclination toward a clerical vocation. In 1856 he moved on to Munich, where he worked under Ignatius Döllinger, the famous church historian. He then studied at Berlin, where he was thoroughly trained by F. A. Trendelenburg in the works of Aristotle. This training was decisive in all that he did afterward, for his psychological and philosophical thinking bore the impress of Aristotle. He also studied philosophy and theology at Munich and later at Tübingen, where he took his degree in 1862. He then entered the priesthood in 1864. Two years later he became *Dozent* in philosophy at Würzburg. For the next few years he busied himself with lecturing and writing papers on the philosophy of Aristotle and the history of science within the church.

During the sixties a controversy of considerable moment arose within the Catholic church concerning the infallibility of the Pope. Ignatius Döllinger, Brentano's former teacher, was a leader of the group within the church that opposed the doctrine. Brentano, too, had strong doubts about this proposed dogma and wrote and published a memoir to refute it, on the basis of which he became something of a leader among the dissident clerics. Then, in 1870 the Vatican Council accepted papal infallibility, making it dogma. Brentano was now faced with that age-old decision, to acquiesce or to become a heretic. In his preface to a posthumously published work, he emphasized that this dilemma was the last of a series of doubts he had about being able to reconcile faith and reason.[2] Before the meeting of the Vatican Council took place, he had doubted papal infallibility without other matters beclouding the issue. After the Council's decision, he still found it untenable, and so, in 1873, he resigned the professorship to which he had been appointed as a priest. He thereafter put off clerical duties and garb. Unlike many of the other priests who left the church at this time, he did not join another church, such as the so-called Old Catholic church, which was sponsored by Döllinger. Nor did Protestantism appeal to him. He remained to his death a devout Christian of simple faith, but without church affiliation.[3]

During the period that followed, without either university or clerical duties to interfere, he produced the book, *Psychology from an Empirical Standpoint*.[4] In 1874 he was appointed, as a layman, professor at the University of Vienna, a post he held until 1880.

In that year a second major crisis arose. He wished to marry a Catholic, which was impossible for a former priest under Austrian law.

He once again resigned his professorship, took citizenship in Saxony, and married. He immediately returned to the University of Vienna, not as a professor, but as a lecturer.

Over these years his lectures were very popular. The hall was always crowded, and subsequent informal smaller discussions were usual; his students often followed him home.[5] Among his students, at Würzburg and at Vienna were such diverse persons as Carl Stumpf, the assiduous student of the psychology of sound; Edmund Husserl, the philosopher and psychologist of phenomenology; Christian von Ehrenfels, the originator of the concept of form quality and founder of the Austrian school of the philosophy of values; Thomas Masaryk, the founder of the Czechoslovakian Republic; and Sigmund Freud, the originator of psychoanalysis. The influence of Brentano upon Freud is still a moot point. He may have been more influenced by Brentano than is generally recognized.[6]

Brentano's students testified to their devotion to him; Stumpf and Husserl were especially glowing in this respect.[7] It is generally agreed that Brentano expressed himself most completely orally rather than in his relatively few publications. He himself apparently believed that his contribution was made more through oral exchange than through the written word.

In 1894 his wife died, and his own health became poor. An eye disorder threatened his sight. In that year he resigned for the last time, never to hold an academic post again. After his resignation he devoted the remainder of his life to study, occasional writing, and informal conversational teaching among his friends and admirers. In 1895–6 he settled in Florence.

During the years in Vienna he had published hardly any psychological works. Shortly before he left, he did write some papers on visual illusions. In 1907 a small but significant book on sense psychology[8] appeared, and in 1911 he published *Von der Klassifikation der psychischen Phänomene*,[9] his nearest approximation to the missing second volume of the *Psychologie* of thirty-seven years before. After Italy entered the war, Brentano, a pacifist, moved to Zürich, where he died in 1917.

ACT PSYCHOLOGY

For Brentano there was no essential schism between philosophy and psychology.[10] In this regard he was returning to the work of Locke, for whom psychology was basic to philosophy. Psychology became the means of rescuing philosophy from the morass into which it had slumped under Kant, whom Brentano considered a mystic to be classed with

Plotinus. The work of John Stuart Mill also influenced him to regard psychology as basic to other fields.

Even the title of his book was firmly rooted in the past. To the associationists, "empirical" meant derived from sense experience, Brentano returned to the Greek meaning. By empirical, Brentano intended an emphasis on activity. As Brett put it," . . . it was 'empirical' in the sense that it was based on the claim that it reached a pure experience and analysed it."[11]

Titchener[12] considered that Brentano's use of "empirical" was related to a consistent and reasoned account of mind, essentially argumentative in nature rather than descriptive, which Titchener considered Wundt's psychology (and his own) to be. Carmichael,[13] on analyzing this argument, reached the conclusion that a more apt term to describe Brentano's approach would be to call it "rational." It would be easy to agree with this position, since Brentano's approach was essentially logical. He presented arguments and offered proofs.

Observation rather than experiment was his primary tool. He did not reject experiment as such. When he disagreed with the results of experiments, he tended to try to destroy them by argument, not by carrying out or suggesting research. In his studies of illusions, his characteristic method of exposition was to suggest that the reader see for himself. Brentano reproduced the illusions, but the reader's visual inspection was the basis on which he was content to rest his case.[14] The conclusions were drawn from observation, not reason alone. To that extent they were empirical. His writing also gave the impression that, once developed, his system was permanently fixed.[15]

As a first approximation, before turning directly to the way Brentano stated his system of psychology, let us try to relate his thinking to Aristotle. Aristotle (p. 60) had taught that sensation received the form of the object, as distinguished from nutrition, which took in the material itself from the object. We eat the nutritive object, the fig; we sense its form without assimilating the matter. In sensing there is assimilation of form, not merely passively but actively, in that sensing actualizes the quality of the object. When we pass beyond sensing to knowing (p. 118 f.)—from color or magnitude to asking *what is* color or magnitude—these universals are actualized by knowing, and knowing as actualized is identical with form.

Brentano was moved by a similar spirit. He wished to find a way of relating the person, the experiencer, to the environment. He insisted that a distinction must be made between the experience as structure and the experience as a way of acting.[16] The quality "blue" and the sensing of blue are different. This latter process is the true subject matter of psychology. Going back to the ideas of Aristotle, it might even be said that psychology is concerned with the experiences the mind carries out when it actualizes blue. The blueness, as such, is merely passive. Looking at blue is a way of experientially doing something. Without going into further details or tracing the development through the thinking of Aquinas, it was in the spirit of these and other considerations that Brentano derived a psychology of the act. This is to say that he stressed activity of the mind at the expense of the content of the mind. Psychology is concerned with the act, not the content. Thus Brentano was promulgating a functional prescription; he conceived psychological categories as activities.

This does not mean that content disappears, nor does it mean that the content with which the mind deals is always real. We refer our ideating to objects whether they do or do not exist. We may ideate blue of the sky or the skin sheen of the unicorn even though in the two cases their epistemological status is different. Nevertheless, they may be the objects in our thinking. Nor is the content of a psychical phenomenon always physical; it may be another psychical act. The act has become the content or object of another act.

On seeing a color, the color itself is not mental; it is the act of seeing that is mental. The color itself belongs to physics. Psychical phenomena *relate* to content, but they are not that content. Nevertheless, to see, something must be seen. It "inexists" in the seeing. Act psychology constitutes an intentionalism, since mind is represented as comprising mental acts that by intention are directed upon some object. Seeing, hearing, and so on are mental acts that must have some object like blue that they "intend." In Brentano's terminology, seeing "intends" the blue that "inexists" within the act of seeing, blue being the "immanent" object of the seeing. "I see blue" is the act of the mental datum, and the blue is this commonest object of the act.

We can define psychical phenomena, says Brentano, by saying that they are phenomena that intentionally contain an object in themselves.[17] Mind points to something outside itself, called by Brentano "intentionality." When we see something, two things take place—first comes the act of seeing, and then the seen object or the content of seeing. The objects are not part of the act. The object intentionally inexists with the act (not actually existing, hence "inexisting," but present by implication). Mental acts refer to something outside of themselves. An act has an object that it intends or is directed upon.

The source of all psychological experience is inner perception. Each of us has an inner perception that supplies the psychological phenomena. Calling the phenomena psychic or subsuming them under soul makes no difference. If we do so, the soul *is* its acts. It can be seen from this that Brentano is neatly disposing of physiology. Psychology cannot be reduced to physiology, since its field is the act.

3 Kinds

Psychic phenomena consist of acts of three kinds—ideating, judging, and feeling. Quite consistently, Brentano arrived at his classification of function by an examination of the various types of relationship a subject has to an object.[18] The first and most ubiquitous relationship is that of having an idea of an object—real, imaginary, past, present, future, and even negative. Hence, there is *ideating*. But in addition, the sheer diversity of kinds of objects ideated makes possible an affirmation or denial of the object. Hence, there is *judging*. Moreover, one may take attitudes toward objects that may be expressed as running the gamut from love (attraction) to hate (repulsion). Hence there is *feeling*. In ideating, something is ideated; in judging, something is judged; in feeling, something is felt. Every act refers to an object or content that inexists within it, no matter what the kind of act.

Despite the ancient sources of Brentano's system of act psychology, it came as a revolt against established ways of thinking, especially those sponsored by Wundt. Brentano's system gained stature and point by being clearly in opposition to Wundt's psychology of content. Wundt saw mind in terms of static elements. He had admitted apperception to his system, but more or less as a reluctant afterthought and not as an integral and primary conceptual tool. Hence, the lines were drawn for a distinction between a psychology of content and a psychology of act, each to have its devoted followers.

Hermann Ebbinghaus (1850-1909)

In about 1876 a student of philosophy and psychology, browsing at a bookstall in Paris, chanced upon a secondhand copy of Fechner's *Elements*. The mathematical approach to psychological problems that it contained came as a revelation to young Hermann Ebbinghaus.[19] From his reading of this book arose his greatest intellectual feat—a conviction that the strictly scientific measurement Fechner had carried through with psychophysics could also be applied to the higher mental processes. Wundt's recently published *Principles* contained his contention of the impossibility of experimentally studying the higher mental processes. Ebbinghaus was probably familiar with this volume.[20] If so, it merely served as a challenge to him, not a deterrent.

EARLY LIFE

Hermann Ebbinghaus was born in Barman, near Bonn, in 1850, the son of a merchant. He studied history and philology at Bonn and then moved, first to Halle and then to Berlin, in the meantime shifting his interests to philosophy. After serving in the army during the Franco-Prussian War, he returned to Bonn for his doctorate in philosophy, writing his dissertation on Hartmann's philosophy of the unconscious. This was in 1873. The next seven years were spent in independent study, first in Berlin, where he followed the not-unusual practice of the philosopher of his time in studying the sciences. After 1875, he spent three years in England and France in private study and in tutoring. It was during these years that he chanced to discover Fechner's book.

RESEARCH ON MEMORY

Without a teacher, a university environment, or a laboratory, and without any inspiration except the general climate of the times, Ebbinghaus plunged into the study of learning and memory, subjects heretofore untouched by measurement and research. Working alone, he saw clearly the difficulties standing in his way, devised the necessary methods and materials and, using himself as the only subject, carried through the research that was to eventuate in his monograph *Über das Gedächtnis*.[21]

He perceived that his self-appointed task required careful preparation and planning. He saw that he could not take over Fechner's psychophysical methods as they stood, because they would be entirely too slow and cumbersome. But he did want to use a method that was in the spirit of Fechner.

Associationists, particularly Brown and Mill, had attached importance to the principle of frequency as a condition of recall. Frequency of repetition of material or number of trials until learning was complete was seen by Ebbinghaus as the essential condition for forming associations. He decided to use the number of repetitions to serve as his measure of learning. Not only was there to be repetition of the same material to the point where it was wholly learned, there must also be repetition of the task, each time with similar but not identical materials, until he could be confident of the accuracy of his findings. In order for variable errors from trial to trial to be cancelled out, Ebbinghaus would use the same procedure again and again, as did Fechner, varying only the particular content to be learned; then he would find an average measure. In deference to the demands of experiment, he went so far as to regulate his habits, following the same rigorous pattern day after day and learning the materials always at the same time of day.

He was familiar with the fact that some pieces of poetry or prose can be learned much more easily than others. Associations already formed with such materials facilitate learning them. Recognizing that differences due to acquaintance with the material to be learned must be eliminated, Ebbinghaus needed homogeneous, equally unfamiliar material for the many learning sessions that he was planning. Thus, although he used poetry and prose to some extent, the majority of his studies were carried out with new materials of his own invention, the so-called nonsense syllables. Two consonants with a vowel between, as in *nuz, lef,* and *bup,* formed these syllables. All possible combinations of German consonants and vowels were prepared by him, and each was put on a separate card. This gave him a reservoir of 2,300 nonsense syllables from which to draw at random to form lists to be learned.

The following specific procedure is representative of what he did. Cards for the twelve syllables on a particular list would be read through by him at a uniform rate of two-fifths of a second (controlled by the ticking of a watch). When the reading of the list was completed, there was a pause of fifteen seconds, which he used for recording the trial. Again and again he would read through the cards until he believed he could repeat them without mistake. At this point he would try to recite them without looking at the cards. If he failed, no matter how few the mistakes, he would record the errors; and then he would read them again. He continued this procedure until he could give the complete list of nonsense syllables from memory without error. Then he considered the list learned. That was the method of "complete mastery," as it came to be called. He now passed on to other lists of syllables. After a given lapse of time, an hour, a day, or a week, whatever his schedule called for, he would return to the originally learned list and ascertain the number of repetitions now necessary to relearn it for complete mastery. There would be a saving in the sense that relearning did not take so many readings as learning did originally. This came to be called the "savings method." Thus if sixteen readings were at first necessary to reach the complete mastery of one correct run-through, and relearning the material twenty-four hours later took only eight readings, then the saving was eight-sixteenths of 50 percent, a measure of what had been remembered for twenty-four hours.

The very first relearning trial also gave him another measure of memory. When the time came to test this first memory of a given list of nonsense syllables, he would find out how many of the syllables he still knew before learning them again. The number still known divided by the total learned was this measure of memory. Suppose twelve syllables were originally learned. At the first relearning trial, say a day later, he remembered four of the nonsense syllables. That meant that four-twelfths or 33 percent was retained.

From these experiments came the well-known Ebbinghaus curve of forgetting. One of the conditions he studied experimentally was the effect of varying the length of time since learning the lists of nonsense syllables. The material would be forgotten very rapidly in the first few hours and then more and more slowly thereafter. When the results were plotted on a chart, they formed a curve that went down very sharply at first, then gradually leveled off. If the material was "overlearned" (that is to say, if Ebbinghaus went beyond bare learning by repeating the material to the point of several correct series in the original learning, instead of one) it was forgotten more slowly. Under these circumstances the plot of the curve would now show a more gradual drop and even after consider- able lapse of time would show more retention of the material than the learning to the level of merely one correct repetition. Later research confirmed these findings.[22] After carefully verifying these and many other findings by repetition, Ebbinghaus finally published his monograph in 1885.

[handwritten marginal note: Positive Effect of Overlearning]

LATER LIFE AND RESEARCH

In 1880, while still carrying on his research in memory, he became *Dozent* at Berlin, and in 1886, a year after his research appeared, was advanced to a rank equivalent to that of assistant professor. During this period he founded the Berlin psychological laboratory, but it was small and not well supported.

Ebbinghaus left the field for others to develop. In 1890, in collab- oration with Arthur König, he founded the *Zeitschrift für Psychologie und Physiologie der Sinnesorgane*, a journal that was needed to represent psychology outside the sphere of Wundt's *Studien*. It is plausible to believe that relative lack of publication was the reason behind his failure to be advanced in academic rank at Berlin to a full professorship.[23] At any rate, in 1894, when Carl Stumpf came from Munich to Berlin as professor, Ebbinghaus moved to a lesser post in the hierarchy of German univer- sities at Breslau, where he founded another laboratory.

Here he made his second major contribution, which, although not equal to the eminence of his studies of learning, deserves mention. The school officials of the city of Breslau called upon him to help solve a problem of fatigue in school children, i.e., to find the time of the continu- ous five-hour school day at which the child was least efficient. Accord- ingly, he devised three tests to be given in a few minutes before each class period.[24] The first and second were rapid addition and multiplication and a test of memory for digits. The third, the "completion method," which was original with Ebbinghaus, was destined to have pronounced usefulness in intelligence tests to come. Ebbinghaus argued that mental ability demands, among other capacities, the ability to combine verbal material into a significant whole. Essentially, the test consists of omitting words (or portions of words) from sentences in a story and asking the subjects to restore the appropriate words or syllables. An example in the spirit of the original ones used is, "Big things are heav ____ than _____ things" with the missing syllable and word to be supplied by the child.

When the students were grouped by scholastic standing into good, average, or poor, the results from the completion test proved markedly superior in discriminating among the groups when compared with the results from the other two tests. Ebbinghaus argued that this measure showed the great importance of a combining function in intelligence. It might be added that the fatigue problem, the impetus for the study, was largely lost sight of, with the question left open so far as the report went.

Alfred Binet, the pioneer in the development of intelligence tests, acknowledged that the success of the Ebbinghaus Completion Test had encouraged him in his conviction that he should use complex tasks to measure intelligence, rather than simpler ones, such as tapping rate or reaction time, hitherto used with little success.[25]

Ebbinghaus wrote two very successful books. The first volume of his general text, *Grundzüge der Psychologie*,[26] was published in complete form in 1902, and a shorter sketch, *Abriss der Psychologie*,[27] was issued in 1908. These became tremendous successes, resembling the *Psychology* of James in their sprightliness and lucidity of style.

The first sentence of the *Abriss* was that often quoted, beguiling half-truth, "Psychology has a long past, but only a short history."[28] Ebbinghaus was acutely aware that experimental psychology had just begun. He had seen its beginnings in the work of Fechner, Helmholtz, and Wundt, all carried out not more than fifty years before his own, and most of it practically contemporaneous with his own work. Present perspective makes it possible to see that preexperimental contributions were also necessary and that they, too, formed an essential part of the history of psychology. Experimental psychology, as we know it, had had but a short history, psychology a very, very long one.

In 1905 Ebbinghaus left Breslau for Halle. Generally in good health, he contracted pneumonia and died suddenly in 1909 at age fifty-nine.

Ebbinghaus published relatively little, although what he did publish was important. He made no systematic contributions. In fact, he cannot be said to have had a system. Nevertheless, he made an important advance in opening a new area of research for psychology. In the process of doing so, he presented a model of experimental control of factors. Before Ebbinghaus, the associationists had speculated on how associations were established. Ebbinghaus started by forming these associations experimentally and then testing their resistance by later recall. It might be thought at first glance that what he did was but a small matter compared to all the sweeping claims of his predecessors. From the viewpoint of modern research, these earlier claims seem grandiose, rather than great. True, they took in much more territory than those of Ebbinghaus. Their originators might be compared to monarchs who added to a statement of their holdings, "and the lands beyond the seas," without occupying these lands. Ebbinghaus not only occupied the territory, he tilled the soil. His discovery of a way to do research on memory, important and highly original though it was, is not his major claim to be mentioned in a history of the great psychologists. Rather, it is his determination to control factors so as to eliminate sources of error and to quantify his results as precisely as possible. He did such careful work in his studies of memory that they are quoted to this very day in contemporary textbooks side by side with later studies, not just for historical interest, but as valid and accurate research findings.

George Elias Müller

George Elias Müller (1850–1934), a student of Hermann Lotze, was a physiologist and philosopher with psychological interests. That Müller was not a student of Wundt's meant that, free of immediate proximity to this overpowering figure, he was able to develop an independent program. In a sense he was a rival of Wundt. Müller became professor at Göttingen in 1881, succeeding Lotze, and held that post for forty years until 1921. Over the years he attracted a number of students, the more prominent of whom were Oswald Külpe, E. R. Jaensch, David Katz, and Edgar Rubin.

Müller undertook extensive criticism and extension of Fechner's work in psychophysics in his *Zur Grundlegung der Psychophysik*,[29] published in 1878, and in *Die Gesichtspunkte und die Tatsachen der psychophysischen Methodik*[30] in 1904. In particular he demonstrated that the fluctuations of the threshold in the same person from day to day are not due to error but are real fluctuations in sensitivity itself. He laid down what he considered to be the fundamental psychophysical axioms of the relationship between perception and neural excitation as expressed in a parallelistic fashion (p. 276). While he also spent many years on problems of color, it is research in learning for which he is most noteworthy.

He was among the first psychologists to work in the research field of learning and memory opened up by Ebbinghaus. He carefully verified and extended Ebbinghaus's findings, which had taken the objective approach exclusively.[31] Ebbinghaus had found just how many trials it took for him to learn or relearn, but he had not recorded introspections about his mental processes while the learning was going on. Müller doubted that Ebbinghaus's account of learning as a mechanical and automatic process was correct as it stood. Accordingly, he added introspective report while applying the methods of Ebbinghaus and found that, instead of learning mechanically, the subjects were very active, using groupings and rhythms, finding meanings even in nonsense materials, and, in general, consciously organizing the material. This activity demonstrated to him that learning is not mechanical and that it requires the combination of introspective and objective methods. He concluded that association by contiguity is not enough to account for learning. An active search for relations is also taking place. A "preparatory set" (Anlage) influences the memory processes. Müller demonstrated that judgment involves not only the expected images, sensations, and feelings, but also mental events incapable of thus being classified. For example, readiness, hesitation, and doubt seem to be present, a class of mental phenomena usually called "conscious attitudes." These findings anticipated work that followed very shortly from the Würzburg laboratory under Oswald Külpe.

Müller also worked through many other learning problems, making methodological improvements, and increased the precision of the equipment used in the study. It was he, along with a collaborator, Friedrich Schumann,[32] who introduced the familiar revolving drum for uniform presentation of nonsense syllables used since that time in various adaptations for countless studies of memory and learning. This is perhaps a small matter, but since it increases objectivity and precision, deserves mention.

Oswald Külpe and the Würzburg School

Oswald Külpe (1862–1915) already has been encountered as a student and assistant to Wundt. After studying with G. E. Müller at Göttingen, he received his degree at Leipzig and stayed on as Dozent and assistant in the laboratory.[33]

His book, published in 1893 and translated in 1895 as *Outlines of Psychology*,[34] significantly bears the subtitle, *Based upon the results of experimental investigation*.[35] He wrote clearly and attractively, but he was still under the shadow of Wundt. Only one aspect of his distinctive views made its appearance. This was his telling criticism of the subtractive procedure on reaction time (p. 283).

In 1894, Külpe became professor at Würzburg. By 1896, with the aid of private funds, he had founded a laboratory there. Its progress was such that in a few years it was referred to as the outstanding laboratory in Germany after Leipzig. Charming and friendly, Külpe attracted many students and visitors, including several Americans, among them J. R. Angell of Chicago, R. M. Ogden of Cornell, W. L. Bryan of Indiana, and W. B. Pillsbury of Cornell and Michigan.

Americans

Külpe's distinctive work in psychology arose from his conviction, contrary to Wundt's, that the thought processes can be studied experimentally. Most of the Würzburg studies were not themselves performed by Külpe; but he was the professor, with all that this meant in a German university of that day, and frequently he served as a subject in the experiments of his students. There was enough integration to speak of this collective effort as the work of the Würzburg school.

"Systematic experimental introspection," to Külpe and the members of his school, meant performance of some complex task, such as that involved in thinking, remembering, or judging, and then rendering a retrospective report of their experiences during the original operation. It was systematic in the sense that the whole experience was described methodically, time period by time period, thus fractionating it. This procedure contrasted vividly with the description of immediate experience demanded by Wundt. To use the Würzburg version of introspection, one must think, memorize, or judge and then turn around and examine how one thought, memorized, or judged. The task was not specified in advance, as it was with Wundtian introspection, so the subject at Würzburg did not know beforehand exactly what he was to observe.

#

Imageless Thought and Related Issues

Closely identified with the Würzburg school is the concept of what came to be called in English, "imageless thought"—the representation of meanings in thinking that do not seem to be conveyed by specific images. Watt, Bühler, and others, in the course of their controlled introspections, supplied many instances of thinking of a definite problem or reaching a conclusion without being aware of any specific mental content of the sort previously identified. Another feature of this work was the influence of the task itself on the subjects.

A capsule description of two characteristic experiments is in order. Marbe, in a study of judgment of weights, found that while sensations and images were present as usual, their existence told nothing about how the subjects made their judgments.[36] The subjects just judged a weight as heavier or lighter, and they usually were right. But they did not know how they arrived at their conclusions; the sensations and images they reported did not describe the process of how they reached their judgment.

Watt[37] studied association in a variety of ways. For example, his subjects were faced with finding a subordinate or superordinate for the word *bird*. They reacted correctly, but often without being conscious of their intention. It would seem that the conscious work had been done not after the stimulus was presented, but earlier, when the instructions were understood. Once they understood, the subjects thereafter gave the response to the stimulus without conscious effort. To account for such findings, Watt emphasized the concept of task (*Aufgabe*). The subjects did not think of the task in terms of searching for the superordinate of *bird* and arriving at *animal;* they just thought "animal." The conscious phenomena obtained in the introspection corresponded closely to the volitional variable previously spoken of in connection with Külpe's early work. Although terms similar in nature are used now more or less indiscriminately for any potentiality in consciousness, to Watt, task meant the purpose, or conscious task, that precedes a later unconscious course of events. The conscious task (*Aufgabe*) brings about an unconscious set (*Einstellung*) in the subject.

Watt (and Ach), in research related to the study of association, held that the organism had a set or, to use Ach's term for it, a "determining tendency" to react in the way the given instruction called for. If, in advance of exposure to material, one has decided to subtract from a "6" and a "4," he will produce the response "2," not "10," which a determining tendency to add would have produced in response to the same visual stimuli. Once the task has been accepted and the set has been adopted, the actual performance runs off with remarkably little conscious content. These determining tendencies, not present consciously during performance, seemed important in volitional activities. The Würzburgers were suggesting that predispositions outside consciousness act to control consciousness.

This work on thought elements was negative in the sense that what the studies found lacked sensory content. It was not until the work of Karl Bühler in 1907 and 1908 that a new element in consciousness was

Marbe

Watt

task: Aufgabe

WATT + Ach

Bühler

announced.[38] His method of conducting introspections was even freer than that of systematic experimental introspection. He used very compli- cated problems, far removed from those of simple addition or subtraction, but always to be answered first with a "yes" or a "no." After answering, the subject gave the fullest possible account of the experiences by which he reached his decision, with questions interjected from time to time by the experimenter. Illustrative were: "Was the theorem of Pythagoras known in the Middle Ages?" "Can we with our thought comprehend the nature of thought?" or "The smaller the woman's foot, the larger the bill for shoes?"[39] The subjects (including Külpe) in their introspections used such terms as "awareness of a consciousness that," but more frequently simply referred to "thoughts." Thought was the new element that Bühler claimed must be accepted if his results were to make any sense. He went on to describe three types of thoughts—consciousness of rule, con- sciousness of relation, and intention. The first type of thinking was used by his subjects most often in solving mathematical, logical, or grammati- cal problems. The second occurred when several parts of a thought required a relation to be established as consequence or opposition, and the third took place when a problem was seen overall and an outcome was to be reached.

It must be emphasized that, while opposed to the Wundtian posi- tion concerning the sensory nature of certain kinds of conscious experi- ence, Külpe and the others were still seeking new *elements* in thought. They were still analytical in their approach.

Their use of analytical methods did not render their interpretations acceptable to the Wundtian psychologists of content who considered what they were doing a caricature of psychology. The reports of their introspections, particularly those of Bühler, drew vigorous opposition, especially from Wundt,[40] who offered scathing criticism, calling their procedures "mock" experiments and arguing that what they called ex- perimental introspection was neither experimental nor introspective. Recollection of what Wundt meant by these operations will show the logical rigor of his criticism, even though one may regret that he could not permit a broadening of the older meaning to encompass the work of the Würzburg school.

Of course, a distinction such as that between the warring views of the Würzburg school and Wundt is never as clean-cut as enthusiasts would like to believe. Wundt had spoken of apperception, although he can hardly be said to have stressed it. From the perspective of today, it can be seen that the views of the Würzburgers and Wundt were not incompatible. After all, the conscious attitudes or preparatory sets of G. E.

Müller had been demonstrated without creating a furor within the ranks of the psychologists of content. In fact, as a student of Müller as well as Wundt, Külpe had probably been influenced by him. But the temperaments of the critics of the Würzburg school would not permit a reconciliation.

Külpe, for his part, both then and later, showed his high admiration and regard for Wundt. Müller also attacked Külpe's methods and results, as did Titchener, a friend and companion from Külpe's Leipzig days. For both, Külpe preserved the highest regard. But the issue had been forced, and a rival school was consequently established.

Külpe's own interpretation of the work from his laboratory is rather hard to specify. He wrote very little on the matter, and his projected description of the psychology of the thought processes was never completed.

Külpe's fifteen years at Würzburg are for the history of psychology his most important. It was not that he lost interest later, for at Bonn, where he went next, he founded a laboratory; and, in 1913, when he moved to Munich, he saw to it that the laboratory allocated to his predecessor was suitably equipped. It was rather that his continuing interests in philosophical problems, particularly esthetics, which seemed to him in no way antagonistic to his interests in psychological issues, came to the fore. He sought to prove that the actualities of conscious experience required independent objects. He never completed the statement of his later views. His student, Karl Bühler, published posthumously his *Vorlesungen über Psychologie* in 1920.[41] What he had covered in the *Grundriss* in 1893 constituted in this new work the content of psychology; the contribution of the Würzburg school was what he called *function*.

The psychological implications of these views led him to a position much closer to that of Brentano. By now Külpe conceived of psychology as *both* content and act (although he called the latter, function) and it is to be regrettable that he did not live long enough to work out fully his own synthesis. To Külpe, content and function are both facts of mental life because they can be demonstrated to be different.[42] They are separable in experience: in dreams there is content but little function; in barely noticing something there is function with little content. They are independently variable: content changes without function when one perceives objects one after the other; function changes when one object is first perceived, then recognized, and then judged. They possess characteristic differences: contents are analyzable in consciousness, observable in introspection, and relatively stable; functions are not analyzable in consciousness (analysis alters the function), are observable in retrospect only, and are relatively unstable. They obey different laws: the laws of content are association, fusion, contrast, and a relation to stimulus and sense organ; function includes the effects of the laws of determining tendency. Külpe was actively engaged in this combined psychological and epistemological enterprise of synthesizing content and function just before the time of his death in 1915.

The work of the Würzburg school was prophetic of the development of a holistic view as separate from the elementalist view of Wundt. Indeed, the Gestalt psychologists who were to come later owed a debt to Külpe for attempting to deal with both act and content.

The results of the Würzburg school were interpreted as relating to thought as such, which was their emphasis. But two other aspects of their achievement are significant today. First, there was the way they stressed volition, or motivation, as we would call it. Task, set, determining tendency, to use their key words, have a motivational connotation today. Motivation was treated by them as a variable affecting the results of thinking, a topic that is very much a part of the modern scene in psychology. The relatively simple kinds of association of the British and of Wundt were not enough to explain the variations in volition that they found from one experiment to the next. Second, it seemed as if behavior depended not only on the elements present in the subject's consciousness, but also on the way he adjusted to the experiment, even though he was not aware of this operation in conscious analysis. These directive tendencies were not evident in consciousness. They were often unconscious in nature; unconscious determinants of behavior were being demonstrated.

Members of the Würzburg school were working at the same time as Freud, but without his ruthless radicalism, they did not cut through to the bold conclusion that many of the experiences they were dealing with were unconscious. Instead, they treated the impalpable phenomena with which they were struggling as a consequence of some vague conscious element.

Overview

It will be remembered that it fell to Wundt to synthesize the first modern view of a scientific psychology. The analogy was suggested that the picture of psychology that left his hands contained some, but by no means all aspects of a modern view. His contemporaries and successors served to broaden the canvas, in terms of both methodological and contentual considerations.

In formulating act psychology Brentano was guided by a functional prescription, in contrast to the contentual prescription to which Wundt adhered. By insisting on the distinction between sensory quality and act, with psychological emphasis on sensing, he effectively committed himself to a contentually subjective position concerning the nature of psychology. ·

Although Wundt had declared it impossible, Ebbinghaus studied experimentally and quantitatively the higher mental process of memory and learning. At the time his approach to learning and memory received little notice except in criticism, but it was objective in the results derived. His was the first major research study, other than those in psychophysics, which would make psychology contentually objective.

G. E. Müller was cognizant of this emphasis in that he criticized Ebbinghaus for his failure to report introspections. By his own research he established what was prophetic of a modern conception of the value of introspection. It might even be called the forerunner of the "new look" in cognitive psychology. Instead of believing that learning is mechanical, as Ebbinghaus's results made it seem, he found that subjects actively searched for meaning and relations, held a preparatory set, and experienced hesitations, fleeting doubts, convictions, and the like, which the plotted curves did not reveal.

Külpe and the others of the Würzberg school broadened the scope of introspection and opened the area of the thought processes to experimental study. The essential change they made was to convert introspection into retrospection—the report of a past experience, rather than a description of an immediate experience. One thought, memorized, or judged, and then turned around and examined what one experienced during the process. The lack of sensory experience during many aspects of the tasks being studied, so-called imageless thought, was one of their major contributions, another was the discovery that various forms of directive tendencies to be adopted before performing the task gave it coherence and direction. As a consequence Külpe found it possible toward the end of his career to conceive of psychology as both contentual and functional.

The founding of psychology, embracing as it does not only Wundt's work but also that of his contemporaries and successors, is noteworthy for certain developments, which may be referred to in prescriptive terms. Without fanfare and with remarkably little explicit discussion, certain guiding methodological attitudes common to other sciences had been accepted as characteristics of the science of experimental psychology. General agreement was reached on nomotheticism, the search for general principles; on naturalism, that these principles are within nature and not in some transcendental realm. Also accepted were methodological objectivism, the use of methods open to other competent observers, and quantitativism, the dependence upon measurement (although without the more sophisticated tools of statistics that we have today). Determinism, the belief that human events are explicable in terms of antecedents, was adhered to, as was empiricism, in the preferred form of experiment. These prescriptions are now so much a part of the procedural approach of the psychologist as to be almost universally accepted. Both deviations and refinements will be encountered in later developments but these prescriptive allegiances form a background pattern for much of what follows.

References*

1. O. Kraus, *Franz Brentano, zur Kenntnis seines Lebens und seiner Lehre* (Munich: Beck, 1919); M. Puglisi, "Franz Brentano: a Biographical Sketch," *American Journal of Psychology,* XXXV (1924): 414–419; Antos C. Rancurello, *A Study of Franz Brentano. His Psychological Standpoint and His Significance in the History of Psychology* (New York: Academic Press, 1968). This last mentioned reference is probably the most authoritative current statement about Brentano and his views.
2. F. Brentano, *Die Lehre Jesu und ihre bleibende Bedeutung* (Leipzig: Meiner, 1922).
3. *Ibid.*
4. F. Brentano, *Psychology from an Empirical Standpoint,* ed. O. Kraus, English ed., ed. Linda L. McAlister (New York: Humanities Press, 1973).
5. J. R. Barclay, "Franz Brentano and Sigmund Freud," *Journal of Existentialism,* V (1964): 1–36.
6. This fascinating issue has a number of ramifications. Some of the references are J. Barclay, *op. cit.;* P. Merlan, "Brentano and Freud," *Journal of the History of Ideas,* VI (1945), 6, 375–377, and *ibid.,* "Brentano and Freud—a Sequel," *Journal of the History of Ideas,* X (1949), 451. John C. Brentano (Professor of Physics Emeritus, Northwestern University) the son of Franz, who had been devoting his retirement years to his

*See p. 19 for description of reference style.

father's works, assured me in personal conversation that Freud was relatively uninfluenced by his father and that, so far as his father was concerned, he broke not only with Freud but also with Breuer as a result of the publicity arising from the case of Frl. Anna O. This implies a closer relationship between Brentano and Freud than E. Jones (*The Life and Works of Sigmund Freud*, Vol. 1 [New York: Basic Books, 1953]), dean of the biographers of Freud, would admit.

7. Kraus, *Franz Brentano.*
8. F. Brentano, *Untersuchungen zur Sinnespsychologie* (Leipzig: Duncker and Humblot, 1907).
9. F. Brentano, *Von der Klassifikation der psychischen Phänomene* (Leipzig: Duncker and Humblot, 1911).
10. G. S. Brett, "Associationism and 'Act' Psychology," C. Murchison, ed., *Psychologies of 1930* (Worcester, Mass.: Clark University Press, 1930), pp. 39–55.
11. *Ibid.*, p. 48.
12. E. B. Titchener, *Systematic Psychology: Prolegomena* (New York: Macmillan, 1929).
13. L. Carmichael, "What is Empirical Psychology?" *American Journal of Psychology*, XXXVII (1926): 521–527.
14. E. G. Boring, *History of Experimental Psychology*, 2nd ed. (New York: Appleton-Century-Crofts, 1950).
15. Titchener, *Systematic Psychology.*
16. *Psychologie*, Bk. II, Chapter 1, Sec. 9 (Herrnstein and Boring, Excerpt No. 112).
17. *Ibid.*, Chapter 1.
18. *Von der Klassifikation.*
19. D. Shakow, "Hermann Ebbinghaus," *American Journal of Psychology*, XLII (1930): 505–518; R. S. Woodworth, "Hermann Ebbinghaus," *Journal of Philosophy*, VI (1909): 253–256.
20. Boring, *History of Experimental Psychology.*
21. H. Ebbinghaus, *Ueber das Gedächtnis* (Leipzig: Duncker and Humblot, 1885) (Herrnstein and Boring Excerpt, No. 95).
22. R. S. Woodworth, *Experimental Psychology* (New York: Henry Holt and Company, 1938).
23. Boring, *History of Experimental Psychology.*
24. H. Ebbinghaus, "Ueber eine neue Methode zur Prüfung geistiger Fähigkeiten und ihre Anwendung bei Schulkinder," *Zeitschrift für Psychologie*, XIII

(1897): 401–439 (Herrnstein and Boring, Excerpt No. 82).

25. A. Binet, "Description d'un objet," *L'Année Psychologique*, III (1897): 296–332.

26. H. Ebbinghaus, *Die Grundzüge der Psychologie* (Leipzig: Veit, 1897–1902).

27. H. Ebbinghaus, *Abriss der Psychologie* (Leipzig: Veit, 1908).

28. *Ibid*, p. 1.

29. G. E. Müller, *Zur Grundlegung der Psychophysik* (Berlin: Grüben, 1878).

30. G. E. Müller, *Die Gesichtspunkte und die Tatsachen der psycho-physischen Methodik* (Strassburg: Bergmann, 1903).

31. G. E. Müller and A. Pilzecker, *Experimentelle Beiträge zur Lehre vom Gedächtniss* (Leipzig: Barth, 1900).

32. G. E. Müller and F. Schumann, "Experimentelle Beiträge zur Untersuchungen des Gedächtnisses," *Zeitschrift für Psychologie*, VI (1893): 81–190, 257–339.

33. R. M. Ogden, "Oswald Külpe and the Würzburg School," *American Journal of Psychology*, LXIV (1951): 4–19.

34. O. Külpe, *Grundriss der Psychologie* (Leipzig: Engelmann, 1893).

35. O. Külpe, *Outlines of Psychology: Based Upon the Results of Experimental Investigation*, trans. E. B. Titchener (New York: Macmillan, 1895).

36. K. Marbe, *Experimentell-psychologische Untersuchungen über das Urteil, eine Einleitung in die Logik* (Leipzig: Engelmann, 1901).

37. H. J. Watt, "Experimentelle Beitrage zu einer Theorie des Denkens," *Archiv für die gesamte Psychologie*, IV (1905): 289–436.

38. K. Bühler, Tatsächen und Probleme zu einer Psychologie der Denkvorgänge, *Archiv für die gesamte Psychologie*, IX (1907): 297–305; 1908: 12, 1–3, 24–92.

39. K. Bühler, quoted in G. Humphrey, *Thinking: an Introduction to its Experimental Psychology* (New York: John Wiley and Sons, 1951), p. 56.

40. W. Wundt, "Kritiche Nachlese zur Ausfragemethode, "*Archiv für die gesamte Psychologie*, XI (1908):445–459.

41. O. Külpe, *Vorlesungen über Psychologie*, posthumously ed. K. Bühler (Leipzig: Hirzel, 1920).
42. Boring, *History of Experimental Psychology*, pp. 451–452.

Chapter 14

Galton:
DEVELOPMENTALISM, QUANTITATIVISM, AND INDIVIDUAL DIFFERENCES

A faith in the timelessness of nature was still accepted by a great majority of men, learned and unlearned alike, in the first half of the nineteenth century. There was, however, a substantial minority who had some conception of an evolutionary process. The fundamental idea of evolution, that living things do change with time, was not entirely novel, having been a part of the intellectual history of man since Anaximandros, a contemporary of Thales. In the centuries before Darwin, the philosophers and scientists of the Enlightenment, Locke, Hume, and Diderot, for example, mentioned only the small gradations they saw as separating plants, animals, and men; they spoke of generation and transformation as well. Philosophers, such as Kant and Hegel, had written of development in a fashion not incompatible with evolution. Lyell had introduced evolution into geological theory; Erasmus Darwin, the grandfather of Charles, had written on evolution; and in 1809, the very year of Charles Darwin's birth, Lamarck[1] had published his theory that the great variety of animal species might be explained by the inheritance of acquired characters, possibly brought about by changes in the environment or through the use or disuse of a part of the body. Herbert Spencer, moreover, was championing an evolutionary point of view prior to Darwin's publication of The Origin of Species in 1859. Nevertheless, the work of Darwin created a veritable scientific revolution that demanded reorganization of all previous thinking. After 1859 no well-informed thinker, unless he were blinded by religious or other preconceptions, could ignore the fact that a developmental view of the nature of all biological phenomena was imperative.

Lamarck 1809

319

Darwin and Evolution

The theory of evolution advanced by Charles Darwin (1809–1882) is too well known to require more than a reminder of its most salient features.[2] Darwin demonstrated that living matter is in a plastic rather than a fixed, immutable form and that the spontaneous variability that each species demonstrates is inheritable. There is a struggle for survival, and the forms that survive have made successful adaptations to the inexorable difficulties they have had to face. The exigencies of the struggle for existence under natural conditions accomplish what every animal breeder who practices artificial selection knows—that certain strains are perpetuated by breeding. Only those forms fittest for their particular environment survive this process of natural selection; the rest die out. Man is no exception; he, too, is the result of this struggle. Purpose, final cause, and supernatural design do not account for evolution. A teleological orientation prominent since the days of Aristotle had been given a definitive rebuttal.

Darwin believed that the variations perpetuated were always slight. Through later research on the mutation of genes, we have learned that the variations are often abrupt and of considerable magnitude. But this later finding does not detract from the importance of Darwin's theory concerning the process of evolution. He demonstrated the process and the range of reasons for it, but not its genetic mechanism.

No summary can give more than a hint of the overwhelming mass of data that Darwin collected. Much miscellaneous biological information, hitherto unrelated, was organized by Darwin. His theory and conclusions appeared irresistible to those who did not find them antagonistic to deep-seated convictions concerning the static nature of living things. As Thomas Huxley said of himself, "How extremely stupid not to have thought of that."[3] And he was by no means alone. There were many who saw in Darwin's evidence a means of organizing and understanding a great amount of otherwise puzzling data.

In relating the Darwinian evolutionary doctrine to religious orthodoxy, fertile sources of controversy appear. Theological disagreement was inevitable, arising from the teachings of the *Book of Genesis*, as were arguments from others who saw man as separated by an impassable gulf from the "brutes." Moreover, there were those who saw in Darwin's work contradictory scientific evidence. The stormy controversy that broke out was one from which Darwin himself held aloof—his temperament was such that speaking sharply to someone made him unable to sleep. He found able champions, however, the greatest of whom was Thomas Huxley. The protest and acrimony died hard, stretching from 1860 and the debate of Huxley and Bishop Wilberforce of Oxford to the Scopes trial, with the anatagonists, William Jennings Bryan and Clarence Darrow, in 1925.

Darwin's second major report on evolution, *The Descent of Man*, appeared in 1871.[4] It was written primarily to present the evidence that the conclusions of the *Origin* also applied to man, a position he had held all along, but that had not been understood by some of his contemporaries. In the *Origin* he had not tried to apply his conclusions to a species taken singly. Now he marshalled the evidence for the evolution of man from some lower form, along with evidence about his subsidiary theme of sexual selection.

Darwin made more specific contributions to psychology. He kept a diary of his infant son, which he began in 1840 but did not publish until 1877.[5] Along with similar work by Preyer, this record was a source for the beginnings of modern child psychology.

Infant biographies — Darwin —Preyer

Darwin also studied emotional expression in animals and man. Sir Charles Bell, the anatomist already known for his differentiation of function in sensory and motor nerves, held that facial movements used in the expression of emotions are primarily expressive, that is to say, their function is to express emotions.[6] Darwin espoused the alternative theory, that facial movements are originally practical, as when an angry dog bares his teeth in action preparatory to biting.[7] Expressive functions, Darwin believed, may be derived subsequently from practical functions. In presenting his argument, he developed three principles of emotional expression and gave illustrations. The first, the principle of serviceable associated habits, was that many expressive movements in emotion are vestiges of originally practical movements. A sneer was seen as a remnant of a response to a malodorous substance, clenching the fists as a vestige of preparation for combat, and being startled as a remainder of a larger flight reaction. The second, the principle of antithesis, was that opposite impulses tend to show opposed movements. When a cat shows affection by arching her back, drawing up her paws, arching her tail, and pointing her ears, these are all movements the opposite of which she would make when about to attack or defend herself. Antithesis is to be found in laughter, which requires expiration of breath, while sobbing, its opposite, requires inspiration. The third principle is related to the direct action of the nervous system. There is the overflow into motor channels that we call "trembling."' These expressive characteristics were acquired from prior practical functions. They then could be inherited. This assumption, of course, was more in line with Lamarckian inheritance of acquired characters than with what is often considered to be Darwinian evolutionary

PRIN. of Emotional Expression

theory. But he is quite explicit in stating that these were originally voluntary movements which turned into reflex actions through habits that are then inherited.

The study of lower animals was shown by Darwin to demand consideration of their drives to action. Study seemed always to lead toward examination of the causes of their activity. Even their more complicated activities often seemed unlearned. To these activities the term "instincts" had already been applied. An important chapter of the *Origin* was devoted to the instincts; Darwin compared and contrasted instinct with habit and showed that instincts are not perfect. Darwin had available to him a variety of accounts of the instincts of animals, particularly domesticated animals, for example, the shepherd's dogs' tendency to hunt hares, the brooding of hens, and the cell-making of bees. Such behavior can best be understood as inherited. Darwin's evidence showed that the animals did not survive if they did not have the proper instincts. Evolutionary theory forced a recognition of the essentiality of understanding the drives to action of both man and beast. The continuance of an instinct approach in psychology was assured.

true but a misnomer →

In effect, Darwin demonstrated that all animals were related, and that they all faced the common problems of adjustment and survival. In *The Descent of Man,* he likened reasoning in man to what appeared to be similar processes in the lower animals. More specifically, he attempted to show that many of man's mental capacities had rudimentary prototypes among lower animals. He also appealed to accounts of primitive man, their susceptibility to praise and blame, for example. If the human body evolved from lower animals, does it not also follow that the human mind developed from more primitive minds? If all animals are related, does it not follow that there will be similarities in behavior and mentality among animals? It was on the basis of such questions as these that the comparative viewpoint in psychology came into being. Psychology was made ready to return to the wisdom of Aristotle, to be concerned with all living things, not with man alone. After Darwin, comparative psychology became recognized as a branch of psychology.

EVALUATION

Despite his great work, Darwin was not a great psychologist. As was the case with Galileo and Newton, Darwin's service was to reorganize the general scientific view and to stimulate others in other sciences—psychology included. Darwin's work stimulated an interest in psychological problems. It was against a background of adherence to naturalism, empiricism, and determinism that Darwin carried out his observations. His more distinctive contributions reinforced developmentalism, functionalism, and dynamicism in biological science. Darwin searched for evidence of development, for evidence of changes with time. A functional prescription was also crucial; he studied activities of organisms, including man, and the ways he adapts to the environment. Development, activity, and adaptation go hand in hand with a dynamic stance; he was interested in change and factors causing change. Variability among members of the same species in psychological concerns, and this prepared the way for the study of psychological individual and racial differences. Almost incidentally, his animal behavioral studies of emotional expression suggested the contentual objectivity of the work in this field in later generations.

The man who helped to develop an almost entirely new aspect of psychology, the field of individual differences, was Francis Galton.

Francis Galton (1822–1911)

Francis Galton was the pioneer who brought about a union between psychological methods of measurement and the theory of evolution, a union that came about because Galton's studies and observations initiated considerable interest in the study of individual differences among men.

LIFE OF GALTON

Francis Galton, a cousin of Charles Darwin, was born near Birmingham in 1822.[8] His large family possessed considerable wealth and had among its members clergymen, physicians, military officers, members of Parliament, and landed gentry. This background afforded Galton connections with a large number of important persons in England at the height of the British Empire. In his autobiography, Galton studs his pages with names, either in indices of their progression through life or in terms of their family connections.[9] For instance, he refers to "Sir Joseph (then Mr.) Hooker," to "Henry Fitzmaurice Hallman . . . the younger son of the historian Henry Hallam . . . and brother to Arthur Hallam . . . , the subject of Tennyson's In Memoriam," and even to his wife as the daughter of the "Dean of Peterborough, previously headmaster of Harrow . . . and before his appointment, the Senior Wrangler at Cambridge. . . . ." In his day, "the Establishment" may have been an allusion to the relation of church and state, but its modern meaning was very much in evidence. It is not denying his great gifts to say that a way of life surrounded him, a way that could lead him to a conviction that eminence runs in families. Others, before and after, had merely accepted this state of affairs, but Galton had the genius to try to explain the obvious.

Following his own and his family's wishes, in 1838 he began as an apprentice to study medicine at Birmingham General Hospital. He rolled pills, made up medicines, attended rounds, and participated in first aid in the accident room. Boldly curious, he decided to discover for himself the effects of the different medicines. Commencing with those under the letter A in the pharmacopoeia, he began taking small doses of each, one after the other. He had reached nearly the end of the letter C when stopped by the effects of croton oil, notorious as an extremely powerful purgative.

After completing a period of experience at this hospital he continued some of his medical training at King's College, London. In 1840 Galton changed his plans and enrolled in Trinity College, Cambridge, for the usual university program. Although deficient in the classics, he managed to keep up in mathematics, the field in which he specialized. Occasionally he wondered at the narrowness of the academic community of Cambridge in that day—faculty and students alike showed no interest at all in what he had learned about biology from his medical education. After a severe mental breakdown had interrupted his studies, he took his degree without working for honors.

In 1845–46, he traveled in the Sudan, and in 1850 he explored Damaraland and the Ovampo country in Southwest Africa. On his return he published accounts of his travels. The novelty and the danger of these trips are manifest when we note that the second trip was taken more than twenty years before the meeting of Stanley and Livingston. In 1854, the Royal Geographical Society awarded him one of their two annual gold medals for exploring the then unknown country of central Southwest Africa. Subsequently, he was elected a Fellow of the Royal Society for the same achievement.

In 1853 he had married. Again, he was immersed in a large and distinguished family, since his wife, in addition to her three sisters, had four brothers, all noted for scholastic or administrative ability. Traveling annually to the continent, visiting at one or another of the houses of his friends, and living in London occupied some of his time. Exploration had become a topic of widespread interest, so he devoted his attention to the preparation of a book, *The Art of Travel,* a practical guide for the explorer. He lectured on the art of camp life to soldiers training for the Crimean War. For several years he tried the life of a country gentleman, riding to hounds, shooting in Scotland, and managing his estate, adding the not-too-incongruous touch to this particular picture of experimenting with electricity. He then turned to the serious study of meteorology. The book that summarizes his findings is said[10] to be the first serious attempt to chart the weather on an extensive scale and to contain the first establishment of the existence of anticyclones. His health gave him much concern, especially since his ill health was a tremendous difficulty in carrying through intellectual activities. Severe bouts of fever would also come unexpectedly.

MENTAL INHERITANCE AND VARIABILITY

During the early sixties his cousin's *Origin of Species* stirred Galton to study anthropology and heredity, interests that resulted in the founding of the field of eugenics. Galton wished to encourage the productivity of the fit while restricting the birthrate of the unfit. To do so, he undertook to demonstrate that human heredity is important and relevant. He wished to study the inherited transmissible qualities of man and hoped that this knowledge would be used for the welfare of mankind. His first publication in this area was a magazine article on hereditary talent and character in 1865.

The first edition of *Hereditary Genius* appeared in 1869, just ten years after the *Origin*.[11] The range of human mental ability from highest to lowest was held to be enormous. Galton not only marshalled evidence about superior persons but also referred briefly to the mentally retarded and mentioned in passing the work of Seguin with idiots and imbeciles. Once variability in ability is accepted, we come to the major issue: Is ability related to heredity?

He specifically acknowledged in his preface to *Hereditary Genius* that, considering his contemporaries at school and in later life, he was surprised to find how frequently ability seemed to depend on descent. Most of his book is occupied with a large quantity of biographical data about eminent men. Since, in a later edition,[12] he expressed regret at having used the word "genius" when he really meant mental ability of high order, we shall use the term "eminent" hereafter. Galton hypothesized not only that there was a general tendency for eminence to run in certain families, but also that there are specific forms of eminence in the sciences, in the arts, in jurisprudence, and in similar fields.

Galton selected his eminent men by the use of biographical sources and then found the number of eminent relations they had. The proportion of eminent relatives that he located much exceeded what might be expected by chance. There were 977 eminent men in his main sample, each judged as so outstanding as to be one man in 4,000. By chance the group might have had one prominent relative. Instead they had 332 close relatives about as eminent as themselves. Although upheld later in a general way, his specific results are subject to many forms of serious criticism. In his own day, his results were taken as unequivocal evidence for the biological inheritance of mental ability. It has become evident since then that this demonstration of eminence running in families can be interpreted as due, in part at least, to similarity of education, socioeconomic status, and social proximity to other eminent (and influential) men. This pedigree method became the favorite tool of eugenics, a social movement aimed at improving human stock, that has generated controversy to this day.

Part and parcel of his relationship with the Establishment was the cavalier attitude taken toward the capabilities of women, and sex differences in general. In his study of eminence, lack of representation of women was not an occasion for either surprise or explanation. This pioneer modern student was heavily influenced by Victorian sexist attitudes.[13] He compared mental and physical traits in men and women, believing that the latter were not only physically weaker but their poorer sensory discrimination was *prima facie* evidence of intellectual inferiority.

Galton did not entirely overlook the influence of environment. In fact, for this reason he later made the first psychologically oriented research study of twins in which he endeavored to separate the influence of heredity and environment. He found that in physical characteristics at least, twins had much more in common with each other than did other nontwin children of the same parents.

His essential thesis in all this was that mental characteristics are inherited in the same fashion and at the same rate as physical characteristics. He won his cousin to this view that intellectual ability is inherited; in 1869 Charles Darwin explicitly stated in a letter to him that on reading *Hereditary Genius,* he had been "made a convert since previously he had believed that excepting fools, men did not differ much in intellect, only in zeal and hard work. . . ."[14]

STATISTICS AND CORRELATION

Before Galton became interested in statistics, the Belgian astronomer Quételet (1796–1874) had obtained the chest measurements of a large number of Scottish soldiers and the heights of French conscripts and found that these two sets of measures not only showed the same shape of distribution when plotted on a graph, but also that they both followed the same shape of distribution as did plots of runs of luck at a gaming table, and the spread of shot around a target.[15] When plotted each measure formed a curve resembling many other common measures with a peak in the center of the distribution, while on each side the scores fall off symmetrically in such a fashion as to make the curve. Laplace and Gauss before him had applied mathematical principles to data on human errors; Quételet extended their normal law of error to measures other than errors. It was Quételet's work with which Galton first became familiar. What Quételet had demonstrated was that human variation in physique follows the same statistical laws as do certain other living and nonliving phenomena.

Inspired by Quételet, Galton took the next step by extending the findings to a psychological characteristic. He found that marks given on carefully administered and lengthy university honors examinations followed the same distribution as did the biological measures studied by Quételet.[16] Galton saw these results not only as interesting in themselves but also as justifying the application of statistics to psychological measures.

He went further and developed one of the most important of all statistical measures, the correlation. In 1888 he gave a report[17] that described for the first time what he called "co-relations," as well as the working out of several basic procedures. He presented by means of graphs the fundamental properties of the correlation coefficient, as we now term it, and even developed a formula for its calculation, but that was soon superseded. Galton applied his method to variations in bodily measurements, showing that stature and head length, for example, and head length and head breadth are correlated. For instance, tall stature and long head length go together, as do short stature and short head length, and also the various dimensions between. As stature increases, head length tends also to increase.

It was with Galton's encouragement and aid that his student, Karl Pearson, later improved on his work and initiated the present mathematical formula for its calculation, the so-called Pearson product-moment coefficient of correlation.[18] This formula worked out by Pearson allowed one to calculate the precise numerical degree of relationship. The values that are to be found range between nearly perfect correlations through zero to nearly perfect inverse correlations. The latter occur when an increase in one score is accompanied by decrease in the other measure. The correlation was to prove an exceedingly useful tool because it made it possible to state results of research in quantitative terms, such as .30 or .61, instead of qualitatively and in "some, but not a great deal of relationship." This formula is now applied regularly, not in psychology alone, but in all fields where statistics are used.

GALTON'S VERSATILITY

For a time after writing *Hereditary Genius,* Galton was absorbed in collecting measures of physical characteristics—height, circumference of head, and so on. According to Pearson, it was in the middle seventies that he came to the conclusion that static, anthropometric measures like those mentioned were not so fruitful to understanding diversity among individuals as are psychometric or psychological measures that relate how individuals *function.*[19] Thus, Galton moved from physical anthropology to psychology.

His psychological contributions are contained in his *Inquiries into Human Faculty and its Development,*[20] appearing in 1883 and based upon work that had occupied him for at least the previous seven years. This collection of studies is strikingly original. But it includes no attempt to unify its contents beyond the theme stated in the title and certain implicit general methodological guidelines that can be inferred—human beings vary enormously, man is a biologically rooted organism that evolved, empiricism is the road to knowledge, observations may be quantified and statistics applied to the results.

Let us take this opportunity to pause and specify some of Galton's diverse contributions as they appeared in the *Inquiries* and later, reserving for a more detailed discussion his major contributions to psychology. In this work, we find articles on spectacles for divers, the breeding of rabbits, gregariousness in cattle, statistical analysis of the efficacy of prayer, visualized movement, composite portraitures, color blindness, outfitting an anthropometric laboratory, the Australian marriage system, dice for statistical experiments, arithmetic by smell, and the speed of trotting horses.

Galton tells how, as a means of studying the diversity of association, he walked along Pall Mall, a distance of about 450 yards.[21] He found that he had developed numerous associations with nearly 300 objects. A few days later he repeated the walk and again was struck with the variety of ideas that welled up, although somewhat chastened by the realization that there was considerable repetition of the associations shown on the first occasion. He compares these associations to a procession of players who, having once marched across the stage, went round by the back to come on again, giving the impression of a larger group than there really was.

On another occasion he tried to work himself into the state of mind of the insane. He hit on the plan of consciously trying to invest everything human, animal, and inanimate he encountered on a walk with the attributes of a spy. By the end of the morning stroll, every horse seemed to be watching him either directly or, just as suspicious, disguising their espionage by elaborately paying no attention! Hours had to pass before this state of mind wore off, and he later discovered it was all too easy to reinstate.[22]

On still another occasion he wished to gain some appreciation of the feeling that a savage might have for his idol, so he selected the drawing of Punch, the traditional cover of the magazine, and pretended with all the fervor he possessed that it had divine attributes, the power to reward or to punish.[23] He was so successful in empathizing with his role that for a long time after the experience he retained for this picture a feeling that a barbarian might have for his idol.

For Galton nothing was too trivial to be counted. He used an audience's yawns and fidgets, per unit of time, as a measure of boredom. He familiarized himself with the ways of wild animals by visiting zoos. It was here he put to good use his invention, the Galton whistle, which gave pitches beyond the audibility of human ears, but not that of various animals.

Three of his contributions to psychology deserve more detailed consideration: his work on mental imagery, on association, and on mental tests. As Galton saw them, these problems involved not only the evolutionary principle but the older traditions of associationism and empiricism.

MENTAL IMAGERY

Galton became interested in the problem of visual mental imagery because he thought demonstrations of it in varying degrees might help to establish an essential difference in the mental operations of different people.[24] After some preliminary inquiries, he devised a questionnaire that he had both students and men from various professions complete. It contained specifications for various situations in which they were to try to elicit images. The most famous of these was the request to recall the scene of their breakfast table that morning. His subjects were to say whether the image they had was dim or clear, the objects well- or ill-defined, and the colors natural or absent; they were to estimate the extent of contents of the field of view, the steadiness of maintenance of the mental picture, and the like.

To his astonishment, many men of science whom he had first questioned about mental images protested they did not know what he was talking about. They strenuously denied having any imagery. In this respect they resembled color blind persons who do not know of their disability. He accounted for this relative absence of mental imagery in scientists by their habits of highly abstract lines of thinking, considering that, if they ever possessed such imagery, they must have lost it through disuse. At the more general levels of society, and among women, boys, and girls, imagery of a clear, well-defined, distinct sort was present. In fact, when Galton feigned disbelief at certain answers, these persons were as surprised by his inability to accept their replies as obvious facts as the scientists were by his claim that such images existed. With more returns available, although similar differences persisted, he found numerous exceptions. Some scientists did have vivid imagery; some persons in the general population lacked imagery.

Frequently, Galton found distinct imagery types. His preliminary finding about the absence of imagery in scientists may have helped to bring about this belief. As a matter of fact, although he had spoken of types in his summarization, Galton stressed that there was a gradation of clarity of imagery from distinct to faint. It was other workers after him who popularized the notion of imagery types as if this had been his major finding. Careful later work demonstrated that Galton was right, and those who came later were wrong in their belief that imagery falls into types. It is more or less normally distributed in the population with the great majority having some, but not much, capacity for it.

MEMORY AND ASSOCIATION

Another problem of even more systematic importance in psychology with which Galton concerned himself was that of association.[25] One phase of his work, the finding of diversity of association, but with repetition, has already been described. This study of the free play of his own associations he did not find particularly fruitful. Much more important was his work on the reaction time necessary to produce associations. Independently of Ebbinghaus he launched this experimental study of memory and association. Words with which to associate, each written on a separate slip, were exposed to his view one at a time. When he had given two associations to each word, he recorded the time taken from a watch. This gave him an association reaction time. He followed the same procedure for each word in turn. Many of his associations were single words, but on some occasions the response took the form of a mental image that had to be described in some detail. He wished to find the probable origin of these associative reactions. Presently it became evident that a large number of the associations came from experiences in childhood and adolescence; in fact, about 40 percent came from this period, about 45 percent from manhood, and only 15 percent from the immediate past. This was perhaps the first demonstration by re-

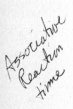

search of the importance of childhood experience on subsequent adult thinking.

MENTAL TESTS

In addition to being the first to study abilities scientifically through estimates of those of eminent men, Galton was also the first to develop certain specific mental tests.[26] In fact, he invented mental tests (although not the term, for that came later). The first phase of his interest in tests was shown in his efforts to develop measures of intelligence based upon sensory capacity, an undertaking that rested on the supposition that discrimination would be highest among the ablest individuals. He offered various anecdotes on the sensory obtuseness of idiots and imbeciles. Galton used highly contrasting groups, the able on the one hand, the idiots-imbeciles on the other, to bring out sensory differences between them. He devised a set of weights for lifting and suggested other measures in the sensory area. Characteristically, although Galton did not collect many data, he clearly implied that intelligence can be measured and that sensory ability is correlated with intelligence. This test of weight discrimination and his measures of association can be seen as mental tests.

As early as 1882 Galton established a small laboratory in London where, for payment of a fee, a person could take a battery of tests—physical measurements, reaction time measurements, and tests of sensory acuity.[27] Each client was given the results, and another copy was kept by the laboratory. Thus Galton, in addition to inventing mental tests, started the world's first mental testing center and in the process became the first psychological practitioner. He had, however, no intention of trying to do more than break even financially and did not succeed even in that.

One of Galton's works, published in 1884, brings out very clearly his interest in the measurement of personality.[28] After suggesting somewhat overoptimistically that intellectual performance had already been "adequately" measured and, more correctly, that temperament and character had been neglected, he offered a variety of suggestions for the measurement of these latter attributes by the cardiograph, the sphygmograph, and blood pressure apparatus employed to test the effect of small emotional shocks. Among a variety of other suggestions, there is one that bears quoting:

The poetical metaphors of ordinary language suggest many possibilities of measurement. Thus when two persons have an "inclination" to one another, they visibly incline or slope together when sitting side by side, as at a dinner table, and they then throw the stress of their weights on the near legs of their chairs. It does not require much ingenuity to arrange a pressure gauge with an index and dial to indicate changes in stress, but it is difficult to devise an arrangement, that shall fulfill the threefold condition of being effective, not attracting notice and being applicable to ordinary furniture. I made some rude experiments, but being busy with other matters, have not carried them on, as I had hoped.[29]

The article makes it clear that he was striving to develop as broad an inventory of human abilities as possible. If the word "personality" had had the meaning then that it does today, he surely would have used it.

Galton was knighted in 1909 and died at Haslemere in 1911. In his will he left funds for a laboratory for the study of eugenics.

EVALUATION

The measurement of individual differences in psychology was launched by Galton. Consider the work on the continent at this time. Helmholtz had given up the measurement of reaction time because the time varied so much from trial to trial. Wundt was not interested in Cattell's self-imposed problem of individual differences in reaction time. Galton had the insight to see that individual differences were not a nuisance to be eliminated but should be investigated for their own sake. He also forged the link between an evolutionary and a developmental outlook in psychology. He was the originator of mental tests. He made the first extensive use of the questionnaire for psychological research. For these reasons, Galton is included among the great psychologists.

Galton continued the individualistic spirit of English nineteenth-century science. He never had a specialty but ranged broadly over a wide number of fields. He was not a eugenicist, nor an anthropologist, nor even a psychologist; he was Galton. Like Boyle and Darwin, he never held an academic position. The brute fact was that Oxford and Cambridge were only beginning to awaken to the continental scientific spirit. They were far from ready to welcome so young an upstart as psychology, far down in the prestige order of the sciences. In Galton's case, it is fortunate that he was not confined within the mould of a professorship, where specialization would have been demanded; yet the advantages of the university were also denied him. There was little of the follow-through in his work that a university setting might well have encouraged. His work—although Karl Pearson was a faithful follower, and an American, James McKeen Cattell acknowledged Galton's profound influence upon him—did not attract students, as did Wundt's in Germany. There was no group of enthusiastic followers to carry on his work in psychology and to clean up details and bring order generally to his thinking, although in this regard his work in eugenics and biometrics fared somewhat better.

Galton's adherence to the developmental, functional, and dynamic prescriptions that characterized the work of Darwin influenced his contributions to psychology. Far more important, however, was quantitativism, the desire to count and measure, that ran as a thread throughout his diverse endeavors, psychological and nonpsychological alike. He made measurement of variability an interesting and important facet of psychological research.

Galton had worked with a profusion of psychological topics but, once a particular study was done, there was no later integration into a larger pattern. Spencer was the contemporaneous synthesizer of psychology and evolution.

Herbert Spencer

Herbert Spencer (1820–1903) was born in Derby, the son of a schoolmaster. Tutored by his father, he was otherwise practically self-educated.[30] As a young man he worked as a surveyor and a railroad engineer. He then secured an appointment as a junior editor of the journal *The Economist* and was launched upon his career as a writer, which was to be his means of livelihood thereafter. At this time Spencer contributed numerous articles to the *Westminster Review*, articles that sketched aspects of what was later to emerge as his philosophical doctrines. He became a friend of many of the leading scientific figures of his age—Huxley, Darwin, and others.

PSYCHOLOGY AND EVOLUTION

Spencer preceded Darwin in his public espousal of evolution. It was about 1840 that he read Lyell's *Principles of Geology.* Its arguments against Lamarck's theory of the inheritance of acquired characters had the effect of leading him to accept Lamarck's position. As early as 1852 he had definitely disassociated himself from a belief in the immutability of species. He developed an evolutionist doctrine in the years immediately preceding the publication of Darwin's *Origin of Species,* but his publications attracted relatively little attention at that time.[31] Before Darwin, Spencer's views were based primarily on philosophical, geological, and anthropological arguments and very little on biological data. When Darwin produced his theory and precipitated a movement, Spencer associated himself with it.[32] Once reinforced by the genius of Darwin, Spencer was caught up in the great new trend, though he preserved his independence and remained very much his own man. Darwin had supplied the detailed proof but was careful not to generalize beyond his data; in his turn, Spencer supplied a universal application, drawing out the implications of the theory so as to extend it over the range of human knowledge and endeavor.

Spencer did this through his *Synthetic Philosophy,* which was a comprehensive system in which he attempted to apply the master concept of evolution to all human knowledge. After failing to secure a state subsidy, he sent out to prospective subscribers a syllabus for his *Synthetic Philosophy,* eventually to encompass ten volumes, and secured enough money to go ahead with its preparation. Once started on the undertaking, he never wavered, working doggedly toward its completion despite frequent ill health and very little money.

Successive parts of *The System of Synthetic Philosophy* appeared from 1862 to 1893. It began with the *First Principles*[33] and proceeded through *The Principles of Biology,*[34] *The Principles of Psychology,*[35] (the second edition), *The Principles of Sociology,*[36] and *The Principles of Ethics.*[37] He continued writing and reviewing through a long productive life and died in 1903.

The main outline of his position is rather easy to present in short compass. The nature of reality is unknowable. All philosophy and science are concerned only with sensible experience (in this sense he was an empiricist of a sort). The sciences work in more restricted areas, while philosophy serves to unify their concepts. The ultimate law of development, which runs through all things, is based on the principle of the conservation of energy, and the task is to specify how this energy is transformed.

There is a unity to all the sciences, and the unity exists in evolution. Existence *is* evolution. Development of man and the stars involves differentiation followed by integration. Everything proceeds from homogeneity toward heterogeneity. "Evolution," he said in that famous rolling Victorian sentence, "is an integration of matter and concomitant dissipation of motion; during which the matter passes from an indefinite, incoherent homogeneity to a definite coherent heterogeneity. . . ."[38] The physical sciences he dismissed after a very general discussion, leaving himself free thereafter to concentrate on the sciences of man. Biologically, life is an adjustment of internal relations to external conditions. As for psychology itself, consciousness accompanies increased correspondence and better adjustment. With increased complexity of structure, there is increased differentiation in consciousness.

It was John Hughlings Jackson (1835–1911) who provided the physiological interpretation for his evolutionary views. As his ardent disciple, Jackson worked out a view that would make the nervous system subject to an evolutionary hierarchy.[39] In this conception the opposite of evolution, dissolution, to use as he did, Spencer's term, accounted for nervous disease. According to Jackson, in neurological disorders higher levels were attacked first and only then did the disorder proceed to lower levels. This hierarchical view naturally led to less emphasis on, if not outright rejection of, exact localization of function in favor of the position that higher and lower levels were involved according to the complexity of function.

Spencer gave considerable attention to association, the elements of which he referred to as "feelings" and "relations between feelings."[40] A feeling is a portion of consciousness with a perceivable individuality and is not further reducible into elements. A relation between feelings on the other hand occupies no appreciable part of consciousness. Take away the feeling units, and relations also disappear. But feelings and relations between feelings still must be kept separate for reasons that later discussion will show.

Feelings include emotions and sensations, the former centrally initiated, the latter peripherally initiated. Spencer also makes a distinction between these real or primary feelings and the "ideal" feelings (i.e., remembered sensations or emotions or ideas of sensations and emotions) on the basis of the greater vividness of the former and the relative faintness of the latter.

Feelings of relation include those of difference, coexistence, and sequence.[41] The feeling of difference is illustrative. This feeling occurs when we pass from one conscious state to another, as when we are aroused from a train of thought by being called to supper. The passage from one state to another creates a slight momentary shock because of the difference between the temporally adjacent states. Similarly, there are relations of coexistence and of sequence in our continuing conscious experience.

Feelings of relation, being a "given" of consciousness, help to reduce the burden on the working of association.[42] These feelings of relation were the result of association itself to Spencer's predecessors. James Mill as we have seen, burdened the mind with an impossible number of associations. As we also know, John Stuart Mill and Alexander

Bain both struggled with this problem, not too successfully. By postulating feelings of relation, Spencer helped to get around this difficulty. The affinity of the relations to the solutions of the problem that the Würzburg school suggested is apparent.

As to the mechanism of association itself, Spencer stressed similarity, but since associations are built up by experience, he could not dispense with the principle of contiguity entirely; he therefore mentioned, as additional conditions of association, vividness and repetition.[43]

Aside from the postulation of feelings of relation, Spencer's position here differs only slightly from the earlier individual versions of associationism. This account, however, is but a pale preliminary to the overall originality of his discussion of other psychological topics.

After a lengthy physiological introduction, Spencer considers the relation of psychology to biology. In the classification of the sciences, psychology appears as a division of biology. Physiological processes are correlated with psychological processes. Adjustment of interactions to outer conditions is a theme Spencer persistently stresses.[44] The life of every organism is a series of adjustments to the environment. Just as in biology, the environment must always be considered in dealing with psychological phenomena. In fact, the environment must be considered just as much as the "correlated phenomena of the organism."[45] For example, for Spencer as they were for Hartley, pleasure and pain are adjustive.[46] If animals find poisonous foods enjoyable, they die. "Survival of the fittest"[47] (Spencer's phrase, not Darwin's) brings inclinations into harmony with environmental conditions.

From the discussion of feelings of relation, it may have been inferred that Spencer emphasized the constant flow of consciousness. There had been some conception of a stream of consciousness in the work of Bain, but Spencer developed the idea much more fully. Interruptions in this flow of consciousness were expressed by feelings of relational difference; coexistence and sequence stressed its continuity.

According to Spencer there are two separable aggregates of consciousness, objective (vivid) and subjective (faint). By objective, he meant the consciousness of what we today would call the present environment, whereas the subjective aggregate deals with our thoughts of situations not physically present. States of consciousness arising from the objective world will show cohesion and continuity, provided we are physically passive. To change this state, we must change ourselves.

At the seashore it is still the sand, the sea, and the pier of which we are aware, despite our sitting through the sunlight of day to the dusk of night with all the changes of experience that this entails. There is no break in the consciousness throughout. By contrast, subjective states are characteristically less vivid and are easily changed. As we sit at the beach, the sight of a book in the hand of a passerby or a sea gull crossing our line of vision may start a new subjective state of consciousness, totally breaking off our reverie, say, about some past triumph. Nevertheless, the objective state of consciousness remains throughout the subjective shifts.

In discussing consciousness in general, Spencer states that changes of a particular sort do occur. Without change, consciousness is impossible. But this is not simply random change. It is orderly change. There is an organization to it.[48] Changes would pass as images do across a mirror, unless there were assimilation, the work of intelligence.[49] So change (differentiation) and assimilation (integration) continually take place. Intelligence is this process of assimilation of impressions.[50] ⟵

Spencer emphasized much more what intelligence *does* than what it *is*.[51] Intelligence is the means of bringing about that adjustment of internal to external relations[52] that had previously been called the definition of life. Intelligence establishes this correspondence to the best of its ability, using its feeling of relation and other activities, such as instinct, perception, conception, memory, will, and the like. In fact, only feelings as such are omitted, since they are not a constituent of intelligence but only its raw materials. Intelligence is to be judged by its remoteness from reflex action.[53] He specified the ways in which intelligence and reflex differ as the relative simplicity, poverty, and rigidity of the latter. When there are limitations of intelligence in an individual, abstract conception becomes impossible.

Mind and intelligence are specifically distinguished by Spencer. Intelligence involves the relational aspect of mind, but this in turn demands the present of the feelings to which the two are related. Intellect consists of various degrees of flexibility in the form of the relations of the mind.[54] Assimilation of a relation to its past kindred is by means of intelligence of operation.[55] Intelligence increases progressively throughout the scale of the animal kingdom.[56] Within the individual, growth of intelligence is shown in three ways: increase in the accuracy with which inner tendencies are proportioned to outer persistences, increase in the number of cases of equal difficulty, and increase in the complexity of coherent states of consciousness answering to coherent complexities in the environment.[57] This is a definition of intelligence of astonishing complexity and subtlety, considering the relatively primitive state of understanding of the nature and function of intelligence current at the time.

We now come to the crucial issue, the means by which Spencer made association an evolutionary doctrine. He held that often-repeated associations develop a hereditary tendency so that the offspring are more likely to inherit a tendency that their forebears had learned.[58] This has a cumulative effect in successive generations. To put it succinctly, there is an inheritance of acquired associations.

This supposition that habits acquired by the individual can be transmitted by means of heredity is, of course, dependent on the validity of the transmission of acquired characters. Later research in genetics has not demonstrated such transmission.

Despite this difficulty, the old quarrel between the empiricists and nativists was in some measure resolved by Spencer's theory. As Boring writes:

> Finally we must note that evolutionary psychology played into the hands of nativism and against geneticism. It is almost paradoxical that such should have been the case. Locke's empiricism led to associationism, and the genetic view of perception, for example, was the natural result. In fact, this view was as often called empiristic as genetic. Nativism, the opponent theory, seemed to go back through Kant to the innate ideas of Descartes, the very view that Locke brought empiricism to combat. Spencer's theory was essentially a resolution of the two views, although, because of the failure of science generally to accept the doctrine of the inheritance of acquired characters, his synthesis lacks the importance that it would otherwise have. Spencer simply substituted phylogenetic origin for ontogenetic origin in many cases. What is empiristically derived in the race may nevertheless be native in the individual, he might have said.[59]

The tabula rasa was banished. The individual, although he may not inherit experiences, does inherit certain organic capacities that make different experiences possible for later members of the species.

For a variety of reasons given in this and earlier chapters, association as we have followed it through the centuries has changed as a doctrine. This is signalized by the use hereafter of different conceptual terms—historically derived from associationism, to be sure, but deserving of a new terminology to accompany the new outlook.

There remains only Spencer's interpretation of pleasantness-unpleasantness. In the various species of animals there is a correlation between the pleasant and the beneficial and the unpleasant and harmful, as noted earlier. Whatever is pleasant, the organism maintains, and this association is inherited; on the other hand, whatever is painful is abandoned. Spencer was saying that there is a selection of pleasant acts that are useful and an abandonment of unpleasant acts that are harmful. He was advocating a version of what became later the law of effect. That rewards and punishments are instigators of behavior was to become a central theme of psychology.

Other philosopher-psychologists than Spencer were profoundly influenced by evolutionary thinking. One of these was James Ward (1843–1925), who wrote the account of psychology for the ninth edition (1885) of the *Encyclopaedia Britannica* and later revised it for the eleventh edition.[60] He is chiefly remembered today for this article, which had a remarkable influence on succeeding generations of British psychologists. His was a combination of phenomenology and evolutionary doctrine. In a manner akin to Brentano he objected to conceiving of the mind as passive. Instead, he saw the mind as active in its judging and perceiving. Mental processes were not Wundtian building blocks; rather, they evolved from an undifferentiated state in the direction of greater and greater differentiation. Mental elements, instead of existing from time immemorial, went through a process of emerging from out of more undifferentiated mental states. There was no combination and recombination of elementary units; instead, there was growth and differentiation where none existed before. His point of view became part of the staple fare of English psychology for generations.

Morgan and Comparative Psychology

In the early nineteenth century, there had been some interest in animal behavior. The concern centered primarily on the question of instinct as contrasted with reason. Meanwhile, biologists and physiologists were becoming interested in the sense organs and the motor activities of various kinds of animals.

With the advent of Darwinism, research with animals accelerated rapidly. It took as its major problem the relation of forms of behavior to the phylogenetic scale of animals, particularly as expressed in the similarity and difference between man and the lower animals, leading to the expression, "comparative psychology."

In the earliest phase, and still for some time to come, the task was conceived of as investigation of mind. G. S. Romanes saw his task as

1882

observing behavior, right enough, but to do so as to be able to draw inference about the animals' mental processes.[61] This he did on the theoretical premise that the degree of differences between man and animal depended on the degree of evolutionary separation between them. He concluded from the evidence he collected that in varying degrees animals do possess the mental characteristics of man. In its earliest phase the question at issue was still seen as the contrast between instinct and reason. Naturally on the side of diminishing the gulf between man and animal, evolutionists stressed finding evidence of "reason" in animals. Their major tool at first was to collect anecdotes about animals, that is to say, the accounts of casual observations of remarkable feats of animals upon which they chanced or ferreted out by questioning farmers, animal breeders, zoo keepers, and the like. Most often the anecdotes unearthed involved behavior that could not be accounted for by instinct, such as a dog's lifting a gate latch without known previous training. Thus it would seem that the dog had reasoned he could get out if he did what he had seen his master do, and accordingly did so.

This particular instance of the dog and the opening of the latch serves admirably to introduce one of the first crude but effective experiments that C. Lloyd Morgan (1852–1936) reported.[62] Morgan considered precisely this behavior of a dog lifting a latch. He agreed that it was not due to instinct but speculated that this behavior could be explained otherwise than by assuming that the dog had reasoned out a relation of the means employed to the end obtained, for he had observed what had happened in his own dog in precisely this instance. He agreed that the person observing the behavior *after* the process was fixed could not be blamed for assuming that it was reasoning that brought about the solution. The surety, smoothness, and celerity with which the dog performed the necessary toss of the catch and then immediately bolted off down the road seemed to indicate reasoning. What actually had happened? Before the dog could lift the latch with his muzzle, Morgan had observed that he would run up and down, sticking his head through the vertical bars at various points, sometimes near the catch, sometimes farther away. He wanted to get out, and in his excitement behaved restlessly. The dog happened to put his head beneath the latch and lifted it during the process. He looked through the gate and then noticed it was open, and bolted down the road. Thereafter, Morgan waited at the gate until his dog's frequent poking, often in the wrong place, eventually lifted the latch. It was nearly three weeks and a dozen repetitions before the dog did it neatly and quickly. Morgan attributes the delay to the dog's failure to relate means and end, commenting that the dog "never had the faintest notion of how or why looking out just then came to mean walking forth into the road."[63]

In addition to such findings, Morgan carried comparative psychology farther by criticizing vigorously the anecdotal work that went on before him, and he supplied more rigorously interpreted instances of observations than his predecessors. As a means of increasing rigor, he formulated a famous interpretive dictum as a guide for the psychologist.[64] His phrasing, which has come to be called Lloyd Morgan's canon, was _Parsimony_ that in no case should a particular animal's activity be interpreted in terms of higher psychological processes if it is interpretable in terms of processes standing lower in the scale of psychological evolution.

The work of Morgan was representative of that of a small but increasing number of persons who were founding the field of comparative psychology. In fact, research studies had been performed even before those of Morgan. Spalding's had been among the first.[65] He took young swallows from the moment of hatching, confined them in cages away from other birds, and released them at an age when normally they would be able to fly. He found that they soon "learned" to fly, despite having never observed the flight of other birds.

In the United States, simultaneously with Morgan, E. L. Thorndike was carrying on his studies with the added controls of laboratory equipment. His pioneer studies on learning in cats, chicks, dogs, and monkeys began to appear in 1898.[66] Major discussion of his work is reserved for later (p. 341). ? _This is 341!_

Later Developments

Accounts of mental development by psychologists, largely due to the pioneering work of Darwin and Galton, began to appear in increasing numbers at the end of the nineteenth and the beginning of the twentieth centuries, particularly in England and the United States. More specifically, studies of mental development in the race and in the individual, studies in child psychology, and studies in animal psychology increased in number and quality.

The evolutionary biological influence on psychology served as a corrective to the earlier almost exclusively cognitive psychology, but it did not change psychology overnight. Evolutionary thinking modified many psychological foci of interest by putting a number of the old problems of sensation-perception and association in different perspectives. It introduced more functional issues, such as those of intelligence as a process and of adaptation to the environment. The old problem of instinct versus reason was now banished, and the new question of the relative influence of instinct and learning was coming to take its place. But psychology remained predominantly introspective.

Emphasis on the adaptability of man to his environment and, indeed, on behavior as such as considerations of psychology inspired the functional and contentually objective approaches of the twentieth century. Meanwhile in France other developments were taking place.

References*

1. J. B. Lamarck, *Zoological Philosophy: An Exposition with Regard to the Natural History of Animals*, trans. H. Elliot (London: Macmillan Ltd., 1914) (1809).
2. C. Darwin, "The Origin of Species by Means of Natural Selection," 2nd ed., in R. M. Hutchins, ed., *The Great Books of the Western World* (Chicago: Encyclopaedia Britannica, 1952), Vol. XLIX, pp. 1–251 (1859).
3. L. Huxley, ed., *Life and Letters of T. H. Huxley*, 2 vols. (New York: Appleton, 1900), Vol. I, p. 183.
4. C. Darwin, *The Descent of Man and Selection in Relation to Sex* (New York: Appleton, 1871).
5. C. Darwin, "A Biographical Sketch of an Infant," *Mind*, II (1877): 285–294.
6. C. Bell, *Anatomy and Philosophy of Expression* (London: Longmanns, Hurst, Rees, and Orme, 1806).
7. C. Darwin, *The Expression of the Emotions in Man and Animals* (London: Murray, 1873) (1872).
8. K. Pearson, *The Life, Letters and Labors of Francis Galton* (London: University of Cambridge Press, 1914–1924); F. Galton, *Memories of My Life* (London: Methuen, 1908).
9. *Ibid.*
10. "Galton, Sir Francis," *Encyclopaedia Britannica* (Chicago: 1955), Vol. IX, p. 989.
11. F. Galton, *Hereditary Genius* (London: Macmillan Ltd., 1869) (Herrnstein and Boring, Excerpt No. 78).
12. F. Galton, *Hereditary Genius* (London: Macmillan Ltd., 1892), prefatory chapter.
13. A. R. Buss, "Galton and Sex Differences: An Historical Note," *Journal of the History of the Behavioral Sciences*, 12(1976): 283–285.

*See p. 19 for description of reference style.

14. Pearson, *Life, Letters and Labors of Francis Galton*, Vol. I, p. 6.

15. A. Quetelet, *Physique sociale* (Brussels: Marquardt, 1869), Vol. II.

16. Pearson, *Life, Letters and Labors of Francis Galton*, Vol. II.

17. F. Galton, "Co-relations and Their Measurement, chiefly from anthropometric data," *Proceedings, Royal Society of London*, XV (1888): 135–145.

18. K. Pearson, "Regression, Heredity and Panmixia," *Philosophical Transactions*, CLXXXVIIA (1896): 253–318.

19. Pearson, *Life, Letters and Labors of Francis Galton*, Vol. II.

20. F. Galton, *Inquiries into Human Faculty and its Development* (London: Macmillan Ltd., 1883) (Herrnstein and Boring, Excerpt No. 79).

21. F. Galton, *Inquiries into Human Faculty and its Development*, 2nd ed. (New York: E. P. Dutton, 1907).

22. Galton, *Memories*.

23. *Ibid.*

24. Galton, *Inquiries*, 2nd ed.

25. *Ibid.*

26. *Ibid.*

27. F. Galton, "Psychometric Experiments," *Brain*, II (1879): 149–162.

28. F. Galton, "Measurement of Character," *Fortnightly Review*, XXXVI (1884): 179–185.

29. *Ibid.*, p. 184.

30. Sources for the details of the life of Herbert Spencer are very meager, a result of his almost complete neglect during the last fifty years or so. To be sure there is his *An Autobiography* (2 vols., New York: Appleton, 1904), but it is more a reworking of a diary than a full-fledged autobiography. This situation has been remedied to some extent by the recent publication of J.D.Y. Peel, *Herbert Spencer: The Evolution of a Sociologist* (New York, Basic Books, 1971). Other details had to be sought in secondary sources, such as E. Nordenskiold, *The History of Biology* (New York: Alfred A. Knopf, 1928); and W. C. Dampier, *A History of Conscience and Its Relations with Philosophy and Religion*, 4th ed. (Cambridge: Cambridge University Press, 1949).

31. Dampier, *History of Science*.

32. Nordenskiold, *History of Biology.*

33. H. Spencer, *First Principles* (London: Williams and Norgate, 1862).

34. H. Spencer, *The Principles of Biology* (New York: Appleton, 1872).

35. H. Spencer, *The Principles of Psychology*, 2nd ed. (London: Williams and Norgate, 1870–1872) (1855).

36. H. Spencer, *The Principles of Sociology* (New York: Appleton, 1876–1879).

37. H. Spencer, *The Principles of Ethics* (New York: Appleton, 1879–1893).

38. H. Spencer, *First Principles*, 6th ed. (London: Williams and Norgate, 1908), p. 321 (1862).

39. J. Hughlings Jackson, *The Croonian Lectures on the Evolution and Dissolution of the Nervous System* (London: 1884), pp. 3–5 (Herrnstein and Boring, Excerpt No. 49).

40. Spencer, *Psychology*, 2nd ed., pp. 64ff.

41. *Ibid.*, Sec. 89.

42. E. G. Boring, *History of Experimental Psychology*, 2nd ed. (New York: Appleton-Century-Crofts, 1950), pp. 241–243.

43. *Ibid.*

44. Spencer, *Psychology*, 2nd ed., Sec. 57.

45. *Ibid.*, Sec. 54.

46. *Ibid.*, Sec. 125.

47. E.g., *Biology*, III, Chapter 12.

48. Spencer, *Psychology*, 2nd ed., Sec. 49.

49. *Ibid.*, Sec. 382.

50. *Ibid.*, Sec. 475g.

51. C. E. Spearman, *Psychology Down the Ages* (London: Macmillan Ltd., 1937).

52. Spencer, *Psychology*, 2nd ed., Sec. 203.

53. *Ibid.*, Sec. 486.

54. *Ibid.*, Sec. 76.

55. *Ibid.*, Sec. 120.

56. *Ibid.*, Secs. 177–181.

57. *Ibid.*, Sec. 188.

58. H. Spencer, *The Principles of Psychology* (London: Smith and Elder, 1855), Part 4, Secs. 173–174, pp. 179–180 (Herrnstein and Boring, Excerpt No. 74).

59. Boring, *History of Experimental Psychology*, pp. 243–244. Reprinted by permission.

60. J. Ward, "Psychology," *Encyclopaedia Britannica*, 9th ed. (New York: Encyclopaedia Britannica, 1886),

Vol. XX (1885) (Herrnstein and Boring, Excerpt No. 113).

61. G. J. Romanes, *Animal Intelligence* (London: Appleton, 1882) (Herrnstein and Boring, Excerpt No. 87).
62. C. L. Morgan, *An Introduction to Comparative Psychology*, 2nd ed. (New York: Scibner's 1904) (1894).
63. *Ibid.*, p. 293.
64. *Ibid.*, e.g., pp. 53, 292 (Herrnstein and Boring, Excerpt No. 88).
65. D. Spalding, "Instinct and Acquisition," *Nature*, XII (1875): 507–508.
66. E. L. Thorndike, "Animal Intelligence: An Experimental Study of the Associative Processes in Animals," *Psychological Review, Monograph Supplements*, II (1898).

Chapter 15

Binet:
FRENCH PSYCHOLOGY
IN THE NINETEENTH CENTURY

From the beginning of the nineteenth century, the French psychological tradition had centered on psychopathological problems. Pierre Janet, one of France's leading psychologists toward the end of the century, was to affirm that the development of "pathological" psychology was most characteristic of France.[1] It follows that the French were both utilitarian and idiographic in outlook in contrast to the Germans, who leaned toward purism and nomotheticism. Even psychologists who had their degrees in philosophy or in one of the sciences were apt to be influenced by these traditions. There were two discriminable groups of psychologists in France at the time—the physician-psychologist interested in abnormal mental phenomena and their treatment, and the academic-medical psychologist who paid some attention to the more conventional aspect of psychology, including its teaching, but who was also drawn into consideration of the same phenomena that interested his medical confreres. Charcot and Bernheim represent the former group; Ribot and Janet represent the latter. Binet, as befits the greatest French psychologist of his time, shared in this tradition but also created one of his own.

Near the beginning of the nineteenth century, France became the first country to begin developing adequate care for the insane and the feeble-minded. One of its leading physicians at the turn of the century was Philippe Pinel (1745–1826).[2] In 1792, he had been appointed superintendent of the asylum at Bicêtre. In the wake of the Revolution came his own particular application of the "Rights of Man" to the miserable patients in his charge, who heretofore had been kept in chains and treated as wild beasts, even to the point of being on exhibit to those who paid a small fee. After a personal plea before the

Pinel → Esquirol
JEAN Itard → Edouard Seguin

Revolutionary Convention, Pinel was permitted to dispense with the chains. He treated his patients humanely and placed them under the care of reasonably competent physicians. His book on mental diseases was a powerful plea for more humane treatment of the insane.[3] Instead of accepting the view then current that the insane were wicked and in the grip of demoniacal possession, Pinel was convinced that brain dysfunction may be related to severe psychological disorders. He knew too little to advance very far, but the conviction was there. Pinel was succeeded in his work by Jean Etienne Esquirol (1771–1840), who worked assiduously at establishing properly run asylums. He also wrote a monumental work on mental diseases, one more rational and descriptive than the barren speculations of most of his predecessors.[4]

Jean Itard (1775–1838), a contemporary of Pinel and Esquirol, was the pioneer in the systematic study of mental deficiency.[5] A teacher of the deaf, he was consulted about the "wild boy of Aveyron" in 1798. The year before, in a woods in the Department of Aveyron, a so-called wild boy had been found by hunters. He was brought to Itard to see if he could be trained to live in civilization, a topic of more than usual interest because of the popularity of the then prevalent theories of the "noble savage." Itard worked long and arduously but could not in any way restore the child to normality. Through much effort, the boy learned a few habits more in keeping with his new environment, but was still unable to take care of himself. Finally it dawned on Itard that the boy was an idiot or an imbecile. He abandoned further work with the child as hopeless, since he shared in the common belief that idiots or imbeciles were but brutes incapable of any sort of training. But his assistant, Edouard Seguin (1812–1880), continued to work with the boy after Itard had given up because he appreciated that the gains made, slight though they were, caused the child to be both happier and better adjusted to society. Afterward, Seguin devoted his career to attempts to train feeble-minded children and eventually was put in charge of a school for the feeble-minded. This was the first institution of its kind; its establishment marks the beginning of training schools for the mentally retarded.

Another source in France making for a medical psychology was an interest in hypnotic phenomena. The history of phenomena of what came to be called hypnotism is at least as old as temple medicine in ancient Greece. Its modern phase begins with the work of Franz Anton Mesmer (1734–1815).[6] After attracting considerable notoriety in Vienna through use of his so-called animal magnetism in treating all sorts of patients, he was ordered to leave the city. He settled in Paris during

Rousseau

the 1780s, where his remarkable cures, especially of what we would now call hysterical patients, made him well known. He thought of animal magnetism as an invisible fluid whose magnetic power he communicated to his patients by making his hands pass over their bodies, after which he assured them that they were cured. Physicians called Mesmer an impostor, and the first of several commissions was appointed by the French government to investigate his powers. One of its members was Benjamin Franklin. The general conclusions of this and later commissions was that Mesmer effected many cures, but was mistaken in attributing to animal magnetism what was actually due to some as yet unknown physiological cause. Whatever else may have been taking place, magnetism as known in physics had nothing to do with these phenomena. The reports, generally unfavorable, were widely disseminated. As a consequence of this unfavorable publicity, Mesmer lost his practice and retired.

For some time after the French Revolution, mesmerism, as it was by then called, led a checkered career, kept alive by a few who used it with little or no understanding of what they were doing. Meanwhile, it was derided as quackery by most physicians.

It was James Braid (c. 1795–1860) in England in 1843, who named the various phenomena "hypnotism."[7] He considered that in hypnotism some sort of change took place in the nervous system as the result of psychological instigation. Braid described hypnotism as induced sleep and considered hypnosis nothing more than a convenient and quick means of throwing the nervous system into a state useful for the treatment of certain disorders.[8] He showed that hypnotism could be produced by focusing the eyes on an inanimate object, a procedure which helped to remove it from the realm of the uncanny. His lack of exaggeration, his caution, and his modest admission of lack of understanding impressed other medical men. The fact that he first expressed his interest in the topic by publicly attacking the mesmerists probably served to provide him with a respectability that the earlier workers had lacked. His work became known in France in the middle of the nineteenth century through a Dr. Azam, a surgeon of Bordeaux. Azam saw its advantage in surgical operations and proceeded to use it in this way. He was followed by others. But hypnosis came into national prominence only with the work of Charcot.

[margin note: Also Esdaile in INDIA. was important]

Jean Charcot

Jean-Martin Charcot (1825–1893), a physician, was appointed professor of pathological anatomy at the University of Paris in 1860.[9]

[handwritten: at Salpêtrière]

[handwritten: CHARCOT]

Two years later, he was appointed a senior physician to the Salpêtrière, a hospital for mental disorders, where he established a neurological clinic. He is often referred to as the father of neurology because of his ability to relate clinical signs present in the functioning of his patients to the normal and morbid anatomy of the nervous system, a correlation that is precisely the basis of neurology today. He carried on important studies of such diseases as multiple sclerosis and spinal paralysis and worked with problems of the localization of lesions in the brain and spinal cord. He was also famous as a teacher, for he was skilled in communicating his knowledge of diagnosis and anatomy to his pupils through case conferences. His fame was international, and students came to him from all over Europe. In 1885–1886 Sigmund Freud worked under Charcot, learning enough from him to refer to him later as "my master"[10] (p. 496).

Charcot was already a well-established teacher and researcher when he acquired his interest in hypnosis. Charles Richet (1850–1935) in 1875 had judged the phenomenon of hypnosis to be undoubtedly genuine. Accepting this statement of a respected colleague, Charcot launched into a period of intense clinical investigation and made his case conferences famous by demonstrating the many phenomena that can be induced by hypnosis. He began to center his attention on patients showing symptoms of hysteria.

[handwritten: Hypnosis + Hysteria]

What are some of the symptoms of hysteria? Somnambulism (sleep walking), fugues (running away without awareness of doing so), multiple personalities, and convulsive attacks are all included whenever organic causes can be ruled out, as are contractures, paralyses, vomiting, deafness, blindness, loss of speech, and anaesthesia of parts of the body.[11] To add to the complexity, the symptoms change even from day to day, for one day a patient may complain of vomiting, and the next day of headache. Mesmer and the mesmerists must have treated a large number of individuals who later would have been in this category. Hysteria is the great simulator of other diseases, such as tumors, intestinal obstructions, lesions of the bones and muscles, as well as organically based blindness and deafness.

Charcot soon compared the phenomenon of hypnosis to artificial hysteria. The patients of Salpêtrière, whom he found to be amenable to hypnosis and especially to very deep phases of hypnosis, were those already diagnosed as hysterics. He soon discovered that the symptoms of the hysteric patient could be modified by hypnosis, and hypnosis came to be the preferred method of treatment for this category of patients. He thus moved against established medical opinion, which still

[handwritten: Hypnosis due to pathological STATE in organism]

regarded hypnosis as somewhere between a theatrical stunt and sheer charlatanism.

At Salpêtrière under Charcot's leadership it was believed that the hypnotic phenomenon arose from hysteria in that only a person with an hysterical make-up could be brought to hypnotic sleep. Based on studying various degrees of the depth of hypnosis, Charcot asserted the existence of three main progressive stages in the depth of hypnosis: lethargy (drowsiness), catalepsy (isolated suggestions can be accepted and acted upon, since there is no interference by other ideas), and somnambulism (ability to carry out complicated activities with no recollection afterward).[12]

His interest in producing deep hypnosis arose from his desire to be absolutely certain of being able to distinguish between true hysteria and simulation of these conditions. Hysteria and malingering are not easy to differentiate, and Charcot was satisfied only with placing his patients under deep hypnosis in order to be sure that faking was eliminated.

Meanwhile another approach to hypnosis was being developed in Nancy by Liébeault and Bernheim.

Liébeault and Bernheim

A country doctor, Ambroise-Auguste Liébeault (1823–1904)[13] had been using hypnosis in his practice without fee with all peasants who would agree to its use, whereas for other forms of treatment they had to pay. Knowing a bargain when they saw one, the peasants flocked to him. It was not until he happened to treat a former patient of the neurologist Hyppolyte Bernheim (1840–1919) that his work received the attention that would place it ultimately in the history of psychology and medicine. This patient, who suffered from sciatica, had not responded to Bernheim's treatment, but he did to Liébeault's hypnosis. The already well-known Bernheim was impressed and became a pupil of Liébeault in 1882 and a few years later wrote a text that made him the leader of the Nancy School.[14]

Together, Liébeault and Bernheim had founded the clinic at Nancy, which was presently to rival Paris as another center for work in hypnotism. These workers, seeing no essential difference between spontaneous and induced sleep,[15] used the suggestion of sleep as the basis for the production of hypnosis. Essentially, the method of treatment of the Nancy school was based upon suggestion. To them, suggestion meant that under hypnosis new attitudes and beliefs were accepted by the patient uncritically, and he would then behave in accordance with these new ideas. During hypnosis, these two doctors would tell their patients that they would feel well or that their symptoms would disappear. In a fair number of instances, the effect was not merely temporary, as might have been expected, but appeared to be permanent.

The clinics of Nancy and Paris became ideological rivals. At Nancy it was taught that hypnosis, at least the mild form of it that was customarily used there, could be induced in nearly all subjects and that it was essentially a passive-receptive state brought about by suggestion. On the other hand, Charcot regarded hypnosis as a pathological state of the organism. At Nancy they challenged the identification of hypnosis with hysteria, arguing that the very stages that Charcot found were the result of specific suggestions. Later findings have tended to support Bernheim and Liébeault rather than Charcot.

Workers at Nancy and at Salpêtriére, far apart as they might have thought themselves at the time, were both laboring with similar groups of patients—the neurotics. No longer was interest in abnormal mental phenomena to be confined to the severely disturbed on the wards of mental hospitals. These men had isolated the neuroses from other mental diseases and in doing so had discovered them.

Théodule Ribot

Théodule Ribot (1839–1916) had perhaps the greatest breadth of interests and certainly was the most well read of the French psychologists of his time. He served as the psychological educator of his countrymen. In 1870[16] and 1879[17] he published books that interpreted English associationism and German experimentalism to his colleagues. In general, French psychologists tended to be skeptical about the value of German experimental psychology and to make only sparing use of associationism. As a medical psychologist in the French tradition, Ribot also systematically explored what was known about the pathological aspects of affective life. He wrote books about diseases of the will, memory, and personality, regarding these abnormalities as products of faulty brain functioning. In discussions of diseases of personality and in his presentation of cases, Ribot stressed dissociation, the splitting of the bonds of consciousness. He also reintroduced evolutionary thinking into French psychology. In 1875 he founded and edited the Revue Philosophique, which was to publish a fair amount of psychological material.

Ribot was appointed Professor of Experimental Psychology in 1889 at the College of France. He was not, however, an experimental psychologist in the sense of having a laboratory. In his strategic position he was to have as students many of the next generation of academically oriented French psychologists.

Pierre Janet

Pierre Janet (1859–1947) studied philosophy and psychology in the Faculty of Letters and then went on to the Faculty of Medicine at the University of Paris.[18] Before completing his medical training, he accepted a teaching post in philosophy at a *Lycée* outside of Paris. At this time he was only twenty-two years old. Eager to advance his career, he became interested in a patient named Léonie, already known to the medical profession for exhibiting both hypnotic and clairvoyant phenomena. After making a careful study of this intriguing combination, he reported that it seemed she could be hypnotized from a distance. Through this case study Janet came into contact with Charcot.

Shortly afterward Janet returned to Paris to study again in both the Faculties of Letters and Medicine, and in 1889 he received his doctorate in letters with a thesis on the psychology of automatic activities.[19] The following year he was invited by Charcot to become director of the psychological laboratory of Salpêtrière, where he tried to bring some order and system into the classification of hysteria and, in turn, to the conceptions of academic psychology. This study became the thesis for his doctorate in medicine, a degree he received in 1892.[20] After teaching at the Sorbonne from 1895 to 1902, Janet succeeded Ribot in the chair in the College of France, which he held until his retirement. He visited the United States in 1906 to lecture at Harvard University Medical School. The lectures were published in English as *The Major Symptoms of Hysteria,* the book for which he is best known in the United States.[21] During all these years, in addition to carrying out his academic duties, he was also a busy practicing physician, specializing in mental diseases. He died in 1947.

Janet himself clearly differentiated his work from that carried on at Salpêtrière. The work under Charcot was primarily neurological, so that paralyses, contractures, and disturbances of the senses were emphasized. Janet, on the contrary, saw hysteria as a *mental disease,* which chiefly consisted of an exaggerated suggestibility; he therefore emphasized mental phenomena—particularly impairments of memory and the presence of fixed ideas. This appeal to fixed ideas was based on the fact that hysterical patients had somehow fastened onto the idea that they were paralyzed or had lost sensitivity. These symptoms were not readily resolved and, hence, were referred to as fixed ideas. Thus Janet was closer to Bernheim in his interpretation than to Charcot, for both Janet and Bernheim saw many of the phenomena of hypnosis and of hysteria as products of suggestion. This resemblance becomes evident when one stops to consider that the behavioral phenomena are similar; for the only difference seems to be that under hypnosis, we know how the behavioral phenomena were instilled, that is, we know their origin, whereas in hysteria we do not.

Psychic energy and its diminution or depletion was a guiding concept of Janet.[22] Feelings of pressure experienced by the patient and consequent feelings of effort served to indicate this diminution of functioning quite apart from behaviors considered as symptomatic of psychic energy. Janet held that we do not know the nature of the energy, but we can study its manifestations. Individuals differ in quantity of energy available to them from both hereditary and environmental origins.[23] Janet cited fatigue, malnutrition, disease, pernicious experience, and inadequate education as the environmental sources responsible for lessened energy. Neuroses are fundamentally due to conditions of low mental tension—an inability to mobilize enough energy to meet the exigencies of life. There was a weakness in these hysterical patients. Illustrative of how weakness came to be postulated is the frequent triviality of the precipitating situation. At age twenty a man found himself near a heavy object as it fell from a window, breaking glass with a sound as of a gun shot. The man became dumb for two months, and twenty-six years later the slightest unexpected noise would still strike him dumb for several months at a time.[24] An even more famous case was observed in Boston, where a young woman, upon being kissed unexpectedly, developed symptoms that kept Morton Prince, an American psychologist, busy for years.[25]

To Janet, personality was a matter of integration. Within the normal individual, this integration of tendencies and ideas is relatively stable; in the hysterical individual this unity is lacking, and in extreme cases a lack of integration may extend to the point of splitting the personality into alternating personalities, most often two, but sometimes more. In these extreme cases a failure of conscious control has taken place. There is, said Janet, a narrowing of the field of consciousness open to the individual. In the contraction of consciousness, the hysterical symptoms are carried on without the individual being consciously aware of them. A rhythmic movement of the arm evokes in the patient no sense that he is doing it; he looks at it as something alien. The arm is carrying out the movement without his volition. The paralyzed leg is an alien "stump," as some of his patients called it, attached to the body, but not part of the person. If double personalities develop, the primary personality may not be aware of the thoughts, feelings, and experiences of the secondary personality. When a fugue occurs, a person may travel, eat in restaurants, answer questions, and generally behave in a fashion that attracts no attention, yet he will, on "awakening," not know where he is, how he got there, or what he did in the interval of the weeks or months during which he lived in the fugue state.

Janet considered that the dissociative split of consciousness came about because of some mental or physical shock. Often he found that the patient's history showed either a long-maintained or a continued series of conflicts. Essentially, hysteria is a contraction of consciousness due to exhaustion of the higher functions.[26] Over all, the dynamic factor is conversion symbolism, the "driving back" of that which is unacceptable in consciousness. The patient tries to get rid of thoughts that are painful or in opposition to moral feelings; he struggles to drive them out of consciousness. When he succeeds in making these experiences unconscious, his symptoms develop with the contraction of consciousness. As a result of clinical investigation, Janet came close to a conception of unconsciousness as a dynamic process. He had spoken of automatic activities as early as 1889 in his doctoral thesis and had discussed the unconscious, but impartial critics see in this usage hardly more than a figure of speech.

As for treatment itself, Janet found that under hypnosis these forgotten experiences can often be recalled to the patient and that the symptoms, the origin of which was unknown, could be traced back to their source and, after hypnotic suggestions, would even disappear (although other symptoms might turn up to take their place).

As might be anticipated, these views created a strained relationship between Janet and Sigmund Freud, whose formulations of a similar nature are discussed later (Chapter 20). Freud saw Janet as working in a similar area but at a superficial level. In turn, Janet claimed that psychoanalysis originated from his and Charcot's work.[27] As an eclectic in psychotherapy, he considered psychoanalysis one among many forms of treatment. Specifically, it served to bring about dissociation of traumatic memories.

Alfred Binet

In early fall of 1904, the Minister of Public Instruction appointed a committee to recommend what should be done about the education of subnormal children in the schools of Paris. The decision to place them in special schools necessitated the development of some means of identifying them. It was to this task, a call that he himself had helped to arrange, that Alfred Binet, then a man of forty-seven, turned his talents and experience to constructing the first intelligence scale.[28] To appreciate properly the nature of his contribution, it is necessary to say something about the years of preparation for the task and the status of psychological testing prior to that time.

LIFE OF BINET (1857- 1911)

Alfred Binet was born in Nice in 1857.[29] He was educated at Paris in law, a subject in which he received his degree in 1878; but his interests in the sciences and in medicine came to the fore, and he abandoned law. While still a law student, he had been attracted to the Salpêtrière where Charcot was the center of attention. Binet's predilection for psychological problems became evident to Charcot, particularly in respect to that burning question of the day, hypnotism. He became an enthusiastic, and, for a time, uncritical, follower of Charcot. Binet took a doctorate in natural science in 1894 with a thesis on the nervous system of insects, but not a degree in medicine. While still working on his degree, Binet had written a book on hypnosis, with Féré,[30] giving a detailed account of its history. This book appeared in 1886. He had studied hypnosis, using such devices as the dynamometer to measure strength of grip and the pneumograph for the recording of breathing rate. A few experiments were reported; these measures were taken in the normal state, in the hypnotic state, and under the effect of various suggestions and compared. The devastating criticism of Binet's work by members of the Nancy School made him lose enthusiasm for the investigation of hypnosis thereafter.

Another book by Binet, also appearing in 1886, was concerned with reasoning.[31] This volume was prophetic of his life-long interest in higher mental processes. In writing it, however, he depended for his sources on a general theory of association, on some incidental findings in hypnosis, and on his knowledge of logic, rather than on research data. Meanwhile, events were making him a psychologist, perhaps partly because of these books.

Henri Beaunis, professor of physiology on the faculty of medicine at Nancy, became the first director of the psychological laboratory founded in 1889 at the Sorbonne.[32] Although in the Sorbonne, the laboratory was administratively not part of the Faculty of Letters but of the École Pratique des Hautes Études. Ribot, who had previously been in charge

[handwritten margin note: with Féré, a History of Hypnosis in 1886]

of the course in experimental psychology but who had no laboratory, moved from the Sorbonne the same year to the chair of experimental and comparative psychology at the College of France. Binet, who was associated with Beaunis during these years, was asked in 1892 to be adjunct director. On the retirement of Beaunis in 1894, Binet became director of the laboratory, a post he held until his death in 1911 at age fifty-four.

Some of Binet's early work stressed the abnormal; he wrote a book on *The Alterations of the Personality*[33] in 1892 and one on *Suggestibility*[34] in 1900. In the same period, he carried on studies in tactile sensibility and optical illusions in a fashion similar to that of his German contemporaries. He studied handwriting, using blind analysis to increase his objectivity. He investigated the thinking of chess players. He carried on a series of studies of suggestion. It was these studies of suggestibility—within the tradition of medical psychology—for which Binet was best known up to this time.

Collaborating with Beaunis, he established in 1895 *L'Année psychologique*, which became the leading French psychological journal.

About 1900 Binet began to study thinking by the use of introspection. His previous book on reasoning had been written without the hindrance of research data. Now in his new work, published in 1902, he depended for data on the reports of the thinking of his two daughters, then of high school age.[35]

As happened later with his studies of intelligence, he failed to be impressed by the necessity of working with minute elements of psychic life and believed that psychological problems of thinking may be attacked globally. (In fact, it is only in keeping with contemporary usage that this may be called a study of thinking. Actually, Binet referred to it as a study of "intelligence.") He asked his daughters to solve problems and then to report to him the steps they took to reach a solution. Often the girls specifically denied the presence of images. In general, these results anticipated and supported the research of the Würzburg School. Like those at Würzburg, Binet found much thinking that could not be reduced to sensory or ideational elements.

Although the girls were similar in their thinking in regard to matters so far described, it also happened that they differed strikingly in their particular ways of thinking and in their personalities—differences to which their father's account devotes considerable attention. Undoubtedly, this study strengthened Binet's interest in individual differences.

He evinced a greater interest in laboratory research than was characteristic of his fellow Frenchmen and wrote a textbook of experimental psychology. Generally, Binet's career with its interest in abnormal phenomena was quite in keeping with the tradition of psychology in his country.[36] Busy as all this work kept him, however, his claim to greatness rests primarily on his contribution to the measurement of intelligence.

MEASUREMENT OF INTELLIGENCE

In 1905 Binet urged that it was necessary to establish an accurate diagnosis of intelligence if the recommendation of the committee concerning placement of feeble-minded children in special schools were to be carried out adequately.[37]

He was sharply critical of medical diagnosis of this condition. Previously, diagnosis of mental deficiency was considered analogous to diagnosis of physical disease. It is not surprising that errors occurred, since no one invariable sign of mental deficiency was known, then or later. For this purpose, Binet drew attention in copious detail to the errors that physicians had made in diagnosis by showing that the same child could carry different diagnoses when evaluated by different physicians, just a few days apart. It was thus that the work of the Parisian committee precipitated the development of the Binet Scale and centered Binet's interest on the problem of the diagnosis of the feeble-minded. It did not create his interest in the problem of intelligence.

For many years before the establishment of the Paris committee of 1904, Binet had had an interest in the measurement of intelligence and individual differences. From 1887, his principal source of subjects for study had been the school children in and around Paris upon whom he had tried out various tests.[38]

With his collaborator and assistant, Victor Henri (1872–1940), Binet published seven papers on individual differences. The crucial paper on tests appeared in 1896.[39] First Binet and Henri reviewed the literature, which was already quite extensive. Without confining discussion to the specific tests they reviewed, it will suffice to say that they were presumably familiar with the work of Galton and perhaps also with the contribution of Ebbinghaus on the completion test to be published in 1897. Also available to them was considerable literature on elementary sensory, perceptual, and motor measures. Narrow phases of mental activity, such as sensory acuity, reaction time, attention span, speed of movement, and the like, had been studied during preceding years. Binet and Henri pointed out that too limited and too specialized abilities were being utilized for a measurement of so complex a matter as intelligence. Moreover, with a problem such as the relation of memory to intelligence to be studied, it would be necessary to examine various kinds of memory, rather than one kind alone. Several variations of memory must be tapped. Binet and Henri proposed that visual memory of a geometrical design, memory of a sentence, memory of musical notes, memory of color, and memory of digits should all be included as tests of intelligence. Recognition of the differences in endowments among individuals indicated the need for tests covering a wide scope. They urged for this purpose tests, not of elementary functions but of the higher mental processes. Among the ten mental processes they proposed to study were 1) *memory*, as already noted; 2) *images*, measured by recalling twelve randomly selected letters exposed to view long enough for two readings at a "natural" rate; and 3) *attention*, divided into duration (reproduction of the length of a line of a given length shown only once) and scope (the ability to count the total number of strokes of two metronomes set for slightly different speeds with gradual increase of the speeds on successive trials until the subject's limit is reached). The other tests were for measurements of imagination, comprehension, suggestibility, esthetic appreciation, moral sentiments, strength of will, and motor skill.

memory

10 Mental Processes

During the years between 1897 and 1905 Binet and his collaborators busied themselves with developing new tests, particularly for the higher mental processes. Théodore Simon (1873–1961), a new collaborator, also collected anthropometric measurements.

In 1905 the first intelligence scale appeared as the joint effort of Binet and Simon.[40] It consisted of a long series of tests they had given to what was for the time a rather large sample of children. Their guiding concept was that of a *scale*—a series of tests of increasing difficulty starting with the lowest intellectual level and extending to that of the average level.

The scale was avowedly a test to be applied rather than just a means of research, for they encouraged others to use their instrument for the measurement of intelligence. They urged prospective testers to secure training from them, stressed the need for uniformity of administration, and warned against permitting coaching of the children tested.

In 1908 they revised and improved the scale.[41] The tests were arranged, not merely according to level of difficulty but according to the age at which presumably normal children could pass them successfully. If on the tryout of a test being evaluated for possible inclusion, it was found that all or nearly all the children six years old failed, the item was obviously too hard for that age; whereas if practically all eight-

Revision 1908

year-olds passed it, it was too easy. The only possibility remaining would be to place it at the seven-year level. This particular test would then have been placed at the seven-year level provided it met the general criterion for placement of a test. The rule was that if 60 to 90 percent of the children at a given age passed a particular test, it was to be considered standard for that age and included in the scale. Thus the first *age scale* was launched. In this way, it came about that children of all levels of intelligence were brought into focus of attention, and the feeble-minded were left merely as a deviant from the normal. A shift away from the relatively specific problem of the detection of feeblemindedness to the more general problem of the measurement of intelligence at all levels had taken place.

Tabulated below are the tests at both ends of the scale grouped according to the age at which the majority of children succeeded on them:

Age 3 Years

1. Points to nose, eyes, mouth.
2. Repeats sentences of six syllables.
3. Repeats two digits.
4. Enumerates objects in a picture.
5. Gives family name.

Age 4 Years

1. Knows sex.
2. Names certain familiar objects shown to him; *key, pocketknife,* and a *penny.*
3. Repeats three digits.
4. Indicates which is the longer of two lines five and six cm. in length.

Age 12 Years

1. Repeats seven digits.
2. Finds in one minute three rimes for a given word—*obedience.*
3. Repeats a sentence of twenty-six syllables.
4. Answers problem questions—a common-sense test.
5. Gives interpretation of pictures.

Age 13 Years

1. Draws the design that would be made by cutting a triangular piece from the once-folded edge of a quarto-folded paper.
2. Rearranges in imagination the relationship of

two triangles and draws the results as they
would appear.
3. Gives differences between pairs of abstract
terms, as *pride* and *pretension*.[42]

Mental Age

By means of the 1908 scale one could find the mental age of the
child, irrespective of his actual chronological age. If he passed the tests
of eleven years, but not those of twelve years, he had a mental age of
eleven years. However, very few children were so obliging as to pass all
tests at one level and fail all of them at the next, so inherent difficulties
of scoring existed that were not cleared up until the next and last revision.

Binet and Simon applied the scale to feeble-minded children and
on the basis of their results, set limits for three degrees of feeble-mindedness: idiot, two years mental age or below; imbecile, between two and
seven years; and moron, above seven years. They recognized that the
classification lacked prognostic value, since they were dealing with absolute limits.[43] That is to say, their definitions did not take into account
the actual or chronological age of the child. Hence, as the child with
the passage of years could continue to grow mentally (although more
slowly than the average child), he might pass from an idiot to an imbecile to a moron.

idiot <2
imbecile 2<7
moron >7

Sometime later this problem was solved by William Stern[44] (1871–
1938), a German psychologist, who suggested the use of an Intelligence Quotient or I.Q., to be found by dividing a subject's mental age
(M.A.) by his actual or chronological age (C.A.). Since the resulting
I.Q. is a ratio, it removed the difficulty of M.A.s as an absolute measure
being used to define degrees of intelligence, including feeble-mindedness. Using the I.Q., a child C.A. four with an M.A. of two would have
an I.Q. of 50 (2/4), as would a child eight with a mental age of four (4/8).
(The use of a decimal result is eliminated by multiplying by 100.) The
I.Q. was adopted by Terman in the United States in his 1916 *Stanford
Revision of the Binet Scales* for which he provided a classification of
degrees of intelligence in terms of I.Q., not M.A. Mental age as an absolute measure was still useful; it was supplemented by the I.Q., which
placed the individual's intelligence relative to his age.

Stern
IQ

*Adopted
by Terman
1916*

Considerable interest was shown in the United States in using the
1908 version of the Binet-Simon Scale.[45] However, Decroly and Degand performed an early significant study in Belgium.[46] They tested a
group of boys and girls in a private school in Brussels to find that,
on the average, their subjects were one and a half years in advance of
the expected standards or norms published by Binet. After a certain

amount of understandable confusion, it was realized that what had been found was the effect of superior social status, since the Belgian children were the sons and daughters of professional men, while the Parisian children on whom Binet's norms were based were from poorer sections of the city. This finding opened up the whole problem of the relation of intelligence to social class.

In 1911, the year of Binet's death, the last of his revisions appeared.[47] He had profited from the research done with the test, restandardized the placement of tests, added some new tests, and discarded others, particularly because they were too dependent upon school information. He also took care of the difficulties of scoring the 1908 revision by making each test at each year worth a certain fraction of a year of mental age, expressed as months of mental age, so that all the tests passed, irrespective of the years at which they were placed, could be added together to get the mental age.

Binet had not attempted to analyze intelligence into parts and then devise tests based on this analysis; rather, he used the combined efforts of a series of promising complex tasks selected as generally relevant to intelligence. Naturally, he had devoted some thought to the nature of intelligence. Throughout the years, he offered, withdrew, and amended a whole series of definitions. We have already seen that he related intelligence to judgment. Probably the most characteristic definition and certainly the definition most commonly associated with his name is that intelligence is a combination of capacities to make adaptations in order to attain a desired end, to maintain a mental set, and to be self-critical.[48]

EVALUATION

Speaking generally, Binet advanced objective measurement in psychology. His work and that of others, with his or similar instruments, demonstrated the superiority of objective measurement over clinical diagnosis carried on without such instruments. The Binet Scales and the later instruments derived from them were quickly demonstrated to be of practical value in educational, social, and medical settings. He also contributed to the more theoretical aspects of psychology by developing a concept of intelligence as a combination of cognitive abilities, and, in the process of doing so, he distinguished intelligence from the specific sensory and motor abilities with which it had earlier been confused by Galton and others.

One criterion of the greatness of a psychologist is the fruitfulness of his contribution in leading to other research. In this regard Binet stands very high. Only one or two other psychologists have stimulated as much research as he did.

Overview

The French psychopathologists saw their patients as *people*— sick individuals in need of care. They saw them as individuals and were interested in them as such as well as in what they could learn about them. An impersonal attitude, natural to study of the generalized human mind, was in the process of being supplemented by an interest in the welfare of the individual. Janet[49] made this explicit in a paper describing his way of investigating the individual's unique characteristics. Binet worked in a similar spirit. He saw children as individuals, extending from his own daughters to those tested for the sake of establishing the norms of his scale. After all, an intelligence test score represents something about a person. Binet and his associates were applying a clinical method by studying their patients not only in order to understand them, but also in order to help them. The French psychologists of the nineteenth and early twentieth centuries advanced the understanding of the clinical method in psychology to a point where Freud and others could carry through the next stage. It seems clear that both utilitarian and idiographic prescriptions were being fostered. Moreover, hesitant steps were being made toward accepting the value of unconscious mentalism, irrationalism, developmentalism, dynamicism, i.e., factors making for change in the individual.

But Binet did even more. While still advocating application of an interest in the individual, he did much to create a means of measurement and also applied it to the higher mental functions, and thus fostered quantitativism.

References*

1. P. Janet, *The Major Symptoms of Hysteria*, 2nd ed. (New York: Macmillan, 1920).
2. W. Riese, *The Legacy of Phillipe Pinel: An Inquiry into Thought on Mental Alienation* (New York: Springer, 1969).
3. P. Pinel, *Traité médico-philosophique sur l'aliénation mentale* (Paris: Richard, Caille and Revier, 1801).

*See p. 19 for description of reference style.

4. J. E. Esquirol, *Des maladies mentales* (Paris: Baillière, 1838).

5. R. Pintner, *Intelligence Testing: Methods and Results* (New York: Holt, 1923).

6. H. F. Ellenberger, *The Discovery of the Unconscious: The History and Evolution of Dynamic Psychiatry* (New York: Basic Books, 1970).

7. *Ibid.*, p. 112.

8. J. Braid, *Neurypnology; or, the Rationale of Nervous Sleep; Considered in Relation with Animal Magnetism* (London: Churchill, 1843) (Reprinted, 1899).

9. G. Guillain, *J.-M. Charcot 1825–1893: His Life—His Work*, trans. P. Bailey (New York: Hoeber, 1960).

10. S. Freud, "The History of the Psychoanalytic Movement," A. A. Brill, ed., *The Basic Writings of Sigmund Freud* (New York: Random House, 1938), p. 943 (1912).

11. Janet, *Major Symptoms.*

12. J.-M. Charcot, *Clinical Lectures on Diseases of the Nervous System*, trans. T. Savill (London: New Sydenham Society, 1889), III.

13. G. Zilboorg and G. W. Henry, *A History of Medical Psychology* (New York: Norton, 1941), pp. 357–378.

14. H. Bernheim, *Hypnosis and Suggestion in Psychotherapy: A Treatise on the Nature and Uses of Hypnosis*, 2nd ed., trans. C. A. Herter (New Hyde Park, N.Y.: University Books, 1964) (1884–1886).

15. A. A. Liébeault, *Du sommeil et des états analogues, considérés surtout au point de vue de l'action de la morale sur le physique* (Paris: Masson, 1866).

16. T. A. Ribot, *English Psychology* (London: King, 1873) (1870).

17. T. A. Ribot, *German Psychology of To-day* (New York: Scribner's, 1886) (1879).

18. P. Janet, "Pierre Janet," C. Murchison, ed., *History of Psychology in Autobiography* (Worcester: Clark University Press, 1930) Vol. I, pp. 123–133; W. S. Taylor, "Pierre Janet, 1859–1947," *American Journal of Psychology*, LX (1947): 637–645.

19. P. Janet, *L'automatisme psychologique* (Paris: Alcan, 1889).

20. P. Janet, *L'état mental des hystériques* (Paris: Rueff, 1892).

21. P. Janet, *The Major Symptoms of Hysteria* (New York: Macmillan, 1907).

22. P. Janet, *L'analyse psychologique* (Psychology analysis.), in English, C. Murchison, ed., *Psychologies of 1930* (Worcester: Clark University Press, 1930), pp. 369–373.
23. Taylor, "Pierre Janet."
24. Janet, *Major Symptoms.*
25. M. Prince, *The Dissociation of a Personality* (New York: Longmans, Green, 1905).
26. Janet, *L'analyse psychologique.*
27. P. Janet, *Psychological Healing: A Historical and Clinical Study,* 2 vols., trans. E. and C. Paul (London: Allen and Unwin, 1925).
28. A. Binet and T. Simon, "Sur la nécessité d'établir un diagnostic scientifique des états inférieurs de l'intelligence," *L'Année Psychologique,* XI (1905): 163–190, partial trans. W. Dennis, ed., *Readings in the History of Psychology* (New York: Appleton-Century-Crofts, 1948), pp. 407–411.
29. By far the most authoritative, analytical and complete biography in any language has been recently provided by Theta H. Wolf. *Alfred Binet* (Chicago, Ill.: University of Chicago Press, 1973).
30. A. Binet and C. Féré, *Le magnétisme animal* (Paris: Alcan, 1886).
31. A. Binet, *La psychologie du raisonnement* (Paris: Alcan, 1886).
32. Personal communication from P. Fraisse to E. G. Boring, February 5, 1962, through the kindness of the latter. There has been some confusion about who had priority in founding the first laboratory in France. Presumably this is attributable to the fact that three independent institutions of higher education all were involved in the events of 1889. Ribot moved to the College of France from the Sorbonne, or the College of Letters of the University of Paris. The same year a laboratory was placed in the Sorbonne under the direction of Beaunis in association with Binet, although it was administered by L'École Pratique des Hautes Études, still a third educational institution.
33. A. Binet, *Les altérations de la personnalité* (Paris: Alcan, 1892).
34. A. Binet, *La suggestibilité* (Paris: Schleicher, 1900).
35. A. Binet, *L'étude expérimentale de l'intelligence* (Paris: Schleicher, 1903).

tale (Paris: Alcan, 1894). For a convincing demonstration of the breadth and depth of his experimental interests, see R. H. Pollock and Margaret J. Brenner, eds., *The Experimental Psychology of Alfred Binet* (New York: Springer, 1969).

37. Binet and Simon, "Sur la nécessité."
38. A. Binet and N. Vaschide, "La psychologie à l'école primaire," *L'Année Psychologique*, IV (1898): 1–14.
39. A. Binet and V. Henri, "La psychologie individuelle," *L'Année Psychologique*, II (1896): 411–465 Herrnstein and Boring, Excerpt No. 81).
40. A. Binet and T. Simon, "Méthodes nouvelles pour le diagnostic due niveau intellectual des anormaux," *L'Année Psychologique*, XI (1905): 191–244.
41. A. Binet and T. Simon, "Le développement de l'intelligence chez les enfants," *L'Année Psychologique*, XIV (1908): 1–94.
42. J. Peterson, *Early Conceptions and Tests of Intelligence* (New York: World Book, 1925).
43. Binet and Simon, "Le développement."
44. W. Stern, Die psychologische Methoden der Intelligenz- prüfung. In F. Schumann, ed., *Bericht über den V. Kongress für experimentelle Psychologie*. (Leipzig: Barth, 1912), pp. 1–102. Chapter 2, trans. G. M. Whipple as *The Psychological Method of Testing Intelligence* (Baltimore: Warwick and York, 1914) (Herrnstein and Boring, Excerpt No. 86).
45. Peterson, *Early Conceptions*.
46. O. Decroly and J. Degand, "La mesure de l'intelligence chez des enfants normaux d'après les tests de Binet et Simon: nouvelle contribution critique," *Archives de Psychologie*, IX (1910): 81–108.
47. A. Binet and T. Simon, *A Method of Measuring the Development of the Intelligence of Young Children*, trans. Clara H. Town (Chicago: Chicago Medical Books, 1915) (1911).
48. Peterson, *Early Conceptions*.
49. Janet, *L'analyse psychologique*.

Chapter 16

James:
THE BEGINNINGS OF PSYCHOLOGY IN THE UNITED STATES

Before the 1880s, there were in the United States only two major psychological traditions—phrenology and Scottish mental philosophy.[1] Despite its errors, phrenology was objective to the extent that it did depend on measurements. It also had a practical aim, so it flourished outside the schools. Its appeal to medical men, for example, has already been mentioned (p. 256) and businessmen and reformers of all persuasions also found it met their needs. If the interest of the latter seems incongruous, it should be remembered that phrenology was a doctrine upholding the changeability of human nature.[2] Hence, phrenology was a minor theme in various activities directed toward other ends: temperance, anti-tobacco, and birth control—to name three which dealt with the control of human nature.

Scottish mental philosophy in the United States, as earlier, was used as a defense of revealed religion. James McCosh, President of Princeton University from 1870 to 1892, and Noah Porter, President of Yale University about the same period, were two of its most prominent exponents. This combination of teaching mental philosophy and serving as president of a college was not unusual. Textbooks were written to review the European literature.[3] There was also a certain amount of original work, but the psychology to come was overwhelming enough to relegate it to oblivion.

In the United States between 1880 and 1895, psychology was transformed in a dramatic fashion.[4] By 1895 there were twenty-four psychology laboratories, three journals, and a flourishing scientific society, many of whose members were full-time psychologists. Only

[handwritten margin notes: Phrenology; Scottish mental philosophy at Princeton + Yale.]

fifteen years before, none of this had existed. The new psychology had obviously arrived.

The antecedents for these sweeping changes were to be found in the system of higher education that prevailed at the beginning of this period and in the reaction in the United States to the German university system.

Higher Education in the United States

educational
component of
faculty was
review

Before the Civil War, one-curriculum colleges were the rule; the emphasis was on Latin, Greek, mathematics, and philosophy. What little instruction given in the physical sciences was offered without laboratory work of any kind.[5]

At that time educational theory was based on a faculty psychology. This phase of Scottish psychology served as a justification for the method of mental discipline. The faculties of the students were to be exercised by those subjects that—to use the words of Jeremiah Day, president of Yale in the early decades of the century—were "best calculated to teach the art of fixing the attention; directing the train of thought; analyzing a subject proposed for investigation; following with accurate discrimination the course of argument; balancing nicely the evidence presented to the judgment; awakening, elevating, and controlling the imagination; arranging, with skill, the treasures which memory gathers; rousing and guiding the power of genius. . . ."[6]

Scientific work was carried on almost entirely outside the colleges in a manner reminiscent of England, but without the saving grace of the well-to-do amateur. The establishment of scientific schools, beginning with those at Rensselaer, Yale, and Harvard, helped to break this exclusion, although these schools were isolated within the colleges. The medical schools also began to contribute, although they did not do a great deal to encourage research. Much of what was done was carried out without the support of universities. Enrollments actually declined as colleges became more and more out of touch with the times; the number of students going abroad to Germany and Austria for graduate study increased.[7] In 1880 there were about as many American graduate students abroad as there were in all of the United States.

The German universities were dominated by the idea of research. The professor had a considerable amount of freedom to work on problems of his own choosing. Within the limits of his field, he could choose to teach what he wished. The student was also free to study what and when he chose. And because of the effectiveness of their research, the German universities were the scientific centers of the world.

Educators reacted vigorously to the example of the German universities. After the Civil War, a strong movement sprang up to extend the scope and improve the quality of university education. Three college presidents in the forefront of this movement were Eliot of Harvard (despite his bias against research), White of Cornell, and Gilman of Johns Hopkins; all were influenced by the German university system in the changes they introduced at their respective institutions. These three schools will figure prominently in the account that follows. In addition, Clark University, whose first president was G. Stanley Hall, was avowedly modeled on European graduate schools. Stanford University and the University of Chicago were also to come into prominence as examples of the new trend. Meanwhile, a gradual reform and reorganization of the so-called graduate schools already in operation was taking place at such universities as Harvard, Yale, and Princeton. These older schools had suffered losses of students, prestige, and the services of some of their abler professors to the new graduate schools.

Reform began by replacing the fixed curriculum with an elective system. This resulted in an increase not only in the number of courses, but also in the number of departments. Most important of all was the establishment of graduate schools to take the place of the fifth year in residence that had previously led to the M.A. Johns Hopkins, which began as a graduate school in 1876, was the leader in this field; it required an independent research project from each student.

In these changes psychology occupied a favored and strategic position. It was one of the new subjects introduced into colleges and universities from the German system. Although psychology was still under the departments of philosophy in German universities, its introduction into the United States often meant the creation of an independent department. It also supplied a weapon to attack faculty psychology. No matter what the differences of opinion among the first American psychologists, they were united in their opposition to faculty psychology. Moreover, the economic and social conditions prevailing under the pioneer spirit made the application of psychology almost a foregone conclusion.

This separation of psychology from philosophy and its recognition as a science meant that a struggle to maintain supernatural values within psychology was by-passed. Hereafter, American psychology was naturalistic in attitude with hardly a dissenting voice.

As Albrecht reminds us, these were years of preparation; actual scientific advances came later.[8] In what follows, not only research articles will be of concern, psychology as a social institution and the men who helped to make it so will be also.

William James (1842 – 1910)

An academician's moment of truth comes when he hears read the citation accompanying an honorary degree. For William James, that moment came at the Harvard commencement of 1903.[9] We do not know his reaction to the award itself, but more accessible is what happened *before* this moment. According to his son, Henry, he went about for days, half in jest, half in earnest, dreading to hear President Eliot pronounce him "psychologist."[10] He was not a psychologist, he insisted, but a philosopher.

Not only did William James vehemently deny that he was a psychologist, he even denied that there was a new psychology. Furthermore, he was not primarily a founder and was certainly not an adherent; he was not even an experimentalist. He founded no system of psychology and was without disciples. He drew his inspiration not from one man or even from one movement, but from a combination of sources, and in a fashion that made it self-initiated. He knew of the developments in German experimental psychology; he assimilated some aspects, rejected others, but was guided by none. He showed similar independence regarding British associationism and French psychopathology. Despite all this, William James was the first great psychologist in the United States.

LIFE AND INTERESTS

James's grandfather came to the United States from Ireland just before the beginning of the nineteenth century. Starting with a modest investment, he gradually amassed a fortune. He had thirteen children by three wives. His son Henry was the father of both William and Henry James. Thanks to his inherited wealth, Henry, Sr., never worked at all in the conventional sense. He devoted his time instead to religious questions. Throughout his life he struggled to give utterance to his deep but unorthodox beliefs. He was especially influenced by Swedenborg, concerning whose doctrines he wrote a series of books, essays, and pamphlets. These made so little impression upon others, however, that William Dean Howells said of him that: "He had written a book about the 'Secret of Swedenborg' and had *kept it*."[11] Nevertheless, wherever Henry went he had distinguished friends. Ralph Waldo Emerson in particular impressed him, though in later life he found Emerson lacking in intellectual coherence and thought his dismissal of the reality of evil too blithe.

William was born in New York City in January 1842. Fourteen months later, his brother Henry was born also in New York City. Their father devoted himself enthusiastically to their education. He alternated between rushing them off to Europe because of his conviction about the "narrowness" of American schools and bringing them home because of an equally strong feeling that his children should be with their own kind. Extensive travel and sporadic schooling in the United States, England, France, Switzerland, and Germany followed for William and Henry and their younger brothers and sisters. They studied with tutors and in various kinds of schools, learning even more from the galleries, museums, and theaters they visited. Unlike the rigors that faced John Stuart Mill in having his education supervised by his father, they had a delightful, unsettling time with their kindly and enthusiastic father.

As befitted their very different personalities, Henry and William later disagreed flatly on the value of their schooling. William regretted its lack of discipline; he believed it had prevented him from developing an ability for orderly reasoning. Henry found it invaluable in stirring the free play of curiosity. There was but a year's difference in age between the two, but William was always the "big brother." He took the lead, responding more quickly and with much greater assurance than Henry. In later years William vigorously criticized his brother's writing, with no complaint or impatience shown by Henry. Eventually, Henry calmly declared his independence, which, in everything but name, had been his all along.

There was a very deep affection between the brothers, though in many respects they were utterly unlike. Henry became a naturalized British subject late in his life. Like many such expatriates, he reflected the stereotype of the formal and reserved Englishman. William, on the other hand, despite his cosmopolitan experiences, remained to some extent the breezy American. H. G. Wells tells a story that neatly illustrates the brothers' differences in this regard.[12] In later years, when they were both famous, Wells came to visit them while they were in England and found Henry very upset. Henry appealed to Wells to tell his brother what *is* and *is not* done. It seems that William had happened upon a small inn with a garden separated only by a high wall from that of a house at which G. K. Chesterton, the British writer, was staying. With American directness William had placed the gardener's ladder against the wall, climbed up, and peeped over. And Henry had caught him at it!

Following the advice of his father who insisted that a hasty decision would be wrong and "narrowing," William took years to decide on the work for which he was most fitted. He tried painting; he spent six months at the studio of William Morris Hunt in Newport, Rhode Island. He quickly realized his lack of promise.

In the autumn of 1861, at the age of nineteen, William enrolled at the Lawrence Scientific School of Harvard University; by now his choice of a career had been narrowed down to the sciences and philosophy. Despite his interest in chemistry, on which he concentrated first, William's teachers observed an impatience that drove him away from accurate and painstaking laboratory determination; this was prophetic of his distaste for such work throughout his life. He soon left chemistry for physiology, anatomy, and biology and enrolled in the medical school, even though he was already convinced that medical practice held no attraction for him.

In 1865 he went with Louis Agassiz to the Amazon as the start of a possible career in biology, but he soon found that he hated collecting. On his return he resumed his medical studies, interrupting them again to go abroad for two years, because he felt that he did not have the stamina to continue the arduous work. Indecision about a career was now complicated by a neurotic depression with insomnia, eye trouble, digestive disorders, very severe back pain, and other symptoms; these lasted for nearly five years. There was even some preoccupation with thoughts of suicide, but he managed to put them aside; he wrote home to his father in a carefully restrained fashion that "thoughts of the pistol, the dagger, and the bowl began to usurp an unduly large part of my attention; and I began to think that some change . . . was necessary."[13] During this trip abroad he mentioned in a letter to a friend that he considered the time had come for psychology to be a science and that he had decided to do some work in it.[14] He also mentioned plans to go to Heidelberg to work with Helmholtz and Wundt, but, whatever the reason, he was to catch only a glimpse of them. His knowledge of their work attests to his general alertness to contemporary developments in psychology. This was in 1868, only eight years after Fechner's *Elements* had appeared.

In 1869, he returned to the United States to take his medical degree. It was obvious to William, to his friends, and to his family that he could not practice, since his back pain precluded standing for long hours. Laboratory work also was out of the question. He resolved that summer to continue to work in "psychological subjects."[15]

A philosophical crisis preceded the beginning of a partial recovery from his various ills. Feeling lost and alone, on occasion becoming panic-stricken in a world that seemed filled with evil, James read the evolutionary philosophy of Renouvier's *Second Essay*, which persuaded him that there was freedom of the will, and that spontaneity is available to him who makes it so. James resolved that his ". . . first act of free will shall be to believe in free will."[16] This apparently delivered him from the clutches of the strict determinism of Mill, Spencer, and Bain and opened up the way to his becoming a philosophical psychologist.

In 1872, he received an offer from President Eliot to teach physiology at Harvard; he accepted. By this time a gradual recovery of his health was taking place.

In 1875, James gave his first course in psychology—on the relation between physiology and psychology; he thus moved closer to his now established goal. James never had instruction in psychology. As he put it, the first lecture he ever heard, he gave himself.

William James founded a psychological laboratory in 1875, the same year that Wundt established his. In retrospect, James himself was not sure whether it was 1874, 1875, or 1876, but the new evidence found by Harper in the references cited[17] shows it was in 1875. One especially compelling item that Harper mentions is the report of the Harvard treasurer of that year, which cites an appropriation to James of $300, for use in physiology. Other evidence, including the nature of the 1875 course mentioned earlier, shows that the appropriation was for equipment for physiological psychology. The laboratory was located at Lawrence Hall. In 1876, James was advanced to assistant professor of physiology. G. Stanley Hall, about whom we shall be hearing presently, arrived as a student in that same year, and took his degree in 1878.

The year 1878 was notable for two events. First, James married Alice Gibbens, a Boston school teacher. She shared his interests and watched over him with untiring devotion. She, and marriage itself, introduced a certain amount of organization into his life that had not been present before. Sensitive and nervous as he was, however, it is hardly surprising that the five children that were born over the next several years occasionally got on his nerves. Moreover, the financial strain of a growing family led James to write a considerable number of popular articles and to give many lectures for the sake of the financial return they brought. The second event of 1878 was his signing of a contract with the publisher Henry Holt for a volume on psychology. At the time he apologized to his publisher that he would have to take two years in which to write it. He actually took twelve!

In 1880 he was made assistant professor of philosophy, a department where psychology more properly belonged. He was admitted to the department but "not without opposition."[18] The thought of a physiologist teaching psychology infuriated some members of the department, who were quite content with the accustomed Scottish variety of that subject.

Despite the lack of a major work, he was advanced to a professor of philosophy in 1885, and in 1889 his title was changed to professor of psychology.

While working on the *Principles,* he traveled abroad, and this further delayed completion of the book. In 1882 a leave of absence from Harvard allowed him to go to Europe, where he made important professional contacts and became a recognized name on the continent. He also formed friendships with several psychologists and philosophers.

The closest friends he made among the European psychologists were James Sully, James Ward, Theodore Flournoy, and Carl Stumpf. It is perhaps significant that none of them received much mention in the earlier chapters on European psychology. The senior European psychologists with whom we are familiar did not appeal to him. Herbert Spencer, despite James's debt to him, was an "ignoramus";[19] Wundt, ". . . the finished example of how much *mere* education can do for a man";[20] and G. E. Müller was "brutal" (a comment made in connection with the latter's highly critical review of a work by Münsterberg).[21] Fechner was viewed ambivalently: on the one hand he was seen both as a source of inspiration and as a kindred spirit;[22] but he was also a source of irritation, because the upshot of his careful work in psychophysics to James was "just nothing."[23] James assessed Hermann Ebbinghaus as "one of their best men."[24] It must be emphasized that with one exception these comments were made in personal correspondence. In his formal writings he gave their work careful attention, even though he made it clear that he did not necessarily accept all their views. He did not reject the findings of experimental psychology *in toto.* After all, many pages of his *Principles* are taken up with this work (even though it is relegated to fine print).[25]

His book was growing in connection with his classroom teaching. In the classroom, as in his writing and conversation with friends, James was charming; his presentation of his material was without obvious order. He was vivacious, so full of humor that one of his students interrupted him one day with the remark, "To be serious for a moment. . . ."[26] His picturesque language and vivid imagery were such that his students remembered them long after the more methodical lectures of others had been forgotten. But for all his delight in the insight of the moment, he did not shirk thinking through thoroughly and laboriously whatever he wrote and said; he would painstakingly present details and scrupulously examine counter-arguments. Writing did not come easy to him, and he worked his material over and over again. His infinite pains, however, were rewarded with a clarity unexcelled in the literature of psychology.

Since university administrators expect frequent publications from professors, he arranged for various chapters or sections of chapters of his forthcoming book to be published as articles. This was the case with his famous formulation of emotion, which was in print in 1884; a year later, the Danish physiologist Lange published a very similar view.

In 1890 *The Principles of Psychology* finally appeared.[27] The delay and the prior publication of parts of it had built up keen anticipation among psychologists. James was scarcely original throughout, but the brilliance of his writing gave new life to old themes. The reviews hailed the book as an important contribution; it was a pronounced success. An observation made some years ago remains true; it is still read by persons who have no obligation to do so.[28] The criticisms offered tended to center on its "unsystematic" or "impressionistic" character. To call the *Principles* unsystematic does not mean that it is disorganized. In fact, it would sometimes appear that what was meant by this charge is that James did not follow the conventional ordering of topics. James believed that the proper starting point is experience as immediately given and as it flows in perception. Hence, unlike others before and after him, he did not start with sensations; for that is not the way in which we experience.

Two years after *Principles,* James published the *Briefer Course,*[29] a condensation explicitly designed to serve as a textbook and to make both him and his publisher money.[30] For many years "Jimmy"—as the book became known in order to distinguish it from its parent—was used as a textbook, for it eliminated many of the digressions of the portlier "James."

Laboratory work was more of a symbol and never a habit with James, despite the rooms used for equipment when he was in the department of physiology and his mention of spending two hours a day in the psycho-physics laboratory that he started in 1885.[31] Both in the *Principles* and in other writings James took a disparaging view of laboratory psychology. In 1894 he commented that the United States was overstocked with laboratories.[32] In the *Principles* James offered the opinion that the results of laboratory investigation were not yet commensurate with the labor involved; in another well-known passage, he remarked that the experimental introspective method "could hardly have arisen in a country where natives could be *bored.*"[33] Elsewhere he said that ". . . brass-instrument and algebraic-formula psychology fills me with horror."[34] In view of his attitude, it is not surprising that except for the study of the transfer of training, he did not contribute experimental results of any importance.

James recognized that laboratory work was useful for psychology, but he wanted to be relieved of responsibility for it. In 1890 he succeeded in raising $4,000 for a psychology laboratory.[35] James had been impressed by the work of Hugo Münsterberg at the University of Freiburg. So he recommended that Münsterberg be offered the directorship of the new Harvard laboratory. The offer was made, Münsterberg accepted it, and the German assumed his new post in 1892. Unfortunately, Münsterberg never became for Harvard the leader in experimental psychology that James had hoped he would be. His first few years of directorship went well. After that, Münsterberg scattered his efforts among a variety of fields—psychotherapy, legal psychology, and industrial psychology, among others—and paid relatively little attention to the laboratory.

First Lab ?

In 1895, G. Stanley Hall, by then a rival psychologist and president of Clark University, stirred up a controversy over the priority of laboratory founding in the United States with his claim of having founded the first laboratory at Johns Hopkins in 1883, along with a statement about the large number of other laboratories organized by his Hopkins and Clark students. As a loyal Harvard man, James issued a claim for priority for his work of 1875.[36] In part, Hall was moved to this claim by an understandable confusion about what constitutes the organization of a laboratory. Is it when research is performed using equipment by the professor? When it is performed by his students? When the university gives space or equipment? Or when the university formally proclaims that it supports a psychology laboratory? Based, as it was, on this last and rather incidental criteria, it would seem as if Hall's claim of priority was unfounded.

Students

The number of psychologists trained by James was surprisingly small. Few doctoral dissertations in psychology were completed under his sponsorship. Hall had worked with him in 1876–1878. From about 1890 onward he had some students who became psychologists, including James R. Angell, Mary W. Calkins, William Healy, Edward L. Thorndike, and Robert S. Woodworth. Their number may have been small, but all of them went on to achieve considerable prominence.

James grew up in an atmosphere of liberalism; topics such as abolition, homeopathy, and women's rights were freely and eagerly discussed, and often championed. When this is coupled with his father's devotion to the teachings of Swedenborg, which formed part of his son's experience, it is no wonder that James expressed a kindred interest in spiritualism. He found mediumship, clairvoyance, and so-called automatic writing carried on without the conscious cooperation of the subject as matters to be approached with an open mind. In the same spirit, he came to the defense of mental healers when they were under the attack of the medical profession. In 1882–1883 James met the Englishmen who were the founders of the new Society for Psychical Research, and when their friendships ripened, their cause became his. He was an eager student; he attended many seances, carried on an extensive correspondence, and published his findings. As usual, *facts* were what he wanted. He was interested not only in the problem of survival after death but also in psychic phenomena and the continuity they formed with those of hypnotism, hysteria, and multiple personality. Did he accept the existence of a residue of reality after charlatanry, suggestion, and abnormal psychology had been eliminated? In speaking of Mrs. Piper, the medium he most thoroughly investigated, he concluded in his final report that there was an external source trying to communicate but beyond this we would have to wait for the accumulation of more facts.[37]

In the 1890s James came to be recognized as America's leading *Pragmatism* philosopher. His work on pragmatism and radical enpiricism was his major contribution. Years before, he had read and admired the works of Charles S. Peirce. Peirce, however, had been virtually ignored. James's writing in both *Pragmatism*[38] and in *The Meaning of Truth*[39] was so persuasive that pragmatism became an important philosophical doctrine. The central theme of pragmatism is that the value of ideas must be tested by their practical consequences. Contrary to what was generally supposed, beliefs do not work because they are true; they are true because they work. This ambiguous usage of "work" was open to various criticisms that were not long in coming. Despite them, pragmatism was a popular success.

James advanced the pragmatic view as one resolving the dilemmas created by the perennial clash between rationalism with its eternal principles and empiricism with its immutable facts. Rationalists are "tender-minded," "intellectualistic," "idealistic," "optimistic," "religious," "free-willed," "monistic," and "dogmatical." Empiricists, in contrast, are "tough minded," "sensationalists," "naturalistic," "pessimistic," "irreligious," "fatalistic," "pluralistic," and "skeptical."[40] His doctrine of radical empiricism was first published in 1904 in an article whose purpose was to deny that the subject-object relation is fundamental in consciousness.[41] Thereafter he elaborated this doctrine in many articles and books. In respect to the subject-object relation, James held that the distinction between one kind of occurrence, "knowing," and another, the object or "known," is false. In the view that he was rejecting, mind or soul, the knower, was in sharp contrast to the object known, which might take the form of a material object or another mind. This dualism of subject and object James rejected in favor of a monism in which the world is neither mind nor matter.

He believed that empiricism needed radical revision because earlier empiricists had accepted a dualism of knower and known; they had also accepted consciousness as one thing and the object as another. Empiricism is correct, James said, in that we learn only from experience, but what we learn from is "pure experience," the one primal substance in which consciousness is *not* a thing but a relation or a process. Similarly, the known is a relation. Both the knower and the known are relations within pure experience.

In 1898 James overtaxed his heart during a climb in the Adirondacks. The following summer, while out for a short walk, he lost his way and again strained his heart. The consequences affected his health to the extent that two years of comparative idleness in Europe was necessary.

In 1899 James published *Talks to Teachers,* which grew out of public lectures given to teachers in 1892 and afterwards.[42] He helped to bring psychology into the classroom by stressing applications to everyday problems. He stressed the individual rather than the social goals of education.[43] He had received, some years before, an invitation to prepare and deliver the Gifford Lectures at Edinburgh, which he gave in 1901–1902. These lectures formed his book, *The Varieties of Religious Experience.*[44] He contended that he spoke as a psychologist and, in so doing, made considerable use of personal documents that recounted religious experiences and paid particular attention to the pathological strain evident in many of them. He insisted, however, that the presence of psychopathological traits in these persons did not vitiate the reality or value of their religious experiences. In fact, he challenged the use of mental stability as a criterion of social value. There is, he said, a type of religious experience that is marked by shallow healthy-mindedness and that denies real anguish. In contrast, there is the religion of the "sick soul."[45] Despite the revulsion that arises in the healthy-minded, James argued that such persons recognize the existence of a wider scale of experience. They recognize evil and pass into a state of agony, but in the process may eventually conquer despair, as a result of which they feel a justifiable optimism in which the world, good and evil, is seen as unified.

After the Gifford Lectures James resolved to forego the "popular lecture style" and do something serious and systematic, but he never managed to keep his resolution. The nearest approach to a formal exposition of his philosophy is the unfinished, posthumously published, *Some Problems in Philosophy,*[46] which, following his directions when he realized it would not be finished, had as its subtitle, *A beginning of an introduction to philosophy*. After talking for years about retiring from his professorship, he finally did so in 1907.

In 1909 G. Stanley Hall, president of Clark University, invited Sigmund Freud as one among many distinguished figures to a celebration in Worcester. James attended, and naturally met Freud. James already believed, of course, in the existence of a mental life of which the individual himself is not fully aware. Earlier, he had praised F. W. H. Myer's view of extra-marginal consciousness as the most important advance since James had begun the study of psychology.[47] The existence of mental events outside of awareness was a very intriguing fact to James, since it seemed such an unexpected peculiarity of human nature. There is, however, a tremendous gulf between Myer's subliminal consciousness and Freud's unconscious. Myer and others of similar interests were looking for subconscious feats; Freud was searching for unconscious motives. In keeping with his openmindedness and his desire to give everyone a hearing, James expressed the hope that Freud would push his ideas to their utmost limit, though he added that Freud impressed him as a man with fixed ideas and that he could make nothing of his dream symbolism.[48]

For the sake of his health, James went to Europe in the spring of 1910. He did not, however, slow down his pace sufficiently to reap any benefit. Despairing of any relief, he turned homeward to die two days after his return, late in August, 1910, at his country home near Mount Chocorua, New Hampshire.

Selected Psychological Views

It would be false to James to present his thinking about psychological matters as an overall systematic point of view.[49] He avoided the outward appearance of system quite deliberately because he believed that to do otherwise would result in an artificial and premature schematization. As Perry[50] remarked, James was an explorer, not a map maker. Only some of his more important and characteristic psychological views can be given. To show the charm and vividness of his style, liberal use will be made of quotations.

THE STREAM OF CONSCIOUSNESS

The starting point for psychology is that which is immediately given—the stream of consciousness. Earlier psychologists, James said, had thought of consciousness in terms of discrete elements, e.g., of ideas and sensations. These elements were then treated as the building blocks for more complicated levels of organization. James could not accept the elements that others presumed constituted the mind. The analytical method that they used seemed unwarranted to him. Experience is what it is; it is not groups of elements teased out of their matrix by introspection. Far from being experienced directly, these elements are the products of a sophisticated discrimination, often arduous in nature.

What is experienced is a flow of consciousness. Consciousness is not a mosaic of separate bits and pieces but something continuous and unbroken. Things shade and merge in space and in time. Consciousness is a stream. This continuity is one of the five major characteristics James attributes to consciousness. To be sure, relative differences exist. There are more stable substantive states of consciousness, which are the most obvious and the usual source of study by psychologists. Very much present, but apt to be neglected, are the vague, fleeting, intangible, unstable, transitive states, such as the feeling of "and" and "but," resembling in some respects Spencer's "feeling of relation." These transitive or relational states help to give consciousness a streamlike continuity. James offers a vivid illustration of what he means by the substantive and relational state.

> Like a bird's life, it seems to be made of an alternation of flights and perchings. The rhythm of language expresses this, where every thought is expressed in a sentence, and every sentence closed by a period. The resting-places are usually occupied by sensorial imagination of some sort, whose peculiarity is that they can be held before the mind for an indefinite time, and contemplated without changing; the places of flight are filled with thoughts of relations, static or dynamic, that for the most part obtain between the matters contemplated in the periods of comparative rest. *Let us call the resting-places the "substantive parts," and the places of flight the "transitive parts," of the stream of thought.*[51]

He then goes on to say

> There is not a conjunction or a preposition, and hardly an adverbial phrase, syntactic form, or inflection of voice, in human speech, that does not express some shading or other of relation which we at some moment actually feel to exist between the larger objects of our thought.[52]

In a similar vein James discusses feelings of tendency, expectation, and intent; these also are elusive. James admits that there may be consciously experienced interruptions in this continuity of the stream of consciousness in sleep, but on waking there is no trouble in reaching back and making connection with one's own stream of consciousness.

Its personal nature is another major characteristic of consciousness. Consciousness "tends to appear" as a part of a personal consciousness. It is not merely a thought; it is *my* thought. There is a personal self that separates by a wide gulf one's consciousness from that of others. James applied the qualifying expression "tends to appear" to this characteristic of the stream of consciousness because he was well aware of the phenomena—such as multiple personalities, automatic writing, and posthypnotic suggestion—that seem to show the presence of secondary personalities.

Still another characteristic, James found, is that consciousness is a state of constant change. He held that we can never have the same thought or conscious state twice. We may think more than once of the same object, but each time we do so we experience it differently because of other experiences that have intervened since the earlier occasion. This is most obvious on occasions that are separated by relatively long periods of time, when we wonder what we could have seen in a given person, book, or idea. It may be convenient to formulate the matter as if ideas were simple and unchanging, but to put it in James's own words, "A permanently existing 'idea' or 'Vorstellung' which makes its appearance before the footlights of consciousness at periodical intervals is as mythological an entity as the Jack of Spades."[53]

Consciousness also has the characteristic of dealing with objects independent of itself. Many earlier psychologists had confused these objects of thought with the thoughts themselves. It was a version of the psychologist's fallacy that they were committing. In its most general form, this fallacy is a confusion of one's individual standpoint with that of the mental fact with which one is concerned. In this particular instance James wrote:

Another variety of the psychologist's fallacy is the assumption that the mental state studied must be conscious of itself as the psychologist is conscious of it. The mental state is aware of itself only from within; it grasps what we call its own content, and nothing more. The psychologist, on the contrary, is aware of it from without, and knows its relations with all sorts

of other things. What the thought sees is only
its own object; what the psychologist sees is the
thought's object, plus the thought itself, plus possibly all the rest of the world. We must be very
careful therefore, in discussing a state of mind from
the psychologist's point of view, to avoid foisting
into its own ken matters that are only there for ours.
We must avoid substituting what we know the
consciousness *is* for what it is a consciousness *of*,
and counting its outward, and so to speak physical,
relations with other facts of the world in among the
objects of which we set it down as aware. Crude as
such a confusion of standpoints seems to be when
abstractly stated, it is nevertheless a snare into
which no psychologist has kept himself at all times
from falling, and which forms almost the entire
stock-in-trade of certain schools. We cannot be too
watchful against its subtly corrupting influence.[54]

In committing this fallacy we start to describe the object, not the thought,
as in the following:

If, for example, the thought be "the pack of
cards is on the table," we say, "well, isn't it a
thought of the pack of cards? Isn't it of the cards as
included in the pack? Isn't it of the table? And of the
legs of the table as well? The table has legs—how
can you think the table without virtually thinking
its legs? Hasn't our thought then, all these
parts—one part for the pack and another for the
table? And within the pack-part a part for each
card, as within the table-part a part of each leg?
And isn't each of these parts an idea? And can our
thought, then, be anything but an assemblage or
pack of ideas, each answering to some element of
what it knows?"

Now not one of these assumptions is true.
The thought taken as an example is, in the first
place, not of "a pack of cards." It is of "the-pack-
of-cards-is-on-the-table," an entirely different
subjective phenomenon, whose Object implies the
pack, and every one of the cards in it, but whose
conscious constitution bears very little resemblance to that of the thought of the pack *per se*.
What a thought *is*, and what it may be developed

into, or explained to stand for, and be equivalent
to, are two things, not one.[55]

Each thought is a unity, just as a soap bubble is a unity. Touch a bubble, and the bubble disappears. So also does a thought. Once gone it cannot be brought back again.

Consciousness also has the characteristic of being selective. It is always rejecting, accepting, uniting, and keeping apart objects and parts of objects. One cannot direct attention toward everything impartially. Monotonous, regular progression, as in the ticking of a clock, is broken up into rhythms, now one, now another; dots scattered on a surface are grouped into a pattern, and then regrouped into a different pattern. One's very sense organs in their threshold limitations are selective instruments. Even more important, we are conscious of only a small portion of the experience open to our sense organs. Helmholtz had reported research on blind spots, after-images, double images, marginal changes of color, and movement of accommodation—studies of visual sensations of which the ordinary run of mankind is not even aware. A tabletop is still "seen" as square, when, from any of our usual particular perspectives, the image falling on the retina is not that of a square; similarly, we see grass as green in bright sunlight and the same shade of green at dusk, though the colors are very different. James contends that, generally speaking, the members of the human race agree more or less on what to notice or not to notice from among all that is available.

me + not me

THE SELF

One matter that we all examine is the nature of "me" and "not me." Each of us has a different view of the matter. To James, the consciousness of self is not an abstract, but a living, breathing thing. As aspects of the empirical self or "me," he distinguished among the material self, the social self, and the spiritual self.

The material self embraces not only one's body but also one's clothes and possessions. In an extended sense, the material self includes the immediate family, the home, and worldly possessions. They arouse the same feelings as the narrower material self, but in varying degrees. When they flourish, we flourish; when we diminish, they diminish.

The social self is more properly spoken of as social selves, since a person has a different social self for every individual who has some sort of image of him. Fortunately, however, the social selves tend to fall into classes to the extent that there are different groups of persons about whose opinions the individual cares enough to show a different side of himself—a family self, a club self, an employer self, a friend self, a lover self. James reminds us that even in everyday speech there is this discrimination among selves: "as a soldier I condemn him, as a father I pity him."

The spiritual self is more intimate than the other two, more subjective in the sense that it is a person's own impression of his skills or faculties—his feeling toward his ability to argue, his inflexible determination, his purity of conscience, his conscientiousness, and his feelings of guilt.

James finds this self in activity, in a person's ways of preparing to meet a situation. Some would consider this self a manifestation of the action of a soul; others would argue that it is a fiction. For James, the activity in the spiritual self, so-called, was actually found to be, not spiritual, but rather a sort of obscure body process generally localized within the head. Attending, accepting, negating, making an effort—all seemed to James to involve these head movements. In this instance, the self is present in these activities but is not the same as these activities. When making an effort to remember, James felt as if there were a pulling in of the periphery, a withdrawal from the world, a rolling upward and outward of the eyes, the exact opposite of fixating. He hastens to add that he is not saying that this is all the spiritual self is for other persons. All he can do is speak for himself. Taken together, the material self, the social self, and the spiritual self form the empirical self.

Within this heterogeneous self, seeds of conflict are going to be sown. There often is a conflict of these aspects of the different selves; one is often confronted with the necessity of accepting one self and forsaking the rest. Here are the inimitable words of James:

> Not that I would not, if I could, be both handsome and fat and well dressed, and a great athlete, and make a million a year, be a wit, a *bon-vivant*, and a lady-killer, as well as a philosopher, a philanthropist, statesman, warrior, and African explorer, as well as a "tone-poet" and saint. But the thing is simply impossible. The millionaire's work would run counter to the saint's; the *bon-vivant* and the philanthropist would trip each other up; the philosopher and the lady-killer could not well keep house in the same tenement of clay. Such different characters may conceivably at the outset of life be alike *possible* to a man. But to make any one of them actual, the rest must more or less be suppressed. So the seeker of this truest, strongest, deepest self

must review the list carefully, and pick out the one
on which to stake his salvation. All other selves
thereupon become unreal, but the fortunes of this
self are real. Its failures are real failures, its
triumphs real triumphs, carrying shame and glad-
ness with them.[56]

Failures in connection with activities germane to potentially available, but nonselected selves, find no place in our self-esteem. A poet may
be complacent about his ignorance of automobile mechanics, while to a
self-made man the lack of a college education may be a source of pride. In
neither instance is that which is lacking a source of self-feeling. The lack
of mechanical knowledge or the lack of a college education is not, to
use James's term, part of their pretensions to success. Our pretensions on
what we do consider part of the self, compared to successes in these
particular areas, decide our self-esteem. In other words, our self-esteem is
a ratio of our successes divided by our pretensions to success.

Over and above the empirical self with all of its subordinate selves
is the Pure Ego, the self or principle of personal identity. Here the problem
is the self as thinker, not as an object of thought. The problem at hand is
whether or not one must go beyond what has already been discussed to
account for personal identity. To James, there is no evidence of absolute
oneness, even though introspectively there seems to be a center of one's
existence that remains steadfast throughout the shifts of experience. This
steadfastness James explained by appeal to the transitive states, the
consciousness of relation of the stream of consciousness. They give the
needed continuity without appeal to something behind experience. This
led James to compare the hypothesis of an immortal soul, or transcendental principle of unity, with the associationist solution that would deny that
there is a principle and that all there is is a stream of passing thoughts. The
upshot of the analysis is the conclusion that, for psychology, with its task
of describing what can be studied within the field of direct experience, it
is unnecessary to take a stand. To introduce a "knower" beyond what has
already been described is to proceed beyond psychology into
metaphysics.

SPONTANEITY OF MIND

James insisted, as did Spencer before him, that the mind did more
than passively adapt to the external environment.[57] The mind has a
spontaneity, a selectivity of its own. Consciousness in the mind is causative; it intervenes in cause-effect sequences. James advanced the argu-

ment that the reality of the intervention of consciousness as causative is demonstrated by our more intense awareness of the functioning of consciousness when obstacles are encountered. When there are no obstacles and things run smoothly, consciousness tends to lapse and habit takes over. Consciousness, moreover, shows interest or attention. It is volitional as well as sensory. It selects and dwells upon some aspects of the experience to which it is open and rejects others. What is selected becomes vital and real; what is rejected becomes unimportant and unreal. Mind is an instrument drawing from the world whatever interests it. Persons differ in that they introspect identical situations in different ways according to their interests. This selectivity of consciousness, presumably due to the action of selective natural evolution, runs as a theme through the chapters of the *Principles* devoted to attention, conception, and discrimination and comparison, and is most explicitly stated in Chapter 5 when James argues against the conception of man as an automaton.

HABIT

Habit is treated by James as a matter of the functioning of the nervous system. The argument shows his strong physiological bent. Habit is due to the increased plasticity of neural matter, which makes it easier for repeated actions to be carried out; at the same time, habit lessens the need for attention to the activity in question. Moreover, habit has enormous social implications.

James's account of habit is the most famous chapter in his book. It received separate publication many years later. The sheer grace of his writing makes quotation imperative.

> Habit is thus the enormous fly-wheel of society, its most precious conservative agent. It alone is what keeps us all within the bounds of ordinance, and saves the children of fortune from the envious uprisings of the poor. It alone prevents the hardest and most repulsive walks of life from being deserted by those brought up to tread therein. It keeps the fisherman and the deck-hand at sea through the winter; it holds the miner in his darkness, and nails the countryman to his log-cabin and his lonely farm through all the months of snow; it protects us from invasion by the natives of the desert and the frozen zone. It dooms us all to fight out the battle of life upon

the lines of our nurture or our early choice, and to make the best of a pursuit that disagrees, because there is no other for which we are fitted, and it is too late to begin again. It keeps different social strata from mixing. Already at the age of twenty-five you see the professional mannerism settling down on the young commercial traveller, on the young doctor, on the young minister, on the young counsellor-at-law. You see the little lines of cleavage running through the character, the tricks of thought, the prejudices, the ways of the "shop," in a word, from which the man can by-and-by no more escape than his coat-sleeve can suddenly fall into a new set of folds. On the whole, it is best he should not escape. It is well for the world that in most of us, by the age of thirty, the character has set like plaster, and will never soften again.[58]

Later he wrote:

Could the young but realize how soon they will become mere walking bundles of habits, they would give more heed to their conduct while in the plastic state. We are spinning our own fates, good or evil, and never to be undone. Every smallest stroke of virtue or of vice leaves its never so little scar. The drunken Rip Van Winkle, in Jefferson's play, excuses himself for every fresh deriliction by saying, "I won't count this time!" Well! he may not count it, and a kind Heaven may not count it; but it is being counted none the less. Down among his nerve-cells and fibres the molecules are counting it, registering and storing it up to be used against him when the next temptation comes. Nothing we ever do is, in strict scientific literalness, wiped out. Of course, this has its good side as well as its bad one. As we become permanent drunkards by so many separate drinks, so we become saints in the moral, and authorities and experts in the practical and scientific spheres, by so many separate acts and hours of work. Let no youth have any anxiety about the upshot of his education, whatever the line of it may be. If he keeps faithfully busy each hour of the working-day, he may safely leave the final result to itself. He can with perfect certainty count on waking up some fine morning, to find himself one of the competent ones of his generation, in whatever pursuit he may have singled out.[59]

ASSOCIATION AND MEMORY

Though James rejected the fundamental presupposition of associationism, namely its atomism or elementarism, he did not reject association itself, despite his denial that it was a matter of simple couplings. He insisted that what is associated is not ideas, but objects. Earlier psychologists had confused the objects of thought with the thoughts themselves—the psychologist's error. The basis of association is through brain processes. Association is a merging of physiological processes in the nervous system, not of discrete bits of ideas.

Contiguity is a way of expressing the basic law of association— objects "experienced together tend to become associated."[60] In keeping with his emphasis on physiology, James preferred to formulate association as the law of neural habit: "When two elementary brain-processes have been active together or in immediate succession, one of them, on reoccurring, tends to propagate its excitement into the other."[61] James was writing on this topic before the acceptance of the neurone theory, and consequently he did little more about the physiological basis of association than to speak vaguely of irradiation of energy over the cortex without making clear the mechanism of spread or connection. James[62] saw associationism as further restricted because the mind, either in keeping with or as an aspect of its spontaneity (p. 385), possesses an innate capacity to perceive relations and categories evolved in the process of rational selection. This was in contradistinction to Spencer's inherited associations (p. 338).

In the course of writing the chapter on memory in the *Principles*, James became intrigued with verifying an opinion he had to the effect that, after memorizing material, one did not develop a better retentive power in general, but merely became more efficient with the particular kind of material on which one practiced. This contention contradicted the view of the faculty psychologists who said that if you cultivate any phase of memory you have a better memory for everything. He decided he would try to find out whether a certain amount of daily training in memorizing poetry would shorten the time necessary to learn an "entirely different kind of poetry."[63] This was the first experiment on the transfer of training; James carried it out first on himself and then on a few of his students. He obtained results more or less in favor of his view; his subjects did not tend to do better on a second kind of material after learning a certain kind of poetry. More carefully controlled studies by others, especially those of Thorndike and Woodworth,[64] demonstrated unequivocally that the doctrine of formal discipline of faculty psychology was false. They found that the amount of transfer of improvement depended mainly on the degree of community of the tasks. Transfer effects are far from general, and for the most part have been found to be confined to closely related activities; this disproves the faculty psychology point of view.

EMOTION

James would have had us reverse the usual way of thinking about the emotions. The customary view holds that perception gives rise to emotion. This in turn brings about bodily expression. James, however, said that the bodily expression directly follows the perception of the emotion-provoking events. The feeling engendered *is* the emotion.

Common-sense says, we lose our fortune, are sorry and weep; we meet a bear, are frightened and run; we are insulted by a rival, are angry and strike. The hypothesis here to be defended says that this order of sequence is incorrect, that the one mental state is not immediately induced by the other, that the bodily manifestations must first be interposed between, and that the more rational statement is that we feel sorry because we cry, angry because we strike, afraid because we tremble, and not that we cry, strike, or tremble, because we are sorry, angry, or fearful, as the case may be.[65]

For evidence he appealed to introspection; if all experiences of bodily symptoms, such as the heartbeat, the tensions in the muscles, and so on, are abstracted, there is nothing left to the emotion. Independently and almost simultaneously, Lange,[66] in studying the circulatory system, reached the conclusion that feelings of vascular change are the essentials of emotion.

Evidence has been brought to bear against the so-called James-Lange theory in the research that was almost immediately stimulated by their work. James's felicitous expression could and did lead to misunderstanding. When he said, ". . . we feel sorry because we cry, . . . afraid because we tremble," he disregarded the fact that we can be sorry without crying and afraid without trembling. This does not alter the fact that some bodily process precedes and is the sensory source of the emotion; that, after all, is the essence of his theory. No one denies that emotions have physical causes, but modern research shows that they are caused by processes in the thalamic region of the brain, mediated through the autonomic nervous system. Nevertheless, James's theory did much to stimulate the research that established the organic basis of emotion.

INSTINCTS

James endowed the human organism with a generous number of instincts, more, in fact, than those of the lower animals. For the beginnings of his catalogue, he drew upon observations of children by Preyer, an embryologist and a pioneer child psychologist. But he went considerably beyond Preyer. He listed sucking, biting, crying, locomotion, and vocalization among the human instincts. They were the more specific forms of instinct, reflexlike in character; they stood in contrast to the broad generalizations sometimes offered as instincts, as when an instinct of self-preservation is postulated. This is not meant to imply that James did not list instincts more complicated than those just mentioned; he went on to include imitation, emulation, pugnacity, hunting, fear, acquisitiveness, play, curiosity, shyness, cleanliness, modesty, love, and jealousy.

According to James, we follow the dictates of instincts because at the time it seems the natural and appropriate thing to do. Every instinct is an impulse to action of some sort but not all instincts are blind or invariable. The sheer possession of many and contrary instincts means that with slight alterations of conditions, now this, then another impulse may be in the ascendant. Pugnacity and timidity, bashfulness and vanity, sociability and pugnacity are paired antithetical instincts that create conditions that make for variability in behavior since they mutually conflict with one another, and at a given moment only one or the other can be manifested. An additional factor making for nonuniformity of expression of instincts is that instincts may be inhibited by habits.

After the work of James, preparing catalogues of instincts became a popular pastime of psychologists, and considerable ingenuity was exercised in getting a complete and logically consistent classification. In today's perspective we consider this a self-defeating form of armchair theorizing because the concept of instinct lends itself to an explanation of behavior akin to that of faculty psychology—we fight because we have a fighting instinct. But in the time of James, appeal to instinct in the human species was a way of calling attention to man's biological heritage, a view that then needed defense. Man as an organism in a world of nature was being defended by an appeal to instinct.

PSYCHOLOGIST OR PHILOSOPHER?

James's opinion of himself as a psychologist and philosopher demands examination. One must be careful to distinguish this more general opinion from that negative one already expressed concerning the value of laboratory work in psychological research.

Philosophy and psychology were freely intermingled by James in the study of perception, thought, will, the self, religion, experience, and association. When, as he often did, he introduced philosophy into his psychology, he recognized it for what it was and made it clear to the reader. At any moment, he was given to yearning to be what he was not. He was an empiricist, a pluralist, a pragmatist, and an individualist, but when set for the moment on any of these, he wished for rationalism, monism, intellectualism, or socialism. No important intellectual problem was to James of such a nature that it could be settled, once and for all. Even against his strongest intellectual antipathies the door was not slammed shut; a crack was left standing open, so if he wished he might later slip through.

Was he a psychologist or a philosopher or both? James himself did not change; he directed his interest to a different aspect of an overall interest. He was aware of these shifts, as in the *Principles* when he speaks of staking his all on being a psychologist, with the significant qualification, "for the time."[67] Nevertheless, he always treated psychology philosophically and philosophy psychologically. It would seem as if he were always both but that one or the other would predominate at a given time, at which point he would castigate his subordinate interest. He was a *psychologist*-philosopher when he worked on his *Principles* and when he said of philosophy, "What a curse philosophy would be if we couldn't forget all about it." He was a *philosopher*-psychologist when he called psychology a "nasty little subject";[68] or when with his usual fine inconsistency, he told his publisher upon completion of the *Principles* that the book proved there was no science of psychology at all and that he himself was "incapable."[69] He was a *philosopher*-psychologist when he was given the honorary degree at Harvard.

One may ask why, if this was what he thought of the new psychology, did he bother with it? First, he was interested in its possibilities for the future and not in its past accomplishments.[70] In this context the *Principles* is a critical survey that helped to give psychology a future. He took a definite strategical position. In writing to Stumpf in 1892 he expressed his conviction as follows: "A psychologist's merit seems to me in the *present* condition of that science to consist much less in the *definitiveness* of his conclusion than in his suggestiveness and fertility."[71] Second, he grew away from it, or as it is perhaps more preferable to put it, his interests in philosophy were strengthened.

Overview

James helped to give psychology an indigenous vitality and a freedom from the narrowing influences of an exclusively laboratory approach; he served to broaden the field to include the whole wealth of human experience. James exercised his great talents as a psychologist and a philosopher in order to separate the two fields. He united these fields in his own person, but he did not wish to keep psychology bound to philosophical assumptions. Instead, he wanted to liberate psychology; he used philosophy as one of his tools. This liberation did not extend to having a separate department of psychology on its own. He was quite content for it to remain in the philosophy department.

But there is the other side of the coin. His very receptivity, enthusiasm, and complexity made for contradiction and confusion. It was his sister, Alice, who perhaps summed up William James and his work most acutely. He had told her that his Chocorua summer house had fourteen doors all opening outward. She commented, "His brain isn't limited to fourteen, perhaps unfortunately."[72]

The thinking of James contained many paradoxes, as Gordon Allport[73] has neatly and succinctly demonstrated. These paradoxes were productive of much thinking in the generations that followed. Precisely because they were paradoxical, they provided intellectual stimulation to individuals of widely different theoretical persuasions.

Some of these paradoxes are found in the preceding sketch of his views. He defended consciousness as operative in the causal chain of events. But for most psychological doctrines he was a strict physiological determinist; his description of habit indicates this. In his exposition of the consciousness of self he dismissed the soul as an unnecessary burden upon psychology. Nevertheless, in dealing with other topics postulating the soul, it became the "least objectionable" of the available hypotheses. There was a selective consciousness within the self by which certain experiences could be disregarded. In discussing habit, on the other hand, any activity, no matter how casual, was seen as being stored up to have its effect. He discussed association in some detail. Despite this acceptance, in his discussion of the stream of consciousness, he denied that two experiences can be identical. This being the case, how can there be partial identity? If not, how can the law of associative similarity operate?

Since James knew these paradoxes could not be resolved in his state of knowledge (and ours), and held that we must look elsewhere for an answer and must not attempt to reconcile the unreconciled. As a fighter for psychology, James wanted psychology to have scope, to embrace all that was applicable to it. He would leave to Judgment Day the synthesis of knowledge, glad that he lived when striving was still possible.

A final summary in terms of the prescriptive adherences that James held to more or less consistently is required. Conscious mentalism as the basis of psychology was forcefully defended, while among his arguments that spontaneous consciousness had a survival value, made provision for both a developmental and dynamic prescriptive adherence. Habit as arising from the functioning of the nervous system was very persuasive in his defense of a dualism of mind and body. But overall, there was a fundamental dependence on a functional adherence—pragmatism, the spontaneous self, self-directing conscious mentalism, habits, emotion, and the role he ascribed to the nervous system were all imbued with a functionalist attitude that pervaded most of his thinking. Mind strives to adjust the organism to the environment, but this does not imply that the function of mind can be rendered exclusively in biological terms. His belief in mentalistic facets, the application of the environment to the mind, which is conscious of its own ends, also makes James a protophenomenologist. It could have made him the intellectual predecessor of phenomenology in the United States.[74] But it did not. Instead, phenomenology came to the United States by a different route (pp. 604 and 610).

References*

1. F. M. Albrecht, The New Psychology in America: 1880–1895. Unpublished Ph.D. dissertation, Johns Hopkins, 1960.
2. E.g., O. S. Fowler, *Human Science of Phrenology* (Philadelphia: National Publishing, 1873).
3. J. McCosh, *Psychology of the Cognitive Powers*, rev. ed. (New York: Scribner's, 1906) (1886); N. Porter, *The Human Intellect, with an Introduction upon Psychology and the Soul*, 4th ed. (New York: Scribner's, 1887) (1868).
4. Albrecht, The New Psychology in America.
5. R. F. Butts and L. Cremin, *A History of Education in American Culture* (New York: Henry Holt, 1953).

*See p. 19 for description of reference style.

6. J. Day, "Original Paper in Relation to a Course of Liberal Education,"*American Journal of Science and Arts,*XV (1829): 300–301.
7. Albrecht, The New Psychology in America.
8. *Ibid.*
9. Biographical material is drawn from H. James, ed., *The Letters of William James*, 2 vols. (Boston: Atlantic Monthly, 1920); F. O. Matthiessen, *The James Family; including selections from the writings of Henry James, Senior, William, Henry & Alice James* (New York: Alfred A. Knopf, 1947); and R. B. Perry, *The Thought and Character of William James: as revealed in unpublished correspondence and notes, together with his published writings.* Vol. 1, *Inheritance and Vocation;* Vol. 2, *Philosophy and Psychology* (Boston: Little, Brown, 1935).
10. H. James, *Letters,* Vol. 2, p. 3.
11. *Ibid.,* I, p. 12.
12. H. G. Wells, *Experiment in Autobiography* (New York: Macmillan, 1934), pp. 453–454.
13. H. James, *Letters,* Vol. 1, p. 96.
14. *Ibid.,* pp. 118–119.
15. *Ibid.,* p. 154.
16. *Ibid.,* p. 147.
17. R. S. Harper, "The Laboratory of William James," *Harvard Alumni Bulletin,* LII (1949): 169–173; R. S. Harper, "The First Psychological Laboratory," *Isis,* XLI (1950): 158–161.
18. G. S. Hall, "Philosophy in the United States," *Mind,* IV (1879): 89–105.
19. Perry, *Thought and Character of William James,* Vol. 2, p. 69.
20. *Ibid.*
21. *Ibid.,* II, p. 117.
22. *Ibid.,* II, p. 586.
23. W. James, "The Principles of Psychology," in R. M. Hutchins, ed., *The Great Books of the Western World* (1890) (Chicago: Encyclopaedia Britannica, 1952), LIII, 348.
24. Perry, *Thought and Character of William James,* Vol. 1, p. 403.
25. W. James, "Principles."
26. E. Boutroux, *The Life and Work of William James* (New York: Longmans, Green, n.d.).
27. W. James, "Principles."

28. Perry, *Thought and Character of William James.*
29. W. James, *Psychology: Briefer Course* (New York: Henry Holt, 1892).
30. W. James, *Letters of William James,* Vol. I, p. 314.
31. Perry, *Thought and Character of William James.*
32. *Ibid.*
33. W. James, "Principles."
34. Perry, *Thought and Character of William James,* Vol. II, 195.
35. *Ibid.,* I, 415.
36. J. M. Cattell, "Early Psychological Laboratories," *Science,* LXVII (1928): 543–548.
37. W. James, "Report on Mrs. Piper's Hodgson-Control," *Proceedings of the American Society for Psychical Research,* III (1909): 470–589.
38. W. James, *Pragmatism: A New Name for Some Old Ways of Thinking* (New York: Longmans, Green, 1907).
39. W. James, *The Meaning of Truth: A Sequel to "Pragmatism"* (New York: Longmans, Green, 1909).
40. W. James, *Pragmatism,* p. 22.
41. W. James, "Does Consciousness Exist?" *Journal of Philosophy, Psychology and Scientific Method,* I (1904): 477–491.
42. W. James, *Talks to Teachers on Psychology: and to Students on Some of Life's Ideals* (New York: Henry Holt, 1899).
43. M. Curti, *The Social Ideas of American Educators* (New York: Charles Scribner's Sons, 1935).
44. W. James, *The Varieties of Religious Experience* (New York: Longmans, Green, 1902).
45. *Ibid.,* Lec. V, VI.
46. W. James, *Some Problems of Philosophy: A Beginning of an Introduction to Philosophy* (New York: Longmans, Green, 1911).
47. W. James, *Varieties,* p. 233.
48. Perry, *Thought and Character of William James.*
49. W. James, "Principles."
50. Perry, *Thought and Character of William James.*
51. W. James, "Principles," p. 158.
52. *Ibid.,* p. 159.
53. *Ibid.,* p. 153.
54. *Ibid.,* p. 129.
55. *Ibid.,* pp. 180–181.
56. *Ibid.,* pp. 199–200.

57. *Ibid.*, pp. 84–94 (Herrnstein and Boring, Excerpt No. 91).
58. *Ibid.*, p. 79.
59. *Ibid.*, p. 83.
60. *Ibid.*, p. 367.
61. *Ibid.*, p. 370.
62. *Ibid.*, pp. 851–865 (Herrnstein and Boring, Excerpt No. 75).
63. *Ibid.*, p. 436.
64. E. L. Thorndike and R. S. Woodworth, "The Influence of Improvement in One Mental Function Upon the Efficiency of Other Functions,"*Psychological Review,* VIII (1901): 247–261; 384–395; 553–564 (Herrnstein and Boring, Excerpt No. 100).
65. James, "Principles," p. 743.
66. C. G. Lange and W. James, *The Emotions,* K. Dunlap, . ed. (Baltimore: Williams & Wilkins, 1922).
67. W. James, *Principles,* p. 200.
68. H. James, *Letters,* Vol. 2, p. 2.
69. *Ibid.*, p. 48.
70. E. G. Boring, "Human Nature vs. Sensation: William James and the Psychology of the Present," *American Journal of Psychology,* LV (1942): 310–327.
71. Perry, *Thought and Character of William James,* Vol. II, p. 180.
72. *Ibid.*, Vol. I, p. 411.
73. G. W. Allport, "The Productive Paradoxes of William James," *Psychological Review,* L (1943): 95–120.
74. B. Wilshire, *William James and Phenomenology: A Study of the Principles of Psychology* (Bloomington, Ind.: Indiana University Press, 1968).

Chapter 17

HALL, CATTELL, AND TITCHENER:
PIONEERS IN PSYCHOLOGY IN THE UNITED STATES

William James was the first American psychologist, but the growth of psychology before and after the turn of the century was not the work of one man alone. James had worthy younger contemporaries in G. Stanley Hall, James McKeen Cattell, and Edward Bradford Titchener, as well as in that group of psychologists who founded functional psychology.

G. Stanley Hall

G. Stanley Hall was much more important in his role as the first organizer and administrator in American psychology than as a contributor to psychological research or theory.[1] But these other functions also had to have a pioneer, and Hall's effect on psychology in the United States must be considered.

EARLY LIFE

Granville Stanley Hall was born of English ancestry in 1844 at Ashfield, a rural hamlet in Massachusetts. The Halls were substantial, hard-working, pious farmers. His parents were unusual only in the extent of their education. His mother had attended the Albany Female Seminary, then one of the very few institutions in the East for higher education of women; and his father had saved his money from some years of farm labor to return to school. Both parents then taught school for several years.

Hall's boyhood was spent on the farm, working hard out-of-doors, except in the winter, when the long evenings were filled with reading aloud by his mother. After doing well in the local rural school, Hall "kept school" for a while himself. His mother had always wanted him to go to college, however, and they finally convinced his father. Hall himself was more than willing. A year's work in a seminary prepared him for Williams, where he enrolled in 1863. It was not until after the Civil War that Hall discovered his father had bribed a physician into certifying him exempt from military service.

At Williams, Hall studied with Mark Hopkins and found diversified interests—associationism, the Scottish school, John Stuart Mill, and the theory of evolution. Without too much in the way of a call, he prepared for the ministry. Consequently, on graduation in 1867, he enrolled in the Union Theological Seminary in New York City. During his year in New York, he explored the city with zest, roaming the streets, visiting police courts, and attending churches of all denominations. He joined a discussion club interested in the study of positivism, visited the theater for plays and musicals, tutored young ladies from the elite of New York, visited a phrenologist, and generally had an exciting year. He was not noted for his religious orthodoxy. After preaching his trial sermon before the faculty and students, he went to the office of the president for criticism. Instead of discussing his sermon, the president knelt and prayed that Hall would be shown the errors of his ways!

One member of the faculty, a foreign-trained scholar who tutored him in philosophy, advised him to seek foreign study. Through the intercession of Henry Ward Beecher, the famous preacher, he received a loan of $500 for this purpose.

In the early summer of 1868 Hall sailed for Europe and made his way to Bonn. After studying theology and philosophy there, he moved to Berlin, where he continued his theological and philosophical studies. In particular he studied Aristotle. He also worked under DuBois-Reymond in physiology; he studied physics, attended a clinic for mental diseases, and satisfied a wide array of other interests. Beer gardens, theaters, and some lighthearted romantic episodes helped to round out his German education.

It was not until 1871 that he returned home, heavily in debt and without a degree. He expected to take up an appointment at a midwestern university, but the administration cancelled the appointment, fearing that his proposal to teach the history of philosophy would be unsettling.

Through a friend he received an appointment as a tutor to the five children of Jesse Seligman, the banker. He remained over a year with the Seligmans, in New York City and at their country places.

Antioch College, a western outpost of Unitarianism, had need of someone to teach English literature. Hall was appointed to this post. Later he shifted to French and German and finally to philosophy. As was not unusual in small colleges he had many extracurricular duties—he served as librarian, led the choir, and took his turn at preaching. In his second and third years he managed to spend most of his time teaching philosophical subjects. He read the first volume of Wundt's *Physiological Psychology* immediately after its publication and decided to return to Germany to study psychology. He started out in the spring of 1876, but he got only as far as Cambridge, Massachusetts. Here he was met with an offer of an instructorship in English at Harvard. He took it, hoping for a chance to transfer to philosophy and psychology. His work in required sophomore English was monotonous and time-consuming, but he found time to work with H. P. Bowditch at the Harvard Medical School and to carry out in Bowditch's laboratory a study on "the Muscular Perception of Space," which he presented as a thesis for the doctorate in philosophy at Harvard in 1878. He also did work with James, whom he got to know quite well. Hall received his degree in psychology upon recommendation of the department of philosophy. After his degree he immediately left for Europe.

Hall first studied at Berlin, where he did a considerable amount of work in physiology. In his second year he moved to Leipzig and became Wundt's first American student. Despite the enthusiasm with which he had looked forward to working with Wundt, the reality does not seem to have been to his liking. Hall attended Wundt's lectures and served as a subject in experiments but seems to have performed no research of his own in the laboratory. Instead he undertook a considerable amount of work in physiology, particularly in the physiology of muscles. He then went to Berlin to work with Helmholtz, only to find him immersed in physics. Nevertheless, he wrote James that he was disappointed in Wundt and had gotten much more out of Helmholtz.[2] Travel to educational centers followed; he had decided that the way to make a living was to apply psychology to education, though when he returned to the United States, he was without a job and had no prospects of getting one.

Meanwhile, he married a girl he had known from his days at Antioch whom he met again in Berlin, where she was studying art. They took a small flat in a suburb of Boston in September 1880. Things appeared bleak until a good fairy in the unlikely guise of President Eliot appeared at their house with the request that Hall give a series of Saturday talks on education in Boston under the auspices of Harvard University. These talks, which were well attended, brought him considerable favorable publicity.

JOHNS HOPKINS YEARS

On the strength of reports of his Saturday morning lectures, President Gilman of Johns Hopkins University invited Hall to Baltimore for a series of public lectures. In 1882 Hall arrived at Johns Hopkins, a school already celebrated for the beginning in 1876 of its bold experiment in higher education on the German plan. President Gilman had been having trouble finding just the right philosopher for his school; he wanted someone who would be both "modern" and favorably disposed toward science, but who would not offend orthodox religious sensibility. For a while there was considerable academic "in-fighting" involving Hall and the two other part-time appointments in a department for which only one professorship was planned. Both the other contestants, Charles S. Peirce and George Morris, were very eminent men in philosophy. Hall was a scientist, and Gilman wanted a scientist, but the scales tipped more in his favor because of his accommodating attitude toward religious orthodoxy. Hall wanted to dissociate psychology from religion, but he held no animosity toward his former field. He remained discreetly silent. In 1884 he was appointed professor of psychology and pedagogics.

After his professorial appointment Hall immediately took steps to separate his work from that in philosophy; he arranged it in such a way that the Metaphysics Club, which had flourished before his time, died for lack of appropriate material for presentation.

In 1883, while still a lecturer, Hall set up laboratory equipment in a private house adjacent to the campus.[3] The next year he was given rooms on the campus. Hall's laboratory at Johns Hopkins opened in 1884, and is often said to be the first formally accepted psychological laboratory in the United States. But this claim is obscured somewhat because the university did not officially list it as a laboratory and its equipment was treated as private property, since Hall later took it with him to Clark University.[4] A rather plausible case has been made that Jastrow's laboratory at the University of Wisconsin, which was founded in 1888, was the first laboratory in the United States that received formal recognition from university authorities.[5] But Cattell speaks of founding a laboratory in 1887 at the University of Pennsylvania,[6] and Jastrow himself acknowledged the priority of Cattell.[7] James's laboratory of 1875 was without formal recognition, but the university did supply space and funds (p. 373). So James deserves to be considered founder of the first psychological laboratory in the United States.

Among Hall's students were James McKeen Cattell, John Dewey, Joseph Jastrow, William H. Burnham, and Edmund C. Sanford—all destined to become prominent psychologists. Cattell and Dewey, however, were only incidentally his students. Cattell was at Hopkins when Hall arrived and left shortly thereafter for Leipzig. Dewey's degree, though taken during Hall's professorship, was for work done under Morris. But Dewey did work in the laboratory and appreciated the significance of the "new psychology." The first Ph.D. in psychology at Hopkins went to Joseph Jastrow. Hall's own degree at Harvard had been awarded in psychology but this was in one sense an afterthought on the part of the philosophy department at the time of completion of the work. Jastrow had enrolled for a degree in psychology, so his was the first Ph.D. in psychology in the United States.

Besides the laboratories of Johns Hopkins, Harvard, Pennsylvania, and Wisconsin, research laboratories were soon started at Columbia, Clark, Cornell, Indiana, Brown, Stanford, Yale, and Chicago. As mentioned before, at least twenty-four laboratories were founded before 1895, though some were small affairs designed only for undergraduate instruction. This was an impressive number, and clearly indicates the rapid spread of the new psychology.

In 1887, while still at Hopkins, Hall established the *American Journal of Psychology*. Its founding was entirely unexpected, though Hall had hoped to found a journal some day. A total stranger walked into his office, suggested he found a journal, and, then and there gave him a check for $500. It later turned out that his benefactor had confused experimental psychology with psychical research and he cancelled his subscription in the second year of publication. This mistake is by no means as foolish as it sounds. The designation "committee on experimental psychology" was used by psychical research organizations as the name for their investigatory bodies.

CLARK UNIVERSITY

By then, Hall was preparing to leave Hopkins for the presidency of the soon to be established Clark University in Worcester, Massachusetts. A wealthy merchant, Jonas Gilman Clark, had decided to endow an institution of higher learning in his home town. Before the school actually opened, Hall had high aspirations for it, higher than could actually be realized. He embarked on a tour of the European educational centers. Hall's letters[8] from Europe addressed to Clark are filled with the ideas suggested to him by these encounters, discussion of the chance of persuading a distinguished scholar to come to Worcester, and the like. He planned to make Clark University a graduate scientific institute, modeled after the German universities and surpassing Johns Hopkins. Research was to be its task, education a necessary accompaniment. Clark University, founded in 1889, began with a faculty organized into a small number of departments with no pretense of covering the remaining fields.

Hall was soon to find that Mr. Clark had ideas different from his own. Naturally reticent, Clark could not or would not commit himself on money matters, and the amount of money advanced was much smaller than Hall had been led to expect. Instead of confiding his troubles to the faculty, Hall chose to keep silent at the time, so he was blamed by them for the tight budget; but years later he was to say that his strongest motive for publishing his autobiography, the *Life and Confessions of a Psychologist,* was his desire to tell the full story of Clark University.[9]

By 1892 faculty dissatisfaction had reached the point where resignations of a majority of the faculty were imminent. Unknown to Hall at the time, the situation was aggravated by the appearance of President Harper of the newly founded University of Chicago, who desperately needed to build a faculty in order to fulfill plans to utilize the Rockefeller millions. A faculty raid of monumental proportions took place, with Harper offering to double salaries. Three Clark men were made department heads of chemistry, physics, and biology at Chicago. At the end of the expedition Harper even offered an appointment to Hall, who, on hearing from him what he had done, told Harper he thought "his act comparable to that of a housekeeper who would steal in at the back door to engage servants at a higher price."[10]

Clark University continued its work, though with a vastly reduced staff. Those faculty members who remained were intensely loyal. Of the twelve men who started the academic year of 1892, there were no resignations for twenty-one years thereafter! Some other money came in, and Hall and the Clark faculty adjusted to this economic level. Finally, near the turn of the century, the bulk of the Clark estate came to the university, divided between the library, the graduate school, and a new undergraduate institution that Hall had opposed but Clark had long advocated. The terms of his will stipulated that Hall was to have no connection with the college as such, though he continued as head of the graduate school.

Fortunately for psychology, President Hall had also made himself professor of psychology and continued to teach in the graduate school all during these years and afterward. He had also brought along Edmund C. Sanford from Baltimore to head the laboratory. William H. Burnham, another Hopkins student, was put in charge of pedagogics, which in this setting meant educational psychology and mental hygiene. Adolph Meyer, later the leading psychiatrist of his time, who was then at Worcester State Hospital, also gave lectures.

Hall's last publication within the conventional limits of experimental psychology (on touch sensitivity) appeared in 1887. His own work thereafter was nonexperimental in nature, but this limitation does not reflect his attitude toward the field and his faith in the advantage of scientific rigor. He eloquently and unequivocally defended laboratory work. His students saw him as the leader of the forces that would make psychology a science. There are many indications, however, that the laboratory was too far removed from life to meet his own personal interests. He was impatient with the slow plodding of laboratory work. Nevertheless, experimental psychology was still his vision of psychology, even though he realized that others would have to carry on the work.

His own teaching struck sparks in all directions. He was at his best in his weekly seminar, held at his home, where students and faculty presented papers. L. M. Terman, who originated the Stanford-Binet Scales of Intelligence and became the leading student of intelligence in the United States for some decades, expressed a representative opinion. "For me, Clark University meant briefly three things: freedom to work as I pleased, unlimited library facilities, and Hall's Monday evening seminar."[11] Hall was the great graduate teacher of American psychology. By 1893 eleven of the fourteen Ph.D. degrees from American universities had been given by him; by 1898 this had increased to thirty awarded out of fifty-four.[12]

FOUNDING OF THE AMERICAN PSYCHOLOGICAL ASSOCIATION

It was Hall's idea to institute the first scientific organization of psychologists, the American Psychological Association, which was founded in July, 1892.[13] He issued the invitations, arranged for a meeting in Worcester, and in general dominated the proceedings. Almost as a matter of course, he was elected the first president. It was at this first meeting that the scientific character of the organization was established. It is impossible after all these years to determine just who was present, but apparently ten to eighteen psychologists were there.[14] James was in

Switzerland, but was included in the twenty-six charter members who received invitations. The first annual meeting was held later the same year. From these small beginnings has come an organization now having a membership of over 40,000. After considerable controversy over the years, it has broadened its functions to include the application of psychology and the advancement of its professional status while maintaining its original scientific goal.

CHILD STUDY AND DEVELOPMENTALISM

A guiding prescription for Hall was developmentalism as expressed in evolutionary theory, which had fascinated him since his student days at Williams. Hall's thinking concerning a whole host of psychological topics was guided by the conviction that the normal growth of the mind occurs as a series of evolutionary stages. Pursuing this aim, he turned to the psychological study of the child through the use of questionnaires, a procedure he had learned in Germany. In fact, in 1881, before leaving Boston for Baltimore, Hall had had a chance at research in the Boston school system. In this study, entitled, "The Contents of Children's Minds," and in subsequent studies, he unearthed a considerable body of miscellaneous information about children's thinking on a variety of subjects.[15] By the end of 1915, 194 questionnaires had been developed and applied by Hall and his students. The topics included anger, dolls, crying, the early sense of self, fears, foods, religious experience, death, conventionality, mathematics, superstitions, and dreams.

Although in present perspective these studies are seen as naïve and poorly executed, they created great public enthusiasm and led to the founding of the so-called child-study movement. Large numbers of parents and teachers turned to the task of applying and interpreting questionnaires. All over the world they uncritically and dogmatically reported their superficial excursions into child development. The sentimentality and general wooliness of the movement led to a reaction against it, both within psychology and from various sectors of the public, and in a few years it disappeared. Nonetheless, the concept of psychological development had been firmly established through this work. The child-study movement served to bring home forcefully the importance of the empirical study of the child, while through its very excessess it made for an increased critical evaluation of research.[16]

In 1893, Hall had founded at his own expense the *Pedagogical Seminary* (now the *Journal of Genetic Psychology*), to which he and his students contributed a large share of the articles. For some years this journal was the chief outlet for research in child study and educational psychology.

It was in his huge work entitled *Adolescence* that Hall stated most completely his particular recapitulation theory of development.[17] He offered the conjecture that in his individual development, the child repeats the life history of the race. For instance, the level of the primitive man is repeated when the child plays at cowboys and Indians.

Theory of Recapitulation

Hall maintained his interest in religion, expressed in speculation and research on the psychology of religion. During the latter years of the century, he offered a course in the psychology of Christianity and encouraged studies in this area by his students. In 1917, he published his own major contribution, *Jesus, the Christ, in the Light of Psychology*.[18] To view Christ as the title implies did not sit well with his former brethren of the cloth.

ATTITUDE TOWARD PSYCHOANALYSIS

Hall was one of the first Americans to become interested in psychoanalysis. The twentieth anniversary of Clark University in 1909 was celebrated with a series of conferences, including the famous visit of Freud and Jung to the United States at Hall's invitation. This invitation was a courageous step in view of the suspicion and dislike that Hall knew to be directed at the whole psychoanalytic movement.

He also showed interest in psychoanalysis by teaching the subject. A report of his teachings for the academic year 1916 included this description of a course he offered:

> Much stress is laid upon the score or two of so-called mechanisms of the Freudian school, its history and development, and epitomes of the works of the chief representatives, along with an account of the two divergent groups of workers represented by Jung and Adler. . . The view taken by these lectures is that the methods of psychoanalysis open up, as nothing has yet done, the more or less unconscious domains of the psyche, and enable us to explain some hitherto insoluble problems and far more yet of the emotional or affective life of man. The chief trend of this course, however, is to show that many of the mechanisms apply not only to ordinary life, but to all the other great emotions besides love, so that not so

much the psychology of sex as that of the deeper
nature of man is considered.[19]

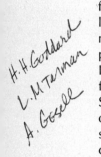

Acceptance of Freud

This last sentence captured his attitude. He was an eclectic, cheerfully
borrowing from Freud what he was as useful and equally without malice
accepting work that contradicted Freud.[20] He could admire Freud, but he
wanted to go beyond the "psychology of sex." As his letters show, he
could never understand why Freud was so intolerant of eclectic borrowing.[21] Freud, of course, saw this behavior as unforgivably inconsistent.
Hall maintained his interest in psychoanalysis throughout his life although in his later years he expressed himself much more negatively
about it. In the last conversation that Cattell had with him, Hall expressed
himself puzzled over why academic psychology so vehemently rejected
psychoanalysis.[22]

In another perspective this advocacy of a hearing for
psychoanalysis was but one of Hall's contributions to what was to emerge
as clinical psychology. Even before arriving at Clark, Hall had been
interested in abnormal psychology. He had taken his students to Bayview
Hospital for the Insane for demonstrations, and for a time he had even
functioned as its superintendent. The presence of Adolph Meyer as a
lecturer in abnormal psychology at Clark University has already been
mentioned. Though commonplace in France, the teaching of
psychopathology to psychologists was most unusual in the United States.
It was Hall's student, H. H. Goddard, who did important pioneer work on
feeble-mindedness; and another of his students, L. M. Terman, with his
Stanford-Binet test, supplied the indispensible tool for the measurement
of intelligence. Arnold Gesell, still another of Hall's students, was responsible for painstaking research on the physical and mental growth of
children. Hall lent his encouragement to this kind of work by giving it
access to publication sources in his journals.

After resigning the presidency of Clark in 1920, Hall continued
writing, and completed his autobiography. Characteristically, he became
interested in the problems of aging and published a volume on *Senescence*[23] in 1922. In 1924, four years after his retirement, he died at his
home in Worcester, Massachusetts, a few months after being elected
president of the American Psychological Association for a second time.
With his death, a romantic and heroic era closed.[24]

OVERVIEW

Some clues as to Hall's stature can be gleaned from the opinions of
a large sample of psychologists who were solicited in connection with a

commemorative statement about him.[25] Despite the veil of adulation that clouds such ceremonies, it is clear that he was primarily a source of stimulation for others, opening up for them areas of study and research. As Titchener[26] put it at about the same time, "He sought to inspire and I tried to train." They shared the goal of research; their difference was in the means used, not in the end sought. A psychologist[27] who worked with Hall at Clark spoke of Hall's conviction that psychology should not set limits for itself and of his desire, "to build the top of the mountain first."

Hall remained throughout his life an intensely agile thinker with boundless enthusiasm for often contradictory views on practically everything. He was a founder so intent on his pioneering that he almost always moved immediately to his next adventure, leaving for others the task of tidying up. He, himself, wondered if his life had not been a series of fads or crazes.[28] He said that Wundt would rather have been commonplace than brilliantly wrong.[29] One suspects that Hall would have reversed the statement for himself.

G. Stanley Hall was versatile and broad in his interests, a pioneer in many areas of psychological endeavor. A considerable number of the psychologists polled considered him to be the pioneer in studies of childhood, adolescence, senescence, and human genetics. Of these, the stimulation he gave to child psychology is most important. In a sense Hall made a gospel of childhood. He lifted childhood to a new plane of importance, focusing on the child as a child, and studying him for his own sake.

An all pervasive developmental allegiance characterized his work. His adherence to a dynamic rather than a static attitude and some appreciation of unconscious mentalism was apparent, but neither was integrated into an overall view in any systematic fashion.

James McKeen Cattell

In the course of an after-dinner speech, James McKeen Cattell[30] once told the story of his boyhood visit to a phrenologist. After inspecting the bumps of his head, the phrenologist proceeded to describe his characteristics, all but one of them were laudatory—according to the phrenologist, Cattell suffered from a deficiency in will power! The eruption of laughter from his friends that greeted his remark seemed to surprise Cattell. In point of fact, many of Cattell's major characteristics centered on this salient trait. Dogged determination, unflagging energy, and resistance to domination by those with what he considered undeserved authority seem to have characterized this American psychologist and scientific statesman.

James McKeen Cattell, encountered earlier as Wundt's self-appointed first assistant and as a student at Johns Hopkins, was born in 1860 in Easton, Pennsylvania, where his father was a professor of classics and later president of Lafayette College.[31] Here in 1880 Cattell took his bachelor's degree. His undergraduate interests were chiefly literary, but these interests changed, and he followed the usual custom of graduate study abroad, going to Göttingen and to Leipzig to study philosophy under Wundt. After a paper in philosophy had won him a fellowship at Johns Hopkins for the years 1882–1883, he returned to the United States, just at the time Hall was organizing his laboratory. In the laboratory Cattell started research on the time taken for various mental activities. This research reinforced his desire to become a psychologist, so he returned to Leipzig the following year. It was on his return to Leipzig that he announced to Wundt that he would be his assistant.

Indications of his independence and firm convictions appeared early. Contrary to the usual custom of being assigned a problem by Wundt, Cattell worked on his own problems in reaction time. He also became convinced that the introspective efforts directed toward fractionation of the reaction time into perception, choice, and the like, then gospel in Wundt's laboratory, was something he could not carry out and which he doubted others could. The situation reached the point where he did some of his experiments at his lodging rather than in the laboratory, since Wundt would not permit subjects in his laboratory who could not profit from introspection.[32] Though somewhat strained, relations between them never reached a breaking point. Wundt and Cattell did agree on the value of the study of reaction time. In Cattell's eyes it was a valuable tool for the study of the time necessary for mental operation and especially for the investigation of individual differences. As early as 1885,[33] Cattell published a paper on the exposure time necessary before perception of colors, letters, and words. It concluded with a discussion of what he called a matter of "special interest," the individual differences he had obtained. Cattell worked prodigiously during the Leipzig years of 1883 to 1886, publishing nine research papers before the next year was out. Studies on the influences of stimulus intensity upon reaction time (1885), the time of word perception (1886), and the association time for various categories (1887) were typical subjects of his research.

After taking his degree at Leipzig in 1886, Cattell divided the next two years between the United States and England. On one side of the Atlantic he taught at Bryn Mawr College and at the University of Pennsylvania and on the other, worked in Galton's laboratory in London and lectured at Cambridge.

Cattell found in Galton a kindred spirit—"the greatest man whom I have known."[34] Contrary to the opinion sometimes expressed, his interest in individual differences, as we have seen, had made itself apparent before his contact with Galton. In fact, his research into individual differences was begun in America before he went to Leipzig. From the tone of his writings, the most specific reason for his interest in variability was the climate of the times in the United States.

In 1888, Cattell was appointed professor of psychology at the University of Pennsylvania. This was the first professorship in psychology, not only in the United States, but in the world. Before him, psychologists had been appointed to the department of philosophy. With Cattell's appointment, the field of psychology had the recognition of its independence from the older discipline. The practice of naming professors of psychology spread rapidly, and before the beginning of the twentieth century there were a considerable number of them. Cattell founded a laboratory at Pennsylvania in 1887, but it was not until 1889 that an adequate laboratory was opened.[35] Although not the first in the country, it did have the distinction of being the first to introduce undergraduates to the methods of experimental psychology.

first lab for undergraduates.

In 1891 Cattell moved to Columbia University as professor of psychology and administrative head of the department; he was also charged with the task of administering the work of anthropology.[36] His rapid rise on the American psychological scene is evident: at twenty-eight, he was a professor at the University of Pennsylvania; at thirty-one, the chairman of the department at Columbia; at thirty-five, president of the American Psychological Association; and at forty, he was elected to the National Academy of Sciences—the first psychologist ever so honored.

Meanwhile, Cattell continued to be active in research. In a paper published in 1890 in *Mind,* the British journal, he coined the term "mental tests"[37] in describing a battery of tests administered to students at the University of Pennsylvania. As distinguished from Binet's later more complex tasks, these involved elementary operations. The basic tests of this series were dynamometer pressure, rate of movement, sensation areas by means of the two-point threshold, just noticeable differences in weight, reaction time for sound, time for naming colors, bisection of a line, judgment of times, and memory span for letters.

tests

At Columbia, Cattell continued his testing program with largely the same sort of tests. After collecting data from several entering classes, an analysis of the results was made by Wissler in 1901.[38] Correlations of the individual test scores with academic class standings were found to be inconclusively low, as were the intercorrelations among the scores of the tests themselves. In sharp contrast, academic grades in the various subjects and overall academic standing were substantially correlated with each other. Results with specific sensory-motor tests, likewise showing negligible correlations with other measures, also emerged from Titchener's laboratory at Cornell.[39] It began to appear that the available psychological tests were relatively useless as predicators of ability. Further exploration along the lines suggested by these studies tended to dwindle. Binet's results, which would later dominate, had yet to be appreciated in the university setting.

In the spirit of the earlier work of Galton, but with vastly improved methodology, Cattell also carried on studies of the nature and origin of scientific ability, using the method of the order of merit. This method is applicable to any set of stimuli capable of being ranked according to some criterion, such as the relative brightness of shades of gray, the problem he first investigated.[40] It could be and soon was applied to such problems as the relative appeals of pictures or of colors. A number of judges would be asked to arrange the items to be evaluated in order of merit. The average ranking for each item was then calculated and a final rank order obtained.

This method was applied by Cattell to the relative eminence of American psychologists in 1903.[41] For obvious reasons, the actual names associated with specific ranks were not published immediately. It was not until 1929 that the order of names was released. Rank number one went to William James, while the next five ranks went to Cattell, Hugo Münsterberg, G. Stanley Hall, J. Mark Baldwin, and Edward Bradford Titchener. Two of these men do not rank among the great psychologists treated here. It will be instructive to pause and examine their careers.

CONTEMPORARIES

Hugo Münsterberg has been met before as James's rather unfortunate choice to head the laboratory at Harvard and as a student of Wundt. His lack of influence can probably be attributed to his new found interest in arguing the case for the application of psychology to fields that did not yet have a research basis from which to operate.[42] His glorification of German contributions in various fields immediately preceding World War I resulted in personal unpopularity and public disfavor. He died in 1916.

James Mark Baldwin (1861–1934), whose most productive period was a ten-year stay at Princeton, was an "international" psychologist, teaching not only in the United States but also in Mexico and finally in Paris, where he died. Interested in theory more than research, he vigorously pursued the theme of the importance of evolutionary doctrine for psychology, including the study of the child.[43] In cooperation with others, he edited a huge *Dictionary of Philosophy and Psychology*.[44] His departure from the American scene as early as 1909 contributed to his relative lack of influence.

LATER LIFE

In further developing the method of order of merit, Cattell asked men acknowledged to be competent in each of the various scientific fields to rate their colleagues in order. Those emerging at the top of the lists for each science were given a star in the *Biographical Directory of American Men of Science*, a source book that emerged from this work. Through the seventh edition the starred men were asked to select the new men for the directory, a technique not followed in subsequent editions. To this day, the directory in its successive editions is a basic reference book, comparable to a specialized *Who's Who*. Though originating in a purely scientific study, its practical value has been considerable.

In 1895, Cattell acquired from Alexander Graham Bell the weekly journal *Science*, which had been having financial difficulties. In its publication, Cattell sought and secured the help of leading scientists throughout the country. After overcoming the financial difficulties, *Science* became the leading general scientific publication in the United States and in 1900 was made the official organ of the American Association for the Advancement of Science.

Cattell and other American psychologists, including James,[45] had decided that the *American Journal of Psychology* was functioning primarily as a house organ for the staff of Clark University and some of their associates. Accordingly, in 1894 in collaboration with J. Mark Baldwin, Cattell founded a rival journal, the *Psychological Review*. In his hands this journal grew into an entire series of journals. Editing a weekly and managing journals takes time, and Cattell's personal research productivity began to drop off.

Robert S. Woodworth and Edward L. Thorndike had joined him at Columbia soon after his arrival and were associated with him for many years. The separation of psychologists at the College and Graduate

School from those at Teacher's College, where Thorndike did his work and where Cattell did some of his teaching, fortunately had not yet happened. It was only later that 120th Street, separating Teacher's College from the main campus, became "the widest street in the world."

During the years Cattell was at Columbia, more psychologists-to-be studied at Columbia University than at any other institution in the United States. By and large, Cattell gave his students freedom to advance on their own; he was available for guidance, but he stressed independent work.

He insisted on a similar independence for himself, arguing that a professor's time, if spent within his areas of competence, should not necessarily be devoted solely to the university and its students. He established his home on a hilltop near Garrison, forty miles from New York, coming to the university only on certain days of the week. Later he equipped a laboratory and an editiorial office in his home. To some extent this served to free him from the interruptions of university life.

Relations with the university administration became strained. He believed that many decisions that were being left to university administrators were properly matters for faculty decision. He not only raised his voice in pursuit of the aim of faculty participation, he also helped to found the American Association of University Professors. During the years of World War I, Cattell wrote a letter to members of Congress protesting the sending of conscientious objectors into combat duty. This unpopular and personally disadvantageous position was one from which he could not in good conscience desist, so he stood by his position. The president and the trustees judged his action to be treason and on this ground dismissed him from the University. Cattell sued for libel, and the case was settled by his receiving a large annuity.

Many of Cattell's most important activities thereafter continued to be, in the best sense of the word, promotional in character. His numerous presidential addresses were often concerned with the growth and the current status of psychology.[46] He also served as a spokesman for psychology to the other sciences in the United States, as his editorships show. He did not hesitate to criticize and to advise in print universities, philanthropic agencies, the Carnegie Institution, and the National Academy of Sciences. He vigorously defended the growth of applied psychology, and psychology as a profession. As early as 1904, he predicted that there would eventually be a profession of psychology as well as a science of psychology.[47] In a similar spirit he organized the Psychological Corporation in 1921 in order to promote the application of psychology.[48] This corporation has grown considerably; it has used its profits to support other research, and it continues to play an important role in professional psychology. Cattell remained active as an editor and senior citizen scientist until his death in 1944.

OVERVIEW

Cattell epitomizes a major movement of American psychology. Never given to theoretical writing, he remained in research for some years of his life, thereafter maintaining a respect for research and an ability to criticize it. His interest in individual differences was instrumental in his working for psychology as a profession as well as a science. His bent toward administration and editing placed him among that small group of men who gave the beginnings of psychology in the United States its characteristic flavor. His wholehearted devotion to both puristic and utilitarian prescriptions did much to advance both. It also served as a living example that they were not irreconcilable attitudes to hold simultaneously.

Edward Bradford Titchener

During the second decade of this century, at Cornell University, an academic ceremony took place each day that the professor of psychology lectured on introductory psychology. Shortly before the class hour the professor inspected the demonstrational material that had been laid out; the staff and assistants gathered in his office, which adjoined the lecture room; the professor donned his Oxford master's gown, which, as he put it, "gives me the right to be dogmatic;" the staff filed through one door to take front row seats, the Professor emerged through another door directly onto the lecture platform. The lecture began.

Such was the grand manner in which lectures were offered by Wundt's most faithful pupil, Edward Bradford Titchener.[49] Trenchant and powerful lectures, they were often the occasion for pronouncements about his system of psychology, and to Titchener's audience of staff, graduate students, and sophomore college students, Titchener's system *was* psychology.

After Wundt's American students returned home, they almost always significantly modified his views according to their particular temperaments or social environment. This was not the case with Titchener. He developed and modified specific details, of course, but in most respects in both teaching and writing, Titchener held to the tradition of Wundt. His contribution to Wundt's theory was a systematic explicitness superior to that of his prolific and erudite master.

Titchener was born in 1867 in the old Roman town of Chichester, England. His father had died shortly after marriage, leaving young Titchener with little monetary security. At fourteen Titchener went to Malvern College, a new but already recognized public school. He continued his studies at Oxford, where for four years he concentrated upon philosophy and the classics. In his fifth year he became a research assistant to Burdon-Sanderson, the physiologist, for whom he was to have a lasting admiration.

Dissatisfaction with what he called the "logical constructions of the English school"[50] was instrumental in drawing Titchener to Leipzig. As he later put it, he heard about psychology at Oxford; he studied it at Leipzig.[51] Upon arrival he found himself a part of an active, enthusiastic group of future psychologists, including a half-dozen from the United States. Meumann, mentioned earlier, was his roommate, and Külpe was *Dozent*. Despite the fact that Titchener's stay at Leipzig lasted only two years, Wundt made a lifelong impression on him.

After receiving his degree from Leipzig in 1892, Titchener returned to Oxford, where for a few months he served as an extension lecturer in biology. To stay on at Oxford would have been his ambition, but Oxford was not ready for psychology. In any event, he had agreed to accept a position at Cornell University, replacing a friend from Leipzig, Frank Angell, who was leaving for Stanford University.

So in 1892 Titchener arrived in Ithaca, New York, on the new campus of Cornell University. He was assistant professor of psychology, but more important, he was in charge of the laboratory that his friend Angell had founded the year before.

For the next few years, Titchener was busy organizing the laboratory, buying and building equipment, carrying out research, writing articles (sixty-two between 1893 and 1900), and gradually attracting more and more students. At first he cooperated personally with every study in his laboratory, but discontinued this arduous practice[52] in later years. His research then came almost entirely through his students; he himself published nothing from the laboratory under his own name alone. His own published research consequently gives no indication of his productivity; it was through his direction of student investigations that the basis for his systematic statements was developed. Under his direction fifty-eight doctorates and many minor studies were conducted. Of the forty-six studies published in the first thirty volumes of the *American Journal of Psychology,* fifteen were on sensation, eight were on perception, six each were on memory and attention, and the rest were scattered over related fields.

What could be more natural than to translate the Master? This he proceeded to do for several of Wundt's works. But he found it hard to keep up with Wundt. Years before, while still in England, Titchener had finished translating the third edition of the *Principles of Physiological Psychology,* only to find that the indefatigable Wundt had written the fourth edition. Titchener therefore started over again, translating completely this new edition—only to find that the prolific Wundt now had his fifth edition ready. This time Titchener translated but six of the twenty-two chapters and, taking no chances, went to press. The rest of the book was never put into English. Titchener also translated works by Külpe, his friend from Germany who had not yet strayed from the path of Wundtian exactitude into the luxurious but overgrown jungle of imageless thought. Moreover, before the new century was six years old, Titchener himself had written his *Outline of Psychology* (1896), his *Primer of Psychology* (1898), and the four important volumes of his *Experimental Psychology* (1901–1905).

His *Experimental Psychology* bears the significant and relevant subtitle, *A Manual of Laboratory Practice;* it was designed to be used in "drill" courses for training in the method of psychology.[53] It is divided into four parts, two instructor's manuals and two student's manuals, one of each devoted to qualitative experiments—sensations, affective qualities, attention, action, perception and association of ideas—and the other devoted to quantitative experiments—thresholds for pressure, tone and sound, Weber's law, the various psychophysical methods, the reaction study of simple discrimination, cognition and choice times, and the reproduction of a time interval. Qualitative experiments, as he saw them, were essentially descriptions of conscious experiences by means of introspection, in which questions of "what" or "how" are asked; quantitative experiments assume that the mental process as such is already familiar from prior examination, and the task is to gather a long series of rather simple observations, which are then expressed through mathematical shorthand in which questions of "how much" are asked. These volumes are probably the most erudite and encyclopedic works on psychology written in English.

Titchener had close friends from his student days whom he cherished through the years. Throughout his life he always had a small group of psychologist friends with whom he kept up a voluminous correspondence. One psychologist had a collection of 212 letters addressed to him from Titchener.[54]

At first Titchener entered into social life at Cornell, but as he grew older, he withdrew more and more from the usual social and university contacts. He became a living legend to some members of the Cornell faculty, who had heard of him for years but had never met him. Punctilious and somehow formidable, he gave deference where he thought it due and expected in turn to receive it from those he thought owed it to him.

His relation with psychologists outside his own group also showed a tendency toward withdrawal. The American Psychological Association, to which he was elected by the charter members in 1892, did not claim him for long. He resigned almost immediately in response to the Association's refusal to support a measure that Titchener considered to be a matter of professional ethics. Moreover, the Association's membership as a whole was by no means as rigorously scientific as Titchener's standards demanded. In 1897 he was host to a meeting of the Association, but he was still not a member. He did rejoin but did not attend meetings, and later again resigned. When the Association meeting was held in Ithaca in 1925, Titchener held an "open house" for those who cared to come to see him at his home.

Beginning in 1904, Titchener organized his own group, the "Experimentalists."[55] It was not an organization in the strict sense; annual meetings were arranged by the director of the laboratory where the group was to meet. Needless to say, Titchener dominated the meetings and had much to do with selecting those invited and the topics included. To this day, the group, now somewhat more formally organized, carries on as a worthy representative of experimental psychology of the purest variety.

The *American Journal of Psychology,* for which Titchener became an associate editor in 1895, served something of the same function for him as did the *Philosophische Studien* for Wundt. However, it was not until 1921, when he became sole editor of it, that it could be employed as his own journal and could therefore serve as a platform similar to Wundt's. Titchener held firmly to his conviction that Cornell graduates in psychology formed a group, unified by their shared psychological orientations and therefore differentiated from the rest of the psychological world. He was staunch in defending his opinions against outside disagreements, yet flexible under self-criticism. In these and other respects he resembled Wundt.

Toward the close of the first decade of the century Titchener prepared *A Textbook of Psychology.*[56] A systematic work in relatively brief compass, this gives what is still the most comprehensive account of his psychology available. After publication of the *Textbook,* Titchener began to prepare an extended statement of his systematic views. This work he found impossible to complete, though its appearance was expected for many years. A part of this work was published as articles in the *American Journal of Psychology,* and republished posthumously as a book.[57]

During the fifteen years preceding his death in 1927, his productivity showed neither the scope nor the depth of his earlier work. Perhaps he had known honorary degrees and the trappings of academic success too early. Perhaps the decline had something to do with geography; Titchener never really became a part of the American scene, and he never considered giving up his English citizenship. He was thus ineligible for election to the National Academy of Sciences, and as a psychologist in the "colonies," he never received his F.R.S. Did this decline in productivity perhaps have something to do with the changing face of psychology? Here the record becomes obscure, and what follows must be seen as an individual interpretation, not necessarily shared by those who knew him personally and perhaps understood him better. As a younger man in a magnificent sort of simplicity, he had seen his particular views as psychology; other points of view, admirable though they might be, were simply not psychology. Except at Cornell and at two or three student-manned laboratory outposts at other universities, psychology as a whole was moving steadily away from him in his later life. Did Titchener simply refuse to watch while psychology irrevocably changed? We cannot be certain, but this might have made him unable or unwilling to continue with what should have been his most important work.

THE POINT OF VIEW OF PSYCHOLOGY

Titchener started with the view that all scientists are concerned with some phase of human experience, and that all knowledge is based on human experience.[58] Biologists deal with living forms and chemists investigate elements. The psychologist studies experience also, but from the special point of view of the experiencing person. Perception, especially the perceptual illusion, is illustrative. For instance, if one sees a stick that is partly in and partly out of the water, it appears bent. The experience as given is that the stick is bent, even though applying a straight edge to it would disprove this. Even "white" as experienced is a mixture of colored lights, none of which is white. But as a datum in consciousness, white is simple in nature. Neither the physical stick nor the multitude of lights are the concern of psychology; the experience is.

Stimulus error. (handwritten margin note)

The psychologist's interest is in the process of experiencing these phenomena.

To confuse the object with the mental process is to commit the "stimulus error."[59] To describe the object in common-sense terms, instead of reporting the conscious content of the experience, is to commit this error. An orange is not an orange so far as introspective report is concerned; it is the hues, brightnesses, and spatial characteristics of a certain stimulus object. Nor should a subject say he is afraid, for this is merely an interpretation; he must describe the conscious content in order to avoid the stimulus error.

For Titchener,[60] mind is the sum total of human experiences considered as dependent on a nervous system. Mind and consciousness are essentially the same, but the latter involves mental processes occurring *now,* rather than the sum-total. Mental experiences are always processes. According to Titchener the most striking fact about these is change. Nothing is stable; everything is in flux, a mosaic in motion.

It is perhaps appropriate to examine at this point what Titchener considered outside the field of psychology. He shared Wundt's distaste for the applied aspects of psychology. Behavior is not the concern of a psychology of consciousness. If experience is the sole concern of psychology, then performance (behavior) is irrelevant. Behavior is worthy of study—as a branch of biology, not as psychology. Titchener objected to what he called "the penny-in-the-slot sort of science," in which consciousness is said to be inferred, when it was always there waiting to be examined.[61] Objective study is always inferential; experience and its study set the pattern. Behaviorism, to which the study of behavior is paramount, is logically irrelevant to psychology. Nevertheless, psychology does obtain information concerning bodily mechanisms from the study of behavior and examines this biological information in the light of psychology.[62]

Titchener's dictum concerning unconscious phenomena was simply that consciousness includes only present mental processes. The unconscious consists of processes not present. Titchener was not concerned with what lies below the surface of consciousness. In fact, he was definite in disparaging psychology as seen by James. Titchener spoke of James's *Psychology* as a "theory of knowledge" and as not psychology at all![63]

INTROSPECTION AS THE METHOD OF PSYCHOLOGY

All science depends on observation. Psychological science depends on observation of conscious experience—in short, on introspection. For Titchener, to "look within" consciousness meant having clear experiences regarded as dependent on the experiencing individual.[64] There is no place in his psychology for the unconscious; his adherence to conscious mentalism was total.

Sometimes this involves hardly more than simple inspection. Consider the following illustration. In front of a subject are two color wheels (motors arranged to spin paper discs rapidly). On one wheel is a violet disc, on the other both a blue and a red disc interlocked so that when the wheel is standing still one sees portions of both the blue disc and the red disc. They are adjustable, so that an increase of either portion is possible. When spun, the second wheel will give a blue-red, that is, a shade of violet. The task of the subject is to adjust as exactly as he can the red and the blue portions until the resulting violet matches the violet of the first disc. The introspection is essentially inspectional; the subject merely reports when the two discs match.

Another illustration may be drawn from the already familiar two-point threshold. When the stimulus separation is very small the perception is that of a single pressure, which is reported as "one." When the stimulus separation is great, there is a report of two pressures. Intermediate between these two extremes the experience of pressure resemble the pattern of a dumbbell, i.e., two pressure points that are joined by a narrower band of pressure. The naïve subject would report "two" because he knows that one round point could not give that particular stretched-out pattern. But in so doing he commits the stimulus error. He has lapsed from the psychological point of view to *infer* what the stimulus must be. The sophisticated introspectionist would report "one," because he perceives a unitary pattern.

The material for introspection may often be more complex. For example, a word is called out to the subject, who then reports the effect it produces on his consciousness. Sometimes conditions get complicated, as in a long, drawn-out observation in which the introspection is delayed until the experience has run its course. Even a short temporal exposure may require a very long description. In both instances the introspector has to use retrospection. Often when he finds he cannot maintain an introspective attitude throughout the course of a complicated experience, he can have the experience repeated as many times as desired, removing the danger of missing some aspect of it.

THE TASKS OF PSYCHOLOGY

The questions of the psychologist are "what," "how," and "why."[65] The task of analysis is to answer the question "what." Consciousness is directly observable. It is composed of simple describable units; the analytical task of the psychologist is to break it down into its simplest components. The task of synthesis is to answer the question "how." The psychologist does this by arranging in order the elements found in analysis in various combinations in order to arrive at the laws of their combination. For example, sensations of tone will blend, but they give an imperfect fusion, as in a major chord; whereas sensations of color fuse perfectly, as when the spectrum mixes to give a simple white. The question "why" gave Titchener more difficulty. One mental process cannot cause another. As evidence Titchener cited that an experience may be due to present stimuli to which one has never before been exposed. He rejected neural processes as the direct cause of mental processes, since the theory conflicted with his already postulated psychophysical parallelism. Titchener solved the problem to his satisfaction by arguing that, while the nervous system does not cause mental phenomena, it may be used to explain them. By introducing the "map" that the nervous system makes, it is possible to systematize our introspective data. The parallel processes in the nervous system explain the mental processes as a map explains the terrain. This is an important theoretical shift from the position of Wundt since the experiencing individual is acknowledged to be dependent on a nervous system that may be used for explanation. This is a position that, it will be remembered, Wundt vigorously denied (p. 276).

STRUCTURALISM

Description of Titchener's system of psychology is sometimes over-simplified. Critics say that he was a structuralist. By that they mean he was concerned with the static elements of experience, not with the functional study of the process of experience, as James and others had been. This is simply not true. There is no doubt that he utilized functional material; the findings of psychophysics, which formed one major segment in his system, can be viewed as dependent on the functions of discrimination estimation. Unequivocally, he accepted the existence of a functional aspect of psychology.

To Titchener, his systematic view of psychology was of psychology simply, with no qualification whatsoever. He did, however, formulate the so-called structural position in an article published in 1898.[66] He noted that in investigating mental structure, a large proportion of experimental psychology corresponds to that branch of biology known as morphology. "Descriptive" psychology, concerned with function, on the other hand, corresponds to physiology. In his opinion, psychology's study of structure must precede its study of function. In justification, he pointed out that while considerable agreement had been reached concerning the postulates of a structural psychology (e.g., among Wundt, Külpe, Ebbinghaus, and, of course, himself), this was not the case with those he considered functionalists, such as Brentano and James, who disagreed among themselves. So he concluded that functional study is neither as accurate nor as scientifically final as structural investigation, and a swing toward a functionally oriented psychology would be regrettable, since there is so much work yet to be done on structure.

Titchener's view has sometimes been referred to as existential psychology, since experiences are studied by him as existences, i.e., as facts deserving of study for their own sake.[67] For example, content that lacks verbal meaning—the nonsense syllables of Ebbinghaus, for example—presents itself to the experiencing person as existential. But a word of caution is necessary. The present-day popular meaning of existentialism has no more relation to the word as applied to Titchener's psychology than does the existentialism of St. Thomas Aquinas.

From the standpoint of those who applied the terms "structural" or "existential," his was a school of psychology. For him, it was simply psychology.

VIEWS ON SOME PSYCHOLOGICAL PROBLEMS

In Titchener's original view, long maintained, elementary mental processes consist of sensations, images, and affections.[68] Each of these three categories contains experiences irreducible to anything simpler, similar in this respect to so-called chemical elements. As a youthful effort, Titchener even calculated the number of sensory elements; he found that the eye supplied somewhat less than 33,000; the ear, less than 12,000, and all the rest about 18.[69] Each of these qualities is a distinct conscious element, blended in various ways to form perceptions and ideas. Sensations are the elements of perception; images are the elements of ideas; and affections are the elements of emotions. In practice, Titchener stressed the study of sensations, minimized the study of ideas, and placed the study of affections somewhere in between.

The Wundtian attributes of quality and intensity were expanded by Titchener to include protensity (duration), attensity (clearness), and extensity.[70] Protensity is self-explanatory. Attensity is introduced as an attribute to lend systematic clarity to the place of attention in psychological experience. Attensity allows a particular place to a sensation in consciousness; clear sensations are dominant and outstanding; those less clear are subordinate and undistinguished. Clear sensations are those to which we attend; attention and sensory clearness are identical. By making attention an attribute, Titchener eliminated the need to appeal to a "power" of attention and at the same time gave attention a systematic place within his system. Extensity is the spatial attribute, the "spread-outness" of the experience.

Titchener later postulated that these attributes might be the data of observation; sensation is only a systematic classificatory device almost without existential reality.[71] Once they become the object of direct study, attributes are the "systematic concepts" that stand up under observation.

Titchener saw no reason to change his basic assumption concerning the primacy of sensation, images, and feelings after examining the imageless-thought controversy[72] (p. 309). In thinking, there may be obscure, fleeting, or faint aspects of experience, but these are still imaginal or sensory elements that are being manifested. To Titchener, conscious attitudes were no more than complex integrations of sensory components, improperly analyzed by the Würzburg group and others. Even if these later proved to be nonsensory elements of meaning, they would be the concern of logic, not of psychology.

Meaning as conscious representation comes about when primary elements are combined in a manner reminiscent of Berkeley. Perceptions, to put it simply, are sensations (and images) with meaning, and this meaning is defined by Titchener as context. Sensations are the core of perceptions, but images and context also contribute.

In order to remain systematically rigorous and parsimonious, Titchener did not wish to introduce perception as still another mental element.[73] Although patterns of clarity, sensation, and attention account for some of the phenomena of perception, there remains an unexplained aspect. Meaning is that something we expect to be accounted for by perception; perceptions are meaningful, we say, when we perceive an apple, a friend, or a sentence in a book. To Titchener,[74] meaning shows itself in context—one mental process is the meaning of another, if it is the other's context. In its simplest form it takes at least two sensations (or images) to make a meaning, one serving as core, the other as context. An illustration would be seeing a strange face (core) and having a visual image of the person's name come to mind (context). Hence one knows what it means (perception). By some process of accretion, presumably associative, meanings as composed of sensory or imaginal contexts accrue to an initial sensory or imaginal core. Thus, context gives meaning in the framing of new perceptions and ideas. Titchener does note an important exception: habitual meanings can occur without conscious context, which means they may be carried unconsciously. In this acceptance of unconscious context Titchener went beyond Berkeley. In addition to the belief that perception has as its core a sensation, the context of which is other sensations and images, he held there was an unconscious context. All three make up the total context.

Feeling or affection received special attention from Titchener's students in the Cornell Laboratory. On the basis of introspective studies carried on in his laboratory, Titchener dissented from Wundt's tridimensional theory.[75] He denied feeling the dimensions of tension-relaxation and excitement-depression, since he found these to be "muscular attitudes." This left to feeling the traditional dimension of pleasantness-unpleasantness.

At one time Titchener held that feeling was a conscious element, distinct from sensation. Work from his laboratory during the last years of his life tended to show him that this view must be modified.[76] Under introspection, feelings turn out to be modes of pressure. Pleasantness is a bright pressure; unpleasantness is a dull pressure. Affective experience from every sense department may take on an increment of bright or dull pressure. For pleasant experiences, terms such as "liveliness," "brightness," "airy" were used by the introspectors; unpleasant experiences were identified as "dull," "heavy," and "hard." Direct appeal to pressure, as such, was evident among all the observers. Feeling was thus related to touch.

But this was not the only change. Even earlier, Perky[77] and Edwards[78] had carried out studies in the Cornell laboratory that had cast doubt on the concept of the image as a separate element.

The studies of feeling and image that made it no longer possible to consider them elements of mental life had appeared too late for Titchener to incorporate into his own systematic publications. This service has been rendered recently by an important paper by Rand Evans.[79] From the papers of Titchener's students, from his correspondence, from notes on Titchener's lectures in the later years, Evans has demonstrated that the goal of systematic psychology was a study, not of elements, but of dimensions of mental life. These dimensions were quality, intensity, potensity, extensity and attensity. Sensations were a major source for qualities but so too were images and affections, although they were not held to be separate elements. Moreover, Titchener softened his heretofore rigid view about the conditions of introspection, allowing even phenomenological investigation a place in psychology.

OVERVIEW

Boring's biography of Titchener, published the year Titchener died, closes with the statement that a century may have to pass before it is possible to assess Titchener's place in the history of psychology.[80] From the present perspective of only some fifty years later, the approach to psychology through introspection seems to have closed with Titchener's death. Not that content of consciousness as a source of psychological data has disappeared. Verbal report and free association are still with us, but a unified, unsupplemented appeal to introspection and nought beside has disappeared. That we have progressed beyond Titchener's views anyone with a sense of history would acknowledge, but this inevitable lesson does not detract from the contribution these views represent.

Wundt and Titchener both thought they had set the pattern for psychology. Actually, their work was but a stage in its history and barely survived Titchener's death. In fact, the remarkable aspect is the speed with which the change took place. By 1930, students of Titchener[81] were arguing that the homogeneity among psychologists is much greater than the differences and that, except for a few diehards, a reconciliation among the warring schools was actually taking place.

A transfer from one culture to another must always be relative and selective, never complete. As any sociologist could have predicted, Titchener's attempt to transfer Wundtian psychology in its entirety proved to be a failure. But it was a magnificent failure.

A rigid contentually subjective view of psychology and an adherence to a conscious mentalism expressed through a search for molecular structures were salient features of Titchener's view of the nature of psychology. This was modified in later years to a view still molecular, but not unrelievedly so, in which dimensions of experience, not the elements, were the object of study. His insistence that psychology is severely puristic, while characteristic enough, was not vital to it. Search for general laws, or nomotheticism, did reinforce this purism.

Functional Psychology

As the name implies, functional psychology was concerned with the mind as it functions. Emphasis on use lent itself readily to the practical and to the struggle to get ahead. Even before its meaning is elaborated, it is easy to anticipate why the temper of the times in the United States would be receptive to this approach in psychology. This congeniality of practical applications of psychology, with utilitarianism, marks a separation of the functionalists from the structuralists. The latter were impatient with such efforts; to characterize functional psychology in terms of use seemed to them tantamount to criticism. The functionalists, however, tended not only to welcome application of psychology by others, but also to engage in it themselves. The lives of some of the functionalists stand witness to this. John Dewey became a leading educator; J. R. Angell became president of Yale University and, on his retirement, an executive of a radio corporation. Lest this lead to a misunderstanding, let it be noted that functionalists were still very much interested in psychology as a science. Here they showed a partiality toward research on learning, perception, and similar processes; they were especially receptive to animal psychology, physiological psychology, and differential psychology.

WILLIAM JAMES AS A FUNCTIONALIST

Functional psychology has many forebears. In the modern era it was James who was singled out by Titchener as a typical functionalist in his 1898 article contrasting functionalism and structuralism.[82] Actually, James was too versatile to be easily labeled. Only when we contrast his views with those of Titchener does it become possible to regard him as a functionalist. As a matter of fact, James had anticipated Titchener by differentiating between a structural and a functional position as early as 1884.[83] He attached no great importance to the distinction, however; in 1890, in his *Principles* he banished it to a footnote.[84]

In what sense was James a functionalist? In the *Principles*, James assimilated psychology into biology and treated thinking as an instrument in the struggle for life.[85] Mental processes were conceived of as activities. Mind was not an entity, but a functional activity of the organism. The biological survival value of mind was stressed; if consciousness had no value it would not have survived. James saw consciousness as useful because it intervened in the cause-effect sequence, resulting in the spontaneity and productivity of the mind. This particular view was accepted and elaborated on by John Dewey in his appeal to consciousness as part of the adjustive equipment of the organism, and Angell[86] used James's already familiar argument that consciousness is not present when it has no utility.

JOHN DEWEY AS A FUNCTIONALIST

Charles Darwin had helped to prepare the way for functionalism by emphasizing adaptation, activities, and individual differences. Galton and Spencer continued this tradition, each in his own way, the first emphasizing individual differences and the second, adaptation. Showing its evolutionary heritage, functionalism saw psychology as the study of the adaptation of the organism to its environment. In the United States there were already familiar kindred spirits, such as James McKeen Cattell and Robert S. Woodworth at Columbia, James Mark Baldwin and, in some ways, G. Stanley Hall. But none of these was identified with functionalism as a separate and distinct school of psychology.

In this narrower sense, John Dewey (1859–1952) was the first functional psychologist.[87] After appointment in 1884 to the department of philosophy of the University of Michigan, he followed the usual custom and taught psychology as well as philosophy; indeed, he published in 1886[88] a somewhat influential text in psychology (with the philosophical presuppositions characteristic of his time). His period as a force in psychology, however, coincided with his stay at the University of Chicago during the years 1894 to 1904. When he left Chicago for Columbia University in 1905, he no longer worked directly in the field, though he did utilize psychology in the larger educational and philosophical perspectives that later concerned him.

It was Dewey's paper of 1896 on the reflex arc concept that served to introduce the school of functionalism.[89] As James before him had attacked psychological atomism by demonstrating that simple ideas have no existential reality in the stream of consciousness, so Dewey found the same doctrine of elementarism lurking in the reflex arc. He was searching for a unifying concept for mental life, and he considered the reflex arc, recently borrowed from physiology, a likely possibility. Despite its promise, detailed analysis led him to reject it for this purpose because of its "patchwork" qualities.[90]

As Dewey saw it, a child's withdrawal of his finger from the flame, often given as the classical example of the reflex arc, does not tell the whole story of what is happening. After an experience of this sort, the visual perception of the flame, previously inviting to the child, is now permanently altered. The stimulus and the response of the burn-withdrawal reflex does not end with the withdrawal. It now serves as the stimulus for another situation that belongs to the same act, instead of being a new occurrence. Every reaction, Dewey argued, is a circuit—adjustment is more than a response to a stimulus: it is a realignment within one's environment. The unitary act completes a circle from sensation through movement to a new sensation that arises out of that movement. Sensation as an "existence" and motion as a response do not account for the psychological facts, which form, not an arc, but a circuit. Dewey argued that reflexes, as well as other forms of behavior, should not be treated as artificial constructs by the abstraction of their sensory and motor phases. It is their significance for adaptation that is crucial. In this way Dewey was making a plea for function as the basis of psychological study.

It was in this spirit Dewey approached educational matters. The child is an active dynamic being, with interests and desires of his own, and ,he task of education was to provide opportunities to learn.

JAMES ROWLAND ANGELL AND HARVEY CARR

Without deliberate intention, the functional viewpoint became crystallized as a school. In some measure this came about through answering attacks made by critics of this viewpoint. When Titchener christened functionalism by contrasting it with structuralism, James Rowland Angell (1869–1949), a former student of James and Dewey's younger associate at the University of Chicago, accepted the challenge and in a paper and a book attempted to present the functional point of view. The University of Chicago was afterwards the major source from which functional psychologists came. It should be emphasized, however, that the Chicago functionalists argued that the heritage of functionalism was of such a broad nature that it was, properly speaking, not a school at all, and they expressly stated that it should not be identified with psychology as taught at Chicago. Despite this disclaimer, most psychologists besides the spokesman for functional psychology and their students were inclined to consider the Chicago psychologists sufficiently different from other psychologists and sufficiently similar among themselves to warrant classification as adherents to a particular school.

In 1906, Angell's presidential address to the American Psychological Association was "The Province of Functional Psychology."[91] He brought together three conceptions of function that he considered acceptable to functional psychologists. 1) Functionalism is concerned with mental operations, the "how" and "why" of consciousness, as contrasted to the "what" of the psychology of mental elements. 2) Mind is a means of mediating between the needs of the organism and the environment. Consciousness, in accordance with the emergency theory of James, is utilitarian, since it serves some end. Because consciousness helps to solve problems, an interest in the applied fields of psychology flows naturally from an interest in it. 3) Functional psychology is a psychophysical psychology that requires that the mind-body relationship be taken into consideration in psychology. The functional psychologist is interested in studying mental processes as a means of adjustment; this in turn implies that the epiphenomenalistic solution, which holds mental activity to be nothing more than a useless by-product, is incompatible with functionalism. Other than this, no special psychophysical position is necessary. This article clearly spelled out the functionalist position, and in this sense was more important than Dewey's paper, which, though it

Angell on Functionalism

showed a functionalist spirit in dealing with a particular psychological issue, did not explicate the conceptions of a functional psychology.

In 1904,[92] Angell wrote a textbook concerned with both the structure and the function of human consciousness, as its subtitle attests. Functional solutions were sufficiently emphasized to make clear what he meant by functional psychology. He still saw the introspective study of consciousness as the principal method, but added the objective observation of the individual's actions as a supplement. Thus the study of behavior was explicitly accepted as a method of psychology.

Harvey A. Carr (1873–1954) had studied at Chicago with Angell. He was appointed to the department of psychology there in 1908. When Angell left, he took over as head of the department, a post he held from 1926 to 1938. During this time he continued the Chicago functionalist tradition.[93] He wrote a text[94] and a book on space perception,[95] both from the functionalist's point of view. During Carr's years at Chicago about 150 psychologists received their Ph.D.s; and their later careers showed the influence of the functionalist spirit.

Carr helped to clarify the meaning of "functional," over which there had been considerable controversy.[96] A charge had been made that "function" had been used inconsistently by the functional psychologists.[97] It was argued that what was sometimes meant by functional were the mental activities, such as seeing, hearing, perceiving, and the like; at other times functional served to indicate use or service for some end, as when we speak of the function of a word. The functionalists, it was said, would apply the word function to an activity, such as breathing or digestion, and later use the word to denote the utility of an activity, as when it is said that oxidation of the blood is a function of breathing. This made it possible to speak of a function of an activity, in other words, of a function of a function, which critics of functionalism saw as an absurd confusion. In replying to this charge, Carr insisted that there is really no discrepancy because at a higher level of interpretation the two meanings are actually the same. The common identity of the two—process and end—is the mathematical meaning of function, as in the expression $y = f(x)$; i.e., "y" is a function of "x." When a mathematician says y is a function of x, he is merely saying there is a contingent relation between them, but he does not specify the precise nature of that relation. Functional psychologists use the term the same way, whether they speak of process or end, act or structure, cause or effect. A contingent relation and a functional relation are synonymous. In this, Carr came very close to contemporary usage. The use of cause and effect, which Carr specifically mentioned as one of these functional relations, later led to statements that psychology is the study of functional or contingent relations between antecedent psychological events and their consequents. A considerable number of contemporary psychologists would subscribe to this definition.

EXTENSION OF FUNCTIONALISM

Clearcut self-conscious allegiance to their school of thought did not characterize the functionalists as it did the structuralists. As has already been mentioned, Columbia University in the person of James McKeen Cattell was sympathetic to a functionalist point of view without being narrowly identified with it. In the next generation, he was ably seconded by Robert Sessions Woodworth, whose position was also more eclectic—in 1918 he saw psychology as embracing both the older tradition of introspection and the newer one of behavior.[98] By 1930, Carr said he dared not list functionalists by name lest some he considered to fall within its scope be "rudely shocked."[99] It is probable that a large number of psychologists of the first three decades of the century who thought of themselves simply as "psychologists" (with the exception of the Titchenerians) were closest in spirit to functionalism. This, however, was a functionalism much more slanted toward behavior than Woodworth intended, because, as the next chapter will discuss, the latter half of these three decades saw the appearance of behaviorism.

References[*]

1. L. N. Wilson, "Biographical Sketch, Granville Stanley Hall, Feb. 1, 1844–April 24, 1924," *Publication Clark University Library*, VII (1925): 3–33; G. S. Hall, *Life and Confessions of a Psychologist* (New York: Appleton, 1923); Dorothy G. Ross, *G. Stanley Hall: The Psychologist as Prophet* (Chicago: University of Chicago Press, 1972).
2. H. James, ed., *The Letters of William James* (Boston: Atlantic Monthly, 1920), Vol. 2, pp. 17–18.
3. J. M. Cattell, "The Founding of the Association and of the Hopkins and Clark Laboratories," *Psychological Review*, L (1943): 61–64.
4. F. M. Albrecht, The New Psychology in America: 1880–1895. Unpublished Ph.D. dissertation, Johns Hopkins, 1960.
5. *Ibid*.

[*]See p. 19 for description of reference style.

6. Cattell, "Founding."
7. J. Jastrow, "American Psychology in the '80's and '90's," *Psychological Review*, L (1943): 65–67.
8. N. O. Rush, ed., *Letters of G. Stanley Hall to Jonas Gilman Clark* (Worcester: Clark University Library, 1948).
9. Hall, *Life and Confessions*.
10. *Ibid.*, p. 296.
11. L. M. Terman, "Trails to Psychology," in C. Murchison, ed., *A History of Psychology in Autobiography* (Worcester: Clark University Press, 1932), Vol. II, pp. 297–332.
12. R. S. Harper, "Tables of American Doctorates in Psychology," *American Journal of Psychology*, LXII (1949): 579–587.
13. W. Dennis and E. G. Boring, "The Founding of APA," *American Psychologist*, VII (1952): 95–97.
14. *Ibid.*
15. G. S. Hall, "Contents of Children's Minds," *Princeton Review*, XI (1883): 272–294.
16. D. E. Bradbury, "The Contribution of the Child Study Movement to Child Psychology," *Psychological Bulletin*, XXXIV (1937): 21–38.
17. G. S. Hall, *Adolescence: its Psychology and its Relations to Physiology, Anthropology, Sociology, Sex, Crime, Religion and Education* (New York: Appleton, 1904).
18. G. S. Hall, *Jesus, the Christ, in the Light of Psychology*, 2 vols. (New York: Doubleday, 1917).
19. G. S. Hall, "Department of Psychology," *Publication of Clark University Library*, V (1917): Nos. 2, 35.
20. J. C. Burnham, "Sigmund Freud and G. Stanley Hall: Exchange of Letters," *Psychoanalytic Quarterly*, XXIX (1960): 307–316.
21. *Ibid.*
22. Cattell, "Founding."
23. G. S. Hall, *Senescence: the Last Half of Life* (New York: Appleton, 1922).
24. Cattell, "Founding."
25. E. D. Starbuck, "G. Stanley Hall as a Psychologist," *Psychological Review*, XXXII (1925): 103–120.
26. E. B. Titchener, "Letters in Memory of G. Stanley Hall," G. S. Hall, "Feb. 1, 1844–April 24, 1924," *Publication Clark University Library*, VII (1925): No. 6, 1–92.

27. Starbuck, "G. Stanley Hall," p. 117.
28. M. L. Reymert, "Letters in Memory of G. Stanley Hall," Granville Stanley Hall, Feb. 1, 1844–April 24, 1924, *Publication Clark University Library*, VII (1925), No. 6, 81–84; G. S. Hall, *Founders of Modern Psychology* (New York: Appleton, 1912).
29. *Ibid.*
30. R. S. Woodworth, "James McKeen Cattell—in Memoriam: Some Personal Characteristics," *Science*, XCIX (1944): 160–161.
31. R. S. Woodworth, "James McKeen Cattell, 1860–1944," *Psychological Review*, LI (1944): 201–209; M. M. Sokal, "The Unpublished Autobiography of James McKeen Cattell," *American Psychologist*, XXVI (1971): 626–635.
32. J. M. Cattell, "Psychology in America," *Scientific Monthly*, XXX (1930): 114–126.
33. J. M. Cattell, "The Inertia of the Eye and Brain," *Brain*, VIII (1885): 295–312.
34. Cattell, "Psychology in America," p. 116.
35. Cattell, "Founding."
36. C. Wissler, "The Contribution of James McKeen Cattell to American Anthropology," *Science*, XCIX (1944): 232–233.
37. J. M. Cattell, "Mental Tests and Measurements," *Mind*, XV (1890): 373–381 (Herrnstein and Boring, Excerpt No. 80).
38. C. Wissler, "The Correlation of Mental and Physical Tests," *Psychological Review Monograph Supplement*, III (1901): No. 6. (Herrnstein and Boring, Excerpt No. 84).
39. S. E. Sharp, "Individual Psychology: a Study in Psychological Method," *American Journal of Psychology*, X (1899): 329–391 (Herrnstein and Boring, Excerpt No. 83).
40. J. M. Cattell, "The Time of Perception as a Measure of Differences in Intensity, *Philosophische Studien*, XIX (1902): 63–68.
41. S. S. Visher, "*Scientists Starred 1903–1943*" in *American Men of Science* (Baltimore: Johns Hopkins Press, 1947), pp. 141–143.
42. H. Münsterberg, *Psychology and Life* (Boston: Houghton Mifflin, 1899); H. Münsterberg, *Psychotherapy* (New York: Moffat Yard, 1909).
43. J. M. Baldwin, *Mental Development in the Child and*

the Race (New York: Macmillan, 1895) (Hermnstein and Boring, Excerpt No. 92).

44. J. M. Baldwin, ed., *Dictionary of Philosophy and Psychology*, new ed., 3 vols. (New York: Macmillan, 1901).

45. Perry, *Letters*, Vol. II.

46. A. T. Poffenberger, ed., *James McKeen Cattell: Man of Science*, I, *Psychological Research*, II, *Addresses and Formal Papers* (Lancaster, Pa.: Science Press, 1947).

47. J. M. Cattell, "The Conceptions and Methods of Psychology," *Popular Science Monthly*, XLVI (1904): 176–186, reprinted, in part, "Retrospect: Psychology as a Profession," *Journal of Consulting Psychology*, I (1937): 1–3.

48. Poffenberger, *James McKeen Cattell*, Vol. 1, p. 498.

49. E. G. Boring, "Edward Bradford Titchener, 1867–1927." *American Journal of Psychology*, XXXVIII (1927): 489–506.

50. E. B. Titchener, *Experimental Psychology: a Manual of Laboratory Practice* (New York: Macmillan, 1901–1905), I, pt. II, vii.

51. W. B. Pillsbury, "The Psychology of Edward Bradford Titchener," *Philosophical Review*, XXXVII (1928): 95–108.

52. *Ibid.*

53. Titchener, *Experimental Psychology*.

54. E. G. Boring, Personal Correspondence, 1960.

55. E. G. Boring, "Titchener's Experimentalists," *Journal of the History of the Behavioral Sciences*, III (1967): 315–325.

56. E. B. Titchener, *A Textbook of Psychology* (New York: Macmillan, 1910).

57. E. B. Titchener, *Systematic Psychology: Prolegomena* (New York: Macmillan, 1929).

58. Titchener, *Textbook*, pp. 2 ff. (Hermnstein and Boring, Excerpt No. 111).

59. *Ibid.*, pp. 202f.

60. *Ibid.*, pp. 9 ff.

61. E. B. Titchener, "The Problems of Experimental Psychology," *American Journal of Psychology*, XVI (1905): 220–224.

62. E. B. Titchener, "On Psychology as the Behaviorist Views it," *Proceedings of the American Philosophical Society*, LIII (1914): 1–17.

63. Boring, "Edward Bradford Titchener."

64. Titchener, *Textbook,* pp. 19 ff. (Herrnstein and Boring, Excerpt No. 111).

65. *Ibid.,* pp. 36 ff.

66. E. B. Titchener, "The Postulates of a Structural Psychology," *Philosophical Review,* VII (1898): 449–465.

67. E. G. Boring, "Titchener and the Existential," *American Journal of Psychology,* L (1937), 470–483; E. B. Titchener, *Lectures on the Experimental Psychology of Thought Processes* (New York: Macmillan, 1909).

68. Titchener, *A Textbook of Psychology,* p. 48.

69. E. B. Titchener, *An Outline of Psychology* (New York: Macmillan Company, 1896), pp. 74–75 (Herrnstein and Boring, Excerpt No. 14).

70. E. B. Titchener, *Lectures on the Elementary Psychology of Feeling and Attention* (New York: Macmillan, 1908), pp. 4 ff.

71. Boring, "Titchener and the Existential."

72. Titchener, *Thought Processes.*

73. Titchener, *A Textbook of Psychology,* pp. 135–136.

74. *Ibid.,* pp. 367–371 (Herrnstein and Boring, Excerpt No. 41).

75. *Ibid.,* pp. 225–264.

76. J. P. Nafe, "An Experimental Study of the Affective Qualities," *American Journal of Psychology,* XXXV (1924), 507–544.

77. C. W. Perky, "An Experimental Study of Imagination," *American Journal of Psychology,* XXI (1910): 422–452.

78. A. S. Edwards, "An Experimental Study of Sensory Suggestion," *American Journal of Psychology,* XXVI (1915); 99–128.

79. R. B. Evans, "E. B. Titchener and His Lost System," *Journal of the History of the Behavioral Sciences, 8,* (1972): 168–180.

80. Boring, "Edward Bradford Titchener."

81. E. G. Boring, "Psychology for Eclectics," in C. Murchison, ed., *Psychologies of 1930* (Worcester: Clark University Press, 1930), pp. 115–127; J. P. Nafe, "Structural Psychology," in C. Murchison, ed., *Psychologies of 1930* (Worcester: Clark University Press, 1930), pp. 128–140.

82. Titchener, "Postulates of a Structural Psychology."

83. W. James, "On Some Omissions of Introspective Psychology," *Mind,* IX (1884): 1–26.

84. W. James, "The Principles of Psychology," in R. M. Hutchins, ed., *The Great Books of the Western World* (1890) (Chicago: Encyclopaedia Britannica, 1952), Vol. LIII, p. 348.

85. *Ibid.*, pp. 6–8. (Herrnstein and Boring, Excerpts Nos. 91, 114).

86. J. R. Angell, *Psychology, an Introductory Study of the Structure and Function of Human Consciousness* (New York: Henry Holt, 1904).

87. E. G. Boring, "John Dewey: 1859–1952," *American Journal of Psychology,* LXVII (1953): 145–147.

88. J. Dewey, *Psychology* (New York: Harper and Brothers, 1886).

89. J. Dewey, "The Reflex Arc Concept in Psychology," *Psychological Review,* III (1896):357–370 (Herrnstein and Boring, Excerpt No. 64).

90. *Ibid.*, p. 358.

91. J. R. Angell, "The Province of Functional Psychology," *Psychological Review,* XIV (1907): 61–91. (Herrnstein and Boring, Excerpt No. 93).

92. Angell, *Psychology.*

93. H. L. Koch, "Harvey A. Carr: 1873–1954," *Psychological Review,* LXII (1955): 81–82; W. B. Pillsbury, "Harvey A. Carr: 1873–1954," *American Journal of Psychology,* LXVIII (1955): 149–151.

94. H. A. Carr, *Psychology: a Study of Mental Activity* (New York: Longmans, Green, 1925).

95. H. A. Carr, *An Introduction to Space Perception* (New York: Longmans, Green, 1935).

96. H. A. Carr, "Functionalism," in C. Murchison, ed., *Psychologies of 1930* (Worcester: Clark University Press, 1930), pp. 59–78.

97. C. A. Ruckmick, "The Use of the Term *Function* in English Textbooks of Psychology," *American Journal of Psychology,* XXIV (1913): 99–123.

98. R. S. Woodworth, *Dynamic Psychology* (New York: Columbia University Press, 1918), pp. 34–36 (Herrnstein and Boring, Excerpt No. 115).

99. Carr, "Functionalism."

Chapter 18

Watson:
BEHAVIORISM

In 1913 an article appeared in an American psychological journal that was the manifesto of a new psychology. Written by a thirty-five-year-old psychologist, John Broadus Watson, it opened with these sentences:

> Psychology as the behaviorist views it is a purely objective experimental branch of natural science. Its theoretical goal is the prediction and control of behavior. Introspection forms no essential part of its methods, nor is the scientific value of its data dependent upon the readiness with which they lend themselves to interpretation in terms of consciousness.[1]

So began the first statement of the goal of behaviorism and the object of attack against it.

This was more than a declaration of independence; it was an announcement of the intention of behaviorism to occupy the entire field of psychology. It was not enough that the study of behavior (contentual objectivity) be lifted to status equal with that of consciousness (contentual subjectivity). Behavior was hereafter to be the only concern of psychology, and its study was to be the definition of psychology. In Watson's view, psychology had failed in its fifty years as an experimental study to establish itself as a science. To reach its rightful place, it must discard consciousness. To quote further: "The time seems to have come when psychology must discard all references to consciousness; when it need no longer delude itself into thinking that it is making mental states the object of observation."[2]

Anything in the nature of mental phenomena was anathema to Watson. It was as if to him the mental were outside this rational world of ours, dwelling in the dark with ghosts and goblins. His conception of the earlier work in psychology was simple and clear; the introspectionists assumed the soul or its substitute (consciousness) to exist and then proceeded to study this airy nothing by introspection.

Watson thought the introspective method notoriously unreliable—as exemplified in the quarrel between the Leipzig and the Würzburg schools over imageless thought. As he saw it, almost all psychology before him was tarred with the same mentalistic brush and was therefore unscientific. He specified that his quarrel was not only with the structural psychology of Titchener but with functional psychology as well, since it also used mentalistic terms and emphases. He did agree that a functional emphasis upon biological significance was laudable, but felt the so-called functionalists still failed to be scientific. They had slipped into an interactionistic position in which they saw mental states as playing some part in the adjustment of the individual. This is nothing more than a relic of philosophy, Watson argued, and the whole issue should and can be ignored by focusing on behavior to the exclusion of all else. He claimed that behaviorism is the only consistent functionalism. The study of functional capacities expressed in behavior is relatively easily and directly determined; references to conscious states in functional terms are not only uncertain, but also trivial and unreal.

One may assume, Watson said, the presence or absence of consciousness as one wishes; it does not affect the problems of behavior one iota.[3] A man has something that may be called consciousness—a psychologist, as a human being, has this something. But so, too, does a physicist, as a human being. But what the psychologist shares with the physicist in this regard is no more part of his field of research than it is that of the physicist.

In 1913 Watson stood almost alone in his behavioristic convictions before his last major publication in revised form in 1930. Seventeen years later,[4] his view had swept through psychology in the United States leaving it, in many respects, a new field.

Pavlov and Russian Physiology

Emphasis upon contentual objectivity had preceded Watson. One generation earlier there had been the work of two Russian physiologists, Ivan P. Pavlov and Vladimir M. Bekhterev. In turn, it was a publication by Ivan M. Sechenov, the Reflexes of the Brain,[5] which Pavlov acknowledged as the single most important theoretical inspiration for his work on conditioning.[6]

SECHENOV

It is generally agreed that Ivan M. Sechenov (1829–1905) founded Russian physiology.[7] After early training in Russia and study abroad with Claude Bernard, DuBois-Reymond, Johannes Müller, and Hermann von Helmholtz, he returned to teach physiology at the St. Petersburg Military Medical Academy and at various other institutions; he spent his last years as professor of physiology at Moscow University.

Early in Sechenov's career, he carried on experimental investigations of the inhibition of reflex movements by the cerebral cortex. This inspired him to show that there was a physiological basis for psychical processes. Thereafter, he labored with the problem of demonstrating that the psyche, rather than being independent of the body, is a function of the brain and central nervous system and is therefore a physiological problem.

His thesis was that psychical activity can be explained by reflex activity. With his physiological orientation he tended to emphasize the receptor and motor (muscular) phases of the reflex psychical processes. All psychical processes are expressed in motor activity of one sort or another.

A few of his characteristic teachings may be mentioned. Sechenov identified reflexes as innate or learned. Learning itself is a process of association. It is implied that contiguity is the most important principle, but that learning is not the primary subject of investigation. Thinking, Sechenov held, was an inhibited reflex. In thinking there is the receptive phase of the reflex, and its transmission; but the end of the reflex, expressed in movement, is absent. In all of this, as Pavlov remarked, Sechenov was developing a theoretical outline.[8] It was Pavlov who took the giant step of submitting his contentions to experimental study.

PAVLOV

Ivan Petrovich Pavlov, the son of a village priest, was born in Russia in 1849, and received his early education in a local seminary.[9] In 1870 he entered the natural history section of the University of St. Petersburg; his specialty was physiology. After obtaining his degree in 1875, he enrolled as an advanced student in the medical school, not with any thought of a career as a practicing physician, but as further preparation for a research post in physiology. His academic success was such that on completion of his thesis, he won a scholarship to Germany, where he worked with prominent physiologists for two years. Nevertheless, it was not until 1890 that he was made professor of pharmacology (later physiology) at the St.

Petersburg Military Medical Academy and head of the physiology department of the Institute of Experimental Medicine. For many years he devoted his research to the processes of digestion. In fact, half of his career was taken up with work on digestion, for which he received the Nobel Prize in 1904. Only after the age of fifty did he study what became known as conditioning. This study covered a span of another thirty years.

The specific impetus for the study of conditioning was a phase of his work on the digestive glands. Using the dog as the experimental animal, Pavlov's general method was a surgical arrangement so that digestive secretions flowed to the surface of the body for collection and measurement. One aspect of his work was the functioning of saliva in digestion. By operation, a salivary duct could be diverted so that the saliva stimulated by meat in the mouth of the dog flowed through a fistula to the outside of the body where it was collected. Prior to 1900, and before working with the conditioned response, he had noticed that a dog secreted saliva before the meat was given him. Further observation showed that this occurred not only when the dog saw the meat, but also when it heard the footsteps of the attendant.

The secretory reflex with the innate response of salivation to food on the tongue had now become "conditioned" to the sight of the food or the sound of the footsteps of the attendant. Pavlov realized that this happened because this sight or sound had been so often associated with the ingestion of food. This is association by frequency of contiguity, as it would be called in associationistic terms. The term "conditioned reflex" was first applied to this phenomenon in 1901.[10]

Pavlov wondered whether he should follow up this new lead into an area that many physiologists would view with disdain, since it was psychic in nature. Some leading physiologists, in point of fact, on hearing of his dilemma, advised him against embarking on the work. On the other hand, he had the example of Sechenov before him. After a long struggle with himself, he resolved to go ahead and to make it a physiological problem by maintaining the role of the external observer with no consideration of introspective findings.[11] This was in 1900 or 1901.

He absorbed himself in his new task. The basic procedures, with the exception of the selection of the stimulus to bring on salivary flow, had already been standardized through his work on digestion. His already extensive laboratory resources were directed to this new problem. When the Soviet government came to power, his research faculties were expanded. An increasing number of associates and assistants joined him. This collaborative effort was an example of coordination of research involving more researchers and extending over more years than anything since Wundt. Over the years, some two hundred collaborators worked with him on problems in conditioning.[12]

The basic model for Pavlov's work was the presentation of two kinds of stimuli: one that was "appropriate," "biologically adequate," or "unconditioned;" another that was "psychic," "conditioned," or "learned."[13] Each reflex has an appropriate (unconditioned) stimulus that brings it on. If the patellar tendon is struck, the knee jerks; if food is placed on the tongue, saliva flows; if the finger is pricked, it is jerked back. In his studies, Pavlov tended to depend on the food powder leading to the salivary response, though other forms were also used. When a response such as salivation becomes attached to a stimulus that formerly did not arouse it, it is said to be conditioned.

Practically any stimulus, Pavlov found, can act as a conditioning stimulus to produce a conditioned response. The salivation to the sight of the food or the sound of the footsteps of the attendant are stimuli for conditioned responses. Sight of food or the sound of footsteps had come to serve as signals, and they now brought about a response formerly elicited by food in contact with the tongue.

Pavlov originally referred to "psychic reflexes," that is, reflexes aroused not by the adequate stimulus of meat in contact with the tongue but by some other form of stimulation that had been presented along with the meat. He almost immediately dropped this term in favor of conditioned responses. Over the years, Pavlov preferred to use as conditioned stimuli the sound of a tuning fork, a bell, and a light flash. These were the stimuli that acquired a new reaction, namely a flow of saliva.

A specific instance might be given. A hungry dog would be led into the experimental room and placed in a restraining harness (to which he was already accustomed). After a few minutes a metronome would tick for thirty seconds, and then food powder would be mechanically introduced into the dog's mouth. Saliva would begin to flow. Every fifteen minutes the same sequence—thirty seconds ticking, then food introduced—would follow. Before many repetitions, saliva would begin to flow while the metronome was ticking and *before* the food was introduced. A conditioned response had been established. A previously inadequate stimulus (inadequate, that is, to produce saliva) would now produce a response formerly elicited only by the adequate stimulus of food powder.

In addition to the study of their formation, conditioned responses were open to all sorts of other quantitative manipulation. Among other phenomena studied by Pavlov are what have been called extinction, reinforcement, spontaneous recovery, generalization and discrimina-

Other important topics

tion, and higher order conditioning.[14] "Extinction" has been studied in the following fashion. After the conditioned response has been formed, the stimulus—the bell, for example—is continued on the trials that follow, but the natural or adequate stimulus of meat powder is no longer introduced. The result is that the conditioned stimulus loses its capacity to elicit the conditioned response. When the adequate stimulus for the conditioned response is not given, it is said to be nonreinforced. Generally speaking, repetition without reinforcement through the meat powder results in a decrease of the amount of salivation from trial to trial until it ceases, that is, shows extinction. Unless periodically reinforced, a conditioned response extinguishes. The extinction may not be permanent, however. After a rest, the application of the conditioned stimulus may again produce a flow of saliva. This is an instance of so-called spontaneous recovery.

Pavlov and his collaborators also conducted experiments on generalization and discrimination. When a stimulus different from the one to which conditioning has already been developed is introduced and produces the conditioned response, generalization has occurred. A "spread" or generalization has taken place. Suppose a sound of a particular pitch has been used to begin to form a conditioned response. Now a sound of somewhat lower or higher pitch is substituted. The conditioned secretion occurs as it did to the original pitch. This is generalization. With continued training, however, the conditioned reflex acquires a certain degree of specificity; that is, it can no longer be elicited by stimuli that differ too greatly from the training stimulus. This is discrimination. This degree of discrimination is obtained without particular effort. This procedure, which consists merely of continuing to present the same stimuli while occasionally interposing stimuli of a different pitch in order to see if it will elicit the response, still leaves a relatively wide band of pitch differences that the dog will treat as the same by salivating when they are presented.

The degree of generalization remaining can be cut still further by training of a specific kind. The task now is to test the limits of the dog's discriminability, that is, to refine still further his discrimination to the point where, despite an actual difference in pitch, no difference can be detected in the dog's behavior. This training in discrimination is done by differential reinforcement; one pitch serves to lead to food, another slightly different pitch does not lead to food. Perhaps food is not presented to the dog after a pitch of 825 vibrations per second, but it is presented after a pitch of 812 vibrations. The dog, after repeated trials, will discriminate between the two pitches by salivating to the latter and not to the former. The pitches selected for illustration are the limits of discrimination for this particular dog, because trying to train him to a pitch difference of less than thirteen vibrations per second (825 minus 812) led to failure to learn. In this connection, Pavlov discovered that some dogs, pushed beyond their limits of discrimination, break down, lose whatever discriminatory ability they have already gained, and become agitated. This opened up still another facet of research, that of the study of experimental neuroses, in which a dog was found to show a variety of forms of abnormal behavior by being driven beyond his capacities.

An already established conditioned response may be treated as if it were unconditioned in order to bring about still further or so-called higher-order conditioning. Suppose a dog has been conditioned to the sound of the tuning fork vibrating at a certain rate paired with the meat powder so that it evokes salivation. The sound of the tuning fork (without the meat powder) is now paired with a sight of a black square, which prior to the experiment produced no secretory response. After paired stimulation of sound and square, the black square will now produce salivation. (Of course, if this were kept up too long, without reinforcement, extinction would occur.) This is second order conditioning. Pavlov also found it possible to go on to third order conditioning, but not beyond it.

Pavlov considered conditioning a cortical, not a subcortical affair like a reflex. As his findings accumulated, Pavlov worked through a theory of cortical excitation and inhibition to account for his results in purely physiological terms. Though his method was seized on avidly, his theory has received relatively little attention outside the Soviet Union, so no attempt will be made to present its details.

It will be remembered that following Sechenov, Pavlov saw this work as a problem in physiology, not psychology. He hardly wavered in his view. It colored his attitude toward what the world called psychology, which can only be described as one of pessimistic skepticism. He believed that psychology could never be an independent science and that its position was "completely hopeless."[15] He believed he had completely excluded it from his own work.[16] Pavlov wished everyone in his laboratory to use physiological terms exclusively; a worker was fined if he used psychological terminology.[17]

Pavlov's attitude toward the Soviet regime was complicated and cannot be adequately summarized in a couple of sentences. For many years he was outspokenly blunt and critical and was once called in by the secret police.[18] On the other hand, he received generous government support for his research, and there is no suggestion of any pressure being put upon him to carry on work along lines selected by the government.

His work was always of his own choosing. Pressure on those who came after him is a different matter.

In 1935 Pavlov gave voice to a changed attitude. In a speech before the Fifteenth International Congress of Physiologists, he spoke of the very favorable position that science occupied in his country and said that as an experimenter himself, he saw his country as an experimenter of an "incomparably higher category."[19] Babkin, a coworker who left the USSR for Canada, believes his change of heart came about due not only to the support of science by the USSR buy also to the fact that he was very much alive to the threat of Hitler, having expressed forebodings on several occasions before this date.

He died in 1936.

BEKHTEREV   *Reflexology*

Something must also be said about the physiologist, V. M. Bekhterev (1857–1927), a countryman, a contemporary, and a rival of Pavlov in the opening years of the century.[20] Independently of Pavlov, he also became interested in the study of conditioning. He, too, worked at the St. Petersburg Military Medical Academy, from which he was graduated. After studying abroad, and after holding a chair in psychiatry at the University of Kazan, he returned to a chair in mental and nervous disorders at the Military Medical Academy, where he later had his own research institute. Bekhterev studied conditioning or as he called it, associative reflexes, through the study of muscular or motor responses.

By motor responses, Bekhterev meant such processes as retracting the finger from an electric shock. The associative reflexes were not the result of any mental process, but they remained reflexes. He became convinced that more complex behaviors could be explained in a similar manner. Habits were seen as the compounding of motor reflexes, and even the thought processes were essentially activities of the speech musculature.

He expressed his convictions in a book, *Objective Psychology,* which appeared in Russian in 1907, was translated into German and French in 1913, and into English in 1932, under the title, *General Principles of Human Reflexology.*[21] The change of title reflected the shift of his point of view. At first he had called his work *Objective Psychology* but later preferred *Reflexology.* It was a plea for a psychology based upon the tools and concepts of physiology with no appeal to subjective processes. Psychology expressed in a study of states of consciousness was simply ignored. Objective study would be sufficient for a complete account of man's behavior.

Thorndike, Behavioral Studies and Functionalism

Another of the sources of behaviorism was animal psychology as studied in the United States. There were also currents in psychology in the United States contemporaneous with Watson that had influenced him, despite his expressed opposition to the views. This was the case with the approaches of Edward L. Thorndike and Jacques Loeb.

Edward Lee Thorndike has already been mentioned as a student of James and as one of the psychologists at Columbia University with Cattell.[22] While at Harvard, he had started research with chickens and, lacking more suitable quarters, took advantage of James's generosity and used the basement of his home as a laboratory. When offered a fellowship at Columbia by Cattell, he took it and continued his work with chickens, "the most educated" pair accompanying him in a basket from Cambridge to New York.

Along with two psychologists at Clark University, Thorndike deserves credit for introducing the modern laboratory type of experiment into animal psychology. Pavlov himself acknowledged that the researches in 1898 of E. L. Thorndike were the first experiments in this general research area, but he added that when he began his own work he was unfamiliar with them.[23]

Thorndike's study of the behavior of kittens in a puzzle box is classic.[24] A series of these boxes, open-slatted affairs, had each a different "combination" that, when learned, allowed the hungry kitten to escape from the box and to secure food placed outside it. The learning tasks for a kitten involved strings to pull, buttons to turn, and levers to press. At first, the kitten's behavior showed excessive activity, clawing all over the box and trying to squeeze through the bars. In this struggle the kitten happened to claw the string or button, and the door opened. In other words, the kitten carried on very actively and randomly until the successful act was hit upon. On repeated trials, gradually, the erroneous, unsuccessful acts were dropped, one by one. Ultimately, when the kitten was placed in the puzzle box, he would immediately claw the appropriate button or string and escape from the box.

This process of learning Thorndike came to call trial and error learning. As the trials succeeded one another, both the number of errors and the time taken to escape decreased. The learning, as expressed in decrease of errors and time, was gradual. He interpreted the results to mean that practice stamps in correct responses and stamps out incorrect ones.

As a result of his studies, Thorndike formulated two fundamental *[handwritten margin notes: "law 1) effect 2) Exercise a) use b) disuse"]*

laws of learning: 1) the law of effect, in which it is stated that any act in a given situation producing satisfaction becomes associated with that situation, so that when the situation recurs, that act is also more likely to recur, and 2) the law of exercise in two complementary parts, the laws of use and of disuse.[25] The law of use says in substance that there is a strengthening of connections with practice; the law of disuse, that there is a weakening of connections when practice is discontinued. Research he conducted[26] many years later convinced him that sheer repetition was unimportant and that reward was much more effective than punishment. The law of exercise is a direct descendant of the old law of association, not association of ideas, to be sure, but rather a connection between stimulus and response. The law of effect is of more dubious parentage, but it is at least partially related to the pleasure-pain or hedonistic principle. Here again, is an objective approach in that functioning has been inferred from behavior. Thorndike did not hold that psychology could dispense with consciousness, but he did hope that much of psychology could be objectified.

Thorndike was not alone in the United States in performing pioneer contentually objective research studies with animals. Robert M. Yerkes (1876–1956), under Thorndike's influence, went down the phyletic scale to study learning and intelligence in the turtle in a setting more a maze than a puzzle box.[27] A Clark University student, Willard S. Small (1870–1943), studied learning using rats and a miniature of the Hampton Court maze and firmly established both the maze as a method and the rat as an experimental animal.[28]

[handwritten margin notes: "Willard S. Small", "Maze"]

Jacques Loeb (1859–1924), the physiologist and one of Watson's teachers, must have had some influence on him, although Watson makes little mention of him (and that disparaging), presumably because of Loeb's failure to reject completely an appeal to the psychic processes. Loeb had revolted against anthropomorphism and sentimentality in interpreting animal activity, but he did not reject consciousness, which he thought to be associative memory or the capacity of the animal to learn from experience.[29] Loeb had announced his theory of tropisms in 1890 and thereafter embarked on mechanistically oriented studies of simple organisms and plants. The classical or narrower theory of tropism conceives of animal behavior as nothing more than a forced movement of a physical-chemical nature. In more general fashion, the theory of tropism has to do with the orientation of the organism in a field of force. According to this view, recourse to such terms as sensation or pleasure is not necessary.

[handwritten margin note: "tropism"]

Though Watson rejected functionalism as a school, he was at the

University of Chicago during its formative years; its emphasis upon activity became part of his heritage. From his point of view he had just as much a quarrel with functionalism as with structuralism. From the present perspective his disagreement with the functionalists was on the grounds that they insisted mental processes were an integral part of psychology. From his point of view they wished merely to study the biological significance of conscious processes rather than to analyze conscious states as did the structuralists,[30] and he found the distinction "unintelligible."[31] In this connection, a case can be made that a good bit of functionalism's conservatism was no more than lip service to the old tradition of psychology as the science of the mind.[32] Much as Watson claimed to reject functionalism, his views shared a fundamental similarity with it; he too stressed function and demanded a larger scope of application for psychology.

During these years there were also other general trends toward contentual objectivity with which Watson was presumably familiar. For example, Cattell in 1904 was so far removed from introspection that he claimed most of the research done in his laboratory "is nearly as independent of introspection as work in physics or in zoology."[33] Cattell cited studies in which no introspective report was asked; for example, studies of reaction time, accuracy of perception, color preference, fatigue, animal and child behavior studies. At about the same time, certain psychologists were even defining psychology as the study of behavior; witness McDougall in 1905[34] and again in 1923[35] and Pillsbury[36] in 1911. Neither one, however, would exclude introspective data from the field of psychology. This was the step taken most effectively by John B. Watson. Others, working in the same climate of opinion but independently of Watson, also presented general behavioristic statements, excluding mind and consciousness from psychology. There was Max Meyer (1873–1967), whose book, first published in 1921, bore the apt title *The Psychology of the Other-One.*[37] Four years later, Albert P. Weiss (1879–1931), who dedicated his book to Meyer, published *A Theoretical Basis of Human Behavior.*[38] These were both statements that in many ways were more erudite and sophisticated than Watson's. But neither one had anywhere near Watson's impact upon psychology.

John B. Watson

John Broadus Watson was born in 1878 on a farm near Greenville, South Carolina.[39] At first he attended rural schools; but when he was twelve, the family moved into Greenville, where Watson attended public schools. According to his own account, he was lazy and insubordinate and never made more than passing grades. Nevertheless, as a sixteen-year-old sub-freshmen, he entered Furman University in his hometown. Its prescribed curriculum of Latin, Greek, mathematics, and philosophy (including psychology) was more characteristic of colleges in the United States before the 1880s than in his own day, except that Watson had some work in chemistry. Here he remained through 1900, leaving with a master's degree.

Being more interested in philosophy than in psychology, and knowing of the fame of John Dewey, Watson enrolled as a graduate student at the University of Chicago. He found Dewey "incomprehensible" and almost immediately lost enthusiasm for philosophy. He continued to minor in the subject however, and took a considerable number of philosophy courses; but, as he himself commented, philosophy somehow did not take hold. In these years the department of philosophy included the courses in psychology, and it was James R. Angell, the functionalist, who awakened his interest in psychology as a career. A second minor, one in neurology, eventuated from his work in the neurological laboratory of H. H. Donaldson, where he made the acquaintance of the white rat. He also took biology and physiology under Jacques Loeb, who wanted Watson to do his dissertation with him. Angell and Donaldson did not consider Loeb quite "safe," so he worked with the two of them instead. His doctoral dissertation used both neurological and behavioral techniques in the study of the correlation of the behavior and the growth of medullation in the central nervous system of the white rat. It was to Angell and Donaldson that he dedicated his first book. In his opinion, these two and Loeb were his most influential teachers.

In the fall of 1903, his degree year, he had a breakdown, with anxiety attacks, inability to sleep without the light on, and comparable symptoms. After a few weeks of enforced rest, he was back to work. In retrospect he saw his breakdown as a valuable experience because it taught him his own limits.

Watson had worked his way through graduate school as rat caretaker, assistant janitor, and fraternity house waiter. On receiving his degree he was offered an assistantship to work with Angell. This he did for a year and then was made an instructor. As others before him had done, he promptly married.

While he taught the usual kind of Jamesian psychology in the classroom at Chicago, his major interest was in the studies he was conducting in the animal laboratory he had constructed in the basement. Familiarity with Lloyd Morgan's work first stimulated his researches in animal psychology; so also, and even more directly, did the work of Thorndike.[40] At this time he was not aware of the work of either Pavlov or ·Bekhterev. Watson was a hard worker and produced a considerable number of studies with the white rat, the monkey, and the tern before he left Chicago in 1908.

He was scheduled to become an assistant professor that year; Johns Hopkins University in Baltimore, however, offered him a full professorship in experimental and comparative psychology and the directorship of the laboratory as well. The advance in rank, a substantial increase in salary, and freedom to vary his teaching from the traditional pattern left him with no choice but to go to Baltimore. During the period between 1908 and 1920, while at Johns Hopkins University, Watson did his most important work. Founding an animal laboratory at Johns Hopkins was one of his first considerations. Several years of research, organization, and writing followed.

In 1913, there appeared the article that was the manifesto of behaviorism. Before it saw print, there had been several preliminary steps. Actually, Watson said, it was in 1903 that he first broached a behavioristic psychology, presumably in conversation with a colleague at the University of Chicago.[41] He goes on to say that he was told it might work with animals, but not with humans. Public expression of his views first occurred in 1908 at a colloquium at Yale University. Four years later, at Columbia at the invitation of Cattell, Watson gave a series of lectures that included the contents of the crucial article.

In 1914, in his book, *Behavior: An Introduction to Comparative Psychology,* he marshalled the available evidence to demonstrate the right of animal psychology to be considered a major specialty.[42] This was an important consideration for Watson. Indeed he admitted in his earliest statement of behaviorism that part of his motivation for a new psychology was embarrassment about the skepticism he met concerning the value and relevance of animal research to psychology.[43] Animal research contributed very little of value to psychology as long as the latter was considered a study of human experience. What Watson wished to combat is represented by the attitude held by Titchener. In allowing for an animal psychology, Titchener had had to appeal somewhat lamely to an analogy.[44] Since an animal shows movements similar to those of a man in similar circumstances, it is possible to reconstruct the animal's consciousness as essentially similar to that of man under these same circumstances. The observations are then cautiously to be interpreted in terms of human consciousness.

The attention actually paid to this translation into mentalistic terms was not necessarily more than perfunctory, but it was done. Even Watson's first publication bore the subtitle, "the psychical development of the white rat." He began to object strenuously to this attitude. Watson went so far as to call interpreting animal behavior in terms of the information it gives about conscious states, "absurd."[45]

Behavior brought out forcefully the advantages of using animals as sources for psychological material.[46] As subjects, animals offer the experimenter the advantage of achieving much more complete control of experimental conditions. Careful control of environmental conditions, such as rest, diet, activity, living conditions, even extending over its entire previous life span, is quite feasible. Known hereditary strains of rats can be studied. Moreover, it is possible to follow procedures too drastic to use with humans.

The manifesto of 1913 lacked a major positive characteristic of Watsonian behaviorism—emphasis on the conditioned response as the methodological tool *par excellence*. Watson had found the German and French translations of Bekhterev and was familiar with the salivary conditioned response studies of Pavlov. So rapidly did he assimilate this material into his approach that he used the theme of the place in psychology of the conditioned reflex (with particular emphasis on the value of Bekhterev's motor reflex) for his presidential address before the American Psychological Association in 1915.[47] At this time he was still under forty years of age.

In 1918, through the facilities of the Phipps Clinic in Baltimore Watson extended his researches to young children. Very little experimental work on human infants had been conducted prior to that of Watson and his coworkers. Baby biographies had been maintained, questionnaires used, and tests developed, but the deliberate manipulative introduction of forms of stimulation demanded by experimental study had hardly been attempted.

Setting aside conditioning for later discussion, Watson's methods of studying hand preference merit mention as illustrative of the other research techniques he used.[48] It is well known that the great majority of adults are right handed. Whether or not this is an instinctive response is the question Watson set out to answer, applying to young infants a variety of ingenious techniques. He measured the anatomical structure of the arm; the time that the infant would hang suspended from a bar by right and by left hand; and the total amount of work done with each hand by an infant. The latter was measured by attaching "work adders" (wheels that turn in one direction when there is movement) to both hands; when the child slashed about with his hands the wheel revolved, pulling up the cord to which a small weight was attached. After reaching toward an object was established in the infant's behavior repertoire, Watson noted the particular hand extended to secure a peppermint stick. The overall evidence tended to show little or no favoring of the right hand over the left hand. He therefore concluded the right-handedness was not instinctive but a matter of social pressure—a form of conditioning.

Psychology from the Standpoint of a Behaviorist, Watson's work, appeared in 1919, was revised in 1924, and revised again in 1929.[49] It was essentially an attempt to extend the methods and principles of animal psychology into the human sphere. The value of conditioning as a method of study was extolled.

In 1920, Watson's academic career came to an abrupt end. Divorce proceedings had been instituted against him, sensational publicity was the result, and he was asked to resign from the faculty of Johns Hopkins. In the same year, he married Rosalie Raynor, with whom he had carried on a research collaboration in the study of infants. Although he knew nothing of the world of business, he made contacts that in 1921 resulted in his affiliation with the New York City advertising agency of J. Walter Thompson. To learn something of the business world, Watson made a house-to-house canvass to find what rubber boots were being worn, sold coffee, clerked in Macy's, and went through every department of the advertising agency. He must have been successful, for he was advanced to vice-president in 1924. He remained with this company until 1936 when he went with William Esty and Company.

He continued contact with psychology by writing popular articles for *McCall's, Harper's,* and *Collier's* magazines. His book, *Psychological Care of the Infant and Child,* published in 1928, was meant for general reading.[50] It was almost inevitable that he would write this book. He had a deep-seated enthusiasm for the practical value of psychology in controlling behavior and his environmentalist position demanded that infancy be seen as an extremely important formative period, for good or for ill. Illustrative of its contents is the question of whether or not children should live in individual homes or even know their parents, since it was these parents who were the major source for faulty conditioning. The avoidance of creating fears by adverse conditioning, the dangers of too much stroking, and the pernicious effect of the hampering of movements are illustrative of the advice he would give parents. In the terminology of a later time, Watson very strongly aligned himself with the regulatory rather than the permissive school of child rearing.

In articles and books, he carried on polemics for behaviorism, including a famous extended argument with William McDougall (1871–

1938).[51] McDougall was a British psychologist who had come to Harvard University in 1920 and from there went on to Duke University. While still in England, he had made notable contributions, particularly in social psychology, but almost from the moment he arrived in the United States, he found himself engaged in a series of controversies. This was unfortunate, but the reason for it is not hard to understand. He was an unyielding supporter of unpopular causes—freedom of the will, psychic research, the inheritance of acquired characters, and Nordic superiority—among others. Opinions contrary to those of the majority of psychologists brought him into conflict with Watson. McDougall is best known through his vigorous espousal of an instinct theory of considerable scope and complexity and for his fervent opposition to a mechanistic interpretation of the behavior and experience of man. Watson issued a sweeping denial of the existence of any instincts whatever in man and became an enthusiastic and rather naïve mechanist. On these issues the battle was joined. When it was over, neither had changed his opinion; each remained convinced of his essential correctness. Later events have shown Watson had the best of the argument.

While in New York City, Watson secured a grant for research on the human infant, and the work was carried out by a research associate. For a time, he lectured at the New School for Social Research. These lectures are the basis for his book *Behaviorism,* a statement of his view in a form suitable for popular reading.[52] In retrospect, Watson conceded that the book was too hastily prepared. The revision of this book in 1930 marked his complete departure from psychology. After that date Watson occupied himself exclusively with work in the business world until his retirement in 1946. He died in 1958.

Characteristic Interpretations of Psychological Problems

In his zeal to remake psychology, Watson attempted to apply the behavioristic approach to a variety of psychological problems. Characteristic are his interpretations of instinct, emotion, thinking, learning and conditioning, and personality. In their study he was guided by the concept of stimulus-response and would limit their study to psychological methods considered acceptable for research.

BEHAVIORISM AND STIMULUS-RESPONSE

Psychology is concerned with the behavior of the whole organism. Physiology, its closest neighbor among the other sciences, is concerned with the functioning of the parts of the body, the organ systems, circulation, digestion, and the like.[53] To reduce behavior to its simplest terms, it is found that the acts of human behavior always involve a stimulus that brings about a particular response. This stimulus is provided by something in the environment, by movements of the muscles, or by glandular secretions. The response follows upon the incidence of the stimulus. If these assumptions are accepted, it follows that the task of psychology is to study the laws of behavior; thus, when given the stimulus, one may learn to predict the response, or, given the response, one may isolate the effective stimulus. In terms of a formula, psychology was the science of S-R, where S refers to stimulus and R refers to response. If the stimuli are of a complex character, it is appropriate to speak of the stimulus situation, which is ultimately resolvable into its component parts. Actually, except in the rarest of instances, we are dealing with situations, not with an isolated stimulus. Likewise, responses involve not only the simple responses that are also studied in physiology, such as the knee jerk or eye blink, but also more complex responses, to which the term "act" may be applied. Usually, what is meant by action is that the organism responds by some movement in space, as in walking, talking, fighting, or eating. Nevertheless, these actions reduce to two forms—motor and glandular responses. Responses may be overt, that is, observable; or they may be explicit or nonovert, that is, nonobservable or implicit. A man may show responses while standing apparently immobile; precise measurement would nevertheless show that muscular and glandular changes were taking place.

Responses, besides being either implicit or overt, are either learned or unlearned. Specification of the extent and nature of both the unlearned and learned responses is necessary. So, too, is the discovery of the laws of acquisition of the learned responses.

Stimulus-response units are, by an extension of their meaning in physiology, called reflexes. They are not to be analysed by the psychologist as minutely as they are by the physiologist. Watson did devote attention to the structures that make behavior possible, but he left to the physiologist the tasks of providing a detailed analysis and unraveling whatever organization takes place within the central nervous system. Brain processes, as such, did not particularly interest him, because of the inaccessability of the brain, that "mystery box," as he called it.[54] Moreover, the brain had been used by earlier psychologists as the repository for whatever they could not explain in mentalistic terms. Behavior involves the whole body, not the nervous system alone, but the muscles and glands as well. Watson's interest was in somewhat larger segments of behavior: what an individual would do in a given situation;

for example, with what hand the infant would reach for the peppermint stick or what his response would be to a loud noise.

While behavior of the whole organism might have been his announced goal, it is now apparent that his approach, problem by problem, was still molecular in character, that is, he was guided by a belief that his behavioral data was to be described in terms of relatively small units. He did not operate at the extreme lower level that he insisted the physiologist did, but used their units in larger assemblages. This will become even more obvious when his conception of personality is presented (p. 460).

PSYCHOLOGICAL METHODS

Methodological objectivism was sought. Watson explicitly states that methods used by the psychologists are: 1) observation, with and without the aid of instruments; 2) the conditioned reflex methods, both secretory and motor; 3) testing; and 4) the verbal report method.[55] Observation is, of course, fundamental and the basis for all other methods. How Watson would use it has been illustrated in his studies of handedness. The conditioned-reflex method is described in a later section. The test methods included use both those instruments already extant and new ones developed, but their results have been treated as behavior samples to ascertain general level of behavior and special abilities. Incidentally, intelligence as measured by tests is nothing more than the capability to form new habits according to Watson.

The verbal report method merits special attention. Speech reactions are observable and therefore open to use by behaviorists. An illustration is the study of the response to warm and cold by a given skin area. The observer must tell when a warm cylinder or a cold cylinder is applied. He responds with the words "cold" or "warm." Sensation, as such, is rejected by Watson because we cannot observe the sensation of another person, but we can observe his verbal report. This response is overt and is recorded as the results of the experiment, just as if conditioning trials had been used. Verbal report, he admitted, is a relatively inexact method, however, which should be discarded as soon as possible. Unfortunately, it is the only one available for some problems.

Some would say this admission of verbal report into behavioristic psychology by Watson simultaneously with his rejection of sensation is nothing more than verbal quibbling. Sensation as experience is not acceptable, but an auditory response heard as a word is permissible. Whether recourse to verbal report was anything more than banishing introspection by the front door, to allow it to return by the back, was hotly debated by Watson's contemporaries. It is evident that he was particularly vulnerable to this criticism. In defense of Watson, although he does not say so explicitly, it is evident he would rule out unverifiable verbal reports as would arise from investigations of so-called imageless thoughts. He did not qualify his statements carefully enough in this regard. He indicated that he would severely limit the use of verbal report but failed to specify how he would do so.

INSTINCT

Watson's views about instincts passed through three stages. He started from a more or less conventional acceptance and ended with a sweeping denial of their existence in humans. In his 1914 book on animal psychology, he devoted a considerable number of pages to discussing instinct, noting, however, that it was a much abused word.[56] Nevertheless, he used it, characterizing it as a series of joined reflexes that unfold as heredity dictates. By 1919, in his *Psychology from the Standpoint of a Behaviorist,* he argued that unlearned behavior can be seen only in young infants because this behavior is quickly overlain by habits.[57] His position at this time was that, if we study infants, we can tease out the processes by which the complex learned behavior patterns, loosely called instincts, have developed.

In his *Behaviorism* of 1925 he flatly rejected the concept of instinct for man.[58] As evidence for his denial of instinct, he offers a catalogue of the reflex behavior repertoire of the human infant, such as sneezing, crying, smiling, turning the head, arm movements, feeding responses, crawling, walking, and handedness. Because of slight structural differences among infants, there are equally slight but significant differences in how these reflexes are performed. Given the individual differences and the capacity for rapid habit formation, we have the basis for what has erroneously been called inherited characteristics.

In showing how habit formation works, Watson considered handedness, which he had studied by the methods outlined earlier. Watson suggests that a dominance present at birth might be due to long-maintained intrauterine position, which makes it essentially a habit either of right- or of left-handedness learned before birth. Most infants show no hand dominance at birth; as he had demonstrated, they use both hands interchangeably. Watson argued that social pressure steps in to establish handedness, through such means as training to shake hands, to wave "bye-bye," and to eat in the customary fashion. Handedness is not an instinct; it is a socially conditioned response.

Not only did Watson claim there were no instincts, he went further and said there were no inherited capacities, temperaments, or talents. In so doing, Watson was taking an extreme environmentalist position. Such was his insistence upon the plasticity of human nature that he wrote:

> Give me a dozen healthy infants, well-formed, and my own specified world to bring them up in and I'll guarantee to take any one at random and train him to become any type of specialist I might select—doctor, lawyer, artist, merchant-chief and, yes, even beggar-man and thief, regardless of his talents, penchants, tendencies, abilities, vocations, and race of his ancestors.[59]

Actually, this extreme environmentalism is not characteristic of the behavioristic emphasis on objective content and methodology and rejection of introspection. Although Watson's stand on instincts was part of his system, it did not follow that it was an integral part of behaviorism. One could be a behaviorist and still reject his interpretation of environmental effect.

EMOTION

To Watson, emotions are not matters of experienced states, but bodily reactions to specific stimuli.[60] The presence of danger as a stimulus causes visceral changes and overt responses. For Watson, there is no appeal to the perception of danger or to the sensory experiences from the internal organs. Nevertheless, emotion involves implicit behavior in these visceral changes, but these changes are, to some extent, overt or visible; this is shown in his study of infants that we will discuss. It is these visceral responses of involuntary muscles and glands that distinguish emotions from other bodily reactions.

Watson was just as emphatic in denying the inheritance of complicated emotional patterns as he was in denying the inheritance of instincts. He gathered his evidence of the stimuli and the responses in emotion from children observed over long periods, some from birth, living in hospitals or in homes that were often visited.

One of his tests of fear was a measurement of the reactions to an animal introduced into the laboratory room with the infant. A friendly, purring cat and a rabbit always produced reaching-out and touching by these infants. Dogs and white rats, while not producing as much in the way of positive responses, provoked no fear. Watson considered these results to be conclusive evidence that the alleged hereditary or instinctive fear responses to furry objects were unfounded.

His most famous study was the search for the stimuli that produce emotional responses. Consonant with his methodological tenets, he not only paid attention to the stimuli, but he also described objectively the responses that the stimuli brought forth. He stimulated each infant in a variety of ways and narrowed down those eliciting emotional responses to a small number. Watson believed he had found evidence for only three emotions in infants—fear, rage, and love. Fear was produced only by a loud noise (made by striking a steel bar with a hammer) and by loss of support (carried out by allowing the child to drop a few inches, or by jerking his blanket). Other situations, such as the presence of furry objects mentioned earlier, or the dark, or a snake, or the thousand and one things of which children are supposedly afraid simply did not at this young age produce fear responses. Watson described the responses of fear as involving startle, a catching of breath followed by rapid breathing, changes in skin color, hand-clutching, puckering of lips and crying, and, if the child was old enough, crawling, walking, or running away.

The only stimulus for rage that Watson found from a wide variety of stimuli was hampering or restricting the infant's movements in one fashion or another, such as holding his head firmly or restraining his movements. The behavior exhibited in response to this stimulus was described as stiffening of the body, holding the breath, and slashing movements of arms and legs.

Love, not as fully investigated as the other two emotions because of the restrictions of convention, was produced by stroking of the skin, by gentle rocking, and by patting. Smiling, cooing, and gurgling were the responses to this form of stimulation.

These were the only unlearned emotional responses that Watson could find, although more cautiously than he is often pictured, he said that the presence of others must be left in doubt. All other emotional reactions, he concluded, have to some extent a component of learning, largely acquired through conditioning during early childhood. Just as the child acquires his motor skills, walking, skating, or typing, he acquires his fears, his loves, and his hates.

Watson's findings on emotions stimulated considerable research interest in the emotional development of children, including many studies that attempted to refute his contentions. A considerable amount of evidence has been collected that fails to confirm the existence of the specific emotional responses advanced by Watson. In 1927, Mandel Sherman, for example, asked observers to judge the emotion displayed by infants under various conditions.[61] When the stimulating conditions, such as dropping or restraint, were available to them, the judgments they offered followed the Watsonian classification fairly well. For example, seeing the infant lose his support, they labeled the response "fear." But in the second phase of the study, when they were kept in ignorance of the particular stimulations applied, and saw only the responses, there turned out to be little correspondence between the names they gave the emotions and those called for by Watson's theory. A final telling blow to Watson's contentions was delivered when they viewed motion picture film so spliced that the stimulus they saw and the emotional reaction that followed were not related. They tended to label the emotion in terms of what they saw as the stimulating condition. That is to say, first seeing the infant restrained, with the emotion shown by the infant response actually produced by a "fear" stimulus, they judged it to be produced by anger. Rather than clear-cut emotional responses in infants, as Watson claimed, according to contemporary interpretation there is a mass of random movements to any strong stimuli out of which individual emotions emerge as the child grows older.

THINKING

To Watson, the most important kind of implicit sensory-motor behavior occurs when the person stands stock still and, after a lapse of time, comes forth with a solution to some problem, the solution being expressed verbally or by some movement of the body, arms, or legs. The implicit behavior prior to the overt action, of course, would be thinking. To Watson, committed as he was to behavior as his datum, this implicit behavior was genuine and relevant.[62] Thinking, he said, is only subvocal talking or muscular habits learned in overt speech that become inaudible as we grow up. After learning to talk by conditioning, thought is nothing more "than talking to ourselves."[63] A bodily response is a word substitute. A man thinks, that is, he makes implicit verbal reactions that do not differ in spirit from the overt movements made by a rat in running a maze. Thinking, to be sure, is more implicit and more economical of time and effort, but this is a difference only of degree. Attach recording devices to the larynx of the thinker, and we get movement that thus becomes explicit. In a young child who is in the process of learning a language, these quantitative differences in amount of movement are even less great. Often children, and occasionally adults, think aloud. The child will say what he is going to do and then do it. Under the influence of social pressure (conditioning), he learns to give up clear articulation for whispering and finally reaches the stage of inaudible or implicit speech, characteristic of the adult. The most obvious source of evidence Watson could not use, namely, that we are sometimes introspectively aware that we do talk to ourselves while thinking. He could hardly bolster behaviorism with an appeal to introspection![64]

Thought is not merely behavior of the larynx or subvocal talking; it involves the whole body as when we gesture, frown, or nod, or when we carry out any movement that stands for an object or a situation. Watson suggested observing a deaf mute's fingers. During his thinking, muscular movements of the fingers will be found, just as there are movements from the larynx of normal persons. Failure always to get positive results from this method Watson attributed to the lack of delicacy of the instruments available. As a matter of fact, use of improved methods has demonstrated that thinking does involve these peripheral muscular factors, but that central or brain processes have also been shown to be present by later research. The judgment of later generations of psychologists is that Watson's theory of thinking as subvocal speech is too schematic and oversimplified.

LEARNING AND CONDITIONING

Watson's views of learning showed progressive change and expansion. In his 1913 article he conceived of behaviorism as using stimulus-response and habit formation but made no mention of conditioning.[65] By 1916 in his presidential address he enthusiastically endorsed conditioning.[66] In his *Behavior* of 1919 the available research on discriminatory maze and puzzle-box learning was described in detail.[67] He called Thorndike's law of effect "highly figurative."[68] Evidently, he saw conscious feeling lurking somewhere in this way of formulating the animal's responses. Watson would have substituted recency and frequency for the influence of effect. The successful act, over a series of trials, was that most frequently performed and, by its position within a trial, was also the one that occurred most recently. He argued that, after all, the animal takes the correct path at least once every trial, while particular blind alleys are skipped in a given trial; the successful path occurs last and is therefore the most recent.

After 1916, Watson emphasized the importance of conditioning. The conditioned reflex became the heir of associationism. He expressed it in contiguous conditioning or a continuation of stimuli accompanying a movement, so that, when this combination recurred, it tended to be followed by that same movement. Watson emphasized repetition while he rejected effect and, consequently, failed to recognize the importance of reinforcement, a key concept in later conditioning theory.

Watson's application of conditioning principles to learning in general and to thinking and emotion in particular now becomes relevant.

Habits are nothing more than complex conditioned responses, such as those involved in playing tennis, in soling shoes, or in exhibiting maternal reactions to children.[69] These habits are integrations of conditioned responses around an activity built up from the available behavior repertoire, starting with innate movements. Movements combine by conditioning into complex acts. Language habits are merely a special case in that, to some extent, they become implicit.

Conditioning is the basis of speech, and speech is the basis of thinking. This bald summary shows why conditioning is important in thinking. Shortly after birth the infant exhibits vocalizations that, after conditioning, are spoken words. The vocalization of the infant of "da-da" is attached to the person of the father; through further conditioning it becomes "daddy." With stronger verbal habits, the child no longer has to say aloud the conditioned response of, "father," selectively conditioned from the more primitive, "daddy." Thinking it alone now suffices. Other words and thoughts develop in a similar fashion. Subvocal speech, or thinking, has been developed through conditioning.

The child's fears and other emotional reactions beyond those given to unlearned responses are brought about by conditioning. Watson and Rosalie Rayner demonstrated this contention by building up a conditioned fear in the laboratory.[70] Their single subject, one of the most famous in psychological literature and therefore deserving of specific mention, was Albert B., a healthy, eleven-month-old infant, raised in the hospital where his mother was a wet nurse. The only fear reactions that he showed were to loud sounds. His reaction to anything at all coming close enough was to reach out toward it and, if possible, to manipulate it. This included animals, such as the white rat. Presented here is the experiment itself, in synoptic form from their laboratory notes, faithful in spirit, but not precise in all details:

> (Eleven months, 3 days)
> 1. Rat introduced. A reached. Just as hand reached, steel bar struck (not visible to A). A jumped violently, fell forward, but did not cry.
> 2. Again A reached; bar again struck. A jumped violently and whimpered. (One week allowed to lapse so as not to disturb child too seriously.)
>
> (Eleven months, 10 days)
> 1. Rat presented without sound. Steady fixa-

tion, but at first no reaching, then tentative reaching, but withdrawal as rat touched.

2–4. Combined stimulation rat and sound. Started, no crying.

5. Rat alone. Puckered face, whimpered and withdrew.

6–7. Combined stimulation. Started and cried.

8. Rat alone. Turned away, fell over, raised himself and began to crawl away rapidly.

(Eleven months, 15 days)

1. Blocks introduced. Reached readily.

2. Rat alone, whimpered.

3. Rabbit alone. Leaned away, whimpered and then cried.

A conditioned fear had been established. A rat to which Albert had previously shown no fear, now brought forth fear. It can be inferred that such fears could inadvertently build up a home, so that a child is being conditioned when he is in bed in the dark and hears a loud clap of thunder, producing thereafter a fear of the dark.

This study did more than demonstrate a conditioned emotional reaction: the two research workers went beyond this to show that the conditioned fear transferred to other previously nonfeared objects. When the rabbit was introduced, Albert showed fear. Other furry things, a dog, a fur coat, cotton, wool, and a Santa Claus mask were introduced, to which fear responses were now shown.

If conditioning can produce fears, can conditioning also be used to eliminate them? In another, later study "unconditioning" was compared with other methods as to its efficiency in eliminating fear responses.[71] The other methods were: 1) disuse (allowing a period of time to elapse without exposing the child to the fear situation); 2) verbal organization (the fear object not introduced, but talking about it with the child); 3) frequent application (introducing fear object, time after time); 4) social factors (introducing other children into the situation when the child is exposed to the fear object). Their evidence, found in a study conducted by Mary C. Jones, is admittedly incomplete, but they showed, to their satisfaction at least, that the method of unconditioning, to be described, was most effective and most free from side effects.

Prior investigation had shown that the child, Peter, three years old, was afraid of white rats, rabbits, fur, cotton, wool, and fur coats. In view of this similarity with Albert B., it should be asserted that these fears were homegrown, not produced in the laboratory. The setting for uncondition-

Peter
3 yrs old

ing was Peter's midafternoon lunch, given to him in a large room. Just as his crackers and milk were given to Peter, a rabbit in a cage was placed in the room but far enough away as to not disturb him. During his snack the next day, the rabbit was brought closer, still without disturbing him. The same routine of bringing the rabbit closer and closer was followed on succeeding days. Eventually, the rabbit could be placed on the table, and then on Peter's lap, still without producing fear. Tolerance now changed to a positive response, shown by Peter's stroking of the rabbit. He was now tested with the other furry objects that formerly had also produced fear. His fears had either disappeared completely, or a tolerance level had been reached. To Watson, this was convincing preliminary evidence that conditioning could be used for eliminating fears in children.

PERSONALITY

To Watson, with his molecular predispositions, personality was a straightforward summation of activities, neither mysterious nor necessitating concepts other than those used before.[72] All actual and potential reactions, verbal, manual, and visceral, go to make up the personality. Personality is the end product of an individual's habit systems. By habit systems Watson meant general, conveniently large groupings of individual habits that cluster together, constituting a useful way of talking about the various constituents of personality. Habits are formed just as described earlier, but now they are grouped to fit the particular topic. In a particular illustration used by Watson, shoemaking (the man's trade), religious, patriotic, marital, parental, arithmetic, general information, special fear, personal, and recreational habit systems are listed. These, of course, are only a sampling of the habit systems that constitute a personality. In another person, a different classification of habit systems would be used, although some of those listed are of a general character applicable to anyone. Since the cross section is taken at a point in time, later or earlier cross sections would show differences because habits are changeable; no individual's personality remains the same throughout life.

In this changeability of personality lies an opportunity for the betterment of mankind. Behaviorism, Watson believed, should stimulate adults to change themselves and especially to be prepared to bring up their children in a scientific way. Will not they "in turn bring up their children in a still more scientific way, until the world finally becomes a place fit for human habitation?"[73]

Overview

Watson's career as a psychologist lasted hardly two decades, and yet his effect on psychology has been pronounced.[74] As even the brief review of earlier work has shown, he did not originate the view that psychology was contentually objective. What he did was to give psychology a direction by making it a cause and by stressing its value in such a single-minded, massive fashion that he could not be ignored. For many psychologists he was a breath of fresh air, clearing away the musty accumulation of the centuries.

A major source of his appeal was that he held to the methodological imperatives characteristic not only of psychology, but also of science in general. He was methodologically objective, as witness his four "suitable" methods. He was naturalistic to the core in trying to rid psychology of its "goblins and ghosts." He espoused a mechanical model. He searched for general laws and, hence, was nomothetic. He stressed quantitative methods. He had no use for other than empirical methods. It never occurred to him to be other than deterministic in outlook.

His pronounced influence also originated from a source he would have denied—he was a functionalist, not in the superficial sense of accepting conscious experience within the ken of psychology, but in the much more salient sense of emphasizing the adaptiveness of psychological activity. In this way he moved *with*, not against, the other dominant aspect of the psychological scene.

A strong adherence to peripheralism arose from his rejection of mental states and his movement away from dependence upon underlying physiological mechanisms, such as the innate bodily processes of the instincts, first accepted and then later rejected (p. 453). A physiological substratum became irrelevant in his later view of psychology. What occurred in the nervous system was either unknown or irrelevant to the study of stimulus and response. He even referred to the nervous system as a "mystery box"[75] many years before the "black box" became another metaphor with the same connotation.

His appeal to others was widened by his eagerly embracing both utilitarian and puristic aims for psychology.

Quite apart from the nature of his formulations, prescriptive and otherwise, his appeal was enhanced by characteristics he manifested— the youthful optimism, the tough-mindedness, and a trenchant, self-confident style of writing—all of which contributed to his great impact on psychology. Each new problem, for instance, emotion or instinct, when first broached, would be introduced by a sweeping denial of the value of earlier work. As he saw it, the "great mass" of literature on emotion lacked a central scientific viewpoint; James's evidence for his theory of emotion became nothing more than "a bit of introspecting," while McDougall's list of emotions was dismissed because no "objective" methods were used to derive them. After the denial, Watson would then make a new start.

By the same token, these characteristics repelled some, or at least moved them to ridicule and satire. As a case in point, his conditioning studies, such as that of Albert B., convinced him that practical control of infant behavior (and by implication, that of the adult) was possible. No doubt motivated by high social motives, his comments on social control through conditioning left him, however, open to satire. The satirization of the social use of conditioning and other aspects of behaviorism in Aldous Huxley's *Brave New World* comes to mind in this connection.

Limitation of discussion up to this point concerning Watson's own research interests and what he stressed in describing behaviorism gives a limited impression of what he admitted to be within its precincts. Accepted as methodologically objective were those methods concerned with reaction time and business psychology.[76] Personality was to be studied by intelligence, achievement, and motor tests; personality questionnaires; and interview techniques. Moreover, he explicitly denied that applied psychology is of less stature than pure psychology. Workers in the areas of application, since they were accorded complete acceptance, could perhaps enjoy, with a touch of glee, his vigorous attack on their more academic colleagues. For all these reasons, Watson affected psychology profoundly.

Some of the consequences of Watsonian behaviorism will be examined when contemporary psychology in the United States is considered.

References*

1. J. B. Watson, "Psychology as a Behaviorist Views It," *Psychological Review*, XX (1913): 158–177 (Herrnstein and Boring, Excerpt No. 94).
2. *Ibid.*
3. *Ibid.*
4. J. B. Watson, *Behaviorism*, 2nd ed. (New York: W. W. Norton, 1930).
5. I. M. Sechenov, "Refleksy golovnogo mozga," trans. as "Reflexes of the Brain," by A. A. Subkov, in I. M. Sechenov, *Selected Works* (Moscow and Leningrad: Gozmedizdat, 1935), pp. 264–322 (1863) (Herrnstein and Boring, Excerpt No. 63).

*See p. 19 for description of reference style.

6. I. P. Pavlov, *Selected Works*, ed. K. S. Kostoyants, trans. S. Belsky (Moscow: Foreign Languages Publishing House, 1955) (1873–1936).
7. Sechenov, *Selected Works*.
8. Pavlov, *Selected Works*.
9. I. P. Pavlov, "Autobiography," *Selected Works*, pp. 41–44 (undated); B. P. Babkin, *Pavlov, a Biography* (Chicago: University of Chicago Press, 1949).
10. I. P. Pavlov, *Lectures on Conditioned Reflexes*, 3rd ed., trans. W. H. Gantt (New York: International Publishers, 1928) (1904).
11. *Ibid.*
12. I. P. Frolov, *Pavlov and His School* (London: Kegan Paul, Trench, Trubner, 1937).
13. Pavlov, *Selected Works*, pp. 76–80 (Herrnstein and Boring, Excerpt No. 101).
14. *Ibid.*
15. *Lectures*, p. 219.
16. *Ibid.*
17. Frolov, *Pavlov and His School*.
18. Babkin, *Pavlov, a Biography*.
19. *Ibid.*, p. 162.
20. A. L. Schniermann, "Bekhterev's Reflexological School," in C. Murchison, ed., *Psychologies of 1930* (Worcester: Clark University Press, 1930), pp. 221–242.
21. V. M. Bekhterev, *General Principles of Human Reflexology*, trans. 4th Russian ed. (New York: International Publishers, 1932) (1907).
22. E. L. Thorndike, "Edward Lee Thorndike," in C. Murchison, ed., *A History of Psychology in Autobiography* (Worcester: Clark University Press, 1936), III, pp. 263–270; Geraldine M. Joncich, *The Sane Positivist: A Biography of Edward L. Thorndike* (Middletown, Conn.: Wesleyan University Press, 1968).
23. Pavlov, *Lectures on Conditioned Reflexes*.
24. E. L. Thorndike, "Animal Intelligence: an Experimental Study of the Associative Processes in Animals," *Psychological Review Monograph Supplement* II (1898): No. 4. (Herrnstein and Boring, Excerpt No. 97).
25. E. L. Thorndike, *The Elements of Psychology* (New York: Seiler, 1905), p. 203.
26. E. L. Thorndike, *The Fundamentals of Learning* (New

York: Teachers College, 1932); E. L. Thorndike, *The Psychology of Wants, Interests, and Attitudes* (New York: Appleton, 1935).

27. R. M. Yerkes, "The Formation of Habits in the Turtle," *Popular Science Monthly*, LVIII (1901): 519–525 (Herrnstein and Boring, Excerpt No. 98).

28. W. S. Small, "Experimental Study of the Mental Processes of the Rat, II," *American Journal of Psychology*, XII (1901): 206–232 (Herrnstein and Boring, Excerpt No. 99).

29. J. Loeb, *Einleitung in die vergleichende Gehirnphysiologie und vergleichende Psychologie mit besonderer Berücksichtigung dir wirbellosen Thiere* (Leipzig: Barth, 1899) (English trans. 1900) (Herrnstein and Boring, Excerpt No. 89).

30. J. B. Watson, *Behavior: An Introduction to Comparative Psychology* (New York: Henry Holt, 1914), p. 8.

31. *Ibid.*

32. G. Bergmann, "The Contribution of John B. Watson," *Psychological Review*, LXIII (1956): 265–276.

33. J. M. Cattell, "The Conception and Methods of Psychology," *Popular Science Monthly*, LXVI (1904): 175–186.

34. W. McDougall, *Physiological Psychology* (New York: Macmillan, 1905).

35. W. McDougall, *Outline of Psychology* (New York: Scribner's Sons, 1923) (Herrnstein and Boring, Excerpt No. 116).

36. W. B. Pillsbury, *The Essentials of Psychology* (New York: Macmillan, 1911).

37. M. F. Meyer, *Psychology of the Other-one: An Introductory Text-book of Psychology*, 2nd ed., rev. (Columbus: Missouri Book, 1922) (1921).

38. A. P. Weiss, *A Theoretical Basis of Human Behavior* (Columbus: Adams, 1925).

39. J. B. Watson, "John B. Watson," C. Murchison, ed., *A History of Psychology in Autobiography* (Worcester: Clark University Press, 1936): III, 271–281; R. S. Woodworth, "John Broadus Watson: 1878–1958," *American Journal of Psychology*, LXXII (1959): 301–310.

40. J. B. Watson, *Psychology from the Standpoint of a Behaviorist*, 3rd ed. rev. (Philadelphia: Lippincott, 1929), preface.

41. *Ibid.*
42. Watson, *Behavior.*
43. *Psychology as a Behaviorist Views It.*
44. E. B. Titchener, *A Textbook of Psychology* (New York: Macmillan, 1909).
45. Watson, *Behavior,* p. 3.
46. *Ibid.*
47. J. B. Watson, "The Place of the Conditioned-Reflex in Psychology," *Psychological Review,* XXIII (1916): 89–117.
48. Watson, *Behaviorism.*
49. J. B. Watson, *Psychology from the Standpoint of a Behaviorist* (Philadelphia: Lippincott, 1919).
50. J. B. Watson, *Psychological Care of Infant and Child* (New York: Norton, 1928).
51. J. B. Watson and W. McDougall, *The Battle of Behaviorism* (New York: Norton, 1929).
52. Watson, *Behaviorism.*
53. *Ibid,;* Watson, *Psychology,* 1929.
54. Watson, *Beviorism,* p. 49.
55. Watson, *Psychology,* 1929.
56. Watson, *Behavior.*
57. Watson, *Psychology, 1919.*
58. Watson, *Behaviorism.*
59. *Ibid.,* p. 104.
60. *Ibid.*
61. M. Sherman, "The Differentiation of Emotional Responses in Infants," *Journal of Comparative Psychology,* VII (1927), 265–284, 335–351.
62. Watson, *Behaviorism;* Watson, *Psychology,* 1929.
63. Watson, *Psychology,* 1929, p. 238.
64. M. F. Washburn, "Introspection as an Objective Method," *Psychological Review,* XXIX (1922): 89–112.
65. Watson, *Psychology as a Behaviorist Views It.*
66. Watson, *Place of Conditioned-Reflex.*
67. Watson, *Behavior.*
68. *Ibid.,* p. 256.
69. Watson, *Behaviorism.*
70. J. B. Watson and R. Rayner, "Conditioned Emotional Reactions," *Journal of Experimental Psychology,* III (1920): 1–14.
71. Watson, *Behaviorism.*
72. *Ibid.*
73. *Ibid.,* p. 304.

74. The best overall evaluation of the contribution of John B. Watson to psychology, in my judgment, is that of Bergmann, *The Contribution of John B. Watson*.

75. Watson, *Behaviorism*, p. 49.

76. Watson, *Psychology*.

Chapter 19

Wertheimer:
GESTALT PSYCHOLOGY

In 1910, the psychologist Max Wertheimer was traveling by train from Vienna to the Rhineland on his vacation.[1] During this journey an idea came to him for a research study that was to result in the founding of Gestalt psychology. Gone were his plans for a vacation. At Frankfurt, he left the train, bought a toy stroboscope, and took it to his hotel room to verify, in a preliminary way, the insight that had just come to him. The stroboscope is a device allowing successive still pictures to be exposed at a constant rate of speed so that movement is perceived. Before the advent of motion pictures, a later development of the same principle, strobo-scopes were relatively common as children's toys. But Wertheimer did not have to use the stroboscope in his formal experiment; the University of Frankfurt placed at his disposal a tachistoscope, a device for regulating the length of time during which a visual stimulus, such as a nonsense syllable or a figure drawing, is exposed. It may also be used to present successive stimuli, separated by short and precisely regulated intervals of time.

What was this epoch-making experiment? It was a problem in the perception of apparent motion, that is, the perception of movement when no movement has actually taken place.[2] Two lines were exposed in two different places on the face of the tachistoscope. Each exposure lasted a very short time and was separated from the next exposure by varying lengths of time. If there was too long a time between exposures, the subject would see the lines successively. If the time was too short, he would see the lines simultaneously. But, when the interval of time between the exposures was at an optimal length, the subject saw, not two lines successively or simultaneously, but *one* line *moving* from one place to another. The visual experience was that of a single line that moved, despite the fact that actually there were two successively exposed stationary lines separated by an interval of time. Variations—such as exposing a vertical line followed by a horizontal line, causing the observer to see a line swinging around through ninety degrees—gave the same result. This apparent movement Wertheimer call *phi phenomenon*. Sometimes an observer reported movement alone, with no line seen; this he called *pure phi*.[3] Although the name was new, the phenomenon itself had been known for years. This seemingly trivial verification of what was already known was to launch a new movement in psychology. It is the interpretation, extending far beyond its ostensible subject, and not the results, that is important.

Wundt's view of psychology will serve as an illustration of what Wertheimer and others would try to combat through this and similar studies. To Wundt, there were various psychological dimensions available for compounding—quality, intensity, pleasantness-unpleasantness, tension-relaxation, and excitement-depression. When these are compounded by association, ideas and perceptions are formed. Wundt had been aware that these compounds had characteristics as a whole, not readily explained by their parts. Somewhat lamely, Wundt's solution depended upon creative synthesis (p. 290). Wertheimer's study arose from dissatisfaction with this elementaristic and associationistic position which left many characteristics of percepts unexplained by their supposedly ultimate components.

Antecedents of Gestalt Psychology

Some of the perplexities of configuration had already been elucidated and explanations had been attempted before Wertheimer appeared in Frankfurt. In *The Analysis of Sensations*,[4] Ernst Mach showed that changes in spatial orientation—such as first viewing a square from one of its sides and then shifting to a corner; or first hearing a series of sounds at one tempo and then hearing them at a faster or slower tempo—did not bring about a radical change in the experience of the overall configuration. Despite wide variation in viewing conditions, a table remains a table, no matter how viewed. Look at a table from one corner with its edge at eye level. Although the retinal image is a complex quadrilateral, you see a rectangle oriented obliquely in space. Mach went on to speak of sensations of space-form and sensations of time-form as kinds of experience in themselves. The circle may change size or color without changing its space-form of circularity.

Mach's conception of sensations of space-form were further de-

ERNST MACH

veloped by Christian von Ehrenfels (1859–1932) at the University of Graz in Austria. He noted that in the visual field certain visual characteristics, such as roundness, angularity, and slenderness are ignored when we deal with sensations.[5] Their occurrence seems to be due to something beyond single sensations. If individual stimuli are changed in the same proportion, these particular characteristics of slenderness, angularity, and roundness are still present. Among the other phenomena that he considered was the effect of transposing a melody. A melody made up of one series of notes is still heard as the same melody when played in a different key. That aspect of perception characterized by the transposition of melodies and proportionate changes in roundness, angularity, and slenderness, von Ehrenfels called *Gestaltqualität* or form quality. These perceptions were based on something more than the sum of the individual lines, and on something over and above the tones. The form quality, however, was treated by von Ehrenfels as another element (although not a sensation), so that, if there were nine notes and a *Gestaltqualität*, there would be ten elements in all—nine sensory and one nonsensory. A variant explanatory principle offered accounted for the phenomenon with "relations between elements." Ehrenfels and the Austrian School of *Gestaltqualität* that developed at Graz held that form qualities were constructed out of sensory data and, since the elements were the ultimate facts of consciousness, they continued an old tradition, rather than beginning a new one.

Other relevant work outside what was to become the Gestalt tradition went on more or less simultaneously with that of Wertheimer. Friedrich Schumann, G. E. Müller's assistant and collaborator in the invention of the memory drum, was Wertheimer's host in Frankfurt; he had already found in studies of visual shape and size perception that analysis of sensory elements was of no help in explaining the results.[6]

The arguments of William James[7] helped in this revolt against elementarism. James had held that elementarism fails to account for the simplest facts of experience. For example, our field of vision is ordered and extended. We see unitary objects of definite extension, form, and size, not a bundle of sensations.

Gestalt psychology was influenced by the continuing phenomenological trend. From the days of Goethe and Purkinje and their observations of color in the early nineteenth century, a phenomenological trend had continued to develop close to the main stream of psychology, although it was not accepted by the dominant tradition. Since phenomenology involved the study of immediate experience, its conclusions were thought to follow directly from the experience. Hering's studies of color and space, for example, essentially demonstrated experimentally, the presence of some color phenomena or visual perception; but Hering did not feel the need to go beyond this demonstration to arrive at quantitative values for his findings.[8]

Before the time of Wertheimer, phenomenology had received increased support and interest because of the work of Edmund Husserl (1889–1938), professor of philosophy at the University of Göttingen, mentioned before as a student of Brentano. He had accepted Brentano's distinction between psychology's contentual area, the act of "seeing" color, and physic's contentual concern of the color object itself, which was an underpinning to Brentano's elaborations of his view of intentionality (p. 301). After a period of positive interest in phenomenology as applied to psychology,[9] Husserl disavowed psychology, especially of the Wundtian variety, and turned to what would be his major life's work, establishing a new approach to ph'losophy based on a description of immediate experience with all its biases, which included keeping the scientific-psychological aspect at the lowest possible level.[10] The realm of consciousness is sharply separated from the material, physical world in this process. The latter, while not denied existence, is said to be irrelevant to the task. Phenomenologically, consciousness is a unique realm not dependent on physical processes. It is paramountly a medium of access to whatever exists. Subjective experience of this sort is used to synthesize a meaningful universe. This is the task of pure phenomenology as Husserl saw it.

In contrast to Wundtian introspection, phenomenology does not search for presumed elements but examines meaning, forbidden to Wundtians as the source of stimulus error (p. 418). For the phenomenologists, elements do not exist, and stimulus error is not an error, but the very core of what they investigate.

Edgar Rubin,[11] a Danish phenomenologist and a contemporary of Wertheimer, emphasized the distinction between the figure—the substantial appearance of objects—and the ground—the general homogenous environment in which the object exists. Perception, he argued, is selective. Not all stimuli are perceived with the same clarity and distinctness. Those perceived with greater clarity form the figure; the remainder provide the ground. The house against the sky, the word or picture on the white page, the recognized face against the rest of the faces in the photograph—all have this relation of figure and ground.

Wertheimer went beyond his predecessors by submitting these convictions to experimental study of a crucial kind. From these experiments, Wertheimer found a new understanding of these perplexing phenomena and integrated the results into a new way of looking at psychological phenomena.

Early Years of Max Wertheimer

Max Wertheimer was born in Prague in 1880; his father had directed and taught in a commercial school.[12] After attending a local gymnasium, he studied law at the university for two and a half years, but shifted to the study of philosophy. He attended, among others, the lecture of von Ehrenfels. At Berlin, he continued to study philosophy and psychology. He studied under both Schumann and Carl Stumpf; the latter was a friend of William James and a specialist in the psychology of music. From Berlin, Wertheimer went to Würzburg, where in 1904 he received his degree summa cum laude. He had worked at Würzburg under Külpe at a time when the Würzburg School was carrying on the revolt, not against elementarism as such, but against the constraints that Wundt put on the elements.

An early research interest, in keeping with Wertheimer's interest in law, was in the association experiment used to detect knowledge that subjects wished to keep secret. He published on this research in 1905 and in later years.[13] The years 1904 to 1910, before his arrival in Frankfurt, are not well documented, but some of his activities in Prague, Vienna, and Berlin concerned psychological matters.

Frankfurt, Phi Phenomenon, Köhler, and Koffka

On his arrival in Frankfurt in 1910, after trying out his hypothesis with the toy stroboscope, Wertheimer sought his old teacher Schumann, who had just arrived at the University of Frankfurt. It was Schumann who placed a tachistoscope at his disposal. His first subject was Wolfgang Köhler (1887–1967) and his second Kurt Koffka (1886–1941). These two men were junior only to Wertheimer in their pioneering contributions to Gestalt psychology in the years to come. Koffka and Köhler had taken their degrees at Berlin in 1908 and 1909, respectively, and were the new assistants in the Psychological Institute at Frankfurt.[14] They had already done some research in psychology, Köhler on hearing and Koffka on imagery and thought. What first united these three was their discontent with Wundtian elementarism. As good subjects should be, Köhler and Koffka were kept ignorant of the purpose of the experiment until after its completion. Sometime in 1911, Wertheimer called them in to explain the experiment.[15] From then on their lives and work were intricately interwoven.

Wertheimer's paper on the "Experimental Studies of the Perception of Movement" appeared in 1912.[16] This single study stimulated over a hundred papers on apparent movement in the next thirty years.[17] By and large, Wertheimer's findings were substantiated. Reverberations from his study extended into other psychological fields, particularly those dealing with memory, thinking, and action.

Several explanations of apparent movement were already current.[18] The traditional view of discrete elements was that each stimulus gives rise to its own sensation and, on the basis of past experience, our perceptions of them are integrated. To be more specific, Wundt attributed apparent movement to the kinesthetic sensations produced by the movement of the eyes.[19] Arranging the experimental setting with suitable pairs of lines so as to require two simultaneous movements in *opposite* directions, Wertheimer neatly ruled out Wundt's theory. Phi phenomenon still occurred. The eyes could hardly move in both directions at the same time, and Wundt's explanation fell to the ground.

The Nature of Phi Phenomenon and Gestalt

Wertheimer argued that the apparent movement generated in his experiment had no counterpart in the sensory elements. Local sensory stimulation could not be responsible for the actually perceived phenomenon. It is this fact that he could not fit into existing theories of perception. A general reevaluation of the basic nature of perception seemed necessary to him.

Whatever it was that Wertheimer explained to Köhler and Koffka in 1911 about his experiment on phi phenomenon, it was not the full blown Gestalt theory.[20] But there is no doubt that what was said seemed to them to challenge the established order. Wertheimer did know by then that the *Gestaltqualität* interpretation was not sufficient and said this in his paper, but a more complete statement had to await later work. Two papers devoted to theoretical statements that were published by Wertheimer in 1922[21] and 1925[22] will serve to explain Gestalt psychology in a preliminary way.

In the phi phenomenon, Wertheimer wrote, the subjects perceived a whole, or Gestalt, not the isolated elements. Von Ehrenfels and the members of the Graz School had been on the right track in raising an important problem; but in depending on a summation principle, they had been wrong.[23] What takes place in each part depends upon the whole.

This is true of all perceptual experience. In our perception of objects, there are characteristics that cannot be attributed to a single sensation. This Gestalt, or whole, is a "given" of perception, not something unstructured. The Gestalt is, in itself, primary and inherent in the process of sensory reception. Wertheimer agreed with James that what the elementarists had found were the secondary products of analysis. What was important was not the mosaic but a dynamic field in which the parts interact through the receptive process. Perception shows a totality, a whole, a configuration, an articulated structure; it is the task of psychology to account for this, not by explaining it away, but by exploring its characteristics as a structure. Gestalt psychology restored the "thing-language," as Brunswik phrased it many years later, to its place in the psychology of immediate experience.[24] For psychology to advance,"a procedure 'from above' is required, *not* a procedure 'from below upward' "[25]; understanding of whole properties must precede consideration of the significance of the "parts." A Gestalt is primary to the parts and is not merely their sum. It now becomes relevant to quote Wertheimer's formal definition of Gestalt: "There are wholes, the behavior of which is not determined **by** that of their individual elements, but where the part-processes are themselves determined by the intrinsic nature of the whole."[26] He was announcing that Gestalt psychology is committed to the molar prescription as the basis for both its research and, as we shall see in a moment, its protest against the psychology of the day.

Sometimes the words "configuration," "structure," and "whole" are used as English translations for Gestalt, but the untranslated term is preferable, since none of these words captures its complete meaning. Two meanings of the German word Gestalt must be specified. On one hand, there is Gestalt as object. A Gestalt is an object that has shape, an entity that in itself has form, such as a chair or table. On the other hand, Gestalt is the property of things, their squareness or triangularity. Gestalt, then, is both the object and the form characteristics of that object.

The emphasis on wholes has sometimes led to a misunderstanding about the Gestalt theorists' precise attitude toward parts in the psychological field and toward the process of analysis. The Gestalt position does not demand, for example, that the *entire* visual field be organized into a *single* pattern. One has to do no more than use his eyes to see that it is not. There are aggregates *within* this field that are *Gestalten*. The Gestalt psychologists do use analysis; they do not object to analysis as such, but only to analysis of sensational elements that have no existence as bits of experience. If there is analysis into *genuine* parts, then this is not only permissible, it is demanded.

Analysis is exemplified by the various laws of *Gestalten*. Each law, in one sense, is a statement of analysis, as is the distinction made between figure and ground. The parts, however, are derived from their meaningfulness in the total context, not from sensory elements. Attitudinal analysis is also possible. An observer may, by adopting a particular attitude, select some parts of the Gestalt and suppress others. This happens in reversible perspective, as in a line drawing capable of being seen two ways, permitting the observer to switch from one view to the other. This is a kind of analysis in which there is a change in the organization of the field, so that the impression one receives is different depending on how one perceives it.

Gestalt as a Psychology of Protest

There was to develop not only a Gestalt theory, but also a Gestalt movement; and these three men zealously propagandized for the Gestalt molar point of view in the years to come. In furthering this aim, however, Köhler and Koffka were much more ready than Wertheimer to systematize their thinking and put it into print.

Gestalt psychology developed in Germany at the same time that behaviorism made its appearance in the United States. Both were psychologies of protest.[27] Unlike the behaviorists, however, Gestalt psychologists did not question the existentiality of consciousness; they doubted the reality of the elements of which other psycholgists said consciousness was constituted. Wertheimer summarized these mistaken beliefs in the "bundle hypothesis" and the "association hypothesis."[28] Sensory elements do not form a bundle, and association does not serve as a means of binding together, because there is not a summative relationship, as the psychologists they were attacking claimed. Gestalt psychology was very much a revolution against the established order in psychology. In its early years, the exposure of the inadequacies of the entrenched position in psychology was almost as important to Gestalt psychologists as their positive contributions. They aspired to nothing less than a complete revision of psychology, but from the figure down rather than the ground up.

Wertheimer and the Principles of Organization

Wertheimer lectured at Frankfurt, where he was *Dozent*, from 1912 until 1916 when he went to Berlin. In 1922 he became an "assistant professor" at Berlin. In 1929 he became professor at Frankfurt, where he was given Schumann's old chair. Relevant publications by Wertheimer were slow in coming. During the war years, he collaborated on research in the development of binaural listening devices for use in submarines and harbor defense installations; these were not particularly relevant to Gestalt psychology.

The influence of Wertheimer on the thinking of other psychologists was considerable although, as Newman remarks, hard to evaluate.[29] His students, one of whom was Kurt Lewin, learned about Gestalt psychology mostly from his lectures and his inimitable conversation. At Berlin and Frankfurt, colleagues and students carried out research theses on a variety of studies.

Kurt Lewin —

Much of what was contained in Wertheimer's lectures during these years did not see print until after the war. A paper on creative thinking that appeared in 1920 (as well as a paper on thinking that appeared as early as 1912), in some respects anticipated his major work in this field, which did not appear for more than twenty years.[30]

In 1923 an important paper on perceptual grouping appeared that requires detailed consideration.[31] In this paper Wertheimer attempted to show that a person perceives objects just as directly as he sees motion in the phi phenomenon, that is, not as clusters of sensations, but as unified wholes. The principles of organization of *Gestalten* that Wertheimer formulated had specific reference to perception, i.e., they dealt with how *Gestalten* were organized. He preferred to use simple visual phenomena—such as dots, lines, or figures made of a few lines—or simple auditory stimuli—individual musical notes, for example—to avoid being charged with confusing the issue with common objects whose sheer meaningfulness would suggest organization. He presented various principles, including the following. There is the principle of proximity—parts close together are perceived together . For example, in the series tap-tap, pause, tap-tap, pause, tap-tap, the two taps together will be perceived as belonging together rather than the last tap before the pause and the first tap after it. Things close together in time tend to be grouped together. To illustrate with space, dots relatively close together are readily seen as a group. Second, there is a principle of similarity. Imagine a soft tone represented thus . while ! represents a loud tone. Then in . . . ! ! . . . ! ! . . . the three soft tones are heard together, as are the two loud tones, and so on. With effort we can hear some other arrangement as . . . ! ! . . . ! ! . . . , but this cannot be long maintained. It should be noted that this visual representation of auditory stimuli functions in much the same fashion as the auditory stimuli it is designed to symbolize. To use another visual illustration, dots of the same shape or color are readily seen as a group, distinct from those of another shape or color forming another group.

Wertheimer was demonstrating that we respond not to isolated stimuli, but to the nature of the setting in which they are found. A considerable amount of work developing these and other laws of form followed. By 1933, Helson[32] was able to isolate 114 separate laws of Gestalten.

Certain illustrations in this later work will make this problem of the laws of organization of Gestalten more meaningful. A principle was borrowed from the research of Rubin, whose investigations of figure and ground have already been cited. In the present context, the differentiation into figure and ground became a law of Gestalt organization.

Still another principle of organization is that of closure. Closure is the tendency to complete a figure, no matter what the sensory modality. Visual forms are included, of course. For example, if a figure is drawn with incomplete lines or small gaps (as are many cartoons and sketches) the perceiver completes it, typically disregarding or not "seeing" its incompleteness. A children's puzzle picture in which the task is to find hidden faces also illustrates closure. The obvious figures that the artist has drawn form some pattern, say a country scene with trees and a brook, which we accept. The figure for which one is to search say a face, is hidden because lines making up the face are incorporated into the country scene. The same illustration supplies another instance of closure. As one searches, there is tension, a sense of incompleteness; when the face leaps into view, closure has taken place. A favorite conversational illustration which Wertheimer would demonstrate in a restaurant, involving the waiter and the bill, was in the same vein. Before being paid, the waiter would be able to state the amount of the bill promptly, when asked, since the transaction had not been completed. Called over again a minute after it was paid, he would not be able to remember the amount. Before payment there was tension; payment made closure. This is the completion principle of closure.[33] But there is another aspect of closure that must be distinguished. This is its perceptual principle. Many superficial accounts of closure use a circle made from short, dashed lines as the example par excellence of completion closure. It is nothing of the kind; it is not seen as an unbroken circle, which completion closure calls for, but as a circle made of broken lines—a broken whole rather than a series of unrelated stimulus points. It illustrates what is called perceptual closure. Though broken, it still has perceptually the appearance of a circle.

Closure is essentially a special instance of the most general of configurational laws, that of *Prägnanz,* the principle that all experienced fields tend to become as articulated as possible. Besides closure, factors of proximity and similarity as well as symmetry and regularity are embraced in this law of *Prägnanz.*[34]

Köhler and the Mentality of Apes

Köhler remained at Frankfurt until 1913 when an opportunity arose to go to the Anthropoid Station of Tenerife in the Canary Islands, where he worked with apes and chickens.[35] Because of the war, he remained there longer than he had intended.

An experiment of Köhler with chicks, performed during these years, though simple, brings out clearly what the Gestalt psychologists were trying to demonstrate.[36] Two shades of gray paper on which grain was scattered were exposed. Hens were trained to take grains from one of these papers, the darker shade of gray. If they pecked at a grain on the darker paper, they were permitted to swallow it; if they pecked at a grain on the lighter paper, they were driven away. Eventually, after hundreds of trials, they learned to peck only at grain on the darker paper. The crucial series of trials was now begun. The darker gray paper of the learning trials was used again, but now it was accompanied by a sheet of a *still darker* gray, instead of the original lighter sheet. If the hens pecked on the original gray, they would be responding to specific brightness; if they pecked at what now was the darker paper, they would be reacting to a total situation or Gestalt, that is, to a relation of lighter-darker. As a rule, the hens pecked at the darker gray, not the particular one on which they had learned to peck. This was a relative response in which "darker of two" was the cue, not the specific gray. The hens reacted, not to a specific element in the learning situation, but to the pattern or Gestalt.

The work Köhler did on chimpanzees while at Tenerife resulted in the *Mentality of Apes,* first published in 1917 and later translated into English,[37] along with another important paper,[38] in 1927. His problem was the investigation of the intelligence of chimpanzees in solving problems. The studies took place in and around their cages and involved such simple props as the bars of the cages, which blocked direct access, bananas for them to secure, sticks to be used to draw in the bananas from outside the cage, and boxes on which to climb.

One study involved a stick hidden by Köhler in the framework of the cage roof. The chimpanzees were allowed to watch Köhler while he hid the stick. Afterward, the animals were taken to their living dormitory for the night. The next morning they were brought back to the cage, and one of them found that there was a bunch of bananas outside the cage. He was already familiar with using a stick to draw them in. As Köhler put it, he looked around as a man would in seeking a tool, but he did not find what he was looking for. After some seconds, his eyes went to the place where the stick had been hidden the night before. The stick was not in sight, but he immediately climbed up to where it was hidden, brought it down, and used it to draw in the bananas.

Another study involved a banana, placed at the level of the cage ceiling, and a box, from which, if moved under the banana, the chimpanzee could jump up to secure the banana. Almost all the chimps solved the problem of moving the box to the correct spot under the banana, climbing up on the box, and jumping to get the banana.

Contrast their behavior with that of a relatively stupid chimpanzee. He had been present many times while the others were learning to use the box as a tool to reach the banana. These other chimpanzees even tried to show him how to use it, but he imitated only parts of their behavior. He would move the box, but, as often as not, away from the food. He would then climb on the box and jump, but not under the banana and, after climbing off the box, would then jump up under the banana. He never formed the Gestalt; for him there were two separate groups, climb-box-jump and jump-under-fruit. He did not relate the parts of the activity to the essential structure of the total situation.

These and similar results were interpreted by Köhler as evidence of insight—the seeing of relations.[39] These *Gestalten* occur in the process of solving problems. There was activity on the animals' part that formed a continuous whole in which everything fell into place. There was continuity, a direction toward a goal, and closure. The insightful solutions they displayed are interpreted as making closure of the gap in the animals' psychological field. Capacity for perception of relations varied in different animals and thus became an indication of intelligence.

Köhler and Physical Gestalten

In 1920 Köhler left Tenerife for a Germany in the throes of economic and social reconstruction. He managed to secure only temporary academic appointments for a year or so. Formal recognition of Gestalt psychology by the academic world, however, come in 1922 when Köhler was appointed to a chair and the directorship of the laboratory at the University of Berlin. He occupied this post until 1935. Presumably the publication of a book two years before, whose translated title is *Static and Stationary Physical Gestalts,*[40] was in part responsible for this major appointment.

To evaluate its significance, it is necessary to return to Wertheimer's original experiment.[41] Wertheimer postulated brain action as a configural total process to account for phi. These processes must be essentially similar for apparent and for true motion, since they are experienced as identical. If two phenomena are perceived as identical, one must assume that they have corresponding brain processes. If the nervous system were organized so that it consisted of interlocking elements, it simply could not account for phi. There must be some correspondence between the patterning of the psychological experience and the underlying brain process. The nervous system has unitary properties, its parts being included in the larger units or *Gestalten*. Wertheimer suggested that the seen movement was a consequence of a physiological shortcut. With precisely the right temporal interval, "physiological cross processes" took place. These were modes of functional interconnection in larger patterns rather than in points on the cortex. The physiological processes had whole properties themselves, which were essentially the same in phi as in real motion.

This point of view was generalized by Köhler in his book of 1920.[42] A theory that physical systems possess Gestalt properties was the consequence, and this theory made it possible for Köhler to offer a transition from psychological to physical systems. The brain process and the perceived object correspond in that they are both *Gestalten*. In relating the mental and physical, Köhler advanced the thesis that the *form* of the mental event is the same as the form of the physical.[43] This is the principle of isomorphism; there is a formal correspondence between the brain processes and the experienced consciousness. This correspondence is not the relation of the object to its mirror image; it is *topological*. These two, the physical process and the experience, are different spatially. There is a formal correspondence but not a literal identity between the phenomenal experience and the brain pattern. In framing a psychophysical isomorphism, Köhler drew not only on Wertheimer's formulation for perceived movement already cited,[44] but also on Hering's anticipation of isomorphism in visual phenomena[45] and Georg E. Müller's use of the principle in formulating what he considered fundamental psychophysical axioms.[46] This last brings out the fact that in his statement of isomorphism Köhler offered his particular solution to the age-old mind-body problem. Isomorphism was his way of integrating the mind with the rest of the world.

Isomorphism, however, was but a phase of a much more ambitious undertaking by Köhler.[47] He was intent on nothing short of demonstrating that biology, chemistry, physics, and even astronomy also involved *Ges-*

talten. It should be mentioned that Köhler had studied physics under Max Planck, whose work in the quantum theory influenced him considerably. Köhler's attempt at model building was a heroic effort, the effect of which is hard to assess. Certainly it was meant to be more than an analogy; and in the contemporary period of psychology, Köhler has had success in utilizing it to further psychological investigation.

Koffka and the Growth of the Mind

Koffka had left Frankfurt in 1911 for a long period of service at the University of Giessen (1911–1927), which was interrupted by visits to universities in the United States.[48]

During these years Koffka wrote the *Growth of the Mind: An Introduction to Child Psychology,* which was first published in English in 1924 and is based upon a work in German that had appeared three years before.[49] Koffka made use of a developmental concept in his account, stressing what he called the convergence theory.

To place convergence theory in its proper setting, it is necessary to say something more about the phenomenological strain in Gestalt psychology. Phenomenology tended to go hand in glove with more sympathetic acceptance of nativism, as distinguished from empiricism. According to Gestalt theory, one does not need to learn to see structures in the sense that the properties of the psychological field are used to explain the events taking place within that field.

A neglected facet of Wertheimer's demonstration of phi phenomenon should be made explicit. It is sometimes charged that Gestalt psychology is nativistic because its position that movement in space is perceived as itself is closer to the position of Hering, the phenomenologist, than to that of Helmholtz, the empiricist. But it should not be ignored that Gestalt psychology fostered the study of learning. Denials of adherence to nativism have been offered from time to time. Koffka[50] thought the misapprehension might have arisen because Gestalt psychology denies that learning is an establishment of specific connection between neurons. He attributed this view to the empiricists, hence admitting that he was anti-empirical, but only in this sense. Koffka accepted a convergence theory, originally proposed by William Stern, in which every capacity is the result of a collaboration of inner and outer conditions of development, so that both share in any psychological process. Köhler,[51] in a relatively recent paper, argued that there is a third kind of process, neither learned (empirical) nor inherited (nativist)— neither chromosomal nor dependent on evolution—but, instead, due to the invariant nature of physical-chemical processes that occur in living and nonliving organisms, such as electrical currents and chemical reactions. These invariant processes are equally unaffected by learning and heredity. They give rise to the general principles of action in matter which include the relation of the organism to space.

Koffka submitted the concepts of reflex and instinct to Gestalt analysis. Consistent with the Gestalt principle of the priority of the whole over the parts, he saw reflexes as derived from instincts rather than the reverse. To illustrate his handling of instinct, Koffka held that one of its most conspicuous characteristics is its tendency to require the individual to work toward attaining some goal. This, in turn, brings closure in a temporal Gestalt.

Although Wertheimer had done earlier work in learning, Koffka's book served to emphasize in a detailed fashion that the learning process is clearly within the sphere of Gestalt psychology. The laws of organization in perception were seen as applicable to learning problems. Köhler's work on chimpanzees illuminated the point. His results were used by Koffka to challenge the theory of trial and error learning, offering insight as a replacement to account for the learning process. The trial and error hypothesis assumes that, in learning, a large number of random movements are made, the correct responses are gradually learned, and the incorrect ones are eliminated. A variety of explanations have been offered as to why this takes place, but at this time, the differentiation between those responses learned and those eliminated was attributed to the respective pleasure and pain that accompanied them.

To Koffka, learning was not a gradual mechanical process, but involved the same principles as perceptual *Gestalten*. Koffka rejected trial and error as a principle for learning, pointing out that the customary puzzle boxes and mazes were apparatuses that forced the animals to trial and error because no other approach was possible under these circumstances. The artifacts of such studies, as well as of those in sensation, were seen as results of the laboratory procedure. To be sure, an obstacle between the animal and the goal must be provided; but it should be of such a nature as to permit intelligent, insightful behavior, if the animal is capable of it. This was the case with Köhler's procedures. The causative relations were open to the animals' observation, and insight resulted. Insight takes the place of practice or repetition as the crux of learning, in the Gestalt description of learning. Practice does have some effect—after the Gestalt has been assimilated, practice makes its execution easier, as is the case when a musician grasps the Gestalt of a composition and with the aid of practice proceeds to play it better.

Gestalt Psychology Comes to the United States

With the rise of Hitler, Gestalt psychology experienced an almost complete transplantation of its leaders to the United States. Gestalt psychology, however, did not entirely disappear from Germany. Under Hitler, psychology as a whole became a minor subject in the German academic hierarchy (p. 558).

Before the migration, psychologists in the United States were not unfamiliar with the Gestalt psychologists' work. They had read their publications, and several visits by leading Gestalt psychologists had been made. In 1922, in the *Psychological Bulletin,* Koffka wrote the introductory statement of the Gestalt position for American psychologists.[52] He used as the medium for his presentation the study of perception, a field in which he was now specializing. Although admirable in many respects, his article unfortunately created the misapprehension among psychologists that Gestalt psychology was little more than a theory of perception—a view not entirely dissipated to this very day. Koffka and Köhler made several visits during the twenties and early thirties. Koffka was the first to settle in the United States, becoming in 1927 a professor at Smith College on whose faculty he remained until his death in 1941. He worked principally on color vision in relation to perceptual organization. Köhler's book, *Gestalt Psychology,* appeared in 1929.[53] In 1934, he lectured at Harvard, returned to Germany, and in 1935, in view of his open defiance of the Nazi regime, decided to emigrate permanently. He became professor of psychology at Swarthmore College, where he remained until his retirement. Between them, Köhler and Koffka carried on more of the polemics for Gestalt psychology in the United States than did Wertheimer.

In 1933, Wertheimer and his family left Germany and came to the United States. In 1934, he became a part of the "University in Exile" of the Graduate School of the New School for Social Research in New York City. This was an affiliation that was to continue until his death in 1943.

Other psychologists more peripherally related to Gestalt psychology also came to the United States. There was Kurt Lewin, who had taken his degree at the University of Berlin after World War I. He arrived in 1933 and did important work related to Gestalt psychology in the contemporary period (p. 594). There was also Kurt Goldstein, the neurologist, who was affiliated with Gestalt psychology in Germany. When he came to the United States in 1935, Goldstein continued to make use of Gestalt concepts in his clinical work.

The reception of Gestalt psychology in the United States was mixed, and it made relatively slow progress. Behaviorism was riding the crest of a wave and the language barrier stood in the way. A philosophical substratum was seen as lurking in the background of Gestalt thinking. The Gestalt critique of introspective elementarism left many American psychologists somewhat baffled. Titchenerian structuralism had passed its peak some years before, and functionalism was asking and answering questions that, in part at least, made people think that the Gestaltists were insisting on fighting over a dead issue. Instead of arguing that they were wrong, some American psychologists said that they were correct but either left it at that or added that they were unoriginal.

A new opponent for the Gestalt movement to attack was readily apparent—behaviorism, with its reductionist tendencies. Gestalt psychology accepted the study of behavior as legitimate, but insisted that the approach to it should be molar, not molecular. Their isomorphic view was opposed to the point-by-point correspondence of the S-R formula. This controversy was accentuated by the disagreement over the validity of introspection, even though this was not the same sort of introspection as that of Wundt or Titchener. Behavior composed of reflexes and conditioned responses was considered to be open to the same criticisms that had been made of the brick and mortar psychology of Wundt and Titchener.

American psychologists who were sympathetic to Gestalt theory seldom went so far as to become complete adherents. Seeing it as valuable, they assimilated it more generally into an eclectic pattern where it served as a needed corrective to a more atomistic approach.

As a matter of fact, criticism had been published before the arrival of Gestaltists in the United States. Helson, a sympathetic critic, had pinpointed what was to be a major criticism, then and later.[54] He argued that Gestaltists had followed the advice of Goethe to a friend on how to solve problems; they had changed the problem into a postulate. He said that the issue of organization in mental life was treated by Gestalt psychologists not as a question to be wrestled with, but as a "given" of nature. This is close to solving a problem by denying its existence.

The ten years between 1933 and 1943 in the United States were busy ones for Wertheimer, but not as quantitatively productive as one might have wished. Burdened as he was with adapting to a new environment and struggling with a foreign language, Wertheimer suffered increasing exhaustion.[55] He continued trying little informal experiments, communicating them to his friends and at meetings of psychologists, but not recording them in published form.

Wertheimer did not live by psychology alone. He devoted time and energy to social issues, logic, and ethics. At the New School for Social

Research he was a member of a heterogeneous group of social scientists, which facilitated the spread of his interests beyond psychology. He saw the Gestalt point of view as extending into other scientific areas where it could help in the understanding of their complex problems. Wertheimer felt deeply the social issues of his time and wrote eloquently and incisively on matters such as the meaning of freedom.[56]

One characteristic of the then current work in anthropology caused him considerable distress. This was the doctrine of cultural relativism, which he combatted vigorously. He discussed ethics in relation to this principle of relativity and pleaded that studies of ethnology, sociology, and cultural history were not enough.[57] The conditions of evaluation themselves need study. This would lead to psychological studies, some of which would use Gestalt concepts. Another paper concerned the question of truth.[58] Science and logic have applied the proposition that truth is correspondent to the object, but difficulty has arisen because it is possible to define an object by one of its parts, making this statement true to the part, but false to the whole. For example, a man who hires another to steal something for him, when asked if he stole, replies, "No,"—he is telling the truth to the question (which is only a part), but he is lying in relation to the whole situation. This error is an instance of a piecemeal view of reality. From this point of departure Wertheimer goes into logistics, the study of relational networks, in which the Gestalt part-whole problem is considered. This paper leads directly to his remaining major contribution to Gestalt psychology, a posthumously published book on thinking.

Wertheimer and Productive Thinking

This investigation of thinking had been an implicit and explicit interest for many years. In fact, Wertheimer's interest in the problem of thinking went back to at least 1912, for it was in that year—in which he also published his historic paper on perception—that he first published on this topic. Since Gestalt psychology is sometimes described as if it contributed only to perceptual problems, it is fitting to emphasize that Wertheimer's interest in thinking was contemporaneous with his interest in perception. His study of thinking culminated in the book *Productive Thinking*[59] prepared for publication after his arrival in the United States. As Wertheimer interpreted it, the main factor in productive or creative thinking is grasping the structure of the situation—the Gestalt. Productive thinking serves to relate the problem at hand, whatever it may be, to the tasks and goals and to the total situation. Analysis goes on, not of parts, but of part-whole relationships.

It would be impossible to capture the characteristic flavor of Wertheimer's presentation without direct lengthy quotations quite beyond our present scope. A summary, no matter how adequate on the surface, is to some extent false to the original. It was characteristic that he gave not a polished presentation leading step by step to the solution, but the raw protocol of both productive and unproductive thinking using a great variety of materials in the process—geometrical figures, numerical manipulations, physical principles, and social situations. Productive thinking has its fumbling and false starts, just as unproductive thinking; but in productive thinking there is a return to the theme without undue delay, a sense of direction, and an ability to isolate essential features. In productive thinking, the given material is seen in a new light, and what was obscure before becomes obvious. Consider Wertheimer's example of the task of computing the sum of the numbers in an ascending arithmetical series, i.e., $1 + 2 + 3 + 4 + 5 + 6 + 7 + 8 + 9 + 10$. If, instead of laboriously adding, as the problem seems to call for, the individual sees that, from the two ends of the series going toward the middle the terms increase and decrease at the same rate, a new approach is suggested. It will be noted that the middle pair are 5 and 6, on one side of which the numbers increase and on the other side decrease by one, giving pairs $4 + 7, 3 + 8, 2 + 9$, and $1 + 10$. Each pair equals 11. There are five pairs of 11 each; therefore, the answer is 55. There is a recentering; a regrouping has taken place so that a new figure-group organization emerges. Instead of a single progressive series→it is seen as two series meeting in the center→←. There has been a reorganization of the field. Once the principle of reorganization has been grasped, the recognition of the particular steps necessary for the solution to the problem can be found.

In productive thinking, habitual ways of using familiar concepts often have to be overcome in order to solve problems in a novel fashion. Especially fascinating in this regard is Wertheimer's account of the thinking that culminated in the theory of relativity. His account was derived from the many hours that he spent with Einstein himself in reviewing, decisive step by decisive step, the thinking Einstein had done in formulating his theory. In this recounting, each step seemed to emerge because it was required for the solution. This new theory had the difficulty of going against the strong Gestalt of the traditional Newtonian system of physics. To produce his general transformation formula, Einstein had to transform his thinking at each stage against the weight of this well-articulated structure.

The relevance of the Gestalt principle to teaching was also shown by Wertheimer; it became the basis for criticism of the emphasis on repetition and routine practice, which had derived its rationale from the associationistic theory of learning. Inculcation of rules and principles by rote memory is rarely productive, Wertheimer held; more often than not, the student's response is a blind repetition of arbitrarily learned materials. This lack of productivity is demonstrated, Wertheimer believed, by the student's inability to solve a variation of the original problem when it is presented to him. When teachers arrange their problems so that the whole is available to the student, insight is more likely to occur.

Overview

Max Wertheimer saw an old problem in a new way and thereby founded a new approach to psychology based on a consistent adherence to a molar attitude. He was joined in this enterprise by two other psychologists, Wolfgang Köhler and Kurt Koffka; but it was he who first saw the problem; it was he who grasped the significance of spontaneous groupings in sensory fields, as Köhler[60] said; and it was he who was the "first founder," as Koffka[61] called him.

Wertheimer never wrote a complete, systematic statement of Gestalt psychology. It is probable that he had no desire to do so, any more than he wished to engage in the endless polemics concerning the value of Gestalt psychology. It was not that he did not care; he did care, but these were tasks for someone of a different temperament. He had a restless, inquiring approach to many aspects of life and psychology, and he was prodigal with his carelessly tossed-off insights. His spontaneity and brilliance resulted in his productive contribution to psychology. Paradoxically, he was compulsively careful about gathering and analysing data. He would publish his results only if the data were crystal clear and the experiment unequivocal. This prodigality and brilliance helped his students to learn more from him than others who depended on the written word for their knowledge of his work.

As a school and movement in psychology, Gestalt psychology was characterized by a pattern of prescriptive adherences. Molarism was salient and, to a somewhat lesser degree, centralism, an emphasis upon what goes on within the organism. Isomorphism and convergence are both instances of centralism and illustrations of how Gestalt psychology relates central factors to peripheral ones. They shared in common with psychologists other than behaviorists an emphasis on conscious mentalism and contentual subjectivism. Nomothetic adherence, also shared, was prominent.

References*

1. E. B. Newman, "Max Wertheimer: 1880–1943," *American Journal of Psychology*, LVII (1944):428–435; W. Köhler, "Max Wertheimer: 1880–1943," *Psychological Review*, LI (1944): 143–146.

2. M. Wertheimer, "Experimentelle Studien ueber das Sehen von Bewegung," *Zeitschrift für Psychologie*, LXI (1912): 161–265.

3. *Ibid.*

4. E. Mach, *The Analysis of Sensations* (La Salle, Ill.: Open Court Publishing Company, 1914) (1886).

5. C. v. Ehrenfels, "Ueber Gestaltqualitäten," *Vierteljahrsschrift für Wissenschaftliche Philosophe*, XIV (1890): 249–292.

6. E. G. Boring, *Sensation and Perception in the History of Experimental Psychology* (New York: Appleton-Century-Crofts, 1942), pp. 247–248.

7. W. James, "The Principles of Psychology," in R. M. Hutchins, ed., *The Great Books of the Western World* (Chicago: Encyclopaedia Britannica, 1952), Vol. LIII, Chap. 19 (1890).

8. L. M. Hurvich, "Hering and the Scientific Establishment," *American Psychologist*, XXIV (1969): 497–514.

9. E. Husserl, *Philosophie der Arithmetik*, Vol. 1, *Logische Studien und psychologische Untersuchungen* (Halle: Pfeffer, 1891).

10. E. Husserl, *Ideas: General Introduction to Pure Phenomenology*, trans. by W. R. B. Gibson (New York: Macmillan, 1952) (1913); E. Husserl, *Phenomenology and the Crisis of Philosophy: Philosophy as Rigorous Science* (1911), and *Philosophy and the Crisis of European Man* (1936–1954), trans. by Q. Lauer (New York: Harper, 1965).

11. E. Rubin, *Synsoplevede figurer* (Copenhagen: Gyldendal, 1915).

12. The major source for biographical details are Newman, "Max Wertheimer," and Köhler, "Max Wertheimer."

13. M. Wertheimer, "Experimentelle Untersuchungen

*See p. 19 for description of reference style.

zur Tatbestands-diagnostik," *Archiv für die Gesamte Psychologie*, VI (1905): 59–131.

14. C. Murchison, ed., *The Psychological Register* (Worcester: Clark University Press, 1929), Vol. II.

15. K. Koffka, *Principles of Gestalt Psychology* (New York: Harcourt, Brace and Company, 1935).

16. Wertheimer, "Experimentelle Studien ueber das Sehen von Bewegung."

17. Boring, *Sensation and Perception*.

18. *Ibid.*

19. G. W. Hartmann, *Gestalt Psychology: A Survey of Facts and Principles* (New York: Ronald Press, 1935), p. 5.

20. B. Petermann, *The Gestalt Theory and the Problem of Configuration* (New York: Harcourt, Brace and Company, 1932).

21. M. Wertheimer, "Untersuchungen zur Lehre von der Gestalt," *Psychologische Forschung*, I (1922): 47–58. Abridged trans. in W. D. Ellis, ed., *A Sourcebook of Gestalt Psychology* (New York: Harcourt, Brace and Company, 1938), pp. 12–16.

22. M. Wertheimer, "Ueber Gestalttheorie," *Philosophische Zeitschrift für Forschung und Aussprache*, I (1925): 39–60 (trans. in *Social Research*, XI (1944): 79–99).

23. *Ibid.*

24. E. Brunswik, "The Conceptual Framework of Psychology," in O. Neurath, et al., eds., *International Encyclopedia of Unified Science* (Chicago: University of Chicago Press, 1955), pp. 655–760.

25. Wertheimer, "Untersuchungen zur Lehre von der Gestalt," p. 55

26. Wertheimer, "Ueber Gestalttheorie," p. 43.

27. Newman, "Max Wertheimer."

28. Wertheimer, "Untersuchungen zur Lehre von der Gestalt," p. 49.

29. Newman, "Max Wertheimer."

30. M. Wertheimer, *Über Schlussprozesse im produktiven Denken* (Berlin: De Gruyter, 1920).

31. M. Wertheimer, "Untersuchungen zur Lehre von der Gestalt," *Psychologische Forschung*, IV (1923): 301–350. Abridged trans. in D. C. Beardsall and M(ichael) Wertheimer, eds., *Readings in Perception* (Princeton: D. Van Nostrand Company, 1958), pp. 115–135 (Herrnstein and Boring, Excerpt No. 43).

32. H. Helson, "The Fundamental Propositions of Gestalt Psychology," *Psychological Review*, XL (1933): 13–32.
33. M(ichael) Wertheimer, Personal Communication.
34. Koffka, *Principles of Gestalt Psychology*.
35. M. Henle, "Wolfgang Köhler (1887–1967)," *Yearbook American Philosophical Society* (1968): 139–145.
36. W. Köhler, "Optische Untersuchungen am Chimpanse und am Haushuhn," *Abhandlungen Preussische Akademie der Wissenschafen (Physische-Mathematische Klasse)* (1915), nr. 3.
37. W. Köhler, *The Mentality of Apes* (New York: Harcourt, Brace and Company, 1927).
38. W. Köhler, "Intelligence of Apes," in C. Murchison, ed., *Psychologies of 1925*, 2nd ed. (Worcester, Mass.: Clark University Press, 1927), pp. 145–161.
39. W. Köhler, "Intelligenzprufung an Anthropoiden," *Abhandlungen Preussiche Akademie der Wissenschaften (Physische-Mathematische Klasse)* (1917), nr. 1. (Hermstein and Boring, Excerpt No. 102).
40. W. Köhler, *Die physischen Gestalten in Ruhe und im stationaren Zustand* (Erlangen: Weltkreisverlag, 1920).
41. Wertheimer, "Experimentelle Studien Ueber das Sehen von Bewegung" (Herrnstein and Boring, Excerpt No. 55).
42. Köhler, *Die physischen Gestalten*.
43. *Ibid.*, pp. 189–193. (Herrnstein and Boring, Excerpt No. 56).
44. Wertheimer, "Experimentelle Studien ueber das Sehen von Bewegung."
45. E. Hering, *Zur Lehre vom Lichtsinne* (Vienna: Gerolds Sohn, 1878), pp. 74–80. (1872–1874) (Herrnstein and Boring, Excerpt No. 53).
46. G. E. Müller, "Zur Psychophysik der Gesichtsempfindungen," *Zeitschrift für Psychologie* X (1896): 1–82. (Herrnstein and Boring, Excerpt No. 54).
47. Köhler, *Die physischen Gestalten*.
48. M. Harrower, "Kurt Koffka: 1886–1941," *American Journal of Psychology*, LV (1942): 278–281.
49. K. Koffka, *The Growth of the Mind: An Introduction to Child Psychology*, 2nd ed. (London: Routledge & Kegan Paul, 1929) (1921).
50. *Ibid.*

51. W. Köhler, "The Mind-Body Problem" in S. Hook, ed., *Dimensions of Mind* (New York: New York University Press, 1960), pp. 3–23.
52. K. Koffka, "Perception: An Introduction to the Gestalt-Theorie," *Psychological Bulletin*, XIX (1922): 531–585.
53. W. Köhler, *Gestalt Psychology* (New York: Boni and Liveright, 1929).
54. H. Helson, "The Psychology of Gestalt," *American Journal of Psychology*, XXXVI (1925): 342–370.
55. Köhler, "Max Wertheimer."
56. M. Wertheimer, "A Story of Three Days," in R. N. Anshen, ed., *Freedom: Its Meaning* (New York: Harcourt, Brace and Company, 1940), pp. 555–569.
57. M. Wertheimer, "Some Problems in the Theory of Ethics," *Social Research*, II (1935): 353–367.
58. M. Wertheimer, "On Truth," *Social Research*, I (1934): 135–146.
59. M. Wertheimer, *Productive Thinking*, ed. M(ichael) Wertheimer, enlarged ed., (New York: Harper & Row, 1959).
60. W. Köhler, *Gestalt Psychology*, 2nd ed. (New York: Mentor Books, 1947), p. 85 (1929).
61. Koffka, *Principles*, p. 18.

Chapter 20

Freud:
PSYCHOANALYSIS AND RELATED VIEWS

While modern psychology was developing in academe, other important contributions were taking place in a quite different setting. Far removed from the psychological laboratory, Sigmund Freud was developing another approach to psychology through the study of personality disturbances revealed through clinical observation. He was learning that behind the conscious and rational person there was another phase of human nature, expressed through the dark, emotion-ridden unconscious motivations of his patients. He used the controls of the clinical method rather than traditional experimentation. After a long period of isolation, he gained a few supporters. Two of these supporters went on to develop their own views, which are both important and significantly different from those of Freud. Consequently, after discussing psychoanalysis as expressed through the life, work, and theoretical system of Sigmund Freud, attention will be devoted to Alfred Adler and his Individual Psychology and to Carl Gustav Jung and his Analytical Psychology.

The Heritage of Freud

In an effort to glorify Freud, some enthusiastic disciples write as if his genius came into the world unaided by an intellectual-cultural heritage. They interpret psychology before Freud as concerned exclusively with conscious experience, while the world waited for Freud to discover the unconscious. Nothing could be further from the truth.[1]

The influence of unconscious psychological phenomena has been a theme throughout the ages, from Plato's sleeping beast through Augustine's limitless room of memory to Aquinas's inability to view the soul apart from awareness of its acts. One can leave aside Descartes,

491

Spinoza, Leibniz, and the others who considered unconscious phenomena in some detail and move directly to the nineteenth century. Fechner was most influential to Freud with his iceberg analogy of the mind, that is, the mind is mostly below the surface and is moved much more by powerful hidden currents than by the winds of awareness. Fechner also introduced a topographical distinction between the sleeping and waking states. Sleep differs from the waking state, not only in intensity of mental function, but also in the activities of different stages. There were others immediately preceding Freud who seriously considered unconscious psychological phenomena, though, perhaps, without any direct influence upon him. Helmholtz utilized unconscious inference. Ebbinghaus wrote his dissertation on Hartmann's philosophy of the unconscious. Even Wundt had to have been aware of unconscious phenomena in order to deny them a place in psychology. Those who came before Freud attached significance in varying degrees to unconscious functioning. Some dismissed unconscious psychological phenomena as curiosa, to be mentioned but then ignored. Others attached a fair amount of meaning, or even importance, to manifestations of unconscious functioning. But none of them grasped the crucial importance of unconscious motivation or found a way to study it. Freud found a use for the unconscious, thought that its exploration might help to explain otherwise inexplicable phenomena, and saw that thoughts and feelings beyond awareness played a role in directing behavior. Moreover, he found a means of studying these unconscious processes.

Among familiar aspects of the intellectual atmosphere that Freud absorbed in developing psychoanalysis were the Helmholtzian view of mechanistic determinism, the Darwinian ideas of development, the French psychopathological view of dissociation, and the Galtonian-Wundtian-Kraepelinian view of association. Factors outside the main psychological tradition were also influential, particularly the writings of Goethe, to which aspects of libido theory are traceable.[2] Freud acknowledged that the theories of Darwin and Goethe's famous essay on nature influenced his choice of a medical profession.[3] Many strands of the past affected his thinking. His genius lay in creating a dynamic interpretation of unconscious motivation.

The Development of Psychoanalysis Through the Life of Freud

The sheer wealth of material available about the life of Freud makes it possible to relate rather closely his personal experiences to the development of his ideas.[4] This is especially pertinent to Freudian conceptions regarding sex, since it is easy to be skeptical of his views unless it can be shown that their sources were not his own biases and preconceptions, but experiences with his patients. Experience with some of his first patients suggested aspects of what emerged as the free association method and helped him in constructing some of his major theoretical concepts.

EARLY EXPERIENCES

Sigmund Freud was born in 1856 in Freiburg, a town in what is now Czechoslovakia but was then a part of the Austro-Hungarian Empire. His father was a wool merchant, and the family background was lower middle class. When Sigmund was four years of age, his family moved to Vienna, where he was to live and work for nearly eighty years.

His high intellectual capacity was recognized early, and it was soon known in the family that Sigmund was destined to be its scholar. Homely but revealing evidence of this is the fact that his study-bedroom was the only one equipped with an oil lamp; the rooms of other members of the household only had candles. A year earlier than usual he entered the gymnasium, from which he was graduated with distinction at the age of seventeen. Reading and studying seem to have filled the greater part of his life during these years. Then and later he read widely. He was interested in problems of social reform and, perhaps somewhat surprisingly, in military history. He had a considerable gift for languages and in maturity knew four or five quite thoroughly.

As for his choice of a career, the only professions open to a Viennese Jew in the 1870s were law and medicine. Freud turned to medicine, not because of any direct or compelling attraction to it, but because he felt that it might give him an opportunity to work on those problems of science that interested him. As was not too uncommon in his time, he took eight years, several more than necessary, to complete the medical curriculum. His penchant for sampling other fields not directly required for his training delayed his graduation until 1881.

This penchant for wide study led him to take several nonobligatory courses in philosophy with Franz Brentano. As a consequence, Freud was thoroughly familiar with Aristotle. The precise relation of this intellectual excursion to his later thinking is still an obscurity in Freud's intellectual development (p. 299). Among his other teachers was the German physiologist Ernst Brücke, mentioned before in connection with the pact sworn against vitalism (p. 261). It was from Brücke that Freud learned to see man as a dynamic system following the laws of nature.

During these years, Freud had somewhat vaguely considered following a medical teaching career. But when he concluded that an academic career was not open to him, he turned to medical practice. Unfortunately, he had rather neglected the clinical phases of medical training. He realized that he would need more experience, so he worked in a variety of clinics and hospitals. He devoted considerably more time to neurology and speech psychopathology than was customary. He carried on research in a variety of problems. Then and later he was a prodigiously hard worker. It is worth noting that his very first research endeavor involved sex—in this case an attempt to determine the precise structure of the testes of a species of eel. The results were inconclusive; in this endeavor, the future discoverer of the castration complex was unsuccessful.

Freud did a considerable amount of microscopic work in Brücke's physiological institute. It was here that he discovered the analgesic power of cocaine, and he just missed becoming the first physician to apply it in eye operations, which turned out to be by far its most useful application in medicine. Freud also became a very competent neurologist and actually coined the term "agnosia," which is still used in neurological clinics. Indeed, he maintained a part-time practice in this specialty until almost the end of the century.

He now had an even more compelling reason for going into practice: he had met and fallen in love with Martha Bernays. The courtship was a stormy one on his side; he exhibited violence, jealousy, and moodiness to a much greater degree than was characteristic of him before or afterwards. Typically, after some fancied slight from a relative of his fiancée, he demanded she no longer see the person in question.

The Freuds' home life was conventional and quite in keeping with the middle-class pattern of the time. Despite the wild stories that were to circulate about his sex life, Freud seems to have been faithful to his marital partner. But with his tremendously lengthy work hours, he saw relatively little of either his wife or his children. His wife did not accompany him on his vacations; he had discovered she could not keep up with his rapid traveling pace, and it seems never to have occurred to him to slow his pace down. To Freud, the place of women was in the home. His social recreations were card games with old cronies and visits to his mother, who lived to an advanced age.

One friendship that developed during these years was to be very important both for Freud and for psychoanalysis. He became intimate with Joseph Breuer, a highly successful, sophisticated, and urbane practitioner whom Freud admired immensely. Breuer became for Freud what today we would call—using Freudian terminology—a father figure. Breuer also helped him in a material way, lending him money and offering him advice, both practical and medical. Naturally, this included discussion of the cases handled by Breuer. One case, which Freud first heard about in 1882, was of crucial significance.

In December 1880, Breuer began to treat Fraulein Anna O. This girl of twenty-one had developed a whole host of symptoms. Hers seemed a classical case of hysteria—paralysis of the limbs, anesthesias, disturbances of sight and speech, nausea, and confusion. The illness had first appeared while she was caring for her severely ill father. She was compelled by her own illness to abandon nursing him. The events during her nursing made a deep impression upon her; but when she was first seen by Breuer, she could not remember them. Anna got into the habit of relating to Breuer the disagreeable events of the day. This provided a release for her pent-up emotions or, as it came to be called, a catharsis. She experienced relief and on occasion even the disappearance of a particular symptom by talking about her troubles. For example, during a period when she could not drink water, despite an intense thirst, she told Breuer that the same thing had occurred for a time when she was a girl. She now remembered that at that time she had seen a much-disliked dog of a governess drinking from a glass. She told Breuer this story in disgust and anger. Afterward, she found she could drink water again without trouble and there was no recurrence of this particular difficulty.

She referred to her sessions with Breuer as the "talking cure" and as "chimney sweeping." Breuer discovered that she was relieved of her symptoms if she was placed under hypnosis and induced to express her dominant feelings and emotions at the moment. It also turned out that what was unconscious to her, except under hypnosis, was some thought or impulse that she found repugnant. Symptoms replaced these thoughts or impulses. When she lived through the traumatic scenes again, without the inhibition of the associated feelings, Breuer found that the symptoms in question were reduced in severity or even disappeared. Her emotions up to this time could not be expressed in a normal way, so the emotions associated with these events had expressed themselves in symptoms. Breuer was so interested in her case that he began to devote more and more of his evenings to working with her. He apparently saw Anna for hours at a time every day for more than a year. He became so engrossed in working with her that his wife became bored at first and later jealous. Unknowingly, Breuer had developed what in later psychoanalytic perspective would be called a countertransference. When he finally realized what was happening, he stopped treating the girl. Anna herself had developed a positive transference: she had transferred to him, as she conceived him to be, the loves and hates that she had felt for her father.

The evening that Breuer told Anna of his decision to stop seeing her, he was called to her home to find her excited and in the throes of hysterical childbirth, which he terminated by hypnosis.[5] This incident was too much for Breuer, who fled to Venice with his wife for a second honeymoon. Freud was very interested in this particular case, finding it exciting and, unlike Breuer, not at all threatening.

In 1885, Freud was granted a small stipend to go to France to work under Charcot. Charcot's influence upon Freud as a result of this visit was expressed in theoretical and procedural influences. Heretofore he had held what might be called an organic point of view; after working under Charcot he became much more interested in the functional aspects of mental disorder.

A casual incident that occurred about this time is of importance. In the course of an informal conversation one evening, Charcot insisted that the etiology of the difficulties of a particular patient, the wife of an impotent man, had a sexual basis.[6] The gist of this incident was repeated for Freud on several occasions with other physicians, but always it was mentioned casually and in passing. Freud began to wonder why this lead was not followed up in a more systematic and serious fashion in the medical literature. Remembering this incident, he was thereafter on the alert for any indication of sexual factors in the etiology of his patients. His knowledge of Anna O. must also have sensitized him to this particular lead.

Freud also learned Charcot's methods, particularly his use of hypnosis in the study of hysteria. Hysteria was a condition not at all well understood. At that time the very symptoms of hysteria made it faintly unrespectable. It was still interpreted by many physicians as a confusing mixture of stimulation, an overwrought imagination, and a wandering womb. Greek medicine had considered hysteria a condition due to womb movement, and, in fact, the word comes from the same root as *hysterectomy*. With this etiology, it was popularly and professionally supposed that hysteria was a condition limited to women. But while working with Charcot, Freud observed instances of male hysteria. On his return to Vienna he insisted on lecturing on this topic. To put it mildly, his views, especially those on the reality of male hysteria, were not well received. He was actually publicly challenged to find a male with the symptoms Charcot claimed for hysteria. Without going into further details, it is easy to see why Freud thereafter disliked the members of organized medicine in Vienna and why they, in turn, regarded him as an unconventional medical practitioner.

In his practice, he had been using electrotherapy. This is not the same as electric shock therapy as used today; it consisted of the application of a painful electric shock directly to the afflicted organ, such as the arm. (In those cases where it was successful, suggestion was operative, as was demonstrated shortly afterward.)

Freud found the results of electrotherapy disappointing, and so turned to hypnosis, a technique still held in disrepute. Its use in his practice hardly added to his professional standing, but his interest was prompted by the power of hypnosis-concentration to bring to the surface forgotten thoughts, and as Breuer and Charcot had demonstrated, this was important for the understanding of hysteria.

Freud modified hypnosis in the direction of Breuer's cathartic method of release of emotions. But gradually he eliminated the hypnotic trance until he arrived at the technique of merely having the patient lie on a couch, touching her forehead, and telling her to start talking. One of Freud's patients one day threw her arms around him. Unlike Breuer's panic over a display of affection, Freud saw this as a matter of considerable scientific interest. He began dimly at first, but with gradually increasing clarity, to realize that somehow effective work with the neurotic depended on a personal relationship between the physician and his patient.

THE METHOD OF FREE ASSOCIATION

During these years it was his custom to question the patient rapidly and in considerable detail and to interject other comments freely as they occurred to him. One of his patients, Fraulein Elizabeth, sharply reproved him for interrupting her flowing thoughts. He saw the validity of her reproof and, gradually, the method of free association emerged. Basic to this concept is a thoroughgoing belief in causality—that all matters, dreams, and thoughts, no matter how trivial, incongruous, and inconsequential, actually had some cause. The value of allowing one's mind to wander had also been discussed by one of his favorite authors, Ludwig Borne. This author had written an essay with the striking title "The Art of Becoming an Original Writer in Three Days." As quoted by Ernest Jones, it concludes as follows:

> Here follows the practical prescription I promised. Take a few sheets of paper and for three days in succession write down, without any falsification or hyprocrisy, everything that comes into your head. Write what you think of yourself, of your women, of the Turkish War, of Goethe, of the Fonk

> criminal case, of the Last Judgment, of those senior
> to you in authority—and when the three days are
> over you will be amazed at what novel and startling
> thoughts have welled up in you. This is the art of
> becoming an original writer in three days.[7]

The method of free association that Freud used hereafter consisted essentially of instructing his patients that the basic rule they were to follow was to say whatever came to mind, allowing no selection and no rearrangement whatsoever. This letting one's mind go, akin to daydreaming aloud, sounds relatively easy to do; but his patients often found it unexpectedly difficult, since either there would be blanks or, violating the rule, they would struggle to rearrange the flow of their thoughts. Freud soon realized that these unexpected difficulties were significant as signs that material meaningful to the patient was close to the surface. He became alerted to the fact that when his patients experienced difficulties in associating, something of significance seemed to be occurring. From this finding arose his insistence that they must follow the basic rule, and the analysis progressed when they did so.

Other aspects of the psychoanalytic method developed during these years. Freud recognized his patients' remarkable unwillingness to disclose painful memories, a mechanism that he called *resistance*. Freud saw a connection between resistance and repression. Repression causes memory gaps or amnesias. The forces that produce repression also produce resistance.

The following example of free association illustrates a purposeful failure of memory, the Freudian significance of which is discussed a little later.[8] It is atypical only in that it occurred during a conversation, rather than in the course of the analysis of a patient. An acquaintance, in conversation with Freud, stumbled over a Latin quotation and omitted the word *aliquis*. Knowing of Freud's contentions on this matter, this acquaintance challenged him to find the reason he had forgotten the word. Freud accepted the challenge. He gave the young man the usual instructions about free associations; the young man responded with what he himself considered to be the faintly ridiculous idea of dividing the word into two parts a *liquis*. The gist of the succession of free associations thereafter was as follows: "reliques—liquidation—liquidity—fluid—an article entitled, What St. Augustine Said Concerning Women,'—St. Januarius and his Blood Miracle." (Freud—"Didn't St. Januarius and St. Augustine have something to do with the calendar?") "Yes, and as for St. Januarius a phial of his blood liquified on the date of a certain holiday, and if it doesn't take place the people get excited. A French general occupying the town once demanded the miracle take place forthwith." Young man hesitates. (Freud—"Why do you hesitate?") "Something too intimate to tell, comes to mind." At this point let us pause and consider the sequence of liquid, liquifying of blood, excitement if it doesn't take place, and the demand that it take place. Ask yourself what it was the young man thought of at this point that was too intimate to mention? I suspect that some of you at least have recognized that the sequence had to do with the menstrual cycle. As the acquaintance admitted, he was hoping for a miracle: a friend of his had missed her period.

Although Freud altered his method of approach during these years, he did not vary the aims of his procedures. His principal endeavor was to bring to the surface of the patient's consciousness the traumatic event that was the presumed pathological starting point. Even when this point was achieved and the trauma revealed, Freud continued further back in time. The memories that these patients were able to produce inexorably went further and further into childhood, as if the patients were somehow attracted to this period of life. The importance that Freud attached to childhood will be brought out later in a more systematic discussion of the psychoanalytic theory.

IMPORTANCE OF SEXUAL FACTORS

Freud found that a remarkable number of his patients' repressed memories centered on sexual matters. This, of course, was long before the importance of sexual factors in psychoanalysis became a matter of common knowledge and could not be attributed to knowledge on the part of his patients that sexual disclosures were expected of them. After trying the method of direct inquiry into these sexual matters, Freud realized that this impeded treatment. He therefore resumed his passive position in treatment, but maintained vigilance to detect the appearance of sexual material.

In the late eighties and early nineties, Freud tried to interest Breuer in publishing material on his patient Anna O. and others treated by Freud. From Freud's point of view, Breuer was inexplicably reluctant. Eventually, however, they prepared and published in 1895 the *Studies on Hysteria*, from which it has become customary to date the advent of psychoanalysis.[9] It included a joint paper, previously published, and five case histories, among them those of Anna O. and Elizabeth. Although *Studies on Hysteria* received some reviews, mostly unfavorable, it created little stir. Only 626 copies were sold in the next thirteen years, for which each author received in royalty a sum equivalent to about $170.

Between 1895 and 1897, bitterness developed between the two collaborators, creating a breach that was never healed; thereafter, they went their separate ways.

In 1896, Freud delivered before a psychiatric and neurological society in Vienna a paper on the etiology of hysteria. In it he referred specifically to his conviction that at the basis of every case of hysteria will be found a premature sexual experience early in childhood. He had become convinced that all his patients had experienced something resembling seduction when they were children; most often the adult seducer was an older relative, often the father. It was this trauma that produced the symptoms. One point that convinced him of the validity of his interpretation was the extreme reluctance of his patients to describe in detail that scene and the feeling of unreality that pervaded it. It was as if, unlike other forgotten material, they really did not remember the experience. This convinced him they were not malingering, because they seemed to protest that, although the reported incident was the truth, they felt somehow it could not have happened. A short time after he gave this paper, the horrible truth began to dawn on him—in most, but not all, instances these childhood seductions had never actually occurred.

A lesser man might have hidden his mistake and tried to forget it. A less clinically acute individual might have "bravely" confessed his error and turned to other more profitable matters. Freud did neither. Instead, he went beyond his mistake and asked the question why their fantasies (for that, of course, was what they were) took the particular form they did. His patients were not lying; they believed their fantasies. Was not the very fact that their fantasies took sexual form evidence that there was a sexual tinge to their thinking, and was he not right to emphasize the sexual basis of their difficulty even though the situations they had described had actually never taken place? Despite the temporary setback, this mistake was later to be seen as an advance. Freud, armed with this new insight, was now ready to explore the whole range of sexuality.

SELF-ANALYSIS

For some time Freud had been developing the conviction that he needed to explore his own personality. It was immediately obvious that the method of free association would be impossible; he could not assume the attitude of the patient, give uncritically his flow of free associations, and at the same time take on the role of the analyst alertly listening to the material. In earlier years some of his patients had spontaneously brought him their dreams for analysis, and he had already done some work with dream interpretation. Consequently, dream interpretation suggested itself to him as a means of self-analysis.

This self-analysis was important to Freud. There is a psychologist, whose identity is irrelevant, who endeared himself to the writer when, as a member of a panel of psychologists giving their learned (and often ponderous) view of their experiences on being analyzed, gave as his principal reason for being psychanalyzed simply that "he needed it." So also did Freud. Quite apart from some of the indications of neurotic difficulties mentioned in passing, there were others; for example, a strong fear of railroad travel. Incidentally, in later psychoanalytic thinking this often symbolized leaving the security of the mother! His neurosis, with its frustrations, insecurities, intensities, impracticalities, uncertainties, and vulnerability to threat, gave way in the course of his self-analysis to that more integrated, assured, persevering person that his disciples were to know.

THE INTERPRETATION OF DREAMS

His self-analysis and the writing of The Interpretation of Dreams, finished in the summer of 1899, went hand in hand.[10] This book is, by general consensus, Freud's most important single work. The procedure that he followed was to record his dream on waking and then free-associate to the material of the dream. He found that his dreams contained material touched off by events of the day that had not been completely worked through to some satisfactory solution. In dreaming, the problem would be taken up again. Dreams represent a disguised effort to bring about a solution. This wishful aspect of the dream he referred to as wish-fulfillment. A person dreams of drinking before waking up thirsty. A medical student, wishing to continue sleeping after being called, dreams he is already at the hospital. Dreams have meaning, and deep-seated desires can be investigated by dream analysis, though dream analysis is but an extension of free association not a substitute for it.

Freud drew a distinction between the manifest and the latent content of the dream. The manifest content is the dream taken at its face value; the latent content is the meaning behind this. The task of interpretation is to go from manifest to latent content. This is a complex task, and only some of Freud's dream symbols can be illustrated. Dreams of falling were seen by Freud as circumlocutions for giving way to erotic temptations; dreams of flying signified longing for sexual accomplishment. Certain images in dreams stand for or symbolize objects and desires from the patient's world in a relatively constant fashion. The more common symbols in dreams tend to repeat themselves from patient to patient—money for feces; journey for death; a king for a father; a tree, a steeple, a sword or a snake for the penis; a box, a book, or a purse for the vagina; or a pair of sisters for the breasts. Common symbols, Freud warned, are not to be interpreted without knowledge of the particular patient's unconscious conflicts; the symbols have usual but not invariable meanings.

In spite of the fact that the book devoted to so-called symptomatic acts was not published until 1904, the subject was of concern to Freud during these earlier years. The theme of this book, "The Psychopathology of Everyday Life," was the interference with conscious functioning by unconscious process.[11] The lengthy illustration already presented on page 498 of the young man who could not remember a crucial word when he worried about the possible pregnancy of his sweetheart is an example of this. A boy who forgets a date with a girl quickly discovers she is an amateur psychoanalyst, when she questions whether he actually did not wish to keep the date. Freud supplied a wealth of illustrations drawn from many areas to emphasize the unconscious significance of common errors: forgetting names; making mistakes in speech, reading, and writing; forgetting intentions; "chance" activities; "clumsy" actions; and the like. Such acts, he found, reveal unconscious desires.

The fact that "chance" acts, mannerisms, and slips of the tongue have unconscious motives opened another route to the understanding of the patient for Freud. Again he had evidence that no act is uncaused. Analysis of actions, along with dream analysis, became subsidiary to free association as a method of psychoanalysis. With these developments we come to the end of both a century and the formative and, in many ways, most important period of Freud's life.

EMERGENCE FROM ISOLATION AND LATER LIFE

In the years 1901 through 1906, Freud began to emerge from the isolation that had surrounded him. As the period began, he was forty-five years of age, his practice was increasing, and in 1902 a weekly discussion group was founded for those interested to learn his conceptions of "psychoanalysis," the term he applied to his approach. Not only were these men young, they were also relatively obscure and just at the beginning of their careers. Alfred Adler, to be discussed later, worked with him during these years. Carl Gustav Jung, who first came to see him in 1907, had already established himself as a promising and potentially important young psychiatrist in Zurich. Unlike most of the others who lived in Vienna, Jung visited Freud and then returned to his practice in Switzerland. For the next five years they were closely associated, and

Freud began to feel that Jung was his spiritual son and the heir to psychoanalysis. It was during these years that Jung suggested to Freud that prospective psychoanalysts should themselves be analyzed, a procedure Freud adopted and that has been maintained since.[12] Otto Rank also joined Freud in Vienna as a disciple at about the same time, while A. A. Brill, his American translator, and Ernest Jones, his biographer, were both in touch with him in 1908.

During these years, Freud published prolifically, including the highly important volume *Three Essays on the Theory of Sexuality*.[13] Just as the interpretation of dreams had made him ridiculous in the eyes of many of his contemporaries, this new volume made him appear prurient as well, for he argued that all children are born with sexual drives. Despite the notoriety that his views were now receiving, other more perceptive individuals showed some appreciation of what he was attempting to do.

The first official recognition on an international scale of Freud's work came in 1909 when, on the invitation from G. Stanley Hall, then president of Clark University in Worcester, Massachusetts, and a prominent psychologist in his own right, he addressed a convocation in celebration of the twentieth anniversary of that university. Although appreciative, he was not too attracted to Hall and spoke of him as having "a touch of king-maker about him," a rather perceptive remark.[14] Many other psychologists were in attendance at these meetings, and Freud met Titchener, Cattell, and James. Jung accompanied him and gave lectures at the celebration. Troubled by a bladder infection and affected by the roughness of some aspects of American life, Freud did not consider the trip an unqualified success and thus maintained his rather uncomplimentary view of the United States. Although the papers that he gave were subsequently published in American psychological periodicals, it probably was somewhat of a blow to him that he did not receive the public attention he had expected.

Two years later, in 1911, came the break with Alfred Adler, one of his earliest associates. Aside from differences of personality, the issue was whether or not Adler's ideas could be incorporated into psychoanalysis. Adler held that man has a tendency to compensate for a feeling of inferiority. In this and other respects, Adler was focusing upon aspects of behavior that demanded consideration of the social environment. At this time Freud could not see how it could be explained in terms of his theoretical position. Differences of opinion between Adler and Freud were aired through the discussion group that by now was called the Vienna Psychoanalytic Society. Both Freud and Adler eventually came to realize that their differences were irreconcilable, and Adler and some of the other members resigned from the Society. Acrimony seems to have existed on both sides, expressed by Adler by forming a separate group of his own. Freud himself was relieved, more than anything else, by this final break with Adler because, rightly or wrongly, he had come to consider him unreliable and recalcitrant.

This was not the case, however, with the break that came with Carl Jung. In Freud's view, very relevant to the issue over which they ultimately separated was the general religious and moral climate of Switzerland. Jung and other Swiss psychoanalysts had for some time shown a tendency to minimize the theoretical importance of the sexual basis of psychoanalytic theory. They had found when they did so that their relations with both their patients and the general public improved considerably. In May 1911 Jung told Freud that he regarded "libido" as a term expressing general, not sexual, tension. After a trip to New York, Jung wrote Freud on how successful he had been in making psychoanalysis acceptable by leaving out matters of sex!

On Freud's part, this was not seen merely as a matter of disagreement about the theoretical importance of sex in psychoanalysis, important though this undoubtedly was; but to a great extent his distress arose from a conviction that Jung's reason for minimizing sex was an intellectually dishonest one. Freud believed that Jung was catering to popular opinion by omitting the sexual factor. Then and later, there was some suggestion that Jung believed Freud's Jewish background had something to do with his overemphasis of sex; this hurt Freud deeply.

In 1914, Jung formally severed his connection with Freudian psychoanalysis by resigning his position as president of the International Association of Psychoanalysis. As Freud put it, they took leave of one another without feeling a need for further meetings.[15] The break was difficult on both sides, but it was inevitable and final. The Jungian side of the story will be taken up later.

The years of World War I interrupted Freud's work to some extent but brought no personal tragedy, unusual hardships, or limitations except in number of patients, food restrictions, and reduced income.

His own interests were moving into the more theoretical channels of "metapsychology," as he called it. Metapsychology was a term coined by analogy with Aristotelian metaphysics—going beyond psychology. He meant by it accounting for a mental process in terms of its dynamic significance, topographical features, and economic significance. He aimed to arrive at a general theoretical structure that would guide psychoanalysts in collecting and meaningfully organizing clinical data.

These contributions will form a major part of the systematic account of psychoanalysis given later. During his remaining years Freud was occupied with a great variety of writings. He continued to make clinical contributions, but much of his time was taken up by metapsychology and the contributions of psychoanalysis to biology, anthropology, sociology, religion, art, and literature. The standard English edition of his works, from *The Interpretation of Dreams*[16] of 1900 through the posthumously published *An Outline of Psychoanalysis,*[17] fills twenty-four volumes.

During the period from 1919 until his death in 1939 Freud was at the pinnacle of his fame. In the years immediately following the war, of course, Europe was in chaos. The International Association of Psychoanalysis and the newly organized publishing house founded in Vienna in 1919 were both in a precarious state.

One of his most faithful and hard-working assistants in these administrative ventures was Otto Rank, who had been a protegé of Freud. Under Freud's urging he had taken a nonmedical university degree preparatory to further theoretical work in psychoanalysis. He had a special flair for the interpretation of myths, legends, and dreams. Rank's book, *The Trauma of Birth,* appeared in 1923.[18] Birth trauma as a source of anxiety was the theme. At first, Rank saw this conception as falling within the framework of conventional psychoanalysis, but his reinterpretation of other Freudian contentions in terms of this theme—weaning as anxiety-provoking because it was a separation from the mother, and the male sexual urge as a desire to return into the mother's body—was not accepted by other psychoanalysts. Many heated arguments began. Because of his fondness for Rank, Freud tried to reconcile his views with Rank's as well as with those of Rank's opponents. The attempt was doomed to failure since Rank saw this as rejection by Freud. Rank had meanwhile developed an increasingly severe emotional disturbance. After several trips to the United States, he finally settled here. His break with Freud was final and complete.

In 1923 the first symptom of cancer of the jaw, from which Freud eventually died, had developed. A series of operations was necessary and he had to wear a prosthesis which interfered with his voice to such an extent that he could hardly be understood. In all, he had thirty-three operations. During these years his daughter Anna was his nurse. He had to reduce the number of patients he saw and take longer summer vacations. He had many financial worries during this period, created by the publishing house as well as the public's ambivalent attitude toward him. Abuse from the medical profession continued. On the other hand, he became a world figure, acquainted with and, in some instances, close friends with prominent individuals, such as Thomas Mann and H. G. Wells.

Meanwhile the International Association was going through a certain amount of controversy. One of the most important sources of contention was the question of the practice of psychoanalysis by individuals without medical training. The American Psychoanalytic Association, which had been formed under medical leadership, was vehemently opposed to so-called lay analysis. Associations in other countries were divided in opinion but generally favorable to the practice of psychoanalysis by individuals who had the requisite training but no medical degree. Freud wrote a book entitled *The Question of Lay Analysis* in 1926.[19] In it he unequivocally supported the position that a medical degree was not necessary in order to practice psychoanalysis, a position from which he never wavered.

In the 1930s Hitler came into power. As early as May 1933, the Nazis made a bonfire of Freud's books in Berlin. By 1934 all Jewish psychoanalysts in Germany who escaped had done so. Freud's friends had been urging him to leave Vienna, but he insisted stubbornly that he would remain. In March 1938 the Nazis invaded Austria. The Nazis had actually taken over Vienna, and storm troopers had broken into his home before he could be persuaded to leave. The Nazis held him in Vienna until his stock of unsold books could be brought back from Switzerland for public burning. The Nazis were persuaded to release Freud partly through the intervention of W. C. Bullitt, then United States Ambassador to France. Freud's arrival in London created a sensation that was given considerable space in the press. During this time his physical health was failing rapidly, but he was still very alert mentally. He continued, in fact, to work almost up until the end. He finished his book *Moses and Monotheism* in 1938,[20] and he died on September 23, 1939.

Theory of Personality

From the work of Freud came a method of investigation, an approach to psychotherapy, and a theory of personality that were major aspects of his metapsychology.[21] His clinical method of investigation has already been discussed. Incidentally it should be added that for verification of findings at first he depended mainly on the same relationships occurring repeatedly among his patients. Later those trained in psychoanalysis added to this store of clinically verified findings. It might not unjustly be called validation by consensus of "informed" opinion.

The difficulty, however, that this creates is a strong tendency to disregard findings of others not trained in psychoanalysis. His approaches to psychotherapy, particularly his method of free association, and dream analysis, have already been presented in some detail. However, further discussion of his investigative methods and approach to psychotherapy will have to be forgone in order to concentrate on his theory of personality.

Any summarization of Freud's metapsychology is apt to give the impression that it is static—a fixed system, frozen into the form in which it is encountered. This is misleading because, to Freud, it was a loosely integrated group of theories which evolved through the years with momentarily important points discarded by the wayside. With Freud, as with others, theoretical formulations outlived their usefulness. They are vehicles to be used in part of one's journey but eventually to be given up when no longer cogent. This same evolution continued after Freud. What follows is an attempt to give a classic picture of psychoanalysis as Freud saw it. By the same token, it cannot be a complete view of contemporary psychoanalysis. An effort is made to present only the orthodox Freudian position, differentiated from the steadily increasing number of neo-Freudians who would assimilate Freud into a larger—typically a social—framework of non-Freudian origin. These latter developments are part of the contemporary picture beyond the scope of this chapter.

THE DYNAMICS AND STRUCTURE OF PERSONALITY

To Freud, personality was essentially a dynamic concept in which mental life was an interplay of reciprocally urging and checking forces.[22] Consequently, it is necessary to examine the nature of these forces and the structures through which their interplay takes place. This is tantamount to saying that there needs to be concern with the dynamics and the structures, or systems, of personality. One form of specification of dynamics can be seen through an examination of Freud's theory of instincts.

THEORY OF INSTINCTS

In accordance with the deterministic and positivistic philosophy of his era, Freud employed the theory of finite energy as the power behind this reciprocal interplay of forces. He maintained that the physiological energy of the human organism, by virtue of Helmholtz's principle of the conservation of energy, may be transformed into energy for psychological activity. Psychic energy and its psychological manifestation, instinct, together emerge as the basic unit in the dynamics of personality structure.

It is a quantum of psychic energy, which functions on transformed physiological energy, linking a body's need to a psychological wish. There are a number of separate bodily needs, each of which gives rise to erotic wishes. These may be identified by referring to the erogenous zones of mouth, anus, and sex organs as centers for different wishes. Taken together, these instincts are the sum total of psychic energy. An instinct has four functional characteristics: (1) impetus, the motor element in the amount of force that it represents; (2) aim, the satisfaction obtained by abolishing the condition of stimulation; (3) object, that through which the aim can be achieved; and (4) source, the somatic process in a body part which eventuates a stimulus.[23]

Freud appealed to the concepts of instinct and energy to give his views on sex a scientific footing and provide a means of describing their interrelationships meaningfully. This formulation occurred shortly after the turn of the century.

About two decades later, Freud faced another problem. The war years forced him to direct his attention to aggressive behavior and the subsidiary problem of understanding it in relation to sex. The theory of the death instinct was the consequence. At this point he held that in representing bodily demands, the instincts follow two aims, the life instinct and the death instinct.[24] Under these two headings, Freud assumed a multitude of instincts, although he never identified all of them specifically nor derived their total number. The life instinct operates for human survival and racial propagation, and includes such categories as hunger, sex, and thirst. The form of energy for the manifestations of the life instinct is called *libido*. The death instinct of Freudian theory, impelling one toward death, is analogous to the catabolic, the breaking-down, processes of the body and is therefore opposed to the anabolic, or building, processes of the life instinct. The death instinct, which has the aim of reducing living things to inorganic matter,[25] is systematically less important and, following Fenichel,[26] will be dispensed with in the account to follow. But aggression is utilized within the framework of libido theory. Aggression is an innate, independent, instinctual disposition.[27]

THE ID, EGO, AND SUPEREGO

Originally Freud conceived of the personality structure in terms of the unconscious, the conscious, and the preconscious (that which is capable of consciousness without special effort). This original focus on conscious and unconscious phenomena was brought about by Freud's concern with hysteria and hypnosis. In hypnosis, for example, there is a clear distinction between what the subject is aware of in the waking state and what he can report in the hypnotic state. The distinction between consciousness and unconsciousness was sufficient at this point to account for the phenomena theoretically. Later, however, he preferred to use the unconscious descriptively as a quality of experience.[28] In the psychoanalytic hour, with the shifting panorama of free association, terms like conscious and unconscious are too bald to be used for behavior that is the result of interacting, supporting, or canceling forces. Identification is difficult when only these results are open to observation. Consequently, in the interest of a greater dynamic emphasis, Freud modified his conceptual scheme.

The structural components of the personality are the inherent system of the id and its derivatives, the ego and the superego.[29] The ego and the superego derive their energy from libido, the primary psychic energy reservoir of the id. The libido, consequently, is not only the basic force for personality dynamics but also the source of organization of the personality structure. Each of these structures must now be examined in detail, and attention must be paid to their interrelationship in the fully developed personality. The course of development of the three structures is reserved for presentation in terms of psychosexual stages.

The id is unconscious[30] and is the oldest of the personality structures.[31] It contains everything that is inherited, present at birth, or fixed in the constitution.[32] This includes the source of the instinctual energy, the libido, which demands discharge.[33]

The libido is expressed in the id through the principle of tension-reduction—the pleasure principle—by which the id operates. A physiological tension occurs in an area of bodily need and is then translated into a psychological wish, the aim of which is to reduce tension. The id obeys the pleasure principle[34] in the seeking of pleasure and avoidance of pain without any other consideration to modify or direct it.[35] The goal of the id is the satisfaction of needs, irrespective of considerations of danger or preservation of life.[36] In the words of the musical comedy song of some years ago, "It wants what it wants when it wants it." There is no consideration of decorum, morals, or modesty.[37]

The id has no direct relation with the external world.[38] Everything we know about the id relates to the ego.[39] Since it is unconscious, it can be known only through the ego, which is conscious. Consequently, while still considering the id, it is necessary to deal briefly with this ego function. The id is known through its intrusions into the consciousness of the ego. Dreams, for example, are an externalization of this internal process in which the id tendencies are partially released during the relaxation of the ego in sleep.[40] Examination of dreams is one way of gaining some dim and frightening knowledge of id sources.[41] According to Freud, the dreams of even the most straight-laced person contain amoral elements, illustrative of the functioning of the id.

The ego includes the conscious portion of the personality structure. The processes of the ego alone are conscious.[42] More strictly, the ego includes the preconscious as well, i.e., that which is capable of becoming conscious voluntarily.[43] The ego is formed by the individual's experience.[44]

In contradistinction to the id, which is guided by the pleasure principle, the ego follows the reality principle.[45] In guiding activities, the ego takes into account the external world and its realities. The ego is the organization interpolated between sensory and perceptual processes and motor activity, of which the individual is aware as his "I."[46]

The instincts of the id press for satisfaction; the ego modifies and channels these drives.[47] Since all libido was originally id, the ego arises from a modification of id.[48] Once it does so, the ego serves as an intermediary between the id and the external world. Here its constructive function is to interpose intellectual activity, which calculates ways and considers alternatives, before allowing the demands of instinct to be accomplished.[49] As an approximation, the ego represents reason, while the id represents the untamed passions; of course, when the latter are represented in consciousness, it is also through the ego.[50] If one were to draw upon the previous history of psychology for an illustration, Plato's fable of the charioteer would come to mind. The ego is in control of voluntary movement and is aware of external events.[51] It stores up experiences in memory; it adapts, it learns, it avoids. Thus it has relation to both the id and the external world.

In summary, ego refers to both awareness of self and the carrying on of executive functions. In following the reality principle, the ego mediates between the imperative pressures from the id, the structures of the superego (described in a moment), and the demands of external reality.

Despite what was just said about ego and consciousness, a portion of the ego is unconscious.[52] This unconscious portion results from repression. Materials once conscious, but unacceptable to the ego, are pushed back into the unconscious.[53] Because of its origin, we call this portion of the ego the repressed. Repression, in eliminating unwelcome impulses from consciousness,[54] is a flight mechanism.[55] That which is repressed has an "upward driving force," that is, an impulsion or drive to break through into consciousness again.[56] The ego, under the influence of external reality, controls its entrance into consciousness, and an interplay of reciprocally checking and urging forces develops in which libido must be expended. Repression requires a continuous expenditure of effort.[57]

Anxiety, by definition, is something "felt."[58] As an affective state it is experienced by the ego and serves it as a danger signal. The id cannot be afraid; it cannot estimate danger, for it knows nothing of the external world. There are three kinds of anxiety.[59] Reality anxiety occurs in the face of the dangers from the external world which are too great to cope with; normal or moral anxiety (guilt) in the face of superego restrictions; and neurotic anxiety in the face of the demands of the id. Anxiety, no matter what its particular form, serves as a signal of danger.[60]

The ego, operating through the reality principle, is capable of investing energy in either an inanimate object, some "favorite" possession, or another person. This energy attachment Freud called cathexis, the sum of psychic energy with which an object is invested.[61] This attachment of energy is analogous to an electric charge.[62] When libido of the ego is invested in an object (including persons) it becomes object-libido.[63] This process of investment transforms ego-libido into object-libido.[64] The reverse also takes place: object-libido can return to ego-libido. Moreover, libido is mobile[65] and can pass from one object to another.

A form of cathexis is operating within the structure per se in the process of ego-id interaction.[66] In checking the id, the ego must automatically expend a great amount of energy. This checking force is anti-cathexis and is the principle that maintains repression.[67]

The so-called ego defense mechanisms need elucidation.[68] Each ego makes use of various characteristic ways of defending itself against anxiety. Since there are a large number of defense mechanisms, the fact that each individual has a characteristic pattern of them, with some stronger than others, allows for a considerable variety in personality structures. Repression, just described, is one of the major ego defense mechanisms. Not only repression but also fixation, projection, introjection, and others serve the same function. Just as repression, they demand the expenditure of libido to keep anxiety from appearing. They maintain "peace and quiet," but in a manner analogous to a garrison keeping an otherwise unruly population in check. At best they maintain a stalemate; at worst they express themselves in the eruptions of neurotic or psychotic symptoms.

An important ego function that does not require this continual expenditure of energy is sublimation. This is the most successful of the various mechanisms in that it allows the discharge of energy to bring about a cessation of impulses without the continued defensive function of the other mechanisms. Sublimations are the socially approved ways of discharging libido without anxiety; they express libido with aims other than sexual gratification. Illustrations may be drawn from the various stages of psychosexual development. A child's oral pleasures may be sublimated by pleasures in speaking, and he may go on to a career as a politician or professor. Interest in anal matters may be sublimated by work in the arts; phallic interests may be sublimated by nature study. Many forms of sublimation, however, would not show the obvious relations just sketched. Sublimation, in fact, takes on protean forms with law, order, social progress, interaction, and achievement as areas of manifestation.

The superego is the third of the personality structures. It serves as the vehicle for the conscience.[69] It develops out of the ego, arising as an aftermath of the Oedipus Complex, a facet of development discussed later. It is organized in much the same manner as the ego and deals with the ego as a strict father would toward his child.[70] The tension this engenders is guilt,[71] which was defined earlier as moral anxiety. The superego serves the special function within the ego of demanding restriction and rejection,[72] and it therefore follows that repression is the work of the superego.[73] Although in conflict in many situations, the superego and ego may function harmoniously; in fact, only when there is a conflict can we distinguish between them.[74] When this happens, the superego serves as a pressure on the ego. It makes the child feel guilty, just as his parents had made him feel guilty. In a more general fashion, the superego expresses the child's moral imperatives, ideals, and the like. It serves to control those sexual and aggressive impulses that would otherwise endanger social stability.

Such are the dynamics and structure of personality as Freud and his followers viewed them.

STAGES OF PSYCHOSEXUAL DEVELOPMENT

Psychoanalytic personality development is conceptualized by Freud[75] as a progression through a series of psychosexual stages. These stages are determined by changes in areas of libidinal localization expressed in changing modes of pleasure findings. They are characterized by differences in object relations, the structural organization of personality, and the appearance of various behavior mechanisms, that is, the ego defense mechanisms. Freud's original notion about psychosexual stages was developed to explain the appearance of sexuality in infancy and childhood and the underlying structure of sexual perversions. One of

Freud's senior collaborators, Karl Abraham,[76] contributed a great deal to the elaboration of the theory of psychosexual stages, especially to its extension to explain character structure in the adult on the basis of the child's experiences in the various stages. Freud subsequently accepted this work, so in this sense it is orthodoxly Freudian.

In the progression from birth to adolescence, there are the oral, anal, phallic, and genital psychosexual stages (with the latter two stages separated by the so-called latency period). Although the stages overlap and characteristics of an earlier stage are not entirely absent before the appearance of later stages, erotic pleasure tends to be localized successively in the particular erogenous zones corresponding to the stages.

THE ORAL STAGE

The oral stage extends from birth to sometime in the second year. In the early oral phase, the mode of pleasure-finding is most concretely expressed in sucking and swallowing or, more figuratively, incorporating, i.e., *symbolically making objects part of oneself*. Sensations of the lips, mouth, tongue, and cheeks are exciting in and by themselves. Freud points to the prevalence of thumbsucking without the reward of food as an illustration of pleasure of and for itself.[77] Sucking is pleasurable and is thus a manifestation of libido. The infant's general mouth-centeredness is also illustrative. "He puts everything in his mouth," says the mother.

At birth the infant makes no distinction between world and ego. Libidinal energy is entirely narcissistic; it is directed toward himself but without awareness that there is a separation of self and world. For example, the mother's breast and body are not distinguished from his own body.

The distinction between the infant's self and the environment comes with the diversion of libido from id to ego functions. This distinction comes about, according to Anna Freud, because his needs are not met immediately.[78] If he could always summon up the breast immediately, there would be no occasion to develop any awareness of "self" and "other" from this experience. But his needs are met only after a delay; the mother, by the very nature of things, fails to respond instantaneously. The inevitable delays in ministering to his wants force a recognition on his part that there is a world "out there" that is not part of "him," from which he is separate. Self and social awareness develop hand in hand, when the world and ego begin to be distinguished from each other.

The mother is the first object of the infant's libido, i.e., ego-libido becomes object-libido as invested in the mother. In nonpsychoanalytic terminology, the child is beginning to form a positive attachment; he is learning in an infantile way to "love" his mother. Some id has been transformed, while the remainder is unchanged.[79] Out of the id, present from birth, the ego begins with awareness of the world.

In attempting to control id impulses, the ego supplements the pleasure principle, previously the only regulating principle, with the reality principle, which requires the individual to take into consideration conditions imposed by the outer world.[80] The first signs of the reality principle operating in infants may be nondramatic and hardly noticeable, but they exist. For example, there are the barest beginnings of tolerating delays in having his needs met when the infant does not cry continually because of hunger pangs. After a signal cry, he may be quiet for a few seconds. As the mother describes it, "Johnny isn't as impatient as he used to be." This toleration is the beginning of conforming to the reality principle.

If the mother is gentle and adroit, the infant's little world is pleasant; if the mother is rough and clumsy, the world is bad, not in any clear-cut, thought-out way, but in a nonverbal "feeling." This last observation goes a long way toward accounting for the fact that difficulties of adjustment can occur in homes that look ideal to an adult. The world of the infant is very small and does not take into account the income of the family, the amount of land surrounding the house, the number of servants, or any other indices so obvious to adult eyes. His world is his interaction with his mother.

Incorporation is important in this oral phase. From incorporation or nonincorporation comes the development of two important personality mechanisms, that is, characteristic ways in which the infant (and later the adult) operates. These mechanisms are introjection and projection. To bring out their nature, a quotation from Blum is pertinent here.

> The first judgement of the ego is said to be the distinction between edible and nonedible objects: the first acceptance is swallowing; the first rejection is spitting out. Introjection is a derivative of the former, projection of the latter. In the early stage of development of the ego, everything pleasurable is experienced as belonging to the ego (something to be swallowed), while everything painful is experienced as being nonego (something to be spat out). . . .
>
> At this point it might be well to attempt to clarify the terms "introjection," "incorporation," and "identification." Introjection and incorpora-

tion are generally used synonymously; some also employ identification in the same way. However, identification usually connotes a type of relationship to objects, in other words, a state rather than a process. Thus, oral introjection is said to be the executive of the "primary identification." By introjecting or incorporating, one achieves a state of identification. Primary identification refers to the first relationship to objects, whereas secondary identification is a later repetition of the earlier one.

Projection starts as a primitive method of getting rid of pain, by attributing unpleasant stimuli to the outside world. It is a sort of reverse introjection—instead of the ego's being perceived as having the object's characteristics, the environment is perceived as having the ego's characteristics. In these early phases of development, the mechanism can function without difficulty. Later it requires a serious impairment of the sense of reality for it to play a major role.[81]

The late-oral or oral-sadistic phase begins at about the age when the eruption of teeth occurs. The modes of pleasure-finding shift. Biting dominates, while devouring and destroying are more figurative expressions. The situation is intensified by the process of weaning, which usually occurs at this time. The child is in pain and is frustrated, and ambivalence makes its appearance. No longer is there unalloyed positive attachment to the mother. The object relation with the mother, heretofore only loving, is complicated by the appearance of feelings of hatred, so both positive and negative feelings are concurrently present. How these problems of weaning affect the infant depends in considerable measure on whether or not weaning is either too abrupt or too early. In either case, trouble of adjustment is to be expected. Anxiety will appear inevitably, but it will be intensified if this source of frustration is not introduced slowly and gradually. Each child fixates, i.e., invests some libido in oral matters; but the amount is determined by the extent of oral gratification.[82] Undue frustration or too much gratification can produce too great a fixation, possibly resulting in less than optimal adjustment later.

The oral stage ends sometime in the second year of life, but oral activities continue to be sources of satisfaction, though in varying degrees from individual to individual.[83] Too great or too little gratification may result in an oral character, with oral preoccupations forming a disproportionate part of day-to-day interests—excessive eating, drinking, kissing, and smoking. There will be not only these excessive mouth habits, but also more symbolic manifestations of orality in attitudes of dependence or assurance. An infant overgratified in the oral stage may in adulthood be sanguinely optimistic that everything, à la Micawber, will turn out all right, while lack of gratification may contribute to the formation of a pessimistic individual, who is passively dependent on others for his feelings of esteem. Frustrations in the late oral stage can result in a host of ambivalent adult attitudes, friendly-hostile, aggressive-submissive, and so on, along with a tendency to exaggerate and swing from one extreme of these attitudes to the other. A tendency toward "biting" remarks is also characteristic.

THE ANAL STAGE

The area of libidinal localization is shifted to the anal region sometime during the second year of life, giving rise to the anal stage. Before examining the phenomena, look for a moment at the situation as the infant might. There is nothing about the odor, texture, or appearance of the feces that is inherently unpleasant. The infant has no innate repulsion. He has created it, and the mother seems to prize it, since she is pleased when he has a movement and concerned when he does not. According to Freudian thinking, defecation is "perceived" by the infant as the giving of a gift. What happens to his gift? The mother flushes it down the toilet! Often he acts out his puzzlement about this strange behavior by toilet play, throwing toys in the toilet, only to retrieve them again.

There are two phases to the anal stage—the expelling and the retaining phases. In other words, pleasure is obtained first from the sheer act of expelling and later from the feeling of retaining a full lower intestine. The more figurative or symbolic pleasures of the first phase are expressed in rejecting or destroying, while pleasures of the later phase are expressed in controlling or possessing. Extending over both phases is a sadistic overlay. Anal behavior used to hurt someone else may be manifest in the more symbolic pleasures associated with both phases. The infant may take pleasure in using expulsiveness as a means of defying the parents, or he may withhold excretion as a means of defiance. Parents may not necessarily agree with the Freudian interpretation, but they will certainly agree that the toilet training period is typically one of struggle and the infant seems to be doing just what has been described!

The child's ego, equipped with self-awareness by the oral stage, extends its prowess in the anal stage away from passive functions toward actively directing his own behavior according to his changing environment. In short, the ego begins to take on executive functions; it is becoming the doer. The infant no longer must induce others to do for him, but begins to do for himself. He learns to keep clean, to walk, and to talk. With these accomplishments, he can begin to manipulate his environment. In learning to talk, he can let his wants be known more efficiently. Speech is also important in ego development; through it he learns to handle himself as well as communicate with others. He now self-communicates. In fact, language is such a wonderful tool that in psychoanalytic thinking it assumes a magical and symbolic significance to the child. An illustration from children somewhat older than the age under consideration is particularly apt. "Sticks and stones may break my bones, but names may never hurt me!" This chant is learned by children for its reassurance value. They have to be reassured that names will, in fact, not hurt them. Parents will attest to the fact that on occasion they do have to tell their children at this age that being called a "garbage pail" does not make them one!

Not only is mastery of motility taking place, but judgment on the part of the ego is beginning to develop as well. Partly dependent upon the growth of speech, judgment is shown through reality testing. The infant tries out everything, in the process of which his behavior would make most mothers modify the old saying to read—"Fools (and little children) rush in where angels fear to tread." However immature his judgment may be, the child certainly is exercising it.

Difficulties of adjustment experienced during the anal stage may also leave their mark on the adult personality in the form of the so-called anal character. According to Freud[84] the triad of characteristics that are associated with the anal character is orderliness, parsimoniousness, and obstinacy. In this context, orderliness refers to scrupulousness in keeping everything just so—socks placed away by color, the desk blotter in its precise place—and finickiness about cleanliness. Parsimoniousness refers to "tightness" with money and other things such as speech. Obstinacy refers to immobility even to the point of defiance and irritability. Scrooge, the character in Dickens, and his present-day comic strip descendants exemplify the anal character. These characteristics are generalized extensions of earlier compliance with the parents' wishes regarding excretion. "Cleanliness," "tightness," and "immovability" suffice to show the rationale of this extension.

THE PHALLIC STAGE

Libidinal interests are shifted to the genital zone at about the end of the third or beginning of the fourth year. Genital interests have been present before this age—erections have occurred and masturbation is not unknown—but the interests are now intensified. Part of this intensification is maturational in character, because physical changes are taking place. This is referred to as the phallic stage. Interests center on the sex organs themselves with touching, looking at, and exhibiting genitals, rather than heterosexual behavior which is characteristic of the genital stage yet to come. Sexual fantasies appear, and, in general, a high value is placed on the sex organs as such. An important consequence of the phallic stage is that boys become more masculine and girls more feminine. As a result, it will no longer be possible to use "he" generically for both boys and girls. The sexes must now be distinguished, psychoanalytically speaking.

An event of tremendous importance takes place during the years of the phallic stage—the formation and, under normal circumstances, dissolution of the Oedipus Complex. Hence, it is both logical and convenient to discuss it at this point. However, unless attention is directed to it, an historical inaccuracy would be perpetrated. The theory of the Oedipus Complex was one of Freud's own unique contributions, dating from the period around the turn of the century, not the later years when the theory of psychosexual stages was formulated.

The high valuation of the sex organs characteristic of the phallic stage is significant in the emergence of the Oedipus Complex, which, as might be expected, takes a different course for boys and girls. Its operation in boys will be considered first.

The legend of Oedipus is best known from Sophocles' trilogy of plays. The essentials of the plot revolve around Oedipus killing his father and marrying his mother. Freud turned to this legend for the name, Oedipus Complex, to describe the symbolic playing out of this same drama in the life of every boy. By the very nature of things, the boy will fall in love with his mother and direct death wishes toward his father.

With the coming of phallic interests, the boy develops feelings and behavior directed toward the mother that, commensurate with his age and physical state, are sexual in nature. In fumbling childish ways he shows his sexual feelings. These advances his mother rebuffs.[85] The father is also seen as having privileges with the mother from which the boy is barred. For example, when the father is away, the boy may have the privilege of sleeping in the mother's bed, but when the father returns, this is not permitted. He becomes jealous, and strong hostile feelings toward the father develop. But mother-son incest is prohibited in almost all cultures, bringing into play a powerful taboo reinforced by the father's authority over the boy. The boy is a rival to an all-powerful father, and he also has feelings against which all society sets its face. Small wonder that he develops anxiety and fears the loss of both his parents' love. Massive anxiety, therefore, makes its appearance. As if this were not enough, he has a more specific anxiety about his sex organ, on which, it will be remembered, he places a high value. This is castration anxiety, a fear from implied or actual threat to the organ that some parents employ. When the boy learns of the anatomical lack in girls, this may reinforce his belief in the reality of castration. The cumulative pressures of these anxieties are so great that he represses his desires for the mother, replacing them with tender affection, while his feelings of hostility toward the father are replaced by identification. The Oedipus Complex is "smashed," but its effects are still there. It has not disappeared, but is under the control, sometimes shaky, of maintained repression.

In the girl the Oedipus Complex takes a different course, because she, unlike the boy, must give up her original pre-Oedipal object choice of the mother and redirect libido toward the father.[86] Moreover, the castration anxiety of the boy is impossible for her since the lack that this implies is already a fact. This lack she notices, and "penis envy" develops. She has fantasies that this castration has happened as a punishment, and she wishes to regain it through the father. This drives her into the Oedipus situation in which the loss may be repaired again in fantasy by having a child through the father. She "loves" the father and therefore "hates" the mother, her rival, whom she also blames for her castration. As a means of solving this problem, the girl learns to identify with the mother. The already existing ambivalence toward the mother aids in this displacement of love to the father. In this way the girl is prepared for the Oedipus shift, events driving her into it, rather than destroying it, as was the case with the boy. Because of the way it was formed, there is less drive for the girl to overcome it as abruptly as does the boy, and, in fact, the Oedipal situation remains in effect with the girl for a longer period and is continued more or less indefinitely.

If one asks, not unnaturally, why this stirring drama which takes place in both boys and girls is not so clearly remembered that it becomes common knowledge of our individual past, the answer, psychoanalytically speaking, is simple. We have repressed our knowledge, and, although it is still operative unconsciously, we cannot consciously recall it.[87]

For both the boy and the girl the aftermath of the Oedipal situation is the formation of the superego.[88] The superego is the heir of the Oedipus Complex in that it arises after the complex has been repressed.[89] Parental influence is again paramount.[90] The child identifies with parental views on manners and morals, or rather with their idealized and purified views.

He makes both their approving and disapproving attitudes his own. These demands are often exacting, beyond his childish capacities of accomplishment. Consequently, he is plagued with feelings of guilt; he has measured himself with this idealized view and falls short.

In adult life, an individual showing disproportionate effects of the phallic stage would have continuing castration anxiety or penis envy. The male phallic character gives the impression of being a devil-may-care, masculine, assured person.[91] Intense vanity, exhibitionism, sensitiveness, and a tendency to maintain the offensive are characteristic. At least fitting the stereotype of the phallic character would be the motorcycle fan, the professional wrestler, and the like. A girl driven by her envy would use her physical charms or other capabilities to overcome the male in any way she could. Actually, both male and female phallic characters are dependent, narcissistic, and unable to have mature heterosexual relations. Sexual conquests are precisely that, not means of relating to other individuals.

With the formation of the superego, the last major constituent of the topographical organization of personality has come into being. The interrelationships among id, ego, superego, and environment are taking on their final form. Earlier in this account, consideration was given to the dynamics and structure of personality. If a strictly developmental sequence of presentation had seemed desirable, that discussion could have been interpolated at this point with relatively little modification.

THE LATENCY PERIOD

The latency period extends over the years five to ten with no new area of libidinal localization making an appearance. It was originally considered a period of sexual quiescence. However, sexual interests are still very much present, but sublimation and other mechanisms are operative, producing a relatively quiet period. Social feelings are extended to individuals outside the family circle at this age. The opinion of their peers looms very large to children in this period.

THE GENITAL STAGE

At about the age of ten, the genital stage is introduced by the prepubertal phase preparatory to physical maturity. During the next two or three years or so, there is a sharp increase in the sheer amount of libido available. As sketched by Anna Freud, regression occurs; libido is redirected to infantile love objects; Oedipal fantasies reappear; aggressive impulses are intensified; habits of cleanliness may be lost; immodesty and cruelty may be apparent.[92] There are no new elements, but rather a revival of tendencies from infancy. A general disruption of id, ego, and superego relationships occurs. When the id is in the ascendancy, means of pregenital gratification predominate; when the ego is the stronger, anxiety results. Criminal attacks that make the headlines of our newspapers, although more often involving a youngster a year or two older, frequently involve what is essentially a failure to hold id impulses in check.

With the arrival of bodily sexual maturity or puberty, there tends to be a dropping away of the sloppy and violent behavior characteristic of the earlier phase and greater refinement and even fussiness may appear. Sexual interests again extend beyond family figures. The boy or girl may behave as if a stranger in his own family, with uneasiness over displays of affection. "Crushes" on persons who are parent substitutes may be of high intensity but short duration, and are quickly forgotten. In general, the disruption of the earlier genital phase gives way to the beginnings of some approximation of the genital character of adulthood.

The normal, genital character of adulthood is one of nonneurotic sexual adjustment with extensive use of sublimation as a constructive means of ego adjustment.[93] Nevertheless, all adults show some effects of the other previous psychosexual stages. Oral, anal, and phallic characters, despite their deviation, are within the normal range of adjustment. In fact, the dividing line between them and the genital character is a matter of degree. In a sense the genital character is an ideal imperfectly achieved by most adults.

It should be obvious that the psychoanalytic theory of psychosexual development places considerable stress on the formative decisiveness of the early years of life. More space has been devoted to the first five or six years of life than to the rest of the first fourteen years through adolescence, and adulthood has received hardly more than a footnote. This proportion of space is in keeping with psychoanalytic emphasis.[94] Adulthood is an elaboration of the events in infancy and childhood.

Overview

A unique pattern of prescriptive emphases is found in psychoanalysis. Idiographicism predominates over nomotheticism. Unconscious mentalism, dynamicism, developmentalism, and irrationalism are intertwined salient factors. Shared with some of the other views of psychology discussed in previous chapters are centralism, contentual subjectivism, and determinism. It is not surprising that psychoanalysis is not completely integrated with the rest of psychology even to this day, despite today's broader acceptance and utilization of the very prescriptions considered central to psychoanalysis. But this greater rapprochement was a development to come in the generations after Freud.

In considerable measure, psychoanalysis has been seen to emerge from Freud's experience with patients. His was a clinical method of both investigation and verification. Through free associations, actions and dream analyses he found individual interpretive clues that he then related to other presumably congruent findings from the same sources, either from the same or other patients. Consistency of the data, either within a case or from one case to later cases, led to increased confidence and ultimately to certainty about them. Conspicuous by its absence was the control that would have been given by experiment or some other method of studying exceptions to his generalizations. His emphasis on sex—extended sex as it were, with ramifications into all areas of human behavior and experience —is at the same time indicative of the emphasis he placed on the instinctual character of man's drives to action. He attached crucial importance to childhood development. The decisive imprint of childhood upon our adult behavior was not only expressed through a psychogenetic emphasis, but was also to be played out in a manner that followed a remorseless, biologically genetic pattern. Similarly, he placed emphasis upon the dark, primordial forces of the id, which had the ego at its mercy.

All of these foci were to be questioned, modified, or amplified in varying degrees by followers and critics. The use of methods other than the clinical, emphasis on forms of motivation other than the sexual, greater emphasis upon experience after childhood, increased emphasis upon the social at the expense of the instinctual factors, and recognition of a greater autonomy of conscious control by the ego all were to come in the period after his death. Psychoanalysis, as a means of investigation, as a method of treatment, and as a theory of personality continued after Freud. To these themes the book will return later (p. 605).

Alfred Adler

Although Alfred Adler disagreed with Freud on many issues, he came from a similar tradition, for he worked in a clinical setting with disturbed individuals. Consequently, the approach to psychology that emerged from interaction with his patients shows much closer kinship with that of Freud than with anything encountered earlier.

LIFE AND EARLIER VIEWS OF ADLER

Alfred Adler was born in 1870 in a suburb of Vienna, the second son of a relatively well-to-do grain merchant.[95] Although his early years had many attractive features, having been spent in the open country, in comfortable circumstances, and with a love of music shared by all of his family, Alfred believed he had had an unhappy childhood. The "villain of the piece" was his model elder brother, whose achievements he never felt he could equal. This brother was his mother's favorite; Alfred was his father's. Alfred suffered from rickets and was watched over with the greatest solicitude. The running and jumping at which his brother excelled, therefore, caused Alfred unhappiness, and he apparently felt himself to be undersized and ugly. In spite of all this, he was a friendly, outgoing child. Adler reports that his decision to become a physician was made at the age of five when he was recovering from an illness that he learned had been almost fatal. He later interpreted this life goal as a means of ending his childlike distress at the fear of death, expecting more from this choice than it could accomplish. More than one facet of Adler's later psychological views may be found in these memories of childhood.

He attended the University of Vienna and received his medical degree in 1895. Two years after graduation, he married Raissa Tinofejewna, a wealthy Russian girl who had come to Vienna to study. An emancipated, outspoken woman whose greatest interest was in the social betterment of her homeland, her independence of thinking and her liberalism formed a considerable contrast to the domestic ideal of Viennese men of his class. As a biographer remarked, it is easier to believe in equal rights for women than to live with a woman who practices them. That they had their difficult times there is no doubt, but in later years while there occurred no change of their respective fundamental convictions, a mellowness seems to have marked their life together.

Throughout his years in Vienna, the cafe, so much the part of the life of that city, was also part of his life. He met his friends and students there, thoroughly enjoying the informality, the jokes, the wine, the food, and the animated conversation. Adler loved people and was charming, friendly, and informal. In turn, many individuals from all walks of life were attracted to him. Socialistic in his political views for a time, he insisted that his psychological views had nothing to do with politics. His political position, however, was but a specific manifestation of a dedication to social betterment, a purpose upon which he acted all of his life.[96]

Adler was familiar with The Interpretation of Dreams, which he believed to be an important contribution to the understanding of human nature. The occasion of his first association with Freud and his precise status in relation to him is a matter of interpretation and uncertainty, as an examination of even a portion of the literature demonstrates.[97] To put it bluntly, the Freudians claim he was a disciple who sought and received membership in the Freudian group. The Adlerians see it as equals joining forces at the invitation of Freud. At any rate, he became a leading member of the group and was named by Freud as his successor as president of the Vienna Psychoanalytic Society and as coeditor of *Zentralblatt für Psychoanalyse*.

In 1907 Adler published his views on organ inferiority and compensation.[98] As an ophthalmologist and then as a general practitioner, Adler had recognized that disease afflicts inferior organs, a point already well known. In his monograph Adler went on to indicate that this inferiority must be considered relative to the environment of the person. Disease is a result not only of organ inferiority but also of external demands upon the organ. Moreover, an outcome other than disease may occur to a person with an inferior organ in a particular environment. One outcome may be to overcompensate for this inferiority through that particular organ. History and literature, Adler points out, are filled with instances where an individual's compensation for a weakness of some sort went beyond this level to overcompensation. Demosthenes, the stutterer who overcame his handicap and became a great orator, is illustrative. To draw upon the legends of the United States, the saga of Teddy Roosevelt, the weakling, and his struggle for physical prowess is well known. Another outcome may be to overcompensate by developing superiority in some other field; Nietzsche, afflicted with a physical infirmity, took up a pen, instead of a sword, and wrote a philosophy of power.

In 1910 Adler[99] went on to explore more fully the notion of overcompensation. He recognized that organ inferiority led to subjective feelings of inferiority, a concept not used in his earlier paper. Often children who have inferior organs and inadequate development manifest it in weakness and clumsiness (as Adler himself showed in childhood), which give rise to feelings of inferiority.

This signalized a shift of emphasis from biology and disease to psychology and the subjective state of the person. For feelings of inferiority, individuals may overcompensate by excessive striving in the area of the felt weakness or some other area, or, instead of striving in either fashion, may become submissive. More specifically, Adler introduced the concept of masculine protest—the striving to be strong and powerful in compensation for a feeling of being unmanly.

Freud had already defined compensation in terms of inadequate sexual developments leading to a need to compensate for this deficiency. Adler was using it to bring a social emphasis to bear on sex. Freud accepted the masculine protest but used it in reference to castration fear and penis envy. While Freud used these findings to indicate the omnipresence of sex, Adler used them to point up the individual's interaction with the world, particularly the social world. In women, the masculine protest occurred because in our social world they are made to feel inferior in countless ways. Men also show the same protest; in their case it is directed against the assumption that men have to be superior, that they have to live up to this demand despite feelings of inadequacy.[100]

This social emphasis was clearly present as early as 1905.[101] In an account, for the general public, of Freud's *Three Essays on the Theory of Sexuality*, Adler asked the question, "What purpose is served when nature equips the infant with sexuality?" His answer was that the passion for satisfaction it engenders forces him to enter relations with the outer world, a very precise foreshadowing of his emphasis on the social aspect of sexuality.

To return to the theme of organ inferiority, Adler realized as his thinking developed that, irrespective of the presence or absence of organ inferiority, this inferiority feeling is a universal fact with children because they are small and dependent on adults. Big, strong people, adults, try to control the child's every movement. Neurotic tendencies develop when manifestations of this inferiority feeling are used by children to excuse them from doing what they are capable of. When this continues into later life, inferiority feeling becomes the Inferiority Complex. The individual may overcompensate or use inferiority as an excuse to give up striving. Inferiority per se, however, is not a sign of abnormality. It is a fact of normal development which occurs when the individual combats his feelings of inferiority by striving to be superior. Aggression then arises, not from felt superiority but from felt inferiority. At this stage of his thinking, Adler said, everyone has a drive toward a superiority in order to overcome feelings of inferiority. As will be seen, this view also changed.

At the time, this work of Adler was seen by Freud as a contribution to ego psychology and compensation, a valuable, although peripheral clue to the neuroses. The charge that Adler's approach is superficial in that it is an "ego" psychology alone (as differentiated from a psychology of id, superego, and ego) is still the basic argument of the psychoanalyst against Adlerian psychology. But at the time under discussion, Adler's views were not seen as a separate system. It was only when it was realized that compensation was being made central by Adler, rather than peripheral, that there was a parting of the ways.

The two put up with one another for some time. Finally, Adler rebelled against Freud's demand that his publications in Freud's *Journal* be censored by Jung. At this juncture Freud wrote the proprietors of the *Journal* demanding that they withdraw either his name or Adler's from the title page. Several meetings of the Vienna Psychoanalytic Society were spent in considering Adler's views.[102] Since Freud and several others of those present argued that Adler's views were impossible to reconcile with psychoanalysis, Adler and a group of his followers withdrew. This was when they called themselves the "Society for Free Psychoanalytic Research," but shortly thereafter they began to refer to their work as "individual psychology." Contrary to the frequently expressed opinion, this was not done in order to stress individuality of personality.[103] Nor does it mean that man moves alone, barred from effective relation with his fellows. In fact, this is the diametric opposite of Adler's position: only within a social matrix do the partial processes of the individual achieve meaning.

Adler later spoke of what he called Freud's mythology of sex and regarded psychoanalysis as founded on the selfishness of a pampered child, containing within it an attack upon moral law itself. In general, Adler objected to the pansexualism of psychoanalysis as expressed in libido theory. Adler also believed, as we have already seen in connection with the "masculine protest" and the sexuality of infants, that the phenomena with which Freud dealt were capable of a nonsexual interpretation. For example, the Oedipus Complex, if it arises at all, comes about from the dependency of the pampered child upon his mother. Sexual feelings exist, to be sure, just as hunger and thirst do, but these biological factors come into psychological prominence only to the extent that they come into the striving for superiority. Adler did not deny the reality of unconscious motivation, although he was inclined to stress ego functions to a greater degree than Freud. He also found dream interpretation useful, although he saw the dream as a vicarious solution to a problem of the individual, a means of planning for the future. The dream had an emotion-producing function, expressed by Adler's reference to dreams as the factory of emotions.

In 1911, a German philosopher, Hans Vaihinger, published a book, *The Psychology of "As If,"* that almost immediately influenced Adler's thinking.[104] Vaihinger advanced the idea that man lives by fictional goals that actually have no counterpart in reality. He said that man creates the fiction that the universe is an orderly determined affair, and, by acting as if it were so, even though the universe may really be chaos, in a sense he makes it orderly. We create a God when we act as if He existed. Although these goals may be falsifications of experience, we act as if they were real; hence, they affect our thinking and behavior.

Adler applied this notion to his more specifically psychological problems, especially the issue of purpose and causality.[105] It will be recalled that Freud established causality as a fundamental principle and laid great stress on constitutional factors and childhood experiences as determiners of personality. Adler found in these conceptions of Vaihinger a means of rebutting this rigid determinism. Man, Adler said, is motivated more by his future expectations than by his past experiences. He behaves as if motivated by a goal. These goals are a part of a teleological design, although they are fictions; they permit the individual to guide his behavior in line with his expectations. The goal toward which a person strives explains his behavior. The goals he "sees" determine what he will do. Not that he is aware of these goals; as a matter of fact, he is largely unaware of them—they are goals that he does not understand. The hidden goals are the essential content of unconsciousness.[106] Adler called one aspect of the fictional goal the guiding self-ideal.[107] It was by means of his unifying principles that the individual found superiority, an enforcement of safeguarding of self-esteem. The neurotic tries to enforce self-esteem by being a "real man."

During World War I Adler served as a physician in the Austrian Army. Afterward, through the intercession of a leading Viennese citizen interested in education, he was given the opportunity of organizing child-guidance clinics in the school system of Vienna. His point of view had expanded to the point where it was applicable to teacher-child as well as parent-child relationships and to normal as well as problem children. His influence on teachers, then and later, was very strong. Unlike Freud, he never insisted on long, drawn-out training for practitioners, and many of the more successful and prominent individual psychologists have come from the ranks of teachers who combined his teachings with educational practices. It is perhaps appropriate to add that for the rest of his life much of his teaching was carried out through public lectures and institutes to which teachers and anyone else who was interested were invited.

In the 1920s Adler's fame spread. In Vienna many students and admirers surrounded him, and he spent much time with them. Lecture tours took him to various countries. In 1926, he made his first trip to the United States, where he was warmly received by the teachers who had attended his European conferences. He made several half-year visits thereafter. In 1927 he was appointed lecturer at Columbia University; and in 1932 he was made professor of medical psychology at Long Island College of Medicine, a connection that continued until his death.

In 1934, Adler decided to make the United States his permanent home. The following year he founded the *International Journal of Individual Psychology*, which was short-lived. Adler embarked in the spring of 1937 on a strenuous lecture tour of Europe, which sometimes called for appearances in two towns in one day. After completing the continental portion of this tour, he had a fatal heart attack while walking the streets of gray, granite Aberdeen.

Adler was a prolific writer who addressed a large number of books to the general public. Since his writings were based on his lecture series, they lack the systematic coherence arrived at only by selection and rearrangement, a task the Ansbachers have carried out admirably.[108]

MATURE SYSTEMATIC POSITION

Adler's systematic views may be sketched against the setting of his earlier conceptualizations of inferiority feeling, fictional goal, and family situation, but in a larger and changed perspective.

To Adler, the individual person exists in a context of social relations.[109] Everyone has an innate urge to adapt positively to the social environment that he experiences. This innate capacity for friendly and loving responses, called "Social Interest," is the most important facet of his striving. Instead of all people being driven by inferiority feelings to strive toward superiority, as Adler had earlier stated, Social Interest was more basic, permitting the normal individual to move toward participation and integration according to his mature view. The neurotic suffers from these feelings of inferiority and has a drive to superiority, but the normal person does not. The normal person, though inferior because by the very nature of things he must be incomplete, shows a willingness as well as an ability to participate that is basic to Social Interest. There are three major social ties, which set for each person three major problems—occupation, social contact with one's fellowmen, and love and marriage. Failure in any or all of these tasks is a failure as a human being. If one fails to adjust to these problems or directs one's life to escaping these tasks, one is potentially neurotic or delinquent. A complete refusal to accept these tasks is a psychosis.

In a variety of other ways, Adler emphasized the social factors that are operative in helping to shape the personality. One expression of Adlerian interest in social factors is his emphasis on the importance of the child's position in the family in relation to that of other children.[110] Sibling relationships of a given child may lead to certain characteristic experiences. To mention only some of the more prominent characteristics: The only child is most often spoiled by the parents, although occasionally hated by them; he tends to dominate the mother and father, be hyperintellectual and overmature for his age, and show considerable adroitness in getting along with adults. The second born not only dethrones the first born, but often ends up dominating him as well as his parents; he also often tends to be somewhat more competitive. The youngest child in the family enjoys the doubtful privilege of never being displaced, that is, of being "little" and "helpless" forever; as a consequence, he often learns to get his way through stealth and guile.

The characteristic way in which a person's individuality is expressed in its environment Adler calls "style of life."[111] The individual's life style is an effort to reach his goals. These styles of life are generalized ways of coping with the problems the individual faces, which are unique for each individual. Everyone has a style of life, but no two are alike. The goals of security, unity, oneness are the same, but the routes to them are different. "Acting out of character" is an everyday phrase that shows recognition of the style of life. In every expression of his personality, man shows a unity, a consistency, which is his style of life.[112]

A way of identifying the life style that Adler found highly useful was to ask a person to recount his first memories. His own early memory of his illness at five years of age and his decision to become a doctor in order to ward off fear of death is illustrative of what he was seeking to find. Incidentally, he checked this particular conviction by asking a sample of doctors for their first childhood memory and found that they most often reported something involving recovery from a serious illness or a death in the family. Conversely, he asked children in families where there had been a death what they thought they wanted to be when they grew up—and the answers most often given were "doctor" or "nurse."[113]

A faulty style of life may arise from three major sources in childhood experiences—inferiorities, neglect, and pampering. Children with infirmities may be handicapped by considering themselves failures. With the aid of understanding parents or by appropriate psychotherapy, they may compensate for these inferiorities and actually transform them into strengths. Pampering may produce a child without social feeling who is self-centered and expects society to conform to his wishes; this results in a clash between the child and society. Neglect in childhood may lead to a style of life in which revenge against society is sought. Pampering or neglecting the child usually results in the individual lacking confidence to meet the demands of life.

The decision to compensate is dependent on individual courage, in addition to parents or psychotherapy and quite apart from these external sources. These particular sources may lead to compensation, or they may not, depending upon the child's interpretation of them and his courage in facing them. He may creatively choose to compensate or he may choose to remain a failure. Adler pointed out that man is not merely the creation of the environmental forces to which he is exposed; there is a creative power in the individual.[114] The individual fashions his own unity; he directs his drives and decides his goals. It is interesting to observe that neglect, pampering, and organic inferiority were all present in Adler's own personality and could have led to inferiority feelings and neuroses. Yet they did not. Adler's forms of compensation, both personally to solve these problems and socially to develop his systematic approach, show his own creative solution.

PSYCHOTHERAPY

A patient comes to the therapist because his life style is incapable of solving his life situation, his particular difficulty being a way of evading conflicts. The fundamental mistake that a patient makes is to draw false conclusions about the world from his early social relations. The goal of psychotherapy is to cut through this erroneous life style and suggest a new one.

The patient cannot change his style of life until he gains understanding.[115] He gains that understanding when his Inferiority Complex is traced to its origin in early childhood maladjustments. More specifically, Adler recommended that the following methods be used: (1) to study the family constellation; (2) to infer from the earliest childhood recollection some of the aspects of the style of life ideal; and (3) to investigate and interpret dreams to see in what particular way, guided by his style of life ideal, he allowed emotions to interfere with his particular style of life.

Needless to say, Adler did not follow the techniques of Freudian therapy. He used a face-to-face situation much more conversational than Freud would have countenanced. He was sympathetic and encouraging in attitude, appealing to the patient's social interest, while at the same time trying to aid him to find a solution through his own efforts. Encouragement was by no means an incidental attitudinal matter—its use was an essential aspect of his therapy. Exaggerated inferiority feeling leading to an Inferiority Complex is, in another sense, discouragement arising from maladjustments and deficiencies. Hence, encouragement is important.

There was a characteristic "openness" to his therapy. His clinics with children were conducted before any and all interested individuals who wished to attend—parents, teachers, anyone. Questioning of the child was direct as if he were a contemporary, although in the simplest of language. On first meeting the child, it was also characteristic of Adler to try to make swift insightful decisions about the child's problem. Seeing a very discouraged child whom he judged had a passionate desire to shine, Adler promptly sat down on a step lower than that of the child. On first seeing a boy with a strong temper, Adler asked what he liked to do. He received the reply, "Play football." Adler said, "It's fine barging into the other boys isn't it?" On meeting a child noted for showing off in class, Adler drew himself up on tiptoes as high as he could, and sank slowly back and said, "I am making myself bigger than I am, just as you do, but there are other ways of doing this than by upsetting the class."

OVERVIEW

Adler shared with psychoanalysis an adherence to idiographicism, dynamicism, and developmentalism but placed less emphasis upon unconscious mentalism and irrationalism. He continued sharing with the rest of non-behavioristic psychology, as did psychoanalysis in general, adherence to centralism and contentual subjectivism, but deviated from both on the issue of determinism. Adler rejected the exclusive influence of what came to be called hard determinism, that is, external objective causation, and added self-determinism, akin to teleological causation.

Adler directed his thinking toward the social sciences and away from biology and medicine. The heart of his teaching was social interest, although, in a restricted sense, his theory was biological in its view of man as inherently a being with social interests. Nevertheless, Adler directed his thinking to the exploration of how the social environment influenced the individual's development and personality.

Freud, to be sure, had found the family and society necessary for the vicissitudes of the libido to unfold, but can hardly be said to have elaborated the influence of specific experiences arising in the family or in society. In contradistinction, Adler made the social setting fundamental. At first he stressed organ inferiority, but in time emphasized the attitude the person adopted toward his defect, and finally arrived at a view in which positive Social Interest was basic. Adler's influence upon other psychologists will be considered in a later chapter.

Carl Gustav Jung

Another former colleague of Freud, Carl Jung, made contributions of such magnitude and originality as to demand detailed consideration.

LIFE OF JUNG

Carl Gustav Jung was born in 1875 in the Swiss village of Kesswil, located on Lake Constance, and grew up at Basle, a university town, where he received his early schooling.[116] The family background was scholarly: one grandfather had been a professor of anatomy and internal medicine at Basle, the other a grammarian, and his father a philologist and pastor in the Swiss Reformed Church. Jung's youthful interests were in philosophy and ancient history. He would have liked to become an archaeologist, an early expression of his continued desire to explore the roots of man's thinking in his historical past.[117] Another current of interest, reflected in his dreams during his student years, led him to the study of the natural sciences. The difficult choice of a profession was limited by the fact that the University of Basle offered no curriculum in archaeology and Jung was not financially able to study elsewhere. He decided to combine his humanistic and scientific interests in the study of medicine, and he received his medical degree at Basle in 1900. After a year or two of clinical experience, he went to Paris for a semester to study psychology with Pierre Janet. In 1903, he married Emma Rauschenbach who, over the years, did much collaborative work with him.

Jung's first clinical appointment was to the Psychiatric Clinic of the University of Zurich and its hospital, known as Burgholzi. In 1898, both had come under the leadership of Eugen Bleuler (1857–1939), the best known psychiatrist in Switzerland. Bleuler's particular interest was in the psychopathology of dementia praecox on which he was to publish a monumental work. He coined the term "schizophrenia" to signalize the revolutionary reformulation he made. He argued that, contrary to the previously held view, so-called dementia praecox was a group of psychiatric reactions, not a single formal disease. Patients so designated were not incurable; mental deterioration did not inevitably occur; and the patients did not lack an affective or feeling life. In 1900, Jung was appointed Bleuler's assistant and, in 1905, lecturer in psychiatry at the university; at the same time he was advanced to physician of the clinic, a position he occupied until 1909.

The first publication of Jung, in 1902, was a clinical study of an adolescent girl who, in somnambulistic states, performed as a medium.[118] It clearly bore the impress of Janet, under whom Jung had worked during the year of its publication.[119]

WORD ASSOCIATION

Beginning in 1903, Jung devoted considerable attention to experiments in word association.[120] The immediate inspiration for his work was a review by the Swiss psychologist, Claparède. Jung stressed the affective determinants as differentiated from the earlier ones, already familiar from the studies of Galton, Cattell, and others who emphasized cognitive aspects.[121] He investigated the emotional preoccupations of his patients and of normal persons through their responses to a specially prepared list of 100 words. To each of these words subjects were instructed to respond with the first word that came to mind. Typical words were "head," "green," "water," "sing," "dead," and "ship." The time it took to respond to a word was noted by means of a stop watch. With some of his subjects a measure of breathing rate was also taken through use of a pneumograph strapped to the chest, while changes in the electroconductivity of the skin caused by sweating were measured by a psychogalvanometer attached to the palm of the hand. If a word produced a long reaction time, an irregularity in breathing, and the onset of sweating, an emotional response connected either with the stimulus word or with the reply seemed indicated. Sometimes the individual is aware of matters brought to light by responses but has chosen to keep them secret, as exemplified in this method's later, relatively widespread use in lie and crime detection. Actually, Jung did apply it in precisely this fashion on the occasion of a theft at one of the hospitals. He used as "complex indicators" the names of objects in a stolen purse, such as "key" or "mirror," which to an innocent person would seem quite neutral in content.

To Jung, the use of the method to detect unconscious problems, however, was much more important systematically. In such instances, the subject's response to a word with signs of emotion but no knowledge of its significance—that is, he was unconscious of its meaning—was still an emotional indicator. Jung asserted that when this happened, a "complex" had been touched.

To Jung, complexes were psychic fragments that had been split off owing to traumatic influences or certain incompatible tendencies. From the association experiments, Jung concluded that complexes interfere with the intentions of the will and disturb the conscious performance; they produce disturbances of memory and blockages in the flow of association; they appear and disappear according to their own laws; they can temporarily obsess consciousness, or influence speech and action in an unconscious way.[122] It is clear that at this time Jung was dealing with the concept of repression, that is, the disturbing effect of pain-producing thoughts when they are repressed into the unconscious. He saw how these repressed contents tended to erupt into consciousness, interfering with the normal processes of associative thought.

RELATIONS WITH FREUD

On reading *The Interpretation of Dreams* soon after its publication, Jung was greatly interested, seeing in it an exposition of the concept of repression from a point of view different from his own, namely, its effect in the formation of dreams. In many ways, Freud's understanding of the complex agreed with Jung's independent observations. Encouraged by Bleuler, Jung began to apply Freud's theories to his patients at Burgholzi. This resulted in his monograph *The Psychology of Dementia Praecox*, published in 1907.[123] His application of psychoanalytic principles to the psychotic was highly original. He was led by his clinical findings to compare the contaminated, disintegrated associations of the dementia praecox patient with those of the neurotic patient's dream life, and he attributed to repression the inadequate and "flat" feeling tone that the former manifested. He applied his own technique of controlled association to these patients and related the two kinds of findings.

In 1906 Freud and Jung began correspondence, and in 1907 Jung made the journey to Vienna to meet Freud; from this meeting came a strong friendship, based upon mutual liking and respect, but which lasted only a few years.

Until 1913, Jung worked closely with Freud, serving as an editor of a yearbook sponsored by Bleuler and Freud and, in 1911, as first president of the International Psychoanalytic Society. Also in 1911 Jung expressed to Freud his doubts about the essentially sexual nature of libido. In 1912 a book, *The Psychology of the Unconscious*,[124] and a series of lectures given at Fordham University, entitled *The Theory of Psychoanalysis*,[125] brought their differences about libido into sharp focus. Although Freud broadened his views later, at this time he conceived of libido as narrowly sexual in nature. Sexual trauma, although no longer interpreted according to the seduction hypothesis, he still saw as operative in the patient's fantasies almost to the exclusion of all else. While Jung recognized the importance of early sexual trauma, he did not give this a central position in his theoretical approach. Libido was understood by Jung as psychic energy that was able to communicate itself on different levels of intensity or value to any field of activity: power, hunger, hatred, sexuality, or religion. But it was not itself a specific instinct.[126] Sexuality was but one of its manifestations. Libido expressed itself in nutrient terms in infancy, in play and social interaction in the years following, and in heterosexual form only after puberty. Jung did not deny that there may be a relationship between nutritive and sexual traits. In fact, libido frees itself from the nutritional only with difficulty, and some individuals never do break the association. The libido, in its progression from nutritional to sexual zones, retains the nutritive traits so abundantly demonstrated by Freudian study. Libido includes the whole range of drives and is all-embracing, closer in spirit to Plato's *Eros* or Schopenhauer's will-to-live than to Freud's more restricted meaning. Psychological trauma, instead of being stressed, was seen by Jung merely as a device of the patient to bring his difficulty into focus. The past experiences of the patient were important to Jung primarily in their usefulness in delineating a pattern to better understand the present needs of the patient.

Even while Jung and Freud were closely associated, between the years 1909–1913, during which time they traveled together to the United States to lecture in behalf of the psychoanalytic movement, Jung could not fully accept what he considered Freud's "dogmatic" view on sexuality. He noted in his autobiography that he alone logically pursued the two problems that interested Freud most: the problem of "archaic vestiges" and that of sexuality.[127] Jung saw the value of sexuality—and this played an essential part in his psychology—as an expression of psychic wholeness. But his main concern was to investigate, over and above its personal significance and biological function, its spiritual aspect and its meaning in myth and religion. Freud saw Jung's divergence as an attempt to desexualize psychoanalysis and thus negate his own efforts; consequently a rift developed between the two. In 1914, Jung officially severed his connection with psychoanalysis by resigning the presidency and, a little later, by giving up his membership in the society. Jung retained his admiration for Freud and, on several later occasions, explicitly acknowledged the importance of his work. Thereafter Jung applied the term "analytical psychology" to his own theories.[128]

EXTRAVERSION AND INTROVERSION

Jung first presented his views on extraversion and introversion at the International Psychoanalytic Congress at Munich in 1913,[129] although he had been thinking about these concepts in his years of practical medical work.[130] He was struck with the fact that among the many individual differences in human psychology, there also existed these "typical" distinctions, and the two types were described in one of his best known works, "Psychological Types."[131] Those individuals who habitually derive their motivations from inner necessity and are preoccupied with the inner life, Jung called introverts. Those individuals who habitually derive their motivation from external factors, including social relations, he called extraverts. Later, he used these two types to explain the differences between Freud and Adler.[132] Freud's view was interpreted as that of an extravert, based on a relation with a sexual object, while Adler's view was introvert, since it was based on the subjective side, the individual, and the will to power. An even more personal reason for his interest is admitted. He elaborated his type theory in an attempt to understand better what brought about his own break with Freud. The essential point of the type theory is that it holds the germ of Jung's recognition that every psychological phenomenon contains implicitly the seeds of its opposite, and that for an understanding of man's complete nature it is necessary to determine the tendencies that are overtly expressed as well as those that are latent.

LATER LIFE

To follow this trend of thinking, Jung realized he would have to devote more time to research into the nature of the unconscious. He gave up his university appointment in 1913 in order to work independently without the restrictions of academic tradition. He could then devote his attention to the significance of myths, legends, and cultural history for the unconscious life of the individual.[133] This interest became most prominently expressed in his contention that, in addition to the individual unconscious, there is a collective unconscious, which expressed through the individual the deeper images and experiences shared by all mankind.

His interest in this problem led him to make field expeditions to study the mental processes of primitive peoples, first in North Africa in 1921, later among the Pueblo Indians of Arizona and New Mexico, and, in 1926, in Africa where he studied the natives of Kenya. Jung also carried on collaborative work with the aid of specialists in philology, mythology, Chinese philosophy, and poetry. An astonishing array of books was the result. Not only did he study medieval alchemical texts, but he also wrote commentaries on Chinese and Tibetan historical documents that had recently become available through translation into German. He also considered modern mystical writings and reported on the phenomenon of occultism.

The results of some of these studies may at first appear puzzling to the modern reader accustomed to a logical exposition of factual material. Consider a book originally appearing in 1944 and published in the English expanded form in 1953, which bears the title, Psychology and Alchemy.[134] Its editors for the English edition assure us that it is of such major importance as to rank with The Psychology of the Unconscious and "Psychological Types." Along with the text, it contains 270 illustrations drawn from prints, beginning with one depicting "the Creator as Ruler of the threefold and fourfold universe"—from a manuscript of 1652—through the allegory of the psychic union of opposites circa 1550, to the phoenix as a symbol of resurrection from a 1702 manuscript. The symbols that Jung found in the works of alchemy were seen by him as a projection of psychic contents into matter. The decoding of these symbols served as a parallel or model for understanding the psychic processes through analysis. He noted that alchemists who were aware of the spiritual aspect of their work states that "our gold is not the common gold," indicating that their search was more than an attempt to turn base metals into gold. For many of those who worked with it, alchemy was a symbolic way to understand nature—to find the philosopher's stone. Alchemy, to use Jung's term, was an "under-current" to the Christianity that ruled on the surface.[135] He went on to suggest that alchemy was related to Christianity as the dream was to consciousness. In this framework, alchemical symbolism is discussed in the book by drawing upon material from several hundred dreams.

In another book, Jung argued that the religious impulse is a fundamental instinct in man.[136] Take away his gods, and man will find others, whether it be by deifying leaders of the state or by the obsessive charging of such things as money or work with godlike qualities. Only with the recognition of good and evil within us can we come to a true understanding of self and have a chance to solve the crises of the present-day world.

Jung resumed academic lecturing in 1933, when he also became professor at the Federal Polytechnical University in Zurich. He remained there until 1942, when he gave up this post for reasons of health. In 1944, Jung was named professor of medical psychology at Basle, a position especially created for him. He held this appointment only a year or so. On relinquishing it, he also gave up medical practice. In 1948, a Jungian training center, the C. G. Jung Institute, was founded in Zurich through the initiative and funds of various persons and institutions who wished to further his work. Honorary degrees and other academic and professional honors came to him from all over the world during the decades of the thirties through the fifties. In 1961 he died at his home in Küsnacht, near Zurich.

SYSTEMATIC VIEWS ON PSYCHOLOGY

Jung considered his systematic position to be growing and changing, and therefore tentative and incomplete.[137] Some of the earlier steps have already been mentioned: how he defined complex, his formulation of libido and its development, his general conception of introversion-extraversion, and his emphasis on the importance of the collective unconscious. These earlier conceptualizations must now be integrated into a larger perspective, involving his mature views on introversion-extraversion, the personal and collective unconscious, the polarities and antitheses, the conscious ego, and the self.

TYPE THEORY

Introversion and extraversion, defined by Jung as attitudes or directions of outlook and interest, are considered collectively in Jungian theory as the direction of libido. In the introvert, there is a turning inward of libido toward the self. In the extravert, libido is directed outside the self to objects and relationships with objects. An introvert is reflective, thoughtful, and tends to be self-assertive; outside influences meet resistance, expressed by the individual wanting his own way. An extravert adapts quickly to his environment, pays attention to objects; his shyness is minimal.

As Jung is sometimes labeled a "type" theorist, the Jungian concept of the average man needs clarification before proceeding to further ramifications of the theory. In the earlier stage of his theorizing, Jung stated that average men form an even more extensive group numerically than do the introverts and extraverts. Although later he would not make this claim, he then saw such a person as influenced more or less equally from within as from without.[138] Even here, however, the introverted and extraverted attitudes, which should be complementary, tended to function in opposition. Jung warned against a rigid dependence on types: "Every individual is an exception to the rule."[139] Man shows not only conformity but also uniqueness.

Without altering the essential meaning of extraversion and introversion based on direction of libido, Jung later went on to treat them as categories superordinate to the four functions, which may be thought of as four possible ways of viewing or dealing with any specific situation. The functions were identified by Jung as thinking, feeling, sensation, and intuition. These functions were selected as basic since they are not further reducible, i.e., thinking is different from feeling and cannot be reduced to it, any more than any one of the other functions can be reduced to another. Each of the four functions may be carried on through either an introverted or an extraverted attitude, depending upon the direction in which the libido is turned.

A theory of two types had given way to a theory of two classes and four types.[140] Feeling imparts value in the subjective sense of rejection or acceptance. Thinking is conceptual and apperceptive, telling us what a thing is. Sensation transmits a physical stimulus to conscious perception. Intuition transmits perception in an unconscious way (as when having a hunch). Sensation and intuition are the perceiving functions, and thinking and feeling the rational or judging functions. To consider thinking as telling us what a thing is causes no particular trouble. But feeling as a judging function seems, at first glance, to be contradictory. For it to make sense requires an unusual separation—but one demanded in Jungian theory—the separation of feeling from emotion and mood. Mood and emotion are not matters of function, but of sensitiveness, which actually is unsettling of judgment. To Jung, feeling has a judging function; it gives a positive or negative value to a thing, and consequently is not an aspect of emotion. Indeed, any function can lead to, but is always distinct from, an emotion. From Jung's point of view, emotion is the result of being hit in a blind spot, a consequence of the individual being touched in an unconscious, usually "defended" area. It is an affect and may be characterized by a measurable physiological reaction.

Only one of the perceiving functions and only one of the judging functions can be dominant at the same time. Either sensation or intuition, thinking or feeling, can be dominant, but not both; for a person either tends to observe consciously what is going on about him, or he unconsciously perceives the details and responds with an awareness that is a synthesis of what he has "seen"; this is experienced by him as an intuitive impression or "hunch." Likewise, either thinking or feeling is dominant, for a person either approaches something with the objectivity that comes from a neutral logical approach, or he weighs it and gives it a subjective value. Since it is already established that either introversion or extraversion can be dominant, but not both, it follows that eight possible combined types emerge up to this point. There may be an extravert (1) with intuition and feeling, (2) with intuition and thinking, (3) with sensation and feeling, and (4) with sensation and thinking. The introvert would show the same four combinations among these variables. It may be well to give examples. A person who is an introverted, thinking, intuitive "type," like Jung himself, with the consequent combination of abstraction and hunch, may be a creative scientist whose brilliant excursions must be checked and elaborated by others plodding behind. On the other hand, intuition and feeling in a setting of extraversion might give a visionary prophet, burning with zeal to lead others but distrustful of logic.

In terms of degree of dominance, one may call an individual an introvert when there are more occasions that this aspect dominates than the extravert. On some occasions he will manifest the unconscious attitude, though sporadically and without finesse, as when an "introvert" in a burst of enthusiasm over something that interests him considerably, say a coin collection, will chatter on and behave as an extravert might, but with no realization that his captive audience is bored.[141] To consider introversion-extraversion alone utilizes only a portion of Jungian theory. One must specify the presence of both one of the perceiving functions and one of the judging functions and then determine whether the perceiving or thinking function dominates the other. Only through this procedure will all of the ramifications of Jungian type theory be employed.

Each person manifests these attitudes and functions in varying degrees but tends to emphasize in one or another of the combinations an habitual attitude and particular functions. The harmonious adjustment of attitude and functions is achieved by few individuals. Usually the predominance mentioned earlier will take place rather than the ideal harmonious development.

At a given moment, although mutually exclusive aspects cannot be operative, nonhabitual, nondominant, latent functions nevertheless appear in relation to a given experience.[142] A type, in the sense just discussed, applies to the conscious psyche. A response always implies a choice, and the response not chosen remains unconscious as a potential rather than actual way of dealing with the situation. This is borne out in the analysis of dreams, through which Jung was able to find evidence that a conscious type of introvert with intuition and feeling dominant will be extraverted with sensation and thinking dominant in his unconscious. The more the individual consciously develops his natural inclination toward one or the other of attitudes and functions, the greater is the unconscious libidinal charge of its opposite. This contrast between the conscious and unconscious facets of an individual's personality runs as a theme through all that follows. It is Jung's conception of the complementary relationship between conscious and unconscious that must now be examined.

THE EGO, PERSONA, AND THE UNCONSCIOUS

The ego, at the center of consciousness, possesses a high degree of continuity and identity, having, as it does, an awareness of "I."[143] It is often regarded by the individual as the center of his personality although, as we shall see, Jung held that this is not the case.

The persona, a term derived from the masks worn in ancient Greek plays, refers to a similar mask figuratively worn by the individual in society, i.e., the expected social role he plays that covers the private personality existing behind this facade. The individual adopts to some extent the characteristics expected in his role—a businessman is energetic, an artist otherworldly, and so on. The persona is the outer layer of the personality, serving as mediator between the exterior world and the other aspects of personality, including the ego and the other even deeper unconscious layers.

The unconscious includes both individual factors in the personal unconscious and dispositions inherited from one's ancestors in the collective unconscious.[144] The personal unconscious is derived from several sources. Forgotten experiences may become unconscious; repression occurs in our more or less deliberate withdrawal of attention, and subliminal perception occurs without the individual's awareness, leaving traces that are to be found in the unconscious. Instead of removing the child's nature, animal-like acquisitiveness, aggressiveness, and lustfulness, education pushes these tendencies back into the personal unconscious, where they live on. Even more important than any of these sources is the fact that the personal unconscious serves to reflect one-sided development, the attitudes and functions neglected in the conscious being active in this area in accordance with the principle of unconscious development of opposites.[145]

The collective unconscious, more or less common to all individuals, is the product of generations past, the deposit of the experiences to which our ancestors were exposed. It contains the wisdom of the ages in which man's innate potential lies and which emerges from time to time in the form of "new" ideas and various creative expressions. Jung attached great importance to the collective unconscious; elucidation of its secrets points the way to the individual's future and relates that individual to the development of all mankind.

The collective unconscious consists of the sum of the instincts and their correlates, the archetypes.[146] These are archaic vestiges or primitive modes of functioning that carry a charge of energy and that may be manifested through their ability to organize images and ideas.[147] "Archetypes are typical modes of apprehension," says Jung, "and whenever we meet with uniform and regularly recurring modes of apprehension we are dealing with an archetype, no matter whether its mythological character is recognized or not."[148] The archetypes themselves are unconscious and should not be confused with their conscious representations in images and ideas,[149] since they are but possibilities of ideas.[150] They are the "a priori determinants" of all psychological experiences.[151] Archetypes are inherited with the structure of the brain, of which they represent the psychic, i.e., nonmaterial, aspect.[152] Despite the contrary opinion sometimes expressed, it would seem as if Jung were talking not about the inheritance of archetypes as acquired characters but about the inheritance of potentialities or predispositions.

These archetypes rooted in man predispose him to react the same way as did his ancestors to experiences common to mankind over all parts of the world, "primitive" and "civilized" alike. Even more important than the sheer frequency of these ever-repeated experiences is their attachment to significant, emotion-laden events—birth, death, marriage, transitional stages of life such as adolescence, and awe-inspiring experiences. An example of this last category is the course of the sun and the change from day to night, impressed upon the mind of each man from time immemorial.[153] What is found in the archetypes is not a scientific explanation but an expression in terms of a worldwide analogy. The conglomerate basic tale that Jung found is that of a god-hero born from the sea, who mounts the chariot of the sun; in the west a great mother awaits him by whom he is devoured as evening comes; in the belly of a dragon he travels the midnight sea and after a combat slays the dragon of the night and is born again.

While almost entirely submerged during the waking state of normal adults, archetypal images tend to emerge in dreams, in adult fantasies, in children, in the delusions of the insane—in whom the individual ego has been overwhelmed by the collective unconscious—and in myths and fairy stories found throughout the world.

It is from these sources that Jung sought his evidence. For example, a dream image that had been reported among his patients would be isolated, and the patient would be encouraged to elaborate upon it until a more complete image was formed.

His general argument for the reality of the existence of archetypes rests on finding that highly complex and detailed representations of them, similar down to the smallest detail, may appear in all parts of the world and at different points in time. Also, the fact that archetypal images are produced by patients who have no conscious knowledge of their existence or significance attests to their universality. In *Psychology and Alchemy*, for example, Jung argued that he had presented evidence demonstrating the existence of the archetypes in man. He found his evidence in the parallels between dream symbols and the symbols of the medieval alchemist. To lend more concreteness to this contention, an illustration of Jung from another source, first published in 1927, follows.[154] Around 1906 Jung observed a paranoid patient who had grandiose ideas and active hallucinations. One day Jung saw him gazing at the sun through the window, making at the same time a curious movement of his head from side to side. He told Jung he wanted to show him something—if one looks at the sun with eyes half shut one can see the sun's phallus and by moving the head from side to side one sees the sun's phallus likewise move from side to side. The patient added that this was the origin of the wind. At this time, Jung saw it as a bizarre incident and nothing more. In 1910, Jung came across the so-called Paris magic-papyrus of the Mithraic cult of many, many centuries ago, which just recently had been deciphered, and he found it contained an account of a vision that the sun had a tube by the movement of which one could tell the prevailing wind. Still later, he found that in medieval art, the tube of the sun was depicted as a sort of hose pipe by which *conceptio im-maculata* reaches Mary in the form of a dove. These widely scattered images, separated by centuries of time and thousands of miles of space, Jung believed were evidence of the working of a collective unconscious.

Jung would not accept the contention that the collective unconscious was a consequence of nothing more than diffusion, a common conception of cultural anthropology, which holds that the scattering of a myth (or any other cultural product for that matter) from a central source occurs by cultural contact with neighboring peoples. Instead, Jung insisted that myth and ritual appeared in similar form the world over because people, no matter where they happen to be, are endowed with certain innate tendencies that result in their thinking and symbolizing in the same manner. This similarity Jung attributed to the collective unconscious. Archetypal images appear in many forms—as persons, supernatural figures, geometrical shapes, numbers. Behind this diversity of form, the archetypes themselves are limited in number.[155] There is the mother archetype, embodying nourishment, and the father archetype, symbolizing strength. All preexisting mothers with their protective nourishing influences combine to form an image; fathers signify strength and authority. Jung finds the mother archetype in the Chinese *yin;* the father archetype is exhibited in *yang.*[156] Archetypes are not always expressed as something readily recognizable as "mother," but there are many more distant associations as with "earth," the warming hearth, the protecting cave, or even the milk-giving cow. So, too, the father archetype is glimpsed in rivers, winds, storms, battles, bulls, and all things that are moving and dynamic.

In contrasting his view with those of Freud and Adler, Jung claimed that his theory was, ". . . based on the principle of opposites, and possibly pluralistic, since it recognizes a multiplicity of relatively autonomous psychic complexes."[157] There is a self-regulative function expressed by these opposites; the libido flows between opposite poles as between the positive and negative poles of an electric circuit.[158]

THE TOTAL PERSONALITY

The psyche, or total personality, is constructed in terms of complementary opposites. It is already apparent that, in his system, Jung recognized several pairs of polarities or opposing forces. When libido flows into introversion, it is withdrawn from extraversion. Similarly, libido directed toward certain functions is withdrawn from the others. The same principle of complementarity holds in the relation of the conscious to the unconscious. Psychic energy is constant, only its distribution is variable.[159] Several other complementary opposites drawn from the theory of the archetypes must be indicated.

The shadow, or darker self, is unrecognized and disowned; the inferior, animal-like part of the personality is rejected by the ego; but it is, nevertheless, present and active although unconscious. As an archetype, it is Mr. Hyde to our Dr. Jekyll, wanting to do everything that we will not permit ourselves to do. When the shadow dominates, as it sometimes does, we speak with more truth than we know in saying, "I was not myself." In archetypical collective fashion, the shadow is expressed by the image of a demon or a witch. The man without awareness of his shadow, statistically a very common occurrence, is the man who believes he is actually only what he knows about himself, and is thereby not a complete individual. He usually projects his shadow, and this becomes evident when he reacts with inappropriate affect to someone who expresses views or values that he consciously rejects. Thus, unreasonable predilections against certain types of persons—xenophobia, racial prejudice—may be partially understood as evidence of the projected shadow. Only by recognizing that not all the evil is outside of the individual himself can a person withdraw the projections and attend to that aspect of the problem that is a part of his own shadow personality.

Jung held that, at a psychological level, masculine or feminine characteristics are exhibited by the opposite sex. Under certain circumstances, homosexuality may be an extreme manifestation of this condition. The personality structure of the man contains elements of repressed femininity, while the woman is largely unconscious of her masculine tendencies. These contrasexual elements in the man are referred to as a feminine archetype, the anima; those in the woman as a masculine archetype, the animus.[160] Characteristically, the man experiences unconscious feminine attitudes expressed through the anima, while the woman experiences unconscious masculine attitudes expressed through the animus. A man first makes a relationship with a woman through the projection of his anima; a woman with a man through her animus. In both sexes, trouble is to be expected in heterosexual relationships if the archetypal image of the opposite sex is too disparate from the love object upon whom it is projected. Discrepancies between real and ideal must be compromised if adequate adjustment is to take place.

The self is to be differentiated from the ego, since the latter is mostly conscious. The self is the central archetype, the archetype of order and the totality of the personality.[161] It embraces not only the conscious, but also the unconscious psyche and is therefore a personality that we *also* are. There is little hope of our ever being able to reach even approximate consciousness of the self, since however much we make conscious there will always exist an indeterminate and indeterminable amount of unconscious material that belongs to the totality of the self.[162]

The self as an archetype is expressed in man's striving to reach psychological unity. For a healthy or integrated personality each of the elements must be permitted to reach its fullest development, and differentiation is therefore necessary. This developmental process is referred to as individuation, or an urge toward self-realization.[163] It does not call for the self to take the place of the ego; if the ego becomes identified with the self it becomes inflated into a sort of pseudo-superman. If the reverse occurs, and the self becomes all-important with a resultant diminution of the ego, the individual will have a very low opinion of himself—he may become depressed or even psychotic. Both ego and self must preserve their intrinsic qualities. The appropriate adjustment occurs when the self acts compensatorily to the ego-consciousness. A continuing dialogue between the two is healthy, not unhealthy, and makes for self-realization. Nevertheless, the self, the midpoint of personality, is the means whereby its various parts are unified. It acts as a balance point for stability and equilibrium.

PSYCHOTHERAPY

Jung's approach to treatment emerged from his theoretical position. The purpose of psychotherapy is to help the patient become a whole man.[164] It is necessary to aid in releasing the hidden potentialities that are being stifled and to integrate them with the already more active and dominant aspects of the personality. Man's religious striving, too, must be recognized and made a part of the integrated harmony between various polarities and systems, separating him from his self. This last point is especially pertinent with older patients. In a complete orientation of consciousness, all the functions should cooperate with one another.[165] Instead of conflict, cooperation between the conscious and the unconscious is sought as a goal of therapy. More specifically, it is necessary for the conscious ego to come to terms with the unconscious components of its personality.[166] For example, there must be a realization that the shadow is present and active. In selected cases the therapist interprets the meanings of archetypes, the deep universals, to the patient. Instead of stressing the sexual etiology of the individual with the intent of uncovering the conflicts of childhood, Jung found it more useful to stress analyzing the immediate conflicts in all of their various ramifications.

OVERVIEW

In common with Freud and Adler, he shared adherence to idiographicism and developmentalism and, with Freud, the depth of unconscious mentalism. Centralism and contentual subjectivism also characterized his position.

Central to Jung's view of development was his emphasis on goals that guide or direct the destiny of man. Man is determined by the past under the principle of causality, but he is also determined by the future (teleology).[167] Man is guided not only by his individual and racial history but by his aims and aspirations as well. Jung's approach is functionally oriented toward the present and future. In this respect, he stands in contrast to Freudian exclusive dependence upon hard determinism.

References*

1. For discussion of this problem and, indeed, practically all aspects of Freudian thinking, H. F. Ellenberger, *The Discovery of the Unconscious: The History and Evolution of Dynamic Psychiatry* (New York: Basic Books, 1970) is unexcelled.

2. S. Rosenzweig, "The Cultural Matrix of the Unconscious," *American Psychologist*, XI (1956): 561–562.

3. S. Freud, "An Autobiographical Study" in J. Strachey, ed., *The Standard Edition of the Complete Psychological Works of Sigmund Freud* (London: Hogarth, 1959), Vol. XX, pp. 7–70 (1925).

4. The standard reference is E. Jones, *The Life and Work of Sigmund Freud,* 3 Vols. (New York: Basic Books, 1953–1957). This is supplemented by Freud's "Autobiographical Study" and by "The History of the Psychoanalytic Movement" (*vide* ref. 6), which are specifically cited when used. Otherwise, Jones is the source.

*See p. 19 for description of reference style.

5. Anna O.'s real name was Bertha Pappenheim. She never married, was very devout, and went on to a career in social work. She became so distinguished in her field that Germany issued a semipostal stamp in her honor in 1954. What has been reported in the text is the "received opinion" as given by Breuer, Jones, and Freud. Quite recently, H. F. Ellenberger has unearthed new evidence reported in "The Story of 'Anna O': A Critical Review with New Data," *Journal of the History of the Behavioral Sciences* VIII (1972): 267–279, which casts considerable doubt that there was either catharsis or a cure.

6. S. Freud, "The History of the Psychoanalytic Movement," in A. A. Brill, ed., *The Basic Writings of Sigmund Freud* (New York: Random House, 1938), pp. 933–977 (1914).

7. Jones, *The Life and Works of Sigmund Freud*, Vol. I, p. 246.

8. S. Freud, "Psychopathology of Everyday Life," in Brill, ed., *The Basic Writings of Sigmund Freud*, pp. 35–178 (1904).

9. J. Breuer and S. Freud, *Studies on Hysteria* (London: Hogarth, 1955) (1895).

10. S. Freud, *The Interpretation of Dreams* (London: Hogarth, 1953) (1900).

11. Freud, "Psychopathology of Everyday Life."

12. M. Fordham, *The Objective Psyche* (New York: Humanities Press, 1960).

13. S. Freud, *Three Essays on the Theory of Sexuality* (London: Hogarth, 1953) (1905).

14. Freud, "Autobiographical Study," p. 51.

15. Freud, "The History of the Psychoanalytic Movement."

16. Freud, *The Interpretation of Dreams*.

17. S. Freud, *An Outline of Psychoanalysis* (New York: W. W. Norton and Company, 1949) (1939).

18. O. Rank, *The Trauma of Birth* (New York: Harcourt, Brace and Company, 1929) (1923).

19. S. Freud, *The Question of Lay Analysis* (New York: W. W. Norton and Company, 1950) (1926).

20. S. Freud, *Moses and Monotheism* (New York: Alfred A. Knopf, 1939).

21. N. Fodor and F. Gaynor, *Freud: Dictionary of Psychoanalysis* (New York: Philosophical Library, 1950). This reference is a convenient source to find

citations of the definitions of some of the crucial characteristics of psychoanalysis.

22. S. Freud, "Psychogenic Visual Disturbances According to Psychoanalytic Conceptions," *Collected Papers* (London: Hogarth, 1924), Vol. II, pp. 105–112 (1910).
23. S. Freud, "Instincts and Their Vicissitudes," *Collected Papers*, Vol. IV, pp. 60–83 (1915); S. Freud, *The Ego and the Id* (London: Hogarth, 1947) (1923).
24. S. Freud, *Beyond the Pleasure Principle* (New York: Boni and Liveright, 1922) (1920).
25. Freud, *An Outline of Psychoanalysis*, Chap. 2.
26. O. Fenichel, *The Psychoanalytic Theory of Neuroses* (New York: W. W. Norton and Company, 1945).
27. S. Freud, *Civilization and Its Discontents* (London: Liveright, 1930), Chap. 6 (1929).
28. Freud, *An Outline of Psychoanalysis*.
29. *Ibid.*
30. Freud, *The Question of Lay Analysis*, Chap. 2.
31. Freud, *An Outline of Psychoanalysis*, Chap. 1.
32. *Ibid.*
33. S. Freud, *New Introductory Lectures on Psychoanalysis* (New York: W. W. Norton and Company, 1935), Chap. 3 (1932).
34. Freud, *An Outline of Psychoanalysis*, Chap. 8.
35. Freud, *Beyond the Pleasure Principle*, Chap. 1.
36. Freud, *An Outline of Psychoanalysis*.
37. Freud, *New Introductory Lectures on Psychoanalysis*, Lec. 2.
38. Freud, *An Outline of Psychoanalysis*, Chap. 8.
39. *Ibid.*, Chap. 2.
40. S. Freud, "Metaphysical Supplement to the Theory of Dreams," *Collected Papers*, Vol. IV, pp. 137–151 (1916).
41. Freud, *An Outline of Psychoanalysis*, Chap. 2.
42. Freud, *The Question of Lay Analysis*, Chap. 2.
43. Freud, *Moses and Monotheism*, Part III, Sec. 1.
44. Freud, *An Outline of Psychoanalysis*, Chap. 1.
45. Freud, *The Question of Lay Analysis*, Chap. 3.
46. *Ibid.*, Chap. 2.
47. *Ibid.*, Chap. 3.
48. Freud, *An Outline of Psychoanalysis*, Chap. 1.
49. *Ibid.*, Chap. 8.
50. Freud, *New Introductory Lectures on Psychoanalysis*, Lec. 3.

51. Freud, *An Outline of Psychoanalysis*, Chap. 1.
52. Freud, *New Introductory Lectures on Psychoanalysis*, Lec. 1.
53. Freud, *An Outline of Psychoanalysis*, Chap. 4.
54. S. Freud, "Repression," *Collected Papers*, Vol. IV, pp. 84–97 (1915).
55. S. Freud, *The Problem of Anxiety* (New York: W. W. Norton and Company, (1936), Chap. 10 (1926).
56. Freud, *New Introductory Lectures on Psychoanalysis*, Lec. 3.
57. Freud, *The Problem of Anxiety*, Chap. 10.
58. *Ibid.*, Chap. 8.
59. Freud, *New Introductory Lectures on Psychoanalysis*, Lec. 3.
60. Freud, *An Outline of Psychoanalysis*, Chap. 1.
61. S. Freud, *Wit and Its Relation to the Unconscious* (New York: Moffat, 1916), Chap. 5 (1905).
62. Freud, *An Outline of Psychoanalysis*, Chap. 2.
63. Freud, *Three Essays on the Theory of Sexuality*.
64. Freud, *New Introductory Lectures on Psychoanalysis*, Lec. 4.
65. Freud, *An Outline of Psychoanalysis*, Chap. 2.
66. *Ibid.*, Chap. 6.
67. S. Freud, "The Unconscious," *Collected Papers*, Vol. IV, pp. 98–136 (1915).
68. A. Freud, *The Ego and the Mechanisms of Defense* (London: Hogarth, 1937).
69. Freud, *An Outline of Psychoanalysis*, Chap. 5.
70. *Ibid.*
71. Freud, *New Introductory Lectures on Psychoanalysis*, Lec. 3.
72. *Ibid.*
73. *Ibid.*
74. Freud, *The Problem of Anxiety*, Chap. 3.
75. The general outline of what follows is dependent upon Freud, *An Outline of Psychoanalysis*, but some of the details are derived from other sources. For example, Freud originally described only one oral phase, but this and other stages were elaborated and, as Freud accepted them, these elaborations are presented.
76. K. Abraham, *Selected Papers on Psychoanalysis* (London: Hogarth, 1927).
77. Freud, *Three Essays on the Theory of Sexuality*.
78. A. Freud, "Some Remarks on Infant Observation,"

in Ruth S. Eissler et al., eds., *Psychoanalytic Studies of the Child* (New York: International, 1947), Vol. II, pp. 11–30.

79. Freud, *An Outline of Psychoanalysis,* Chap. 4.
80. Freud, *The Question of Lay Analysis,* Chap. 3.
81. G. S. Blum, *Psychoanalytic Theories of Personality* (New York: McGraw-Hill Book Company, 1953), pp. 46–47 (Reprinted by permission).
82. Fenichel, *The Psychoanalytic Theory of Neuroses.*
83. *Ibid.*
84. Freud, *New Introductory Lectures on Psychoanalysis,* Lec. 6.
85. R. L. Munroe, *Schools of Psychoanalytic Thought* (New York: Dryden Press, 1955).
86. *Ibid.*
87. Freud, *New Introductory Lectures on Psychoanalysis,* Lec. 3.
88. *Ibid.*
89. Freud, *An Outline of Psychoanalysis,* Chap. 8.
90. *Ibid.,* Chap. 1.
91. Fenichel, *The Psychoanalytic Theory of Neuroses.*
92. Freud, *Ego and Mechanisms of Defense.*
93. Fenichel, *The Psychoanalytic Theory of Neuroses.*
94. Freud, *Moses and Monotheism,* Part III, Sec. II.
95. P. Bottome, *Alfred Adler, a Biography* (New York: G. P. Putnam's Sons, 1939). This has been considered standard for many years. It must, however, be supplemented by a more recent statement which fills in some of the gaps and makes some corrections. This is the account by C. Furtmüller (*vide* ref. 96, pp. 311–393).
96. H. L. Ansbacher and R. R. Ansbacher, eds., *Superiority and Social Interest: A Collection of Later Writings by Alfred Adler* (Evanston: Northwestern University Press, 1964) (1928–1937). Editorial introduction.
97. Furtmüller, in Ansbacher and Ansbacher, eds., *Superiority and Social Interest;* A. H. Maslow, "Was Adler a Disciple of Freud? (A note)," *Journal of Individual Psychology,* XVIII (1962): 125; H. L. Ansbacher, "Was Adler a Disciple of Freud? (A reply)," *ibid.,* XVIII (1962): 126–135; E. Federn "Was Adler a Disciple of Freud? (A Freudian view)," *ibid.,* XIX (1963): 80–82.

98. H. L. Ansbacher and R. R. Ansbacher, eds., *The Individual Psychology of Alfred Adler: A Systematic Presentation in Selections from His Writings* (New York: Basic Books, 1965), pp. 23–35 (1907–1937).

99. *Ibid.*, pp. 45–52 (1910).

100. R. Dreikurs, *Fundamentals of Adlerian Psychology* (Philadelphia: Chilton Book Company, 1950).

101. A. Adler, "Die sexuelle problem in der Erziehung," *Die neue, Gesellschaft,* I (1905): 360–362.

102. K. M. Colby, "On the Disagreement between Freud and Adler," *American Imago.,* II (1951): 229–238.

103. Dreikurs, *Fundamentals of Adlerian Psychology.*

104. H. Vaihinger, *The Psychology of "As If"* (New York: Harcourt, Brace and Company, 1925) (1911). (Sections excerpted in Ansbacher and Ansbacher, *Individual Psychology,* pp. 77–87).

105. A. Adler, *The Neurotic Constitution* (New York: Moffat-Yard, 1917).

106. Ansbacher and Ansbacher, *Individual Psychology.*

107. Adler, *The Neurotic Constitution.*

108. Ansbacher and Ansbacher, *Individual Psychology;* Ansbacher and Ansbacher, *Superiority and Social Interest.*

109. A. Adler, *What Life Should Mean to You* (New York: Blue Ribbon Books, 1937); H. L. Ansbacher, "The Structure of Individual Psychology," in B. B. Wolman and E. Nagel, eds., *Scientific Psychology: Principles and Approaches* (New York: Basic Books, 1965), pp. 340–364.

110. *Ibid.*

111. A. Adler, *The Science of Living,* H. L. Ansbacher, ed. (Garden City, N. Y.: Doubleday and Company, 1969); H. L. Ansbacher, "Life Style: A Historical and Systematic Review," *Journal of Individual Psychology,* XXIII (1967): 191–212.

112. Adler, *What Life Should Mean to You.*

113. H. Orgler, *Alfred Adler: The Man and His Work: Triumph over the Inferiority Complex* (London: Daniel, 1939).

114. Ansbacher and Ansbacher, *Individual Psychology.*

115. A. Adler, "Individual Psychology," in C. Murchison, ed., *Psychologies of 1930* (Worcester: Clark University Press, 1930), pp. 395–405.

116. J. Jacobi, *The Psychology of C. G. Jung,* rev. ed. (New

Haven: Yale University Press, 1951); F. Fordham, *An Introduction to Jung's Psychology* (London: Penguin Books, 1953).

117. C. G. Jung, *Memories, Dreams, Reflections* (New York: Pantheon Books, 1961), p. 84.

118. C. G. Jung, "On the Psychology and Pathology of So-Called Occult Phenomena," *Psychiatric Studies* (New York: Pantheon Books, 1957).

119. Fordham, *An Introduction to Jung's Psychology*.

120. R. A. Clark, "Jung and Freud: A Chapter in Psychoanalytic History," *American Journal of Psychotherapy*, IX (1955): 605–611.

121. C. G. Jung, *Studies in Word Association* (New York: Moffat-Yard, 1919).

122. C. G. Jung, "Psychological Factors in Human Behavior," *The Structure and Dynamics of Psyche* (New York: Pantheon Books, 1960), p. 121.

123. C. G. Jung, *The Psychology of Dementia Praecox*, trans. by A. A. Brill (New York: Mental and Nervous Disease Publishing, 1908).

124. C. G. Jung, "The Psychology of the Unconscious," *Two Essays on Analytical Psychology* (New York: Pantheon Books, 1953).

125. C. G. Jung, "The Theory of Psychoanalysis," *Freud and Psychoanalysis* (New York: Pantheon Books, 1961).

126. C. G. Jung, "The Concept of Libido," *Symbols of Transformation* (New York: Pantheon Books, 1956), p. 137.

127. Jung, *Memories, Dreams, Reflections*, p. 168.

128. Jung, "The Theory of Psychoanalysis."

129. C. G. Jung, "Psychological Types," *Contributions to Analytical Psychology* (London: Kegan Paul, 1928).

130. *Ibid.*

131. *Ibid.*

132. *Ibid.*

133. Clark, "Jung and Freud."

134. C. G. Jung, *Psychology and Alchemy* (New York: Pantheon Books, 1953)

135. *Ibid.*, p. 23.

136. C. G. Jung, *The Undiscovered Self* (Boston: Little, Brown and Company, 1957).

137. Jacobi, *The Psychology of C. G. Jung*, foreword.

138. Jung, "Psychological Types."

139. *Ibid.*, p. 303.

140. H. Gray and J. B. Wheelwright, "Jung's Psychological Types, Including the Four Functions," *Journal of General Psychology*, XXXIII (1945): 265–284.
141. Fordham, *An Introduction to Jung's Psychology*.
142. Gray and Wheelwright, "Jung's Psychological Types."
143. Jung, "Psychological Types."
144. C. G. Jung, "The Conscious Mind, the Unconscious and the Individuation," *Archetypes and the Collective Unconscious* (New York: Pantheon Books, 1959), pt. 1.
145. Blum, *Psychoanalytic Theories of Personality*.
146. C. G. Jung, "Instinct and the Unconscious," *The Structure and Dynamics of the Psyche* (New York: Pantheon Books, 1960), p. 138.
147. C. G. Jung, "On the Nature of the Psyche."
148. *Ibid.;* Jung, "Instinct and the Unconscious," pp. 137–138.
149. *Ibid.*
150. C. G. Jung, "Mind and the Earth," *Contributions to Analytical Psychology* (London: Kegan Paul, 1928), p. 110.
151. Jung, "Instinct and the Unconscious," p. 133.
152. Jung, "Psychological Types."
153. Jung, "Mind and the Earth."
154. *Ibid.*
155. Jung, "Instinct and the Unconscious."
156. Jung, "Mind and the Earth."
157. C. G. Jung, "Introduction to Kranefeldt's Secret Ways of the Mind," *Freud and Psychoanalysis* (New York: Pantheon Books, 1961), p. 329.
158. Jung, "The Psychology of the Unconscious."
159. C. G. Jung, *Modern Man in Search of a Soul* (New York: Harcourt, Brace and Company, 1933).
160. Jung, "Mind and the Earth."
161. Jung, *Memories, Dreams, Reflections*, p. 386.
162. C. G. Jung, "The Relations Between the Ego and the Unconscious," *Two Essays in Analytical Psychology*, p. 175.
163. Jung, "On the Nature of the Psyche."
164. Jung, *Psychology and Alchemy*.
165. Jung, *Contributions to Analytical Psychology*.
166. Jung, "On the Nature of the Psyche."
167. C. G. Jung, *Analytical Psychology* (New York: Moffat-Yard, 1916).

Chapter 21

RECENT EUROPEAN PSYCHOLOGY

During the same early decades of this century that saw the development of schools, other events important to the history of psychology were taking place. Moreover, some developments in psychology in the very recent past must be expressed in a report of the thinking of a few contemporary psychologists. Despite hopes that psychology will become a science with a universally agreed-upon content, national differences are still so important that it is necessary to order discussion to national-linguistic boundaries. In this chapter German, French, Russian, and British psychology of the recent past is discussed, while the next chapter is devoted to events in the United States.

German Psychology

For examination of one potent intellectual force in recent and contemporary German psychology it is necessary to return to a contemporary of Wundt, Wilhelm Dilthey (1833–1911).[1] Although he was an important and popular professor of philosophy at the University of Berlin, his posthumous influence was even greater. In considerable measure this was because Dilthey's views were in accord with the pervasive background of German Romanticism, widespread in Germany but with relatively little influence beyond. His views gained momentum during the rise of experimental psychology in Germany but commanded a dominant position in Germany after the death of Wundt.

Dilthey[2] drew upon the philosopher Wilhelm Windelband's (1849–1915) distinction between the natural and cultural sciences (Geisteswissenschaften) that led to a spirited and widespread conflict over whether to conceive of psychology as a cultural science or as a natural or empirical science. Empirical psychology is inadequate, argued Dilthey, in its study of the elements of consciousness. Instead, the total structure of the mind must be understood. Dilthey and his supporters referred to this "structure" in a new sense diametrically opposed to the structure of Wundt and Titchener. The search for elements is a pseudo study in an attempt to develop a natural science. It should be replaced. As he put it, the proper task is not the study of the bricks and mortar but of the overall architecture of the completed structure which shows how it relates to the parts. Disclosure of development in order to understand the dynamics of the mind is still another task. Dilthey thus opposed considering psychology a natural science. He held that natural sciences explain and psychology has no need for explanations, since the mind acts as a unit. What is needed is not to explain details, but to understand the mind as a whole. There is, nevertheless, a cultural science psychology. This psychology, Verstenhende-psychologie in his terminology, is a descriptive or understanding endeavor, not an explanatory science.[3]

His original bitter attacks on psychology were met by spirited rebuttals, such as that of his former pupil, Ebbinghaus[4], who argued that his view was directed against antiquated representatives of empirical molecular psychology, such as Herbart, rather than the contemporary views of psychology. However, by and large, experimental psychologists at the turn of the century, and for perhaps two decades thereafter, merely shrugged their shoulders and went on with their work.

It was only in later years that Dilthey's views became increasingly a threat to experimental psychology. Philosophers more and more were influenced by Dilthey's antagonism to experimental psychology. Psychology, academically speaking, was still in the philosophical faculty, which was usually within the division of the humanities. Decisions about new appointments and the direction psychology was to take therefore rested with those suspicious of experimental methods.[5] A decline in the power and prestige of psychology as a natural science became evident. Wundt's explanatory psychology, indeed any positivistic psychology, began to lose ground, and with this decline there was an increase in the influence of a psychology in agreement with Dilthey's position.

It is now fitting to return in time to Leipzig after Wundt's retirement. It was Felix E. Krueger (1874–1948) who succeeded Wundt in 1917 to that oldest of psychology's chairs, the one at Leipzig. Disregarding certain nuances of difference, he established what has been called Ganz-heitspsychologie, totality psychology, holistic psychology, and the Leipzig Gestalt School.[6] German psychologists had always referred to Gestalt psychology in terms of its original university setting. Thus the work of Wertheimer, Koffka, and Köhler was referred to as the Berlin Gestalt School. The Leipzig Gestalt School accepted the integrated whole or Gestalt concept, but it owed perhaps as much or more to the oldest of Gestalt schools, that at Graz, Austria (p. 469). They also were influenced by Dilthey's concepts of totality and structure. Krueger and his associates accused the Berlin School of limiting itself to cognitive processes and consequently neglecting the all-embracing totality of the life of feeling. Moreover, this school placed considerably more emphasis than the Berlin school on understanding the psychological phenomena of the mind in the light of its development, and they insisted that the scope of psychology be broadened to include social and cultural factors.

Although Dilthey had denied that experimental psychology would be a natural science, as indicated before he did accept the notion that psychology of personality could be classificatory and descriptive provided it was molar in nature. Rationalistically derived insights from this view he sketched in terms of broad areas of human activity.

This point of view was adopted by Eduard Spranger (1882–1963), a student of Dilthey and a philosopher at the University of Berlin, who first published in 1913 on personality types expressed in attitudes or values.[7] Types of men were differentiated according to the attitude which predominated in the individual. These attitudes, which are expressed as aims, are the economic, the theoretical, the esthetic, the religious, the social, and the political. The economic man aims at the political and utilitarian; the theoretical man aims at cognition; the esthetic man, the artistic values of life; the social man, the rights of other individuals; the political man, power. These are ideal types and do not occur in pure form. Instead, there is a mixture with varying degrees of strength in the individual. While Spranger was content to present his theory in a rationalistic, impressionistic, insightful fashion, Gordon Allport[8] in the United States saw it as the starting point for empirical investigation and developed a test of values.

Ernst Kretchmer (1888–1964), whose work on physique and character in a descriptive view first appeared in book form in 1921, is perhaps better known in the United States.[9] It is unfortunate that the available English translation is so out of date as to give only a caricature of his views.[10]

Undoubtedly the world's foremost graphologist was Ludwig Klages[11] (1872–1956); *Handschrift und Charakter,* his most celebrated book, first appeared in 1917, and during the next fifty years went through twenty-six editions.[12] Suspect in the United States because of its intuitive character, graphology is still widely used throughout Europe, both as an individual tool of appraisal and, more commonly, in conjunction with other devices. His psychological theory based on the information provided by graphology was a variant of the so-called characterology next discussed.

Characterology is a prevalent European approach to personality. Thomae catches at least some aspects of the term's meaning when he defines character "as the structural aspect of personality, the inner conditions of overt behavior that are, to a certain extent, constant."[13] An approach to characterology still prevalent in German psychology is stratification theory—actually a variety of approaches that stress a hierarchy or hegemony among distinct mental processes. The leadership in stratification theory may be said to have been shared by two German psychologists, Erich Rothacker (1888–1965), late of Bonn, and Philipp Lersch of Munich, who first published simultaneously and independently in 1938.[14] The debt to Freud's theory of ego, superego, and id is both obvious and acknowledged.[15] A debt to philosophical ontology, though not obvious, is also not unexpected. But an appeal to brain research is perhaps a surprise. Here the emphasis is on the different psychological functions found in the new brain (cerebrum) and the old brain (brain stem). The theories of stratified levels of personality call not for development as a steady growth, but for the superposition of one layer of personality on another.[16] They also hold that psychology occupies a position between the natural and social sciences and is by no means exclusively confined to experimental methods.

Interest in characterology continues unabated, particularly in Germany and Austria. A general statement by Hubert Rohracher[17] of Vienna has been extremely popular. An attempt to reconcile the American and German approaches of personality has been made by Hans Thomae[18] of Bonn, while a masterly appraisal of contrasting trends in European and American personality psychology has been provided by G. W. Allport[19] of Harvard.

One Swiss psychologist writing in German must be mentioned. Influenced by both Freud and Jung, Hermann Rorschach[20] (1884–1922) carried out many clinical studies with his ink-blots between 1911 and 1921. Although for years similar material has been used in the study of imagination, Rorschach's contribution was to conceive of these blots as a means of studying personality by analyzing the interpretations made of these ambiguous figures.

The influence of World War II on psychology, or any other human activity for that matter, cannot be dated between declaration of war and the signing of a cease-fire agreement. It extended through most of the thirties and all of the forties. Metzger[21] estimates 40 percent of German psychologists were lost to Germany as a result of the Nazi's rise to power.

The scholarly journals ceased publication. A bibliography of German literature prepared after the war by Wellek[22] tells the story. By 1943–1944, except for Swiss publications in German, there were no psychological articles, and the handful of books published were propaganda glorifying the ideal type, the Nazi. It took years for the flow of publications to again resume.

German psychology, even today, is only slowly recovering from the circumstances prevailing before and during World War II.[23] The number of professorial chairs is still small. Psychology departments continuing to function as parts of larger faculties—either the humanities or the natural sciences, which for very different reasons may view psychology askance—handicaps their further independent development.

Not surprisingly, traditional laboratory studies are few compared to both Germany in the past and the United States in the present. Effects so minute as to require elaborate statistical manipulation interest German psychologists only infrequently.

After the war, younger representatives of the Leipzig Gestalt School, such as Albert Wellek,[24] late of Mainz, continued that tradition. While upholding the school's emphasis on totality, he emphasized its relation to stratification theory just discussed. In so doing he stressed the breadth that a humanistic emphasis gives and considered that, while experimentation has a place, it is a relatively limited one.

In the more rigorous Berlin Gestalt tradition, the senior representative for three decades or more had been Wolfgang Metzger (1899–1973) of Münster. His 1968 statement of the current status of Gestalt psychology is the most systematic, orthodox treatise available in any language.[25] His own research is best represented by his volume on visual perception.[26]

The stress on learning problems, so obvious in the United States, is absent in Germany.[27] On the other hand, in contrast to the United States, there is considerably more research interest in problems of the will, aesthetics, graphology, and expressive movements in general. Some research in perceptual problems is carried on, especially that cast in the phenomenological mold. There is also continued interest in a particular kind of personality study, referred to previously as characterology.

There is evidence that in the last few years a spirit of greater empiricism yet still showing the strong influence of philosophy has been developing in German psychology. This is vividly expressed in the twelve-volume summary of psychology, Handbuch der Psychologie, originally under the editorial auspices of Philipp Lersch of Munich and Friedrich Sander and Hans Thomae of Bonn,[28] but involving a large and representative sample of German psychologists.

One particular account of German psychology is admirable for its catholicity and lack of doctrinaire emphasis. This is in the compact volume edited by Peter R. Hofstätter of Hamburg and part of the Fischer "Lexikon" series.[29]

French Psychology

The University of Paris, with which are affiliated in intricate ways the Sorbonne, the Collège de France, and the Ecole pratique des hautes études, dominated psychology in France to an extent almost inconceivable in the United States where there are perhaps ten universities of at least roughly the same degree of excellence. In relatively recent years it has been renamed Universitaires de René Descartes.

The dominant figure for over 50 years in French psychology from 1911, when he succeeded Binet as head of the Sorbonne psychology laboratory and assumed editorship of L'Année Psychologique, until his death a few years ago, was Henri Piéron (1881–1964). He had been trained in both philosophy and physiology, but was explicit that work in physiology had the greater influence.[30]

Some years before Watson's pronouncements on the matter, Piéron had insisted that behavior or conduct is the only proper subject of psychological investigation, with which he would combine a physiological substratum. This did not mean he would have abandoned psychology and become a physiologist. Both the total reaction (psychology) and the partial reactions (physiology) of the organism are essential. His books exercised considerable influence. One, on the senses, with emphasis on sense physiology, is a standard reference.[31] His interest and contributions extended over all of French psychology. He was active in fostering psychotechnology[32] which embraced the industrial and school psychology of personnel selection and vocational guidance, in animal psychology,[33] including work with insects, and in psychophysics.[34]

Georges Dumas (1866–1946) was the editorial catalyst who twice integrated the state of French psychological science into multiple-volumed series, first in the 1923–1924 Traité de psychologie[35] and again in the 1930–1941 Nouveau traité de psychologie.[36] Some research and theories originating in other than French speaking locales was included, but it was miniscule. Another French series, edited by Paul Fraisse and Jean Piaget,[37] which began to appear in 1963, like the American (p. 588) and German (p. 559) series, aims to summarize and evaluate research and theory. Some of the volumes have been translated into English.

In certain respects, Albert Michotte (1881–1965), who taught at Louvain from 1905 to 1956, was to Belgian what Piéron was to French psychology.[38] Of almost identical life-spans, they both published over a sixty-year period and both they and their universities dominated psychology in their respective countries. In their research interests and attitudes toward psychological problems, they parted company, however.

Michotte had worked a half year under Wundt at Leipzig and another half year with Külpe at Würzburg, while teaching experimental psychology at Louvain the other half years. His Würzburg background led to his occupation, before World War I, in problems of volition, using Külpe's approach of systematic experimental introspection. However, the evidence amassed during this period by Wundt, Titchener, and others on the inadequacy of the method led him to abandon his approach. After the war, he turned to problems of perception of movement and rhythm, with introspective reports being limited to the presence or absence of the phenomena in question.

It was his studies of the perception of causality instituted by his interest in Gestalt principles that attracted greatest international interest. Michotte took up the Humean problem of the conditions that prompt us to believe a sequence of events is causally connected. The action used was simple but effective—one thing seems to hit another and thereby "cause" it to move. A rotating disc behind a slit, with appropriately painted stripes, allowed systematic variation of time, position, and velocity. Phenomenological overtones are apparent in his conception that his work showed the fundamental structures of the phenomenal world being linked with identifiable conditions of stimulation. "Causality," "reality," and "permanence" (i.e., of the world), he contended, are at least preshadowed at the level of perception. These studies culminated in a book first published in French in 1946 and now available in English.[39]

Swiss-French psychology had been initiated by Théodore Flournoy (1854–1920), who had studied with Wundt.[40] In 1893 he opened a laboratory at Geneva, the first to be attached to a faculty of science. One of his students was his cousin, Edouard Claparède (1873–1940).[41] In 1901 they founded the *Archives de Psychologie*. Claparède established the Jean Jacques Rousseau Institute for the study of the school child in 1912 and a little later was given a professorship at Geneva.

The greatest of all Swiss psychologists, Jean Piaget, became interested in natural history while still very young (his first paper was published in a local scientific journal when he was ten years of age).[42] Before he was twenty-three, he had worked with mollusks and their classification, maintained copious notebooks, studied philosophy and science, had a religious crisis, published a novel, and obtained a doctorate in science. In 1918, he went to study psychology and psychiatry in Germany. During the next two years he studied at the Sorbonne, where he became acquainted with Simon, Binet's collaborator. He worked in Simon's laboratory school, ostensibly on the standardization of Burt's tests for reasoning, but he was actually exploring the reasons for each particular child's failures by exposing them to verbal tasks involving concrete relations of cause and effect. Submission of a psychological article (his third) to Claparède for publication in the *Archives* resulted in a call to be the Director of Studies at the Institute Jean Jacques Rousseau. So in 1921 he moved to Geneva, where he continues to work to this day. At present, he is professor of psychology, director of the Psychological Section of the Institute of Education, director of the Center for Genetic Epistemology, and editor of the *Archives de Psychologie*.

The author of perhaps sixty books and a proportionate number of monographs and articles (to say nothing of the hundreds of studies his contentions have stirred in others), his enormous productivity defies adequate summary or even citation in short compass. To complicate matters still further, Piaget writes as if each new book were to be read only by those who had faithfully read and digested his previous works.

The first of two broad phases to his work centered on the development of the cognitive abilities of the child.[43] He followed the conversational method first used in Simon's school, proceeding in a clinical-genetic fashion that would liberate the child's thinking to enable him to show not just what he does, but what he could do if given the opportunity. The mass of information he has revealed about cognitive development—how the child forms concepts of space, time, number, reasoning, and causality—is extremely revealing. His blithe, seemingly unpremeditated excursions into the child's intellectual development do show an overall plan to study the stages by which a particular form of cognitive process is individuated from experience, how it changes with further experience and yet is still related to previous stages.

Piaget's studies of child psychology, especially the earlier ones, were considered quantitatively unsound and based on far too few subjects by American standards. Many of his pronouncements on child experience and behavior served as a challenge for more careful research by others. Often his statements were found to be, not so much wrong, as much too sharply demarcated as to the age ranges involved.

In recent years he has devoted attention to a second major phase: work in so-called genetic epistemology, which is an attempt at integration of psychology and epistemological philosophy, with the central theme being the study of the way in which the individual constructs his knowledge during his development. Related problems of the philosophy of science, such as application of the techniques of symbolic logic to thought structures, have also received his attention.

His latest book to appear in translation[44] is characteristic of his approach to domains of thought—number, causality, and the like—in its study, through a series of experiments and then generalization, of how children grasp consciousness of what they are doing. An excellent secondary account, available for both phases, has been prepared by John H. Flavell[45] of Minnesota.

To turn to the very recent past, in France, Professor Piéron remained active until the time of his death in 1964. Piéron's successor at the Sorbonne as editor of *L'Année Psychologique* and to his position of dominance in experimental psychology was Paul Fraisse. His research has centered on the perception of time and rhythm.[46] Another successor to Piéron is the Professor and Director of the Laboratory of General Neurophysiology of the College of France and (loosely translated) "coeditor" of *L' Année Psychologique* Alfred Fessard. In the tradition of Piéron, Fessard continues work on the neuropsychological bases of memory and learning but centers his specific research on brain potentials.[47] He shares with Fraisse the senior position in French experimental psychology.

Borrowing from Clark's study[48] on the rise of the French university, the term "cluster" may be applied to the various groupings of about a dozen individual psychologists with a minimal core of shared intellectual and academic beliefs, both at their own and other French universities. They work together, try to place their men in strategic appointments, university committees, and journals. There are clusters other than the experimental ones for which Fraisse and Fessard share direction.

The psychopathological tradition so prominent in earlier French psychology has become psychoanalytic in orientation. A psychoanalytical society was founded in Paris in 1924 and psychoanalysts now occupy chairs at the Sorbonne.[49] After Janet's death in 1947, one of these, Daniel Lagasche,[50] became professor of Pathological Psychology. He also teaches social psychology through a special laboratory devoted to the topic.

Another cluster centers on Pierre Oleron,[51] whose research shows the influence of both Binet and Piaget in stressing utilization of symbols in the development of intellectual activities. He also does research on child development.

French concepts of characterology, including Henri Wallon's contributions and work drawn from the philosophy of René La Senne[52] (1882–1954) are sympathetically examined and placed in a more psychological framework by René Zazzo[53] of Paris. He also works in the Piagetian tradition with children.[54]

There is a philosophically oriented cluster with Jean-Paul Sartre, the French existentialist philosopher, as its pioneer.[55] His study of the imagination bearing the subtitle "A psychological critique" is more psychologically oriented than most of his works which are concerned primarily with the philosophical problems of being and existence. Essentially it evaluates interpretations of imagination in associationism, Ribot's and Binet's work, and discusses and finds wanting the Würzburg School. But in France the greatest positive utilization of psychological principles and findings is to be found in the writings of Sartre's erstwhile collaborator and friend, Maurice Merleau-Ponty (1908–1961), late professor of philosophy at the College de France. Political and philosophical differences estranged them, and Merleau-Ponty's increasing familiarity with and use of psychological facts and principles resulted in his writings[56] being more influential in psychological thinking of both France and the United States. A phenomenally based philosophy of existence had led him to psychology. His fundamental phenomenological orientation is expressed in his choice of perception as the crucial problem. Perception is the way of relating experiences to objects, a way of coming to terms with the world. Consequently, it is considered fundamental to all psychological problems.

In Belgium a self-realization theory of personality with emphasis on its interrelation with Christian philosophy has been the center of focus for Joseph Nuttin[57] of Louvain (now called "Leuven").

A short history of psychology prepared by Maurice Reuchlin[58] is available.

Russian and Soviet Psychology

Russian psychology, too, had its Wundtian, G. I. Chelpanov (1862–1936), who had received his training at Leipzig. He served as director of the Psychological Institute of Moscow, which was founded in 1911, and he founded the first Russian psychological journal. The Wundtian tradition was considered idealistic and hence anathema to the victors of the 1917 Revolution, to which Chelpanov[59] made adjustment in various Marxian oriented publications in the twenties.

An assistant to Chelpanov, Konstantin N. Kornilov (1879–1957) remained on at Moscow University, weathering several changes in the ideological climate. In the twenties, he developed a psychology in line with dialectical materialism, which he called reactology.[60] Following Marx, he said that social existence determines consciousness. Psychic life cannot be reduced to simple mechanistic motion. Hence, reactology was not confined to mere behavior, but centered on the subjective content of reactions. This view, dominant for a time, had a rapid demise. In the early thirties, the Communist cell of Moscow University reached the conclusion that reactology was too passive for the activism of Lenin, Marx, and Engels. Although reactology disappeared with hardly a trace, Kornilov did not. He returned to educational psychology, moving to the Institute of Pedagogy. As early as 1927, he published a textbook based on dialectic materialism, compiled over the years in collaboration with others, and he wrote a series of textbooks and continued as a senior Soviet psychologist until his death in 1957.[61]

Research on conflict or disorganization of human behavior was carried out during the twenties by A. R. Luria, who used hand movements and associative responses into which conflict situations were interjected; under hypnosis, for example, a subject would be instructed to think of some "indecent" word as the response. The book containing the results of this research was translated into English in the early thirties and established its author as the senior Soviet psychologist in American eyes.[62]

Another psychologist who became rather well known at the same time was L. S. Vygotsky (1896–1934), who published an article about his test of concept formation in the United States in 1934, the year of his death.[63] His more general and theoretical statement concerning the relation of thought and speech to intellectual development was posthumously published. Many years later it was translated into English.[64] This general line of research was used particularly with the genesis of thought and speech in children. Psychological development is social in nature and language development is crucial to it. Practical application in education with the handicapped eventuated.

During this period the Pavlovian tradition as a field of physiology was still very active, expressed, for example, in the work of Konstantin M. Bykov[65] (1886–1959). Psychologists, however, were not involved in this research because it was still considered the province of physiologists.

In the thirties, political pressures were very strong; Luria, for example, criticized Western or bourgeois psychology as primitively biological or idealistical.[66] In 1936 a decree of the Central Committee condemned mental testing, which then largely disappeared. In the early forties military efforts were paramount.[67]

As a discipline, psychology was officially called to task in 1950 for not paying sufficient attention to Pavlov's work.[68] Previously, Pavlov's work had been considered to lie in the area of the physiology of higher nervous activity. Research was carried out in biology faculties and very definitely was outside psychology. So rapidly did an adjustment occur in the thinking of psychologists that within two years Soviet psychologists held a Pavlovian session of their own. This decree shows that Soviet psychology is clearly under control. In evaluating its effect, however, we have been assured by at least one of our Soviet specialists, Gregory Razran,[69] late of Queens, that this change does not materially interfere with the empirical advances in psychology.

Based on the number of papers delivered at the National Congress between 1959 and 1963, psychological research more than doubled in that period.[70] The 1963 papers were almost equally divided between "applied educational research" and "basic research." In turn, the basic research could be subdivided into three approximately equally important areas—engineering and information theory, traditional experimental, and comparative psychology.

In recent years, we have not lacked English translations. *The Annual Review of Psychology* publishes periodic assessments.[71] An English language journal, *Soviet Psychology and Psychiatry*, translated pertinent articles. Recently, this journal has split, giving each of the two fields its own journal. In 1966 there was a special issue worth mentioning specifically. Josef Brozek of Lehigh University and others reported on current psychological work and the books translated, and gave bibliographies.[72] Between 1964 and 1966, thirty-four monographs and books were translated from the Russian. A two-volume statement of psychological science and an even more recent handbook are available in English.[73]

The cognitive processes expressed in developmental terms, language usage, the thought processes, and information processing have been the concern of Alexei N. Leontiev,[74] his country's spokesman at International Congresses, professor and head of the department of Moscow University, and recipient of the Lenin Prize for Science.

Anatoli Smirnov,[75] director of the Institute of Psychology of Moscow University serves as editor of a projected six-volume survey, *Foundations of Psychology*. The first volume appeared in 1971 and is devoted to both a history and survey of the field. Presumably, the series is to serve the same functions as the comparable German, French, and American multi-volumed surveys of the decade before.

Outside of the Soviet Union the mistaken impression has arisen that psychology is still dominated by Pavlovian thinking. In spite of frequent introductory remarks praising Pavlov in practically any kind of psycholog-ical publication, the reported research content ranges over almost as wide an area as in contemporary publications in the United States, despite differences in emphases. In a volume[76] of translations from the journal literature of the sixties, there were detailed summaries from hundreds of publications, the areas covering not only psychophysiology and neuropsychology but also child psychology and learning and areas not much stressed in the United States—labor psychology, aviation psychology, military psychology, and the psychology of sports. Other very active research areas, although not represented by articles in this particular publication, are cybernetics and thinking. A current statement by Rahmani[77] on the status of Soviet psychology has the virtue of being devoted to this wide spectrum of psychological activities.

British Psychology

As we have seen in Chapter 14, experimental psychology was slow to be established in British universities. During the early decades of this century, laboratories were just beginning to be founded; chairs (i.e., professorships) in psychology, so important as sources of academic power, were yet to be established.[78] The first of these was the chair founded at Manchester in 1919 and held by Tom H. Pear. Charles Spearman held the Grote Chair of Mind and Logic at University College, London, until 1928; Cambridge had its first chair in 1931, but Oxford was not to establish one until 1946. The first occupant of this chair was George Humphrey[79] (1889–1966), an Oxford man and a Canadian, who had taught in both his native country and the United States. He did what he could to fight the good fight, but on reaching Emeritus status, he retired to Cambridge.

The British Psychological Society, founded in 1901, still had fewer than 100 members in 1918 (although this was due in part to very restric-tive requirements for membership).[80] At the outbreak of World War II, the total lecturing staff in psychology at British universities numbered only about thirty.[81] As a consequence, work by physiologists and statisticians loomed large in these years. Names such as Hughlings-Jackson (p. 335), Sherrington, Head, and Spearman come to mind as representative of the period, and of these only Spearman was a psychologist. This is reflected in the account to follow.

The long life of Sir Charles Sherrington[82] (1857–1952), Nobel prize laureate in physiology, covered much of the period that saw the emergence of modern psychology. First at Liverpool (1895–1913) and then at Oxford (1913–1935), he not only carried on distinguished work in neurophysiology, but also lent his prestige and facilities to the developing field of psychology. He did much to establish the bases of our knowledge of neural functioning. His major work, *The Integrative Action of the Nervous System*, first appeared in 1906 and was reprinted in 1947.[83] In it, the reflex was examined, not as it functions in isolation, but as the unit of functional integration in which it came under control of high levels of neural action. His task was to work out the mechanisms involved in this integration. The discovery of reciprocal innervation led him to work out many of the details of excitation and inhibition, particularly showing that the latter, too, is an activity. In his Liverpool laboratory, psychologists served as research men and lecturers, as did Robert S. Woodworth and Cyril Burt.

Henry Head (1861–1940), a disciple of Hughlings-Jackson (p. 335) and Sherrington's friend and contemporary, did for sensation what the latter had done for reflex action. He also worked directly with psychologists—not only with W. H. R. Rivers, mentioned shortly, but years later with F. C. Bartlett (p. 571). In 1905 and 1908, Head,[84] with W. H. R. Rivers (1864–1922), ethnologist and early teacher of experimental psychology at Cambridge, published research on the cutaneous sensibility of injured nerves and found that a dissolution, in Jackson's meaning of the term, occurred. Head did this by cutting nerves in his arm and studying the loss and then return of sensibility. On the basis of these and other observations, he postulated three levels of sensibility—"deep" sensibility, responsive to pressure and movement; "protopathic" sensibility, responsive to extremes of heat, cold, and pain; and "epicritic" sensibility, accurate and discriminating for all forms of cutaneous stimulation.[85] These levels of sensibility were considered to support the Jacksonian doctrine of evolutionary levels.

His other major research concerned speech disorder and culminated in *Aphasia and Kindred Disorders of Speech,*[86] which appeared in 1926. One facet of the work was his concept of vigilance, which accounted for the level of efficient alertness that keeps automatic actions under control.[87] Lowered vigilance occurs when neural disorders or debilitating disease cause loss of this controlling function. For example, a sick child loses vigilance when he wets the bed, which was previously prevented because of control by a spinal reflex. This concept was not developed by Head in any detail, but did stimulate considerable research by others later.

This tradition of physiological work intertwined with psychological aspects did not cease with the passing of Sherrington and Head. It was continued by Edgar D. Adrian, who worked on the refractory period of the nerve fiber and more generally, as the title of one of his major works indicates, *The Mechanism of Nervous Action.* [88] He took advantage of the availability of vacuum tubes to amplify the small electrical charges that corresponded to individual nerve impulse passage. It led to his conclusion that no radical differences exist in the nature of the nerve impulses in either different kinds of sense organs or different parts of the brain.

After a considerable period of reading and reflection while serving in the military service, Charles E. Spearman[89] (1863–1945) decided at the age of thirty-six that psychology was the field he wished to pursue. So at the beginning of this century, he turned to Leipzig and obtained a degree with Wundt, Krueger, and Wirth. Although he admired Wundt as a person, he did not have the same feeling toward his work, which he characterized as being too centered in sensation. The several years that followed his degree he spent in more or less casual but intensive postdoctoral work with Külpe, Müller, and physiologists. In 1907, he accepted appointment at the University College, London, and in 1911 was made professor, a position he held until 1931.

He saw his major task as nothing less than finding the fundamental laws of psychology.[90] While familiar with the doctrine of association and its claim to establishing such laws, he was not satisfied with their formulation. He believed that the associationists had ignored the mental power of knowing relations and generating items of knowledge not known before. Old relations in new situations, he believed, can bring about the generalizing of new plans of behavior. In point of time, this theory came after some earlier work he had done in statistics, supplying it with a theoretical substratum. Inspired in part by Galton's work, he published two seminal papers in 1904.[91] In the first of these, he provided a necessary safeguard for the correlational analysis of mental traits by showing the need to take into account and make allowance for the measurements' degree of reliability. This was a precaution previously unappreciated. In the second paper, he concluded from a statistical study of intercorrelations of test scores of a heterogeneous group of school children that all intellectual tasks use a single capacity—general intelligence or "G"—plus whatever capacities are specific to each of the tests involved. This was the famous two-factor theory of intelligence, which was to be the center of vigorous study, pro and con, for many years to come.

Central to his factor theory was what he termed the hierarchy of the specific intelligences, that is, a systematic interrelation of the correlation coefficients "such as to allow the table of correlations to be arranged with the highest values in one corner and with the other values regularly decreasing in both horizontal and vertical directions."[92]

The Abilities of Man,[93] published in 1927, contains the most comprehensive account of the work he and his associates had done, along with a vigorous criticism of what he called "rival doctrines." After demonstrating to his satisfaction that G and s exist, he proceeds to relate them to response speed, attention, perseveration, conation, and the like. It was on the basis of its scope, as he saw it, that he was led to write an article[94] in which G is offered as a school to end schools; he claimed that application of the general theory of two factors isolates the factors, while use of the subtheories explains them. In England the history of factor analysis can be told in terms of the reaction of others to his proposals and findings.

While serving as Wilde Reader in Mental Philosophy at Oxford, William Brown (1881–1952) took the position that, although Spearman's studies of factor analysis were an epoch-making advance, he nevertheless disagreed with his interpretation of the significance of the hierarchical order in matrices of correlation coefficients. He was joined in this critique by Godfrey H. Thomson (1881–1955), who collaborated with him in the second and third editions of The Essentials of Mental Measurement.[95] The gist of their argument was that the hierarchical order could be produced by random overlap of group factors without any general factor being present. Thomson, located at Edinburgh University from 1925 on, continued this effort in a very successful general and remarkably nonpartisan statement of factor analysis, The Factorial Analysis of Human Ability.[96] He was also concerned with the development of intelligence tests, evaluation of the educational significance of intelligence, and a general furtherance of educational psychology.[97]

R. A. Fisher (1890–1962), a Cambridge mathematician, did his major research through an agricultural research station. He was sharply critical of the work of Karl Pearson and the psychologists who used his statistical procedures, since they were based on assumption of infinitely large samples. In research in the field, he argued, small samples are the rule. He proceeded to supply means of calculating exact sample distributions. In 1922 he published a paper that provided a rigorous statistic for measurement,[98] and in 1925 he published the first edition of Statistical Methods for Research Workers,[99] which appeared in 13 editions by 1963.

While his procedures had many ramifications, probably the most characteristic and widely known is the null hypothesis: one sets out to test the logical contradiction of the hypothesis being tested. The null hypothesis, then, is that there is no difference greater than chance. If the null hypothesis be disproven, then a difference has been demonstrated.

The work of Fisher and other British statisticians came into common use in psychology relatively slowly because it originated in agriculture and called for difficult and even seemingly paradoxical mathematics. Wide application of small sample statistics, both in Britain and the United States, was essentially a post-World War II phenomena.

Beginning in 1931, and for many years thereafter, the chair of psychology at Cambridge University was held by Sir Frederic C. Bartlett[100] (1886–1969). Directing, one of the very few British advanced graduate programs, Bartlett exercised tremendous administrative and educational influence. For about a quarter century he edited the *British Journal of Psychology*. In his laboratory were trained many of the present holders of chairs in British universities.

As for personal research, a major study of his, *Remembering,* significantly bore the subtitle *A Study in Experimental and Social Psychology*.[101] He tells us that early in his career he became dissatisfied with the use of nonsense syllables on various grounds: these stimuli are still meaningful, their use creates an artificial situation, and, on the response side, their use ignores the influence of a subjective attitude toward the material. Consequently, for his research, material from everyday life was used. Following up on some of Head's physiological theorizing concerning postural change, Bartlett and some of his students after him insisted that past experiences were not replicated, but gave rise to a personal schema, a model of ourselves which constantly changes but with which we meet subsequent experiences.[102] In the forties two of his students, R. C. Oldfield and O. L. Zangwill,[103] summarized not only the results of Bartlett's schema approach but also the earlier position of Head.

In view of Bartlett's importance in shaping the thinking of British psychology (other than in the statistical area), it might be well to pause and examine the other major intellectual influences at work. James Ward (p. 339) had died as recently as 1925, and his evolutionary views and conception of the mind as active were still part of the thinking of most British psychologists. Another potent influence was William McDougall. Long after his departure for the United States in 1920, he influenced British psychology, particularly through his *Social Psychology*, reprinted twenty-four times between its first appearance in 1908 and McDougall's death in 1938.[104] Both "instinct" and "sentiment" as promulgated by him were concepts much used by British psychologists. Psychology defined as the science of mental life was still entirely acceptable. The existence of a conscious self was accepted as central by all psychologists. Cognition and will were still favorite subjects of research.

Sir Cyril Burt[105] (1883–1971), Spearman's successor at University College, London, came to the post in 1931 with the most varied background of interests and experience of any British psychologist since Galton himself. He had been McDougall's student at Oxford. McDougall knew of his interest in the work of the then still living Galton, and encouraged him to work in standardizing tests. A period at Würzburg followed. This, in turn, was followed by a period at Liverpool with Sherrington. At Liverpool, Burt taught medical students and continued his research on tests. His experiences during the next twenty years in one way or another involved work with mental tests and statistical procedures. He served as a clinical psychologist in the first official British child guidance clinic. During World War I, he was employed by the National Institute of Industrial Psychology. Only after this varied experience was he appointed to the chair at the University College, a post he held for twenty years. His research was similarly varied, but true to the statistical tradition, his most important work was The Factors of the Mind, published in 1941.[106] He took the position that all factor methods are either approximations to or linear transformations of the same set of theoretical values. Consequently, reconciliation among the methods is possible. In considerable measure, this represents the present position. He was also a strong advocate of the overwhelming importance of heredity upon intelligence.

James Drever, Sr.[107] (1873–1950) for many years represented Scottish (as differentiated from British) psychology. Trained at Edinburgh (and later London) he represented psychology at the only one of four Scottish universities at which psychology was then on an equal footing with the other arts subjects. Financial circumstances had required him to spend many years teaching school. This, coupled with the pioneering reforms in Scottish education, including the requirement that all teachers receive training in psychology (this innovation was as early as 1905), brought him an appointment in education, and, in a few years, a laboratory in educational psychology. His interests, however, were considerably broader than this seems to imply; he did much work in general psychology, on instinct, for example.[108] After World War I, he transferred to the psychology department, and in 1931 he was made professor of psychology, the third such chair in the British Isles. While continuing his other interests, he added juvenile delinquency and the psychology of the deaf.[109]

On his return from Canada just before World War I, Ernest Jones,[110] (1879–1958) a Welshman met before as Freud's biographer, introduced psychoanalysis to London, and in later years became Britain's principal national and international spokesman on psychoanalytic matters.[111] Two other world leaders of child psychoanalysis, Melanie Klein[112] (1882–1960) and Anna Freud,[113] practiced and taught in London for many years. There would be little quarrel with the statement that they more than any other brought the psychoanalytic study of the child from its position of relative obscurity during Sigmund Freud's lifetime to a point where it is now equal to adult psychoanalysis.

In British psychology the major general development after World War II was probably the increased number of graduate students and the opening of several new universities in various parts of England.[114] Wider latitude for individualized programs, rather than following the traditions of "Oxbridge," seems apparent. A new generation of younger psychologists occupies the forty or so chairs. Leadership is not so concentrated in a few individuals as it had been.

Oliver L. Zangwill,[115] met earlier in connection with Bartlett and Head (p. 571), is at present director of the Psychological Laboratory of Cambridge and editor of the Quarterly Journal of Experimental Psychology and, besides conducting his own research on physiological psychology with emphasis on cerebral dominance,[116] directs the research of a considerable number of students, including an occasional American.

A rigorous experimental approach to the dimensional study of behavior, particularly personality assessment, is very prominent at the University of London and the associated Maudsley Hospital under the direction of Hans J. Eysenck.[117] By and large, the research is programatic in that he and his associates deal with research directed toward a common objective in which the entire organization participates. Factor analysis is the favorite statistical devise. There are, of course, psychologists working in Britain in the statistical-measurement tradition of Burt and Thomson, of whom Philip E. Vernon,[118] earlier of London and now of Calgary, is an outstanding example. He has concerned himself with personality assessment among other fields.

International Cooperation

International cooperation among psychologists originated in Europe, so it is proper to say something about it at this point.

International conventions as a means of cooperation and interchange of information are by no means a recent innovation. The oldest are those of the International Congresses of Psychology, the first of which occurred in Paris in 1889. So far there have been twenty-two. They now occur at three-year intervals. Since 1951 they have been organized by the International Union of Psychological Science, which includes among its constituent members national associations of psychology.

The International Union aims to improve communications among psychologists of all nations, to encourage exchange of research workers and students, and to collaborate with other international organizations on matters of mutual interest.[119] It has sponsored a directory and a journal. The second edition of the *International Directory of Psychologists*, which appeared in 1966 under their auspices, lists biographical data for psychologists exclusive of the United States.[120] Twenty thousand questionnaires were mailed out and some 8,000 replies received.

The *International Journal of Psychology* began in 1966 published under the International Union's auspices. Two other journals serve the same ends, although in more specific ways. *Acta Psychologica* started in Amsterdam in 1935 and serves as a forum for European psychology. A feature is periodic accounts of current research in the various European countries. *Psychologia*, an international Oriental journal of psychology, began publication in 1951. It serves as a channel of communication between East and West and a forum for international discussions. These three journals, though respectable enough, have not achieved anywhere near the readership one might have expected from their international character.

Other organizations of psychologists extend beyond national boundaries. The International Association of Applied Psychology, founded in 1920, functions in the same manner as the International Congresses. The Inter-American Society, founded in 1951, promotes communication among psychologists in North and South America.

There are also frequent international congresses devoted to more specialized interests, both intradisciplinary and interdisciplinary. A recent psychological journal listed for that year international meetings on psychology and meditation, group therapeutic techniques, sexology, language disabilities, Piagetian theory, intercultural education, acoustics and speech, history, suicide prevention, group psychotherapy, mental health, psychoanalysis, behavior therapy, and the study of twins.

Overview

A major contribution that European psychology has made to the United States is the migration of Europeans to the United States, which supplied the first generation of both psychoanalysts and Gestalt psychologists. Other imports that travel well are certain seminal theories:

Wundtian, Freudian, and Pavlovian, in the past, and, most recently, theories based on Piaget's work. European scholars are frequent U.S. visitors and there has been an increased flow in recent decades from the United States in the other direction.

The research interests followed and the prescriptive attitudes adhered to by contemporary European psychologists almost defy brief summarization. A few outstanding aspects of research interests and some major manifestations of prescriptive adherence may be sketched.

The battle of the schools, so obviously compelling in the United States, hardly influenced European psychology, although there were some psychoanalysts and Gestalt psychologists. Somewhat comparable ideological differences were found in the arguments between Europeans supporting psychology as an explanatory science and those who saw it as a descriptive, holistic venture.

Ties with acknowledged philosophic assumptions are characteristic of continental psychology. This relation is obvious in Germany, perhaps less so in France, but overwhelmingly so in the Soviet Union where compatibility with dialectic materialism is still the essential characteristic.

European psychologists did not take a militant stance concerning objectivity of method and content that characterized neobehaviorism in the United States, consequently they were less preoccupied with these issues.

The Germans showed a reserve about elementaristic reduction and consequently tended to be molar in attitude. They showed an even stronger reservation concerning methodological objectivism. Insistence on more exactly controlled research has made some inroads, especially through the work of the younger men who had part of their training in the United States.

In an international symposium devoted to national trends in psychology Wolfgang Metzger[121] offered a very able summary of German psychology. Phenomenology, he held, is still a strong intellectual current. It will be remembered that it is founded on what might be called faith in the validity of observation. Phenomena, to the observer, are what they are. In keeping with this attitude, a psychological test is often a means of refining observation, of accumulating experiences, not a method for collecting scores for later statistical manipulation. In personality study, an analysis of style rather than measurement of definitely established characteristics marks the work. This phenomenological emphasis reinforces what would be considered in the United States a lack of a rigorous approach to research.

In the recent past, French social and child psychology has been relatively open to international influences, and a continued international flavor is apparent in its psychoanalytic interests. But in many areas of experimental psychology, it has tended to expand upon research developments within its linguistic boundaries of France, Switzerland, and Belgium. The study of perception is characteristic of this problem. Developmentalism is a major theme in French and Swiss psychology, not only in Piagetian work but in almost all of the "clusters" identified at the University of René Descartes.

For Soviet psychology one can do no better than summarize Rahmani's concluding remarks.[122] He indicates that Soviet psychologists have expressed three attitudes toward Western psychology. During the earliest stage of development of a distinct Soviet view, some Western schools of psychology were regarded as compatible with Marxism. Between the end of the 1940s and the first half of the 1950s, an overall negativistic view prevailed. The current period is characterized by the incorporation into a dialectic framework of certain specific theories of Western psychologists and neurophysiologists. Neurocybernetics, the broader approach to cortical localization, the study of perception through information processing, nonassociationistic approaches to problem solving, and the use of sociometric analysis are some of the indications of the wider platform for rapprochement between Russian and Western scholars. Rahmani goes on to say that this does not mean Soviet psychologists are sacrificing their adherence to a dialectic materialistic philosophy. Their general endeavor is always to produce a materialistic psychology. In so doing, Soviet psychology is cast in a framework distinct from that of Western Europe and the United States.

Britain has made considerable strides in research since World War II in a relatively wide number of fields. In many respects the research resembles that of psychology in the United States, but with less emphasis on a militant methodological objectivism or adherence to the doctrines of any of the schools and less interest in learning as the central issue. In test development its work is as rigorous as that done in the United States. Contributions by and collaborations with physiologists have been and continue to be important. In this and other ways there is greater similarity between psychological activity in Britain and the United States than between either country and that of the continent.

After an examination of recent psychology in the United States in the next chapter, broader developments will be examined in the Epilogue.

References*

1. W. Dilthey, *Gesammelte Schriften*, ed. H. Mehl et al. 12 vols. (Stuttgart: Teubner, 1914–1958) (Variously reprinted).
2. W. Dilthey, "Einleitung in die Geisteswissenschaften," in *Gesammelte Schriften*, 5th ed. (1883), Vol. 1.
3. W. Dilthey, "Ideen über eine beschreibende und zergliedelrnde Psychologie," *Sitzungsberichte Akademie der Wissenschaften in Berlin*, II (1894): 1309–1407. Reprinted in *Gesammelte Schriften*, Vol. 5, pp. 139–240.
4. H. Ebbinghaus, "Über erklärende und beschreibende Psychologie," *Zeitschrift für Psychologie*, IX (1896): 161–205.
5. W. Metzger, "The Historical Background for National Trends in Psychology: German Psychology," *Journal of History of Behavioral Sciences*, I (1965): 109–115.
6. F. Krueger, *Über Entwicklungspsychologie, ihre sachliche und geschichliche Notwendigkeit* (Leipzig: Engelmann, 1915); F. Krueger, *Zur Philosophie und Psychologie der Ganzheit: Schriften aus den Jahren 1819–1940*, ed. E. Heuss (Berlin: Springer-Verlag, 1953); F. Sander, "Structure, Totality of Experience, and Gestalt," in C. Murchison, ed., *Psychologies of 1930* (Worcester, Mass.: Clark University Press, 1930), pp. 188–204.
7. E. Spranger, *Lebensformen*, 8th ed. (Tübingen: Niemeyer, 1950) (1913); E. Spranger, *Types of Men: The Psychology and Ethics of Personality*, trans. 5th German ed. (Halle: Niemeyer, 1928) (1913).
8. P. E. Vernon and G. W. Allport, "A Test for Personal Values," *Journal of Abnormal and Social Psychology*, XXVI (1931–1932): 231–248.
9. E. Kretschmer, *Körperbau und Charakter*, 25th ed. (Berlin: Springer-Verlag, 1967) (1921).
10. H. J. Eysenck, "Cyclothymia and Schizothymia as a Dimension of Personality" (I. Historical review; II. Experimental), *Journal of Personality*, XIX (1950): 123–152; XX (1952): 345–384.

*See p. 19 for description of reference style.

11. L. Klages, *Handschrift und Charakter*, 26th ed. (Bonn: Bouvier, 1966) (1917).

12. Speaking of twenty-six editions for Klages's book gives me the opportunity to indicate that often a new German edition is nothing more than a new printing without change of content. It also allows me to apologize for sometimes failing to give the latest edition to a particular book in the German literature.

13. H. Thomae, "Problems of Character Change," in H. P. David and H. von Bracken, eds., *Perspectives in Personality Theory* (New York: Basic Books, 1957), pp. 242–255, 243.

14. E. Rothacker, *Die Schichten der Personlichkeit*, 5th ed. (Bonn: Bouvier, 1952) (1938); P. Lersch, *Aufbau der Person*, 7th ed. (München: Barth, 1956) (1938).

15. P. Lersch, "The Levels of the Mind," in David and von Bracken, eds., *Perspectives in Personality Theory*, pp. 212–217.

16. A. R. Gilbert, "On the Stratification of Personality," in *ibid.*, pp. 218–241.

17. H. Rohracher, *Kleine Charakterkunde*, 7th ed. (Vienne: Urban and Schwarzenberg, 1956).

18. H. Thomae, *Personlichkeit: Eine dynamische Interpretation*, 2nd ed. (Bonn: Bouvier, 1955).

19. G. W. Allport, "European and American Theories of Personality," in David and von Bracken, eds., *Perspectives in Personality Theory*, pp. 3–24.

20. H. Rorschach, *Psychodiagnostics: A Diagnostic Test Based on Perception* (New York: Grune and Stratton, 1942) (1921); H. Ellenberger, "The Life and Work of Hermann Rorschach (1884–1922)," *Bulletin of the Menninger Clinic*, XVIII (1954): 173–219.

21. Metzger, "The Historical Background for National Trends."

22. A. Wellek, ed., *Gesamtverzeichnis der deutschsprachigen psychologischen Literatur der Jahre 1942 bis 1960* (Göttingen: Verlag für Psychologie, 1965).

23. Metzger, "The Historical Background for National Trends."

24. A. Wellek, *Ganzheits Psychologie und Struckturtheorie*, 2nd ed. (Bern: Francke, 1969) (1955).

25. W. Metzger, *Psychologie: Die Entwicklung ihrer Grundannahmen seit der Einführung des Experiment*, 4th ed. (Darmstadt: Steinkopff, 1968) (1954).

26. W. Metzger, *Gesetze des Sehens*, 2nd ed. (Frankfurt am Main: Kramer, 1953) (1936).

27. Metzger, "The Historical Background for National Trends."

28. P. Lersch et al., eds., *Handbuch der Psychologie*, 12 vols. (Göttingen: Verlag für Psychologie, 1959–1967).

29. P. R. Hofstätter, ed., *Psychologie* (Frankfurt am Main: Fischer, 1957).

30. H. Piéron, "Henri Piéron," in E. G. Boring et al., eds., *A History of Psychology in Autobiography* (Worcester, Mass.: Clark University Press, 1952), Vol. IV, pp. 257–278.

31. H. Piéron, *Aux Sources de la connaissance: La sensation, guide de vie*, 3rd ed. (Paris: Librarie Gallimard, 1955) (1945); H. Piéron, *The Sensations, Their Functions, Processes, and Mechanisms* (New Haven: Yale University Press, 1952).

32. H. Piéron, et al., "*Methodologie psychotechnique: Traité de psychologie appliquée*" (Paris: Presses Universitaires de France, 1951).

33. H. Piéron "Psychologiezoologique," in G. Dumas, ed., *Nouveau traité de psychologie* (Paris: Alcan, 1941), Vol. 8(1), pp. 1–255.

34. H. Piéron, "Les echelles subjectives. Peuvent-elles fournir la base d'une nouvelle loi psychophysique?" *L'Année Psychologique*, LIX (1959): 1–34.

35. G. Dumas, ed., *Traité de psychologie*, 2 Vols. (Paris: Alcan, 1923–1924).

36. G. Dumas, ed., *Nouveau traité de psychologie*, 8 vols. (Paris: Alcan, 1930–1941).

37. P. Fraisse and J. Piaget, eds., *Traité de psychologie experimentale*, 9 Vols. (Paris: Presses Universitaires de France, 1963–1967).

38. A. Michotte, "Albert Michotte van den Berck," in Boring et al., eds., *A History of Psychology in Autobiography*, Vol. IV, pp. 213–236.

39. A. Michotte, *The Perception of Causality*, 2nd ed. (New York: Basic Books, 1963) (1946).

40. H. F. Ellenberger, "The Scope of Swiss Psychology," in David and von Bracken, eds., *Perspectives in Personality Theory*, pp. 44–64.

41. E. Claparède, "Edouard Claparède," in C. Murchison, ed., *A History of Psychology in Autobiography*

(Worcester, Mass.: Clark University Press, 1930), Vol. I, pp. 63–97.

42. J. Piaget, "Jean Piaget," in Boring et al., eds., *A History of Psychology in Autobiography* Vol. IV, pp. 237–256.

43. J. Piaget, *The Language and Thought of the Child* (New York: Harcourt, Brace and Company, 1928); J. Piaget, *The Child's Conception of Physical Causality* (New York: Harcourt, Brace and Company, 1930).

44. J. Piaget, *The Grasp of Consciousness: Action and Concept in the Young Child,* trans. by Susan Wedgwood (Cambridge: Harvard University Press, 1976) (1974).

45. J. H. Flavell, *The Developmental Psychology of Jean Piaget* (Princeton, N. J.: Van Nostrand, 1963).

46. P. Fraisse, *Les structures rhythmiques: étude psychologique* (Louvain: Publications Universitaires de Louvain, 1956); P. Fraisse, *The Psychology of Time,* trans. by Jennifer Leith (New York: Harper & Row, 1963).

47. A. Fessard, "Mechanisms of Nervous Integration and Conscious Experience," in J. F. Delafresnaye, ed., *Brain Mechanism and Consciousness* (Oxford: Blackwell, 1954), pp. 200–236.

48. T. N. Clark, *Prophets and Patrons: The French University and the Emergence of the Social Sciences* (Cambridge: Harvard University Press, 1973).

49. M. Reuchlin, "The Historical Background for National Trends in Psychology: France," *Journal of the History of Behavioral Sciences,* I (1965): 115–123.

50. D. Lagasche, *La Psychoanalyse,* 9th ed. (Paris: Presses Universitaires de France, 1969) (1955).

51. P. Oleron, *Les activités intellectuelles* (Paris: Presses Universitaires de France, 1964).

52. R. La Senne, *Traité de caracterologie* (Paris: Presses Universitaires de France, 1945).

53. R. Zazzo, "Current French Concepts of Characterology and the Study of Character," in David and von Bracken, eds., *Perspectives in Personality Theory,* pp. 101–108.

54. R. Zazzo, *Conduites et conscience: I. Psychologie de l'enfant et methode genetique* (Neuchatel, Switz.: Delachaux and Niestle, 1962).

55. J. P. Sartre, *Imagination: A Psychological Critique,* trans. by F. Williams (Ann Arbor: University of

Michigan Press, 1962); P. J. R. Dempsey, *The Psychology of Sartre* (Cork: Cork University Press, 1950).

56. M. Merleau-Ponty, *Phenomenology of Perception*, trans. by C. Smith (New York: Humanities Press, 1962) (1945): M. Merleau-Ponty, *The Structure of Behavior* (Boston: Beacon Press, 1963).

57. J. Nuttin, *Psychoanalysis and Personality: A Dynamic Theory of Normal Personality*, trans. by G. Lamb, 3rd ed. (New York: New American Library, 1962) (1953).

58. M. Reuchlin, *Historie de la psychologie*, 6th ed. (Paris: Presses Universitaires de France, 1967).

59. G. I. Chelpanov *(Psychology and Marxism)* (Moscow: Russki Knizhnik, 1924); G. I. Chelpanov *(Objective Psychology in Russia and America)* (Moscow: Dunov, 1925).

60. K. N. Kornilov, "Psychology in the Light of Dialectic Materialism," in C. Murchison, ed., *Psychologies of 1930* (Worcester, Mass.: Clark University Press, 1930), pp. 243–278; G. Razran, K. N. Kornilov, "Theoretical and Experimental Psychologist," *Science*, CXXVIII, (1958): 74–75.

61. K. N. Kornilov *(A Textbook of Psychology in the Light of Dialectic Materialism)*, 5th ed. (Moscow: Giz, 1931) (1927).

62. A. R. Luria, *The Nature of Human Conflict*, trans. by W. Horsley Gantt (New York: Liveright, 1932).

63. L. S. Vygotsky, "Thought in Schizophrenia," *Archives of Neurology and Psychiatry* (Chicago), XXXI (1934): 1063–1077.

64. L. S. Vygotsksy, *Thought and Language*, trans. by E. Hanfmann and G. Vakar (Cambridge: M.I.T. Press, 1962) (1934).

65. K. M. Bykov, *The Cerebral Cortex and the Internal Organs*, ed. and trans. from 3rd Russian ed. by W. Horsley Gantt (New York: Chemical Publishing, 1957).

66. A. R. Luria, "The Crisis in Bourgeois Psychology," *Psikhologia*, I-2, (1932): 63–88.

67. R. A. Bauer, ed., *Some Views on Soviet Psychology* (Washington, D.C.: American Psychological Association, 1962).

68. L. Rahmani, *Soviet Psychology: Philosophical, Theoretical, and Experimental Issues* (New York: International Universities Press, 1973).

69. G. Razran, "Soviet Psychology and Psychophysiology," *Behavioral Science,* IV (1959): 35–48.
70. G. Razran, "Growth, Scope, and Direction of Current Soviet Psychology: The 1963 All-Union Congress," *American Psychologist* XIX (1964): 342–347.
71. E.g., J. Brozek, "Current Status of Psychology in the USSR," *Annual Review of Psychology* XV (1964): 493–594.
72. J. Brozek and J. Hoskovec, "Curent Soviet Psychology: A Systematic Review," *Soviet Psychology and Psychiatry* IV (1966): 16–44; J. Brozek, J. Hoskovec, and D. Slobin, "Review in English of Recent Soviet Psychology: A Bibliography," *Soviet Psychology and Psychiatry* IV (1966): 95–99; J. Brozek and J. Hoskovec, "Soviet Psychology in English: Translations of Books," *Soviet Psychology and Psychiatry* IV (1966): 100–104.
73. B. G. Anan'yev et al., eds., *Psychological Science in the USSR,* 2 vols. (Washington, D.C.: U.S. Joint Publications Research Service, 1961, 1962); M. Cole and I. Maltzman, eds., *A Handbook of Contemporary Soviet Psychology* (New York: Basic Books, 1969).
74. A. N. Leontiev *(The Origin and Initial Development of Language)* (Moscow: Akadimya Nauk, USSR, 1963).
75. A. A. Smirnov, ed. *(Foundations of Psychology,* Vol. 1. *History and the Current Status of Scientific Psychology)* (Moscow: Prosvescheniya, 1971).
76. J. Brozek and D. I. Slobin, eds., *Psychology in the USSR: An Historical Perspective* (White Plains, N.Y.: International Arts & Sciences Press, 1972).
77. Rahmani, *Soviet Psychology.*
78. A relevant history of British psychology that can be recommended is L. S. Hearnshaw, *A Short History of British Psychology: 1840–1940* (New York: Barnes and Noble, 1964).
79. G. Humphrey, "Five Years in the Oxford Chair," *British Journal of Psychology* XLIV (1953): 381–383.
80. Beatrice Edgell, "The British Psychological Society," *British Journal of Psychology* XXXVII (1947): 113–132.
81. Hearnshaw, *A Short History of British Psychology,* p. 208.
82. R. Granit, *Charles Scott Sherrington: An Appraisal* (London: Nelson, 1966); Judith P. Swazey, *Reflexes and Motor Integration: Sherrington's Concept of Inte-*

grative Action (Cambridge: Harvard University Press, 1969).

83. C. Sherrington, *The Integrative Action of the Nervous System* (New Haven, Conn.: Yale University Press, 1947) (1906).

84. H. Head, W. H. R. Rivers, and J. Sherren, "The Afferent Nervous System from a New Aspect," *Brain* XXVIII (1905): 99–115; H. Head and W. H. R. Rivers, "A Human Experiment in Nerve Division," *Brain* XXXI (1908): 323–450.

85. H. Head, *Studies in Neurology* (London: Frowde, Hodder and Stoughton, 1920), Vol. 1.

86. H. Head, *Aphasia and Kindred Disorders of Speech*, 2 Vols. (Cambridge: Cambridge University Press, 1926).

87. *Ibid.*, Vol. I, pp. 479–487 (Herrnstein and Boring, Excerpt 52).

88. E. D. Adrian, *The Mechanisms of Nervous Action: The Activity of the Sense Organs* (Oxford: Clarendon Press, 1932).

89. C. E. Spearman, "C. Spearman," in Murchison, ed., *A History of Psychology in Autobiography*, Vol. I, pp. 299–333.

90. *Ibid.*

91. C. E. Spearman, "The Proof and Measurement of Association Between Two Things," *American Journal of Psychology* XV (1904): 72–101; C. E. Spearman, "General Intelligence, Objectively Determined and Measured," *American Journal of Psychology* XV (1904): 201–293 (Herrnstein and Boring, Excerpt 85).

92. Spearman, "General Intelligence," p. 231.

93. C. E. Spearman, *The Abilities of Man: Their Nature and Measurement* (New York: Macmillan Company, 1927).

94. C. E. Spearman, "G' and after—A School to End Schools," in Murchison, ed., *Psychologies of 1930*, pp. 339–366.

95. W. Brown and G. H. Thomson, *The Essentials of Mental Measurement*, 3rd ed. (Cambridge: Cambridge University Press, 1925) (1911).

96. G. H. Thomson, *The Factorial Analysis of Human Ability*, 4th ed. (London: University of London Press, 1950).

97. G. H. Thomson, "The Trend of National Intelligence," *Eugenics Review* XXXVIII (1946): 9–18.

98. R. A. Fisher, "The Goodness of Fit of Regression Formulae and the Distribution of Regression Coefficients," *Journal of Royal Stat. Soc.* LXXXV (1922): 597–612.

99. R. A. Fisher, *Statistical Methods for Research Workers*, 13th ed. (New York: Hafner, 1963) (1925).

100. F. C. Bartlett, "Frederic Charles Bartlett," in C. Murchison, ed., *A History of Psychology in Autobiography*, Vol. III, pp. 39–52.

101. F. C. Bartlett, *Remembering: A Study in Experimental and Social Psychology* (New York: Macmillan Company, 1932).

102. *Ibid.*, pp. 199ff.

103. R. C. Oldfield and O. L. Zangwill, "Head's Concept of the Schema and Its Application in Contemporary British Psychology. I, II, III, IV." *British Journal of Psychology* XXXII, XXXIII (1941–1942, 1942–1943): 267–286, 58–64, 113–129, 143–149.

104. Hearnshaw, *A Short History of British Psychology*, p. 212.

105. C. Burt, "Cyril Burt," in Boring et al., eds., *A History of Psychology in Autobiography*, Vol. IV, pp. 53–73.

106. C. Burt, *The Factors of the Mind: An Introduction to Factor Analysis in Psychology* (New York: Macmillan Company, 1941).

107. J. Drever, "James Drever," in Murchison, ed., *A History of Psychology in Autobiography*, Vol. II, pp. 17–34.

108. J. Drever, *Instinct in Man: A Contribution to the Psychology of Education*, 2nd ed. (London: Cambridge University Press, 1921) (1917): J. Drever, "The Classification of the Instincts," *British Journal of Psychology* XIV (1924): 248–255.

109. J. Drever and M. Collins, *Performance Tests of Intelligence: A Series of Nonlinguistic Tests for Deaf and Normal Children* (Edinburgh: Oliver and Boyd, 1936).

110. E. Jones, *Free Associations: Memories of a Psychoanalyst* (New York: Basic Books, 1959).

111. E. Jones, *Papers on Psycho-analysis*, 5th ed. (London: Baillière, Tindall & Cox, 1948) (1912, reprinted 1961).

112. M. Klein, *Contributions to Psychoanalysis, 1921–1945* (London: Hogarth Press, 1948).

113. A. Freud, *The Ego and the Mechanisms of Defense* (New York: International Universities Press, 1946) (1935): A. Freud, *The Psycho-analytical Treatment of Children* (London: Imago, 1946).

114. C. Monchaux and G. H. Keir, "British Psychology 1945–1957," *Acta Psychologica* (Amst.) XVIII (1961): 120–180.

115. O. L. Zangwill, "The Cambridge Psychological Laboratory," *Bulletin of the British Psychological Society* XXXXVIII (1962): 22–24.

116. O. L. Zangwill, *Cerebral Dominance and Its Relation to Psychological Function* (Edinburgh: Oliver and Boyd, 1960).

117. H. J. Eysenck, *The Scientific Study of Personality* (New York: Macmillan, 1952).

118. P. E. Vernon, *Personality Assessment: A Critical Survey* (New York: John Wiley & Sons, 1964).

119. R. W. Russell, "The International Union of Psychological Science," *International Journal of Psychology* I (1966): 65–72.

120. H. C. J. Duijker and E. H. Jacobson, eds., *International Directory of Psychologists*, 2nd ed. (Assen, Netherlands: Royal Vangorcum, 1966).

121. Metzger, "The Historical Background for National Trends."

122. Rahmani, *Soviet Psychology: Philosophical, Theoretical, and Experimental Issues.*

Chapter 22

RECENT PSYCHOLOGY IN THE UNITED STATES

Before considering previously neglected aspects of the history of psychology in the United States, something must be said about the sheer magnitude of the contemporary field to serve as a general background for what follows.

The United States now leads in psychological science. Although by no means the only index of this leadership, more than half the world's 75,000 psychologists are in the United States. From the meeting in 1892 of a handful of psychologists in Worcester, Massachusetts, at the behest of G. Stanley Hall, the membership of the American Psychological Association had grown by 1945 to a respectable 4,500. In the more than 30 years since then, the number has reached over 40,000. With increased numbers has come a tendency toward increased specialization. Sheer size has forced the Association to separate into divisions organized around some general or specialized scientific or professional interest. Representative of the former are the division devoted to experimental psychology, evaluation and measurement, developmental psychology, personality, social psychology, and the history of psychology, representative of the latter are the divisions devoted to teaching and clinical, industrial, educational, and school psychology.

There has been a considerable increase in the United States in the number of psychological journals, the chief source of research reports. From the *American Journal of Psychology* and the *Psychological Review* of the eighties and nineties, the publications owned by the American Psychological Association have increased to 21. Another 50 or so journals are considered of sufficient interest to psychologists for their publishers to offer special rates. Including the literature from abroad, the *Psychological Abstracts* in 1975 abstracted about 25,000 individual reports of research and opinion judged by its editor to be of interest to psychologists. Other indications show that the quantity of research is not merely increasing, but increasing at an accelerated rate; that is, as time passes, the rate of increase increases, not merely the number of studies. Of books there is no end. In 1975 the journal of reviews, *Contemporary Psychology*, received nearly 1,500 books whose publishers hoped would be acceptable for review. Disregarding half of them as either trash or the result of a mistaken view of what would interest psychologists still leaves about 750 books that might be reviewed. It is plausible that foreign language books in psychology, not all of which are sent to *Contemporary Psychology*, especially the Slavic and Japanese language publications, would include another 400 worthwhile volumes. To keep up with the literature of the entire field of psychology would require reading 69 articles and over three books a day. Small wonder that specialization within psychology has occurred in America to a much greater degree than in other countries.

In 1959, a summary and evaluation of research activity in psychology reached a new high point. This was the year that the first volume of a comprehensive survey of psychology as a science made its appearance. Plans to survey the methodological, theoretical, and empirical status of psychological science in the United States from about 1930 to the time of publication were begun in 1952 by the American Psychological Association. Sigmund Koch, then of Duke University, served as editor with the support of an advisory panel drawn from the Association. Eighty carefully chosen contributors to *Psychology: A Study of a Science* were each invited to write on a specialized topic to which he had made a direct and substantial contribution. Since practically no one refused, the men selected were clearly of first rank in the judgment of their peers on the advisory panel. Six volumes appeared between 1959 and 1963. The collection still stands as the most comprehensive and authoritative overall view that we have of psychology in the United States.

In considering psychology in the United States in past chapters, temporal unevenness has occurred. While the schools were flourishing, there were many psychologists whose research was independent of their doctrines. Attention must be given to them and a severely limited number of contemporary psychologists. For choosing the latter, selectivity has obviously been exercised. Of the 45,000 current members of the American Psychological Association, the research and theory of barely more than ten are considered.

It is also necessary to examine the recent theoretical activities occurring among the schools and attention must be paid to other contemporary theoretical currents—humanistic influences, the existential approach, and the phenomenological method and theory.

Research Contributors

During the same years that interest in the schools of psychology reached their heyday in the twenties, thirties, and forties, there were other contributions relatively removed from the clamor of tongues. For these were the decades in which Lashley did his research on the role of cerebral localization in learning; Thurstone applied the factor analytic approach to psychometrics; and only a little later Allport, Murray, and still later Rogers formulated their views on personality; Murphy presented his systematic views of social psychology and related them to personality; Lewin developed his field theory approach to social psychology; and, perhaps collectively even more significant, Hull and Guthrie and, somewhat later, Skinner carried on their studies of learning. Studies of learning did have some behavioristic implications, but their significance as research, independent of the schools, is far more important. Finally, it was the period in which arose a new theoretical orientation which could be applied irrespective of school affiliation—so-called operationism.

LASHLEY AND PHYSIOLOGICAL PSYCHOLOGY

The way for Lashley's work was prepared by Shepard Ivory Franz[1] (1874–1933). Around 1900, Franz had combined the method of studying animal learning with that of the surgical extirpation of brain tissue which he used in a series of studies. Typical was the study published in 1915,[2] in which he attacked that most firmly established of all "facts" of localization, Fritsch and Hitzig's localization of motor functions (p. 257). His results showed that there was considerable lack of precision to cerebral localization. His findings, however, were seen as hardly more than negative; no more general significance was attached to them.

Research performed by Karl S. Lashley (1890–1958), first with Franz at St. Elizabeth's Hospital, then at the University of Minnesota, and finally under the auspices of the Behavior Research Fund in Chicago, led to his appointment at the University of Chicago, and in 1935 to a call to Harvard directly at President Conant's behest.[3] Conant, the story has it, was seeking "the greatest psychologist in the world."

What was the research that brought on his rapid academic rise, to say nothing of the presidency of the APA and membership in the National Academy of Science before he was forty years of age? It concerned the effect of differential extirpation of the rat's cerebral cortex on intelligence (learning ability). To appreciate the significance of this rather pedestrian-sounding problem, it is necessary to refer to the neurophysiological interpretation of learning then current. At that time, learning in the nervous system was seen as a matter of isolated neurones and synaptic resistances forming reflex paths with detailed localization of function in the cerebral cortex. The accepted rough model of the brain's function was that of the electrical switchboard. Changes at the synapses in a network of neurones had come to be the physiological equivalent of what started at the psychological level as association of ideas. It still was a strongly molecular point of view. Begun about 1920, Lashley's research culminated in his 1929 publication, *Brain Mechanisms and Intelligence.* [4] In it, he reported overwhelming evidence for much less localization of function in the cortex than had heretofore been accepted and further demonstrated that large lesions affect learning more than small lesions. For these results, he supplied a conceptual framework involving "equipotentiality" and "mass action." Equipotentiality is the capacity of the intact portion of the brain to continue to carry out the function previously served by it and the extirpated part of the functional area. Mass action, while indicating a functioning of an area as a whole, serves as a reminder that there can still be proportional reduction of efficiency in complex functions. The reduction is in proportion to the extent of the injury. Considerable evidence for modes of organization rather than isolated single specific pathways and reactions was found in a series of experiments.

A widespread misconception of the significance of his results came about at least partly because of Lashley's manner of presenting them. He was interpreted as saying that what happens in the nervous system is guided by mass action, that when any area of the cortex is removed, another area can carry out its functions. What, under this interpretation, is left for physiological psychology to do? Based on a general acquaintance with his findings, an antiphysiological trend set in, and psychologists lost interest in physiological research, even coming to see the nervous system as irrelevant to psychology. "Behavior theorists," to use a loose but sufficiently apt term, could trace part of their skepticism concerning physiology directly back to Lashley's work. I say "part" because, after all, they did make tremendous progress in their studies of behavior with a DNS (disregarded nervous system).

This loose interpretation of his results ignored what a more careful examination would have shown. He was not denying localization in the summary fashion attributed to him. What he was saying was that localization was both less precise than and different from what previously had been conceived—and considerably more complicated. In some cases equipotentiality held; in others, it did not. Mass action was not always a factor. Mass action and equipotentiality are more evident in complex problems and less so in simple ones, which leaves plenty of scope for physiological-psychological research.

THURSTONE AND FACTOR ANALYSIS

To a considerable extent, factor analytic research in the United States was derived from earlier work in Great Britain. In this area of research, at least one man in the United States reached the stature of Spearman, Thomson, and Burt. This was L. L. Thurstone (1887–1955).

L. L. Thurstone had taken a degree in electrical engineering at Cornell, worked as an assistant to Thomas Edison, and taught engineering before he turned to graduate work in psychology in 1914, studying both at Chicago and the Carnegie Institute of Technology.[5] He had done so, he tells us, to pursue an interest he had developed in studying learning as a scientific problem. Somewhere along the line, however, his interest shifted to factor analysis and psychometrics.

After teaching for seven years at Carnegie Institute of Technology and carrying out some research in Washington, he returned to the University of Chicago, where his interests in factor analysis came to the fore. Instead of repeating Spearman's question about the presence or absence of a general factor, he asked how many factors must be postulated in order to account for a matrix of correlations. Consequently he saw no reason to call one factor more general than another. In this setting, the G of Spearman came to be seen as a "second-order" factor emerging in correlational study only after the first order multiple-factors. It was the multiple-factors obtained, not G, which he considered in order to account for the obtained correlations. By and large, however, his results are not so much in opposition to those of Spearman as an extension of his work. His principal publication was the *Vectors of Mind,* published in 1935.[6] As he continued to work with his approach, it became more and more complex and the data collected became more and more extensive. As a consequence, the earlier book was rewritten in more extended form to appear in 1947 with a new title, *Multiple-Factor Analysis.*[7]

ALLPORT, MURRAY, AND ROGERS AND PERSONALITY

Personality was and is an amorphous field, to which it is hard to set boundaries or even say precisely what it includes. But in the thirties great strides were made toward bringing order and clarity to the field in the attempted integration of its various widely scattered aspects by Gordon W. Allport and a program of in-depth research by Henry A. Murray.

Gordon W. Allport (1887–1967) was graduated from Harvard in 1919.[8] He had come to college with an already formed conviction that guidance of conduct would be for him what could be described as "diffusive sympathetic affections." It is significant in this connection that his first faculty appointment at Harvard in 1924 was as instructor in social ethics; and his last before final retirement in 1967 was as professor of social ethics. For the intervening years, except for a short digression to Robert College of Istanbul and to Dartmouth, he was in the psychology department at Harvard (and, on its reorganization and split, the department of social relations).

He found that within psychology, his social interests best related to the question of personality and how it should be studied. With really remarkable consistency, he has maintained this focus from his doctoral dissertation on traits of personality in relation to social diagnosis and his first article on the topic of personality and character. "Trait" and "Organization" and "Development" characterize his approach; the individual's characteristics cannot be divorced from the pattern they form because they both develop over time. It was his *Personality: A Psychological Interpretation,* which appeared in 1937, that established the modern concept of personality as an area of thought and investigation.[9] Later works, extending in time beyond 1945, followed the same path. His work has been eclectic in the finest sense of the term. If he has not succeeded in integrating the diverse strands of personality, it has not been for lack of ability or devotion to the task, but because the field is not yet ready for it.

Henry A. Murray, director of the Psychological Clinic and professor at Harvard, arrived at his faculty appointment at Harvard in 1926 by a series of idiosyncratic intellectual experiences that perhaps ideally fitted him for the work he has carried on.[10] After being graduated from Harvard in 1915, with one and a half lectures (by Professor Münsterberg), thus completing his formal training in psychology, there followed medical school, a surgical internship, years of biochemical research, a short but important relationship with Jung, and then the Harvard appointment.

He has always lived by his theories personally, a point recognized in his own section in *A History of Psychology in Autobiography,* in which the first two references mentioned are labeled "Autobiographical and Theoretical."[11] His *Explorations in Personality,*[12] published in 1938, recounted the work he carried out with a considerable staff of unusually talented associates, including Erik H. Erikson, Donald W. Mackinnon, Saul

Rosenzweig, and Robert W. White. They used an in-depth approach in a multi-pronged simultaneous attack on as many aspects of personality as their resources afforded. Harvard undergraduate subjects were assessed by several investigators, each working independently and each using his own particular technique. The data from all sources on a particular individual were interpreted by one investigator before the assembled group of investigators who criticized his efforts. Discussion continued until a consensus was obtained. This procedure was used for all forty subjects. These results, in turn, were subjected to a synthetical interpretation based not only on Freud's system but also on the contributions of such diverse theorists as Jung, McDougall, Adler, and Lewin. From this came a conceptual system for assessing a personality in terms of his motives (needs) and the environmental forces bearing·upon him (press). It was from the results of this study that much of his later work emerged.

The major vehicle for Murray's research was *The Thematic Apperception Technique*,[13] a projective device in which subjects told stories in response to pictures which were mostly perceptually clear in details but permitted wide interpretation of what was happening and would happen afterward. Individual personality portraits emerged from the kinds of stories told, for example, from the various themes emphasized.

The other major projective technique, the Rorschach Test, was brought to the United States in the late twenties with Samuel J. Beck[14] as a pioneer who has continued to be a leading figure. His careful, meticulous research with intrinsically subjective material is a model of its kind.

During the present decades, enthusiasm for projective devices as measures of personality has been somewhat chastened and more restrained. This is due to the sharply critical conclusions that emerged from rigorous study, despite protests from protagonists that many of the studies were inappropriate.

During the decades of the forties and fifties, Carl R. Rogers[15] was occupied with developing an approach to counseling and therapy and later with quantitative research on the effect of psychotherapy.[16] After some years a theory of personality and interpersonal relations emerged from this work which stressed the role of self-concept in self-actualization.[17] Rogers became convinced that his patients must change their self-structures by themselves if improvement was to occur.

The individual's self-concept regulated his behavior and his view of his psychological environmental reality. A patient's views of that environment was distorted; if he changes his concept of self, environmental distortions may disappear or be modified.

MURPHY AND LEWIN AND SOCIAL PSYCHOLOGY

Prior to this period, social psychology had evolved from a man retiring to his study to spin out a system for which empirical illustrations were then selected. A few modern textbooks had appeared that depended on the instinct concept, such as McDougall's, and which enjoyed the popularity in England mentioned earlier. But they still fit the description just given.

Gardner Murphy received graduate training at Harvard and Columbia, where he took his Ph.D. in 1923.[18] He was associated with Columbia until 1940, when he moved to the College of the City of New York. Although he published in the history of psychology,[19] it was his work in social psychology that marked his Columbia days.[20] His prior decision to make it his specialization, his teaching responsibilities, and his share in the overall graduate program at Columbia directed him toward this area. He came to the field with an already firmly established eclecticism, which included the conviction that findings from both the biological and the social sciences were important to social psychology. It became a challenge to him to utilize comprehensively both the social and the biological research literature. This resulted in his definitive *Experimental Social Psychology* of 1931, revised in 1937 with the collaboration of not only his wife, who had participated in the original venture, but also Theodore M. Newcomb.[21] Personality development, which Murphy is convinced is an integral aspect of social psychology, became an increasing concern. Indicative of the consistency of his viewpoint in his work in social psychology, his major work in personality bears the subtitle "A Biosocial Approach to Origins and Structure."[22]

Kurt Lewin (1890–1974) did graduate work at Berlin, and his thinking bears definite relation to that school of Gestalt psychology.[23] But his later views, especially those formulated after he arrived in the United States in 1932, are sufficiently distinctive to merit separate discussion. While teaching at the State University of Iowa and then as director of the Research Center for Group Dynamics at the Massachusetts Institute of Technology, he established what has come to be known as field theory. His point of view is most conveniently summarized in the posthumously published collection of his writings, *Field Theory in Social Science,* edited by Dorwin Cartwright.[24] What is field theory? He characterized it as "a method of analysing causal relations and of building scientific constructs."[25] The psychological field is always contemporaneous. If past experiences are still effective, they are part of that field. The psychological task is to identify the general variables that determine behavior at a given moment. In the life space (the psychological, as differentiated from the physical environment) of the individual, the various psychological phenomena are interdependent. In the view of a considerable number of social psychologists, Lewin made a conceptually illuminating success of applying his method and these concepts to such problems as "intention," "frustration," "regression," "resistance," and "conflict." The very nature of the problems listed also emphasizes that field theory extends beyond the boundaries of social psychology.

HULL, GUTHRIE, AND SKINNER AND LEARNING

This generation of research workers on learning had to come to terms with the findings of Thorndike (p. 443) on trial and error learning and the law of effect and Pavlov (p. 437) on conditioning and the influence of contiguity and reinforcement. It came to be seen that the crucial issue was that either reinforcement or contiguity was essential for learning. The work of Clark Hull supported the former, the work of Edwin Guthrie the latter.

It was during his years at Yale University that Clark L. Hull (1884–1952) carried out his collaborative investigations of learning that made reinforcement central.[26] He had received his graduate training at Wisconsin and had taught there before moving to Yale University as a research professor in 1929. At Yale, his weekly research seminar became one of the major training grounds for many of the present generation of eminent psychologists. Either in connection with the seminar or through other means Kenneth W. Spence, Neal Miller, John Dollard, Robert Sears, Ernest Hilgard, and O. H. Mowrer were associated with him.

The basic statement of the theory of behavior proposed by Hull is given in his *Principles of Behavior*[27] published in 1943. It was modified in his *Essentials of Behavior*[28] of 1951 and extended in *A Behavior System,*[29] published the year of his death.

In his autobiography, he stated that he:

came to the definite conclusion around 1930 that psychology is a true natural science; that its primary laws are expressible quantitatively by means of a moderate number of ordinary equations; that all the complex behavior of single individuals will ultimately be derivable as second laws from (1) these primary laws together with (2) the conditions under which behavior occurs; and that all the behavior of groups as a whole, i.e., strictly social behavior as such, may similarly be derived as quantitative laws from the same primary equations.[30]

To implement these aims of objectivity and quantitativity, he developed statements about learning in terms of postulates, corollaries, and equations in a hypothetico-deductive framework using carefully defined symbols. A postulate or corollary led to the formulation of empirical predictions for a particular kind of learning situation, such as multidirectional maze learning.

After two preliminary postulates, his third had to do with the key principle of primary reinforcement. To quote:

> Whenever an effector activity (R) is closely associated with a stimulus afferent impulse or trace (s) and the conjunction is closely associated with the rapid diminution in the motivational stimulus (S_D or S_G), there will result an increment (Δ) to a tendency for that stimulus to evoke that response.[31]

Another of his postulates, which numbered seventeen in all, had to do with habit formation, utilizing the variable of the number of reinforcements. Others concerned primary motivation or drive, stimulus generalization, reaction potential, and experimental extinction.

Hull's theoretical formulations led to many empirically testable propositions and a tremendous amount of research, which it is impossible to summarize here. One or two conclusions may be briefly mentioned.[32] Contiguous repetition does no more than generate inhibition; all improvement in learning depends on reinforcement and the basic element in reinforcement is reduction, either positive (food) or negative (escape from injury). Reward and punishment have the same primary reinforcing quality.

Kenneth W. Spence (1907–1967), late of Iowa and Texas, not only extended Hull's research while modifying his view in some particulars, but also served as a stimulating collaborator.[33] At first, Spence concentrated on discrimination learning; then he turned to the investigation of the assumptions of a theory he had formulated concerning very simple learning.[34] Relatively recently Frank A. Logan[35] presented an authoritative statement of the "Hull-Spence" approach to learning.

Edwin R. Guthrie (1886–1959), from 1914 until retirement in 1946 at the University of Washington, interpreted learning as dependent upon contiguity of stimulus and response.[36] His training at the University of Pennsylvania had been primarily in philosophy, his thesis being in symbolic logic. His interest in psychology and behaviorism had come from philosophy; he was especially interested after he heard E. A. Singer read a paper on minds as observable objects. His early collaboration on an elementary textbook with Stevenson Smith, a behavioristically oriented colleague, served as part of his postdoctoral training in psychology.

It is fitting that someone trained as a philosopher kept association doctrine alive; his basic principle of learning was contiguity restated in conditioning terminology: taken together, two events temporally contiguous—stimulus and response—are the single sufficient condition for learning.[37]

He even insisted that repetition is not necessary. A single, contiguous occurrence is sufficient. To answer the obvious question of why it often seems to take many trials for learning to occur, he answered that the same complex of stimuli is not present on each trial. The simplest learning situation is, in reality, so highly complex as to be different in each trial. Each time the response is made, the stimulus situation is slightly, but according to his position, crucially different. Repeated trials only bring about an increase in the number of cues conditioned to response. If the stimulus situation had been identical, then one trial would have sufficed.

Motivation, though often present, is not a necessary condition of learning. When present, it is a part of the present stimulus pattern and thus enters into learning. But motivation is but one kind of stimulus condition; its absence does not prevent learning.

His first paper on this topic concerned conditioning as a principle of learning.[38] In it he mapped out much of this theoretical system but without presenting the evidence. Thereafter, he sought evidence and was not at all hesitant to use anecdotal material open to him, as had his associationistic forebears, and to press into service research by others that seemed to support his position. He never had many students, so very few research studies were conducted under his auspices. In 1935 his book *The Psychology of Learning* appeared, which was revised in 1952.[39]

Guthrie's and Horton's study of cats in a puzzle box will serve as an illustration of the type of evidence marshalled.[40] While they found the expected trial and error behavior, they also observed what they called "stereotypy." This was the strong tendency for cats to repeat the precise movements leading up to and including the escape movement. These routines were repeated by individual cats, each with his own routine, trial after trial. This they interpreted as evidence in favor of contiguity learning. The pattern of escape movements is repeated because it eventually removes the animal from the box, thereby preventing new and contradictory associations from being formed. Variation from the pattern, which appeared as new solutions, could also be interpreted by the contiguity principle. Entering the box from a slightly different direction or angle set up what was essentially a new learning situation that required a new escape response. Guthrie summarized his mature views on contiguity in a chapter published the year of his death.[41]

B. F. Skinner[42] of Harvard, to be encountered again in the discussion of neobehaviorism, has outstripped all of his rival learning specialists in the enthusiasm he has stirred among other research workers following his lead, both in the positions sketched earlier and in what he and his students have incorporated in the name of their division of the American Psychological Association, "The Experimental Analysis of Behavior." The same group has also sponsored journals. His studies of animal performance used rats conditioned to bar pressing and, later, pigeons conditioned to pecking at a disc.[43] The particular kind of conditioning with which he worked, operant conditioning, he defined in his *Schedules of Reinforcement* both as an operation and a process. As an operation, it consisted of arranging conditions so that a particular reinforcer follows the emission of a particular response. As a process, there was a consequent increase in the rate of occurrence of responses possessing these particular properties.[44]

It should be noted that it is reinforcement of response that is under discussion. Instead of reinforcement being correlated with stimuli, in operant conditioning the response is correlated with reinforcement. Pressing of the lever by the rat leads to food, but not the sight of the lever (or the sound of a bell as in classical conditioning).

STEVENS AND OPERATIONISM

In the United States during these decades, the most influential new theoretical orientation was operationism. It was the work of a Harvard physicist, Percy W. Bridgman[45] (1882–1961), published in 1927, which triggered this interest and acceptance. In physical study he argued that a concept was the same as the corresponding set of operations by which it was found. To illustrate he gave the example of length. What is length? To find out, we perform certain operations and "the concept is synonymous with the corresponding set of operations."[46] Psychology was ready for operationism; so much so that four years before Bridgman, E. G. Boring, reflecting an already widespread cliché, wrote a paper for a national magazine which pointed out that it could be argued that "intelligence is what intelligence tests test," an operational definition before operationism.[47] On this and other grounds, the climate of opinion was receptive to operationism.

S. S. Stevens, in a 1935 paper, called psychologists to adopt "an operational base of psychology."[48] This was followed in 1939 by a book by Carroll C. Pratt that gave the history of operationism and considered its implications for psychology.[49] About this time, operationism had been seized on avidly and a flood of articles began to appear. Besides the rigor this theory introduced into psychologists' research activities, it provided a graceful retreat from the excesses of the "schools" that by this time were embarrassing psychologists.

Operationism is wider than a behavioristic outlook. It can be and is used in situations where conscious experience was traditionally considered to be involved, as in studies of sensation and perception, and it could even use mentalistic terms, provided they are operationally defined. A research situation is arranged, the observer reports what he sees—the perception is the reaction. The subjective had been translated into the objective because they were now public operations. From the operational reports of one investigation another research worker can go and do likewise, thus verifying or not, as the case may be, that the operations lead to the claimed result. Operationally, consciousness becomes discriminative behavior.

Operationism itself had a relation with positivism, specifically with a particular approach to the philosophy of science, namely, logical empiricism, which about this time was attracting considerable interest in the United States with the arrival of European refugee philosophers of science, especially those who had been associated with the so-called Vienna circle, which included Rudolf Carnap and Herbert Feigl.

It was again S. S. Stevens who first acquainted American psychologists with this particular orientation. He mentioned it in the paper devoted to the operational basis of psychology already referred to, and more explicitly in a paper a year later;[50] following Bridgman's lead, he showed that the relativity theory associated with the name of Einstein arose from fundamentally the same problem and reached the same solution—that the observer needs some way to come to terms with the operations that go into the determination of his research findings and Einstein was dealing with operations and not physical properties.

With acceptance of operationism and to some extent positivism, psychology's relation with physics was made respectable. There was a relation, too, with an influential point of view in philosophy of science. From the same perspective, since psychological observations enter into *all* scientific endeavor because the scientist's position inevitably is that of an observer, then psychology, as Stevens argued, is propaedeutic to all science. Although the last point was not taken too seriously, all this gave psychology what seemed to be a more assured position in the scientific hierarchy. But more important tnan giving theoreticians the comforting sense of unity with the other sciences and with the philosophy of scien :e, it gave the research men a tool.

Stevens's research is in the operational vein. Following the grand tradition of Fechner since the early thirties, Stevens, as both a Harvard graduate student and faculty member, worked in psychophysics primarily through the study of pitch, frequency, and loudness of tones.[51] His singleness of purpose was signalized some years ago when he arranged to have his title changed to professor of psychophysics. In a broader area, he did much to clarify for the psychologist the various kinds of scales of measurement available for use and thereby helped to avoid their misuse.[52]

The concept of the intervening variable appeared at about the same time as operationism. E. C. Tolman referred briefly to "operational behaviorism" as representing his view as early as 1936, but in a relatively obscure publication which could not have had the effect of Stevens's papers of this same period.[53] The central theme of this paper was the functional and mathematical dependencies of "intervening variables" on the other variables. He then pointed out the necessity of using operational means of specifying these intervening variables. Discussion of intervening variables in his presidential address[54] before the American Psychological Association, published in 1938, gave his position the wider audience his earlier paper had lacked. Thereafter, the concept of intervening variables was integrated with operationism in a way that made the two central to theoretical endeavors of the time.

The loosening of the grip that operationism then had on much psychological thinking came in the postwar years with the realization that operationism was a methodology, not a means of selecting significant problems. It was recognized that, if a particular psychological problem was amenable to operationalism so much the better, but this did not rule out studying other problems where it did not apply.

Aftermath of the Schools

In the decades after the thirties, changes occurred in the schools. Structuralism had already ceased being a viable force as a school before the forties. But the functional spirit continued after the disappearance of the self-conscious school of functional psychology. Many contemporary psychologists without professed allegiance to any school are often close to the functionalists in their stress on activities as utilities, acceptance of the application of psychology and the contingent meaning of function. This functional cast to modern psychology was reinforced by Watson's adherence to it despite his expressed opposition to functionalism as a school. Contemporary functionalism is most clearly expressed in studies of learning.

The other schools, behaviorism, Gestalt psychology, and psychoanalysis, still showed vitality in that they may be differentiated from psychology in general.

BEHAVIORISM

When viewed from the perspective of the schools, both Hull and Guthrie were "later" behaviorists. That is, they were members of the postpioneer generation who, while accepting many of the tenets of behaviorism, concerned themselves much more with a particular research area—in this case learning—than with speaking out in favor of the adoption of a behavioristic outlook on psychological matters. Since they devoted most of their efforts to the study of learning, their work was discussed in that setting. Neither was really too enthusiastic about the doctrinaire aspects of behaviorism. In fact, Hull rather avoided calling himself a behaviorist.

A good case could be made for considering the work of Edward C. Tolman in the setting of learning discussed in the previous section. He was devoted to research on learning more or less independent of the schools. But his behaviorism, his molarism, and his purposiveness outweigh his contributions to the cognitive theory of learning, which has variously been described as involving sign-Gestalts, sign-significances, or expectancies. According to his autobiographical statement, he stresses in his work not learning, but a formulation of these other concepts. This was done, however, in a fashion much less militant and strident than the earlier generation of behaviorists.

Edward Chace Tolman[55] (1886–1961) had been a graduate student at Harvard. In the main, his training had been in the Titchenerian vein and his encounter with Watson's *Behavior* in Yerkes' course in comparative psychology was both a stimulus and a relief, for he had already been troubled about the inadequacies of introspection. He took his degree in 1915 and in 1918 moved to the University of California at Berkeley where he remained. On arriving at Berkeley, his choice of a new course to teach was comparative psychology and he was soon embarked on research in learning in rats. He concluded that Watson held oversimplified notions of stimulus and response and, influenced by his exposure to Gestalt (he had spent some time in Giessen with Koffka), he began to develop his particular views of psychology. Since he conceived psychology as dealing with something larger than muscle contractions—with behavior as behavior, as he stated it—it was not surprising that he borrowed from his philosophy teacher at Harvard, R. B. Perry, the notion that purpose and cognition, while essential to understanding behavior, can still be basically descriptive.

With this as some of the background, he published in 1932 his *Purposive Behavior in Animals and Men*.[56] One should say immediately that "purposive" was being used in the descriptive sense already mentioned. In more detail, he saw it as an urge to get to or away from a type of goal object, shown by persistence and the tendency to use the shortest route. By taking this position, he was calling attention to such matters as the readily observable fact that if on reaching the food box the rat finds no food, he tries other ways of finding it. A series of trials, not a single trial, shows that blind alleys are eliminated and the shortest possible route is finally adopted—the animal is learning a route to a goal, the means to an end. "Learning the maze" is for Tolman decisive evidence of goal seeking. This definitely was *not* a teleological use of the term. In contrast to molecular behavior, which had to do with the underlying physiological activity, Tolman emphasized the molar behavior of men and animals acting in respect to ends.

From the original appeal by the first generation of behaviorists—Watson and the rest—psychology passed through the stage of the "later" behaviorists just discussed. The present period is that of the neobehaviorists. Edward Chace Tolman, considered as a "later" behaviorist, now emerges as a neobehaviorist. Other leading neobehaviorists are Kenneth W. Spence, late of Iowa and Texas, and B. F. Skinner of Harvard.

The language of intervening variables, it will be remembered, had been coined by Tolman as a later behaviorist. Similarly, Hull, Skinner, and Spence involved themselves in some way with this terminology in conceptualizing their work as behavioristic psychologists (as did other psychologists of the "prevailing eclecticism"). In the early forties, a variety of concepts—"symbolic constructs," "hypothetical constructs," and "hypothetical entities"—roughly related to Tolman's intervening variables were being used more or less interchangeably, thus creating considerable confusion.

In 1948, Kenneth MacCorquodale and Paul E. Meehl[57] published an extremely significant paper that attempted (and, as later events showed, in some measure succeeded) to bring order into this confusion of terms. They made the distinction between hypothetical constructs, which involve hypothesizing a process or event that is not itself observable (such as events within the nervous system), and intervening variables that do not involve such hypothetization but abstract the empirical relationships without surplus meaning being involved.

Tolman, more than others, represents the neobehaviorist position. He shared the widely held opinion that "grandiose" systems, such as his own, are at least temporarily out of step with the present. His title for his article in the Koch volumes is the "Principle of Purposive Behavior,"[58] but the article is devoted almost exclusively to specification of his position on learning. There is no mention of behaviorism as a system other than his skeptical comment just mentioned. The structure of his system is stated in terms of independent variables (past and present), intervening variables (means-end readiness, expectation, and perceptions), and dependent variables. His intervening variables, he cheerfully admits, share in the surplus meaning of the hypothetical constructs as the term is used by MacCorquodale and Meehl.

Kenneth W. Spence also used the variable approach in formulating his view of behaviorism.[59] This he stated in terms of response variables, stimulus variables, hypothetical state variables (the intervening variables of Tolman), and (possibly) organic variables leading to different types of empirical relationships that yield empirical and hypothetical laws.

In many ways B. F. Skinner shows a more militant and certainly less "liberal" point of view about how to behave as a psychologist. Overall theories are premature, according to Skinner; even intervening variables that had been tolerated by Skinner in his early work of 1938,[60] he argued against in his Science and Human Behavior of 1953.[61] The variables we have available for scientific analysis are operations performed on the organism from without, such as water deprivation and a kind of behavior, say, drinking. The inner condition "thirst" (what would be called a hypothetical construct) is useless in trying to control behavior because we cannot manipulate it as we·can the operation from without, that is, the water deprivation. Skinner would do away with all such intermediaries entirely.[62] Since theories depend upon these intermediaries, it is quite logical that he would also dispense with theories. Psychology as a field, he holds, is still inadequate for theorizing and we must collect many more data. The nearest approach to a theory he tolerates is the assumption that there is order to be found in behavioral data. Functional analysis of these data with a single kind of organism, with adequate controls, but dispensing with statistics except for counting, since statistics hide more than they reveal, characterizes the way he carries out research.

GESTALT PSYCHOLOGY

There are differences of opinion among psychologists about the present status of Gestalt psychology. In varying degrees, Gestalt theses about perception have been absorbed in psychology, not to the exclusion of other views, such as those derived from contemporary learning theory, but to the extent that they remind psychologists they must always reckon with the configurations, patterns, and equipotentialities involved in perception. As an experimental phenomenon, there is no longer any question that the whole cannot be reduced to its parts and the parts are changed in different contexts. It is significant that we can still speak meaningfully of Gestalt psychologists. Non-Gestalt psychologists would say that what was unique and worthwhile within the movement has merged with psychology as a whole. Gestalt psychologists, including Köhler,[63] are not so sure that the assimilation has been quite so successful. They point to the continued appeal of additive connectionism to some psychologists as a flagrant instance of nonintegration. Another one of the new beginnings in psychology has largely merged into the field but, just as there are articulated objects within a larger field, Gestalt thinking is still distinguishable within that field. Attempts of non-Gestalt psychologists to translate Gestalt concepts into the terms appropriate for other approaches have recently been critically examined by Mary Henle and found to be unsuccessful.[64]

Whether it be meant as a source of praise or of disparagement, it is generally agreed that Gestalt psychology has helped very much to keep alive conscious experience as a legitimate interest of psychology. The status of the systematic views of Köhler has recently been examined both by an interpreter and by Köhler himself.[65] Important in itself, it is relevant at this juncture because it shows how Köhler regarded psychology as a science of both behavior *and* experience. Experiences, rather than responses, are correlated with stimulus variables.

In the United States, a younger generation of psychologists with strong allegiance to Gestalt principles has come to the fore. One of them is Mary Henle of the New School of Social Research who edited a valuable collection of recent papers on Gestalt approaches to general theory, cognitive processes, social psychology and motivation, and expression and art.[66] Other psychologists, whose papers are included, are three of the leading psychologists working in the Gestalt tradition. Rudolf Arnheim of Sarah Lawrence works primarily with problems of aesthetics,

Solomon E. Asch of Rutgers University, Newark, with social psychological problems, and Hans Wallach of Swarthmore with perceptual and cognitive problems.

PSYCHOANALYSIS

Quite possibly the most important theoretical development in psychoanalysis since Freud's death in 1939 has been the extension of the concept of the ego. Although other theoreticians contributed to this, the work of a particular trio of psychoanalysts, Heinz Hartmann, Rudolf M. Loewenstein, and Ernst Kris (1900–1957), is most prominent.[67] In classic psychoanalytic theory, the ego was considered as deriving from and securing its energy from the id. This contention is now qualified by extending the sources for both its derivation and its energy. The ego is seen as being less at the mercy of the id, and some autonomous aspects are even attributed to it. Both id and ego are seen as arising from a more or less undifferentiated substratum, rather than the ego arising from the id alone. This autonomy of the ego permits some independence from instinctual demands and makes learning, in the more usual and conventional sense, relevant to psychoanalytic thinking. Development is no longer seen as entirely id-instigated. The ego, moreover, is defined by its functions—control of motility, perception, reality-testing, and thinking. This allows some psychological functioning to be conflict-free and less a ceaseless struggle against primitive id forces. Conflict-free avenues of adaptation to reality, instead of being peripheral, are now conceived of as central, and every adaptation or instance of learning need not be attributed to conflict and related means of functioning. These modifications of psychoanalytic thinking open the way for rapprochement between psychoanalysis and psychology in general.

Some psychologists have contributed to the theory of psychoanalysis and also interpret it in a fashion that would bring out its relation to the general, nonanalytic psychology. The papers of David Rapaport[68] (1911–1960), late of Stockbridge, are outstanding in their effort to make psychoanalysis a complete and unified theory of individual and social behavior coextensive with psychology. Robert R. Holt and the late George S. Klein[69] of New York University have worked toward the same end. Integration of psychoanalysis with psychology and anthropology has been attempted with special success in the field of child development by Erik H. Erikson[70] formerly of Harvard, another prominent psychologist-psychoanalyst.

In many respects, Freudian psychoanalysis remains apart from the main body of psychological science. Its origin in the treatment of adult neurotics, its investigatory method of free association, its insistence on the primacy of unconscious sexual factors, its development of its own terminology, and its derivation of most of its personnel from the ranks of physicians show how this separation came about and how it is maintained.

Collectively, psychoanalysts resist any move toward integration with the rest of psychology. It may be protested at this point that Rapaport, Klein, Holt, and the other psychologists whose contributions toward rapprochement were considered surely are moving in this direction. But what about most psychoanalysts, physicians within medical settings and their affiliated training institutes and those in private practice? It is not that they oppose a rapprochement, they are indifferent and perhaps hardly aware that an attempt is being made in this direction.

Freud and his followers were convinced of the validity of their contentions by the sheer wealth of supporting data from case after case. Become psychoanalysts, they said to critics, and you, too, will be convinced. In reply, the nonpsychoanalytic psychologist is apt to ask that they go beyond this piling up of positive instances and apply much more frequently than in the past the method of experiment. Admittedly, this is a difficult task, but it is necessary before psychoanalysis becomes an integral part of the mainstream of psychology.

As various surveys show, there has been no lack of attempts at experimental verification of psychoanalytic propositions as well as an extensive literature examining the extent to which psychoanalysis meets the canons of the scientific method. These critics include E. R. Hilgard[71] and Robert R. Sears of Stanford and B. F. Skinner of Harvard. Others, writing with more of a psychoanalytic allegiance, such as Merton Gill, Lawrence Kubie, and Heinz Hartmann,[72] have emphasized the relation of theory to method in an attempt at reconciliation. A valiant in-depth attempt to integrate Hull's learning theory and some aspects of psychoanalysis was made by John Dollard of Yale and Neal E. Miller, now of Rockefeller.[73]

Some psychologists contend that almost all of the research studies of psychoanalysis are at fault in that in most instances they do not measure what they purport to. Even when the results support psychoanalytic contentions, it is not clear that it is any more than an analogous relationship. Reliable, general, secondary sources are available.[74]

THE NEO-FREUDIANS

The so-called neo-Freudians show two major characteristic differences from modern psychoanalysts in the major Freudian tradition.

While accepting many Freudian tenets, they decisively reject other salient features of Freudian thinking. They put much more emphasis on the
influence of social factors on personality development. Karen Horney[75]
(1885–1952) was most explicit on points of agreement and disagreement.
She accepted the doctrine of unconscious motivation, strict determinism,
the pervasive influence of emotion upon formation of attitudes and
behavior, and the concepts of conflict and repression. On the other hand,
she considered that libido theory was unsubstantiated; needs grow, not
out of instincts, but out of a child's need to cope with a difficult environment; the Oedipus Complex is not a biological imperative, but stems
from describable conditions in the family environment. Penis envy she
rejected, and the phenomena subsumed under this rubric she saw as
being aroused in women by the superior status given to masculine
qualities in our culture.

A contemporary neo-Freudian, Erich Fromm,[76] sees man as primarily a social creature whose major characteristic is precisely his independence from instincts. Although influenced by Freudian thinking concerning psychosexual stages, he sees character structure most adequately
defined in terms of social characteristics and developed such concepts as
the receptive person, the exploitative individual, the marketing
personality—showing by the very terminology used the emphasis he put
on the influence of social factors.

THE NEO-ADLERIANS

Alfred Adler anticipated the psychological temper of the present
day in emphasizing the influence of social factors on personality and
development. To be more specific, it will be remembered that Adler
emphasized ego functions, denied the primacy of the sexual drive, insisted that attention be given to the individual unity of each person,
wanted psychology to look at man from an ethical point of view, and
counseled a more active role in psychotherapy. One of the more general
reasons that psychologists have been responsive to Adlerian thinking is
its strong functional character. In these emphases, Adler was prophetic of
much current thinking, not only among Adlerians but also among neo-
Freudians and many other psychologists. The followers of Freud moved
closer and closer to these views of Adler as time passed, without surren-
dering their more specifically Freudian tenets.

Although her evaluation may be more than usually colored by
personal feelings, Alexandra, Adler's daughter, claims that the theory of
individual psychotherapy has changed relatively little.[77] She therefore

looks to and writes about applications in psychotherapy, such as its use in conjunction with drugs.

While it may be that no radical innovation has been introduced in psychotherapy or even in the principles on which it is based, there is no question that greater systematization of principles has been introduced since Adler. This was exhibited in Chapter 20 by the greater order brought into Adlerian concepts by the Ansbachers (p. 528). An even more recent effort by H. L. Ansbacher of the University of Vermont shows the continued progress made in this area.[78] Without doing violence to Adler's thinking, he shows that there can be expanded interpretation which places it in a newer framework, as with the interpretation of the fictional goal as an heuristic device or a construction by the psychologist interpreter to provide himself and the patient with a conceptual tool to help modify the latter's behavior. The unconscious is interpreted by him as largely a similar construction.

For all these reasons, present-day interest among psychologists has increased. Formally organized groups are to be found, particularly in New York, Chicago, and Los Angeles. There is a flourishing journal, the *Journal of Individual Psychology*. Editorially, it has recently broadened its scope to include related phenomenological, field, and socially-oriented approaches.

While systematic, controlled research is not entirely absent, particularly on various facets of the psychological influence of sibling position, there is no question that a greater research orientation, other than clinical, is still very much needed, as illustrated recently with specific research suggestions.[79]

THE NEO-JUNGIANS

The number of individuals interested in analytical psychology has increased considerably. Jung's books are popular, and commentary in magazines and newspapers has brought his name before the public. There are three formal institutes—in Zurich, London, and New York.[80] There are other clubs and societies in London, the West Coast, and Chicago. In 1955, the first Jungian journal was founded in London, the *Journal of Analytic Psychology*. In 1958, the first international congress was held in Zurich. His influence upon scholars in diversified fields has been great. Individuals as varied as theologian Paul Tillich, historian Arnold Toynbee,[81] novelist Philip Wylie, critic Lewis Mumford, and anthropologist Paul Radin acknowledge their intellectual debt to Jung and his views.

And yet from psychologists there is silence. Relevant articles, even in criticism, are almost nonexistent. Only one eminent psychologist, Henry A. Murray, has acknowledged a debt to Jung, but he has taken pains to point out he is not a Jungian. How is this lack of identification to be accounted for? Aside from research of Jung's earlier and admittedly less theoretically important work in word association and introversion-extraversion, almost no research has been conducted in the major psychological tradition. Some Jungians' conceptions have been adapted to others' frameworks, such as complex and introversion-extraversion, but they are out of their Jungian context. Essentially the validity that Jung sought and the neo-Jungians continue to seek is that of mutual corroboration among psychological, archaeological, anthropological, and mythological material. Instances of cross-comparison are sought and woven into an intricate tapestry. Hardly any way for research, as most psychologists understand the term, has yet been found. Until this can be accomplished, Jungian thinking will stand apart.

HUMANISTIC INFLUENCES

A humanistic strain is evident in contemporary psychology in the United States. Humanism is more evocative of a mood or attitude than anything more precise. It is fitting that it does not keep mannered company, for its lack of exclusiveness is precisely what it stands for. There is a realization on the part of some psychologists that man is human in that, as an individual, he has worth and value. They oppose defining man by appealing to nonhuman analogy. Instead, their model is man as he knows himself.

One concept of humanistic doctrine is that there is more to life than science and that, moreover, this "something more" should be integrated with science. This was the hope that C. P. Snow[82] held out in his well-known contrast of the two cultures of scientific technology and the humanities. But there is another aspect—scientific research carried out in the humanistic vein, a task to which Irwin L. Child[83] of Yale has recently addressed himself. He shows with as varied topics as morals, art, hypnosis, social attitudes and opinions, extrasensory perception, schizophrenia, and psychotherapy that humanistic insight may be combined with appropriate research methods. A variety of psychologists, past and present, have been calling for the leaven of humanism. Some of the more representative are Gordon Allport,[84] late of Harvard, Carl Rogers[85] of the Center for Studies of Persons, Abraham Maslow,[86] late of Brandeis, and Adrian van Kaam[87] of Duquesne. Examination of their reasons for this call shows that they are divergent, though in one way or another they are pleas for an added breadth to psychology. It should be added that the majority of psychologists meet this appeal with profound indifference.

THE EXISTENTIAL THEORY

Similarly attitudinal and not without significant overlapping of allegiance with humanism and phenomenology is the approach known as the existential. The philosophy of existentialism has roots going back to Kierkegaard and defies short summarization. It is sometimes discussed as a philosophical psychology, not only because it is thought to have intellectual roots in an array of philosophical doctrines, which is true, but also because it is conceived as not going beyond philosophy, which is not true. As a leading protagonist, Adrian van Kaam,[88] puts it, existential psychology regards existential philosophy as consisting of hypothetical constructs from which testable propositions may be deduced. So far, this is more a statement of policy than of accomplishment.

A useful introduction specifically for psychologists is available, edited by Rollo May,[89] to which sympathetic critics not entirely committed to the position (Maslow, Rogers, Allport) contribute papers.

THE PHENOMENOLOGICAL METHOD

In addition to the Gestalt utilization as preparatory to experiments, phenomenology had two independent introductions in the United States. One strain continued the European tradition in the person of Robert MacLeod[90] (1907–1972), late of Cornell University, who had worked with David Katz (p. 307). Psychological phenomenology, as he conceived it, came about from looking at the facts of experience without presuppositions, identifying the entities of that phenomenal world, and, when satisfied that due care had been taken in this process, proceeding empirically. His role has primarily been to call attention to the importance of the methodology rather than to apply it to data-collecting research. In some measure his Cornell colleague, James J. Gibson,[91] in his research on perception, works in that spirit in the setting up of experimentation. The second strain of phenomenology in the United States was apparently a more or less independent effort with hardly any knowledge of the European work. The first statements were a 1941 paper by Donald Snygg[92] (1904–1967) and a 1949 book by Snygg and Arthur W. Combs.[93] The theme was the exploration of the phenomenal field of the individual, with behavior pertinent to it, and the major consideration was the self of that individual. Carl Rogers is primarily interested in psychotherapeutic activity and research. His 1942 statement of his approach to psychotherapy,

Counseling and Psychotherapy, ignored theory. Somewhat belatedly in his 1951 *Client-centered Therapy*[94] he adopted a phenomenal approach which leaned heavily on Snygg and Combs. He posited that in psychotherapy the way the client as an individual self perceives the objects in his phenomenal field is the crux of the changes that take place in the course of that psychotherapy. A masterly survey of the history of phenomenology in psychology is available through the work of H. Spiegelberg.[95]

Overview

It is appropriate to present an overview in the form of a summarization of the prescriptive adherences of the still viable schools. This provides an opportunity to examine the schools' relations with each other, heretofore not discussed. Particular emphasis is placed on agreements and disagreements about the significance of particular prescriptions. What a school opposes, what is prominent in other schools, sets in sharp relief their positive adherences. Independent evidence will be used which may be compared with what was said previously about behaviorism (p. 435), Gestalt psychology (p. 467), and psychoanalysis (p. 491.) It is unnecessary to consider either structuralism or functionalism. Before the time in question, Titchenerian structuralism had disappeared as a school. Functionalism, as a school, had been replaced by a general functional spirit throughout most psychological endeavor.

In 1974 A. H. Fuchs and G. F. Kawash[96] reported a study on the prescriptive dimension of these schools. They took as their point of departure the definition of a school as a set of interlocking prescriptions, generally with an acknowledged leader. They had members of the Division of the History of Psychology complete on the seven-point rating scales degree of significance they believed adherents of the schools to attach to each of 36 prescriptions. One of several forms of results they report are mean ratings on 36 prescriptive dimensions.

In order to reduce their wealth of data to a form appropriate for summarization, it is necessary to be selective. Since indicators of positive adherence were sought, it was decided to report those prescriptions which allowed each school to be represented by at least its three highest rated prescriptive adherences. Gestalt psychology has the fewest relatively high mean ratings. To allow three, it was necessary to go down to a mean of 5.50, the lowest value to be taken as indicating strong positive adherence. Inspection of the standard deviations shows that one can generalize that 5.50 is at least one standard deviation above the median of means for positive adherence of each school. Using the value of 5.50 as the cut off, behaviorism had twelve salient positive prescriptive adherences and psychoanalysis had eight. Since there was some slight overlap, twenty prescriptive dimensions suffice. Not only are positive adherences, listed in italics, reported, but also the mean ratings for the other schools on those particular prescriptions are reported, which allows comparison across the schools.

To clarify discussion, results are presented in two tables. Table 2 is devoted to methodological prescriptive attitudes—those that indicate the methodological approaches which they favor. Table 3 concerns contentual prescriptions—those that indicate their preferences as to the contentual nature of the field.

It can be observed from Table 2 that a number of methodological imperatives loom large for behaviorism, judging from the impressive number of strong prescriptive adherences. Methodological objectivism was rated the highest of all, followed by determinism and nomotheticism. When empiricism, inductivism, mechanism, naturalism, and quantitativism are added to these, it is seen that the major dimensions of the methodological approach of modern science in general, not psychology alone, are epitomized by their prescriptive attitudes.

Gestalt psychology is not so much antithetic to these prescriptions as it is more muted, less enthusiastic, less committed. It does share with behaviorism considerable enthusiasm for nomotheticism.

Psychoanalysis shares with behaviorism a positive methodological commitment to determinism, but sharply parts company with both behaviorism and Gestalt psychology in its stress of idiographicism, though it also supports nomotheticism to some degree. The other sharp contrast between behaviorism and psychoanalysis is the latter's very low rating on quantitativism. Not as methodologically objective as either behaviorism or Gestalt psychology, it does resemble Gestalt psychology in the unitalicized ratings of methodological dimensions not yet mentioned.

Turning to Table 3, behaviorism, contentually speaking, is committed to contentual objectivism, molecularism, monism, and peripheralism. It is rated as showing no adherence to contentual subjectivism and unconscious mentalism and low in all the others with the exception of developmentalism.

Gestalt psychology is viewed as not taking extreme positions, except for positive adherence to centralism and to molarism and a rejection of molecularism, peripheralism, and unconscious mentalism.

Psychoanalysis stands apart contentually. It shares positive adherence with Gestalt psychology in centralism, and its positive adherence to

Table 2   Average Rater Judgments on Methodological Prescriptive Attitudes for Three Schools of Psychology as Found by Fuchs and Kawash (1974)

SCALE	SCHOOLS OF PSYCHOLOGY		
	BEHAVIORISM	GESTALT PSYCHOLOGY	PSYCHOANALYSIS
Determinism	6.66	4.72	6.15
Empiricism	6.28	4.57	4.12
Idiographicism	2.37	3.56	5.97
Inductivism	5.91	4.68	4.18
Mechanism	6.33	3.56	3.68
Methodological Ob-jectivism	6.85	4.50	2.50
Naturalism	6.51	5.35	5.19
Nomotheticism	6.46	5.50	4.57
Quantitativism	6.28	3.34	1.68

Table 3   Average Rater Judgments on Contentual Prescriptive Attitudes for Three Schools of Psychology as Found by Fuchs and Kawash (1974)

SCALE	SCHOOLS OF PSYCHOLOGY		
	BEHAVIORISM	GESTALT PSYCHOLOGY	PSYCHOANALYSIS
Centralism	3.07	5.75	5.82
Contentual Objec-tivism	6.43	3.43	2.78
Contentual Subjec-tivism	1.40	5.10	5.93
Developmentalism	4.75	3.91	5.87
Dynamicism	3.85	4.85	6.01
Irrationalism	2.58	3.09	6.48
Molarism	2.82	6.44	5.19
Molecularism	5.73	1.79	2.60
Monism	6.22	3.88	3.56
Peripheralism	5.58	2.68	1.98
Unconscious Mentalism	1.63	2.85	6.81

dynamicism and contentual subjectivism is shared with somewhat weaker enthusiasm on the part of Gestalt psychology. It is unique in its stress on unconscious mentalism, developmentalism, and irrationalism. Not characteristic of psychoanalysis are adherences to contentual objectivism, molecularism, monism, and peripheralism, all of which are strongly adhered to by behaviorism.

A final word must be said about contentual objectivism and contentual subjectivism for all three schools. The guiding attitude toward the very nature of the field is reflected in which attitude is accepted. Two of the schools show salient adherence to contentual subjectivism—psychoanalysis and Gestalt psychology; one shows salient adherence to contentual objectivity—behaviorism. Contentual objectivism is judged to be rejected by psychoanalysis; lesser adherence is shown by Gestalt psychology. Contentual subjectivism is rejected by behaviorism. This issue of conflicting attitudes will return in the *Epilogue*.

The results just reported from the Fuchs and Kawash study are in overall agreement with the historically derived overview of these schools presented in previous chapters.[97]

References*

1. S. I. Franz, "Shepard Ivory Franz," in C. Murchison, ed., *A History of Psychology in Autobiography* (Worcester, Mass.: Clark University Press, 1932), Vol. II, pp. 89–113.
2. S. I. Franz, "Variations in the Distribution of the Motor Centers," *Psychological Monographs* XIX, 81 (1915) (Herrnstein and Boring, Excerpt No. 50).
3. D. O. Hebb, "Karl Spencer Lashley: 1890–1958," *American Journal of Psychology* LXXII (1959): 142–150.
4. K. S. Lashley, *Brain Mechanisms and Intelligence: A Quantitative Study of Injuries to the Brain* (New York: Dover Publications, 1963) (1929) (Herrnstein and Boring, Excerpt No. 51).
5. L. L. Thurstone, "L. L. Thurstone," in E. G. Boring et al., eds., *A History of Psychology in Autobiography* (Worcester, Mass.: Clark University Press, 1952), Vol. IV, pp. 295–321.
6. L. L. Thurstone, *The Vectors of Mind: Multiple-Factor Analysis for the Isolation of Primary Traits* (Chicago: University of Chicago Press, 1935).
7. L. L. Thurstone, *Multiple-Factor Analysis: A Development and Expansion of the Vectors of Mind* (Chicago: University of Chicago Press, 1947).
8. G. W. Allport, "Gordon W. Allport," in E. G. Boring and G. Lindzey, eds., *A History of Psychology in Autobiography* (New York: Appleton-Century-

*See p. 19 for description of reference style.

Crofts, 1967), Vol. V, pp. 3–25.

9. G. W. Allport, *Personality: A Psychological Interpretation* (New York: Henry Holt Company, 1937).

10. H. A. Murray, "Henry A. Murray," in Boring and Lindzey, eds., *A History of Psychology in Autobiography*, Vol. V, pp. 285–310.

11. *Ibid.*, p. 308.

12. H. A. Murray, *Explorations in Personality: A Clinical and Experimental Study of Fifty Men of College Age* (New York: Oxford University Press, 1938).

13. C. D. Morgan and H. A. Murray, "A Method for Investigating Fantasies: The Thematic Apperception Test," *Archives of Neurology and Psychiatry* XXXIV (1935): 289–306.

14. S. J. Beck et al., *Rorschach's Test*: I. *Basic Processes*, 3rd ed., II. *A Variety of Personality Pictures*, III. *Advances in Interpretation* (New York: Grune and Stratton, 1948, 1961, 1945).

15. C. R. Rogers, "Carl R. Rogers," in Boring and Lindzey, eds., *A History of Psychology in Autobiography*. Vol. V, pp. 341–384.

16. C. R. Rogers, *Client-centered Therapy: Its Current Practice, Implications, and Theory* (Boston: Houghton Mifflin, 1951).

17. C. R. Rogers, "A Theory of Therapy, Personality, and Interpersonal Relationships, as Developed in the Client-Centered Framework," in S. Koch, ed., *Psychology: A Study of a Science*. Vol. 3. *Formulations of the Person and the Social Context* (New York: McGraw-Hill, 1959), pp. 184–256.

18. G. Murphy, "Gardner Murphy," in Boring and Lindzey, eds., *A History of Psychology in Autobiography*, Vol. V, pp. 255–282.

19. G. Murphy, *Historical Introduction to Modern Psychology*, rev. ed. (New York: Harcourt, Brace and Company, 1949) (1929).

20. G. Murphy, L. B. Murphy, and T. M. Newcomb, *Experimental Social Psychology: An Interpretation of Research upon the Socialization of the Individual*, rev. ed. (New York: Harper and Brothers, 1937) (1931).

21. *Ibid.*

22. G. Murphy, *Personality: A Biosocial Approach to Origins and Structure* (New York: Harper and Brothers, 1947).

23. A. J. Marrow, *The Practical Theorist: The Life and Work of Kurt Lewin* (New York: Basic Books, 1969).

24. K. Lewin, *Field Theory in Social Science: Selected Theoretical Papers*, ed. D. Cartwright (New York: Harper and Brothers, 1951).

25. K. Lewin, "Defining the 'Field' at a Given Time," *Psychological Review* L (1943): 292–310; Lewin, *Field Theory in Social Science*, p. 45.

26. C. L. Hull, "Clark L. Hull," in Boring et al., eds., *A History of Psychology in Autobiography*, Vol. IV, pp. 143–162.

27. C. L. Hull, *Principles of Behavior: An Introduction to Behavior Theory* (New York: Appleton-Century-Crofts, 1943).

28. C. L. Hull, *Essentials of Behavior* (New Haven, Conn.: Yale University Press, 1951).

29. C. L. Hull, *A Behavior System: An Introduction to Behavior Theory Concerning the Individual Organism* (New Haven, Conn.: Yale University Press, 1952)

30. Boring et al., *A History of Psychology in Autobiography*, p. 155.

31. Hull, *A Behavior System*, pp. 5–6.

32. E. R. Hilgard and G. H. Bower, *Theories of Learning,* 3rd ed. (New York: Appleton-Century-Crofts, 1966) (1948).

33. H. H. Kendler, "Kenneth W. Spence: 1907–1967," *Psychological Review* LXXIV (1967): 335–341.

34. K. W. Spence, *Behavior Theory and Conditioning* (New Haven, Conn.: Yale University Press, 1956); K. W. Spence, *Behavior Theory and Learning: Selected Papers* (Englewood Cliffs, N. J.: Prentice-Hall, 1960); H. W. Kendler and J. T. Spence, eds., *Essays in Neobehaviorism: A Memorial Volume to Kenneth W. Spence* (New York: Appleton-Century-Crofts, 1971).

35. F. A. Logan, "The Hull-Spence Approach," in S. Koch, ed., *Psychology: A Study of a Science.* Vol. 2. *General Systematic Formulations, Learning, and Special Processes* (New York: McGraw-Hill, 1959), pp. 293–358.

36. F. D. Sheffield, "Edwin Ray Guthrie: 1886–1959," *American Journal of Psychology* LXXII (1959): 642–650.

37. E. R. Guthrie, *The Psychology of Learning*, rev. ed. (New York: Harper and Brothers, 1952) (1935).

38. E. R. Guthrie, "Conditioning as a Principle of Learning," *Psychological Review* XXXVII (1930): 412–428.

39. Guthrie, *The Psychology of Learning*.
40. E. R. Guthrie and G. P. Horton, *Cats in a Puzzle Box* (New York: Rinehart and Company, 1946).
41. E. R. Guthrie, "Association by Contiguity," in Koch, ed., *Psychology: A Study of a Science*, Vol. 2, pp. 158–195.
42. B. F. Skinner, *"Particulars of My Life"* (New York: Appleton-Century- Crofts, 1976).
43. B. F. Skinner, *The Behavior of Organisms: An Experimental Analysis* (New York: Appleton-Century-Crofts, 1938); B. F. Skinner, *Science and Human Behavior* (New York: Macmillan Company, 1953); B. F. Skinner, *Cumulative Record: A Selection of Papers*, 3rd ed. (New York: Appleton-Century-Crofts, 1972).
44. C. B. Ferster and B. F. Skinner, *Schedules of Reinforcement* (New York: Appleton-Century-Crofts, 1957).
45. P. W. Bridgman, *The Logic of Modern Physics* (New York: Macmillan Company, 1927).
46. *Ibid.*, p. 36.
47. E. G. Boring, "Intelligence as the Tests Test It," *New Republic* XXXIV (1923): 35–36. Reprinted in E. G. Boring, *History, Psychology and Science: Selected Papers*, ed. R. I. Watson and D. T. Campbell (New York: John Wiley & Sons, 1963), pp. 187–189.
48. S. S. Stevens, "The Operational Basis of Psychology," *American Journal of Psychology* XLVII (1935): 323–330.
49. C. C. Pratt, *The Logic of Modern Psychology* (New York: Macmillan Company, 1939).
50. S. S. Stevens, "Psychology: The Propaedeutic Science," *Philosophy of Science* III (1936): 90–103.
51. S. S. Stevens, "The Attributes of Tones," *Proceedings of the National Academy of Science* XX (1934): 457–459; S. S. Stevens, "Volume and Intensity of Tones," *American Journal of Psychology* XLVI (1934): 397–408; S. S. Stevens, "A Scale for the Measurement of a Psychological Magnitude: Loudness," *Psychological Review* XLIII (1936): 405–416.
52. S. S. Stevens, ed., "Mathematics, Measurement and Psychophysics," *Handbook of Experimental Psychology* (New York: John Wiley & Sons, 1951), pp. 1–49.
53. E. C. Tolman, "Operational Behaviorism and Current Trends in Psychology," *Proceedings of the 25th Anniversary Celebration of the Inauguration of Gradu-*

ate Studies at the University of Southern California (Los Angeles: University of Southern California Press, 1936), pp. 89–103.

54. E. C. Tolman, "The Determiners of Behavior at a Choice Point," *Psychological Review* XLV (1938): 1–41.

55. E. C. Tolman, "Edward Chace Tolman," in Boring et al., eds., *A History of Psychology in Autobiography*, Vol. IV, pp. 323–339.

56. E. C. Tolman, *Purposive Behavior in Animals and Men* (New York: Century Book Company, 1932).

57. K. MacCorquodale and P. E. Meehl, "On a Distinction Between Hypothetical Constructs and Intervening Variables," *Psychological Review* LV (1948): 95–107.

58. E. C. Tolman, "Principles of Purposive Behavior," in Koch, ed., *Psychology: A Study of a Science*, Vol. II, pp. 92–157.

59. K. W. Spence, "The Methods and Postulates of 'Behaviorism,'" *Psychological Review* LV (1948): 67–78.

60. Skinner, *The Behavior of Organisms.*

61. Skinner, *Science and Human Behavior.*

62. B. F. Skinner, "Behaviorism at Fifty," *Science,* CXL (1963): 951–958; also in T. Wann, ed., *Behaviorism and Phenomenology: Contrasting Bases for Modern Psychology* (Chicago: University of Chicago Press, 1964), pp. 79–108.

63. W. Köhler, "Gestalt Psychology Today," *American Psychologist* XIV (1959): 727–734.

64. M. Henle, "On Gestalt Psychology," in B. B. Wolman and E. Nagel, eds., *Scientific Psychology: Principles and Approaches* (New York: Basic Books, 1965), pp. 276–292.

65. W. C. H. Prentice, "The Systematic Psychology of Wolfgang Köhler," in Koch, ed., *Psychology: A Study of a Science*, Vol. I, pp. 427–455; W. Köhler, *The Task of Gestalt Psychology* (Princeton, N. J.: Princeton University Press, 1969).

66. M. Henle, ed., *Documents of Gestalt Psychology* (Berkeley: University of California Press, 1961).

67. H. Hartmann, "Ego Psychology and the Problem of Adaptation," in D. Rapaport, ed., *Organization and Pathology of Thought* (New York: Columbia University Press, 1951), pp. 362–398; H. Hartmann,

"Comments on the Psychoanalytic Theory of the Ego," *Psychoanalytic Study of the Child*, V (1950): 74–95; H. Hartmann, E. Kris, and R. M. Loewenstein, "Comments on the Formation of Psychic Structure," *Psychoanalytic Study of the Child* II (1947): 11–38; H. Hartmann, *Essays on Ego Psychology* (New York: International Universities Press, 1964); H. Hartmann, "The Mutual Influences in the Development of the Ego and the Id," *Psychoanalytic Study of the Child* VII (1952): 9–30.

68. M. M. Gill, ed., *The Collected Papers of David Rapaport* (New York: Basic Books, 1967); D. Rapaport, "The Structure of Psychoanalytic Theory: A Systematizing Attempt," in Koch, ed., *Psychology: A Study of a Science*, Vol. III, pp. 55–183.

69. R. R. Holt, "Ego Autonomy Re-evaluated," *International Journal of Psychoanalysis* XLVI (1965): 151–167; G. S. Klein, "Consciousness in Psychoanalytic Theory: Some Implications for Current Research in Perception," *Journal of American Psychoanalytic Association* VII (1959): 5–34.

70. E. H. Erikson, *Childhood and Society* (New York: W. W. Norton and Company, 1950).

71. E. R. Hilgard, "Impulsive Versus Realistic Thinking: An Examination of the Distinction Between Primary and Secondary Processes in Thought," *Psychological Bulletin* LIX (1962): 477–488; R. R. Sears, "Survey of Objective Studies of Psychoanalytic Concepts," *Social Science Research Council Bulletin* LI (1943); B. F. Skinner, "Critique of Psychoanalytic Concepts and Theories," *Scientific Monthly* LXXIX (1954): 302–307.

72. M. M. Gill, "The Present State of Psychoanalytic Theory," *Journal of Abnormal Social Psychology* LVIII (1959): 1–8; L. S. Kubie, "Psychoanalysis and Scientific Method," *Journal of Nervous and Mental Disorders* CXXXI (1960): 495–512; H. Hartmann, "Psychoanalysis as a Scientific Theory," in S. Hook, ed., *Psychoanalysis, Scientific Method and Philosophy* (New York: Grove, 1959), pp. 3–37.

73. J. Dollard and N. E. Miller, *Personality and Psychotherapy* (New York: McGraw-Hill, 1950).

74. R. L. Munroe, *Schools of Psychoanalytic Thought: An Exposition, Critique and Attempt at Integration* (New York: Dryden Press, 1955); G. S. Blum,

Psychoanalytic Theories of Personality (New York; McGraw-Hill, 1953).

75. K. Horney, *New Ways in Psychoanalysis* (New York: W. W. Norton and Company, 1939); K. Horney, *The Neurotic Personality of Our Time* (New York: W. W. Norton and Company, 1937).

76. E. Fromm, *Man for Himself, an Inquiry into the Psychology of Ethics* (New York: Rinehart and Company, 1947); E. Fromm, *The Sane Society* (New York: Rinehart and Company, 1955); R. I. Evans, *Dialogue with Erich Fromm* (New York: Harper & Row, 1966).

77. A(lexendra) Adler, "Adlerian Psychotherapy and Recent Trends," *Journal of Individual Psychology* XIX (1963): 55–60.

78. H. L. Ansbacher, "The Structure of Individual Psychology," in Wolman and Nagel, eds., *Scientific Psychology: Principles and Approaches,* pp. 340–364.

79. J. B. Rotter, "An Analysis of Adlerian Psychology from a Research Orientation," *Journal of Individual Psychology* XVIII (1962): 3–11.

80. E. W. Arluch, "Training Facilities of the C. G. Jung Institute, Zurich," *American Psychologist* XV (1960): 626–629.

81. A. Toynbee, "The Value of C. G. Jung's Work for Historians," *Journal of Analytic Psychology* I (1956): 193–194.

82. C. P. Snow, *The Two Cultures and the Scientific Revolution* (London: Cambridge University Press, 1959).

83. I. L. Child, *Humanistic Psychology and the Research Tradition: Their Several Virtues* (New York: John Wiley & Sons, 1973).

84. G. W. Allport, "Scientific Models and Human Morals," *Psychological Review* LIV (1947): 182–192.

85. C. R. Rogers, "Some Questions and Challenges Facing a Humanistic Psychology," *Journal of Humanistic Psychology* V (1965): 1–5.

86. A. H. Maslow, "Humanistic Science and Transcendent Experiences," *Journal of Humanistic Psychology* V (1965): 219–227.

87. A. van Kaam, "Existential and Humanistic Psychology," *Review of Existential Psychology and Psychiatry* V (1965): 291–296.

88. A. van Kaam, *Existential Foundations of Psychology* (Pittsburgh, Pa.: Duquesne University Press, 1966).

89. R. May, ed., *Existential Psychology* (New York: Random House, 1961).

90. R. B. MacLeod, "Psychological Phenomenology: A Propaedeutic to a Scientific Psychology," in J. R. Royce, ed., *Toward Unification in Psychology* (Toronto: University of Toronto Press, 1970), pp. 246–266.

91. J. J. Gibson, "Perception as a Function of Stimulation," in Koch, ed., *Psychology: A Study of a Science*, Vol. I, pp. 456–501; J. J. Gibson, *The Senses Considered as Perceptual Systems* (Boston: Houghton Mifflin, 1966).

92. D. Snygg, "The Need for a Phenomenological System of Psychology," *Psychological Review* XLVII (1941): 404–424.

93. D. Snygg and A. W. Combs, *Individual Behavior: A New Frame of Reference for Psychology* (New York: Harper and Brothers, 1949).

94. C. R. Rogers, *Counseling and Psychotherapy: Newer Concepts in Practice* (Boston: Houghton-Mifflin, 1942); Rogers, *Client-centered Therapy*.

95. H. Spiegelberg, *Phenomenology in Psychology and Psychiatry, a Historical Introduction* (Evanston, Ill.: Northwestern University Press, 1972).

96. A. H. Fuchs and G. F. Kawash, "Prescriptive Dimensions for Five Schools of Psychology," *Journal of the History of the Behavioral Sciences* X (1974): 352–366.

97. Considerable agreement may be discerned between the overview analysis of positive prescriptive attitudes of behaviorism provided in historical context in Chapter 18 and the results from the Fuchs and Kawash study. Two prescriptions were identified in their study that did not receive explicit attention: induction as a methodological commitment and monism in the contentual area. Purism and utilitarianism, both very evident in behavioristic concerns, did not survive the cut-off score for any school and, consequently, was not reported for the Fuchs and Kawash data. Otherwise, there was agreement.

    In the account given in Chapter 19 of Gestalt psychology, the predominance of the molar prescription was emphasized throughout. Centralism, conscious mentalism, and nomotheticism were also salient. Three of these were rated most highly in the rating study. Conscious mentalism, the fourth stressed in the chapter, did not receive a high enough rating in any school to be included in this summary data. However, in view of the importance attached to phenomenological preparations to experiment by Gestalt psychologists, it is still considered crucial.

The account of psychoanalysis in Chapter 20 is in complete agreement with the rating study. Of the eight salient prescriptions, two methodological and six contentual from the rating study, all are included in the discussion in Chapter 19, and no others.

EPILOGUE: JUST YESTERDAY

Consideration of "just yesterday" in psychology comes dangerously close to implying omniscience and confusing history with prophecy. Contemporary psychologies are too close to us to permit objective analysis. It is wise to consider trends, not individuals, though it will be convenient in a few instances to refer to eponyms, that is, to individuals as representative of trends, e.g., Skinnerianism. Moreover, presentation of trends permits brevity, which an epilogue demands. It is hoped that the broad strokes of the brush used nevertheless will permit summarizations of the details to which the earlier account stands witness.

The contemporary status of psychology as a science is an issue that demands attention. Since the time of Wundt 100 years ago, psychologists have been dominated by naturalistic, empirical, quantitative, nomothetic, and determinist prescriptions in their considerations of methodology. To be sure, some voices were raised in opposition to each prescription, with those who adhere to idiographicism the strongest and most widespread, but there is a relatively firm basis of agreement among psychologists. These prescriptions also guide the workers in other sciences. Methodologically, psychologists resemble scientists in other fields.

Psychology, nevertheless, is still a field, or fields, divided. There are no overarching theoretical contentual guidelines that embrace the thinking of even the majority of all psychologists. Psychologists continue to disagree about the fundamental nature of the field. Contentual subjectivity and contentual objectivity provide the most crucial area of disagreement.

As a science, modern psychology of the last 100 years has gone through three major contentual stages. In the last half of the nineteenth century it was contentually subjective in orientation, as the science of consciousness with introspection as its major method, and possessed a

623

relatively distinctive area of science all its own. When contentual objectivity in the form of behaviorism emerged in the early decades of this century, it temporarily submerged contentual subjectivity (which in reality never disappeared). And, finally, from the fifties on it has been a science in which contentual objectivity predominates and subjectivity is counterdominant but very much viable.

Since there would be little disagreement about the dominance of contentual objectivity in contemporary psychology, it is perhaps most appropriate to examine the question of the restored counterdominance of contentual subjectivity.

What gave the impression that psychology as a science of experience had disappeared was the disappearance of the structuralist school. Wundtian-Titchenerian introspection is gone, not because the investigation of conscious experience is necessarily barren, but because the method they used was, quite properly, shaped for the content categories they were investigating, and these elements of consciousness proved to be barren and were abandoned. Contentual subjectivism in other guises, then and now, is still very much with us. A significant segment of contemporary psychology is concerned with experience.

Even in its heyday in the twenties and thirties part of the overwhelming dominance of contentual objectivity was illusory and provincial. Then and now, psychoanalysis was contentually subjective. So, too, was most of the continental psychology then current, for example, the continued neo-idealistic stream of influence sketched as resulting in the overthrow of Wundtian psychology. Phenomenological investigation, preparatory to experiment in Gestalt psychology as practiced here and abroad, is and was contentually subjective. If anything, in recent years the appeal of the phenomenological method in other forms has been increasing. A case in point is research and theory outside the Gestalt school in so-called cognitive psychology, in which conscious experience is, tacitly, at least, considered saliently dynamic.

Objection to or adherence to the salience of contentual subjectivity, no matter which side of the question an individual psychologist may take, cannot be dismissed as a solution for the field, though it may be one's own personal solution. Broadly put, psychology is conceived either as a science of behavior and experience or as a science of behavior. There is no firm consensus and therefore no universally agreed on contentual basis.

Kuhn, a historian of the natural sciences, has supplied a pertinent background for further discussion.[1] In the course of an account of revolutions in science, he speaks of mature sciences as reaching the level of a universally scientific achievement, serving as a model and held at a particular temporal period. In a "Postscript" now attached to his original publication, he states that the dimensions of this model are symbolic generalizations, shared beliefs, shared values, and exemplars or concrete problem solutions. There is no question that both aspects of method and content enter into these scientific achievements. He refers to these models as paradigms. A paradigmatic science is one whose practitioners agree on as a model during a period of normal science when they add details to the research problems generated by it but do not change and seldom even question the fundamental model itself. When research anomalies to the heretofore accepted model cannot be resolved, a reconstruction of the science occurs, which he refers to as a scientific revolution. Examples of scientific revolutions are, for astronomy, the Ptolemaic (earth-centered) paradigm giving way in the revolution which made contentually central the Copernican (sun-centered) paradigm and, for physics, the Aristotelian paradigm giving way to the Newtonian dynamic paradigm, which in turn was superseded by the Einsteinian paradigm.

Kuhn uses the key concept of the paradigm in several degrees of breadth, so that part paradigms apply within a given segment of a science. Both the paradigm, the methodological and contentual definition of a field of science, and a part paradigm, in which a local, not a global revolution established the paradigm, will be utilized in the discussion to follow, but with emphasis on the importance of the former to our task of conceptualizing psychology as a science. To quote from a previous paper:

> In all of its meanings, a paradigm has a guidance function. It functions as an intellectual framework, it tells them what sort of entities with which their scientific universe is populated and how these entities behave, and informs its followers what questions may legitimately be asked about nature.
>
> What are the consequences in those sciences that lack a defining paradigm? Foremost is a noticeable lack of unity within a science, indications of which Kuhn acknowledges as one of the sources for his paradigmatic concept, which arose in part from his being puzzled about "the number and extent of the overt disagreement between social scientists about the nature of legitimate scientific methods and problems,"[2] as compared to the relative lack of such disagreement among natural scientists.[3]

All science at one time, and some sciences to this very day, Kuhn argues, lacked a defining paradigm. To use his term, they were or are preparadigmatic. He illustrates with the history of electricity at the time of Franklin when there were almost as many views about the fundamental nature of electricity as there were experimenters. As each gained supporters, a period of schools was created. Then one of the schools eventually triumphed, when it was agreed by the researchers that it was better than its competitors, and that school became a paradigm. Other schools disappeared, partly because of conversion of individual scientists and partly because of the death of their protagonists. What little Kuhn said about how a preparadigmatic science functions was admittedly schematic. He did suggest that it is or was guided by "something like" paradigms. This "something like," it has been suggested throughout this book, is prescriptions.

Such, then, are some of the aspects of Kuhn's theory of scientific revolutions. What are seen to be the implications for psychology? Psychology, it would seem, is a preparadigmatic science. It still lacks universal agreement about the nature of its contentual model, the crux of a paradigmatic science. Little supporting review is necessary at this point—witness the opposition between views highlighted by that between contentual objectivity and contentual subjectivity, the debate over other fundamental issues, the continued presence of the schools of psychology, the national differences in psychology in the United States and European countries which have negligible differences in, say, physics and chemistry. These differences, which point to lack of agreement about a contentual model, are still very much part of the psychological scene.

Skinnerian neobehaviorism, as evidenced in the preceding chapter, is at present but a part paradigm. Neobehaviorism does not function as a paradigm because it does not meet the criterion of general acceptance as the contentual basis for psychology, even though methodologically it subscribes to major prescriptive adherence of the sciences in general. It does not appear to have the support of even the majority of psychologists; it cannot be applied in a way that affords adequate explanations for many phenomena considered to be psychological in nature.

On the question of the adequacy of neobehaviorism as a paradigm, there are two discernible attitudes—that the current inadequacy will be remedied in the future by further research, making the stand on the reality of the paradigm a matter of faith; and, equally a matter of faith, that the approach will always be inadequate as a contentual base for psychology. There is a further opinion which hinges on a value judgment—that many phenomena may be ruled out as irrelevant to the psychology that is to be; i.e., given time and further elaboration of research findings, under the rubrics of the neobehavioristic system, some problems considered essential by opponents will be proven nonessential, for example, contentually subjective matters will no longer be a concern for psychologists. The opposition, also making a value judgment, argue that this state of affairs will not come about. Only future events will indicate whether neobehaviorism is or is not a potential paradigm and whether or not the uneasiness that we now experience presages the coming revolution in psychology.

Psychology may someday achieve the hallmark of a mature science and become a paradigmatic science, instead of a prescriptive one, with the disappearance of contentual theoretical schisms, national differences, and disagreements about the fundamental nature of the field that serves to divide rather than unite it. There will always be controversy but, when a mature paradigmatic science, it will be controversy about research and not about fundamental principles that will divide the field. Because of current lack of agreement, psychology is still guided by prescriptions which permit the existence of contradictory, even currently irreconcilable currents, in the thinking of psychologists.

Those of us who live in the present, but are aware of our past, are witnessing and partaking in the events which will be crucial for that future goal—that continued desire to know expressed by Aristotle so long ago.

References*

1. T. S. Kuhn, *The Structure of Scientific Revolutions*, 2nd ed. enlarged (Chicago: University of Chicago Press, 1970) (1962).
2. *Ibid.*, p. 4.
3. R. I. Watson, "Psychology: A Prescriptive Science," *American Psychologist* XXII (1967): 435.

*See p. 19 for description of reference style.

INDEX OF NAMES

INDEX OF SUBJECTS